The Reaper's Line

The
Reaper's Line

LIFE AND DEATH ON THE MEXICAN BORDER

LEE MORGAN II
Special Agent—U.S. Customs Service

RIO NUEVO PUBLISHERS
TUCSON, ARIZONA

Rio Nuevo Publishers®
P.O. Box 5250, Tucson, Arizona 85703-0250
(520) 623-9558, www.rionuevo.com

Library of Congress Cataloging-in-Publication Data

Morgan, Lee, II.
The reaper's line : life and death on the Mexican border / by Lee Morgan.
    p. cm.
ISBN-13: 978-1-887896-97-9
ISBN-10: 1-887896-97-X
  1. Drug traffic—Mexican-American Border Region. 2. Violence—Mexican-American Border Region. 3. Illegal aliens—Mexican-American Border Region. 4. Law enforcement—Mexican-American Border Region. 5. Morgan, Lee, II. 6. Government investigators—Mexican-American Border Region. 7. Border patrols—Mexican-American Border Region.
I. Title.
HV5831.M46M67 2006
363.28'5092--dc22
[B]
                              2006010102

Design: Karen Schober, Seattle, Washington

Printed in Canada.

10   9   8   7   6   5   4   3   2   1

For my loving wife and best friend, Betty Morgan.
You saved my life, in ways you will never know. I love you more
today than yesterday, but less than tomorrow.

With special thanks to Anna and Matt Magoffin,
and retired Assistant U.S. Attorney Randy Stevens,
for their unwavering support during the
writing of this book.

Contents

Prologue

For twenty-eight years I've been under the spell of a fabulously infatuating mistress. She could excite men like no other I had ever seen. On a good number of nights she thrilled and teased me. Every morning when I awoke I looked forward to gazing upon her tantalizing beauty as she basked naked in the desert sun. She could be as hard as steel, or as soft as a newborn calf's breath. During the winter months she turned as frigid as a witch's tit in the Arctic. And during the sweltering summer she could lather up with sweat like a French whore in church on Sunday.

In the blink of any eye her charm could lull a man to sleep, or leave him stranded on the brink of death. Her spell upon me could no more be broken than that which links a child to its mother. I once tried to leave her, but her distant beckoning brought me back after several years. My lust for her nearly cost me my family, as well as my life.

My aging mistress has gone by many names. To Mexican suitors she is sometimes known as La Frontera or La Línea. You may better know her as The Border.

In the never-ending corridors of global turmoil, the U.S.-Mexican border is emerging as one of the most violent places on earth. No one really knows the exact body count, but since 1995, it is estimated that somewhere between 3,500 and 4,000 Mexican citizens alone have met their end while attempting to cross the border illegally. And the number of people murdered on the border since the drug wars began is probably five times that total, or more. But because of the involvement of corrupt, closemouthed Mexican officials in such murders, there will never be a complete accounting of those bodies or where they are all entombed. Aside from furtive homicides, gunfights between dope smugglers and agents of the U.S. Border Patrol and U.S. Customs Service are becoming an everyday occurrence. Not since the days of bandit revolutionaries like Pancho Villa has the U.S.-Mexican border run so violently red with blood.

One of the things that the U.S. government has never learned or understood about the Mexican drug wars is this: You must be as dedicated to stopping the drug lords and smugglers as they are to getting their deadly poisons through the border. The shootings, vehicle chases, rammings, and murders described in this book are testimony to their fortitude. You have to understand that these people are willing to die in order to dig themselves out of their shanties and break the inherent Mexican chains of poverty. They would rather die going for it, than live without it. That's the oath they swear in blood. It is obviously more motivating to them than the oath to protect our country that our politicians and federal agents take. Until we are motivated enough to die protecting this country from Colombian and Mexican dope lords, we will lose the drug wars!

You don't know narcotics agents like me, because there are only a few of us compared to the numbers of the FBI and DEA (Drug Enforcement Administration). I was a special agent of the U.S. Customs Service, Department of Treasury—or so it was known until reorganization under the Department of Homeland Security in 2003—and that's how I'll refer to it through most of this story. Agents like me are not to be confused with the blue-uniformed U.S. Customs inspectors who man the ports of entry and sometimes irritatingly "toss your luggage" after you've been abroad. We are the plainclothes investigative branch of the service. Although we are few, we wear many hats when not working narcotics interdiction on the border. U.S. Customs special agents investigate smuggling of international firearms and weapons of mass destruction, "trading with the enemy" violations, money laundering, child pornography, and violations of the Neutrality Act, to just name a few of the federal laws we enforce. And Treasury agents are often called upon to protect foreign dignitaries, U.S. presidential candidates, and the President of the United States, as well as others who dwell near and around Capitol Hill.

I began my federal law enforcement career on the U.S.-Mexican border in 1974. It was the deadliest year in the history of U.S. law enforcement, with 271 officers being cut down in the line of duty. I was ordered to a little town called Douglas on the border in Cochise

County, Arizona. While nearby Wild West-renowned Tombstone was recognized as "the town too tough to die," Douglas had the dubious reputation of being known as the roughest border town the Arizona Rangers had to tame at the beginning of the twentieth century. And by the end of the same century, the dirty little border pueblo had gotten so rank that out-of-town assassins were literally being buried in the backyards of their intended victims.

For a law enforcement officer, living in Douglas could be the equivalent of living in the pit of Lucifer's most sordid assortment of putrid temptations. If the devil's advocates have an inkling that you're a lawman of weak moral fiber, they will shove dirty money in your face until they completely own your soul. Their women and wine will be at your beck and call. Their lavish cocaine-laced orgies and promises of unlimited wealth have perverted and ruined the lives of a substantial number of lawmen I have known. Douglas is a place where greed, corruption, murder, and the resulting paranoia flourish like tumbleweed seeds in souring horse manure. It is a place where the illegal trafficking of drugs, as well as human cargo, is a way of life—and death.

Douglas and Cochise County are one of the main pipelines for drugs coming into the U.S., taking second place only to Miami. In this historic Old West county where the guns of Geronimo and Wyatt Earp once roared, the Chiricahua Apache wars of a hundred years ago have given way to the Mexican drug wars. The only difference between the two is that the latter has produced, and will continue to yield, a higher number of rock-and-sand-covered graves.

During the drug wars of the last quarter of a century in Cochise County, there was once a handful of men willing to go up against some of the most ruthless death-dealing outlaws this part of the Mexican border has ever known. Although hopelessly outgunned and outnumbered, these U.S. lawmen had the nerve to make a stand in the face of unprecedented official corruption. They faced a foreign and domestic criminal element so powerful and violent that the East Coast mob pales by comparison. This is their story.

I dedicate this book to the handful of lawmen and soldiers, both living and dead, that I have had the honor and privilege to have fought alongside. To the living I respectfully tip my hat. To the dead I pay an enduring homage.

Author's Note

I wrote this book because I wanted to leave a recorded history of a group of U.S. lawmen who made a stand. Some of them survived to tell their story.

This book is written chronologically, as an investigator would do a report for court. At times there are digressions on topics of special interest, especially when my shameless Texas storytelling gets the better of me.

Because this book is true, it required graphic language to authenticate criminal acts, gunfights, and deadly duels. There is no way to soften or "window dress" the inherent ugliness of life and death on the Mexican border. Read at your own peril. Cry when you must, and laugh when obliged.

A few of the names in this book had to be changed. But there is one consistent name that demands no alias. The Reaper.

1

The Reaper and the Beast

Human beings are created by their environments.

—attributed to CHARLES DARWIN

I WAS BORN IN 1951 under a bright crescent moon in Wharton, Texas. For those of you who haven't ever seen God's country, Wharton is located about seventy miles southwest of Houston in the pecan and oak forests. As a kid I read in some old high-school geography book that our area was designated a semitropical zone. If you aren't driving through a thicket of trees and mosquitoes, you'll find yourself crossing some of the most fertile prairies in Texas. The grass grows so lush and tall in that part of the country that it's easy to flat-out lose a newborn calf in it. The soil is so black and fertile that a feller can spit a watermelon seed on the ground on his way into town and on the return trip he can pick a big, ripe melon. Well, you may have to wait a tad longer than that. But I guarandamntee you won't have to wait more than a day or two.

During my formative years of, say, about three to ten years old, I spent a great deal of time on the old Morgan ranch in Fort Bend County being raised by my grandmother, who was widowed shortly after my birth. Even though Grandpa Morgan had passed on, his sons and the black folks that lived on the ranch kept the place running pretty efficiently for years. If you're questioning the black folks part, let me tell you something. It hasn't been all that long ago down in Texas that things got changed for the former sons and daughters of Confederate slaves. In fact, when Grandma was busy with ranch work, she sent me to one of three wooden shacks located behind the main ranch house where three black families were practically born and raised on the premises. The weather-beaten shack where I spent most of my childhood days was the abode of my "Mammy May."

May was probably about thirty or thirty-five years old. She was a pleasantly rotund ball of love through and through. I remember when I got dropped off on May's porch to be watched for the day, she would reach down with a smile as wide as Texas and scoop me up in those large, fleshy arms of hers as if I weighed no more than a small sparrow. Then she would draw me into her warm bosom and squeeze me so tight I thought my belly button would bust. The whole time she was hugging her little added chore for the day, she would be softly singing the gospel to me. Mammy May loved her little white boy unconditionally. And I loved her back without knowing there was any kind of difference in the world between us.

When I wasn't tailing May around her shack as she did her daily tasks and cooking, I would be outside playing with her four girls and boys. We would spend most of the day either swimming in the cattle's watering holes, riding horses bareback, or playing cowboys and Indians in the hay barn. It wasn't until I started school that I knew that there was a difference between being black and white. Then I learned about segregation not only in our local school system, but even our family doctor's office, where there were separate waiting rooms and facilities for black and gringo folks.

No kid is born a racist. He is directed on that sordid, rotten path to hatred. And I reckon I really can't lay the blame at the doorsteps of my parents and ancestors because it was all handed down to them as the same narrow-minded bigotry that I was now being tutored in. But a few years later, as an eighteen-year-old kid in Vietnam, I would learn that there were two things that made us all the same. Our blood was the same bright red color, and death made no bones over the shade of the wrappings that held your blood in check. I reckon I became the first generation of Morgans to teach our children not to judge men solely on color of skin. And even though she has long passed away along with my beloved grandmother, I still love Mammy May with all my heart and soul.

When I wasn't spending time with Grandma Morgan and Mammy May, my parents were rearing me in a pretty tranquil farming and ranching community on the other side of Fort Bend County. It was one of those close-knit rural societies where everyone either knew each other or they were related, whether they knew it or not. Most folks were of German, Czech, or Polish descent, and they liked to refer to themselves proudly as Bohemians. They were a good, simple lot whose only fault, if you want to call it that, was that they did a good bit of beer guzzling on every possible occasion. Weddings, funerals, country fairs, and harvest celebrations would damn near throw the Anheuser-Busch breweries into hops and grain shortages. The French may tout their prowess at wine drinking, but no one in the world can hold a candle to the beer swizzling a Bohemian can get down to when he sets his mind on it.

My father, Lee Morgan, was one of the hardest-working men you would ever want to know. He loved my German-blooded mother with all of his heart, and was full of those honorable virtues and qualities that are becoming shamefully antiquated today. His steadfast integrity and sense of independence were the norm for Texans back in those days. I reckon it's characteristics like these that seem to set Texas folks apart from the rest of the Union.

Growing up on a Texas ranch with his two brothers, my daddy intended to make a living for his own family the same way. Now, if you know anything about ranching and farming, you know it's a crap shoot at best. First, there's the goddamn weather to consider. If you're not getting enough rain, you're getting too much. And if the Almighty's droughts, floods, or freezing weather don't do you in, there are diseases, rustlers, quicksand, bloodthirsty coyotes, and ferocious packs of wolves to worry about. And if that ain't enough, then there's the fluctuating price of beef itself. So when the risky cattle market crashed back in the early 1950s, my daddy gave the gambling up to become a "company" man working for Texas United Gas, a natural-gas pipeline outfit.

But his two odds-playing brothers stayed in the cattle business, and that's where I spent most of my summers as a young pup. If we weren't working a herd of cattle on the flat green prairies, we'd be cutting and raking next winter's feed in the hay fields. And if we weren't doing that, you could find us planting, irrigating, or harvesting fields of life-sustaining brown rice.

It was a good way for a kid to grow to manhood. My cousins and I spent many a hard day working on those rich Texas ranges. But we found time to enjoy the adolescent mischief we were entitled to as young bucks. During the summer in the rice fields there was always a black water moccasin snake to be hunted down and sent to his maker. In the same fields during the winter we could look forward to plenty of prime duck and goose shooting. And on the prairies where we ran the cattle, there were an infinite number of quail and doves that hadn't yet been properly introduced to Grandma's frying pan.

During the spring and fall we'd saddle up to bring the cattle in for vaccination, worming, cutting, branding, and shipping. My uncle Billy (William) Morgan ran cattle on the prairies and down along a stretch of the muddy brown Brazos River. Now, the prairie-raised bovines weren't too much of a problem to round up and herd into the work pens and old wooden chutes. But those four-legged critters down along the Brazos were some of the wildest sons of bitches a horse and rider ever would have to chase after.

The brush grew so thick and matted along the Brazos river bottom that a rancher couldn't get into that cursed country to see his cattle but once or twice a year. When we did ride in, we had to send "cow" dogs ahead to drive the savage locos out of the tangled thickets. And when the dogs finally did get the untamed beasts out into clear open ground, Katie bar the door, because disaster was just itching to break loose. Being that the beeves hadn't hardly ever seen open space, they would damn near stampede full pace on you at the drop of a hat. It was during one of those stampede chases that my mare went down with me and I paid the price with a broken collarbone. I considered a busted clavicle damn lucky compared to the alternative of being trampled to death. But poor ol' Uncle Billy didn't see it that way. He blamed himself so hard that he never hardly let me sit a horse over at his ranch after that.

One of my favorite jobs working the chutes was grabbing the cattle in the nose with steel tongs and holding their heads up for worming and vaccination. To control a half a ton of beef by the nose gave a feller an awesome feeling of power. One of my most hated jobs was throwing and holding calves down for castration. Not only did they fight like the dickens, but I always had this sympathetic identification with their plight. I guess it's just a natural male thing!

We as youngsters always looked forward to reaching the end of a field during the summer cuttings. Whether we were cutting hay or rice, our uncles would try to see to it that we were all together after finishing up a field. To celebrate, Uncle Cotton (Lawrence) Morgan, the self-proclaimed alcoholic in the family, would bring out a couple of Texas-size ice chests loaded down with frosty cold Pearl and Lone Star brews.

We'd have been sweating in that Gulf Coast heat and humidity all day long like mules at the end of a plow. The chaff from the hay and rice would be sticking into your hot, wet skin like needles in a pincushion. And there wasn't a place on your body that was given sanctuary from the incessant itching. Not even beneath your balls. But when you grabbed that ice-cold beer, leaned up in the shade against a now-silent, cooling tractor, and looked back over that cut field into an orange and purple Texas sunset, it all seemed so perfectly right. You knew your life had a definite meaning and purpose. You knew hard work had its own God-given reward. But most important of all, a feller knew the pride in being born a Morgan, and a Texan.

I lived right in the middle of cotton fields and cattle pastures on the outskirts of the Needville village limits. The whole neighborhood consisted of about twelve or fifteen households, which translated to about ten of us boys who were knocking at the gates of puberty around the same time. We became a pretty close group, always playing football, baseball, and army. Although I liked all of the guys, my next-door neighbor grew to be my best buddy in the whole world.

Ray Leissner and I had been inseparable since about the time we were able to walk and crawl up on a horse. His father was a big, beer-drinking German who farmed rice. Mr. Leissner was one of those mean-looking, six-foot-plus, two-hundred-and-fifty-pound, brawny, hairy-chested men who just naturally scared the ever-living shit out of me and Ray when he was pissed off. Now and again Ray and I would pull some really good boners. Just outright stupid dumb shit. Like wrecking a tractor during a puberty-inspired race that you can be damn sure wasn't even close to being authorized by his dad.

When we weren't floating the Brazos or hunting on the farm, I liked to stay pretty close to the Leissner home. Ray had an eighteen-year-old sister who was one of the most beautiful Southern Belle specimens a boy would ever lay eyes on. Of course, never mind the fact that I was still counting my sprouting pubic hairs. At the ripe old age of about thirteen I figured I had already become a semipro at rating girls. And as far as I was concerned Kathy Leissner rated eleven out of a possible ten. She had sparkling blue eyes and hair the color of mesquite-blossom honey. When Kathy smiled she could light up the whole room. She had a petite, slender frame complemented by an ample bosom. Calendar-girl material for sure.

During the last couple of years before Kathy left for college, I would go out of my way to get a glimpse of her whenever visiting the Leissner household. I knew from my youthful pursuit of an education via *Playboy* magazine that Kathy had a figure that was comparable to any "bunny." Her radiant smile always seemed to make my legs turn to jelly. It was your typical schoolboy-crush-on-the-older-woman thing. Fantasies all adolescent boys love to drool over, but in their hearts they know their time has not yet arrived.

In 1965, Kathy brought home her college boyfriend. Much to my adolescent disappointment, it was later announced that the couple was engaged to be married. Charlie was a blond, blue-eyed former

U.S. Marine. Because he was still in the active Marine Reserves, Charlie wore his short-cropped hair high and tight in a true military cut. He often told Ray and me that he had been a frogman for the Marines. Whether that was true or not, I really can't say. But I can tell you that the guy was in great shape and he spent a lot of his free time working out. He had bulging triceps and biceps that he loved to flex for his admiring public, us kids.

Ray and I would sometimes catch Charlie in the backyard of the Leissner home with a death grip on a steel pipe. We'd watch as he would strain for thirty-second intervals against both ends of the pipe as if he were trying to bend it. All the veins in his arms and neck would bulge while he grunted and screamed like he was in some kind of a fit of anger. The Marine called it isometric exercises. But in retrospect, a shrink would probably have called it the release of hostile aggression.

From where we stood, Ray and I thought Charlie should have a place reserved on the all-American hero list next to John Wayne or Superman. He emanated the characteristics of a poster Marine mixed with the cool awareness of the Fonz. But for all of those neat qualities Charlie possessed, the Marine also had this weird, distorted glow about him that as a young boy I would be hard-pressed to explain. It was as if he were wrestling with a satanic seed deep inside of him. He was continually struggling to keep this masked unknown from springing forth. Yet, at the same time, Charlie managed to force a smile, projecting the façade of a happy, wholesome all-American boy. We didn't know it then, but Charlie was fighting to keep the lid on a growing, gnawing turmoil of gothic proportion.

Ray and I were already reading every GI Joe comic book we could get our hands on. So it was only natural that the Marine found us to be an easily captive audience. We would spend hours on end listening to Charlie's stories about military service and his training. Every time we heard Kathy and Charlie were coming home from college, Ray and I would stop whatever we were doing during our hero's arrival.

During one of their fall visits, Charlie was playing football with us on the Leissner lawn when a neighbor's dog was accidentally run over by a truck. The terrified pet was hopelessly torn up as he lay bleeding in the middle of the road, pitifully yelping in high, ear-piercing screams for someone to put him out of his misery. The neighbors had come out to see what all the fuss was about when Charlie, acting like a true hero, went into action.

While most of the adults were losing their marbles and screaming for somebody to do something, Charlie dropped the football and calmly walked over to the trunk of his car, which was parked in the driveway. From the trunk he retrieved what I can only remember now was some kind of a World War II .30 caliber military assault carbine or rifle. It may have been either a semiautomatic M1 Carbine or its larger brother, the M1 Garand rifle. Ray and I watched as our hero coolly and quickly loaded the rifle and hurried off toward the howling dog.

Out of kids' natural curiosity to see bad shit and gore, we started to chase after Charlie. When he saw us tagging along, he stopped and turned with the weapon held across his chest. He hesitated and curiously stared at us as if he was making some kind of a secret difficult decision before speaking. With his thumb brushing back and forth over the rifle's safety, he firmly told us that we couldn't go with him. As he spoke, there was no doubt in my young mind that I was making eye contact with someone, or some *thing*, I didn't yet know or understand. At this age, I was too young to know the dark side of the soul. I had yet to interact with or meet the Beast.

We waited exactly where Charlie told us. A minute or two passed and we heard one shot ring out. The howling ceased. Now that I look back on it, I realize that Charlie was the only adult who showed no emotion whatsoever during the mini-crisis. It was business as usual when he capped the pet. He was a pretty cold character, this Marine of ours.

The next day Ray and I asked Charlie if he would let us shoot the rifle. Sure, we had fired small-caliber weapons and shotguns a hundred thousand times during our hunting escapades. But this was a real soldier's high-power rifle and that was a new barrier for Ray and me to bust through. Charlie's eyes seemed to sparkle with pleasure, knowing all too well that we worshiped him as our big brother and newly adopted expert military advisor. Even though Ray and I had read all those GI Joe comic books, we figured a little tutoring from a real Marine could never hurt us.

The next day, bright and early, we departed Ray's house in Charlie's car en route to the Leissner-farm lakes. As we left I remember seeing Kathy standing in the driveway throwing us a kiss as the wind tossed her hair across the nape of her neck. I swear, she looked just like one of those glamour girls on the cover of one of those cosmetic magazines. Fantasizing the kiss was just for me, but knowing damn good and well it wasn't, I figured I couldn't have lost her to a better man than Charlie.

Once we got off the highway, Charlie further endeared his young worshippers by letting us take turns driving on the back gravel roads leading to the farm. I had never had a brother, much less a big brother. So to me, Charlie was the perfect big brother. Here's a guy who was over twenty years old, could almost drink beer legally, had been a frogman in the Marines, was in college, was dating my heartthrob, *and* he was going to teach Ray and me to shoot a real military rifle. For a fourteen-year-old boy in the sticks of southeast Texas, just short of getting your first piece of ass, it couldn't get much better than this.

We drove up to the edge of the lake and Charlie pulled several different rifles from the trunk of his car. He started Ray and me out on a small .22 caliber carbine and let us work our way up to his high-power rifles, which included a .30 caliber semiautomatic M1 Carbine. While Ray and I were blasting away at floating cans with the rifles, Charlie was shooting turtles in the lake with a .357 caliber revolver with a four-inch barrel. I didn't know it then, but I now know that I was witnessing some of the best handgun shooting I would ever see in my lifetime. This guy was popping the heads off snapper turtles with a friggin handgun at some thirty-plus yards! Charlie was without a doubt an extraordinary shot.

After he had made a dent in the lake's snapper population, Charlie gave Ray and me some introductory instructions on the sight picture of his revolver. We sat by the lake as he lectured us on the safety and correct use of the weapon. Now, I don't know about Ray, but a strange sensation ran up and down my spine as I watched Charlie admiringly fondle the pistol. As he ran his fingers over the pistol and taught us what each part's function was, his eyes seared straight through us, as if we weren't even there and he was looking beyond us into a destiny that my young, naive mind couldn't even begin to comprehend.

A few months later I would realize what was on Charlie's mind that day. Up until this point in my sheltered country existence, my life was never put in jeopardy. But that day with Charlie, I had unknowingly gazed into one of the deepest and darkest secrets of the Grim Reaper. His ever-changing identity.

It is impossible to know exactly where he's hiding or even when he's ready to reveal himself. He can lurk behind the eyes of a loved one, or deep inside a stranger's soul. He can come upon you at any hour of the day he desires. There's only one thing about him that you can bet on. One day, when you least expect it, he will spring forth in a last accounting for the precious time you've had on earth. So spend your time well, my friend. Try not to concern yourself over his whereabouts. It won't do you a damn bit of good. He will find each and every one of us when he's of the mind to.

On August 1, 1966, I was sitting on top of an old green John Deere tractor in a hay field near Katy, Texas. Uncle Billy called the ancient machine "Poppin' Johnny" because of the way the motor would run a few rough strokes and then backfire. With the loud popping came a shooting flame and puff of black smoke up the exhaust directly in front of the driver's seat. Then the old tractor would jerk as if was gasping for air before running the next few strokes and repeating the whole noisy process again.

I was holding onto the teeth-rattling steering wheel for dear life as I made my rounds on the tough old ride. I was raking up rows of Coastal Bermuda hay to be baled on the following day. It was a pretty summer day to be in the field working. Not a cloud in the sky. As the sun shined down on my fifteen-year-old face, I looked up from the hay rows to watch the enormous black crows flying in and out of the oak trees that edged the field.

On most of these summer days, Uncle Billy drove me out to Poppin' Johnny in his bone-jarring old Ford pickup and just dropped me off. He'd head off to another pasture to tend to the cattle and I'd be there all day long by myself, just raking up rows of hay. I loved it. It was a little lonely in a way, but I always had the crows to keep me company. Sometimes the crazy sons of bitches would even become downright playful with me. I'd be minding my own business, plugging away on Poppin' Johnny, unable to hear a damn thing over the straining motor. Then out of the corner of my eye I'd catch a glimpse of something overhead and look up just in time to see one of the screeching black bastards diving down on me like a World War II bomber. They never even came close to putting a claw on me, but they did make the day interesting.

I had been going about my business of raking and dodging dive-bombers for several hours when I looked up over the tractor and saw Uncle Billy's Ford coming. I knew something was up because he was driving hell-bent for leather through the middle of the field and I had never seen him do that before. I throttled Poppin' Johnny back and pulled it to a stop. When my uncle pulled up and got out of the Ford I could tell by the look on his face there was trouble, big trouble.

Uncle Billy by nature is an easygoing, tall, lanky Texas cattleman. He's one of those salt-of-the-earth men who doesn't get rattled by natural disasters or even a friggin nuclear holocaust. He believes in God Almighty and the life-giving power of the soil. And if his own sure-footed firmness wasn't enough, he compounded it by marrying an Osage Indian lady who is the epitome of calmness. So when I saw the alarmed look on this pillar of stone's face, I knew the worst of nightmares had happened.

Uncle Billy stepped out of his truck and took long, urgent strides over to the side of the tractor. He looked up at me and said, "Boy, come on down from there and get on in the truck. You gotta go over to Ray's house and stay with him." I protested that I hadn't finished turning all of the hay over into rows yet. But he waved it off and said it was a matter of no importance right now. I climbed on down from the tractor and got into the truck. It wasn't until we had driven across the field and turned onto a gravel road headed to the ranch that he got the gumption up to tell me why Ray needed me to come stay with him.

On this particular beautiful Texas day, while I had been enjoying the company of the black bombers in the hay field, Charlie was in the process of fulfilling a twisted fate known only to him and his Beast. Unleashed, the sinister Beast within Charlie took him on one of the goriest bloody murdering sprees in our country's history. Charlie Whitman had crawled up into a tower on the University of Texas campus in Austin and entered history as the first mass murderer and terrorist recorded in the United States. He had forever been transformed into the infamous "Texas Tower sniper."

And give the devil his due, as if this wasn't bad enough, Charlie committed more unspeakable transgressions that would permanently mar Ray, and break my young heart as well. On the same day, before leaving his residence and firing his first shot from the tower, Charlie used a large, razor-sharp hunting knife to horrifically murder his mother and his wife. Our beloved Kathy had been violently ripped from our hearts forever.

Texas lawmen eventually broke through Whitman's deadly blazing fusillade of lead and made their way up the stairs, where the insane killer had barricaded himself in a defensive position on top of the campus tower. In what could only be described as the most terrifying close-quarter gun battle in Austin's history, Whitman was taken out. He had murdered sixteen innocent people and wounded another thirty-one individuals during his ninety-six-minute terrorization of the University of Texas campus. The majority of Charlie's killing and maiming had been accomplished with uncanny marksmanship, using a semiautomatic .30 caliber M1 Carbine. For all I know, it could have been the same weapon that Charlie had taught Ray and me to shoot a few months prior.

When I arrived home from the hay field, I saw that the Leissner house was surrounded by news-media assholes. I had never been to a full-fledged circus, but I imagined it couldn't have much over the show I was witnessing around Ray's home. There were television cameras and monitors with flashing lights set up all along the perimeter of the residence. Talk about circle the wagons in your own defense. A microscopic mite couldn't have gotten through those bloodthirsty buzzards.

I got Ray on the phone. We made plans for him to sneak out his bedroom window and meet me in the tree house we had built between our houses years ago. It was the same tree house that we had watched Kathy and Charlie's wedding reception from a couple of years earlier, the beginning of their new life together. From this same tree house we now watched what for all practical purposes would be the death of the Leissner family.

My little buddy would never be the same. A stagnant sadness would linger in his eyes for years to come. A kid once bubbling with life fell subdued by a tragedy that he would carry with him the rest of his life. The deplorable, gut-wrenching event left Ray drifting in a tortured existence for quite some time. Although years later he would start smiling and laughing again on the outside, you knew that his soul would always be permanently scarred on the inside. He hurt, and I hurt for him.

A subsequent autopsy of Whitman's body revealed a tumor in his brain the size of a walnut. On the fringes of adult conversations, Ray and I would later listen to family and friends as they talked about Charlie's history of seeing a shrink. Evidently he had told the doctor that he had terrible headaches that were so maddening in force they made him want to kill huge numbers of people. Some folks tried to blame the whole thing on the unchecked tumor. Others said Charlie just wanted to be famous. Ray and I sat there stoically listening to all of this adult bullshit, which attempted to rationalize the unknown. We didn't know what to think about the whys or what-ifs. What we did know was that we were extremely lucky to be alive.

A few years later the madness continued to take its toll. Mr. and Mrs. Leissner divorced and went their separate ways. Oddly enough, as an adult, Ray would move to Austin and make it his home.

Charlie had once given me one of his Marine utility caps as a token of our friendship. It had his name and rank stenciled in black ink on the inside of the bill. Before the Austin massacre, it was one of my most cherished boyhood treasures. It had come from my former hero. After the murders, my parents quietly crept into my room one night while I was sleeping. I haven't seen the Marine cap since. To this day when I ask my folks what they did with the cap they shake their heads in silence. In fact, since that fateful day in 1966, my folks have never spoken the name of Charles Whitman in my presence. I really believe they thought that because Charlie was once my boyhood idol, I would somehow pattern my life after him. It was as if they were scared that he could somehow influence me from beyond the grave.

Three years later I joined the U.S. Army and volunteered for Vietnam. My parents had a hard time dealing with my decision. Like most folks, they wanted their son to go to college and dodge the war along with the hundreds of thousands of other chickenshits. But I was young and restless and had obviously inherited my Texas Ranger forefathers' spirit of adventure. And the call of a war halfway around the world intrigued me. And you want to know the crazy part of all this? I would continue to cheat death, and I would do it as a government-employed assassin. I would become a sniper on the Fifth Infantry's recon hunt-and-kill teams. The name and call signs of the teams? The Grim Reapers. I kid you not. Ain't life (and death) a kick in the ass?

In Vietnam, and later on the Arizona-Mexican border, I would learn a lot more about the Reaper and his intended purpose. I came to understand that as the Lord's Angel of Death, the Reaper was actually a good rather than an evil. Sometimes, given the right situation and circumstances, he's even a welcome relief from the woes of our sometimes afflicted existence. But the one deliverer of death I came to know and despise was the Beast, that sick, tiny portion of Lucifer that resides in the darkest, deepest center of our souls. The Beast is a wickedness that can spring forth in an evil rage if we allow his chains to be broken. He can be triggered by war, mental illness, physical pain, and a whole host of other miseries. The Beast lies dormant within each and every one of us. And believe me, you'll rue the day he breaks the chains if you allow him to do so.

I met my own Beast and successfully grappled with him in Vietnam. But even in the name of personal survival in the jungle, I regret having been forced to view his disgusting presence within my own soul. Since the war, there's not a day that goes by that I don't check and reinforce the chains I've got the bastard enclosed with. I sincerely pray that you never have to meet your own Beast.

Now, to answer your gnawing question, the answer is a definite and resounding NO. I did not intentionally set out to follow the insane footsteps of a young Marine I once knew by becoming a sniper in Vietnam. That was for the most part the U.S. government's decision, not mine. But by the same token, I believe that there may be some truth in what Darwin once said: You are a creation of your own environment. And between Texas, Vietnam, and the U.S.-Mexican border, I reckon I've been created into an old government agent with some pretty good tales to tell.

As it says in Matthew 13:39, "The enemy who sowed them is the devil [the Beast], the harvest is the end of the age, and the reapers are the angels."

2

The Quickening

For everyone shall be seasoned with fire.

—MARK 9:49

There is no hunting like the hunting of man, and those who have hunted armed men long enough and liked it, never care for anything else thereafter.

—ERNEST HEMINGWAY

LIKE MANY PRIOR GENERATIONS of young men, I was defined and shaped by war. I'm not crying about it, that's just the way things worked out. In 1969, I was eighteen years old when I enlisted in the U.S. Army and volunteered for Vietnam. Why volunteer? Because being a spectator was not my idea of experiencing life. It was a "go for it" John Wayne attitude with me. In the late '60s everybody was jabbering about why we should or shouldn't be in Southeast Asia. Everybody talked about it, but few were willing to answer their country's call to arms. As a youngster I wanted to see it for myself. It was an attitude that would catapult me mentally from an eighteen-year-old kid to a forty-year-old adult in a Mach speed two-year time warp.

As a kid in the woods of southeast Texas, I was never really good at anything in particular, with the exception of hunting. This was a skill that was about to be honed and fine-tuned in Vietnam, where I was trained as a sniper by the 101st Airborne Division in Phu Bai. After my training I was placed on an LRRP (long-range reconnaissance) hunt-and-kill team with the Fifth Infantry Division operating out of Quang Tri Province in the I Corps near the Demilitarized Zone (DMZ). The DMZ between North and South Vietnam was supposed to be the border separating the communist regime in Hanoi from the American-supported money-hungry puppet democracy in Saigon. It would be the first of two borders that I would risk my life defending. I would come to know and understand these invisible political barriers as the "Reaper's Lines."

The elite Vietnam-era recon hunt-and-kill teams were unique in U.S. military history. Such teams were never used before or after Vietnam. Our Fifth Infantry six-man teams included rangers, recondos, jungle experts, snipers, special forces, and a mercenary who was attempting to regain his U.S. citizenship after previously hiring out to foreign governments. In 1970, we even had CIA spooks mixed into the Reaper teams.

With great stealth we performed death-defying hunt-and-kill missions neutralizing particular targets for the CIA. Such tight-lipped operations were ordered by the Military Assistance Command Vietnam (MACV) compound in Quang Tri, where we often met with the spooks for pre- and post-mission briefings. Outside of the spooks themselves, we were probably the most deadly assembled group of specialists in all of Nam at the time. So I reckon I would have to say in all honesty that my first job with the government was that of an extremely low-paid assassin.

It was a hell of a year. It's often said by combat vets of all wars, "I wouldn't take a million bucks for the experience, but then again, I wouldn't take a million bucks to go back!" And I reckon that's a fair statement.

They talk about the eye of the tiger. Let me tell you that ain't a pimple on a fat man's ass when you've been in the mouth of the Beast. I've seen the blackest of nights in the jungle become fully illuminated with muzzle flashes from screaming men in panicked fits of pure, raging, unleashed barbarism. I've seen the mind-boggling carnage that Cobra gunships with their Gatling guns and rapid-fire rockets can rain down on human flesh and bones. I've seen the Reaper boldly walking triumphant over smoldering, blood-soaked battlefields. He only paused to tally his only reason for existence: the body count.

Because we had special warfare skills, the CIA tried to recruit Reaper team members to stay as civilian mercenaries toward the end of our tour in Nam. Along with the one we had on our team, we knew the other mercs because we shared the same chopper pad for insertions into the jungle from our firebase. They were an extremely sadistic, gruesome group, virtual walking representatives of pure hell who had sold their souls to war and the Beast. The repulsive part was that most of them actually enjoyed the killing. Any sane soldier knows that the taking of a human life is no cause for celebration. Although it is a necessary evil of war, the effort to justify it is a catalyst for daily battles in your mind. Some eventually lose these battles and themselves in their struggle to cope with the weight of the Beast. If you ever must take a life, it will rightly haunt you until you meet your maker. It's nothing to be proud of.

On July 28, 1970, my last year as a teenager, our Reaper team was running a CIA-directed op near Khe Shan. As the ever-present slimy leeches sucked our life juices, we crept down a humid jungle trail in chest-high elephant grass. We were doing just fine when, just like turning off a radio, the birds ceased chirping and the animals stopped moving off our flanks through the jungle. And then it was too late to do a goddamn thing about it.

We ended up facing off with a large contingent of Ho Chi's best NVA (North Vietnamese Army) soldiers. Since I was the first on point, my eyes snapped into an immediate death lock with the NVA closest to me. We both knew it would go to the one with the quickest reflexes. A trigger squeeze later, basic survival instinct had taken hold as smoke filled my wide-open eyes and gunpowder burned my nostrils. The NVA lost. What happened next, my insane childhood Marine firearms instructor could have identified with.

After Ho Chi's soldier kissed mud, my basic instinct to simply survive surrendered to the raging Beast that we all have inside of us. The son of a bitch didn't hesitate in unleashing hell on the next two NVA soldiers in line on the trail. And I, the human being outside of the Beast, never again looked into my enemy's eyes before pulling the trigger. From now on, he was just a target wearing a bright, shining red star on his pith helmet.

During the forty-five-minute firefight that followed, between our Reaper team and the death-spitting Cobra Gatling guns that we called in to keep our asses from being massacred, the CIA body count would later claim somewhere between eighty and a hundred NVA soldiers. Amid the dead and dying, there were bright trails of flowing blood, bloody air bubbles, and human tissue breaking in all directions through the elephant grass after the smoke cleared. I went from nineteen to forty years old in one single day. And in that same day, I made more promises to God than I can ever live up to.

Now, you would think that such a high number of kills in a single encounter would bother you. No. What bothers you, what haunts you, what replays in your mind every day for the rest of your life, is this: the first one. I looked into the window of this guy's soul, and in the suspended pump of one heartbeat, I saw surprise, hate, and a resignation to his life. It is hard to precisely explain what you see in a man's eyes when he knows he's in the moment of his last conscious act on earth. To this day I still see the guy's round face and wonder who he *really* was. A loving father, an artist, or maybe even a devoted schoolteacher? Did he leave a family behind? Did his kids turn out exceptionally bad because I denied them their father? I reckon these haunting questions are my penance with the Lord for pulling that trigger.

If any good can come out of our continual destruction of each other as human beings, it is this: The war burned into my brain an unsurpassed appreciation for life. At times we were so tired, so scared, so wet, so completely miserable from leeches, dysentery, and gut-wrenching fear that death was a valid option. When you've reached the point of saving your last grenade as a quick out for yourself (torture was not an option), you've learned to accept Old Man Reaper as the

Lord's guide to a better place. Once you've been to the extreme hopeless bottom of humanity, and if you're able to rise above it all and somehow survive, there isn't much that can ever hurt you again. To explain it in more eloquent words, the rest is pure fucking gravy.

I returned from Vietnam to Texas in 1971 and married my highschool sweetheart. I entered college but left after a couple of semesters because of the ever-present war protesters and my unexplainable, driving unrest. Over the next three years I rousted about working fifteen different jobs, mostly as a roughneck on drilling rigs or a heavy-equipment operator. Nothing seemed to fit. Everything was so out of place. If it hadn't been for my beautiful wife, I probably wouldn't have amounted to much more than a diseased-liver barfly on his way to an early grave in the backwoods of Texas.

Betty and I had met in the rural high school we both attended in Fort Bend County. She was a blue-eyed, blonde, farm-raised beauty with a constant, sincere smile bubbling from her face. Her eyes always sparkled with a fondness and zest for life that could make even the grayest winter days bright. She carried a lively bounce in her step and a happy tune in her voice. In fact, her speech was more like a soothing coo that washed all over me and put me at peace. These were qualities that would prove essential to our young marriage upon my return from Vietnam.

Every job I tried seemed too boring, and every day drudged mundanely by. I was starving for something emotionally, but couldn't quite put my finger on it. It was similar to constantly drifting around in a slow-motion haze. I had heard and read about other combat vets going through similar scenarios. Some shrinks said that we had a "death wish" because we carried the guilt of our dead buddies on our shoulders. Bullshit! You can ask almost any combat vet from World War II, Korea, or Vietnam, and he will tell you, "Hey, I'm sorry Joe got killed. I feel really bad for his family. I think about him a lot." But deep down inside we're all silently glad it was Joe and not us. Maybe some survivor's guilt goes with it. But a "death wish"? No way. I don't buy that crap.

No, I kept searching for the answer to the restlessness and finally figured it out fifteen jobs and three years later. It was the insatiable adrenaline rush ignited by "the hunt"! I missed the thrill of being on the edge between life and death. When you go into combat as an eighteen-year-old kid and live on the edge, day and night, you get hooked on the adrenaline. In a way it's comparable to being a heroin addict or a crackhead, I reckon. You've developed a quenchless thirst. It's not about the killing or dying. It's about the excitement of hunting and, sometimes, even being hunted.

So after coming to grips with my "addiction," I had to decide how I was going to make a living without necessarily doing something stupid like becoming a zombie-like merc for the CIA. I wrestled around with it for a while and decided on law enforcement. But where in law enforcement could I use my Vietnam skills of tracking and hunting men? From all the places it could have come, the answer announced itself from the wall of a post office. No, not bounty-hunting off reward posters. But something that in a strange kind of way would prove to be similar.

The U.S. Border Patrol, a federal law enforcement agency with a structured paramilitary-inherited background, was looking for recruits to become agents in defense of our frontiers. Their duties included "patrolling the U.S.-Mexican border and tracking and arresting illegal aliens discovered crossing the border." I would later learn that aliens were just the tip of the iceberg down south on the frontera. Dope smugglers, burglars, border bandits, homicide suspects, communists, and violent fugitives from all countries and agencies were a few of the bad guys on the list of violators a Border Patrol agent may encounter during his day. Although those criminals weren't mentioned in the employment flier, they would be the ones I would come to prefer to hunt over the regular illegal aliens who were just crossing to feed their families.

Other than going from a jungle to a desert, this was perfect for me, the way I saw it. It was what I had been trained to do. It was to be my life. At the time I didn't know it, but for the next twenty-five years I would hunt and track criminals up and down the southern border for the U.S. government.

I was sent to the U.S. Border Patrol Academy in Los Fresnos, Texas, in November of 1974. I was pleasantly surprised when I learned that about 50 percent of our 160-man class were Vietnam veterans. Now, one can expect to have a lot of infantry soldiers, better known as grunts, going into this line of work. But I was surprised to learn that we also had helicopter pilots and even a jet-fighter jockey from the war in our class. Maybe I had underestimated this adrenaline-junkie theory of mine!

At the academy we studied the Spanish language and both criminal and immigration laws, practiced the use of firearms and hand-to-hand combat, and ran for miles every day wearing spit-shined combat boots. During the five-and-a-half-month training, the BP instructors managed to squeeze in a two-week training exercise down on the Rio Grande near McAllen. They bused us down and detailed several trainees out to each veteran BP agent for night patrolling along the famous old Rio.

It was just after sundown when two other young cherries and I got hooked up with our training agent near the edge of the muddy, swirling tributary that divided the "haves" of the north from the "have nots" of the south. Within the first hour on duty, two events happened that foreshadowed both the fatal and the funny sides of my infatuation with my soon-to-be mistress, the Mexican border.

First, the two idiot trainees I was with ran into each other in the dark on the way to their assigned surveillance locations. After scaring the shit out of each other, they drew down, screaming and threatening to kill one another if one of them didn't drop the gun that he was precariously aiming at the other. Thank God for small favors. Just before the bullet swap got under way the cherries figured out they were both wearing the same goddamn uniform! The best I can say about this fiasco is that both trainees were recent college graduates and not Nam vets.

Second, I went out to take a dump near the edge of the river and a group of five illegal aliens swam across the river, got out, and walked straight into my squatted bowel-release position before I could get my new green jeans pulled up. So with one hand holding my pants up somewhere between my knees and dick, and the other hand palming a .357 Magnum trained on the Mexicans, I paraded them over to my training officer like a young bird dog proudly fetching a duck for his master. The training honcho studied my first-ever arrest scenario before proclaiming in a long Texas drawl, "Boy, if this is any indication of your future, ya'll got a hell of a career ahead of ya'll in this here outfit." Without a doubt, that Texas Border Patrol agent was prophetic. I was about to have the time of my life!

I graduated from the Border Patrol Academy in March of 1975. Betty and I were stationed in Douglas, Arizona, where we would remain for the next five years. As far as border towns go, back then Douglas was a clean, quiet, friendly town of about 15,000 people that relied on the copper mining industry. The town is located about 120 miles southeast of Tucson in Cochise County. This part of the border was to be my training ground. It was here that I would learn about the Mexican people, their culture, and their values. It was here that I would learn how to survive the next twenty-five years of my federal law enforcement career.

"Red" Smith was one of the agents who graduated from the Border Patrol Academy and came to Douglas with me. At a towering six feet, five inches, the twenty-eight-year-old redheaded gringo was covered with freckles from head to toe. He had been a uniformed police officer near the Mexican border in El Centro, California, before coming on duty with the U.S. Border Patrol. We seemed to get along pretty well and I learned quite a lot from Red about the frontera and law enforcement in general.

Red and I were partnered up one cold, dark winter's night during February of 1976. We had been assigned an area on the border just west of the old Phelps Dodge copper-smelting operation near Douglas. For a Border Patrol agent, the smelter provided both a blessing and a curse. The bad part was the ever-present foul air you were forced to inhale. The gray smoke left a sulphur taste in your mouth comparable to sucking on the wrong end of a matchstick all day. The good part was that during the night, the Phelps Dodge train that circled the perimeter of the operation's slag pile would continually dump these two- or three-ton buckets of bright orange, glowing liquid ore over the hundred-foot-high waste bed. It lit up the frontera's darkness with a brilliant, burning flow of manmade "lava" that could be seen for miles and miles.

On this particular evening, Red and I were sitting on a trail just north of the border to ambush a group of marijuana backpackers we had information on. About two in the morning we decided to pull the plug on the operation and go 10-7 (off duty) for the night. For whatever reason unknown to us, it looked like the mules weren't going to make it across the line that night.

Red and I left our surveillance spot in the brush and started to walk south on the trail to check it for tracks in the event somebody had skirted around our position. It was a pitch-dark night with no moon and not much help from the cloud-covered stars. I took the lead on the trail as Red followed me within an arm's length. I was armed with my government-issued .357 revolver and a .12 gauge pump shotgun loaded with buckshot. Red had the same issued .357 pistol, but for a shoulder weapon he was carrying an outlawed .30 caliber M1 Carbine with a thirty-round banana magazine for extra firepower.

It was against official Border Patrol policy for us to have the M1 Carbine. Now, you may ask, why would we want or need to carry such a weapon? Well, have you ever heard the military phrase "peace through superior firepower"? Or how about, "If he's got a .22 I want a .44"? It's all about having the upper hand on your opponent in a gunfight.

Just ask former Border Patrol agent Jesse Shaw. He had been on duty in California on the border a few years earlier when he walked into the middle of ten determined dope smugglers who were armed with .45s, .38s, and 9mm handguns. When the shootout started Jesse took cover behind a sand hill. He initially started blazing away at the bad guys with his government-issued .357 Magnum revolver. The smugglers took their sweet time about closing in on Shaw. After all, the odds were ten to one in their favor. They waited and cautiously counted the lawman's shots. After Shaw had busted six rounds downrange, the smugglers figured to rush him when he was reloading. When they made their rush on poor ol' Jesse, they didn't count on him carrying an unauthorized .30 caliber M1 Carbine with a thirty-round banana clip. Out of ten outlaws, five got picked up by the Reaper for final delivery that night. No matter what official policy says, it all comes down to firepower and survival in the end.

As Red and I walked south on the desert trail I began to hear the faint sound of rocks being kicked. I quietly stopped and reached back in the dark, touching Red on his chest as he trailed in close behind me. I whispered to him that we had movement on the trail directly south and out in front of us. Red and I listened to the noise for about thirty seconds and both decided it must be cattle moving about in the brush.

We started to walk up the trail again when it hit me like a ton of bricks! I stopped and pulled Red to his knees with me on the trail. It had just dawned on me that this particular rancher had moved his cattle to a different pasture the month prior. By this time the kicking of rocks turned into definite heavy footsteps and the mules were walking right down our throats. They were no more than two or three yards from us on the trail when we stood up to challenge them. We were so close to the bastards that I could actually hear them gasping and wheezing from the strain of the heavy contraband they were humping on their backs.

"Halt, U.S. Border Patrol!" was about all I got out of my mouth before the smugglers capped the first round and all hell broke loose. The first shooter was so close to me that his muzzle flash temporarily blinded me when the round went precariously zipping between Red and me. My heart started pounding so hard that I could feel the building pressure and hear the thumping in my ears. The adrenaline started rushing and it came as a temporary relief to such a junkie. It felt great! Back in the saddle again! Okay, calm down. Feed off the adrenaline and think. Be cool. While these guys are losing their marbles and blowing holes in the dark, you have to ride the adrenaline flow and think!

The mules had started the gunfight and Red and I were determined to instruct these assholes in the error of their ways. I opened up first with the .12 gauge pump and tore up every bit of rock- and mesquite-infected real estate the scumbags were standing on. I emptied my shotgun by pumping five buckshot rounds in rapid succession in the direction of the muzzle flash that had blinded me. I heard the mules screaming and breaking brush as Red took my lead position with his M1 Carbine. As I stepped aside we took several more rounds of incoming fire from the retreating mules.

As soon as I was out of his field of fire, Red started warming up his carbine's barrel. At the same moment, I was dropping the now empty shotgun and pulling my revolver, and the smelter train made a timely delivery of glowing orange slag. In the instant of fullest illumination, I glanced at a weird, twisted side profile of Red's face. The freakiest things happen in gunfights. You sometimes see a particular defined vision that sticks in your memory or subconscious years later. No matter how many years may go by, it's as though it happened yesterday.

Red's expression was reminiscent of a guy with a hard-on at the moment of deepest penetration. In a way what I saw gave me confidence and a positive attitude that we'd win this little scrape. Red was smiling in sheer ecstasy! I swear to God I had never seen anything like it in all the firefights I had been in during the war. The son of a bitch had this wicked-ass smirk on his face as he was ripping through his thirty-round banana magazine. His "no fear" face was downright comforting. It made me feel warm and fuzzy all over.

I started cranking revolver rounds off at the bodies now brightly silhouetted by the orange molten slag being dumped by the Phelps train. When Red ran out of ammo for his carbine, he jerked his revolver and went to work with it. We kept putting lead downrange until the incoming fire had subsided. We stopped to reload our revolvers and could hear the mules breaking brush as they headed off toward Mexico, whimpering and groaning from their wounds.

We called for backup on our walkie-talkies and waited in the dark for about five minutes before we moved forward on the trail. When we were sure the mules had fled the area, we used our flashlights to search for narcotics and/or bodies. Abandoned on the trail we found one smoking revolver and six hundred pounds of marijuana in burlap bags. We piled the dope up like a wall and planned to use it like a mini-fort in the event the assholes wanted to reload and make another run at us before our backup arrived. But from what we could hear of their crying and moaning as they scurried south, Red and I were pretty sure they would be licking their wounds down south instead of coming back for more.

After backup arrived we searched the area and found a couple of blood trails headed south into Mexico. The revolver we had seized with the dope had a half-spent cylinder, which definitely indicated that shooter had been hard hit. It's just a fact that a bad guy isn't going to drop his still partially loaded weapon in a gunfight unless he's going down.

A few days later the local DEA Office in Douglas got information from one of their informants in Mexico that confirmed our blood trails. The informant said that the Mexican Mafia had buried two mules on the Sonora-Chihuahua border a couple of days after the gunfight. The mules had been shot up pretty bad with .12 gauge buckshot and .30 caliber rounds. I was kind of sorry to hear that the dickheads died, but I took comfort in knowing that Red and I didn't start the lead-swapping rodeo. It was their decision, and a bad decision it was. They knew damn good and well who we were when they went up against us.

What did I learn from my first gunfight as a federal agent? Well, I learned that as usual the REMFs are wrong and the grunts know what they need in the field to get the job done. What's a REMF? Well let me back up and gently explain the term and its origin to you. Without sugar-coating it too much, a REMF (pronounced "remph") is a Rear Echelon Mother Fucker. In Vietnam they were found in the MACV compound headquarters, where they were safe in their bomb- and bullet-proof cement bunkers. Did you know that for every combat soldier in the jungle in Vietnam, there were eight support personnel (REMFs) in the rear? No wonder we lost the war.

You probably know a few REMFs yourself. In civilian lingo they would probably be known as the Monday-morning quarterbacks, the guys who want to know why you didn't do this or that when you got ambushed. One of my favorite answers was always, "Well, it was pitch-dark, I was trying to save my ass, and sir, I don't think I recall seeing you out there." It seemed to shut them up most of the time.

You can also find REMFs in Washington, D.C., in all of the administrative offices of each federal law enforcement agency. These are the guys and gals who never have been on the receiving end of a gun barrel or angry fist. They're the ones who send out policy and directives like the one that said we shouldn't have been carrying our life-saving .30 caliber M1 Carbine. They would rather see the field agent get whacked than violate a smartly typed piece of paper titled "POLICY."

Now, don't get me all wrong. I understand that somebody has got to captain the ship and do the paperwork. I'm not completely against management, especially if it is good management. The thing about the REMFs that rubs me the wrong way is that they don't take enough, if any, input from the agents in the field who put their lives on the line every day to enforce the laws of the land. We're the ones who should decide what type of equipment we need, not some needle-dick paper jockey riding a desk in D.C.—especially a needle-dick idiot who has never been in the field.

Years later, when I would be serving as a special agent with the U.S. Customs Service, I would see a first-hand example of such idiocy. I had just been issued a company-owned weapon that was brand spanking new, a Colt AR-15 semiautomatic carbine in .223 caliber. It was perfect for border enforcement, being that we had been going up against a lot of smugglers armed with AK-47 assault rifles at that time.

I had been issued the Colt carbine for about a year when the REMFs ordered me to turn it in. When I questioned the directive I was told that we were being issued new .223 Steyr Aug automatic rifles. I, and a lot of other good experienced field agents, wanted to know why. We had brand new AR-15s and even some of their fully automatic sisters, the M16s. Both weapons were highly effective. They had been proven in combat in Vietnam, and not only do U.S. forces still carry similar versions today, but so do most other law enforcement organizations in the country.

On the other hand, the Steyr Aug is prone to jamming and other malfunctions. And any combat vet can tell you that the Steyr Aug has no target acquisition. Which, simply put, means that you have to take the Steyr Aug down from your shoulder to reload it. With the AR-15 or M16 you can reload it from the shoulder position while you watch your target. Try taking your weapon down from your shoulder to reload during a real firefight and see how quick you lose sight of your opponent. The next thing you know the guy has flanked you and is blowing the side of your head off.

I asked a few more questions about the transition to the Steyr Augs and learned that we were exchanging two or three Colts for every one Aug. Sounds fishy? You bet it does. It smacked of somebody high up getting a kickback from the Steyr Aug manufacturer in Austria, or the company that imported them into the U.S. Hmm. Now let's think about this a minute. U.S. Customs is responsible for the enforcement of all weapons that are imported into or exported from the U.S.

It was also rumored that one of the reasons we were given the Steyr Augs was that the head honcho REMF, the U.S. Customs Service commissioner at the time, was into Steven Seagal movies. And yes, you've probably already guessed it. Seagal, who allegedly had been dubbed an honorary U.S. Customs officer by the commissioner, had recently done a movie in which he cut down a lot of bad guys with a Steyr Aug on the ever so influential silver screen. The commissioner thought it was the neatest state-of-the-art .223 he had ever seen, and the rest is history.

You the taxpayer pay for such lunacy, and we the field agents suffer under it. This is just one example of wasted government money and field decisions being implemented from REMFs, some two thousand miles away, who don't have a clue about what it's like in the mud-and-blood thick of it all. Over the next twenty-five years I would witness some unbelievable bureaucratic bullshit. But let's pull the reins in a little before I get too far ahead of the story.

In 1978, as the learning process continued, my first official encounter with the FBI taught me what Hoover's boys were all about. I had been lying in the brush one night on surveillance near the border fence about one mile east of Douglas. The Douglas City Police Department had been having a lot of horrific home invasions and burglaries in the Douglas neighborhoods just north of my location. The tracks from the previous robberies indicated that the perpetrators were illegal-alien criminal types entering from Mexico.

It was about 9:00 p.m. when I heard southbound footsteps on the trail where I was sitting at the base of a dark thicket of thorny mesquites and cactus. I stood up and turned my flashlight on the suspects as they neared me. They were crouching in the dark as they approached. There were two guys dressed in dark clothing with bulging white pillowcases over their shoulders. They froze when I put the light on them and announced my challenge.

After ordering them to drop their stolen loot I observed something that made the hair on my neck snap to parade attention. I guess they figured they had come too far, and risked too much, to break the fruits of their crime on the rocks. They gently placed the pillowcases on the ground at their feet and stood up brandishing eight-inch blades in my face. Their actions indicated that I was about to be disposed of in short order so that they could proceed uninhibited in furtherance of their criminal shenanigans. They thought of me as a mere short-term inconvenience, a Border Patrolman to be whacked on their way home into the protective bosom of old Mexico. The border fence and their freedom was no more than fifty yards away. The adrenaline rush rejuvenated my will to survive as the first one made his move.

To stick or slash me, he had to cross five or six yards to close the distance. As soon as I saw the glint of the blade I jerked my revolver from its holster. He couldn't see it until I shoved it forward next to my flashlight. When he saw the pistol he hesitated. I couldn't really see his eyes but I knew the son of a bitch was sizing me up. He was trying to decide from my demeanor and voice if I had any balls. He was rolling the dice in his mind, wondering if I had the guts to pull the trigger. Up until this moment, he still wasn't sure.

The bandit again started to advance at which time I purposely and slowly cocked the hammer on my revolver. I wanted him to hear it. I wanted him to think about it. To think about his impending death, his own mortality. The never-ending darkness. I wanted him to know without any doubt that the cocking of the hammer would be the last thing he would ever hear on God's green earth if he kept coming. It worked.

When the asshole froze I heard him suck in his breath and hold it in rapt anticipation of his Armageddon. I ordered him in Spanish to drop the knife. The Mexican bandit was so petrified that his goddamn hand never moved from mid-air. The guy was as stiff as a resident mannequin in a New York City Macy's. Without moving any other muscles, the prick opened his fingers and the knife fell blade-first into the ground, ominously pointing the direction one of us was about to go.

After the scumbag got rid of the knife, I ordered him to take a couple of steps forward and lie face-down on the ground. One down and one to go. The second burglar was still standing about five yards down the trail brandishing his blade. He had been directly behind the first guy the whole time, which virtually placed him at the end of my gun barrel. After the way things had gone with his buddy, I only had to tell him one time to drop the blade and he complied. About now I thought things were looking up as far as controlling the situation. It's funny how things can get flipped around so quick!

The second outlaw dropped his blade and started to walk toward me as ordered. The only problem was that when I told him to stop he kept coming at me. At the same time, like they were synchronized into each other's heads, the first burglar jumped to his knees and dove for my legs. I took one step back and drop kicked the sorry prick like an NFL pro kicking a game-winning field goal. My combat boot caught him square in the face, causing him to belly-flop like a fat old toad with his legs and arms going toward the four corners of the earth.

By now the second guy had flanked me in the dark and had jumped on my back, putting his arm around my throat in a choke hold. With his other hand he grabbed my cocked revolver and tried to bend it from its forward-extended position back up toward my throat and face. While we fought for control of the hair-trigger revolver, the "toad" caught his breath and made another crawling effort for my legs. Well, things were looking pretty grim about now. The possibility flashed through my mind that Betty would be collecting my life insurance policy and some new tall, dark, handsome son of a bitch would be laying claim to my favorite rocking chair.

The official version of the fight would later read something like, "I used those self-defensive methods taught in the academy, and only the necessary force to subdue and arrest the suspects." Yeah, right! In other words, I lashed out in a frenzy with every ounce of strength I could muster to save my ass. I kicked the "toad" so hard and continuously that he would later be taken to the hospital with broken ribs that punctured his lungs. These two boys messed up when they woke my Beast up. It was just gonna get uglier and uglier.

Still struggling with the second asshole over the revolver, I decided the best move I could make was to give him what he wanted. I pulled my gun hand back toward both our heads and jerked my head hard to the side as I pulled the trigger hoping to catch him in the face. Miraculously the round missed him, but the concussion from the .357 did knock him loose. The Mexican bandit went flying off my back as I violently pivoted on both feet doing a 180-degree turn. With the revolver as an extension of my arm, the gun barrel caught the outlaw across the top of his skull, laying his scalp wide open. He bled like a stuck hog in a slaughterhouse. I couldn't tell you if he screamed or not because I was near deaf for several days after capping the Magnum so close to my head.

Later that evening both burglars were taken to the county hospital, where they were taped and sewn back together before being thrown into the Cochise County lockup. They were later convicted of numerous burglaries, and they each received about thirteen years in the Arizona state penitentiary for all the jobs they had pulled. As far as being charged for assault on a federal officer, namely me, let me tell you how that turned out.

Since the Border Patrol is part of the Department of Justice, it was the FBI's responsibility to investigate and secure prosecution of the burglars for assaulting a fed. But as a new kid on the block, I found that the investigation can be a two-edged blade. The FBI also investigates and prosecutes officers who violate civil rights of U.S. citizens and/or aliens from other countries.

A few days after I got my hearing back I was at home, off duty, when there was a knock on the front door. It was an FBI agent from Tucson. He told me he was investigating the burglars for assault on a fed and he would like to interview me about the fight. Not knowing much about federal investigations at this point in my somewhat young career as a patrol agent, I invited him in and offered him some coffee.

The agent told me that he would like to ask me some questions, at which time he started to advise me of my rights to remain silent and have counsel present. Naturally the bells rang and the lights flashed and I was pissed off to no end. Hey, what is going on? I had already been before a shooting review board at the chief BP agent's office in Tucson. After reviewing the facts of the shooting, the chief himself had told my union representative that I would have been justified in offing both of the scumbags.

And now I was being treated like a suspect for defending my own life while performing my federal duties of protecting our borders. Hey, people, are you folks home out there? Are you listening to what I'm saying is happening on your U.S.-Mexican border? The guys who are trying to keep you safe and enforce our laws are being treated like criminals. It's supposed to be the other way around! We're not the ones burglarizing your homes and eating your tax money up by riding the welfare rolls!

Needless to say, the burglars were never charged with assault on a federal agent that I'm aware of. The only convictions they received were from the Cochise County Attorney's Office for the burglaries. So it's kind of obvious that the FBI never really intended to go after them. How do I know that? Because years later as a special agent for the U.S. Customs Service, it was my responsibility to investigate and prosecute the assault of U.S. Customs Service inspectors and employees. And any time one of them was assaulted, no matter how slight, as long as he was in the performance of his duties we would prosecute those responsible to the full extent of the law. Why? Because in spite of its problems, the U.S. Customs Service did believe in enforcing the laws and taking care of our personnel. I believe it's a lesson the FBI would be well-served to learn.

During my five years of service with the Border Patrol I was in a couple of other shootings and numerous high-speed pursuits. The adrenaline kept me pumped, but I didn't care for being in uniform. I sucked up as many college hours as possible during my off-duty time, with a major in criminal investigations. When I had enough credits, and time in uniform, I applied to become a special agent in the anti-smuggling unit of the U.S. Immigration Service. I was accepted and spent the next seven years working undercover in Puerto Rico, the Caribbean Basin, and eventually back in Arizona.

During my tour in Puerto Rico I was detailed to the Cuban-Haitian Task Force when Castro dumped his prison garbage on us in 1980. I was one of many special agents who were sent to interview the Marielitos in an effort to differentiate the habitual from the petty criminals. Once we identified the badasses we shipped them to the federal pen in Atlanta, because they were deemed just too dangerous to be released on the American people.

These immigrants were the dregs of the civilized world. I'm sorry if you think I'm not sensitive enough on the Cuban issue. I admit having become somewhat callous over the years. But what else can you say about human beings who throw their own feces and feminine menstrual discharges at you when you walk in to interview them? It didn't matter if you were a federal agent or a civilian employee giving them assistance in finding a home. If you walked through the barracks in the performance of your sworn duties when the Cubans were pissed off, these animals would throw shit and blood at you! Hell, sometimes they weren't even pissed off, they just did it because they didn't like gringos.

Fifty percent of the Cubans I interviewed admitted to having been in prison for murder. About 25 percent said they were jailed for drugs, robbery, or theft. The remaining 25 percent claimed to have been held as political prisoners. But out of the ones claiming to be political, very few in fact were.

I was at the Task Force location at Fort Indiantown Gap, Pennsylvania, investigating a series of Cuban homicides, when the riots broke out. The Cubans were being housed in the barracks of the fort, where they were surrounded by barbwire perimeters and guarded by a handful of ill-prepared U.S. Army regulars. When the shit hit the fan, all available Immigration and Naturalization Service agents and U.S. Marshal deputies responded to assist the soldiers.

When we arrived at the skirmish line, which surrounded the barracks, it was a nasty worst-case scenario of total mayhem. The soldiers were fighting the Cubans with batons in an attempt to keep them from breaking out of the camp. The situation had gotten so far out of hand that the Army placed troop-carrier trucks behind the skirmish line to be used as ambulances for the soldiers. I was shocked to see how many injured soldiers were already being hauled off to the post hospital.

The agents and marshals were the only armed federal presence at the riot. We were spread out behind the soldiers to give them assistance as the situation deteriorated. And the way the riot was escalating, it looked like deadly force was imminent if we were to keep from losing the fort's armory to the Cubans. We were told that the Army regulars needed to hold the line for several hours until the 101st and 82nd Airborne Divisions arrived. The Army had wisely activated the Airborne gung-hos at the first inkling of the impending riot. But these troops were hundreds of miles away.

I was backing up some soldiers on the line when one of them was grabbed by a group of glazed-eyed screaming Cubans. The murderous maniacs drug the young soldier away from the skirmish line into the camp toward the barracks. The Cubans then encircled their victim and began to pulverize the lone soldier with their fists and feet. I pulled my weapon and got as close to the downed soldier as I could without leaving the line. It was then that I saw a demonical looking bastard take a long, sharp shank from beneath his shirt and start to move in on the young soldier for the kill. Without thinking about it, I did what had to be done.

I left the security of the skirmish line and ran dead center into the middle of the frenzied Cubans. I fired several rounds over their heads, catching them by surprise and moving them back away from their victim. I next aimed my revolver at the chest of the shank-yielding devil-eyed prick and growled in Spanish, "If he dies, you die!" The son of a bitch backed down. I kept my weapon trained on the guy with the shank as I bent over to recover the bleeding soldier.

I had successfully grabbed him by the collar of his fatigue shirt and had begun to drag him back toward the skirmish line when a sudden jarring sensation riveted my body. It was like an all-engulfing shock wave that washed over and all around me. A loud ringing in my ears wouldn't stop. Everything went into slow motion as a warm, flowing liquid covered my head and face. For no reason that my brain could comprehend, my legs had suddenly gone limp and failed me.

I remember being on my knees with my hands cupped around my revolver. As I looked down at my weapon, blood was flowing over it, filling my cupped hands. The last thing I remember was the sensation of being dragged by the scruff of my neck. Just before I blacked out I wondered where the Reaper was spending the evening.

When I regained consciousness I found myself sprawled among other bodies in the back of a troop carrier. A U.S. Army medic was cleaning the blood out of my eyes and off my face. In what seemed like a foreign language, although it was English, the medic explained to me that my scalp was severely lacerated and my brain was in a state of shock. Through the garble I was able to grasp that a group of armed agents had rescued me and the soldier. I mumbled something asking about the condition of the soldier. The medic told me the guy would probably live. Then I slipped back into never-never land.

The next time I woke up I was in an Army hospital on the fort. There were screaming, bloody bodies on gurneys all around me. Time didn't seem to matter. Everything was still going in slow motion. I obviously wasn't going anywhere and I really wasn't in any pain that I could tell. In fact, I couldn't feel anything, which is what I found peculiar about the whole thing. To this day I firmly believe that if you ever get beaten to death, you better pray to God that they start with some serious blows to your head. If they do, trust me on this because I know, you won't feel the rest of it!

After I was X-rayed, some Army doctor finally showed up and started sewing my scalp back together. As he stitched he explained that I had apparently been hit from behind with a pipe or possibly a large rock. He said that I had a fractured skull and a concussion. When he was done putting forty-odd stitches in, he told me to go to a hospital with better facilities the next day to be re-examined. He then released me to some agents who wheeled me out and drove me to my motel room, where I crashed on painkillers from the quack, combined with booze from my buddies.

The next day I went to a civilian hospital with a terrible headache and an itching on the top of my head that wouldn't stop. As the physician examined me it was obvious that he had to control his laughter concerning the sewing job the Army doctor had done. He told me he was going to have to re-crack the wound and re-stitch it because the military clown had sewn my hair inside of my scalp. I guess with all the bodies the Army quack was dealing with during the riots, he was a bit rushed.

I was told the next day that the riots had ceased once the 101st and 82nd Airborne had been flown in. The other agents told me that the paratroopers hit the skirmish line and kicked ass until the Cubans humbly retreated to their barracks like whipped dogs. As for me, I would be in recovery for a while and was sent back to Puerto Rico to finish my tour of duty with the anti-smuggling unit.

In 1982, Betty and I were shipped back stateside, taking a duty post in Phoenix, Arizona, with the Immigration and Naturalization Service (INS) anti-smuggling unit there. I worked a lot of undercover operations under one of the best special agents the INS has ever had. Jim Rayburn taught me more about undercover and criminal investigations than I would ever learn in all of the combined federal law enforcement academies I attended over the next twenty years.

Special Agent Jim Rayburn was born and raised in Texas on a cattle ranch. He was a red-headed, small-statured Irishman with fiery green eyes. Jim had also seen combat as a youngster in Vietnam. This Texas Mick was about ten years my senior and he, too, had begun his federal law enforcement service as a young Border Patrol agent in Arizona. He was known to be a tenacious agent who would accomplish any mission the chief tasked him with. When the chief needed someone to initiate a unit to combat the alien-smuggling business, Jim was the man he called on. Make no mistake about it, Jim Rayburn was the father of both the U.S. Border Patrol and the INS anti-smuggling programs.

For the next five years I trained and worked under Rayburn. Through informants, we would be introduced to members of alien-smuggling organizations and penetrate the conspiracy. Posing as alien smugglers, we would pick up loads of aliens from the U.S.-Mexican border in Arizona for transportation and delivery all over the United States. In essence, I reckon we were actually undercover "slave runners."

It was during these years that I learned working undercover can really mess your head up and take you off track from reality. You leave a little piece of your soul in each case as the years go by. When you end an investigation and "surface" from the role-playing, it's your secret. You don't want anyone trying to take a part of it from you. It's not to be shared with prying minds. You feel that if you keep the secret you won't have to leave the case and it can go on and on. You don't want to let go.

I remember I would come home from working weeks or months undercover and Betty would immediately start asking questions about where I had been and what I had been doing. I actually resented the questioning because I wanted to jealously guard this secret life of mine. I didn't want to share it with her. And that, my friends, is messed up! When an agent starts treasuring his undercover life more than his real life, it's time for him to get into some other type of investigations.

Based out of the anti-smuggling unit in Arizona, we traveled undercover anywhere from New York to Florida on the East Coast, and Washington to California on the West Coast. Acting under direction of the U.S. Attorney General's Office, we "sold" human cargo to businessmen, farmers, and ranchers in just about every state. After all of the money negotiations and payoffs were on tape, we arrested the modern-day slave traders and prosecuted them under federal laws for conspiring to smuggle illegal aliens. Our investigations made front-page news and brought on congressional inquiries concerning the alien-trafficking trade.

In the *Miami Herald* and *USA Today,* we splashed the words "peonage" and "indentured servitude" in an effort to dramatize the plight of the smuggled aliens. The only thing that came out of it was that Hoover's boys used it to grab some headlines for the FBI, claiming that should be their jurisdiction. Over the next twenty-five years I would see more of this jurisdictional bickering between all of the most powerful federal law enforcement agencies. To the federal government REMFs, the crime-and-victim issue is secondary to the jurisdictional issue. Why? Because the more jurisdiction an agency has, the more funds it gets from Congress. The more funds the agency gets, the more "Indians" it gets. The more Indians it gets, the more chiefs it needs. The more chiefs it has, the more power it gains. Get the picture?

Rayburn was so wired with informants that he once learned that Geraldo Rivera was going to smuggle himself into Arizona with a group of illegal aliens and use the operation as a news segment on *20/20*. So Rayburn put his spies to work in the alien-smuggling arena until we learned the where and how of Rivera's operation. We then had ourselves introduced to the smuggling ring and worked it out so that we would actually be given the job of picking up the group of aliens that included Rivera.

In this lawman's life of ours, it was a another long night of tedious hours sitting on the Mexican border listening to the coyotes howling off in the distance. We were supposed to hook up with the smuggling guide and his group at midnight at a prearranged location in the arid desert west of Nogales. Trying to bide our time until zero hour, we played the usual "dream on" head games about how easy this deal should go down. If the thing went like it was set up, we would have met the smuggler, loaded the aliens and Rivera up, traveled a safe distance off the border, stopped the truck, opened the back and announced, "Federal agents! Will the real Geraldo Rivera please stand up!" But that would have been just too goddamn easy. No, Murphy's Law always finds a way to screw up your investigation. And if it ain't Murphy kicking your ass, you can damn sure count on the smuggler himself screwing up your bust. After all, that's part of his criminal-element job description: to make a border agent's life miserable.

Sure enough, Rivera must have picked the only dumbshit smuggler in the Mexican state of Sonora that on this particular night, with Jim and me dreaming of an easy bust, could not have found his way to the kitchen for a taco in his own one-room hut. In the dark of the night, the outlaw missed the load site by a staggering distance. The reporter and his group of aliens never showed up at the rendezvous location. So now, in addition to everything else to deal with in the wonderful world of human trafficking, we have to wonder about a *20/20* celebrity newsman missing in action on the Arizona-Mexican border. Fucking great! Another twenty-four hours without sleep.

Early the next morning, Rayburn sent some of his Border Patrol buddies on horseback to start tracking the desperate group across the desert before someone ended up in the hospital or, worse yet, the morgue. As the agents were heading out on their hunt, one of them radioed that he had seen a reservation Native American going down the road in a pickup truck with a couple of bewildered-looking hitch-hikers in the back. It looked like we had located Rivera and his cameraman. Rayburn figured that they were headed into the closest desert pueblo to telephone, so that's where we headed too.

After using the only pay phone in a one-store, one-horse border town, Rivera walked outside, where Rayburn and I made contact with him. After we identified ourselves as federal agents, Rayburn told the reporter that we knew who he was and what he was up to. Rivera got a bit huffy with us until Rayburn's friendly Texas drawl toned him down. When Rivera figured out his secret little operation had been Arizona bushwhacked, he turned on that wiry mustache-accented, wry smile of his and said, "I'm impressed with your intelligence network. Who gave me up?" Then you could see his wheels start turning. Rivera wanted to cut a deal with us.

We ended up in negotiations for the next two weeks with Rivera and his network producers over the filming of a documentary they wanted to do on alien smuggling and the inhumane labor camps these unfortunates are forced into. They would make an offer and our Justice Department REMFs in D.C. would counter the offer. The whole time, Rayburn and I were caught in the middle of the stupid squabble as we listened to Rivera cry on the left hand and the Justice REMFs cry on the right hand. No one ever agreed on the ground rules for the documentary, so it never was aired.

Rayburn and I agreed that the documentary exposing the virtual slaving and abuse of the Mexican aliens was needed to expose the truth about the disgraceful situation. And we even found Rivera to be a likable, determined little feller, even if he was what we considered to be a Back East Yankee type. But on the other hand, we didn't have time to sit on our thumbs waiting for CEOs and REMFs to cut a deal that would please all of the high-rolling bosses. We had real slave-dealing smugglers to fry and this bullshit was taking way too much time. So in the end, we left Rivera hanging and twisting in the dry Arizona wind while we continued our pursuit of America's worst flesh merchants.

In 1986, the U.S. Congress passed the Immigration Reform Act, which was a crying shame of a sellout of our country. Congress insanely decided that the only way to fix the illegal immigration crisis was to make all illegal aliens go away "on paper." So how do you do that? Simple. You legalize all the illegals in the country with one swift stroke of the pen. By doing this Congress thought the problem would be solved forever.

What Congress never told the public was that by law, every newly legalized alien could, and would, petition to bring his entire family over from foreign soil. So if you legalized five million illegals, and they each had a family of four, you just brought twenty million new mouths to feed. That was a conservative estimate. A lot of the illegal aliens I've arrested had families of eight to ten children.

The whole thing got friggin ridiculous. The Phoenix INS Office supervisors had a meeting to explain the new immigration laws to us in an effort to make us believe it was in the best interest of the country. After their sales pitch about how monumental the new laws would be, I asked a sarcastic question that was about to end my career with the INS. "Being that I'm an anti-smuggling agent I would like to know the following. If we're going to legalize all of the illegals that are already here, then are we going to release all of the alien smugglers from prison that brought them over, being that the people they smuggled are now legal?"

Without fanfare I was ordered to immediately shut up and sit down. Obviously, the supervisors knew the new law was a sham as did most of the agents. I thought to myself, if the REMFs at INS head-quarters didn't care enough to fight Congress over the old laws we enforced, then why should I give a damn about enforcing their chicken-shit new immigration laws? I knew it was time to find a different set of federal laws to enforce. For me, the excitement had just been drained out of the anti-smuggling unit. I was really going to miss Jim Rayburn.

As an agent with the Border Patrol I had always loved to chase dope smugglers. For the last seven years I had dreamed of getting back to the border. After thirteen years with the Border Patrol and INS, I decided I would spend the rest of my life enforcing narcotics laws on the frontera. The only question now was which agency, DEA or U.S. Customs?

The next day I visited the DEA and U.S. Customs offices in Phoenix. The choice was simple. DEA wanted to bust me back in grade and send me to one of the "dirty dozen" offices in Los Angeles, Houston, Chicago, Miami, New York City, and I didn't even listen to the rest before I walked out the door. On the other hand, U.S. Customs would allow me to keep my grade and send me to the border, in Douglas, Arizona. Perfect! Blessed with Rayburn's investigative tutoring, my experiences as a Border Patrol agent, and a tour of duty in Vietnam, I was ready for the drug wars.

I didn't know it at the time, but I was about to drop off the ledge into a sordid, evil world of more drugs, money, murders, and corruption than I thought was possible to see in a lifetime.

3

Interdiction

UP UNTIL 1987, the U.S. Customs Service had a wider role in the patrolling and interdiction of drugs on the border. However, between 1987 and 1988, Customs revamped its priorities and decided to phase out its patrol officers along the U.S.-Mexican fence in favor of adding more special-agent positions to its primary law enforcement unit, the Office of Investigations (OI). Apparently due to the ever-changing faces and whims of the D.C. REMFs, the Customs Service felt this to be a necessary step in competing with the DEA, and even later the FBI, for its fair portion of the continually expanding drug war's budget.

For about two decades before I entered duty with the U.S. Customs OI, the investigative unit had been searching for its own place on the federal law enforcement turf. The branch had been the primary federal drug-investigative agency before the birth of the old Treasury Department's Bureau of Narcotics and Dangerous Drugs (BNDD) in 1965. The Customs OI worked pretty much hand in hand with its sister agency, the BNDD, until it was dissolved on July 1, 1973, giving way to the present-day DEA under the Department of Justice.

Ever since the DEA came into existence, the U.S. Customs OI had been battling for its rightful place in the war on drugs. Under Justice Department policy, the OI was relatively restricted to working narcotics interdiction investigations along our country's international borders, as per a memo of understanding between the Customs Service and the DEA. Once the Customs investigation left the border and was destined for the interior of the U.S.—Chicago for example—under the existing agreement between agencies, DEA demanded the final say in the case. DEA, as a small compensation for being under their thumb, allowed the Customs agents to work with them on the investigation in the interior U.S. as long as it was made very clear that DEA retained the final word.

Can you believe this crap? The whole damn country is flooding with drugs all around us—the inner cities, the schools, barrios, ghettos, suburbs—hell, they're even growing marijuana in the rural farm areas throughout the Bible Belt. But DEA will not allow any other federal agency the full narcotics investigative authority that DEA is empowered with by statute. And that's the key word in this whole ridiculous drug war mess: POWER! That's what it always boils down to with the federal government and its bureaucratic, money-grubbing, egotistical REMFs. My house is bigger than your house.

Like a childish bully not wanting to share his bat with other members of the ball team on the same sandlot, DEA is overly protective of its authority to investigate domestic and street drug operations. Now, as far as I'm concerned, that's just fine. If I had wanted to work piddly-ass street dope and live in New York City or Chicago I would have joined DEA to begin with. No, give me the wide-open Arizona spaces and the big border loads with the U.S. Customs Service anytime.

But still, where that may be all right for me, in the end our country still comes out the loser over the issue of federal agents becoming mired in their jurisdictional bickering. Our very survival as a nation is hanging in the balance, and the drug wars have no room for such lost time and disgraceful disservice to our citizens.

The U.S. Customs Service, the oldest federal law enforcement agency in existence at the time I joined, was formed in 1789. We always worked smuggling interdiction pursuant to our authority, which is written into law by Congress. There's nothing DEA can do about it. Every year we surpassed DEA in total narcotics seizures for heroin, marijuana, and cocaine. For example, during fiscal year 1997, the U.S. Customs Service accounted for 72 percent of all heroin, 66 percent of all cocaine, and about 45 percent of all marijuana that was seized within the United States. Every year this Treasury agency seized more dope than *all* other federal law enforcement agencies combined.

And every year, because we made DEA look so bad in total drug seizures and arrests, the DEA attempted to place more constraints on our narcotics authority and investigative duties by keeping us tied to America's outer perimeters. It may sound stupid, but it's true. Why do you think Dallas Cowboys owner Jerry Jones fired a winning coach like Jimmy Johnson a few years back? That's right. Because Johnson outshined him big time!

Upon returning to Douglas, I found it to be somewhat a different community from the one I had departed in 1980. During the seven years I'd been absent, the Phelps Dodge Mining Corporation had shut down its mining and smelter operation and had all but left town. With the largest area economic contributor gone, the Douglas residents had been left high and dry without gainful employment, and things began to look pretty bleak. And as we all are aware, desperation has histori-cally been the excuse for many a good man to go bad.

With Douglas's economic base rapidly deteriorating, the enter-prising Colombian and Mexican drug cartels were quick to identify the large, idle labor force in the dinky little border town. The Colombians wasted no time in moving in and taking full advantage of the residents' lack of legitimate income. People learned they could make quick, easy money operating dope stash houses, driving dope loads across the bor-der, being lookouts, laundering money, and performing other drug-facilitating activities. Not only did the Colombians boost the Douglas economy, but the little neighboring Mexican town of Agua Prieta, just across from Douglas, had tripled in size while I was gone. Other than a few Mexican factories, which paid each of their laborers the peso equivalent of six U.S. dollars per eight-hour day, there wasn't much else supporting the booming little border town other than dope smuggling.

We had a horrific growth of corruption subsequent to the unprece-dented Colombian invasion of this area. On both sides of the border, in Douglas and Agua Prieta, we had dirty cops and federal officers smuggling dope day and night. It didn't take long for me to realize that we, the honest agents, were more the abnormal than the normal in Douglas. You could see it in people's eyes as they peered at you when you walked the street or drove around the block. This was their town to smuggle dope in, and you had no business, federal agent or not, telling them it was against the law. You were a hated aberration. You weren't normal. Values had flipped upside-down in these two neighboring border towns.

From the honest badge-carriers, I quickly learned the good guys from the bad guys. I fell into a pretty secure group of trustworthy federal agents and local cops who continually worked together on investigations. We would later be formed into the present-day Border Alliance Group (BAG), which is a federally funded narcotics interdiction and investigative task force. As a group, we were required to be ever so vigilant of the rotten badges that surrounded us. You couldn't drop your guard even if it was just for a minute. The tarnished badges were always trying to get close to us to find out what we were investigating. Like a surgeon wielding a scalpel on cancerous tissue, we cut the bastards out of any meetings or narcotics-interdiction operations we conducted.

To complement the corruption problem, the violence and drug-related homicides had also skyrocketed. Agua Prieta was averaging at least one drug-related murder per day. For a city with a population of about 100,000, I would say that's a fairly high batting average for the Reaper. It had gotten so dangerous in the area that the DEA, which had an office in Douglas from 1974 until about 1985, closed its doors, tucked its tails between its legs, and pulled its agents completely off the border! The nearest DEA agents were now stationed some 120 miles northwest of Douglas in the relative safety of Tucson. With the growth of the Customs OI in Douglas, we subsequently moved into the old DEA building, where we began to make a do-or-die stand against the dominant drug lords.

From the Phoenix Customs OI, I got some good leads on a major narcotics-smuggling organization to start working on when I returned to Douglas. The Agua Prieta-based organization was run by a strong-willed homicidal Mexican bitch named Yolanda Molina. I took the information to the BAG members and we surmised that the best plan of attack would be twofold. We would first and foremost pursue and seize all their dope loads we could learn about. The second effort would be more devastating: find where they hid their filthy money and seize it as illegal proceeds under the newly written anti-racketeering laws. It was during this case that I would hook up with a soon-to-be lifelong friend, Lawson "Butch" Barrett.

I had previously known Butch from the '70s in Douglas. He was with the Treasury Department's old Customs Patrol when I was with the Justice Department's Border Patrol. Butch had been born and raised in the dirt streets of Douglas and the border. He had joined the Navy, spending some ten years sailing the world, with a pit stop in Vietnam. In Nam he did a year tour as a machine-gunner's mate on a Navy river boat. Although it may have been officially deemed a naval boat, a better description of the vessel Butch was on would be a fiberglass receptacle for incoming VC and NVA lead, rockets, and other incidental explosives.

Butch and I spent a lot of time over the next few years on surveillances together. Surveillance can sometimes be a really boring, time-consuming necessity. Time can pass at a snail's pace while you watch your own goddamn fingernails grow and pubic hairs turn gray. And sooner or later, because of the duration and boredom, Butch and I would end up swapping some pretty hairy war stories. Now, I've seen my share of hell when the shit hit the fan in the jungle. But Butch saw some really *bad* shit. Try to imagine floating in a body of water so thick with bloated bodies that you actually had to lance the corpses with a bayonet on the end of a stick so they would sink, just in order to get your boat upriver! Now, that's some heavy-duty *bad* shit. The stench alone would make most grown men, much less boys, puke their guts out.

When we started working together as U.S. Customs special agents, Butch was about thirty-eight years old and the top of his head already looked like a polar cap. He was one of those guys who would never grow gray gracefully, because he had been white-haired since about thirty. A lot of the local folks, including me, thought that he was a clone of Kenny Rogers. The only difference was that unlike Butch, Kenny probably didn't have a tattoo on his ass in a big, stamped circle proudly proclaiming "Grade A Beef." That was always one of the entertaining things about Butch that I would look forward to during our many "choir" practices over a few brews after work. No matter who was present, males, females, or in between, when Butch got silly rolling-around drunk he would drop his pants and moon everybody with a "Grade A Beef" ass!

Butch and I went after every smuggled load of dope we could find, hoping that it would link us to the Yolanda Molina organization. If the load linked up, we would feed the information to the BAG members for conspiracy charges. If it didn't, no big deal. We still got somebody's load of dope and we kept learning more and more about the different Agua Prieta organizations that made up the cartel as we stumbled down the dangerous path of dope interdiction.

One of the things we learned was that if you keep investigating any dope-smuggling organization long enough, sooner or later it will link up to almost every other dope-smuggling organization in the geographical area you're working. We learned that even though these outlaws were willing to spill each other's guts over a dope load, or even kill each other over a competitive business deal, the overriding factor in the end was always the greed. And as long as there's money to be made, they will hook up sooner or later, even if they hate each other to the grave. And that, my friend, was a weakness that we would eventually exploit. Greed, hate, jealousy, and revenge are a most volatile mixture, leading to complete destruction from within.

We eventually recruited some of Yolanda Molina's own immediate family members, who felt that they weren't receiving their just proportion of the smuggling profits. From them we learned what we needed to intercept the smuggled dope loads and sift our way through the muddy business of the laundered money. We also learned how the Agua Prieta drug cartel was structured and how it functioned. Some of the information was so outlandish, so completely unbelievable, that we took it with a grain of salt and a wait-and-see attitude. In the end, it was shockingly all true.

We learned that the Mexican Federal Judicial Police (MFJP) were the biggest dope smugglers and facilitators of drug traffickers in the Douglas/Agua Prieta area. In brief, it worked like this: As a commander of an MFJP group in any state of Mexico, you can bid for a border station by offering a large bribe to the Mexican Attorney General's Office in Mexico City. Once your bribe is accepted, you're halfway home to making millions of dollars.

So let's say as an MFJP commander you get assigned to Agua Prieta. Once in Agua Prieta you learn there are eight or so major drug-smuggling families or organizations. You also learn how much *mordida* (bribe) each family was paying the last commander to be allowed to smuggle so many tons of marijuana or cocaine per month into the U.S. Once the new commander knows what each family was being charged before he arrived, it is up to him to decide if he wants to raise or change the price for a ton of smuggled marijuana or cocaine. It's all negotiable.

Such up or down "mordida" contract negotiations are done through a designated Mexican attorney that all of the families use to reach out to the new commander. Once the amounts for each family are agreed upon, the MFJP commander is responsible for making sure the dope gets from the families' warehouses to the border fence for crossing. For a little additional charge, the commander and his heavily armed agents will actually help smuggle the dope across the border and deliver it to a specific destination within the U.S.

And if you're really a greedy son of a bitch, there's even more greenbacks to be made. The MFJP does not permit any outside "wild-catting" or freelance smuggling anywhere in their area of the border unless the MFJP has been paid off. So if you're a small-time smuggler, and you get caught trying to backdoor these bastards, they'll ram it up your ass and break it off in a most brutal fashion. Not only will you lose your dope, but you'll be tortured, murdered, or at the very least thrown in prison for as long as they damn well please to keep your rotting ass there. And don't worry about your dope. The MFJP is going to sell it to one of the Agua Prieta cartel's families at a bargain-basement price.

We also learned that the cartel had such a good deal with the MFJP that they would assist them in their public-relations façade directed at both the Mexican and U.S. government REMFs. If marijuana sits too long in a warehouse it will sooner or later develop mildew, rendering it worthless on the U.S. market. The dope families freely deliver the worthless grass to a communal warehouse owned and operated by the MFJP. When the warehouse is full, the MFJP trots out the Mexican and U.S. news media and directs them to the warehouse for a cooperative international press conference. As the MFJP burns the moldy dope and brags to the press about how dedicated it is to the war on drugs, the gullible reporters and photographers are climaxing in true Kodak flashing-bulb fashion. Like grandma always said, "Waste not, want not."

By strategically placing an informant inside the MFJP office in Agua Prieta, we began to receive information on ton-size loads of marijuana being smuggled out of Mexico into Arizona through the mountains east of Douglas. To interdict the loads we had to find the dirt roads the smugglers were using and place our agents on long-term surveillances. We knew the informant was giving us the straight and narrow. We just had to put our time in and wait until the deal popped.

After a couple of weeks or so of surveillance, our agents observed a new blue four-wheel-drive Ford F-250 truck with a camper shell as it cut and drove through the border fence in the desert of the San Bernardino Valley. Butch, several other Customs agents, and I responded to intercept the Ford where we knew it had to come out on a highway about twenty miles north of the border, near Geronimo's final surrender location, known appropriately as Apache, Arizona.

After racing up the highway at 100-plus mph while dodging vehicle-demolishing deer and cattle, we arrived just in time to catch a glimpse of the dust trail the Ford truck was leaving as it came barreling onto the highway from the desert. Butch and I activated our red lights and sirens in an effort to stop the smuggler. As expected, the outlaw punched his engine out, balls to the wall, and the chase was on. We were fast approaching our first real encounter with an MFJP designated shooter sworn to protect the Mex feds' load of dope.

The smuggler driving the blue Ford fully accelerated his rig, which had a monstrous 460-cubic-inch motor. He hauled ass north on the highway, approaching speeds of 115–120 mph. Butch was driving a small Customs-issued Ford Mustang with an interceptor motor, which is comparable to those used by numerous state highway patrols. In other words, this was one of the fastest little packages law enforcement could get its hands on.

Butch tried to pass the guy and get ahead of him on the blacktop in order to block his flight. When Butch pulled alongside the large Ford truck, the outlaw attempted to run the little Mustang off the highway by clipping the Mustang's passenger side door and fenders. Butch reacted by jamming his brake pedal to the floor and allowing the Ford truck to shoot past him at the speed of sound. Butch temporarily lost control during the maneuver and he ended up skidding between the side of the highway and the ditch before he could get the Mustang back under control. At those speeds, it's certain that Butch would have been toast if the guy had brushed him any harder.

I was driving a Customs-issued Dodge Ram truck following Butch as we continued warping up the Arizona highway, headed for the badlands of New Mexico. We were in radio contact with a couple of our other agents, who had gotten north of the Ford truck before he came out of the desert onto the highway. They informed us that around a curve in the highway, about two miles north of our pursuit, they had set up a roadblock. Butch and I snuggled up on the smuggler's rear end to force him into their awaiting arms as we approached the curve.

When the asshole rounded the curve and eyeballed the roadblock he came down hard on his brakes, leaving Butch and me in a blinding cloud of smoke jetting from the rear of his pavement-burning tires. The smuggler cut his wheels 180 degrees, making a left turn off the highway into a roadside ditch. He was going to make a run for the freedom of the open desert when he gave me a broadside target as he turned. Considering this guy had just tried to whack Butch using his truck as a weapon, I had no qualms about doing the same to him.

Butch was unable to control his Mustang's speed and he overshot the guy on the highway. Through the burning-rubber smoke and spewing rocks, I got a fix on the bad guy's driver-side door. Like a jet fighter jockey locking his targeting mechanisms on the enemy, I aimed the front bumper of my Dodge at the door and stomped my gas pedal to the floor for maximum impact. The outlaw jerked his head toward the oncoming fatal collision and the look in his eyes was that of pure "Oh shit!" Screaming, the son of a bitch tried desperately to dodge a direct hit.

As I turned my front wheels into his door for the shot, the smuggler's 460 cubic inch proved to be quite a power plant. He juiced the 460 and flew past me before I could solidly connect with a crippling blow to his door. Without the impact to slow me down, this virtually left me at full speed heading into deep gravel on the side of the highway. It was like throwing a punch in a fist fight as hard as you can, and the guy you plan on connecting with ducks. You have all this force built up with no impact, leaving your ass slicing air and pulling you off balance. And that's just about what happened with my truck. My front wheels got caught in the gravel and my own bullet-fast velocity flipped my truck over, leaving my young ass in deep doo-doo.

Well, so far this was turning out to be a pretty shitty day! I was upside-down in the cab of my truck, skidding down the side of the highway at Mach 1. I was looking out of my quickly shattering windshield at cattle and horses that appeared to my bewildered mind to be zipping by with their hooves pointing toward the sky. When the Dodge came to a stop I was completely blinded by blood, which now covered my face and seeped into my eyes. I bet you're thinking things can't get much worse, huh? Guess again!

As I was hanging upside-down, bleeding from a lacerated forehead, a fleeting childhood thought passed by. When I was a little boy I used to watch my grandmother tie chickens upside-down on a clothesline and cut their heads off. Before becoming that night's fried supper, the decapitated chickens would flutter all about, spewing blood in all four directions until they finally came to rest, limp from their death throes and dripping their last drops of life.

Then I began to smell an ominous odor of gasoline vapors mixed with smoke. Realizing I, too, was about to join the legions of grandma's fried crispy critters, I struggled to turn myself right-side-up and grab a door handle. My hopes of survival quickly dissipated when I found that the door was crumpled in and not going to budge a single inch.

The adrenaline was picking up so I had plenty of energy yet to try my last available option. I rolled my sweat- and blood-soaked body around, placing my back on the dash, and kicked like a colic-stricken Kentucky mule at the back windshield. The more I kicked the more I smelled the deadly mixture of gas and smoke. The more I smelled the flammable mixture, the harder I kicked. Ain't adrenaline a grand thing? It's the body's self-produced natural narcotic. I reckon I wouldn't have ended up in this predicament if more folks would learn to enjoy adrenaline instead of putting man-made chemicals and crap up their noses.

I knew my time on this earth would be short if I couldn't get the goddamn windshield to give. So after kicking the glass barrier hard enough to earn muscle spasms in both legs, I palmed my .45 Colt from my shoulder holster and cut loose a stitching line of glass-shattering lead. The next time I kicked, the windshield broke loose and fell out onto the side of the highway. I rolled out of the cab, gasping for fresh air but free of my potential crematorium. Then Customs agent Bob Schofield pulled up in his government Jeep Cherokee 4x4 and started to mop the blood out of my eyes as he questioned my physical condition.

Hardly hearing a word Bob had said, I shrugged his inquiry off and demanded that he give me the keys to his Jeep. I was so pissed at the dope smuggler in the Ford that I completely ignored my own wounds. At the moment, they were a trivial matter compared to the thought of locking steel around this outlaw's wrists.

I told Bob he could either jump in the Jeep if he was coming with me, or stay at the side of the highway if he wanted. I didn't care which. I knew the way I looked probably scared the hell out of Bob. And I wouldn't have blamed him if he didn't want to ride at Mach speeds through the open desert with a raging lunatic with nothing but revenge on his mind. But I was determined to run this son of a bitch to ground, come hell or high water. As we saddled up in Bob's Jeep and started off, my Dodge truck blew up in a fierce fireball and began to burn to the ground. Wiping the blood from my eyes, I sullenly thought about the hours of explaining and paperwork that was going to cost me with the D.C. REMFs.

Bob and I sped into the desert, crossing through several different ranches. We passed several thirty- to forty-pound bales of marijuana that had apparently been jarred loose from the Ford truck's camper as it bounced through the rough country. I was driving the Jeep full-throttle like a madman on a suicide mission. We were bouncing across the desert floor so hard that Bob's head hit the ceiling of the Jeep's interior every so often when we careened over clumps of brush and ravines. Every time Bob would try to lean over and wipe the blood out of my eyes, I would hit another rock or hole, throwing him out of his seat. He finally said "Forget it," and strapped his butt down with his seat belt.

We kept chasing the smuggler through the brushy desert, going through several more ranches and crossing into some pretty prime grazing pastures. He had already knocked the fences down, leaving loose barbwire for us to cross over and through. I don't know if it was him or us, but one of our vehicles' undercarriages kept scraping the busted fence wires, causing sparks in the combustible dry grass. During the chase Bob and I had been a trifle too busy to look behind us until one of our agents on the radio brought it to our attention. We had caught about twenty miles of U.S. Forest Service land on fire!

So far we had crashed and totally destroyed my truck, burned part of a state highway, damaged Butch's Mustang, torn down several different ranchers' fences, and now we had managed to burn some of the best grazing land in Cochise County! All of this and we had only been chasing the bastard for about fifteen minutes. I predicted that if we went at this rate for an hour, it would be a distinct possibility that we may want to give what's left of southeastern Arizona back to Mexico by the time we finished. I figured I would be on Social Security before I ever got all of the explaining and paperwork done.

Bob and I finally balled up so much loose barbwire around the Jeep's drive shaft and axle that the 4x4 just plain-ass gave up the ghost and stopped. We radioed Butch that our vehicle was dead in the water and we would continue on foot, following the trail of fire being left by the fleeing outlaw.

Meanwhile, Butch and some other agents had been watching the fires and had been able to anticipate where the Ford would hit the next dirt road in a particular Chiricahua Mountain canyon. They headed off in that direction and found the truck abandoned in the rugged canyon where it was boxed in. The smuggler had escaped on foot into the same outlaw-coddling Chiricahuas that had safely harbored Geronimo and the Clantons years ago. The Ford left behind was found to contain about 1,800 pounds of marijuana along with some scattered pistol and rifle ammunition.

Bob and I walked out of the desert to the canyon, where we met Butch and the other agents. Everybody picked out a clean-up assignment. Bob and the other agents dealt with the fires and my smoldering Dodge left on the side of the highway. Butch got stuck with driving me to the Cochise County hospital for stitches to close the seeping wounds in my forehead. And I got saddled with suppressing an insatiable appetite for revenge.

As we left, one of our Customs Blackhawk helicopters from Tucson was just making it to the scene. While the bird made passes back and forth through the burning valley, its twirling blades whipped smoke up into familiar circular, curling funnels. Butch and I looked back across the destructive path of the chase and separately reminisced about Vietnam. It's so weird how similar a Southeast Asian jungle and the southeast Arizona desert can turn out to be at the end of a hard-fought battle. The only things missing were our youth and the smell of napalm.

About a year later I would have surgery on my left arm from injuries incurred during the rollover. But that ain't a pimple on a fat man's ass when you consider what happened to the dope smuggler that same year. Armed with arrest warrants after learning his identity, our U.S. Customs and BAG agents surrounded him and some of his petty cohorts at a ranch on the west side of Douglas down near the border fence.

It was a fine, sunshiny day, if memory serves me correctly. And I hope the outlaw enjoyed the nice clear day because it turned out to be his last on this planet. While being surrounded by our agents, the son of a bitch decided he couldn't do time in prison. So in lieu of incarceration, he skullcapped himself by eating the business end of his own .357 Magnum before we could break the door down and take him into custody. Brains spread all over the inside of the walls of a house, or on the front bumper of my truck ... it didn't matter to me as long as the job got done. I reckon a feller could say that revenge comes in a lot of different flavors.

We didn't have to wait long for the next fight. A month or so later the informant from the MFJP office in Agua Prieta contacted us with information about another large load of marijuana. He said that this one would be heavily guarded by armed MFJP agents, who had instructions to kill any U.S. law officers that got in the way. The informant said that the MFJP agents would get the load up to and through the border fence, where a driver named Machichi would take over. The informant said that Machichi would be heavily armed and that he often bragged to his *compas* (buddies) that he would never be taken alive in the U.S. I guess the Mexican agents sent this determined maniac with the load because they were pissed off about losing the last 1,800 pounds to us.

A new kid to the U.S. Customs OI in Douglas, Special Agent Allan Sperling, and I would use this information to open the door on Machichi's life. We learned that he had been a petty thief on the streets of Agua Prieta as a kid. As Machichi grew up he graduated to larger, more violent crimes, which eventually attracted the admiring attention of the Mexican authorities. In and out of jail, the one-time Sonoran street urchin was eventually recruited by the MFJP to smuggle loads of dope for them. And the feller really didn't have much choice. If he refused they would simply throw him back in jail until he said he would drive for them. After all, who's he going to go to about it? The cops?

Machichi was known to keep a cache of assault rifles in Mexico. To surpass his brag of never being taken by U.S. lawmen, he now upped the ante by spreading it around Sonora that he would kill any U.S. officer who tried to arrest him when he was smuggling dope. The mouthy braggart was a skinny twenty-two-year-old young man with oily, straight, brown shoulder-length hair. His high-cheekboned Apache face featured two yellow, snaggled buck teeth protruding from beneath a scraggly mustache complemented by an equally scrubby goatee. When you looked at a photograph of him it was easy to see that his searing eyes were partially crossed over his long, pointy nose. I guess the best description of the guy would be that of a pissed-off ferret. What can I say? Desperados come in all nationalities, shades, shapes, and sizes.

The informant gave us the time, place, and date the load was coming. We were waiting near the highway on the Chiricahua side of the San Bernardino Valley when Machichi came rolling out of Mexico and across the desert with his dope load. He was driving a white and yellow Ford F-250 4x4 pickup with a camper. An unknown partner was sitting on the passenger's side of the truck's cab, riding shotgun. You almost had to admire the contempt the bastards had for us. Not only did they use the exact same road through the desert out of Mexico, but the truck was exactly the same as the last one except for the color. But there was one deadly difference between these two dope loads. The last guy wasn't a maniacal shooter like Machichi.

Machichi stopped the yellow Ford about a quarter of a mile short of the highway when he saw Sperling and me waiting up ahead for him. The outlaws foolishly attempted to hide the truck behind a large mesquite tree for several moments. Little did we know it at the time, but they were using these precious seconds to lock and load their automatic assault rifles with the intent of whacking us if at all possible.

A cat-and-mouse game was initiated. Machichi slowly drove from behind the mesquite and turned away from us, creeping out into the desert. When Sperling and I inched our separate government vehicles toward the smugglers they again paused and looked us over. Except for the vehicles, it was similar to lawmen and outlaws circling about each other in the dusty streets of Tombstone a hundred-plus years ago. They were sizing us up. Looking for a chink in our armor. Waiting to see who was going to make the first fatal move.

After a couple more slow stop-and-peek maneuvers, Machichi hauled ass away from us into the desert, leaving a cloud of dust behind. He hadn't found what he'd been looking for: an easy way to hit us. Sperling and I gave pursuit by accelerating off the highway and running our 4x4 vehicles through a barbwire fence. We pushed our vehicles hard through the open country, bouncing them over rocks, digging huge chunks of earth up as we closed on Machichi and his partner. Before we overtook the speeding Ford, Sperling and I decided that we would split up and each take different sides of the smugglers' vehicle. Being careful of a possible crossfire situation, Sperling pulled his vehicle to the driver's side and I cuddled mine up on the passenger's side.

As we bounced along, Sperling aimed his .45 semiautomatic pistol at Machichi, screaming for his surrender. On the other side of the Ford, I got so close to the passenger I could see the beads of sweat dripping from his panic-stricken face. He was fumbling with an assault rifle, trying to get the barrel out of his window at me. I placed my pistol in my left hand and grabbed the steering wheel with my right. I leaned out my window, fully extending my weapon within a couple of feet of the passenger's face as we continued racing through the desert. I yelled to the asshole that I would blow his face off if he brought the barrel of his rifle up.

Like I've said before, I hate to cap a guy when I don't absolutely have to. I gave this young man the option of living or dying. It would be his last day in the Arizona-Sonoran Desert if he chose poorly. God-fearingly correct in his decision, the outlaw dropped his assault rifle to the floorboard and raised his hands above his head.

Upon seeing that his shotgun rider didn't have the gumption to exchange lead with us, Machichi became enraged and started cussing and fumbling for his own weapon. As he tried to get his weapon up over the steering wheel toward Sperling, I capped a .45 round past Machichi's face in front of the windshield. Machichi turned pale as he dropped his gun, stopped the Ford, and raised his hands.

Sperling and I pulled our .12 gauge pump shotguns and approached our respective bad guys with extreme caution to pull them out of the truck. My guy was so scared that his knees buckled on him when he stepped out. He went face-first into the dirt on his own power, or should I say lack of power. Let me tell you, this outlaw did no honor to the bad men that once roamed this area of Cochise County.

I cuffed the coward behind his back as he lay facedown, whimpering like a baby. That was one of the characteristics of a good number of these Mexican dope smugglers. They were real badasses until it came down to the nut-cutting. Then, when the moment of true balls arrived, most of them capitulated. But Machichi was about to prove there's always that one asshole in the crowd that has to be different.

Machichi came out with his hands up, going into a sly act of pleading for his life at the end of Sperling's gun barrel. As Sperling approached him to take him into custody, Machichi dropped his hands and pulled a hidden weapon from the truck seat. Sperling's youthful speed allowed him to close the distance before Machichi could squeeze the trigger. Sperling butt-stroked the asshole across the face with his shotgun. The dope smuggler belly-flopped to the ground along with his proclamation of never being taken alive on U.S. soil. As he lay painfully squirming in his own blood, we cuffed and shackled him like the wild animal we considered him to be.

When we were satisfied that everything was under control, Sperling and I took time for a chew of tobacco while the adrenaline receded and we calmed down from the fight. We then radioed other agents that everything was Code Four. We secured the crime scene, photographing the dope and weapons where they lay. We attempted to give Machichi a bit of first aid, but he was too belligerent to accept it. We figured he could see a doctor after we got him booked into the Cochise County Jail.

We took the two smugglers back to the office, where we examined and weighed their load of marijuana. The camper contained 1,275 pounds of dope, which would mean a mandatory five-year sentence for both smugglers plus an additional five years for being armed during the commission of their crime. Sperling and I inventoried the rest of the gear in the cab of their truck. For each weapon there were an additional four fully loaded magazines. They also had a camouflage net large enough to cover the truck, camouflage military uniforms, U.S. military-issued night vision goggles and binoculars, military-issued topographical maps, and, last but not least, enough spare ammunition for the Gulf War. Plenty of firepower. You might say it was Machichi's equivalent of a gringo *turista's* American Express card. He never left old Mexico without it.

While Sperling and I were doing paperwork, a couple of young agents just out of the academy volunteered to take the two outlaws to the *cárcel* (jail). The two agents were already aware of the suspects being armed and resisting arrest. But we stressed that they had to be especially careful with Machichi because he was considered an escape risk plus an all-around badass. After all, this was the asshole that liked to brag in Mexico that he would never be taken alive on the U.S. side of the border. Forewarned that Machichi was a maniac to be dealt with, the two agents took him out of the office cell and placed him in their vehicle for transport to the Cochise County lockup. It was the last time I would ever see Machichi alive.

While Sperling and I were in the office killing trees in support of our never-ending paperwork and reports, we heard one of the two transporting agents come up on the radio with a heart-pounding urgency in his voice. The guy was screaming and cussing in rapid machine-gun-fire Spanglish. Sperling and I looked at each other, already knowing in our guts what kind of a fiasco had transpired. As we listened to the high-stressed screaming for assistance on the radio, we could only pray that Machichi didn't kill anybody during his escape.

Machichi had somehow slipped his cuffs, popped the lock on a door, crawled over the top of an agent as he pounded the shit out of him, and beat feet for Mexico, which was about two blocks from where he made his break. The stupid son of a bitch didn't know it at the time, but he was running toward his own death.

Put the informant's information with all of the military supplies Machichi had in his truck and it adds up to definite MFJP involvement. It would be extremely interesting to hear one of these two pukes sing. We didn't have Machichi anymore, so we tried to make a deal with his shotgun rider to see if he would roll. Machichi's partner was identified as Julio Estrada Contreras, a cokehead punk from the barrios of Agua Prieta. Sperling and I took Contreras before the prosecuting assistant United States Attorney in Tucson, where a deal was cut with his defense attorney. For a couple of years off his ten-year sentence, he provided us with some very useful and enlightening information.

Contreras said that he and Machichi were running dope at the direction of corrupt MFJP agents stationed in Agua Prieta. He said that the Mexican agents had placed him and his partner under orders to shoot any U.S. law officers who tried to seize their coveted load of narcotics. Machichi told Contreras before they left the border with the load that he wasn't going to be taken alive if they ran into any trouble. Contreras said if one agent responded they were prepared to whack him in an ambush. However, being that two agents had arrived, he and Machichi drove further out into the desert to find the right location to make their stand. They were attempting to reach some rocks they thought would make a good defensive position when Sperling and I jumped them.

Contreras said that as they approached the rocks, Machichi was screaming at him to shoot us. After saying this, the young smuggler dropped his head and stated that he couldn't pull the trigger on us because he was scared to death. He said that he could see in our eyes that we would not hesitate to kill him if he made a move with his rifle. It was a compliment to our aggressiveness and a point to be learned by all cops. The best defense is an aggressive offense! In this case it not only saved our lives, but neither did we have to take a life.

This singing young bird went on to say that the Agua Prieta cartel knew everything about the Douglas U.S. Customs special agents. He said that the cartel hires spies to follow and observe the agents in their daily routines. They knew what government and personal cars each agent drove. They knew what time we got home in the evening, what time we went to sleep, and what time we left our residences in the morning to go on duty. He said that they even knew what color and kind of bikes our children rode.

Contreras told us everything we ever wanted to know about how the cartel is structured and how it laundered its money. This information would eventually be used in finding and seizing some $2 million hidden in U.S. banks by the Yolanda Molina family. As for Machichi, the MFJP jailed him back in Mexico for the loss of its load of precious merchandise. And that was the least of his problems.

The MFJP eventually figured that Machichi knew too much about them and their intimate operations with the drug lords of the Agua Prieta cartel. Machichi had now become a liability. The cartel knew that U.S. Customs would have a warrant of arrest issued for Machichi after his daring escape from custody. It was obvious that he was a direct link to 1,275 pounds of MFJP-protected marijuana. Drivers were a dime a dozen. On the open market in Mexico, I figured that Machichi's life was worth about one well-worn peso.

Subsequent to learning of Machichi's incarceration, Sperling and a Cochise County Sheriff's detective paid the outlaw an unannounced visit at the Mexican jail in Agua Prieta. The U.S. lawmen had back-doored the MFJP by getting a friendly Agua Prieta cop to sneak them inside the jail's walls. For a nominal fee, of course.

During the prison cell meeting, Sperling graphically explained Machichi's plight to the inmate. Machichi had one of two choices to make. Either cooperate with the U.S. government in a case against the MFJP, in which case he would remain alive under our witness protection program, or remain in Mexico until the Mex feds whacked him. Machichi arrogantly cursed the U.S. lawman while countering that his honorable Mexican *compadres* would never betray or harm him. Sperling had tried to throw the outlaw a life-saving rope. Machichi chose to cut the line and take his chances.

Machichi's maggot-infested remains were later found protruding from a shallow, sandy grave covered with lime in the Sonoran Desert a few miles outside of Agua Prieta. The Agua Prieta cop who had assisted Special Agent Sperling in bypassing the Mexican prison's security ended up as a cremated crispy critter when his patrol car mysteriously burned to the ground on the outskirts of the Sonoran drug city. It was apparent that Mexican witnesses to the Machichi-MFJP link were now being systematically eliminated. Sperling and I would spend months watching over our shoulders and wondering if the Mex feds would come looking for U.S. lawmen who knew of the same relationship.

As for Machichi's unfortunate demise, I guarandamntee it would be safe to say that the Mex feds weren't going to take the chance that the Sonoran outlaw might one day be taken alive in Arizona. How ironic. His ending was exactly what Machichi himself had always bragged it would be.

4

The Horse Patrol

THE BEAUTIFUL, WIDE SAN BERNARDINO VALLEY is located in the south-eastern corner of Cochise County, Arizona. From the U.S.-Mexican border the valley stretches north to Rodeo, New Mexico, and south into Sonora, Mexico. It is bordered on the west by the Chiricahua Mountains, which take their name from Cochise's and Geronimo's Chiricahua Apaches. On the east the San Bernardino is bordered by the Peloncillo Mountains and their brooding Mexican sisters, the Sierra Madres. These magnificent mountain ranges are part of the Continental Divide, which cuts north through the middle of the U.S. to Canada.

The valley floor itself is a high desert region rising more than 4,000 feet above sea level. The terrain is predominately made up of a reddish, dark-brown lava rock that, depending on the position of the sun, can turn a blackish lavender. The underlying lava-rock soil supports sparse, precious prairie grass mixed with tumbleweeds, cactus, yuccas, and greasewood bushes. As you move west or east toward the bordering mountains, the valley floor gives way to gently rolling hills that eventually creep up to the base of the majestic Chiricahuas and Peloncillos.

The near-10,000-foot Chiricahuas on the west side of the valley, and the somewhat lesser Peloncillos on the east, are covered with beautiful green oak and towering pine trees. Off in the distance from the middle of the valley floor, both ranges have a dark bluish, cooling appearance, which tends to place your mind at ease with the world. The valley is sparsely populated, with a few ranches that have been passed from generation to generation. Along with the lazy grazing cattle, it is not uncommon to see herds of mule deer and antelope roaming in search of forage through the valley.

In the 1880s this area of Cochise County was frequented by desperados, such as the O.K. Corral's Clantons and some four hundred other hard-core outlaws on the run from Texas and other frontier areas. These bad men included such celebrities as Clay Hardin, who killed forty men by the time he was forty years old, compared to Billy the Kid, who only laid twenty-one men in their graves by the youthful age of twenty-one. Others on Arizona's most-deadly list included killers like Clay Allison, Luke Short, Johnny Ringo, and Curley Bill Brocious.

In Skeleton Canyon, which sits on the east side of the San Bernardino Valley in the Peloncillos, Old Man Clanton, his boys, Ringo, and Curley Bill ambushed and murdered some nineteen Mexicans traveling in what was known back then as a muleteer pack train. The outlaws made off with what is believed to have been about $75,000 in silver bullion. In retaliation, the victims' relatives later ambushed and cut down Old Man Clanton and five other Texas cowboys as they rode through Guadalupe Canyon, on a well-known Peloncillo outlaw trail that crossed the border frontier into Mexico.

Now here we are some 120-odd years later starting into a new millennium, and the only real changes are that the outlaws and lawmen have flip-flopped the use of the canyons, and the favored pack trains are composed of horses and an extremely different type of mule. Nowadays, special agents of the U.S. Customs Service are ambushing and arresting Mexican dope-smuggling horse trains and backpacking human "mule" trains in both Skeleton and Guadalupe Canyons. The only other real difference that can be seen is the type of illicit merchandise being smuggled. Instead of running silver across the border, the Mexican horse trains and "mules" now smuggle "white and green gold." Not a precious metal, but a vegetable type of "gold." I reckon it doesn't matter much. Both bullion and dope come from the soil.

In the spring of 1987, U.S. Customs Service Special Agent Butch Barrett and I formally introduced the use of horse-mounted agents to the newly created U.S. Customs Service Office of Investigations. Horses had previously been used by U.S. Customs patrol officers. However, the Treasury Department had foolishly phased out both the patrol officers and the horses. We didn't know it yet, but Butch and I were about to set a new precedent for special agents. And if a feller was to cut new territory, you couldn't find a better partner to do it with than a tough old Arizona native boy like Butch.

We had been finding the tracks of dope-smuggling mules who were backpacking north through the San Bernardino Valley after crossing the U.S.-Mexican border near the historic ranch of former Cochise County Sheriff "Texas" John Slaughter. The smugglers attempted to hide their tracks by brushing them out with greasewood branches. Butch and I would usually find the brush-outs in that area when they crossed a county-maintained dirt road known as Geronimo Trail.

We monitored the smugglers' movements by cutting their sign back and forth through the valley for a couple of months before we could really anticipate their next illegal border crossing. When we were ready we decided to ambush the dope smugglers at the northern-most end of their route, where they would drop their contraband off near a highway about ten miles north of the border. Butch and I picked the right time frame and waited at the stash site, where we expected the load to be picked up early in the morning. We concealed our vehicle about a half mile off the highway in some mesquites, where we quietly waited.

It was a beautiful night in the valley. The sky was clear, allowing you to see absolutely every star God has ever thrown into the universe. The Milky Way was so prominent it looked like a soft footpath that was placed with great thought between the constellations in an effort to keep the stars from being trampled on. The light from the stars caressed the dark peaks of Geronimo's Chiricahuas on one side of the valley, and the outlaw-favored Peloncillos on the other. The starlight appeared to give the ancient mountains a holy definition that brought them to near life. Somewhere down deep inside, you felt that the valley's sole purpose on earth was to give these mountains a place to forever reign over. People, both good and bad, will come and go through this part of the country with the passing of time. But these mountains will be here long after we're all just dust blowing in the wind. When you accept that fact, you're one step closer to becoming one with nature and our Lord.

As Butch and I sat there and waited, it got so quiet that you could damn near hear your own friggin hair grow. The stillness of the desert flows over your body from head to toe. It fills your ears with silence as it brings an inner peace known and understood by few. As you stand and gaze straight out into the darkness you are so consumed by the muteness of it all that you start to wonder if you've actually gone deaf. You feel as though you're in some sort of a strange vacuum at the bottom of a dark, deep mine shaft. As you listen to your own heartbeat keeping you company, you wonder if death can possibly be more serene.

The silence was eventually broken. Off in the distance several packs of coyotes began to alternately call across the valley, communicating their jurisdictional tribal intent to each other. We listened as each pack hunted and surrounded its evening meal for the kill. When a pack surrounds its prey, it calls back and forth, bouncing spine-tingling howls off the canyons that border the valley floor. It doesn't matter if you're standing with one partner or a whole damn troop of soldiers; coyotes on the hunt can conjure up the spookiest sounds you'll ever hear in your entire life.

At about 4:00 a.m. Butch and I watched with night-vision goggles as a car approached the drop site and killed its motor and headlights. In the distance, we could hear some low whistling and whispering going on between the driver and the dope smugglers as they searched for each other in the dark. We then heard the opening and closing of the car's trunk, which usually means the dope's been loaded and the driver is ready to rock 'n' roll. A couple of seconds later we heard his motor violate the desert stillness as his headlights pointed north on the highway.

Butch fired up our government ride and we started slowly picking our way through the lava rocks and brush as we headed for the highway. On the blacktop we opened up the motor in pursuit. Slipping down the highway without headlights, we used our night-vision goggles to negotiate the road for a sneak attack. We wanted to take the outlaw by complete surprise and hit him with the headlights and emergency flashers at the same time. We had done it many times before, and believe you me, it confuses and scares the shit out of criminals so bad that they make big-time mistakes that get them busted. Besides, when you and your partner are all alone out there in the middle of no-man's-land, it's all about stacking the deck as much as you can. A few things about outlaws may have changed since the Clanton days, but there is one remaining constant: The majority of these criminals are ready and willing to either kill you or die trying to protect their merchandise. Count on it.

We caught up to the loaded car within about five minutes and pulled up close to the car's rear bumper. Butch then turned on our red lights and siren with the anticipation of a high-speed pursuit. We couldn't believe it. The guy actually pulled over and gave up. This driver definitely wasn't a member of the majority mentioned above. What can I say? It's nice to meet a puss on occasion. Well, for a change of pace, that was the good news. The bad news was that the puss locked himself in the car and wouldn't come out! I reckon at this point you could say that the doper took himself hostage.

After a few minutes of "self-hostage" negotiations, and maybe a wee bit of cursing and car door kicking on our part, he unlocked his doors and surrendered. He was found to be in possession of about 300 pounds of marijuana in the trunk of his car. Butch and I figured that he had met with about six mules back at the load-up site, carrying about fifty pounds each.

We transported the puss and his dope load back to our Douglas office and put on a pot of coffee. We got all of the paperwork done and booked the driver into the local jail until we could get him before a federal judge in Tucson. As the sun started to rise over the Peloncillos, Butch and I finished off the coffee. The caffeine kicked in and we began to feel pretty peppy considering that we'd been up all night. Not yet ready to call it a day, Butch came up with another adrenaline-rushing plan that had to be acted on ASAP if it was going to work.

With a mischievous little gleam in his eye, he reminded me of a kid who couldn't wait for Christmas morning. He caught me as I was headed out the office door and asked me if I still had my horses at my place. Before I replied I knew what he was thinking. We're going mounted on horses after the mules! What a leap back into the Old West this would be. I tried to think of a reason why the REMFs in D.C. wouldn't let us chase these guys on horseback. But the more I thought about it, the more I wondered why the Customs Service or the Border Patrol hadn't used more horses to get the job done in this part of the country before now. It only made common sense! I guessed we had just outdistanced ourselves in modern amenities and technology.

We jumped in our war-weary pickup truck and raced over to my adobe casa shortly after sunrise. We didn't waste any time hooking up the two-horse trailer and side-arming the saddles and tack into the bed of the truck. Loading the horses into the trailer, we headed toward the load site we had been surveilling the night before. As soon as we arrived we unloaded the horses and rushed to get suited up for the ride. We put on spurs snug against our boots and slid into thick leather chaps for protection from the desert's infinite population of thorns. We pulled our hats tight to our heads with stampede strings to keep the wind from blowing them to hell and back. We holstered our pistols above our chaps in gunbelts and placed .30 caliber Winchester repeating carbines in our saddle scabbards. After checking our saddle-bags for food and water we turned to make ready the horses.

After getting saddled, Butch and I picked up the smugglers' trail from the load site and urged the horses up into a steady trotting gait. Sometimes the trail that the mules were heading south on was in an easy-to-follow direct line. At unexpected intervals, the outlaws would veer off in a zigzagging pattern, trying to hit track-concealing patches of lava rocks. As we stayed on their trail, we rode through century-old Apache hunting camps. The uncaring dope smugglers ahead of us were trampling and breaking cherished, centuries-old historical pieces of pottery and artifacts without a second thought. All the outlaws thought of was getting their merchandise to the silver-laden markets of America's big cities.

When the terrain permitted, Butch and I spurred the horses into a sweat-lathering gallop. We made good time until we hit a brushy area filled with squatty greasewoods and prickly pear cactus. The going got so difficult that the horses started jumping over brush instead of walking through it to avoid being stuck by the thorns. Eventually Butch and I would have to stop every mile or so and use fencing pliers to dig out and forcibly extract the thorns from the horses' bleeding forelegs and chests.

After tracking the mule train south toward Mexico for about five or six miles through the San Bernardino Valley, we saw that the Mexicans had split up. Three of them headed west toward the Chiricahuas and the remaining three trotted off east for the Peloncillos. Butch and I figured that they must have seen the dust trail from our horses and surmised that some mounted lawmen were quickly gaining on them.

By now a U.S. Customs Service Blackhawk helicopter had caught up to us and we were in radio contact with the pilot as he streaked overhead. We decided to split up, with Butch taking the Peloncillo group and me taking the Chiricahua-destined trail seekers. As we separated, the helicopter let us know that he'd search the valley until he got low on fuel and had to return to base. As the chopper flew off into the sun I couldn't help but wonder what Cochise or Geronimo would think about their former enemy, the U.S. Cavalry, now being airborne as the U.S. Air Cavalry.

We kept on our respective trails, while the cool morning passed into the warming afternoon. The Blackhawk had departed after never really contributing any useful information to Butch or me. Most of the older agents will tell you this as a God-given fact. In the end, after taking away all the machines, computers, and modern technology, the old way is the best way. Tracks don't lie. They don't give false testimony. They speak for themselves. If you can learn how to read them, how to interpret them, they'll tell you the true story. It's that simple.

My mare was getting pretty lathered up when Butch radioed me on the walkie-talkie. He was riding a twelve-year-old sorrel gelding quarter horse that answered to the name of Cougar. Now, I knew

Cougar could be an ornery, mean, stubborn son of a bitch when the mood struck him. He's thrown more than his share of good riders. But Butch had previously ridden Cougar on deer-hunting trips and they had always come to terms with each other. In other words, Cougar had never yet unassed Butch from the saddle. So I was somewhat surprised when Butch radioed me and said that he was having trouble with the old gelding.

Butch said that he had been going along fine on the trail of his group of outlaws when Cougar just stopped dead in his tracks and froze. He said the gelding wouldn't budge no matter how hard he put the spurs to him. I asked Butch if Cougar had his ears up or down. I knew that if his ears were laid back he was about to pitch a fit and go rodeo with Butch all over the Sonoran Desert. But if his ears were up it probably meant that he was alerting to something ahead in the brush.

Butch radioed back that Cougar's ears were up and his eyes were trained straight ahead toward a mesquite thicket. It didn't take an experienced lawman too long to do the math on the situation. He studied the mesquite thicket he was about to ride into, cracked a smile to himself, and whispered on the radio, "Hey, I got a couple of mesquites here with boots and tennis shoes growing out of the bottom of the higher limbs."

Cougar had done a fine job for Butch. They had avoided being ambushed and possibly killed by the desperados lying in wait ahead. Butch rode up and took the three assholes out of the mesquites at gunpoint. They were all armed with razor-sharp, throat-slitting Buck knives. They would've no doubt sent Butch to the morgue that day had he ridden unaware under the mesquite tree where the outlaws were treacherously perched.

After having them peel their clothes back for a further weapons inspection, Butch chained them together with leg irons and handcuffs. He then marched the chain-linked outlaws out of the valley toward Geronimo Trail with old trusty Cougar studying their every move like a starving dog ready to pounce on a piece of fresh raw meat. Later that day over a beer with our other agents, Butch, in all appreciation, would rename Cougar. He would be known from this day forward as "Radar."

After Butch radioed me that he was Code Four with his group of dope smugglers in custody, I continued on my trail, still bound for Geronimo's Chiricahua Mountains. It was only about thirty minutes later that I was somewhat puzzled by the disappearance of the group I was tracking. They had endeavored to cross a dry sand wash but hadn't come out on the other side. Their tracks stopped. It's times like these that you really begin to wonder about UFO sightings and their alleged kidnappings!

I cut back and forth trying to pick up the outlaws' tracks on both sides of the desert wash. Nada! There were tracks of wiry javelina pigs and mule deer, but nothing human in the area. I got pissed off and frustrated, thinking I had to have miscued while I was following their trail. I decided to sit still on my mare for a minute or so and think about the last track I had and what mountain or land marker the Mexicans were bearing on.

As I sat still looking at the sand draw I noticed my sorrel quarter horse mare was getting a bit antsy. Wendy was only about five years old and you can expect a horse that age to be a little skittish yet. When I was training her as a two-year-old she had once launched my ass with ten toes and ten fingers to the stars after she spooked to a rattlesnake that had taken her off guard. But this time she was doing a jig that I'd never seen on her dance card before. She kept throwing her nose in the air and snorting toward the draw. She would shift her weight on her rear, back and forth between her legs. But the whole time she kept her front legs square center toward the draw signaling me that there was imminent danger ahead that I couldn't see.

I went with Wendy's instincts and pulled my pistol from its dust-filled holster. I took aim into the middle of the sand draw, cocked back the .357 Magnum's hammer, and bellowed in Spanish, "Stand up with your hands up, you sons of bitches!" For a few moments it looked as though I was acting on a fool's hunch. But after a few seconds I saw the sand start to shift as if a gopher or rattler was just under the surface. I yelled again for the outlaws to stand up and surrender or meet their maker.

If you think I was surprised, you should've seen Wendy when the bastards came rising up out of the ground like some damn evil decomposing corpses. Wendy pitched and jumped a couple of times while I tried to keep a bead on the Grateful Dead crew. These guys had sand in their noses, eyes, ears, hair, everywhere. It was probably even up their butts and under their nuts. The only part that convinced me they were alive was the circles of moisture around their lips and eyelids. Other than that they looked like three stiffs that ought to be laid out in a Sonoran funeral parlor!

Without dismounting Wendy, I took handcuffs and leg irons from my saddlebags and threw them to the three Mexican desperados. I had them put the irons on each other in a way that hooked 'em up like mountain stream trout on a stringer. After they were all secured, Wendy and I pushed them on up toward Geronimo Trail until we met up with Butch and his formerly treed outlaws. The following day, six more dope smugglers went before the judge and that was pretty much the way the use of horses by Customs special agents in Cochise County was reborn in the latter part of the past century.

The horses proved so effective that the Customs Service eventually gave us four horses that had been forfeited to the government as proceeds from a money-laundering investigation. As time went along we even were able to get horse trailers and saddles that had been seized from dope smugglers or their financial investors. We started the whole horse program using dopers' money without having to hit the taxpayer up for a dime.

U.S. Customs Special Agent Allan Sperling had just wrapped up the Machichi case as the horse program was getting off the ground. Sperling had recently entered on duty with us directly from the Pima County Sheriff's Department, where he had served as a range deputy outside of Tucson.

Sperling was raised on his grandfather's working ranch in northern Arizona. His folks were divorced when he was fairly young, giving rise to his restlessness. The youngster joined the Navy when he was seventeen by lying about his age. He volunteered for the elite and secret Submarine Service and later attempted to get into the Seal teams. That in itself should tell you something about his drive and mental determination. However, the Submarine Service was considered a priority by the Department of the Navy, and they would not release Sperling from that commitment to join the Seals. After his service with the Navy, he returned to Arizona and eventually became a range deputy.

When Sperling entered duty with us he was about thirty years old with a country boy's smile. His small, sturdy frame sported bulging, muscular forearms that resemble those of the cartoon character Popeye. He was a good-humored Arizona cowboy in every sense of the word. You never saw him wearing anything other than cowboy boots, belted jeans, a Western shirt, and a black felt Stetson with his own genuine hand-braided stampede string woven out of groomed horsehair. His skin was always tanned from the sun, while his face bore the traces of many dust storms and rancorous barroom brawls. The first time Butch and I met Sperling we knew he would be the man to head up our horse patrol.

Over the next few years we used the horses for a variety of law-enforcement purposes along the Mexican border in Cochise County. On one occasion we seized 277 head of smuggled cattle from shipping pens on the border near the Douglas Port of Entry. We even got a call from the Cochise County Sheriff's Department to find a body. Now, you might wonder what's so peculiar about that call for assistance? Well, this body was headless. Yes, I mean decapitated. It seems a dog had been found near an adobe-mud house in the desert feasting on a human head and no one knew where the hell the pup's supper came from. Sounds like a job for the horses, doesn't it? Wrong!

We trailered the horses out and dropped off near the border east of Douglas, where we found the Cochise deputies waiting for us. After being briefed, we backtracked the head where it had been dragged by the dog across the dry dirt and rocks. Before we found the body we could smell the odor left by the Reaper. The decomposing cadaver smelled so foul that it nearly knocked us out of our saddles. No matter how many times you've encountered it before, it's a smell that you can never really get used to.

I was riding Wendy and Butch was straddling Radar when we approached the body. And Sperling? Well, he was riding his favorite horse, the infamous Nevada, a former renegade mustang from the Bureau of Land Management (BLM). The BLM had transferred Nevada to us because he kept pitching everybody into the dust. Up until this day no one had been able to stay on the rank son of a bitch without being thrown or trampled near to death. Not wanting to be around Nevada when he blew, Butch and I decided to ride up ahead of Sperling so we wouldn't be in the mustang's way when the rodeo started.

We spotted the body lying in the greasewoods about fifteen yards from the border fence. It looked like an old man, probably from Mexico or South America. According to his tracks and what we could surmise, the *viejo* (old man) had crossed the fence, taken his clothes off, and folded them neatly in a pile as if he knew his final hour was upon him. It looked like he just lay down, placing his hands across his chest, and then expired like he had planned it that way. I pondered it a bit and figured that maybe he just wanted to die in a country that he longed to have been born in. Or maybe, he just wanted to die in a country that would perhaps give him a decent burial before stray starving Mexican dogs devoured the remainder of his once-sacred flesh. I reckon only the good Lord knows the answer for sure.

While Butch and I passed the chewing tobacco between us we calculated the foul, oozing, gaping, dark hole between the body's shoulders. Then we settled back in our saddles and waited for the rodeo. Sperling was just riding up and we could see that Nevada was already winding up to pitch a fit. I bet Butch five bucks that Sperling wouldn't stay in the saddle after Nevada smelled the corpse. We stuffed our mouths with tobacco and waited for the show to start like a couple of old buzzards guarding their roadkill.

The wind must have died down because Allan rode right up to the body before Nevada smelled it. The last thing I remember seeing Nevada do was halt cold in his tracks and lower his short, stocky neck between his front legs. I swear it looked to me like the bastard started to glow just before he went vertical. It was like a heat-seeking SAM missile just being launched.

Now, Butch and I knew a little bit about international law. But we just weren't too sure who should be held responsible for the destruction of a perfectly good section of U.S.-Mexican border fence. Was it Nevada? Sperling? The rotting corpse? Or how about the spectators in Mexico who were waving their hats and urging Sperling to stay on his crazy, glazed-eyed steed as he made several illegal entries back and forth between their country and the U.S.? I gladly gave Butch the five bucks and chalked it up to an admission fee well worth the price. After all, we had just had front-row tickets to what may have been the only completely international saddle-bronc riding event in rodeo history!

In June of 1992, we began to find horse tracks coming out of Mexico near Guadalupe Canyon that traveled north and south through the San Bernardino Valley. Sperling, Barrett, and I mounted our horses and cut the trail where it illegally crossed the border fence. We followed the tracks of four shod horses to a dope stash site on Highway 80 near Apache, Arizona. It took us about six or seven hours on a one-way trip eighteen miles north. This meant that the smugglers were making a thirty-six-mile round-trip within about a twelve- or fourteen-hour time span. Since the summer nights allowed about nine hours of darkness, we knew their Achilles heel would be getting back into Mexico before sunup.

Since the horses were shod with iron shoes, we placed electronic magnetic ground sensors on their trail where they would pass through a saddle in the Guadalupe Canyon area during their smuggling trip north. We didn't have to wait but a couple of days until the sensors were activated and we had a shot at confronting the outlaws. The only problem was that we were working a different load of dope on the other side of Cochise County. We knew we were too far out of pocket, but we wanted to give it a good go anyway.

After busting the other dope load, Sperling and I headed over to the San Bernardino Valley with our horses in tow. But as luck would have it, we got in on the trail too late to have a good shot at going up against the dope-smuggling riders when they were northbound. The only option we had was to follow the tracks on their return trip south into Mexico. We felt that this would help us learn where they were cutting the ranchers' fences, what water holes they stopped at, and other habits a hunter needs to know about his prey.

The southbound tracks appeared to be no more than an hour or two old. To quickly gain on the smugglers, Sperling and I used an old U.S. Cavalry method of hunting Apache renegades during the Indian Wars. One of us would stay on the tracks while the other would gallop up about a half a mile or so. When the forward rider re-cut the trail he would signal the back rider to gallop up and take his position. We repeated this "leap-frogging" as we closed the distance between us and the outlaws. Our mounted effort must have put some pressure on the smugglers, because their tracks indicated they were pushing their horses extremely hard. We eventually came up on one of their southbound horses down and dying about three miles north of the border.

The bay gelding was completely lathered in sweat as he lay near death, gasping for air. He still had his saddle on, which meant that we were probably fairly close to having caught the shitheads. And shitheads is just what these guys were! They nearly rode this horse to death and then left him to die without having the decency to take his saddle and bridle off so that the animal could at least attempt to fend for himself. The gelding's ribs and flanks were bleeding from having been incessantly ripped by the sharp rowels of the Mexican spurs. In addition, he had his hide rubbed off down to the red, raw flesh, which was now protruding from his shoulders. It was apparent from such wounds that the smugglers had strapped way too much of the heavy dope load on the poor animal during the northbound run.

As the flies gathered on the horse's flesh, and the accompanying buzzards started their circles of death, Sperling dismounted and forced himself near the abandoned animal. I've seen Sperling cry like a baby before when he had to have a veterinarian put a sick horse to sleep. He's the type of guy that can be tough as nails on a criminal when he deserves it. But on the other hand, he will go out of his way to render aid to a hurting animal.

I knew that these shitheads had just made a mistake that would eventually bring them down. They had pissed off one of the last lawmen in Cochise County you'd want to start dogging your trail. To Sperling, they were no longer just mounted dope smugglers. According to Sperling's own personal law book, these Mexican desperados had now descended to one of the lowest form of outlaws on earth: low-life, scum-sucking horse abusers who had worn out their welcome in Cochise County!

Before the flies and buzzards could finish their natural tasks, Sperling worked with the gelding and got him on his feet. We removed his saddle and bridle, but he was still too weak to travel. Luckily he was near a water tank, where he could eventually get a drink after gaining some strength. Sperling returned to the water tank off and on over the next few days. He fed and doctored the gelding until his survival was ensured. When he was satisfied that the horse was going to make it, Sperling turned his attention to hunting down the criminals.

Sperling already knew most of the ranchers in the San Bernardino Valley. For the most part these folks are salt-of-the-earth people whose families have ranched for generations and generations in the valley. In fact, these ranches go so far back in Arizona history that some of them still don't have the modern amenity of electricity run out to them yet.

Knowing he could depend on such folks, Sperling set about asking them for help in finding out who the mounted smugglers could be. Through the ranchers' pipeline of contacts south of the border, he was told about a Mexican vaquero named Ignacio Ledesma who lived in Sonora just south of the San Bernardino Valley. Sperling learned that Ledesma had worked as a cowboy on most of the ranches in the valley. This would have allowed him to learn the country and study the route he would use to smuggle dope out of Mexico into Arizona. Ledesma was described as a rock-hard, tough-as-nails forty-five-year-old Mexican desperado who could survive an indefinite period in the mountains using his basic instincts and savvy. He would prove to be a formidable adversary.

Armed with this information, Sperling watched the sensor monitor day and night for any signs of activity on the Guadalupe Canyon outlaw trail. After about two weeks, the outlaws' horses tripped the magnetic sensors at about 8:00 p.m. one evening. Sperling radioed me that the horses were on the way north with a load of dope. We had already made plans that I and some other agents would drive ahead to the stash site near Apache and set up surveillance. Sperling would trailer our horses to a drop-off site on Geronimo Trail, getting south of the smugglers.

The plan was to let the mounted smugglers drop their dope load near Apache and ride off unmolested southbound into the dark. The other agents and I would wait for the load vehicle and arrest the pickup guy when he took possession of the dope. I would then haul ass to Geronimo Trail, meeting Sperling with the horses. Sperling and I would mount up, ride up into the mountains near the border, and surprise the riders just after sunup on their return trip into Mexico. It sounded like a great plan, right? Yeah, but Murphy's Law was about to come into play. Anything that can go wrong, will go wrong.

It was about midnight or one in the morning when I heard the sound of shod horses' hooves clicking across the volcanic lava rocks near Apache. The clicking hooves got louder and louder as the horses neared my position. I was about a quarter of a mile from the stash site, hiding near some shipping corrals on a Chiricahua cattle ranch. It was a pitch-dark night with the voluminous summer rain clouds blotting out any hope for much-needed light from the stars or the moon. I could hardly see my own hand in front of my face, much less the outlaw riders sneaking their contraband up near the highway. I sat perfectly still in the dark and cupped my hands behind my ears like megaphones. Between the howls from the ever-present packs of coyotes, I listened intently for any sound being made by the smugglers or their mounts.

After about five minutes, I heard the horses' hooves start to move across the volcanic beds again. The clip-clopping hooves faded off into the distance, going south toward old Mexico. Their clicking cadence dissipating into the darkness reminded me of some mystical Western legend. Like in the folklore of the ghost riders in the sky, I never even saw their figures in the dark. I radioed Sperling and the other agents that the dope had been dropped off and the "ghostly" riders were returning to Mexico. All we had to do now was wait on the pick-up vehicle to arrive and take possession of the dope.

We waited for several hours before a van showed up. The guy stopped at the stash site and turned his headlights off. I could hear him opening and closing doors on the van. Then his headlights came back on and he started to drive north on the highway. I radioed the other agents the take-down phrase for rapid action, "It's show time, boys!"

Like banshees from hell, several USCS agents fired up their trucks and came barreling down on the van from different hills in the San Bernardino Valley. Upon seeing the rapidly approaching agents, the driver of the van braked to a screeching halt on the highway. I couldn't help but laugh to myself while thinking that the outlaw probably soiled his pants. But it turned out that the joke was on me. When we opened the van it was empty!

I stood there in the dark on the side of the highway and tried to put the pieces of the puzzle together. I knew I had heard the horses come north and depart south from the stash site. Why wouldn't they have dropped the dope? What went wrong? Did the riders have night-vision goggles allowing them to spot our surveillance in the dark? None of it made any sense. I looked at the driver's boots. They were dusty. He had evidently been walking out in the desert. So, why didn't he pick up the load?

It was now getting close to sunup, which presented a couple of problems. First, I wasn't going to be able to drive down south and meet Sperling in time to help him intercept the returning riders. Second, Sperling couldn't jump the outlaws if we didn't have the dope. Without the dope as evidence, all we would end up with was a couple of illegal aliens who would probably claim they were riding horses at night when they inadvertently crossed the border. And as far as the judicial system was concerned, that was at best a minimal misdemeanor offense. We knew that this was our one and only chance to arrest these assholes because the driver of the van would later tell Ledesma that we had been waiting at the stash site. Needless to say, they wouldn't roll the dice again after that.

THE HORSE PATROL 93

Sperling called me on the radio and asked what was going on. I told him that Murphy's Law was kicking us in the ass and it didn't look like he was going to be able to grab Ledesma and his partners for any real violation of law. The radio was silent and Sperling gave no indication of replying. I could just picture him sitting there on his horse, steam pouring out of his ears, as he spit his chew of tobacco all over the desert. A once-in-a-lifetime law-enforcement opportunity was going up in smoke. I knew what he was thinking because we had jawed about it before. It was one thing to nail these assholes because of their cruelty to animals. But the other thing was historically juicy.

Here it is 1992. We're approaching the turn of the twenty-first century and this could damn well be one of the last few times in our history that mounted U.S. law officers in Arizona get to chase outlaws down on horseback! At least in our careers, our lifespans, we probably wouldn't get to do it again.

I got my head out of my ass and tried to figure out where the dope could be. I had to find it before sunup! The riders were probably within half an hour of Sperling's ambush. Okay. Let's start with the driver and where he stopped at the stash site. I went back to the stash site and found his boot tracks. I backtracked him out into the desert. His tracks seemed to meander around in the area with no real direction or intent. I kept following him around while I cursed the numerous black lava rocks that I kept tripping over. The sun wasn't completely up yet, but daylight was beginning to break. I've never had an ulcer before, but one was coming on damn fast.

Sperling radioed me that he had the riders in his binoculars about one mile from his location near Guadalupe Canyon's infamous outlaw entrance into Mexico. He said that they would be coming through the mountain gap where he was waiting in about ten minutes. Should he jump them or give them a round-trip ticket back into the old country? I radioed that he had a red light until further notice. I knew we were getting close to the nut cutting, but we had ten precious minutes left to keep looking for the hidden dope.

I was walking through and around the black lava rocks when I jammed the toe of my boot into a soft, spongy piece of black soil that buckled my knees. I hit the ground, landing on my stomach like a sack of potatoes. In the faint light I could barely see that the black dirt wasn't what it seemed to be. No wonder the van driver didn't have the dope. He couldn't find the shit! It was bagged in black military duffel bags and Ledesma had hidden it between the lava rocks. Hell, I don't think you could've even seen the stash if you had been standing on it in broad daylight!

I radioed Sperling that we had seized about five hundred pounds of marijuana and that he had a green light to take the riders down. I also informed him that he would have to do it alone. There was no way any of us could get south to him in time to be of any use. Sperling radioed back that he understood the situation and he was going to confront the smugglers on his own anyway. I knew he could handle it, but you always worry about one of your partners when he doesn't have any backup in a deadly situation like this.

Sperling, being the smart desert border rat he is, used every advantage nature could give him for his ambush. In the saddle of the mountains he had picked to make his stand, he found a depression to hide his mount. In an admirably Apache fashion, Sperling then cut and broke mesquite tree limbs to form a crude but effective blind for himself and his horse to hide behind. He had the sun to his back and he was on the higher ground. This meant that when the smugglers rode up the trail through the saddle the sun would be in their eyes. It was everything a lawman could ask for against a superior number of outlaws.

As the riders approached the saddle, Sperling counted four horses with two riders. He was unable to tell if anyone had handguns, but he was pretty sure they at least didn't have rifles. The lead rider was dressed in a black long-sleeve Western shirt with leather leggings covering his jeans down to his boots. From the heels of his pointed-toe Mexican riding boots hung the blood-crusted, long-shanked, flesh-tearing spurs. Atop his head sat a faded dark sombrero. Sperling figured this lead rider to be Ledesma. He knew if the riders split up Ledesma would be his first priority to bring in. He waited until Ledesma was no more than ten yards away when he drew his .45

automatic Colt and rode onto the trail blocking the outlaws' path into their sanctuary of Mexico.

Ledesma's weather-worn face turned into a perfect medical journal's description of sheer panic. He jerked his reins back so hard that his horse reared high up on his hind two legs. The outlaw wheeled his mount around and dug his sharp spurs into the horse's ribs while screaming and urging him into a dead run off the side of the mountain. By the time Sperling saw the second rider, he had already cut the pack horses loose, and it was a pandemonious sight to behold. There were riders and horses whipping dirt and rocks up in a hellacious storm of fear as they attempted to get down the mountain and as far away from Sperling as possible.

Thinking of the Mexican gelding that Ledesma had abandoned to die a slow, painful death, Sperling gave chase after the bastard. Being that his mount was fresh, he knew he would have no problem overtaking the smuggler's horse, which had just made a thirty-six-mile trip. He watched as Ledesma got to the bottom of the mountains and then turned east toward a flat mesa that would take him around the yucca-covered side of the mountains into Mexico. Sperling knew exactly where he could intercept the outlaw before he made it south. He rode hell-bent for leather up through the saddle of the mountain and turned east too, following a ridge line. Sperling coaxed his mount through the rocks and off the opposite side of the mountain that the smugglers had taken. After a several-minute dead run he drew near Ledesma and his mount as they were going through the flatland toward the border fence.

Sperling ran his horse parallel to Ledesma's and caught up to him. When they were side by side running at full speed Sperling screamed at the smuggler to stop. Ledesma gave Sperling a snarling glare showing his contempt for the lawman. Sperling jerked his .45 from its holster and pointed it at the sneering bastard's chest and again ordered him to stop. Instead of yielding, Ledesma spurred his mount harder as he bent forward aligning his body along the horse's neck. The more the smuggler dug his barbaric spurs into his mount, the more Sperling wanted to bring the bastard to justice.

Sperling looked south over the top of his lather-soaked horse and saw that the border fence was about a quarter of a mile away. The son of a bitch was going to make it into Mexico if he didn't figure out a way to pull him in quick! At this point Sperling figured he had given this asshole every chance to come peaceable. Enough was enough! He aimed his .45 in front of Ledesma's mount and fired several times, throwing lead into the ground. Ledesma wasn't expecting it when his horse came to a skidding halt in the dirt. Like a rock being shot from a slingshot, Ledesma went right up over the top of his horse's head and ended up face first on the gravel-covered desert floor. The outlaw's once-snarling face was now transformed into a rock-scraped, bloody pulp of defeat.

Sperling dismounted and picked up what was left of the now submissive Ledesma from the ground. He handcuffed Ledesma and then forced the sullen bleeding bastard back up into his sweat-soaked saddle. After ripping the punishing Mexican spurs from Ledesma's boots, the Customs agent took his prisoner's horse by the reins and led Ledesma north through the valley to his eventual incarceration in the Cochise County Jail. Ledesma would later be found guilty of marijuana smuggling charges for which he was sentenced to five years in a federal prison. As for the animal abuse offense, Sperling figured justice had been served when Ledesma's horse dumped him on his butt-ugly face just short of Sonora. As Sperling later reflected on the arrest, he knew that former Cochise County Sheriff "Texas" John Slaughter would have been pleased. Once again, mounted law and order had prevailed in one of the last outlaw strongholds in the Old West.

5
The Agua Prieta Cartel

AS EXPECTED, WE LATER LEARNED from informants that Ledesma's horse operation was financed and operated by members of the Agua Prieta cartel. Most fingers kept pointing us in the specific direction of Yolanda Molina and her husband, Antonio Hernández. Both of them had criminal records in Arizona dating back to the late '60s or early '70s. Yolanda had been busted for petty shoplifting in Douglas, while Antonio had gone down while transporting a couple hundred pounds of grass near Tucson. But from humble beginnings some of the best criminal minds take hold and grow.

Over the years the Mexican couple saved their grimy pesos and *plata* (silver, money) until they could invest in some hundred-hectare dope fields in Sonora and Colima. They kept reinvesting and turning profits back into the business until they eventually were worth enough to gain a position of influence with judges and the Mexican Federal Judicial Police (MFJP). Once Tony and Yolanda were making enough profits to keep these politicos on the payroll, they were on their way to becoming part of the Agua Prieta cartel.

The Douglas U.S. Customs Service special agents continued to knock down numerous Agua Prieta cartel loads of marijuana and cocaine between 1987 and 1989. During this two-year period we identified those loads that belonged to the Molina family, which predicated our targeting of them as our first bite to be taken out of the cartel. Knowing that the best way to really hurt them was to take their money, we located about $2 million of their narcotics proceeds, sitting right in front of us in Douglas banks.

The dope cartel of Agua Prieta was now making so much money that the Douglas banks, which used to have to ship money to Agua Prieta's banks for factory payroll purposes, were now seeing a reversal in their procedures. In 1987, for the first time ever, the Douglas banks received $7 million from Agua Prieta to be deposited in the U.S. Federal Reserve. This was more or less the beginning of the Mexican dope lords' takeover of Agua Prieta and Douglas. The face of the border was about to become bloodier than at any other time in Arizona's tenure as a state. The cartel would eventually rival Pancho Villa's army as the most ruthless armed force ever on the frontera between Douglas and Agua Prieta.

Tutored by some scum-sucking dope-defense attorney, the Molina family had made a feeble, unsuccessful attempt at laundering the money and rolling it over through different accounts in various Douglas banks. But in the end it was always deposited in some distant relative's name, making it pretty easy to identify. Besides, they weren't really scared that anything was going to happen to the money. No lawmen had ever hit any of the Agua Prieta and Douglas dope organizations in their financial midsection. But the cartel's impunity was about to come to a screeching halt.

Butch and I took the case to the federal prosecutor, the Assistant United States Attorney (AUSA) in Tucson, where much to our surprise it was turned down. The AUSA handling the case told us not to return to his office until we had witnesses ready to testify that they "muled" the money into the U.S. illegally at the behest of the Molina family. The AUSA added some other investigative demands, but it always came down to having informants or cooperating defendants testify before he would authorize seizure warrants for the money and property.

We tried to explain to the pencil-neck attorney that we already had a hefty body count of murdered informants that could be attributed to the cartel. We argued that it would be literal suicide for anyone to take the stand against the cartel in court. But this particular

AUSA wouldn't listen to our pleadings. He was the typical "safe at home" REMF. He had never had to view the tortured body of an informant for identification purposes. I'm sure that white-collar proper gentleman never woke up at night in a soaking wet sweat after seeing the remains of such a body. I can only imagine that it must be nice to work 120 miles away from the border's violence in a federally protected building.

Now, don't go slapping all the AUSAs in Tucson with this guy's label. The majority of them are some of the hardest-working prosecutors you'll ever meet. These guys and gals work for peanuts compared to what they could make defending dope smugglers. These are the rare few attorneys with enough self-respect to put morals before mammon. They believe in the law and have a conscience about where the money that's feeding their children comes from. If we didn't have folks like these AUSAs, the whole country would be screwed. However, the luck of the draw for federal prosecutors in this investigation didn't get me to first base. It was time for some tricky legal maneuvering. It was time to call Special Agent Arturo Bernal.

I had known Bernal since 1974 when he was a Cochise County Sheriff's deputy and I was a Border Patrol agent. He worked his way up the ladder, earning a position as a detective assigned to the Border Alliance Group. After retiring from the Sheriff's Department, Bernal was hired by the Arizona Attorney General's Office as a special agent. After he entered on duty with the state, the Attorney General assigned Bernal to our office in Douglas, where we had worked together on dozens of dope cases. However, Bernal's most notable investigative forte was financial forfeiture and money-laundering cases. And that was just the caliber of ammo we would need for the weapon we were presently loading.

Bernal, another border rat like Butch, had been born in Douglas. He knew most of the people in the area and his contacts on both sides of the border were impressive as well as secretive. He was a good-humored fellow who wore a continual smile on his slightly rounded face. His receding dark-brown hair accented his high forehead, and he always reminded me of that little happy smiley-face Pac-Man guy who was so popular in the '80s. His integrity was rock-solid, honest to the bone. He was one of the few agents I worked with in Cochise County that I truly trusted with my life.

Like Butch and me, Bernal had served a year in Vietnam. He spent his time in the bush with an Army artillery unit on a firebase. Although he had lived through some shit, he didn't talk about it much. When Butch and I swapped war stories, Bernal would always hang around and listen. With that combat vet's familiar faraway stare, he would contribute a few words to the conversation. But for the most part he was content to listen to Butch and me chew the fat while he gazed out the window, going back in time to younger days.

I often thought that Bernal may have had problems dealing with the war, because he never said much about it. But I later learned that was just his style. He was a quiet, reserved, and observing type. Always giving that smile, he would diligently study people when they talked. It was almost as if he was trying to get inside their heads to see what made them tick. These were just some of the steady qualities I always admired about Bernal.

Bernal was pretty much up to speed on the investigation when I approached him with the AUSA's final words. He had been helping Butch and me for the past two years. About 50 percent or better of the intelligence we gathered for the case had come from Bernal and his contacts in Mexico. I explained to him that the AUSA had declined to prosecute the case and asked him if he could get the Arizona Attorney General to take a shot at it. Bernal didn't let any grass grow under his feet. Within a couple of days we were in Phoenix pitching the case to State Prosecutor Kip Holmes.

Holmes was the Arizona Attorney General's right-hand man for forfeitures. Holmes, a former police officer, had written most of the present Arizona laws on racketeering and money-laundering. He was the primo source on the subject and I figured we might as well get from the number-one guy what was wrong with our investigation. I had never before done a civil drug-proceeds and money-laundering type of case. So at least it would be a good lesson for this country boy. Live and learn, as they say.

Bernal and I presented our evidence to Holmes using some flow charts, maps, and time-linking data. A little razzle-dazzle went along with it, but nothing more than the AUSA in Tucson had gotten. After the presentation, Bernal and I sat down and waited to hear the same old song and dance we had heard from the federal prosecutor. Boy, were we surprised! Or maybe I should say that Holmes was the surprised one. His face was frowning with a questioning twist to it when he asked us if we were sure the AUSA didn't want the case. We kept insisting that the feds wouldn't accept it, and Holmes couldn't understand why. He kept looking for the proverbial skeleton in the closet, I guess. After a long, drawn-out sigh, Holmes looked Bernal and me in the eyes and said, "Boys, tell me what's wrong with the case."

When we told him what the feds had said at our last meeting about "don't return without testimony or confessions," Holmes's face turned into an evil, sharp grin. He knew the feds had just missed a golden opportunity to score some big points for the good guys because they were too lazy to do a little legwork. As he sat there thinking of the unlimited possibilities this investigation would give him to kick open the dope doors in Douglas and Agua Prieta, he reminded me of a high-school kid being asked by the prom queen if he would please use a rubber the next time. Needless to say, Holmes took the case on face value, saying that we had more than enough to seize the Molina family's money and assets.

Due to all of the corruption and leaks in Douglas, the special agent in charge of my office agreed with Attorney General Holmes that Bernal and I would remove our files and evidence from Douglas and spend the next two weeks in Phoenix at the AG's office. Under Holmes's tutoring and watchful eye, Bernal and I wrote a hundred-page affidavit and summary report explaining the Agua Prieta cartel's structure and the Molina family's position in it.

In the affidavit we detailed the movement of thousands of pounds of cocaine and marijuana and connected the proceeds to twenty-three bank accounts, several houses, numerous vehicles, and a ranch on the U.S.-Mexican border. When we were done, an Arizona Superior Court judge issued seizure warrants for all of the narcotics proceeds belonging to the Molina family that we could uncover in the U.S. Armed with the seizure warrants, Bernal and I went back down to Douglas and coordinated the largest federal narcotics bank raid in the history of Cochise County. It had never been done before, and it has never been done since.

On February 2, 1989, a clear, cold winter morning, we dispatched teams of USCS agents, DEA agents, Border Patrol agents, detectives of the Cochise County Sheriff's Department, officers of the Douglas and Bisbee police departments, and state troopers of the Arizona Department of Public Safety. The teams hit a savings-and-loan company and all three major banks in Douglas with seizure warrants for twenty-three bank accounts and numerous safety-deposit boxes. After the teams entered the banks, near pandemonium broke out in the streets of the little dope-smuggling border town. People were lining up on the sidewalks trying to get a peek through the banks' windows. Others were calling the banks to make sure *their* accounts weren't being seized or frozen.

Natalia Molina, one of Yolanda's sisters who lived in Agua Prieta, was present during the service of the search and seizure warrants on one of the Molina residences in Douglas. While our agents were searching the house she became belligerent and visibly pissed off as she stormed about threatening to sue everybody who looked like he carried a badge. She arrogantly stated that she had talked to the Douglas police chief, Alvaro Fragoso. She really messed up and opened new doors to the investigation when she implied that she had some kind of pull with the chief. To cast further doubt on Chief Fragoso, she called him on the phone and then turned to one of the searching USCS agents and said that the chief wanted to talk to him.

The Customs agent picked up the phone, identified himself, and asked to whom he was speaking. The man identified himself as Douglas Chief of Police Fragoso. The chief asked what kind of warrants were being conducted and wanted to know why he wasn't informed of the investigation and enforcement action beforehand. The agent explained that it was a need-to-know investigation that had obviously been kept low-key until now. The last thing the chief wanted to know before hanging up was if Natalia was going to be arrested. Now, isn't this interesting? The Douglas chief of police is on a first-name basis with one of the cartel member's sisters, and he's worried if she's being arrested. Why?

And while we're talking about upstanding political figures that the Molina family dealt with in Cochise County, let's not forget Justice of the Peace Joe Borane in Douglas. During the course of our investigation, before the seizure warrants were secretly issued in Phoenix, Bernal photographed Yolanda Molina and one of her most trusted money mules, Benjamin Loreto, as they departed Judge Borane's office. We were later informed that the meeting was private, personal business being conducted between the judge and Yolanda behind closed doors. According to our source in the judge's office at that time, this was not a "judicial" discussion or matter. And if it wasn't, then what kind of meeting *was* going on between the Cochise County judge and one of the leading members of the Agua Prieta cartel?

When we were done drilling the deposit boxes, we ended up with about $1.8 million. Maybe that's not an extremely large amount as far as some crimes go, but in this little corner of Arizona and Mexico it was the biggest thing since Pancho Villa tried to take Agua Prieta in 1915. Why? Because it had never before been done, and the Mexicans had trouble understanding words like conspiracy and racketeering. As icing on the cake, we seized a border ranch of about 1,600 acres that had been "straw purchased" by the Molina family from a Douglas real estate company run by Judge Joe Borane.

On February 7, 1989, five days after the seizure, Ben Loreto's son visited Bernal and me at our office. Ben Jr., who was at that time an Arizona Department of Public Safety officer, told us that he believed we did in fact have a good money-laundering case on his dad. Ben Jr. attempted to suck Bernal and me into enough conversation that we would reveal whether we had additional criminal charges on his father concerning narcotics smuggling. We didn't take the bait, leaving Ben Jr. to dangle and dive for cover. He departed our office unaware he was being tailed. He was followed to Judge Borane's office, where our well-placed source told us another closed-door meeting took place.

Isn't it peculiar how much contact we've seen so far between the Molina family, the Douglas judge, and the Douglas chief of police? Do you still wonder why Bernal and I had to write our affidavits and reports 250 miles away in Phoenix?

As can well be expected, the Molina family became enraged and embarked on a snitch hunt. Their bought and paid-for Mexican Federal Judicial Police *comandante* in Agua Prieta was a greedy, squinty-eyed little weasel named Pizarro. A rash of killings by the MFJP in Agua Prieta occurred after the Douglas bank seizures. Of course the MFJP, the hired dope smugglers and assassins that they are, labeled the shootings justifiable when they gave their official reports to the Mexican newspapers. They usually had some prefabricated bullshit story to present to the press to cover their tracks. It usually went something like, "Agents of the Mexican Federal Police proceeded to arrest the suspect in the performance of their duties, and in the course of such lawful arrest, the suspect resisted said officers, thereby forcing them to shoot him dead." But if the truth be told, members of the Mexican government have murdered a lot of innocent people while digging for our informants over the years.

During this particular murdering spree, the MFJP got lucky and hit on at least two of our informants. Concerning one of them, the Mexican newspaper quoted Comandante Pizarro as saying that his men had to kill the guy because he was armed and barricaded in his apartment. Well, Bernal and I reviewed the autopsy photographs and it seems to us that it would be hard to initiate a gunfight if your legs are bound and one of your hands is secured by handcuffs. That's right! We received autopsy photos smuggled out of Mexico, and it was plain to see the rope and cuff marks on the poor sucker's legs and wrists.

But it doesn't matter one little hair either way, even if you know the truth. The lies the MFJP tells the Mexican news media are the official way it happened. End of story. It's their piss-pot of a country and we can't say shit about what goes on from our side of the border. Besides, every year that passes, the U.S. government recertifies that the Mexican government is a worthy and honest ally in the war on drugs. And every year, the U.S. taxpayers' money gets funneled to the hands of some of the most corrupt, murderous bastards in the world: the Mexican Attorney General's Office and the MFJP. We fear and/or hate what we don't understand. To know the Mexican people is to love them. After living most of my life on the border, I have come to admire the Mexicans, although I despise their outlaws and corrupt government.

After our informants got whacked, Bernal and I waited day after day until Molina's main money courier, Ben Loreto, was detained at the Douglas Port of Entry for questioning as he was entering the U.S. While he was being held by U.S. Customs inspectors, we jumped on the opportunity to interview him about his relationship with the Molina family and Judge Borane. As it turned out, the Cochise County judge had married Ben Loreto's niece from Agua Prieta.

We arrived at the port of entry and learned Loreto was being detained in one of the holding cells. We accessed the cell and started hammering away at the guy for any kind of an admission to his involvement. He seemed to be breaking over when he said he would talk to me, and only me, alone. As you probably know from watching episodes of shows like *Kojak*, usually this means a crook is about to give it all up. So Bernal graciously dismissed himself, leaving me in the cell alone with the cartel member. Loreto walked up real close to me and got damn near nose to nose. I figured, Great! This is it! He's going to roll over and we'll have a live cartel witness to give Attorney General Holmes. It'll be like chile sauce on the enchilada, better known to ya'll Yankees as icing on the cake!

Standing face to face, the dude looked all around to see if anyone could hear and then he said, "I was sent to tell you, they're going to kill you and Bernal." Now, you can imagine, this is not the kind of confession I was waiting to hear. In fact, not believing what I had just heard this son of a bitch say, I asked him to repeat it. All he would say is, "You heard me the first time."

I went what is known in cop talk as 10–8. In civilian terms it would be something like going ballistic. Here I am, a U.S. government agent, in a U.S. government installation, and I'm being threatened by dope smugglers who are protected by the Mexican government, which is in turn certified by the U.S. government as being our allies in the war on drugs. And on top of it all, the threat is being delivered by a cartel member who is related to a Cochise County judge who conducts business with them!

Keeping in mind that the Agua Prieta cartel falls under control of the same shitheads that kidnapped and murdered former DEA agent Enrique Camarena in 1986, Bernal and I started piecing other information together. Before this, we had heard from some of our well-placed informants in Mexico that Yolanda Molina was so pissed off that she was planning to hit us. But we thought that, like most crooks we've dealt with, she was just running her mouth off for credibility purposes within the cartel. So was it time to start ducking and sliding? I didn't think so yet. Then later, another nail was driven into the coffin lid.

DEA called and said that they had an informant who had recently been at a doper meeting in a southern town in Sonora. This informant was complaining to his dope bosses about a lack of work and that he needed to make some greenbacks. The bosses told him he could make some money by getting some shooters together and taking a trip up north to Douglas. They said that there was a valid contract out for "Morgan and Butch Barrett." According to the bosses, the sponsor of the festivities was alleged to have been Yolanda Molina. The contract was open to any shooter who could fill the bill.

The immediate reaction of the USCS Internal Affairs bosses was to move us out and as far away as possible from Douglas. But that wasn't the way Butch and I saw it. Do you have any idea how stupid that is? What kind of a position does it leave the rest of your agents in? If we knuckled under here and now, before it's over, the cartel would learn that they could eventually get the whole U.S. Customs Service to leave through intimidation. And if the threats alone would work, they would take the next step of murdering an agent or two to get the whole federal government to leave Douglas like the DEA did in the late 1970s. No, it would only open the door to an escalating level of unending bullying if we ran. We told Internal Affairs we were staying and standing.

So, besides checking beneath our vehicles before we hit the ignition key, what else could we do to help ourselves out? As luck would have it, we got some badly needed help without even asking for it. In fact, you might even say we got some brotherly help from beyond the grave.

Through open court records, a limited amount of the information concerning the threats was released and picked up by the media. The newspaper buzzards splashed the threats all over the news in Phoenix, Tucson, and Cochise County. Having done their homework, the reporters even made the correct leap when they said that the assholes making the threats on us were connected to the shitheads who kidnapped and murdered Enrique Camarena. And when the big dope bosses down south got wind of this, they had no choice other than to shut the contracts down. Why? Because they couldn't afford another U.S. agent murdered in Mexico or on the border. The last time it cost them a fortune in narcotics profits.

Not only did the U.S. shut down the border when Camarena was reported missing, but the dope cartels had to pay additional protection money to the MFJP because of all the U.S. State Department heat that was put on Mexico City concerning the agent's murder. So if anyone were to ever ask me, I would have to say that without a doubt Camarena's death was not in vain. Like the deaths of our Texas heroes at the Alamo, Enrique Camarena would be a constant reminder to Mexico of their major national disgraces and defeats.

Camarena had just come back from the grave to save the lives of other U.S. agents. What better way to ward off an assassination than to publish the suspects' names, their past transgressions, and their future intended targets? Considering most judges and prosecutors in Arizona were now aware of the death threats, Butch, I, and even Bernal slept a lot better. In my humble opinion, Camarena's dedication to duty, and his ultimate sacrifice to his country, had made most U.S. agents untouchable at this point.

On March 20, 1989, one of our remaining informants in Mexico called Butch and told him that he had seen his cousin, Efraín Valdez, being kidnapped by the MFJP in Agua Prieta. The informant was allowed one brief visit with Valdez, severely beaten to near death.

During the visit an MFJP agent was continually present, preventing Valdez from telling his cousin what exactly he had been picked up for. As the informant left, Comandante Pizarro told him that Valdez would be transferred to the Nogales MFJP office for interrogation on March 27.

On March 27, 1989, Butch called USCS special agents in Nogales to see if Valdez had arrived at the MFJP office. All efforts to locate Valdez proved futile. He never arrived. More important, we now knew that the MFJP had never intended to transfer him anywhere other than to a shallow, lime-coated grave. Valdez was about to become a number in the ongoing snitch-hunt. Not having been completely idle during this investigation, the Reaper was now about to go 10–8 big time.

Depending on which investigative information you go with, there were several causes of the oncoming messy slaughter. One, the cartel was cleaning out the U.S. government's snitches on both sides of the border. Two, some misguided individuals had stolen one hundred kilos of cocaine from the cartel. Three, the same misguided individuals stole a ton of marijuana from the cartel. But any way you cut it, the St. Valentine's Day massacre in Chicago would be small-scale in comparison to the shit about to take place in Agua Prieta and Arizona.

Valdez was of particular interest to us because he was married to one of Yolanda Molina's sisters. He was one of the Molina family's main organizers for putting mule trains together. He would often lead the narcotics-laden backpacking smugglers into the U.S. himself. Before leaving Agua Prieta with Molina's dope load, he would tell his cousin where the load was destined. Unbeknownst to Valdez, his cousin would then relay the destination of the dope to us, thereby putting U.S. Customs in control of taking the load down. So you see, for all practical purposes, Valdez was an informant of the U.S. Customs Service.

On March 27, 1989, five bodies were found tortured and executed in Tucson. One of the bodies was identified as Pablo Fimbres, a resident of Douglas and a known narcotics mule for the Molina family. This discovery prompted me to pay a call on homicide detective Tom Petropolis of the Pima County Sheriff's Office in Tucson.

Petropolis was a slender hombre with black, curly hair and all the expected facial features of his Greek heritage. He was an experienced homicide dick with a somewhat cocky attitude. I would later learn that along with not being liked by a lot of his colleagues, he had a serious gambling problem.

Petropolis and I jawed a bit about the different possible motives for the murders. We indulged in the usual investigative cop talk about who done it, where, why, and how. I was mostly interested in the Fimbres connection to the Molina family. Petropolis gave me two of his theories pieced together from informants and evidence to date. One, there was a load of coke that had been ripped off from a cartel heavy. Two, somebody was concerned that some unknown snitches were giving up too much good information on the cartel's activities, including their banking practices. Petropolis dwelled on the fact that their laundered money had never been seized from the Douglas banks before our operation. We had hit them below the belt and they were pissed off about it.

On March 30, 1989, twelve bodies were discovered in the bottom of a water well on Los Alamos ranch, several miles west of Agua Prieta near the border. The Mexican government asked for assistance from Arizona's Pima County Search and Rescue Unit because the Mexicans didn't have the expertise and equipment needed to extract the bodies from the bottom of the well. Petropolis, not officially allowed to conduct an investigation in Mexico, accompanied Search and Rescue to "offer his assistance" to the Mexicans. After all the dead bodies he had previously seen in his many years on the job, Petropolis was still profoundly shocked at what he saw at the Los Alamos ranch. It was satanic.

As we had expected, Efraín Valdez's was one of the tortured and mutilated bodies to be recovered from the well. You want to talk about some gross, putrid shit, these bodies resembled anything but humans. The slimy skins and raw flesh of the corpses were covered with flies and maggots crawling up and down their oozing nostrils and leaking skulls. The horrendous stench of death hung in the air above the beaten faces that now resembled those of blowfish instead of human beings. Their rotting cheeks were grotesquely swollen out of proportion to the rest of their faces. It was almost like they were trying to hold their breath, like they had taken their last, desperate gasp of air before being dumped into the well to suffocate under the weight of the torsos to follow. Their open eyes, some protruding out of their sockets, were testimony to a slow, agonizing end of life. Some of their mouths were gaping in a now silenced terror, reminding me of the dying screams I had heard as a youngster in Vietnam.

Their assassins had covered the bodies with lime in an effort to speed up the decomposition process. The lime had caused some of the skulls to weaken, allowing the expanding, festering brains to pop out through the top of the head. Some of the females' fingers had been cut off and tossed on the ground for the coyotes and dogs to feed on. Only animals kill like this! And that is just what the cartel is made up of. Dope-smuggling, greedy, pathological, murdering pieces of shit.

Looking at the blood-splattered walls in the house, you had to wonder if all of the victims were present when the torturing started. Think about it. It's one thing to know you're going to be whacked. If you believe in God, depending on the person and his faith, it may not be too hard for you to cross over. But to watch and listen to others before you, squirming and screaming in unspeakable agony, that's a whole different level of mental torture. Can you imagine being bound and gagged, knowing you're next, and watching body parts being cut and ripped off another human right in front of your eyes?

Before the bodies were pulled from the Well of Death, I'd sometimes gone unarmed when I was off duty. After the well, that changed permanently. After the well, I never took the trash out from my own kitchen without having a pistol on me. I think Barrett and Bernal may have altered their lifestyles also, but I never asked them. I know some may think it was paranoia on my part. But do you realize how stupid it would be to get whacked because you didn't take the proper precautions after you had been told someone was hunting your ass?

One day at the office Butch and I slowly broached the subject of being taken, cut up, and whacked. A DEA informant reported that Yolanda Molina and the Agua Prieta cartel had put a hefty price on our heads. We tried to fool ourselves into believing that it couldn't and wouldn't happen to us. Deep down inside, we knew better. It could happen to any one of us tomorrow. During the conversation, Butch brought up a valid point. He said that if they want you, sooner or later they'll get you. It's virtually impossible to stay on your toes twenty-four hours a day. You could never tell when they may send a vanload of kidnappers, or just one trigger. However, we all agreed that there was one advantage to being continually armed: It would make them kill you. If they had intended on grabbing you for a night of fun and games, you could pull your piece and make them whack you in a gunfight. This way you would cheat them out of their pleasure of making you scream all night while they slowly dissected you.

I don't know if I ever talked about it with the other agents, but I knew we had to come up with a plan in the event one of us or one of our family members got grabbed. I thought about it a lot, and this may sound insane, but it would be the only option that would work. Considering that a man would do just about anything for his family and partners in a crisis, maybe you won't call me a madman when you hear the plan.

First of all, you must understand that the federal government, as a whole, isn't going to do much to help you. DEA borrowed one of my informants when Special Agent Camarena was kidnapped in 1986. The informant was almost murdered by the MFJP when he came very close to learning where Camarena was being held. Rayburn and I had to call U.S. Ambassador John Gavin's office to get the informant out of a Mexican hospital. With the base of his skull crushed by the butt of an AK-47, he was physically crippled and mentally marred for the rest of his life. To this day, when I visit with him, he'll start crying, remembering the events of his own kidnapping and torture.

I know from talking to the informant that DEA did everything it could to save its agent. But I believe that the rest of the federal government as a whole did not do enough, or all it could have done. I don't believe that we brought all of our resources on line to save Camarena's life. Don't you think that if the U.S. government had employed its existing CIA and NSA agents in Mexico, we could have located Camarena before his death? I think so.

So acting on what I had learned from the informant, and what I knew about our own government, I came up with a plan for a worst-case scenario.

As soon as we learn that one of our agents, spouses, or children has been grabbed by someone from Mexico, we'll have to go with the assumption that it's the MFJP in some shape or form. That would be about a 99.99 percent accurate guess. And if they don't have the victim, believe me, they'll know where he's being held. Next, pay a business call on the MFJP comandante in Agua Prieta, inviting him to meet you at the border for mutual cooperation on the investigation. At the border, you grab the comandante and his sub-comandante in full view of the public on both sides of the border. Staying right at the borderline at the port of entry, you shoot the sub-comandante in the kneecaps, dropping his ass half in the U.S. and half in Mexico.

While he's lying there straddling the border and bleeding to death, you put your gun to the comandante's head and politely ask him to send his MFJP thugs to pick up and return your agent. You put a time limit of thirty minutes on your request. If you don't get your agent back in thirty minutes, you execute the sub-comandante and kneecap the comandante, starting the game all over again. I guarantee that you'll get your agent back within the next thirty minutes. And you know what? Being that you're standing in the middle of the border, half in the U.S. and half in Mexico, both countries' courts are going to have a fit trying to figure out your prosecution.

Is this the raving of a warped mind? I think not. Desperation and love are high motivators. And I swear with God as my witness, before I would live the rest of my life knowing that I could have tried this option to save my wife, kids, or partners, I would go ahead with it. Think about it. After the unleashed barbarism at the Well of Death, what possible measures could be considered too extreme to save your loved ones or partners from being butchered by such sadistic thugs?

On March 31, 1989, the word was put out from the MFJP to all U.S. law enforcement that one of the main suspects in the Well of

Death murders was Hector "Tombstone" Fragoso, the owner of Los Alamos ranch. If you hadn't already guessed it, Tombstone was the first cousin of the former Douglas police chief, Alvaro Fragoso. And don't forget that Chief Fragoso was on a first-name basis with the Molina family. We already knew through numerous other dope investigations that Tombstone was an enforcer and assassin for the cartel. More specifically, he was a bodyguard for a cartel relative of the Molina family, Clemente Soto-Peña. In addition, we knew from other sources that Tombstone and the well-dumped Valdez were known associates working together in the dope-smuggling business for the Molina family and Clemente.

On April 2, I was contacted through DEA by MFJP Comandante José Luis Larrazola-Rubio, who had been sent to Agua Prieta to investigate the Well of Death murders by the Mexican Attorney General's Office in Hermosillo, Sonora. It seemed that Comandante Larrazola had received information through his own investigation that the Molina family was responsible for the twelve bodies on Los Alamos ranch. Larrazola was requesting that I meet with him in Agua Prieta for a joint investigation.

Now, with Mexican officials, it's never what they say that you have to worry about. It's what they don't say. Larrazola was telling me he had information concerning the Well of Death and the Molina family. But what he didn't ask was what he really wanted to know: how long Bernal and I had been working the cartel and how much dirt we had accumulated on them. In other words, he was on a Mexican fishing trip in the desert.

Accompanied by a couple of DEA agents, I crossed over to Agua Prieta from Douglas and met with Comandante Larrazola at La Hacienda Hotel, near the border. On the way, I couldn't help but remember the last time I was in Mexico with Larrazola's corrupt affiliate, Comandante Rafael Pizarro. The story began with the arrest of Joaquín Carrizoza, a former U.S. Customs Service informant.

On November 15, 1988, Carrizoza attempted to drive a van through the Douglas Port of Entry from Agua Prieta, Sonora. As he entered the inspection lane to await his turn to clear Customs,

Carrizoza got cold feet and began to perspire. By the time the smuggler pulled up to the Customs inspector for clearance, his eyes were bulging and his carotid artery was visibly thumping in the side of his fat outlaw neck. He was too much of a coward to ever be a successful dope trafficker.

The U.S. Customs inspector took one look at Carrizoza's self-incriminating face and instinct told him something was wrong with the guy. Don't pass Go, don't collect $200. Carrizoza was told to pull over to the side of the Customs garage for an intense inspection of his van. Knowing that this meant they would discover what he was carrying, Carrizoza hit the gas pedal and flipped a U-turn, successfully fleeing back into Mexico. Just inside the sanctuary of the Mexican boundary, Carrizoza jumped out of the van and high-tailed it into one of the numerous, crowded, dust-filled Agua Prieta barrios.

Allan Sperling, some other special agents, and I hauled ass to the port after being radioed of the incident. When we got there the van was still sitting just inside Mexico on the street. We crossed into Agua Prieta and smooth-talked a Mexican Immigration officer into letting us examine the van before the MFJP crooks arrived on the scene. We used a battery-operated drill to core into the van's floor, where we hit a soft, mushy substance. When the drill bit was extracted from the floor it was covered with Lucifer's white plague.

Okay, so we knew who the driver was and we could always pick him up later when he returned to the U.S. The immediate problem was that the evidence to prosecute Carrizoza was in Mexico and we knew damn good and well that the Mex feds would want to keep the coke so they could resell it to the highest cartel bidder. Before the MFJP arrived, we returned to the U.S. with our little sample of coke, hoping to use it as an ace in the hole at a later date. We knew the Mexican Immigration officer wouldn't tell the MFJP that he had let us take a coke sample from the van. They'd have his ass in their next slice-and-dice torture session if they found out he'd let us cross the border on official business.

The following day we set up a meeting with MFJP Comandante Rafael Pizarro at his office in Agua Prieta. Knowing that this sordid son of a bitch worked for the drug cartel, we went to the meeting armed to the teeth. Not only was Pizarro a crooked cop, we also knew that he had recently murdered one of our best informants. I'd have to say at best odds, we gave ourselves a fifty-fifty shot of coming back from this one with more holes in our bodies than we came into the world with.

At the meeting, Pizarro graciously allowed us to photograph the van and some four hundred pounds of cocaine that his Mexican feds had taken out of the false floor and stacked next to the van. We told Pizarro that the U.S. government needed to take custody of the cocaine as evidence against Carrizoza, who would soon be in our custody. Pizarro promptly stated that the coke was now the property of the Mexican government. And the prick had no qualms about letting us know he *was* the Mexican government in Agua Prieta.

Then, oddly enough, Pizarro tried to barter with us. Since Carrizoza was in fact a Mexican citizen, the comandante wanted us to arrest Carrizoza in the U.S. and repatriate him over to the Mexican government for prosecution. I figured that Pizarro had learned Carrizoza was a former U.S. Customs informant. He knew he could coerce or torture a great deal of valuable intelligence out of Carrizoza if he could get his hands on him. Having no intention of ever giving Carrizoza up, we countered that it would be easier to take the coke load and lock it in our evidence vault until we found Carrizoza.

Pizarro didn't want to relinquish custody of the treasured white cash cow. He had probably already been paid one or two hundred thousand dollars for protecting this load, but he knew he could double his profits by resale to the highest-bidding Agua Prieta cartel member. We then asked him if we could take samples of the load in an effort to satisfy our government's prosecution requirements. Obviously becoming agitated by our tenacious investigative efforts, Pizarro firmly said no. Since negotiations were rapidly deteriorating, we pulled out our hold card. We sprung it on Pizarro that we really didn't need another sample since we had obtained a small one from the van before the arrival of his agents. This treacherous motherfucker's face turned twelve shades of red and purple at the same time! No one spoke a word. You could've heard a church mouse fart from two blocks across the plaza. The meeting got so preemptive with the smell of death that a maggot would have gagged.

Here we go again, without brakes, down the narrow road of a classical Mexican standoff. I can't count how many of these macho scenarios I've had to endure over the years with these fucks. But if I had learned anything from the past encounters it was this one un-spoken golden rule of the engagement: The first guy to blink was gonna get butt-fucked.

Pizarro stood up from his plush executive high-back chair and slowly leaned across the dark, smooth wood of the meeting table. His eyes took on the glow of a lunatic's during electric-shock therapy. With his hand teasing the top of his holstered .45 Colt, he gritted his yellow teeth and blurted out, "Well, maybe I should just arrest you gringo *culos* (assholes) for illegally exporting cocaine from my country."

Ah, shit! Well, the day had started out pretty good but it was rap-idly going to hell in a handbasket! Still sitting, not wanting to give him any sign of being intimidated, I leaned toward Pizarro as my right hand slid under the table and into the top of my boot. As my clammy hand palmed the hidden .38 Special in anticipation of the Reaper's visit, I coolly replied, "Do what you gotta do, but remember, our peo-ple know we're here in your office." I could see the wheels starting to turn behind his ion-charged eyeballs.

Pizarro thought about it for a few seconds. Where is the profit in this? What do I gain by murdering the *gabachos* (gringos)? What do I gain by even throwing them in my jail? Nada. The profit is in the resale of something I already possess. It was a no-lose situation for the Mexican federal commander. First, he could make hundreds of thou-sands off the sale of the coke load. Second, if they patronized the gringo feds, President Clinton would recertify the Mexican govern-ment and give them millions of tax dollars.

Pizarro cracked a weak, tight-lipped smirk, as if the whole thing was a joke. But the color of his face didn't change much as he attempted to play down the challenge by breaking into a somewhat forced grin. To ease the tension, he offered us all a cold beer and his hand dropped away from his .45. Friendly dialogue resumed and Pizarro acted as if he had never made the threat at all. I've said it once and I'll say it again, if you don't understand your enemy you're gonna lose!

By the time we were done negotiating, we received ten samples of the cocaine to be taken back to the U.S. for evidentiary purposes. But back to the subject of the Agua Prieta cartel and our meeting with Comandante Larrazola ...

When we drove into the hotel's parking lot, other than lacking the tents and artillery, it resembled an armed military encampment. There were about one hundred armed MFJP agents dressed in new, freshly ironed, black military fatigues guarding the entire center of the hotel. They were Larrazola's own special enforcement unit from Hermosillo, known as Los Tigres. It was apparent that they had ordered all civilians out of the hotel in order to assume it as their temporary headquarters in Agua Prieta. It was easy to tell where Comandante Larrazola was by the concentration of heavily armed agents. The knights were guarding the king.

After identifying ourselves, the DEA agents and I were invited into the comandante's room, where we were properly introduced. Larrazola was very tall for a Mexican. He was light-complected with contrasting dark features. His hair and mustache were very neatly trimmed, and when he opened his mouth it flashed full of gold-capped teeth. Larrazola's black military fatigues were spotless, and when he spoke it was immediately apparent that he was a highly educated tyrant. I knew this was going to be a whole different breed of crook compared to others I'd thrown.

Larrazola told me that he believed that the Molina family had ordered the people in the well murdered and that he needed a copy of my U.S. investigative reports. He went on to explain that my narcotics smuggling reports would be the link he needed to tie the Molinas to the murders. I kept wondering what he was talking about. Why did he need that kind of U.S. investigative material concerning narcotics smuggling when he was conducting a multiple homicide investigation in Mexico? Besides, everyone in Agua Prieta knew that Tombstone and a couple of others had murdered the twelve on the orders of the

Molinas, Clemente, or other members of the cartel. While I was contemplating what this asshole really wanted, he finally got to the question that he had been dancing around.

Comandante Larrazola asked me if I had evidence or reports that implicated MFJP comandantes Pizarro or Flores, and if I did, could he have copies of such reports. So here's the real, deep-down goal: covering the crooked agenda of the Mexican Federal Police. That's what this whole meeting was about. Damage control for his buddies, not to mention the rest of the Mexican government! What? Did I look that stupid? This asshole must have thought I was a REMF from D.C. Or was it that my reports could possibly deter such future U.S. aid? Is that what Larrazola and the Mexican government were really worried about?

I turned to Larrazola, looked him right in the eye, and remembering that the king was surrounded by his knights, and that I was merely a guest in his castle, I lied like a snake in the grass. I told Larrazola that his MFJP comandantes in Agua Prieta were as honest as the day was long. He didn't think to ask me if I was speaking of Arizona or Antarctica days, and I wasn't waiting for the door to hit me in the ass on my way out of the motel room. With a diarrhea-choking smile, I bade adios to the bastard, wondering if the DEA agents and I would make it out of "Camelot's" parking lot alive.

On April 10, 1989, Special Agent Bob Scofield and I intercepted and interviewed Guadalupe Molina, the wife of Efraín Valdez, at the Douglas Port of Entry as she was entering Agua Prieta. During the interview Guadalupe admitted that Yolanda Molina was her sister but she never would admit that Valdez was her husband. We showed her copies of her children's birth certificates that we had previously subpoenaed from the Cochise County hospital. The birth certificates clearly stated that Valdez was the father of her children.

Guadalupe finally admitted that Valdez was her husband but she refused to answer any questions concerning his murder. The bitch was cold and indifferent to any line of questions we pursued about her husband's death. For a recently widowed woman, she sure as hell wasn't showing any signs of grieving. It was like, oh well, such is life in a dope-smuggling family. No big deal. My husband was murdered making a living in our profitable, endearing family business. When we asked her about Valdez's funeral arrangements she became evasive and nervous. That one simple question was a catalyst that would show us how powerful the Molina family could be in Mexico.

On April 29, some nineteen days after we questioned Guadalupe Molina, the Agua Prieta radio stations and newspapers announced the discovery of Efraín Valdez's decomposed body in the desert about ten kilometers south of Agua Prieta. Shit! This had to be one of the most mobile corpses I had ever heard of. We know for a fact, according to informants and prior Mexican newspaper articles, that Valdez's body was discovered on March 30 coming out of the Well of Death. But because the Molina family knew that we had questioned Guadalupe, and that we were piecing the puzzle together, they had the MFJP "replant" Valdez's body outside of the Well of Death reunion. Hell, they even bought the radio air time and cooperation of the Mexican papers to orchestrate the rediscovery folly! Like I said before, it's their piss-pot country and they can get away with whatever they can pay for. That's all it takes in Mexico. Money.

On April 21, Tombstone Fragoso was arrested by a task force of law-enforcement officers near Three Points, Arizona, where he had been hiding in a mobile home. Since up until this point of the investigation there was not enough Mexican evidence to charge him with homicide, Tombstone was detained for being an illegal alien in the United States.

On April 25, Bernal and I interviewed Fragoso at the federal prison in Tucson. Now, we had previously heard about the red-hair dye job Tombstone had tried in an attempt to alter his appearance when he was on the run. And we had also been told that the "do" didn't quite work out. But I never in my wildest dreams could have imagined how comical Lucifer himself could look in bright orange clown hair. If it was ever possible to breed the fallen angel's seed with a clown, I guess this is what the results would have to look like.

Bernal and I knew that if we laughed or even smirked at the hairdo, Tombstone would get pissed, put us on his death list of who to do in the future, and call off the interview. So in order to keep from

cracking up we concentrated on staying away from the hair by looking him in the face and eyes. And that in itself was enough to bring us
back to stark reality about this rat bastard. Tombstone possessed cold,
dark brown, never-ending eyes from hell. I'd seen such eyes before in
Vietnam. His eyes held the same blank, thousand-yard stare of mercenaries and soldiers who bathed themselves in the lust of killing. The
only difference was that Tombstone's eyes held a special satanic quality that in my opinion set him closer to the devil's hand than even the
mercs and soldiers. It was the same hidden evil I had seen only once
before in my life. It made me wonder about the possibility of rein-
carnation. The Beast was as strong in Tombstone as it had been
decades ago in a young Marine I once knew: Charles Whitman.

As Bernal and I sat across the table from the killer during the
interview, he would use his dead eyes in an attempt to intimidate us.
He'd stare straight into your face when you were questioning him. He
would never blink or disengage you by moving his head left or right. It
was as if an evil cosmic force were trying to sear through to the very
core of your soul. It had a message. The Beast wanted to tell you, "I've
just enjoyed torturing and murdering a dozen worthless people. You
mess with me and you're next!" Tombstone wasn't just strong *with*
the Beast. This homicidal maniac *was* the Beast.

Tombstone was a killing machine with arms as big as most men's
thighs. His hands were twice as big as most I've seen, and he had a
chest and set of shoulders like an NFL linebacker. In short, nature had
given him the right equipment to be an assassin and enforcer for the
cartel. And these twelve in the well were by no means even close to his
total kills. Over the years we had heard about his murderous feats in
Mexico. And the exact tally? I wouldn't want to put a number on it
other than to say this: During the debriefing of several different
informants and cartel defendants, it has been said on more than one
occasion that Tombstone has whacked so many folks that they had to
be buried standing up instead of the traditional lying down. That's
right. They say that the Agua Prieta field where his victims were
buried was not large enough to lay everyone out. So, like those little
Vienna sausages in a can, they are buried side by side, standing up

with lime poured over them. Fifty? A hundred and fifty? No one knows for sure, simply "multiple."

Tombstone was definitely one of Mexico's primo mass murderers, according to what we knew about him. And I later told Bernal that if the son of a bitch escaped and we ever had to deal with him, we should seriously consider sneaking up behind him on a dark night, in a dark alley, praying that God had struck him blind, then blowing his brains out from behind. And if that ain't plain enough for you I'll say it straight up: Discretion is the better part of valor, and that means simply knowing when you cannot defeat the Beast face to face. Believe me, this son of a bitch is not of the civilized world.

Bernal and I pushed on through the interview, trying to justify the idea that we were making a deal with Satan himself for testimony against the Molina family. Tombstone, not wanting to return to Mexican justice, probably thought that he could stay in the U.S. and buy himself some time by half-ass cooperating with us. He admitted that he was an associate of Valdez and that he and Valdez both trafficked in narcotics for the Molina family. He acknowledged that he was an enforcer for the cartel and that MFJP Comandante Flores had picked up Valdez for questioning on or about March 20. He even stated that he was present in Guadalajara at the torturing of DEA agent Camarena. But as could be expected, he would never roll on whacking the twelve souls at his own ranch outside Agua Prieta.

As the questioning continued, he always kept steering away from his involvement in the Well of Death. At one point he even told us that MFJP Comandante Flores had murdered three "mules" in Agua Prieta because they were suspected of stealing cartel-owned dope. Every time we went back to the subject of the Molina family he seemed more than willing to give us answers. When we were done questioning him we gave him a cigarette and tried to put him at ease. We worked on hitting his vanity button, getting him to boast about his murderous deeds in Agua Prieta. His willingness to roll on the Molina family was about to appear.

It seemed that in 1985, the Molina family and the head of the cartel at that time, Clemente Soto-Peña, had gone in as equal partners on a hundred-ton field of marijuana down south in Michoacán. The Mexican Army seized the field and held it ransom, threatening to burn it. Clemente paid the Army a $1 million ransom, with the Molina family promising to reimburse Clemente for their half. Later the Molinas tried to stiff Clemente for the $500,000 and Clemente sent Tombstone to collect the debt.

As Tombstone was telling us this story, his voice became steady and bitter. His eyes took on a new, deadly glow, and we could even see the muscles in his thick neck and face start to tighten with the surfacing Beast. It was plain that there was no loss of love between him and the Molinas, and we even began to think that if this murdering piece of shit could tell any simulation of the truth, this may be it.

Tombstone continued that when he arrived at the Molina palace in Agua Prieta they had somehow been tipped that he was coming. He said that when he went up to the front door and knocked on it, they opened fire through the door, hitting him in the chest with a .223 M16. He offered proof of his story by ripping his jailhouse shirt open, revealing the scars the bullets left going through his chest and out his back. How the lucky devil survived is beyond me. Bernal and I later verified the accounts of the shooting through an informant who was present when the gunfight occurred. For once in his unwarranted existence, Tombstone may have been telling the truth.

By now this son of a bitch was getting spooky. He had whipped himself up into a pretty good frenzied lather while pitching his side of the Molina shooting story. Not wanting to see the other side of the Beast, if there is such an unimaginable thing, we decided to leave while the leaving was good. Bernal and I winked at each other knowing that we had plenty of the bastard's testimony to make our financial charges against the Molina family stick. We excused ourselves from the wicked one's presence and told the guards to tighten his chains down before they tried to move him back to his cell. Before we departed, we apologized to the guards for leaving them with an enraged, orange-topped Tombstone. Bernal and I could only think to suggest tranquilizers, being that immediate execution was illegal!

On May 10, 1989, Comandante Larrazola and a detachment of his Los Tigres hit the Molina palace in Agua Prieta. Yolanda and her husband, Antonio, were taken into temporary custody and flown in an MFJP helicopter to an unknown location. They were returned to their residence three hours later; there, Comandante Larrazola was seen to receive a large suitcase filled with a purported million-dollar ransom. We later learned that Larrazola had told the Molinas that he was being pressured by U.S. authorities to arrest them for the twelve bloated floaters in the well. However, a little gratuity on their part would ensure that Larrazola weathered the storm. What did I say earlier about a piss-pot of a country? And I mean country, not the Mexican people.

Tombstone was later deported to Mexico, where he was tried and convicted of the twelve murders. The Mexican government has no death sentence, although I find that somewhat curious being that their own federal agents continually murder people. Anyway, Tombstone was sentenced to thirty years in prison. As of this writing, I am told by my Mexican sources that he is let out of prison on the weekends and holidays to travel in Mexico as he pleases. You have to understand the Mexican bought-and-paid-for judicial system. Thirty years is a long time and even Lucifer is entitled to his lustful pleasures. Convicted and sentenced or not, he's still a Mexican cartel member with the usual national privileges.

No other members of the cartel were ever indicted or tried for ordering the murders. Comandantes Pizarro and Flores were given other MFJP commands somewhere in Mexico, where they were eventually assassinated by drug lords they either crossed or betrayed. Comandante Larrazola was also murdered, from what I've been told. But not before he spent most of the million dollars he screwed the Molina family out of.

About nine years after the Well of Death tragedy, a member of the Mexican Department of Justice (PGR) left Mexico under the threat of death. The PGR agent sought refuge in Tucson, where he began writing his memoirs. This officer broke ranks with his *compas* when he publicly denounced the Mexican government and its federal agents as being corrupt and under the control of drug lords. According to him, a Sonora state police investigation revealed that the twelve corpses were traffickers in the employ of Yolanda Molina. The mass murder, probably the worst in Sonora's history, was a direct result of a war between the Molinas and the Fragosos over two issues. The first, a load of seized dope that Tombstone had lost in Arizona. The second, Tombstone was ferreting out the informant who arranged to have the lost dope load intercepted. If that indeed was the case, I reckon Efraín Valdez pretty much fit the bill.

After Bernal and I testified before an Arizona state grand jury, warrants of arrest alleging racketeering and operating a continuing criminal enterprise were issued for Yolanda Molina and Antonio Hernández-Peña. But as long as they remain in Mexico and pay bribes or ransoms to the MFJP comandantes, they will never be arrested on either side of the border. In fact, I hear that as multi-millionaires, they now own eight ranches and numerous palaces in Mexico. But competition can be a wondrous and terrible motivator in Mexico. Several more Molina family members and scores of cartel folks were whacked between 1987 and December of 2000.

One of the Molinas who went down during the cartel wars was an informant Butch and I had planted right in the middle of the Agua Prieta cartel. Tony Molina, one of Yolanda's own brothers, met the Reaper after being taken down by three rounds from a 9mm on December 7, 2000. A good friend of mine and Butch's, Tony was "Pearl Harbored" in Agua Prieta by one of his sister's own shooters. Evidently, the dope-peddling bitch finally learned of our hidden relationship with her own blood. The scorn of a woman can be a terrible thing. But let me tell you, the scorn of a pissed-off Mexican cartel bitch is tenfold that. But like most of her family and other cartel members, one day she too will be stuffed down the pit of a bottomless well that no doubt will extend into the bowels of Lucifer's abode. Like I always say, they may get away from us, but they will never be able to evade God's judgment.

Although the dozen bodies from the Well of Death were buried in April of 1989, they would never be completely laid to rest for some of us. Bernal, Butch, and I are still looking over our shoulders, especially in light of Tony's recent demise. But Detective Petropolis doesn't worry about it much anymore. Several years after the investigation, he committed suicide in Tucson. Some say it was over his gambling debts. Some say other reasons. But nobody will ever know the last thoughts that rambled through his troubled mind. What do you think they may have been? Bloated, black, decayed faces with protruding, glazed eyes?

In 1990, the Arizona Superior Court in Cochise County upheld our civil seizures of the Molina bank accounts and real properties in the U.S. After summary judgments were ordered we ended up with a total of $2.2 million including interest. The Arizona Attorney General awarded the forfeited money to Cochise County for the construction of a badly needed new jail and sheriff's office. Ten years later the same jail that Bernal, Butch, and I helped build would be used to incarcerate one of the most corrupt, notorious judges Arizona has ever known, The King of Douglas.

6

The Douglas Tunnel

IN JANUARY OF 1990, right on the heels of the Well of Death, the shit hit the fan again. The U.S. Customs Service had begun to seize a lot of large loads of cocaine that were being smuggled through the Douglas Port of Entry. Some of the loads were hit by our Customs agents as they were being transported to stash houses in Phoenix, Tucson, and Los Angeles. Some of the loads were being busted by honest U.S. Customs inspectors right in the port of entry as dirty U.S. Immigration inspectors were trying to help the smugglers get it through. We were seizing five hundred to seven hundred pounds of coke a couple of times a week, and we knew that was just a drop in the bucket compared to what was getting through.

The Agua Prieta cartel had hooked up a coke connection with Amado Carrillo, who was better known at that time as *El Señor de los Cielos* ("Lord of the Skies"). Amado had endeared the Mexican traffickers to the Colombians by accumulating an impressive air fleet that smuggled tons of cocaine every week from Colombia to Mexico for transshipment to the U.S. With the tons of coke came a serious corruption problem, which still has a stranglehold on the numerous federal, state, and local law-enforcement agencies on the border today. No one agency can be singled out for the blame. But because the U.S. Customs Service and the U.S. Immigration Service are in charge of border inspections, they became infiltrated by the some of the most corrupt inspectors in the history of our great nation.

The Lord of the Skies wasn't a dumb son of a bitch by any stretch of the imagination. He recognized that it was senseless to risk his coke loads trying to cross them through the Arizona deserts or mountains, exposing them to numerous narcotics interdiction efforts. All he had to do was have the loads driven through the U.S. ports of entry right under the nose of the U.S. government. All it took was a little bait, usually in the form of a voluptuous 38-24-36, and some hard-cash negotiations. When you owned your own U.S. inspector at the border port of entry, there was no worry about losing the load. Hell, you didn't even have to put the shit in false compartments or try to hide it under other merchandise. All you had to do was go to one of the cartel's cocaine warehouses in Agua Prieta, throw a six hundred-pound load in the back of a big old LTD or Grand Marquis, and head for the port of entry. As long as you knew the right time and the right inspection lane where your "dirty badge" was on duty, the rest was an elementary-school cakewalk.

What Carrillo and the cartel didn't count on were U.S. Customs inspectors like Dale Demmerly, Mike Humphries, and George Campos. These guys were three of the most trusted inspectors I have ever known. And not one of them could stomach what was going on at the port of entry in Douglas. Guys like these weren't willing to turn their heads for any amount of money. And believe me, when people are shoving hundreds of thousands of dollars in your face just to look the other way, you've got to be made of integrity from the guts out. It's not something that is learned or developed. You're either born with it or you're not. It's that simple.

And believe me, folks, the dirty money was there for the taking. Through informants and wiretaps we were able to learn that the going price for a load of cocaine to be smuggled through a dirty inspector was about a $1,000 per kilogram. That's right! For allowing just one three-hundred-kilo load of coke to pass through your inspection lane, you could get over a quarter of a million dollars from the cartel. Can you imagine making $250,000 for simply winking your eye and waving your hand at the right moment?

But guys like Campos and his buddies put a crimp in the dirty inspectors' style. They would watch the scumbags on the primary inspection lanes as they waved suspected loaded vehicles through. Then the good guys would pick these vehicles off for a secondary inspection just before they completely cleared the port. This roving secondary inspection proved extremely effective. We were able to seize large coke loads and arrest drivers who led us to the crooked inspectors' doorsteps. Some of the dirty badges got life imprisonment. Others got thirty years. The cartel had to come up with an alternative smuggling scheme because we were flushing both their dirty feds and future profits down the toilet at the same time.

Buddy Harrison was a veteran Customs agent at the Douglas office. He was a somewhat rounded, pot-bellied forty-year-old with a receding white hairline and steel-blue eyes that darted back and forth when you talked to him. He was one of the rudest loudmouth guys you would ever meet in your life. I very seldom saw him meet anybody that he didn't piss off within two or three minutes. It didn't matter if it was a suspect, a prisoner, or another cop. He was an overbearing son of a bitch some people considered to be an incurable grump. The other agents jokingly called Buddy our public-relations guy. If there was some law-enforcement outfit we would rather not work with, we would send Buddy to spend time with them on an operation. We would never hear from that particular agency again.

But despite all of his shortcomings in tact, he was by far one of the best special agents in any of the federal agencies that I have ever worked with. The guy had a knack for coming up with the best informants, the best investigations, and the largest seizures. I learned to cut through all of his foul behavior and found a soul that would give the shirt off his back if it would help you. Sometimes I just had to sit back and marvel at the guy. He was a six-foot-high pile of contradictions. The mouth would be cursing to the ear but the heart would be compassionate in its action. Go figure!

In about March of 1990, Harrison started getting information from one of his snitches about a secret narcotics smuggling tunnel being built underneath the border between Agua Prieta and Douglas.

The information was so far-fetched that no one really believed it at first. But Harrison stayed with it and his investigation began to yield some very credible facts.

For instance, a new money man had suddenly appeared in Agua Prieta from nowhere. Using the name of Rafael Camarena, he claimed to be a building contractor with access to unlimited funds backed by the Mexican government. Camarena spread the word in Agua Prieta that he was there to build affordable housing for the impoverished Mexican people. He started meeting all of the right people on both sides of the border, including Judge Joe Borane. In a matter of weeks, Camarena had purchased commercial property in Douglas right on the border from Judge Borane.

The commercial lot was located just inside the U.S. about a hundred yards from the international boundary fence, at the intersection of F Avenue and International Avenue. Camarena had proposed to build a truck-shipping warehouse on the property. I guess everyone thought it was just a coincidence when Camarena bought a house in Agua Prieta, again on the international border, directly across from his commercial property in Arizona. That is, everybody but our one and only PR guy.

Harrison smelled a rat in the woodpile and he started chopping through the shit in search of the vermin. By placing an individual near the operation, Buddy put the puzzle together. Camarena was constructing a three-hundred-foot tunnel that ran from his house in Mexico to his warehouse in Douglas. Harrison also learned that Camarena was just a puppet and display piece for the Agua Prieta cartel to hide behind. When Judge Borane sold the property to Camarena, he was in effect dealing directly with the cartel. But it wasn't his first time in bed with the rat bastards. Don't forget about his past dealings with Yolanda Molina.

Harrison eventually learned that the tunnel was built with the assistance of thirty to forty Mexican Indian laborers brought up from the interior of Mexico. The cartel used these Indians for a lot of reasons. They are a predominately petite people, with the average male being just under five feet tall. So they would be a natural for working in small, confined areas. They are strong and hardy, never having been spoiled by modern conveniences.

All their lives they have been farming with their hands, digging and cultivating the earth with no real modern farm implements to speak of. Most of them can't even speak the national language of Mexico, Spanish. Instead they speak an Indian dialect and usually rely on a Spanish interpreter when they leave their remote, mountainous homeland. In effect, because of their own language barriers and previously limited contact with the outside world, the cartel would hold them incommunicado on the border in Agua Prieta.

In other words, they were the perfect little slaves. They took orders, never asked questions, didn't know where they were, and couldn't effectively communicate with the other Mexicans in Agua Prieta. It really didn't matter that they couldn't speak the language, according to what we later heard from our informants. The whole time the tunnel was being built, the Indians were held as virtual prisoners in a guarded, enclosed warehouse on the outskirts of Agua Prieta. They worked on the tunnel day and night, rotating around a twenty-four-hour schedule. They worked and slept under armed guard. In the end, according to our sources, the entire workforce was taken somewhere in the mountains outside of Agua Prieta and forever silenced in a swift, premeditated act of "necessary disposal." To this day no one knows where their mass grave is located. That is to say, no one in the civilized world as we know it.

So what do you think? Could the building of such a tunnel between two sovereign nations have been conducted without the knowledge of the Mexican government? If you believe so, I've got a couple of moon rocks, never touched by human hands, that I would like to sell you! The answer is in the question itself. If Harrison and the rest of our agents on the U.S. side knew about it, how in the hell could the MFJP agents on the Mexican side of the border not know about it? And you can bet your next Social Security check that if the Mexican federal agents knew about the tunnel, they also knew about the genocide of the little Indian folks.

During the construction of the tunnel from Camarena's house, dozens of dump trucks traveled from his house to the outskirts of Agua Prieta. They removed ton after ton of dirt from beneath Arizona and attempted to pass it off as swimming pool construction at Camarena's residence in Mexico. If that wasn't fishy enough, what about the bright yellow school buses that brought the Indian laborers, day and night, back and forth, to and from Camarena's residence? This highly unusual activity was taking place in one of the most police-patrolled areas of Agua Prieta, the international border.

Getting the information about the hows, whys, whos, whens, and wheres of the tunnel was the easy part. Now we had to figure out how to legally get inside without the smuggling operation finding out and getting hinky on us. We figured the best way to proceed was with sporadic surveillance of Camarena's warehouse activity in Douglas. We would wait for an opportunity and tag along behind tractor-trailer rigs as they departed the warehouse north for Tucson or Phoenix. It became apparent that the rigs' drivers were making "heat" runs in an effort to identify any law enforcement surveillance team following them. We knew that we had to take our time with the investigation because these guys had put a lot of money and time into their narco-tunnel and they weren't going to give it up easily. We settled in for a long-term investigation. We had visions of a black ops (covert operation) entering the tunnel with a court order and placing audio and video inside the tunnel and warehouse. It was going to be fantastic!

During our surveillance, the Douglas office was contacted by Customs special agents from the Phoenix office. We weren't surprised when they reported that they had urgent information concerning a tunnel in Douglas. If Harrison's informant was telling him about it, you had to figure sooner or later somebody else was going to hear from another snitch.

Knowing that Harrison's guy was on the inside of the tunnel operation, we were pretty sure that the Phoenix agents' source of information wouldn't be nearly as accurate. We humored the Phoenix dudes on the phone and they eventually invited themselves to our office for a sit-down. During the meeting they tried to tell us that the tunnel ran from Agua Prieta under Douglas for about ten blocks to the Yellow Front clothing store at Pan Am Avenue and Tenth Street. We rolled our eyes and chuckled about how far off their information was. Their bubble busted when they found out that Harrison already knew the tunnel's location. To add insult to injury, we told them they were off the target by a good nine or ten city blocks. You ever see the look on a guy's face when he thinks he's about to land the first punch but instead he gets suckered and loses his wind? When I saw that look on their mugs I knew things were gonna get messy. The green-eyed demon was coming out to dance.

The Phoenix agents got real defensive about their information being wrong and asked why we hadn't distributed our information within the service. As expected, it turned into an argument with us telling them that we were already working the investigation and we had chosen to not disseminate any written reports for security reasons. Hey, we lived and worked on the U.S.-Mexican border in Douglas and not in some cushy office in Phoenix where you have the luxury of privacy! Our daily activities in Douglas are an open book to the cartel's counter-surveillance teams. And even after we explained this to our buddies from Phoenix, they took it as though we had insulted their intelligence as "interior" agents versus border agents. With Douglas agents in the driver's seat of the investigation, the Phoenix guys were gonna be pissed no matter what.

At the time, the resident agent in charge of the Douglas Customs agents was a great guy who had been brought in from Yuma. Steve Mercado was a forty-year-old Hispanic. He sported a slightly balding head over his medium frame. His full black beard and mustache accented his light complexion, giving prominence to his nose and smile. He was a jovial guy with menacing, inquiring eyes that measured you immediately upon meeting. Although Steve had only been with us for about six months, all of the Douglas agents had bonded with him. If you had ever met the guy, you would have liked him right off the bat.

The resident agent in charge of the Phoenix agents was Bill Gately. The resident agent in charge of the Nogales agents was Dave Hayes. They were both wired in heavily with the special agent in charge for the Arizona District in Tucson, Thomas McDermott. These three guys were the highest political power in the U.S. Customs

Service in Arizona. For whatever reasons they may have had, they picked Mercado for the job in Douglas. When they introduced Mercado to us, they impressed upon us how much confidence they had in Steve. We were instructed to follow his guidance and pretty much jump when he snapped his fingers. But none of those directives meant much to the Douglas agents.

I don't know when REMFs will ever learn, but you just can't order agents to respect and blindly follow anyone. It doesn't matter if the guy's title is resident agent in charge, special agent in charge, or commissioner of customs. A leader has to earn respect. Mercado's mettle was tested in our presence on quite a few occasions. After a time, we would have followed him into the lower regions of hell because we wanted to, not because we were ordered to.

Once the tunnel was known to both the Douglas and Phoenix offices, Mercado became a liability to McDermott, Hayes, and Gately. These three guys wanted to take control of the investigation away from Mercado because we all knew the tunnel was going to be a big international media deal. To a couple of true investigators like Harrison and Mercado, this meant an enormous, once-in-a-lifetime, complex case. To them it was going to be a bust to be proud of the rest of their days. But to the other three politicians it was simply a platform for national television exposure. After the media got hold of it their promotions to Customs headquarters in Washington, D.C., would be all but guaranteed. There would be elbow-rubbing with celebrities, and maybe even eventually a book or two.

The problem now was how to get rid of Mercado and take over his office. It had to look professional and fall within the parameters of management needs. If you don't understand the term "management needs," it's a catch-all phrase that pretty much means the big federal bosses can do what they want with your life. You see, as special agents, we are forbidden to have representation by any labor unions. In essence you are left at the mercy of management for promotions, transfers, lateral reassignments, and temporary reassignments. In other words, if the needs of the service dictate it, your ass could end up doing some piddly job in Egypt.

The three power guys had to come up with something to roll over Mercado with. They sat down with him in the Douglas office and asked him for Agent Harrison's reports on the tunnel investigation to date. I'm not sure if they were going to steal all the information we had on it or not. What I do know is that they would use that as a chink in Mercado's armor. Harrison had only kept rough handwritten notes up until this point, choosing not to write a report for service-wide distribution. He and Mercado had wanted to keep the whole thing quiet and wait until we had something really solid that would legally take us into the tunnel. It would be all the technical glitch that McDermott, Gately, and Hayes would need to hang their hats on.

Never mind that we had to move slowly because the Agua Prieta cartel had counter-surveillance watching our office. It wasn't like we could just leave the office and make a drive-by of the warehouse with the underlying tunnel. You had to drive a few blocks in the opposite direction and double back. The whole investigation to this point had purposely been conducted at a snail's pace to hide any suspicion that we knew about the tunnel. We didn't want to show our hand until we were ready to hit the tunnel hard. We knew it would be a one-shot deal when the time came.

But because there weren't official up-to-date reports concerning our surveillance of the warehouse, Mercado was shamefully removed from his position as the Douglas Customs Service agent in charge. He was supposedly "temporarily reassigned" to assist the FBI on a wire-tap in Tucson. The day he loaded the trunk of his vehicle with his clothes and items from his office was the last day we would ever see him in his official capacity as our boss in Douglas. After the "temporary" assist with the FBI, he was basically forced to accept a demotion and return to his old position as a regular special agent in Yuma. It was all bullshit, because Mercado had simply been in the way of REMFs who wanted to make "guts and glory" headlines on television.

Under McDermott's protection, Gately and Hayes rushed our office with their agents and their authority as bosses of the Arizona District. For the Douglas agents these were some pretty demoralizing days. They looked for someone to turn to after Mercado was shit-canned. I was the guy in charge when Steve wasn't around. It was a hard place to be but I couldn't hide from it. But the problem was, when the Douglas guys looked to me for stability, the three juice guys noticed it. It's not enough that you have to fight well-armed, deadly, mean mother dopers down here. Now I was going to have these three juiced political jerks on my case.

We couldn't meet in our own office, so the Douglas agents would always radio for me to come out and meet them somewhere in town or in the desert. The meetings weren't really subversive. It was just that the boys had to bitch their concerns and grievances to me about the loss of Mercado and the subsequent invasion of our area of responsibility. I was once told by an experienced Army infantry captain that troops aren't happy if they're not bitching. He added that it was the times the boys were extremely quiet that you had to worry about. So I figured the gripe-and-bitch sessions were good therapy for the guys.

Well, it didn't take too long before one of Gately's Phoenix agents bumped into the boys and me meeting in the desert. I was radioed to return to the office, where Hayes and Gately were waiting for me in Mercado's now-vacant office. I was ordered on the carpet and the door was slammed behind me. Their first approach was bribery. I was told, in no uncertain terms, that if I would just go along with the program and keep the Douglas agents in line I would step right into Mercado's job as the agent in charge.

Imagine that! These two guys had originally hired me and had a pretty thorough background check done on me when I came over from the Department of Justice. You think they would have found out a little about my morals and values before they tried that move. I reckon over the course of my years I've pretty much busted most of the Big Ten written on the broken stone tablet. But I have never taken advantage of a messed-over friend's misfortune.

The shit hit the fan when I turned their offer down. The gentle bribing wasn't successful, which called for a shift in course. I was accused of leading an insurrection and was threatened with charges of insubordination. I was ordered to get a handle on Harrison because they wanted to take control of his informant. That was one of the things Gately was always good at: taking control of the case agent's informant and then taking control of the entire investigation. I think it was a method of operation he would use years later in Los Angeles during the Customs money-laundering "Casa Blanca" case.

When they got through chewing my ass you would have thought I would know enough to keep my mouth shut, being that my job was hanging by a friggin thread. Forget it! Like Butch Barrett always said, "I was looking for a job when I found this one!" I lost my cool big-time and jumped back with my own tongue-lashing. What hypocrites! You were the guys who hired Mercado and brought him down here. You were the guys who told us to respect and follow him. But what you didn't count on was the fact that Mercado would endear himself to us in ways guys like you will never understand. Mercado was a personable fellow. He could soothe your soul in troubled times and raise hell with the best of them in good times. He would have never had to resort to this type of boot-on-the-neck management.

Now we had an understanding. A truce. I wasn't going to be intimidated or run off. If they wanted a piece of my ass I was standing right dead center in front of them. Now that the air had been cleared, I hoped we could get back to work on the investigation. While all of this jockeying for position was going on, I wondered who was crossing dope through the tunnel.

I and several other agents were sent to Tucson to work on an affidavit for the legal installation of listening devices within the tunnel and warehouse. Such authorization to eavesdrop would put us in total control of the underground facility. By setting up for a long-term investigation with wires and microphones, we could ensure the indictment of most of the tunnel conspirators. Not to mention the fact that we would be almost literally reading their mail. We would have advance information on when cocaine loads were coming up into the warehouse and in what trucks they would be smuggled. We would also be privy to the loads' recipients and destinations. We presented these ideas to the U.S. Attorney's Office in Tucson and they wholeheartedly concurred with our plan of attack.

We had been working on the "wire" affidavit for several days when the most unexpected, idiotic order I ever heard McDermott issue came down. We were told to cut the meat of the affidavit to the bone and prepare it for an immediate search warrant in lieu of a long-term consensual monitoring warrant. We were going to break in and raid the tunnel. It was premature. It was stupid. Without listening devices on the inside there was no way of telling what we would walk into. Now we wouldn't be able to tell beforehand if there was a ton of cocaine or a ton of dynamite waiting for us. Don't you just love it when REMFs and politicians get involved?

Harrison called the U.S. Attorney's Office and vigorously complained. They, too, had a hard time believing McDermott's decision. However, until arrests have been made or evidence has been seized, the U.S. Attorney's Office has no business telling the special agent in charge of the Arizona District how to run his investigations. Everyone in law enforcement was talking about it when they heard we were going in prematurely. We had so far only followed one tractor-trailer out of the warehouse to a residence near Chandler, about thirty miles south of Phoenix. Customs agents had seized about 2,200 pounds of cocaine and identified some of the lower-level players at the unloading. But no one had been arrested and charged for the ton-plus of coke.

To make matters worse, Camarena had been alerted up in Chandler and he was headed south for Mexico after the 2,200-pound load had fallen. Before he could cross the border the Douglas agents located him and were ready to pop his plump brown ass. Harrison was tailing the asshole when he was ordered to let him go into Mexico unmolested. The orders came directly from the three juice guys. We never could figure out why they gave Camarena a free round-trip ticket into Mexico. Especially if they already knew we were going to do an immediate search warrant instead of a long-term investigation. We would've had the guy either way you cut it. Whether we came up with more coke wouldn't matter. Any fool could tell that the tunnel would surface in Mexico at Camarena's residence. That would be all the proof to hang him that any jury would need. But since he crossed into Mexico we knew that meant the odds would be slim to none that we would ever see him again.

After that fiasco, we eventually got a federal judge to sign our search warrant and we gathered at the Douglas office to ready for the entry. Now that Camarena had gone south, it was a sure bet that the bad guys knew we were going to hit the tunnel pretty quick. So if they wanted to, they had plenty of time to leave some rocking-good-time booby traps. And would you like to guess who was nominated by the juice guys to be the first agent down the tunnel? You got it on the first guess! I wasn't sure if it was because of my combat experience or if they were still pissed at me. Whatever, I double-checked my wife's annuity on my life insurance policy before we headed off for the grand entry.

We cut the lock off the warehouse door with bolt cutters and made our entry, armed to the teeth. The younger agents were ready to rock and roll, but the old hands knew nobody would be waiting for us. We were more concerned with the possible traps that the cartel had left behind. The warehouse was empty with the exception of some construction equipment and wooden pallets. In the center of the cement floor, on the south side of the building, was an iron-bar drain. Acting on the informants' information, we used the bolt cutters to get through the iron.

Once we had a hole large enough to slip through, we took turns dropping down, discovering a small, cement-lined room about ten feet by ten feet just under the warehouse surface. In the northeast corner of this little holding room was a cement-lined shaft that descended straight down into the dark earth for about thirty feet. A steel ladder was attached to one of the shaft's four walls. Using flashlights, we could see water at the bottom of the shaft. We had no idea what may be waiting for us either beneath or beyond the water.

Not knowing exactly where the tunnel began, or how deep the water may be, one of us had to climb down the shaft to assess the situation. The guinea pig had already been selected. I slung the shotgun around my neck in front of me so that it would dangle toward the bottom of the shaft. Although it was rather cool underground, beads of sweat stung my eyes as they rolled off my forehead and fell into the black shaft. Right about now, I figured the pucker factor of my ass-hole would have been about the size of a copper-coated BB.

As I climbed onto the ladder, McDermott looked down at the water in the shaft and said one of the dumbest things I'd ever heard in my entire life. "Lee, it looks to me like that water is about one day old." Now folks, like most of you, I gotta tell you that in my lifetime I've seen muddy water, salt water, stagnant water, icy water, steaming water, fresh water, and even bloody water. But I don't *ever* recall see-ing one-day-old water!

You know, it's funny how you remember the dumbest shit when you're about to enter the unknown. In the worst way I wanted to tell the guy, "Geez, I don't know, Tom, I've never seen one-day-old water before!" But I didn't say a word. He was the number-one boss in the Arizona District and I knew that if I had mouthed off and later come out of the tunnel alive, he would make me wish I *was* dead.

I started down knowing that I would be completely on my own if there was an ambush or trap waiting at the bottom. There was no way anybody up on top could have gotten to me in time if the shit hit the fan. It helped a bit knowing that Barrett, Harrison, and Sperling were there. I knew they would get me out if at all possible. Even if it was after the fact, they'd get my body out and back home.

Not wanting to be a better target than I already was, I started down without the use of a flashlight. The humid air in the shaft smelled musty. It was as dark and dank as the hold of an old seagoing cargo freighter. At the bottom of the ladder, a thick wooden plank had been placed on rails above the water. I stepped onto the plank and cautiously squatted down to wait for my eyes to adjust to the dark-ness. It was as still and as quiet as a goddamn graveyard. I could tell I was at the entrance of a concave hole that ran south toward Mexico. I still couldn't see very well, but I knew this had to be the beginning of the tunnel.

It wasn't until this point that I realized how stupid it was to have taken a shotgun. Oh, sure, it would clean out any opposition I may have run into in these tight quarters. But what about the concussion effects on the walls of the shaft and tunnel? There was no way of guessing how stable this structure could be. After all, it wasn't as if it was built by the U.S. Army Corps of Engineers!

When my night vision kicked in, the tunnel's entrance began to take shape. I sat there in silence, straining to hear any voices or movement. After a few minutes I was convinced there was no one in the immediate vicinity. I turned my flashlight on to see what exactly I was up against. I examined the walls. They appeared to be firmly reinforced with steel. I next looked down at the water, trying to figure out how far it was to the bottom of the tunnel's floor. As my eyes focused on the bottom through the water, I saw what appeared to be some kind of an orange line. I studied it a few seconds until my brain registered the threat. I held my breath and my heart skipped a couple of beats. On the bottom of the floor, lying in about two or three feet of water, was an electrical cord!

You couldn't ask for a more perfect ambush. The Agua Prieta cartel could've literally gotten away with murdering U.S. agents without even firing a shot. No noise, no fuss, no mess, no nada! Hell, they wouldn't even have to blow the tunnel with explosives. Just like hot-wiring fish in the rivers back home in Texas. It's as illegal as hell, but it gets the job done.

I kept looking at the wire and wondering if it was hot. Like I said before, I was standing on wood supported by metal rails. I ran my eyes down the rails and saw that they were already in the water. This was a hell of a time to try to remember high-school physics. Talk about the value of a good education! For the life of me, and I mean that literally, I couldn't remember if wood would serve as a conductor between two charged metal rods or not. On top of that, I wasn't sure one way or the other if the bottom of the wood was wet. Ain't life a bitch!

Well, like they say, when in doubt test the waters. I figured I should've fried by now if the wire was hot. So like a little kid testing his bath, I shoved my hand in and out of the water as fast as I could. Looked like the boys in Mexico hadn't paid their electricity bill. It turned out that "day-old" water was as cold as a corpse's ass.

I stepped off the plank and sank in water up to about my nuts. I recited the Lord's Prayer in my mind as I waded into the tunnel. The dimensions were about five feet high by four feet wide. I had to stoop over so my head wouldn't hit the rough cement above me. I eased down the tunnel in the dark without turning my flashlight on. It was absolutely pitch dark. I couldn't have seen my hand on my nose if I had tried. I was relying solely on my equilibrium and flat foot placement to stay right-side up. I imagined this was sort of what it would be like to be a blind, drunk hunchback.

As I continued, the water seemed to keep rising. It wasn't that the floor was going down, or that I was getting deeper like wading off into a lake. As far as I could tell, or rather I should say feel, my footing remained level and constant, yet the water was rising up to my chest. I stopped so I wouldn't make slish-sloshing waves and listened. I heard the unmistakable sound of more water gushing down the tunnel. I turned the flashlight on and saw that a few yards ahead of me the water appeared to be flush with the tunnel's ceiling as it was rapidly advancing my way. I'd never encountered claustrophobia before, but we were quickly becoming acquainted. I *hate* tunnels!

I did an about-face as the rising water caught up with me. The dopers in Mexico had either heard me coming or they had a lookout who saw our search-warrant team make the entry. Either way you slice it, I had walked, or should I say waded, into a perfect no-weapon-required ambush. Let the gringo get midway in the three hundred-foot tunnel, and somewhere between Arizona and Mexico drown him like a rat. That's one thing I'll have to give the Mexican dopers. They have always been so creative when it comes to killing folks. Why waste lead and gunpowder when water is cheaper? They're such a thrifty bunch.

If I hadn't had been a young man with good lungs and a kick-ass underwater swimming routine, I probably wouldn't have made it out of that underground tomb. The closer I got to the bottom of the shaft, the lower the water got in the tunnel. I tell you it was a jubilant puppy that hit the plank and scudded up that ladder. I had never before thought of daylight as a privileged commodity. That had drastically changed in the last few minutes.

We didn't want to try to swim through the tunnel without knowing what the exact distance was. The MFJP had been brought onboard the investigation only after we had entered the tunnel on the U.S. side. Arizona Attorney General Agent Bernal, who was our liaison with the Mexican prosecutor's office, directed the MFJP to meet us across from the warehouse on the border at Camarena's residence in Mexico.

During the meeting we told them the tunnel was flooded and we needed to access the Mexican-side shaft from Camarena's house. They agreed to let us cross through the border fence and meet them at the house. Before it was over, we had cops from the Douglas Police Department, the Cochise County Sheriff's Department, DEA, the Arizona Attorney General's Office, and the U.S. Border Patrol joining us at Camarena's house in Agua Prieta.

Now, here is where some strange coincidental shit happened. During the search for the tunnel access at Camarena's house, I'm going to guess there were about a hundred U.S. and Mexican cops in and around the house. We were all looking for the hidden access to the shaft and tunnel. Harrison already knew how to open the tunnel's access because his informant had told him what to look for. He couldn't go directly to it because it would burn his snitch. So Harrison just lay back to see if anyone else knew how to open it. And if they did know, how did they know? It was going to be interesting to see.

One guy out of all those cops was "lucky" enough to find the answer. It was a common-looking water faucet in the backyard. When you opened the valve, the pool table and floor in Camarena's game room raised up into the air on hydraulic lifts, allowing you access to the same kind of little cement holding room that we found under the drain in the Douglas-side warehouse. Would you like to guess who the guy that found the secret valve was? Douglas police chief Alvaro Fragoso. Yeah, the same guy whose first cousin, Tombstone Fragoso, starred in the Well of Death production. The guy probably never won a dime in Las Vegas before. Yet somehow, out of a hundred cops with thousands of possible household switches, valves, and gadgets, Chief Fragoso chose to turn the faucet in the backyard. I reckon this is the one day he should have gone to Vegas!

It's a nasty little international dope business we have in Douglas, ain't it? Let me see if I can recap all of this for you. Douglas Judge Borane wheels and deals in real estate with Agua Prieta dope cartel member Yolanda Molina. And not to forget, her hands had blood on them from the Well of Death homicides. The judge also went hand-in-hand in a real estate transaction with Camarena, selling him the tunnel warehouse property for a whopping 472 percent profit. Fragoso, who was alleged to be having an affair with Yolanda's sister, had replaced Judge Borane as chief of police in Douglas. Yep, I'm sure of it now. It was just totally coincidental that Chief Fragoso knew where to find that silly valve!

It didn't take the news media too long to smoke the rodents out. They jumped on Judge Borane with sharpened claws. When they ripped into his ass about selling the tunnel property to Camarena, his well-rehearsed response was something like, "How was I supposed to know the guy was a dope smuggler? It's not like it was tattooed on his forehead." That's pretty weak coming from a guy who has dealt with criminals all of his professional life. That's like a doctor being sued for malpractice saying, "How was I supposed to know the guy was sick? It wasn't tattooed across his forehead." Come on, people! You don't get to be chief of police, and even later a judge, without being able to sort out the good guys from the bad guys.

The news industry flourished for about a month in Douglas. The tunnel was splashed all over the country and even worldwide. Washington REMFs you would never see in the field in a lifetime were out by the dozens. Everybody was posing in the tunnel for pictures and making movies. Gately, Hayes, and McDermott were continually in the company of the news media and brass. The juice guys even ordered all the Douglas agents to participate in a reproduction of the tunnel raid to be aired over and over on *Unsolved Mysteries*.

It would be eleven years before anyone was prosecuted for construction of the tunnel and the seizure of 2,200 pounds of cocaine. And it was well before that that Tom McDermott was promoted to Director of Smuggling Investigations in Customs headquarters back in D.C. He would later be sent as the U.S. Customs Service attaché to

London, where he subsequently had a nervous breakdown. He later wrote an article in the Customs Service news magazine about mental illness. Was the article an excuse for how messed up the management of the tunnel investigation was? I don't know. All I can tell you is that, until this day, I have still never seen "one-day-old water."

In 1997, I got a telephone call right out of the friggin clear blue. Dave Hayes, who had retired in Alpine, Texas, was on the other end of the line. There was positively no loss of love between us, so I knew the call had to be business-related. Without exchanging greetings, I listened as he told me that some people were looking at problems about the tunnel investigation. He never made it perfectly clear to me, but I guessed that he had been implicated in some kind of wrongdoing. He danced around the issue until he couldn't dodge it anymore.

When he finally got to it, he asked me straight out if I would ever tell anyone, or testify, that there were criminal actions taken by him or the other two managers during the tunnel investigation. I responded that I didn't agree with how they had handled the investigation, and particularly the removal of Mercado, but I did not believe there was criminal intention to derail the investigation.

I didn't gloat about the phone call. However, I did get a good deal of satisfaction from it. It proved that the three juice guys knew they were wrong, and it vindicated Steve Mercado. A little late, but better than never. I haven't heard from Hayes or the other two since.

In 1999, senior Special Agent Grant Murray of the U.S. Customs Service in Tucson located Rafael Camarena. We had been working with the *America's Most Wanted* television series when we got a call that Camarena was sitting in a Mazatlán jail under an assumed name serving five years for smuggling cocaine into Mexico from South America. The only reason he was arrested was because the Mexican Navy caught him and his organization unloading coke from a mother ship onto runners. Camarena and his boys foolishly opened up on the Mexican Navy, and, well, even Camarena is going to be slapped on the hand for firing on the sovereign Republic of Mexico.

One of our special agents attached to the Customs attaché in Mexico went to the Mazatlán prison to take a look at the tunnel king for identification and extradition. Our agent faxed us a photo with a report that Camarena was being treated like a god in the Mexican minimum-security lockup. Imagine that. Fire on the Mexican Navy and you get five years in the equivalent of a country club and golf course.

A couple of days after we identified Camarena and started the extradition process, Camarena's attorney was whacked as he crossed a street outside his office in Mazatlán. The poor sucker was hit thirty-eight times by two shooters spraying lead from AK-47s. The overkill was a two-fold warning. First, the tunnel people and Amado Carrillo thought that the attorney had a part in fingering Camarena. Second, it was a clear message to any Mexican judges that the same would happen to them if they signed any goddamn gringo extradition papers.

Before we could get a provincial warrant for his extradition from Mexico, we had to have a positive ID on the guy. To that end agent Murray and I went to see Judge Borane with a photo of Camarena, being that they had been business associates and friends.

It was absolutely hilarious when Murray and I hit the door to the judge's chambers. He was sitting behind his grand desk talking to another Douglas judge who was in his black robes. I looked over at the visiting judge, shoved my badge in his face, and announced we were federal agents here to speak with Judge Borane in private. Not only did this other judge promptly and politely excuse himself, but he was in such a rush to get away from us and out of Borane's chambers that he got his robe caught in the door when he slammed it during his exit. I actually had to open the door to unwrap his honor's black robes so he could continue his escape.

When we turned to continue with Judge Borane, he became as white as the sheets the Klan folks bleach up special for a Saturday-night cross-burning session. His speech was slurred and stuttering, his knees were buckling, and his voice was cracking when he asked, as if in a plea to appease us, "What, what, can, can I do for you boys?" The crooked son of a bitch thought we were there to arrest him for sure. Hell, when we showed him a photo of Camarena for the ID we both thought the judge was gonna pass out on us. It was good for a chuckle or two, although it wouldn't amount to a hill of beans.

Arizona DPS would later beat us to the punch on putting the old boy in jail. And I reckon that's all that matters with any outlaw in the end.

After Judge Borane identified the photo we informed him we would probably be calling him into federal court concerning his relationship with Camarena. That was, if we ever got Camarena out of Mexico. The Mexican government agreed to let us extradite Camarena when he ended his Mexican sentence in May of 2001. However, they did warn us that Camarena had a right to appeal their decision to a Mexican judge. And after what happened to Camarena's attorney, I didn't think there would be a judge in all of Mexico that would go up against the cartel. This beautiful country is becoming more and more a carbon copy of narcoterrorist-controlled Colombia.

On June 12, 2001, eleven years after we discovered America's first known international drug-smuggling tunnel, special agents of the U.S. Customs Service extradited from Mexico and took physical custody of Rafael Camarena.

On February 19, 2003, after pleading guilty to federal charges of conspiracy and cocaine trafficking, Camarena was sentenced to ten years in prison. Others are still on the run. And more, some in Douglas and some in Mexico, are still looking over their shoulders.

7
The King of Douglas

THE FRONTIER TOWN OF DOUGLAS rose up out of the tumbleweeds and dry winds in 1901. Canvas tents and adobe shacks sprung forth after the Phelps Dodge Mining Corporation announced it would be building a smelter in the area to process the ore taken out of its Bisbee copper mines. The town took its name from the Phelps Dodge president, Dr. James Douglas. It was built at the southern end of the Sulphur Springs Valley in Cochise County, right up against the U.S.-Mexican border. About twenty miles to the west of Douglas lie the Mule Mountains, which cradle Bisbee. Several miles to the east of Douglas are the haunting Perilla Mountains. And about twenty miles to the north are the famous oak- and pine-graced Chiricahua Mountains, which were home to Cochise and Geronimo not too many summers ago.

As in most newborn mining towns of those days, the economic boom in Douglas attracted the usual riffraff and felons that drifted the frontier, preying on honest folks for easy money. With Agua Prieta, Sonora, being no more than a stone's throw away, outlaws were afforded an avenue of quick escape into Mexico when they anticipated confrontation from lawmen who would arrive unannounced in

Douglas. In the beginning, there were more saloons and whorehouses than any other businesses in the adobe town. Killings and gunfights were a daily spectacle of some interest to passersby. The gunmen and gamblers enjoyed the anonymity the border gave them as the area's notoriety for lawlessness flourished. Such a sordid reputation predicated the arrival of a newly formed group of hard-line lawmen.

In 1902, the Arizona Rangers moved their headquarters into Douglas to clean the mess up. At the time, Douglas had one saloon for about every hundred citizens. The Rangers concentrated most of their efforts on the gambling and prostitutes located in the red-light district of Sixth Street. Because of the pleasures to be had on Sixth, the Mexicans dubbed it Calle Verde, which in English translates to Green Street. A lot of illicit money from gambling and prostitution flowed through this den of iniquity. Even today, keeping one foot firmly imbedded in its violent Wild West history and the other in a questionable future, Douglas has one sign on the street that bears both names side by side: Sixth/Green.

In 1902, according to statements made by Arizona Ranger Captain Thomas H. Rynning, Douglas was rowdier and tougher than Tombstone when he and his Rangers settled in to clean up the little border town. Rynning said that the worst smugglers, cattle thieves, and murderers from both sides of the U.S.-Mexican border called Douglas their home. Bad men with plenty of notches carved on their pistols operated the dance halls. Half of the deputy sheriffs were themselves crooked gamblers and killers who allowed robberies and murders to become commonplace in the dusty streets of the beleaguered tiny pueblo.

In addition to the Green Street criminal activity, the Rangers inherited some larger federal problems. The Yaqui Indians of Mexico had been on the rampage, killing a number of Mexican citizens down south. Their murder rate had been enhanced by the use of modern firearms such as Winchester repeaters. Such weapons were only manufactured and sold in the United States. However, the economics of supply and demand soon opened opportunities for border smuggling. The Mexican government complained to the U.S. State Department and, as always, shit rolls downhill. The Rangers were charged with the job of disrupting the southbound gun smuggling, in which merchants of Douglas, Bisbee, and Naco were involved to some degree.

When the Rangers departed Douglas for Naco in 1907, they left in their wake a legacy of gunfights and graveyards. One of the more colorful outlaws the Rangers cut down in a blazing shootout in the Douglas Cowboy Saloon was the brother of the infamous Texas Sam Bass. The outlaws who were able to survive the Rangers' tenure either crossed deep into Mexico or completely left Arizona to get out of the lawmen's jurisdiction. After enough lead had been dispensed, with some simulation of law and order being restored, Ranger Captain Rynning called Douglas the meanest place in the territory that he had ever cleaned out. He made particular reference to Green Street as having been the most troublesome area during his enforcement operations in Douglas.

After the Rangers departed, the little smelter town slowly grew over the next few years. In 1911, about six thousand U.S. troops were sent to Douglas to guard the border when Mexican General Red López laid siege to Agua Prieta. Political turmoil in Mexico spawned reoccurring revolutions, resulting in Pancho Villa riding against Agua Prieta in 1915. For three days Villa and his soldiers assaulted Agua Prieta. One of the old bandit's favorite military tactics was mass attack by infantry at night under the cover of darkness. As far as that Mexican tactic goes, Villa's dope-smuggling descendants and illegal crossers have perfected the skill, as they now routinely invade the U.S. from Agua Prieta every night!

Villa was unsuccessful in his bloody attempts to take the shanty-filled Mexican pueblo, but it still caused a great deal of concern across the fence in Douglas. Some residents departed for the northern part of the territory until it was safe to return. Others demanded protection from the federal government, resulting in the stationing of the U.S. Army's Arizona District Mexican Border Patrol in Douglas until 1920. Subsequent to the disbandment of the Army's Mexican Border Patrol, the present-day U.S. Border Patrol was born in 1924, and that hard-boiled organization has been attempting to protect our international boundaries ever since.

Arizona state Prohibition was declared in 1914 and, as could be expected, new life was breathed into the Green Street red-light district. With the Arizona Rangers not only gone from Douglas but totally disbanded due to state politics, liquor smuggling enriched the proprietors of the Sixth/Green Street bars and houses of ill repute. Once again, morals were pissing backwards and it was getting a little too raucous for decent folks to walk the streets of Douglas. On October 10, 1917, a Douglas committee hired a young deputy sheriff as a special patrolman with orders to disinfect Sixth/Green Street. This young patrolman was soon to be a Douglas legend.

Officer Percy Bowden was a big, round-faced, robust country boy. He did such a great job mopping up the Sixth/Green area that he was promoted from patrolman to chief of police in Douglas on June 15, 1920. It has been said that Bowden was the longest-serving chief of police in the nation when he hung his spurs up in 1972. And where most people may have viewed this as a good thing, the reality of it was quite different. Understandably, the residents of Douglas admired the lawman because their streets were once again safe to travel. The women and children could go out at night without worrying about being robbed or molested. You could even walk home dead drunk without being mugged. For the most part, the killings and murders stopped and the border town returned to a peaceful existence.

I've talked to people who said that Bowden was viewed by Douglas residents as just barely falling short of a king during his reign. His word was the law. He endeared himself to his constituents by doing a favor for a favor. If you were an auto mechanic and got caught driving drunk, a dismissal of the charges was forthcoming as soon as you tuned up the motor in Bowden's car. And the people of Douglas knew about such arrangements. They learned that the law could be traded with. And that was just the beginning of an entrenched corruption that has lasted damn near a century in Cochise County's Douglas, Arizona.

It's dangerous when any man, woman, or agency is given too much power, and worse yet, too much *time* in power. That was the problem with Bowden. Douglas residents were willing to turn a blind eye more and more. And as they did, Bowden took more and more.

The gambling, liquor, and prostitutes he was supposed to have cleaned out never really ceased altogether. They may have been thinned out some, but the remainder were kept for the most part out of the public's eyesight.

Back rooms continued operation and guaranteed Bowden a fair skim of the green. If a complaint was lodged concerning gambling or prostitution, Bowden's men would investigate the allegations and make a quite visible raid of the establishment. However, such shows were performed only after a warning had been dispatched to the proprietor of the business. With the illegal activities being put on the back burner, officers would walk through the establishment professing to the public that they found no violations.

It has even been alleged that upon the death of an old black madam known as "Nigger Patty," Bowden, knowing where she secreted her ill-gotten gains, slipped into the deceased's premises and cleaned out the till from beneath the old gal's hard-worked mattress. When asked about the money he was later seen slipping into his police station desk cabinet, his only reply was that the funds were "evidence." According to a relative of the witness, the "evidence" never again surfaced for air.

On June 9, 1957, Bowden hired a new young patrolman he had known since the patrolman was a kid. For the next fifteen years, Bowden took Joe Borane under his wing and mentored him on how to become a king. Borane rose through the ranks and received Bowden's approving nod when the time was right. On June 6, 1972, Bowden retired, and on the same day, Borane was sworn in as Douglas chief of police.

Power begets power. If you're a political power from one area, and you need help for votes in another locality, you reach out to that one name that rises above the rest. It doesn't matter if you know the guy is a crook or not. As long as he has the community's recognition, he's your man to go to. It's similar to Wyatt Earp. Everybody knows his name as a lawman, but not everyone knows he was a bullying outlaw himself. I would guess this is somewhat the manner that Bowden became a friend of U.S. Senator Carl Hayden. In retrospect,

Borane must have excelled in Bowden's school of king training. He too, over his tenure, managed to ingratiate himself with Arizona Governor Rose Mofford and a former U.S. Senator from Arizona who is alleged to be linked by marriage to a crime syndicate out of New York.

After ruling Douglas as the chief of police from 1972 to 1979, Borane fell from power after an FBI investigation of his professional conduct and shady financial dealings. However, like most power brokers and politicians, Joe managed to escape prosecution. He even ended up somehow landing on his feet after the investigation and went on to become the Cochise County justice of the peace in Douglas. This sucker was one of those guys who could fall into a tub of shit and come out smelling like a rose every time.

Over the years Judge Borane's popularity, as well as his wealth, which is estimated at about $5 million, has grown by leaps and bounds in the Douglas area. In the late 1960s Joe was even honored with a song written by a local convicted arsonist and drug dealer named Miguel Moreno. The *canción* (song) was released on a 45 rpm record. Although the ballad gives no last name, it is titled "Cocaine Joe" and there is little doubt among the residents of Douglas and Agua Prieta of the hero's surname.

In 1986, Judge Borane was driving a vehicle when he said he took his eyes off the road to adjust the radio and subsequently lost control. The vehicle rolled over several times, killing Borane's passenger, Robert Moreno. Borane was taken to the Douglas hospital, where Arizona DPS officers tested his blood and found that it contained .17 percent alcohol. In the state of Arizona, anything over .10 percent is legal grounds to charge a person with intoxication. I bet I don't even have to tell you the rest of the story now, do I? Do you think that a judge is going to get nailed like a regular guy? Especially a judge so above the law as Joe Borane?

Not only did the investigating officer's report read that Judge Borane was operating a motor vehicle while under the influence of an intoxicating beverage, it also went on to say that he was the driver at the time of the accident that resulted in the death of Moreno. The results of the investigation were presented to a Pima County prosecutor. The prosecutor declined prosecution on the basis that there was no probable cause to take a blood sample at the time Judge Borane was admitted to the hospital.

When I came back to Douglas in 1987 as a special agent with the U.S. Customs Service, the resident agent in charge was Jake Price. He was a Texan by birth, tall in stature, wide in girth, and a borderline alcoholic. He was a very good friend of Borane's and continually told me, as if it was his life's calling, that the rumors about Borane's criminal activity were untrue. Price always said that Joe was a good, honest man who had amassed a fortune in real estate by just being extremely lucky. Price would attempt to get me into social settings where Borane was present so that we could mingle. Jake told me, in no uncertain terms, that if I wanted to succeed politically in the Douglas area, I needed to become one of Borane's "people." Jake made the pitch time and again, but I never would take a swing at the ball.

In about 1987 or 1988, U.S. Customs Special Agent Robert Scofield, while working under Price's supervision, began an investigation into the alleged narcotics smuggling of a man named Daniel Wood. Scofield found that Wood had been previously convicted of felonious land-fraud charges. Without going into any allegations of wrongdoing that I don't know for a fact, I can only tell you what Price told Scofield. After reading Scofield's investigative report of Wood and how he was in cahoots with Judge Borane, Price jerked Scofield's ass into the office and ordered him to shut the investigation down. Price said that although Wood was a convicted felon, he was still, all in all, a pretty good old boy. Daniel Wood was, and still is, a close friend and business associate of Judge Borane.

In 1988, the U.S. Customs Service authorized building a new office for the special agents in Douglas. Price was instrumental in the selection of the site and the construction company, both of which came under Judge Borane's purview. Despite the screams of protest by Butch Barrett and me, Tucson-based Customs Special Agent in Charge Tom McDermott went with Price's recommendation. The only thing I can say about this foolish decision is what you've heard me say time and again: REMFs never listen to the guys in the dirt, living the job, and paying the price.

The new U.S. Customs Office of Investigation was subsequently built on land owned by Judge Borane. The selected construction company was owned by Borane's brother-in-law, Joseph Agers, who was convicted in 1978 on felony land-fraud charges. If it wasn't so funny it would be sad for me to tell you who Agers's defense attorney was: Robert Hirsch, who would also become Agua Prieta cartel member Yolanda Molina's defense attorney.

In 1988, Agent in Charge Jake Price retired from the U.S. Customs Service Office of Investigations in Douglas and became the new Douglas city magistrate. And considering that Price's wife had just gone to state prison for embezzlement, leaving a dark cloud hanging over his head about just how much he knew of her activities, that's a pretty good trick to get appointed as judge by the city council. Everyone in town knew that Judge Borane had used his influence to help his old federal guardian step into the position, thereby satisfying past favors. Hell, there was so much back-scratching going on here that when Price was low on money, he sold his house to Borane and Joe allowed Jake to continue living in the damn thing.

A short time after he became Douglas city magistrate, Jake Price was taken into custody for drunken driving over in Hidalgo County, New Mexico. He posted bail after sobering up and returned to Douglas in a state of depression. Jake went to Joe with his problem and instead of telling Jake to get a good lawyer and face the consequences, Borane did what most power brokers would do in a situation like this: He called Cochise County Sheriff Jimmy Judd, a man who may not have had much finesse, but you would never meet a more honest and diligent lawman. In brief, Borane asked Judd to abuse his authority by calling the Hidalgo County sheriff and getting the charges against Price dismissed. In brief, Judd told Borane to pound sand up his ass. A couple of months later, Price died of a heart attack before going to trial in Hidalgo County.

In February of 1988, M&M Realty, operated by Alejandro Morales and Humberto Montaño, opened its doors in a downtown

Douglas building owned by Judge Borane. Alejandro Morales has been a longtime friend and associate of the judge. Morales is a convicted narcotics smuggler who had been indicted in a conspiracy with Yolanda Molina's relative and well-known narcotics boss, Clemente Soto-Peña. Humberto Montaño, Borane's personal accountant, has also been a lifelong friend of Joe's. One of the first land transactions they ever consummated was the February 29 sale of the San Jose Ranch to a member of the Agua Prieta cartel.

The San Jose Ranch lies about ten miles east of Douglas and about fifteen miles west of Naco. It sits right on the border across from La Morita ranch in Mexico, which was owned by Yolanda Molina. According to our sources, the only reason that Molina wanted to purchase the San Jose was to facilitate her dope-smuggling operation. For obvious reasons, short of having a tunnel, it's a Mexican dope smuggler's dream come true to own both adjoining sides of the border.

On February 29, Ben Loreto Sr., whom agent Arturo Bernal and I had been investigating for money laundering under Yolanda Molina, walked into the M&M Realty office and purchased part of the San Jose Ranch for $113,400. On the same day, Loreto turned around and sold the same property to Evaristo Molina Santa María for $151,200, a $37,800 profit. On October 26, the same procedure was repeated for the purchase of another portion of the ranch. Loreto bought this section for $200,000 and sold it the same day for $220,000 to Jesús Daniel Hernández. In addition to a little money-washing going on here, Yolanda set up her own private international dope-smuggling avenue. You see, Jesús Daniel Hernández is her son, and Evaristo Molina Santa María is her father. You ever wonder why Mexicans have such long adjoining names? Well, if you're a dope smuggler, it's a good tool to confuse gringos while you hide your property and assets.

During our investigation of the Molina cell of the Agua Prieta cartel, Bernal and I learned some other interesting things about the relationships within this particular group. We already had been told that Ben Loreto Sr.'s niece was married to Judge Joe Borane. But we didn't yet know that Loreto's son was an Arizona Department of Public

Safety pilot. And in that capacity, Ben Loreto Jr. was the pilot who flew Arizona Governor Rose Mofford around the state. In fact, after learning that we had his father under investigation, Ben Jr. came to our office and admitted that his father was doing business with suspected dope trafficker Yolanda Molina. When we refused to elaborate on the charges, Ben Jr. departed our office in a huff, and our agents followed him straight to Judge Borane's office.

It wasn't too much longer after this that Bernal and I were at a couple of different social functions and we bumped into the Honorable Joe Borane. I swear Joe was one of the ugliest guys I've ever known. But he must have shaved every morning in a broken mirror, because he really fancied himself as a ladies' man. Born of Lebanese descent, Joe had a crinkled hook-bill nose that sat under a wrinkled, receding-hairline forehead. He was one of those guys with nervous energy who just couldn't sit still. According to informants, his antsy behavior was on regular occasions cocaine-induced.

Borane's dark eyes would continually dart back and forth, looking all around when he entered a room. And if you knew anything about Joe you knew what he was searching for. Opportunity. The opportunity to meet someone he could either make money with, or off. And with Joe, it didn't matter if you were a convicted felon, a senator, a drug kingpin, or some other kind of crook. If there was a chance to make money he was there ready to snuggle up to you. Hell, at one time the good judge even attended an event in Agua Prieta where he became godfather to a drug lord's child and the chosen godmother who was standing across from the judge was herself a well-known federal dope-smuggling fugitive. Judge Borane's hypocrisy knew no bounds.

My skin crawled every time I had any contact with this guy. At one of the aforementioned social functions Joe approached Bernal and me in his usual charming manner and tried to make chitchat. And that's one thing about Judge Borane: He always started out with the same endearing line, "Well, hello, *my friend*." If you knew anything at all about Bernal or me, you would know that we would rather eat five pounds of cactus thorns and shit sharp needles than be called one of Borane's friends. So, already pissed off by that "friend" bullshit, our hackles rose. Seeing that it was a very awkward moment, Joe started to excuse himself.

But before he left, he had to make a stab at keeping us near him. Either the man can't take rejection very well, or he's always thinking of future enterprises and how you can help him. He invited us to a couple of gatherings at his home. The judge was trying to rope us into his circle. He had lost Price and he needed to fill that federal protection void. He needed to keep an eye on us and have us near to pump us for information. By his demeanor we knew that he probably suspected we had an investigation involving him. He just wasn't yet sure how deep we had gone and how much we knew.

Speaking of his circle, Bernal and I analyzed this group of unsavory characters and found that out of eight friends and associates that Borane surrounded himself with, six had been arrested for narcotics or land-fraud felony violations, and two were dope-trafficking suspects. One of the six arrestees was a Douglas police officer who had worked alongside former officer Borane under Chief Bowden. The way we figured it, this was how Joe was always able to insulate himself from being implicated in any wrongdoing or criminal activity. He obviously had learned a great deal during his many years in law enforcement and presiding as a judge.

It's a fact of law that knowing that a guy did a crime and proving it in court are not two, but three entirely different animals. There's the defense lawyer's truth, there's the prosecution's truth, and then there's the real truth. Very seldom does the real truth survive the judicial process. So if you're the ringleader of an organization, and you have your number-two guy and your number-three guy commit a crime, you have two layers of protection between you and the real truth. As long as you didn't do any overt acts, number two and number three have to take the fall for you. And that's the way it all appears with M&M Realty and the many times they dealt with crooks. And over the years, Montaño and Morales were always taking the heat for the judge during criminal investigations and news interviews.

On February 2, 1989, Bernal and I seized the Molina bank accounts and their ranch in Cochise County. Well, Judge Borane didn't wait too long before making a stab at damage control. One day my office phone rang and sure enough he was on the other end of the line. Joe said, "Lee, you know there's this guy that's at the courthouse in Bisbee trying to get a copy of your Yolanda Molina affidavit." I replied, "Yes, and what's the problem with that?" Joe countered, "Well, I just thought you should know about it." There was a long pause here and I waited to see if he would commit to asking me to violate the law. After a few seconds of silence I replied, "Your Honor, those affidavits are public records and anyone can review them. Besides, you don't have any problems of your own in the affidavit, do you?" Again there was silence for several seconds and Joe finally responded, "I don't know, I thought you could tell me." I replied, "No, I can't say anything about the investigation, but just like any other civilian you, too, can go to the courthouse and ask to review the documents." We said our adioses and hung up.

First of all, I found it extremely interesting that a piddly-ass county justice of the peace in Douglas was getting information on who was asking for what affidavits from the Arizona Superior Court in Bisbee. Second, Bernal and I now knew that Joe figured out he was in the affidavit and this phone call was about two things. First, he wanted to know how bad he was going to get hurt. Second, if we had ever owed him a favor, it was being called in now to stop the affidavit from being released. I think if I had played my cards right and hung a little bait out, the judge would have been indictable for obstruction of justice by the end of our conversation.

Another M&M Realty debacle, in February of 1988, was the sale of the infamous Douglas drug-tunnel property from Judge Borane to Enrique Camarena. If ever there was a time that the judge could have been indicted, this was it. He and M&M Realty sold Camarena property at a profit that was so mind-boggling, 472 percent, only a fool with a lobotomy wouldn't have known some kind of criminal enterprise was being hidden. Borane had originally purchased eighty acres of undeveloped desert sand and a commercial lot in Douglas. The eighty acres were about a mile north of town. The commercial lot was right next to the border fence on Pan American Avenue, just a hard spit away from Mexico. He bought both properties for about $24,000 by his own estimate. He sold this same property for $280,000 and couldn't remember a thing about the transaction when he was questioned by the U.S. Attorney's Office in Tucson.

In a 1991 sworn deposition in front of Assistant U.S. Attorney Cindy Jorgenson, Judge Borane testified that he could not remember when and where he first met Enrique Camarena. He testified that he could not remember how the real estate deal was put together. He testified that he did not remember sitting down with Camarena and signing the sales contract. He testified that he did not remember the terms of the sale or what he had received as a down payment from Camarena. He testified that he did not remember personally receiving any money and he didn't even know if he had yet been fully paid for the property. And last, but not least, the Honorable Joe Borane went on record to testify that he was not involved in preparing any of the documents.

Now that last one is a humdinger of a disclaimer. Remember what I said before about insulating yourself from criminal wrongdoing? Borane just piled everything on the backs of his number-two and number-three fall guys. And they did in fact take a good deal of heat. But one of them decided not to fry entirely alone. Montaño was deposed by the same assistant U.S. Attorney and he gave a completely different story under oath. He said that Borane received direct payments from Camarena and that the property had been paid for in full. Montaño said that a deed of reconveyance had been filed showing that the judge had been paid $280,000. But being the good patsy he was, Montaño finished up by saying something to the effect that any discrepancies in the sale of the tunnel property were entirely his fault. Who gives a shit? Not only do we know Borane was involved up to his eyeballs with Camarena, but now he's hiding about a quarter of a million dollars of income from the government!

The agents who investigated the financial part of the tunnel case never located this money. But more important was the fact that Borane had been caught lying to the federal government while under oath. And that, my fine feathered friends, is called perjury, plain and simple. However, like I've said before, attorneys don't hurt attorneys, and they sure as hell aren't going to burn a judge. In her final analysis of the case, Assistant U.S. Attorney Cindy Jorgenson stated that Judge Borane was not forthcoming with the final disposition of the payments for the tunnel property. To regular folks like us, that means the crooked son of a bitch lied about his laundered drug money from Camarena! She further stated that, although there existed clear indication that Judge Borane's activities during the sale of the land were questionable, the investigation was being closed due to a lack of *interest* to prosecute on the part of the U.S. Attorney's Office. Notice that she did not say it was due to the lack of *evidence*.

Now, who said our boy didn't learn well from Bowden? It comes in handy now and again to have favors owed you from a U.S. senator, or maybe even a governor. If that had been citizen Joe Blow sitting there fibbing under oath to the U.S. Attorney, he would have been cuffed up and hauled off as quick as shit rolls down a goose's leg. I mean, here is a guy who admits he was the godfather to Enrique Camarena's child, which is a big deal in the Mexican culture. He admits that he visited Camarena's house, where the tunnel began in Mexico, on several occasions. But somehow Joe Borane, a man who was intelligent enough to become chief of police and judge, can't remember what happened to $280,000 or any of the particulars concerning silly little things like contracts or sales agreements. In fact, when later asked, he couldn't even remember the months or years that he visited Camarena's house in Mexico. I guess if I had frequently visited a friend whose face would soon be broadcast on *America's Most Wanted*, I would also try to lose my memory.

So during the first month of the history of M&M Realty, the boys became squarely involved in two of the largest federal and state criminal drug-smuggling and money-laundering investigations in the history of Cochise County. Well, I reckon it was easy enough to understand what was going to transpire next.

In 1994, a couple of years after the tunnel investigation was completed, agents of the Arizona Attorney General's Office and investigators from the state real estate office pounced on M&M Realty. As soon as the agents walked in, Alex Morales telephoned Borane, who arrived in minutes. Joe went into Morales's office and instructed him to cooperate with the investigators. As the agents reviewed files and documents in the office, the judge just stood there and hatefully glared at them, never saying a word. He departed after about thirty minutes of watching what the investigators were digging through. The state agents later reported that it was obvious Borane acted in a manner consistent with that of a controlling interest and that the review of records indicated the business was probably being used to launder money from illicit proceeds.

The state interview of Alex Morales proved to be quite entertaining. Part of the reason the real estate investigators had gone down to M&M was that they wanted to explain to the Realtors that under state law they were obliged to inform the appropriate authorities about any suspicious financial transactions or customers. Morales smartly asked the agents to define a suspicious person or transaction to him. This formerly convicted dope smuggler said that he couldn't be expected to abide by such laws because he had no way of telling who was suspicious. Morales went on to imply that if a suspicious customer hadn't yet been arrested by DEA or U.S. Customs, he was to be considered okay, and he would continue to deal with him.

Well, it seems like we've heard this same line of shit before. In fact, I would have to say that the judge trained his number-three insulator real well. During a news interview of Borane during the tunnel investigation he was quoted as saying something like, "How am I supposed to know what a dope smuggler looks like? It's not like they have doper written across their forehead." Nice schooling of your boy here, Judge. But it didn't hold water. The state investigator got in Morales's face and said, "You want to know what suspicious is? How about the sale of the San Jose Ranch and the tunnel property in 1989?" Morales's face dropped somewhere under his balls.

By the way, if it wasn't enough that Morales himself was a convicted dope smuggler and should know one when he sees one, how about his sister? Subsequent to the seizure of Yolanda Molina's property and the San Jose Ranch, Customs agents arrested Morales's sister with two hundred-plus pounds of marijuana that she was trying to smuggle through the Naco Port of Entry. I wonder if she wouldn't have qualified in Morales's real-estate dealings as "suspicious" had she brought a grocery sack of cash in.

After the state investigator returned to Phoenix to write up his report, he was called into the office of Edwin J. Ricketts, the deputy commissioner of real estate for Arizona. Ricketts asked the agent just how deeply Judge Borane was involved in the investigation. The agent acted dumb and asked Ricketts why he wanted to know. Ricketts, who was an appointed deputy commissioner under Governor Rose Mofford, replied that he and Joe went way back. Some days later Borane was seen by state employees in Deputy Commissioner Ricketts's office in Phoenix. Ain't the horseless carriage a wonderful thing? Back in Bowden's day it would have taken a lot longer to get from Douglas to Phoenix to hide Madam "Nigger Patty's" mattress money.

The state agents also discovered that M&M Realty was paying bills for a Mexican real estate office in Agua Prieta also named M&M. It was reported that the M&M building in Agua Prieta was owned by Vicente Terán, who was the town's mayor. Before Terán became mayor of Agua Prieta, not only did he live as a next-door neighbor to Judge Borane in Douglas, but Bernal and I also knew he was laundering money through Agua Prieta cartel member Yolanda Molina's U.S. bank accounts. In fact, we had found that one of Yolanda's brothers was depositing large amounts of cash into Terán's business. But even before he was laundering money for the Agua Prieta cartel, and was a next-door neighbor of Borane, he was doing interesting things back in the days when Joe was chief of police in Douglas.

Vicente Terán had been arrested on January 21, 1974, by the Tucson Police Department for the unlawful offer to sell marijuana and attempted armed robbery. What that means is that Terán and some other dope mopes were prepared to whack undercover Tucson narcs when they tried to rip them off during a marijuana buy. In fact, to show you Terán's propensity for violence, during his police interview he admitted to having worked under dope smuggler Francisco "La Rata" Cornejo, who shot a DEA agent in the neck during undercover negotiations in October of 1973. There was no doubt that Terán was prepared to cap the undercover narcs had they not arrested him before he could make his move.

Terán eventually posted bond and fled into Agua Prieta, where he took refuge with the Agua Prieta cartel. Terán became a fugitive from the Arizona courts and American jurisprudence system for eleven years. As he hid in Mexico, his attorney entered a guilty plea in his behalf and the Arizona Superior Court convicted and sentenced the future mayor of Agua Prieta to serve one to two-and-a-half years in the state prison upon being taken into custody.

On September 11, 1985, some eleven years later, presiding Superior Court Judge Thomas Meehan vacated Terán's sentence "in the interest of justice" and dismissed the indictment. The dismissal was partially based on the fact that Terán had stayed out of trouble for eleven years and he had given the Tucson Unified School District a $12,000 van (from the half a million a year he was making in dope). The other reason for allowing the rat to skate was that numerous prominent Douglas and Tucson businessmen testified on Terán's behalf concerning his good character. Now, don't make me slap you in the face to figure out what high-up lords, judges, or senators may have testified for the boy. If you missed the horse when it galloped by, you won't ever be able to survive the border in Douglas and Agua Prieta.

So during the time Terán remained a fugitive in Agua Prieta, and was a good boy as far as not crossing into the U.S. and trying to rip off narcotics agents goes, he amassed quite a little fortune working with the Agua Prieta cartel in old Mexico. It is believed that today he owns some nine ranches in Mexico worth a million dollars each. He owns several businesses in Agua Prieta including the Terán Plaza, which just happens to house Borane's Mexican affiliate, or maybe I should say extension, of M&M Realty. And you wonder how he got so rich over the past few years, don't you?

According to folks in Agua Prieta, in 1993 Terán was seen back and forth in Sonora with one of the biggest murdering drug lords that ever raised his nasty head up from the desert sands: Amado Carrillo. Terán and Carrillo spent a lot of time together in Agua Prieta and on

Carrillo's ranch down south. From what I understand, they both even hobnobbed with the assistant governor of Chihuahua in Ciudad Juárez before Amado was eventually murdered in 1997 over the control of his narcotics-smuggling empire.

To demonstrate what the mayoral position in Agua Prieta entails, during the 1990–1991 narcotics-tunnel investigation I interviewed the then mayor of Agua Prieta, Bernie Meza. Meza told me that he was taking $5,000 per month from Enrique Camarena in bribes. The money was to guarantee protection while Camarena set up his operation and built the tunnel. You have to understand, certain positions in Agua Prieta are expected to guarantee cooperation and assistance to both Colombian and Mexican drug lords. Such positions generally include, but may not be limited to, the commander of the Federal Judicial Police, the chief of police, the federal prosecutor, the mayor, and the chief of the Sonora state police.

When Terán was elected mayor of Agua Prieta in 1997, the word was put out all over Sonora that dope was going to run two ways through Agua Prieta and Douglas. Freely and rampantly. I don't know about you, but I've never been in this predicament. What are you supposed to formally call someone like Vicente Terán when you meet him as a public official? Mayor? Your Honor? Or how about Ex-Convict? Ex-Fugitive? According to the court, all of Terán's wrongdoings have been dismissed. But you know something? I bet you a dime to a doughnut that those Tucson undercover cops, after looking down Terán's gun barrel some twenty-four years ago, have a whole different idea about this piece of shit who called himself Mayor of Agua Prieta.

In 1997, with ex-convicted drug smuggler Vicente Terán becoming mayor of Agua Prieta, guess who comes home from Phoenix to run for mayor of Douglas? Yes, Judge Borane's one and only little brother, Ray Borane Jr. And you ask where he has been all these years? Where else but up in Arizona's capital city, where he had been the assistant Arizona state school superintendent under Governor Rose Mofford. While we're on the subject of the governor's office, let's not forget about the commissioner of real estate. In 1995, pursuant to the 1994 state investigation into the alleged money-laundering by

M&M (&B) Realty, Morales had his broker's license suspended for a whopping sixty days and paid a measly $4,000 fine.

In about 1983 or 1984, the Phelps Dodge Corporation shut down its smelter operations in Douglas and practically fled town. They were the largest employer in town. In fact, as previously stated, the smelter was the only reason Douglas ever came into existence. Ever since the smelter had gone into operation, just about everything that developed in this town was orientated to make money from Phelps Dodge or its employees. Most everything was an augmentation or personification of Phelps Dodge. For all practical purposes, the corporation had become the center of the universe for Douglas.

So when the universe died, you would expect the same for its dependent town. Not so; even without any other real industries here, Douglas has managed to not only hang on, but to actually grow. The little town has a new, large shopping center and a smorgasbord of fast-food joints. In comparison, Agua Prieta has probably tripled its population to more than 100,000 people, including prospering citizens of Colombia. Which brings me to the point. Douglas and Agua Prieta are living off a false economy. If it wasn't for the dope trade, this area would become a virtual ghost town in a matter of days.

In 1998, John F. Kennedy Jr. shocked the residents of Douglas when he dared to tell the truth in *George* magazine. Douglas's guts were laid open for the nation to pick over and inspect when Kennedy's article on corruption listed Douglas as the third most corrupt city in the entire U.S. And when you consider that this little town has a population of about 15,000 people, that's quite an infamous accomplishment. You know things have to be pretty messed up for such a podunk desert pueblo to catch the eye of the nation.

Some of the citizens of Douglas puffed up their chests and acted indignant and insulted. Some of the merchants were interviewed by reporters and it all got pretty hilarious. One of the proprietors of a downtown business went as far as to say on television that Kennedy had done a great disservice to Douglas, and that he was going to vote Republican from now on. I mean, here are people who on a daily basis make their living selling dry goods or whatever to people who predominately make their living smuggling dope.

Now, I'm not saying the merchants are crooks because of who their customers are. They can't help it that the money in this town is mainly narcotics-generated. I'm just saying let's at least face the reality of the situation. We don't need to lie to ourselves about what's going on in this town. How can you explain that we have the highest unemployment rate in the state, yet people are driving $40,000 pickup trucks and buying houses with grocery bags full of cash?

But the Douglas merchants were just part of the responding circus. You should have heard the bitching and moaning coming from the Borane brothers. They were writing letters demanding apologies from Kennedy and defending the "honor" of Douglas. I guess if I was profiting from a false economy and a stranglehold on the "business," I would also pitch a fit when it was brought to the attention of the nation. I mean, after all, Bowden knew how to keep things low-key and backdoor. He never would allow his dirty laundry to be aired out in public like this.

Mayor Borane wrote a letter to the editor of *George* that almost left me rolling on the floor when I read it. He started out by saying he was shocked and totally disturbed by the magazine's lack of moral responsibility. He also wrote that the slipshod, facile, and elementary method of reporting the article was not only reprehensible and unconscionable, but an embarrassment to all capable and professional writers who do their own research and substantiate reported information. The mayor ended his letter by writing that Douglas did not appreciate the indiscriminate and damaging intrusion of *George* magazine.

Well, in response to that I rest my case on this: Agent Bernal, Agent Barrett, Agent Scofield, and I have been narcotics law enforcement officers in this area since about 1974. We have accumulated a total of about one hundred years of experience on the job between us. We have done more investigative time and research substantiating narcotics-smuggling allegations and information than anyone in the history of Douglas, Cochise County, and Agua Prieta. When Judge Borane or Mayor Borane talk about being shocked and disturbed about the lack of moral responsibility, that's like the pot calling the kettle black.

In June of 1998, the Arizona newspapers were buzzing with front-page stories about the gunfights between narcotics smugglers and border agents near Naco and Nogales. If the articles weren't about shootings they mentioned the increasing risk to lawmen and the number of murdered bodies being found on the border. On one of these front-page articles, the Douglas *Daily Dispatch* included a column concerning the proposed 1999 defense-authorization bill, which was then in the conference committee in D.C. The bill included an amendment to allow armed U.S. soldiers to aid the Border Patrol and Customs agents in controlling the border. Do I have to tell you what Mayor Borane's response was? Get ready for a good laugh.

During his interview with the reporter, all Mayor Borane did was bitch and moan about how the people in Congress don't know how we live down here on the border. He said that they don't have any idea what our relationship is with Mexico. No shit! If Congress knew the truth they would probably double the proposed number of troops *and* drug agents! After reading the article I couldn't tell if the reporter had interviewed the mayor of Douglas or the mayor of Agua Prieta, who would have been representing the interest of the Agua Prieta drug cartel.

I mean, all the newspapers were talking about the increased assaults and the recent murder of a Border Patrol agent by dope smugglers, and Mayor Ray Borane responds that he doesn't want any law-enforcement officers getting help from the military! He spewed bullshit like, "We'll have troops down here with no cultural sensitivity and there would be a language barrier. It would send a horrible message to the people in Mexico. We would be deploying troops to keep them out of here, as if they were terrorists." Borane went on to say, "You know, I was in Russia last summer, and seeing all of those armed military men was unsettling. It's not a good feeling." What a crock of horseshit!

First of all, in essence, I guess Mayor Borane is trying to convince us that those military-trained, armed-to-the-teeth, dope-smuggling Mexicans we federal agents go up against on a daily basis are not terrorists! Not to mention the fact that every single time they smuggle a load of dope they violate the sanctity of our border by making an armed invasion into our nation.

Secondly, Mayor Borane, as a part of his normal international functions, must go to Agua Prieta and have meetings with Mayor Terán on a regular basis. And yet he does not say one iota about the fact that numerous armed Mexican troops occupy the plaza in the middle of Agua Prieta. Not to mention that we U.S. agents frequently see the Mexican Army patrolling with their machine guns up and down the border on their side of the fence.

So, if Mexico has armed troops on the border, and that's obviously not offensive to Mayor Borane, why would it be considered so inappropriate for Douglas to complement the U.S. drug agents with the help of U.S. troops? After all, the INS conducted a survey that revealed that 89 percent of Arizona residents were in favor of having the U.S. military patrol the border. I reckon that must mean that Mayor Borane is only speaking for the remaining 11 percent minority. I always thought our form of government adhered to the concept that our elected public officials worked in the best interest of the majority.

Such corrupt agendas must be stripped bare of political complications and made available for public inspection and scorn. It is said that history repeats itself. If that is true, here is some food for thought. I once saw written on the kilo bricks of a smuggled cocaine load the following words: "This Is Our War on the North Americans." Now, think about this. Politicians left our Arizona border defenseless in 1909 with the disbanding of the Rangers. It may be possible that similar, even more cynical, forces are at work today seeking to assist the other side in opening our borders.

Between 1998 and 1999, all hell broke lose in Douglas as far as illegal immigration and dope smuggling were concerned. The U.S. Customs Service recorded a 44 percent increase in seized dope, going from about fourteen tons in 1998 to more than twenty tons in 1999. In addition, our arrests of narcotics violators in Douglas alone rose by 77 percent, going from 149 defendants in 1998 to 264 defendants in

1999. And on the U.S. Border Patrol's side of the house, their agents were arresting about 1,500 illegal entrants per day. At that rate of apprehension, in a little over a week, they were picking up the equivalent of Douglas's entire permanent population!

Now, while most people in the county were screaming for more Border Patrol agents and assistance from the U.S. military forces to help deter the invasion, Douglas Mayor Ray Borane was saying no to such action. He insisted that would only militarize the border and make matters worse. No, what he wanted was to open our borders and give all potential illegal aliens work permits to travel anywhere in the U.S. they wanted to go. And in echoing rhetoric, Agua Prieta Mayor Terán agreed time and again. In fact, they were so repetitive of each other it got downright difficult telling who the Mexican mayor was and who the Arizona mayor was. They were like mirrors.

Meanwhile, the FBI snuck into town when no one was looking. An undercover agent set up a military-surplus store in one of Judge Borane's rental properties downtown and a two-year sting operation was put into motion. You have to remember that the FBI had made a run at the judge in the 1970s, and although they managed to get the boy fired from his prestigious chief-of-police position, they didn't get enough evidence to prosecute the man they eventually came to nickname "The King of Douglas."

In September 1999, after a two-year investigation conducted by the FBI, the U.S. Customs Service, the Cochise County BAG Unit, DEA, and Arizona DPS, unannounced search warrants were served on M&M Realty, the Justice of the Peace office in Douglas, and the Douglas City Magistrate office. While the officers and agents were busy executing the warrants in Douglas, Judge Borane was arrested in Tucson as he was walking down the street illegally carrying a concealed .25 caliber pimp's pistol in his coat pocket. He had previously been indicted by a grand jury after being caught on tape conspiring with the undercover agent to possess and smuggle cocaine, launder narcotics proceeds, and fix speeding tickets. At the moment of his arrest the crooked bastard sassily told lawmen, "You don't have a thing on me. You can't prove a thing." From his contemptuous attitude it was apparent that the last twenty-five years of corruption he had gotten away with was now weighing heavily on his shoulder as a boasting chip.

The search of the judge's chambers at his Justice of the Peace office yielded two things of particular interest to me. First, the man's vanity was shown to glow white-hot by the fact that he kept an original 45-rpm record of the ballad of Cocaine Joe in his desk drawer. It must have been a proud trophy for him to gloat over while cloaked within his black, soiled robes. The hypocrite must have reveled in the knowledge that he had the power to sentence others for crimes he committed while sitting well above the law.

The second was an envelope from a maximum-security federal prison for lifers up in Illinois. The outside of the letter was marked as "legal mail," which restricted it from being opened and read by federal corrections officers because this is supposed to be a privileged communication between a convict and his attorney. Being that it was addressed to a judge, I guess the feds figured that was also protected under our present courts' rulings.

In the envelope was a handwritten letter from a former U.S. Customs inspector named Don Simpson. We had busted Simpson back in 1990 when we caught him smuggling ton-loads of cocaine through the Douglas Port of Entry. The dope loads were linked to Amado Carrillo, Vicente Terán, Yolanda Molina, and other members of the Agua Prieta cartel. Along with the letter the federal convict wrote to Judge Borane was a U.S. Customs Internal Affairs memorandum of information dated October 26, 1986. The memo was written by a special agent after he debriefed an informant who alleged that Judge Borane and Inspector Simpson were smuggling dope together. The accompanying handwritten letter from Simpson told Borane who the informant was, where he lived, and that he could expect to find him at a certain horse race. In my opinion, these documents were mailed by the corrupt ex-fed under the disguise of "legal mail" to the judge as either a request, or a reminder, to have the informant whacked. If there was ever a doubt in my mind that Judge Borane was guilty of association with the kind of people that had DEA agent Camarena murdered and contracts of death put out on Bernal, Barrett, and me, the evidence was now cast into stone.

The case on Judge Borane would have gone all the way to the wall had it not been handled by the FBI. It seemed that the Ruby Ridge and Waco fiascos had followed Hoover's boys into Arizona. Remember how I told you that you really get turned around and lose touch with reality when you're working undercover? Well, it turned out that the FBI undercover agent began to think he really was a free-spirited bad guy when the FBI cut him loose. I reckon he discovered that the Mexican *chulitas* (cuties) were pretty amorous under the influence of a bottle of tequila and a romantic Cochise County moon. One thing led to another and before the agent knew what he had gotten himself into he was balling a single mother and her daughter from Douglas's underground dope-smuggling community. What can I say in his defense? Well, how about this. Being a man with a diamond-cutting woody these days is rough. Thinking with the little head instead of the big head has gotten many an undercover agent into a world of shit.

A few months before Judge Borane got busted, Arizona Department of Public Safety Agent Jesse Gutierrez and I busted the owner of a Douglas mortuary for smuggling five hundred pounds of cocaine from Agua Prieta to the funeral parlor using one of their death wagons as transport. During the mortician's sentencing in Tucson, he brought it to the attention of the federal judge and the U.S. Attorney that his sister and niece were sleeping with the FBI undercover agent in the Borane case. After that little bomb went off in the courthouse, you could have heard a needle-dick mouse fart in the basement bomb shelter thirty feet below.

Subsequently and quite understandably, the federal prosecutors didn't want to have anything to do with the case. Why? Because the defense attorney for Borane would have had a field day "Furmanizing" the FBI agent on the stand. His questioning would have gone something like this: "Are you an *honest* agent of the FBI?" Naturally, he would reply that he indeed was. Next question, "Aren't you married?" The next question, "Did you cheat on your wife?" The next question, "Do you believe as an FBI agent that it is morally proper to have sexual relations with a mother and her daughter at the same time?" And it would all go downhill from there as far as a jury's perception of the veracity of the FBI undercover agent was concerned.

This was the second time in twenty years that the FBI had tried to rope Judge Borane, and they were still throwing an empty loop. So after the Hoovers screwed the case up, the feds dumped it to be salvaged by the Arizona Rangers' descendants, the Arizona Department of Public Safety. I kind of thought that to be poetic justice, being that the original cleanup of Douglas started with these lawmen nearly a century ago anyway. In the end the FBI walked away from the King of Douglas with a 0 and 2 record.

What do you expect from a federal agency that has the worst conviction rate in all the federal law-enforcement community? A 1999 Justice Department report cited that the FBI got only one conviction out of every four cases. A third of the cases they presented to the U.S. Attorney's Office were declined because of weak evidence or because they did not meet the standards of federal interest. The same study reported that one half of the FBI's convictions were drug or bank-theft cases, which *local* lawmen could handle. On the other hand, the FBI seemed to spend less time on cases where it has primary or exclusive responsibility. In national-security cases, in 1997, they only produced twelve convictions; in official corruption cases (like Judge Borane), 233; civil rights violations, 99; and embezzlement, 66.

On May 31, 2000, after pleading guilty to two Arizona state felony counts of tampering with a public record and fraudulent schemes and artifices, violations that carried a possible four-year prison sentence, Judge Joe Borane was sentenced to serve ninety days in the Cochise County Jail. Now, if you can believe this one, the sentencing Superior Court judge allowed the disgraced public official to be released daily from 7:00 a.m. to 6:00 p.m. so he could manage his millions in properties and businesses! According to court records, Judge Borane's income properties were grossing a little more than $500,000 per year, and it was imperative that he be released during the day because he was unable to find anyone in Douglas to manage his properties for him. While serving such an indulgent "sentence," the crooked judge could be seen every day driving his luxurious Jaguar back and forth between his jailhouse bed in Bisbee and his businesses in Douglas.

There's no doubt that title and position will always count for something in Cochise County, I reckon. But if there is any justice here, it is this: Judge Joe Borane served his ninety days of bedtime incarceration in a jail that Cochise County built with money Bernal and I seized from the Agua Prieta cartel's drug lords, with whom Borane had conducted "business." In addition, the sentencing judge ordered that Joe Borane could never again hold any kind of public office. Not even dog catcher! The King had finally fallen from power.

Keeping true to Mexican border ballads and folklore, one star falls and another rises brilliantly on the horizon. On the same day Borane was sentenced, Agua Prieta Mayor Vicente Terán resigned from office to run for the Mexican Congress. He retained control of Agua Prieta and the cartel's interest by putting his wife into his vacated position as acting mayor. According to my sources in Mexico, there was no doubt that with all of the Colombian and Agua Prieta cartel's financial backing, Vicente Terán, and his spouse, would be a shoo-in for both positions of authority.

On June 2, 2000, the Mexican people broke the Partido Revolucionario Institucional (PRI) party's corrupt seventy-one-year rule of their republic. On a high note here, newly elected President Vicente Fox of the Partido Acción Nacional (PAN) was said to have no connections to narcotics traffickers, unlike Mexico's previous presidents.

On a low note, however, with assistance from his sordid narcotics associates, former Agua Prieta Mayor Vicente Terán was elected to the Mexican Congress as the senator representing Sonora under the PRI banner. A man who years before was armed with a 30.06 rifle, handcuffs, a phony badge, and a can of mace when he attempted to rip off U.S. drug officers. A man who worked for drug traffickers who had the determination to shoot a DEA agent who got in their way. A man who admitted during his post-arrest interview that he was making hundreds of thousands of dollars a year trafficking narcotics. A man who is a millionaire ten times over as a result of the illicit drug trade. A man who as a Mexican senator can now advance the agenda of the Agua Prieta cartel as well as those of other Mexican and Colombian drug lords. Think about that the next time our president recertifies the Mexican government as an "ally" in the war on drugs, thereby funneling them millions of your tax dollars!

With the election of Terán, the Mexican government was just one step closer to being completely taken over by narco-terrorizing drug lords. In fact, what do you want to bet that Vicente Terán will one day be president of Mexico? According to my sources in Mexico, that is the Colombian traffickers' dream plan to facilitate streamlining the North American drug market.

Know this: There are many unholy political alliances up and down the U.S.-Mexican border that are similar to what we have here in Douglas and Agua Prieta. These corrupt international relationships, for either political or financial reasons, seek to destroy the very fiber of our Yankee existence. I would guess that at the minimum, Mexico is no more than ten or fifteen years away from being controlled by billionaire drug lords with ties to communist guerrillas just like Colombia is now. And when that happens, our backyard on the U.S.-Mexican border is going to flow red with blood as if we were back in Vietnam.

How Douglas will fare in the future is anybody's guess. We did get rid of Borane and Terán, only for them to be replaced by another Borane and Terán. Much to no one's surprise, Terán's wife won the Agua Prieta mayor's election on July 2, 2000. And Douglas Mayor Ray Borane is still ruling the sheep today in this shithole part of Cochise County.

In July 2001, one month after U.S. Customs special agents extradited and took custody of Douglas Tunnel suspect Rafael Camarena, one of our Douglas agents made an interesting observation. At a local watering hole, sitting at a table in a low-voice conversation, were former Judge Joe Borane, former Douglas Police Chief Al Fragoso, Mexican Senator Vicente Terán, and Douglas Mayor Ray Borane. If you could have only been a fly on the wall for a moment ...

In all probability, Douglas will never be completely cleaned up. Maybe it's because no one really wants to see the little border town break its historic chains to the past century—a century of lawlessness, bloodletting, smuggling, illicit monies, and of course the corruption that the Mexican border just seems to naturally breed deep down in her rotting womb.

8

The Big Sandy Wars

WHEN I RETURNED TO THE "WORLD" from the smoldering jungles of Vietnam in December of 1970, the U.S. Army was thoughtful enough to station me in the snow-covered Rocky Mountains of Colorado at Fort Carson. Now, don't ask me what REMF general had that brain-fart of an idea. But that's just what they did with kids whose blood was water-thin and whose parasite-infested bodies looked anorexic. It made no sense at all other than the fact that it was "the Army way."

One of the great things I learned about Fort Carson after the first month was that they didn't mess with you too much. And the reason for that was the boys they were dumping there were worn-out combat veterans the Army was unofficially semi-retiring until their end of service came up.

After several months of being on the post I noticed several soldiers wearing shoulder-patch insignias of infantry divisions I was unfamiliar with. I knew their divisions hadn't been in Nam, yet they were strutting about with the Army's coveted combat-infantry badge sitting proudly on their chests. Curiosity finally got the better of me and I stopped a couple of these soldiers to inquire why they were wearing combat badges if they hadn't been in Nam. To my utter surprise, the boys explained to me they had been on the DMZ line separating North Korea from South Korea, where they had experienced more than their fair share of firefights and mortars.

I was dumbfounded to learn that any such combat was taking place in Korea during 1969 and 1970. I would also go out on a limb here and bet that most of the American public had little or no idea that our soldiers were in firefights over there during those years. And now I'm going to tell you about yet another DMZ where mortal combat is going on that you may not know of, another north-south-separating DMZ where nightly armed patrols invade and probe U.S. soil, a DMZ where hostile actions and armed encounters are an everyday occurrence. Yes, I'm speaking of the U.S.-Mexican border in Cochise County. And one of the most dangerous portions of this DMZ line is a place drug agents have nicknamed the Big Sandy.

The infamous Big Sandy is a volcanic-rock and white-sand wash that cuts through Cochise County as it parallels the U.S.-Mexican border. The wash originates in the Huachuca Mountains and drains into the San Pedro River at the base of the Huachucas. The rugged peaks of the Huachucas majestically rise some 9,000 feet above the colorful Arizona desert floor. Some years ago these mountains were designated by the federal government as part of the Coronado National Forest. In the late evenings the Huachucas cast an ominous shadow east over the San Pedro River valley. This area of Cochise County is historically significant because it was traveled in 1540 by the famous Spanish explorer Francisco Coronado.

Since the early 1970s, or, more accurately, the beginning of dope smuggling as we know it, the Big Sandy area has been one of the most prosperous and coveted routes employed by dope smugglers. They continually return to the area because it affords them abundant natural cover and quick access to main Arizona highways going north into the U.S. The Huachuca Mountains and the San Pedro River valley are covered with lush, green scrub-oak trees, cottonwood trees, yuccas, century plants, manzanita bushes, and knee-high bear grass. In a border area that is predominately a flat, open desert terrain, you can easily understand why the smugglers would rather snuggle up to the dark secreted canyons that extend into the U.S. from Mexico at the southern slope of the Huachucas.

In the fall of 1995, Douglas U.S. Customs Service agents began to receive reports from the U.S. Border Patrol about an aggressive dope-smuggling organization using the Big Sandy. Customs Special Agent Doran Womack and I met with BP agents to see what information they could supply. We learned that the BP agents were losing a lot of suspected dope-laden vehicles that outran them in desperate attempts to avoid arrest. In some cases during the attempted stop, the dope vehicle would purposely ram the agent's vehicle, putting him out of service. Death or injury to BP agents was imminent, and they needed some serious help ASAP.

To make matters worse for the Border Patrol, one of their agents in California had recently been in a high-speed pursuit that resulted in civilian fatalities. Ever fearful of the news media, the Border Patrol hierarchy at headquarters in D.C. issued a nationwide non-pursuit policy for Border Patrol agents. In the event a suspect vehicle would not stop after activation of red lights and siren, the agents were to immediately terminate contact and let the vehicle go unmolested on its merry way north into the U.S. In addition, these same agents were warned that they would be given days off without pay if they failed to adhere to the new non-pursuit policy. It was a demoralizing mandate, to say the least. Enthusiastic agents were being told to virtually lie down and allow the criminals to run over them.

Needless to say, this unwelcome news took the piss and vinegar out of a good many young, gung-ho BP agents. Hell, it even aggravated the shit out of the older agents. And they weren't alone. There wasn't a law-enforcement officer in Cochise County who could believe any administrators of an enforcement agency would have conceived such a stupid policy without first studying the ramifications. It was indicative of leadership that has never been in the field doing the job and living the life of a border agent.

Again the REMFs at headquarters in D.C., at a safe distance from the reality of the drug war, had made a decision that would put narcotics-interdiction border agents in Cochise County in harm's way.

It didn't matter what agency you were with. When the word got out to the dope smugglers about this new non-pursuit policy, they would start running and ramming into any law officer who attempted to apprehend them. I didn't know it yet, but Womack and I would soon enough be victimized by the new REMF policy.

Doran Womack transferred into the Douglas U.S. Customs Service Office of Investigations from his home state of Georgia in 1993. He had previously served as a special agent with the Georgia Bureau of Investigations, where I'd heard he had done some serious ass-kicking as a law enforcer. The Douglas agents quickly dubbed him a "swamp rat" transplant who probably wouldn't last long in the Arizona climate. They were dead wrong. This short, stocky forty-two-year-old Vietnam veteran not only thrived in the desert, but he certainly surprised the older Arizona agents when he demonstrated an ability to track and cut sign with the best of them. To this day I still can't figure where he picked the skill up. Maybe he tracked gators in the swamp mud back home before coming west.

It was rumored that in his younger days Womack spent most of his off-duty time as a bouncer in various raunchy hell-raising Southern redneck bars. I'd heard that he had broken a few jaws and other assorted bones in true rebel bar-brawling fashion in those days. But all good times must come to an end. Womack eventually met a sweet little Georgia peach who cured him of his rompings. She drug him to a Southern Baptist church, where he got religion. In fact, the tobacco-chewing reb later became an ordained deacon. With all the shit the Douglas agents got into, I figured Womack was definitely just what we needed. The way the decks were usually stacked against us in favor of the border outlaws, it could never hurt to have an agent on first-name basis with the Lord.

After learning about the Border Patrol's problems, Agent Womack and I donned our camouflage fatigues and spent weeks conducting a reconnaissance of Big Sandy. We found where the smugglers had cut the U.S.-Mexican border fence and were driving their narcotics-laden vehicles through the sandy draw. In an effort to surveil the smuggling activity, Womack and I crawled and grunted up and down the

Huachuca Mountains until we found the right spot for a concealed observation post. Armed with 8x56 power binoculars, chewing tobacco, and the patience of an old sniper, we bivouacked in the mountains as our other investigative duties permitted.

From our vantage point in Arizona we could see twenty-five or thirty miles into Mexico. It was a breathtaking view that only a painting or photograph can fully capture. For miles and miles the San Pedro River's cottonwood trees formed an oasis in the desert as the river snaked north into the U.S. and south into Mexico. During autumn the cottonwood leaves were turning a yellowish gold, further accented by a clear blue Arizona sky. The floor of the river valley was engulfed by a sea of green mesquite trees, which were home to an abundant dove population. Whitetail deer cautiously fed between the trees with an occasional call from the ever-present coveys of brown- and white-vested mountain quail. It was hard to believe such a beautiful setting harbored some of the most undesirable dregs of our society— dope smugglers!

During the second or third day of the surveillance I saw something in my binoculars that made me question my ability to judge time, distance, and travel. I didn't want to say anything to Womack yet, so I low-crawled over to him and asked for a chew of tobacco. As Womack reached for his chew I detected a puzzled expression on his face. He threw the chew pouch to me and asked in his Southern drawl, "Ya'll seen anything move yonder down by the fence?" I replied, "Yeah, I think so. What do you see?" Womack paused, put his binoculars to his eyes, and squinted. He looked toward the fence for a few seconds and said, "I know ya'll gonna laugh, but I think there's a bush about three feet high and four feet wide that looks to be creepin' east to west on the border fence!"

Both having fought in Vietnam, we recognized this for what it was. However, we had never seen one move this creeping slow before. He was good, real good. Whoever this guy was, there was no doubt that he was an elite military-trained individual. He wasn't really wearing a gillie suit, which is a camouflage-netted cover commonly used by snipers or recondos. This was more of a portable hide like the ones used by our own Special Forces soldiers. In fact, being that it appeared to be a hide lent credence to the presence of more than one body. Womack and I strained our eyes for about eight hours watching this hide. When we finally called it a day the hide had only moved about a hundred yards from east to west along the border line. We figured in the next few days we would eventually see the hide drift slowly across the border fence and start reconning north toward Big Sandy.

After a couple of days off duty, Womack and I returned to the same observation location in the mountains. We were unable to locate the hide but we did observe a black Chevrolet Suburban as it drove through the San Pedro River valley in Mexico and traveled north to the border fence just beneath our position. We watched as several figures, dressed in black combat-fatigue uniforms, exited the Suburban and bent over in a sneaking crouch toward the border fence. The driver secreted the Suburban in the brush in Mexico as the men in black uniforms scampered into Arizona.

Womack and I became somewhat alarmed when we saw that the men were armed with military assault rifles. As we continued our surveillance we realized that these were probably Mexican soldiers or federal agents. Their orderly movements indicated that they were on patrol looking for U.S. ground-implanted electronic-sensor alert devices. Such electronic "bugs" are commonly used by the Customs Service and Border Patrol to detect illegal entries into the U.S. from Mexico. Now, let me be perfectly clear about this. These armed black uniforms were not patrolling in Mexico. They had invaded our country and were conducting military combat maneuvers on U.S. soil!

It appeared that the intruders were attempting to activate the sensors in an effort to learn the U.S. agents' response time, or, worst-case scenario, to ambush the agents upon arrival. After lying in the brush for about half an hour without any response from U.S. agents, the Mexicans returned back across the border to their Suburban and departed south into Sonora. Womack and I knew the shit was about to hit the fan in the next few days. We also figured we'd better check with some informants about who we were about to go up against.

Womack knew an informant from the San Pedro River valley in Sonora. He had busted the guy a couple of years back with a load of grass and he owed Womack a favor. Womack had helped the guy get a lenient sentencing in court because he had promised to help us with information when we needed it. And if there was ever a time we needed a payback it was now. Womack got up with the guy and he made good his promise to repay his debt.

The informant told Womack that a U.S. Marine deserter, known as "Rambo," was in charge of training the smugglers in the black uniforms. He said that Rambo commanded a drug trafficking-financed training camp hidden in the Sonoran mountains near the San Pedro River. The training camp was protected by the Mexican Army and federal agents. It was off-limits to any local or state Mexican authorities.

A subsequent investigation by Womack revealed that Rambo had in fact at one time been a member of the Marines Special Response team from Camp Pendleton, California. It was alleged that he had shot a Department of Defense security guard when he was caught stealing the night-vision goggles and weapons the black uniforms were now using.

The informant went on to tell Womack that the training camp consisted of barracks, firing ranges, a recreational area, and a driving track, all enclosed by a hot electrical-wired perimeter. He said that the trainees were instructed in the use of various automatic assault rifles, patrolling, evasive maneuvering, and vehicle-ramming techniques.

The trainees were also instructed in the use of camouflage and concealment methods for reconnaissance purposes. Upon graduation from the training camp, the students who exhibited the most propensity for violence, and the willingness to get the job done at whatever the cost, were given positions smuggling dope for the Mexican federal agents.

Womack and I believed this information was valid, considering our previous observations of the black uniforms' movements. We set the wheels in motion to have the U.S. Army's Special Forces teams give us a hand. Sperling had been doing a lot of joint training and operations with the Green Beret teams and we knew he could get them in if anybody could. The only problem was the time limitation.

Because of REMF red tape, it would take Sperling about a month to get into Big Sandy with his snake-eating buddies from the Army. For now we were on our own.

After debriefing the informant, Womack and I were back at it the following day. We had been on our observation mountain for about five or six hours when a Border Patrol vehicle made a routine pass by the Big Sandy. As soon as the agent departed, Womack and I saw Mexican scouts in black uniforms miraculously appear from under the brush on the border fence. The scouts made their entry into Arizona and eased their way toward Big Sandy. They were heavily armed and carried handheld two-way radios. As Womack and I witnessed this armed invasion of U.S. soil, I could only speculate what the average citizen would say about President Clinton giving our tax dollars to the Mexican government to fight the war on drugs.

As the Mexican scouts started their reconnaissance mission, Womack and I got ready for war. We scrambled into our bulletproof vests, placed extra handgun magazines in our gear, and cocked and locked our shoulder weapons for the long haul. You know it's funny, but no matter how many times over the years I've done this, my mouth is always dry about right now. Don't get me wrong. In a situation like this, you're more alive and focused than at any other time in your life. You know it's fixing to get real hairy, but your mouth just seems to turn into a damn cotton-ball factory. So what do you do? Well, that's one of the benefits of partnering up with Womack. He always had a good, fresh chew of Red Man tobacco, a border agent's time-tested cure for the cotton mouth.

After the scouts reconned and cleared the Big Sandy area they radioed the driver of a white and maroon Chevrolet 4x4 Blazer that had been covered with brush and waiting out of our sight just inside old Mexico. The Blazer ripped out of the brush through the border fence and entered the Big Sandy as if the devil himself was chasing the load. As soon as the Blazer hit U.S. soil, Womack and I radioed for backup and slid down the mountain to our vehicles for the chase.

Womack and I caught up to the Blazer at a Texaco gasoline station just off Highway 92, about ten miles north of the border. We were near Sierra Vista, on the eastern slope of the Huachuca Mountains. Our backup hadn't arrived yet and we passed the Blazer as he was parked between the gas pumps. We talked it over on the radio and decided to hit the guy while he was dead in the water instead of trying to stop him when he was mobile on the civilian-crowded highway. I pulled my unmarked pickup truck in front of the Blazer, bumper to bumper. Womack pulled his pickup truck to the back of the Blazer, bumper to bumper. We had the guy squeezed in, or at least it started out looking like that.

I was looking straight at the driver's face just before all hell broke loose. He was wearing U.S. military-issued green camouflage combat fatigues and a matching Ranger cap. He had short brown hair and was wearing dark sunglasses. His fatigues were ironed and pressed and displayed divisional insignia that I was unfamiliar with. He was a Hispanic male of about twenty-five. He had a small American flag dangling from his rearview mirror. He looked as if he could have possibly been a soldier from the U.S. Army's Fort Huachuca in Sierra Vista. In fact, the guy looked so patriotic that for a minute, I thought Womack and I had the wrong goddamn Blazer!

I placed my badge against my truck's windshield and pointed to the driver telling him not to move. I couldn't see his eyes because of the dark glasses, but I knew he was locked in on my every movement. I started to open my truck door to get out when the world exploded. This guy went straitjacket bonkers! He took that big four-wheel-drive Blazer and started ramming my truck and Womack's truck back and forth like a friggin one-ton jackhammer. He was frantically going from drive to reverse at full throttle. There were pieces of metal shrapnel and broken glass flying everywhere! It was equivalent to being smack dab in the middle of a demolition derby without a helmet or any other protection.

Civilians at the gas station were running for cover and screaming bloody murder at the top of their lungs. I was being slammed back and forth so bad that I couldn't grab my handgun from my shoulder holster for fear I'd accidentally shoot myself or some innocent bystander. Every time I saw him coming at me I swear it seemed like the Blazer was being magically transformed into a monster of biblical proportions. It was growing bigger and bigger and BIGGER! The guy's Blazer had so much thrust and weight on our little government trucks that he bounced us out of his path. When he finally broke free the son of a bitch launched off warping south on Highway 92 toward Big Sandy and Mexico.

Womack and I squealed out of the gas station in a cloud of burning rubber, pursuing the Blazer. Our vehicles were badly damaged in the front ends around the radiators and engine compartments. We were smoking a bit but we weren't losing any vital engine fluids that we knew of. We could see the Blazer was leaking coolant, and as we pulled close to his rear bumper our windshields became covered with it. We were traveling at about 110 mph when we saw a school bus coming from the opposite direction. The Blazer had thus far been screaming down the highway with total disregard for human life and property. He commandeered the middle of the highway, running innocent people off the road. When we saw the school bus approaching, we knew we had to back off so this prick would feel a little less pressured. We lost some ground on the Blazer but the bus passed by without incident.

The Blazer made the turn off Highway 92 and headed south toward Big Sandy and Mexico. Womack had fallen way back because of the bus. I had barely managed to keep the Blazer in sight. I chased him down into Big Sandy, eating his dust as we ripped through the desert wash. I wasn't able to overcome the deficit in distance the school bus had cost me. The bastard beat me through the border fence into Mexico by about four car lengths. I started to slow down and turn around at the line.

Before I could get my vehicle turned around at the border fence, I made a mistake that almost cost Womack and me the ultimate price. I had unwittingly driven straight into a well-designed ambush. There were two black uniforms off on my left flank armed with TEC-9 machine pistols. On my right flank were four black uniforms proudly showing me their AK-47 assault rifles. And me, well I'm left in the middle with a large lump in my throat. I think I had swallowed my chewing tobacco at about the same moment I realized this was probably my last day on God's green earth. While my mind was deciphering the trap, I had a brief vision of my wife and sons standing alone at someone's funeral services. At the same moment, I shivered from the ghostly, soft touch of the eternal darkness I sensed was creeping up behind me.

These assholes leveled their weapons at me before I could grab my shoulder weapon. I rolled out of my pickup and used the back of the truck bed for cover. I aimed my .45 pistol back and forth between them wondering who was going to cap the first round at this party. Now, to some people this may have seemed foolish, but I've always believed that the best defense is a strong offense, and so far I've survived by that reasoning. Besides, Mexicans would just as soon shoot a coward in the back as look at him. It's a cultural macho thing that you better come to grips with pretty damn quick if you expect to win life-threatening confrontations on the border.

I'm standing here in the true sense of the phrase "Mexican stand-off," and a couple of things are racing through my mind other than just bladder control. I can't get to the radio and warn Womack. I'm worried he's going to coming busting up out of Big Sandy at any moment trying to find me and the Blazer. If that happens, this tenuous little no-shoot face-off is going to turn into a gigantic fucking firefight. In that event, the unsuspecting Womack is going to get the deadliest surprise of what may be left of his short life via his front windshield. The second thing I'm worried about is that the hard full-metal-jacket ammo those Mexicans are probably carrying is going to penetrate right through the bed of my truck like a hot knife through warm butter. It was most definitely adrenaline prime time!

Knowing the truck wasn't going to protect me, and that I had to do something before Womack got ambushed, I decided on the best five-second plan I could muster up. I came out from behind my useless cover and jumped up in the open bed of my truck. I leveled my .45 at the closest black uniform and waited for his decision. If he wanted to dance, I was going to make him think I wanted to lead!

Our eyes locked together, giving new meaning to the cop-lingo term "eye fucking." Neither one of us would blink for fear of missing the start of the party. I wasn't going to fire the first round because it would have certainly been suicidal. In addition, Womack would have been whacked just as sure as the sun rises in the east and sets in the west. The way things were shaping up, it looked like tomorrow's sun might be doing just that without me and Womack.

After a few seconds the "eye fucker" received a mumbled radio transmission from a walkie-talkie clipped to his uniform. From behind the butt of his AK assault rifle I could see a faint smile start to form on his mouth. He chuckled in a low growling voice and told me in Spanish, "You're a crazy son of a bitch, gringo. Besides, we already have the *pinche* load back. *Nos vemos* [see ya], gabacho." He then called his dogs off at about the same time Womack came skidding up to the standoff. The smugglers backed away into Mexico as they kept their weapons leveled on Womack and me. They eventually retreated into the brush like a pack of rabid coyotes slinking back to the sanctuary of their dens from a nightly hunt. It was over for now, but it was a long way from being finished. The "eye fucker" knew it and I knew it.

Over the next year our Customs agents, Border Patrol agents, and Border Alliance Group officers seized tons of marijuana and cocaine in the Big Sandy area. It was easy to tell that some of the dopers we arrested were military trained. They were always pre-stripped of any identification or documents, but their mannerisms and clothing indicated they were either Mexican soldiers or Mexican federal agents. To lend credence to these observations, we also received intelligence that a secretive sect of "civilian" snipers was beginning to train with the Mexican Army. One could only surmise that these assassins were bought and paid for by drug lords who were associates of the Mexican Army's commanders.

During this part of our investigation, U.S. Bureau of Land Management Special Agent Lisandro Montijo and I received information that the Mexican Army was bivouacked right on the border fence at the San Pedro River, in direct violation of an old treaty between the U.S. and Mexico. Posing as environmentalists, we tossed our weapons and equipped ourselves with shovels and cameras, intending to make contact with the soldiers. I for one wanted to document the Mexican

Army's contemptuous disregard for the treaty their government "honorably" signed with the U.S. Besides, we figured what the hell. We might as well get photos of the enemy we had been going up against day and night.

We found the little assault-rifle-toting boogers brushed up under mesquites and bedded down in the thick bear grass where the San Pedro crosses the border. Although they were camped on the Mexican side of the line, it was plain as day to see they had repeatedly invaded the U.S. because their boot tracks went north and south through the international fence. We made contact with the group's lieutenant at the fence line and explained we were biologists on an environmental mission for the U.S. Fish and Wildlife Service.

While agent Montijo visited with the lieutenant, I pulled a 35 mm camera out of a ditty bag and started taking shots of the river valley's indigenous plants and birds with the troops in the background. When the camera started whizzing, the lieutenant's troops came down with a sudden case of shyness. They quickly turned their backs to me and retreated into their encampment's protection. But not before I got all of them and their weapons on film.

Agent Montijo continued jabbering with his new-found friend and gleaned some interesting facts about the Mexican soldiers. We learned that the average infantry trooper makes about a hundred dollars a month. From this paltry salary the soldiers must provide their own basic needs of canned food, a place to sleep (nylon two-man tents or tarps from Wal-Mart), their own blankets, even their own toiletries and razors. The only things the Mexican Army provides to the men are uniforms, weapons, and ammunition.

So do you really have to stretch your imagination to believe that a good number of these soldiers would be willing to desert the Mexican government, rifles in tow, and "soldier up" on the payroll of a rich drug lord for ten or twenty times the amount the Mexican service was paying them? Not at all! It happens every day in the Mexican military service, according to my informants and observations.

Although the dope seizures were numerous, they weren't coming easy. We had to chase and fight for each one. Numerous vehicles belonging to both dopers and U.S. agents were rammed and destroyed during this year. Gunfire was exchanged on several occasions. A lot of agents were getting jittery.

Maureen Johnson, the only female Customs agent we had in the Douglas office at the time, both entered on duty and resigned in this same year. One of the last things she said to us before leaving was, "You guys have more excitement in one morning than most people have in a lifetime." You know, I had never really thought about it until then. But she's probably absolutely right. I guess if you do so much of any one thing it just becomes second nature to you.

Maureen's resignation and departure didn't stop the interdiction war by any stretch of the imagination. It raged on into the next year. We continued to have armed encounters and subsequent face-offs on the border, but up until this point there hadn't been a really good thirst-quenching shootout. All the agents knew it was just a matter of time before somebody got killed. After all, history usually repeats itself, and Cochise County had been home to violent men like the Earp brothers, Doc Holliday, "Texas" John Slaughter, and, last but not least, Geronimo.

It was the day before Thanksgiving, 1996. A crisp, clear, beautiful, sunny November day. Womack and I were driving toward the Huachuca Mountains when we intercepted a Border Patrol radio transmission indicating electronic sensor alerts had been activated in the Big Sandy area. We kicked our pickup trucks up and arrived at the intersection of Highway 92 just in time to encounter the suspect vehicle as it was turning north on the highway from the Big Sandy area. It was a two-tone green Dodge Ram 4x4 pickup truck being driven by a Hispanic male wearing a white straw cowboy hat. The same white straw hat that most of the Mexican mafia dopers like to fancy themselves in. It's like a sailor with a tattoo. You just know he's going to have one somewhere on his body.

I followed the Ram truck north on the highway toward Sierra Vista as Womack attempted to set up a roadblock at the turn-off back to Big Sandy. We both knew that this guy would flip and run south for Mexico as soon as we attempted to stop him. When Womack radioed me that he was set up my mouth started to taste a bit like cotton.

I pulled my truck in behind the Ram's rear bumper and activated my red lights and siren. The driver looked at me in his rearview mirror, took his hat off, and set the hat on the seat next to him. It kind of reminded me of a guy taking his hat off just before a fight so it doesn't get stomped on and stained with blood.

The driver then slowed down on the side of the highway and pretended to make an effort to stop. As he slowed, he suddenly cut his front wheels, crossing the highway into the oncoming traffic, and put the pedal to the metal on the accelerator. As he streaked back past me southbound I could see him talking on a two-way handheld radio. Let the games begin!

I radioed Womack we were running his way and approaching speeds of about 120 mph. I stayed on the Ram's bumper and couldn't believe what I saw him do. When this guy wasn't talking to his cohorts on the two-way radio, he was taking swigs out of a bottle of tequila! Yes, indeed, Womack and I had come up against the Mexican equivalent of a "party while you race" Mario Andretti.

At the turn to enter Big Sandy the tequila speed demon almost lost it as he attempted to brake from 120 mph to take a 30 mph turn. He was actually going for it, and just about up on two wheels, when he saw Womack was waiting to take his tires out with "stinger" tire spikes. He opted not to make the turn and almost flipped the Ram again as he over-corrected his direction at about 40–50 mph. After he got all four wheels back on the ground and gained control of the Ram, I saw him take another swig from his tequila bottle. What a gutsy bastard!

We shot down the highway through the valley at speeds approaching Mach 1 toward the San Pedro River. I knew by now that he had probably received radio instructions from his people in Mexico to make for the border fence in the river. I also knew that his black-uniformed compas were probably moving to that location to receive him and protect the dope load at all cost to life or limb. Yeah, it was getting pretty close to pucker time!

Sure enough, when he got to the San Pedro River turnoff he started to slow down, looking to turn south on a dirt road that parallels the river. I was right on his rear bumper when he started braking down from about 120 mph to turning speed. Now, if you've never raced cars or been in a high-speed pursuit you may think, no big deal. All you have to do is apply the brakes and you're going to automatically slow down. Wrong!

When you're tearing a hole in the earth's atmosphere at this kind of speed you get tunnel vision. All you can see and comprehend is what is directly in front of your vehicle. Everything off to both sides is just a blur in your peripheral vision. You're concentrating on his rear bumper while you're being sucked up in his wind drag. Once you're in his wind drag, the vacuum just seems to catch you and your brakes don't do shit to hold your catapulting vehicle back.

And that's exactly what I got into. My front bumper and grill guard rode up onto his back bumper and we became virtually locked together like two rattlesnakes fucking in the Arizona sun. I couldn't get loose of him and he couldn't shake me.

As he attempted to turn off the highway I cut my wheels in the opposite direction to break free of him. Our momentum spun both trucks around a couple of times and launched us off the highway in separate directions. We came to a stop in a plowed dirt field with a cyclone of dust all around us. My head was spinning like I'd been on a three-day drinking binge. I struggled to regain my balance and look around while trying to get oriented on up, down, and sideways.

I saw that we had torn down numerous county and state road signs, mailboxes, fences, and a small ranch shed. About the only thing we hadn't completely destroyed yet was each other. But by the look in Tequila's desperado eyes, he wasn't giving up the ghost just yet. He put his vehicle in drive and floored the gas pedal. The motherfucker was aiming his vehicle at the driver's-side door of my truck!

I mumbled a prayer to Chevrolet and punched my accelerator in reverse gear. The Ram caught me before I could get out of its path. He delivered a glancing blow into my door so hard that I bit through my tongue. I cut my wheels sharply and opened up the motor while doing a 360-degree turn. I came back around and slammed him as hard as I could in his truck's bed on the passenger side. The Ram's gasoline tank exploded in fire. All I could see through the flames engulfing my windshield was the Tequila kid's ass and elbows as he evacuated his burning truck. He then made an Olympic-class dash for Mexico and never looked back.

I put my truck in reverse to back away from the burning Ram and discovered I had a bit of a dilemma. My front end was hung up under the rear bed of the Ram and the fire was beginning to get up under my engine compartment. Smoke started to fill the cab of my truck as I felt extreme heat encasing my legs. I prayed and cursed while gunning the motor and flipping back and forth in drive and reverse. I was just about to abandon my truck to the fire when the Chevrolet broke loose from the Ram. I turned my anger to the fleeing Tequila kid, who I figured couldn't have gotten very far on foot.

I drove out of the plowed field and into a mesquite-strangled part of the river valley, which continued south into Mexico. Maneuvering the truck between the mesquites, I saw Tequila as he was beating feet south for the border. I skidded the truck to a stop in front of him, cutting off his escape, and caught up to him on foot. I didn't even think of stopping for all the bullshit formalities they teach at the federal enforcement academies. Stop! I'm a federal agent! You're under arrest! Raise your hands and lie prone on the ground! That's all textbook and movie bullshit.

When a crook is running for the border he's one of the most desperate men you'll ever go up against. It doesn't matter if he's a suspect for homicide, burglary, dope smuggling, or what. If he can get across that fence into Mexico he's a free man. No court, no trial, no prison. And knowing that makes every imaginable type of criminal more dangerous when he's headed south. He'll try to take out anybody who attempts to stand between him and his immediate freedom.

I caught up to Tequila and tackled his ass with all the weight I could bring to bear. This was the first time that I had seen him up close. He was Hispanic, about twenty-five to thirty years old, and of good, muscular build. He was probably close to six feet tall and weighed between 180 and 200 pounds. He had short military-style hair and was clean shaven. He wore a black shirt and black jeans with some type of military combat boots. So what do you think? Mexican federal agent? Mexican soldier? Or was this the one and only Rambo? Take your pick. Either way I knew I was in for a fight for my life.

It was a classic good guy versus bad guy free-for-all. None of that unbelievable television kung-fu martial arts crap. We wrestled, beat, kicked, bit, and gouged each other until we were both out of breath and exhausted. It may not have rated much with the World Wrestling Federation, or boxing heavyweights like Holyfield and Tyson, but when all the grunting and screaming was done, Tequila was in custody and I was sitting on top of his worthless hide.

Completely out of air and drained of almost every ounce of energy, it was all I could do just to remain on top of Tequila. After all that had happened, I couldn't find my handcuffs. They were probably buried in the sand somewhere in today's "Desert Storm." I removed my leather belt from my jeans and hogtied the scumbag bastard the best I could until help arrived.

A Border Patrol agent found my location in the mesquites before Womack arrived. He lent me a pair of handcuffs and I shackled Tequila up. I started to relax a little and come down from the adrenaline heat of the moment. I thought I had weathered the storm in good form. I was wrong. This hadn't even been the main event yet. A tenfold worse nightmare was just around the goddamn corner.

Without Womack arriving, I had to put my trust in the Border Patrol agent who had just arrived. He was from the Naco BP station and I really didn't know him or his reputation that well. I later learned from some Border Patrol and DEA agents that this guy didn't want to get into any trouble or end up testifying in any court. In short, he couldn't be depended on. I sure as hell wished I'd had this information before meeting this particular BP agent.

I escorted Tequila to my truck. The motor was still running from when I had bailed out into the middle of the fight. I walked Tequila around to the passenger side, where the BP agent had opened the door. I placed the suspect in the passenger seat and asked the agent if he could keep hold of the asshole until I walked around and got in the driver's seat. The agent stood inside the open truck door next to Tequila with his hand wrapped inside the outlaw's arm. I asked the agent twice if he had control of the suspect. Both times the agent said it was no problem.

I started to walk around the back of my truck when I heard the BP agent start screaming, "Hey, hey, hey, you son of a bitch!" I looked through the back window of my truck and saw Tequila fighting his way over piles of equipment into the driver's seat. I couldn't believe it! This fucking agent hadn't even grabbed the scumbag, much less thrown a blow into one of his chops. The agent absolutely just fucking froze up. He appeared to be scared to death of tangling with Tequila.

I sprinted around the driver's side of my truck just in time to grab a piece of the steering wheel as Tequila punched the engine, taking off for the border. He dragged my ass alongside of the truck through cactus and yuccas as he accelerated toward a large mesquite tree. My left hand had a death grip on the steering wheel. With my right fist I began punching this son of a bitch in the side of his rock-hard head until a steady stream of blood was rolling down his face. I swear if I could have gotten my hand to my weapon I would have blown his shit-for-brains out!

In horror I glanced forward at the mesquite tree and then back at Tequila's determined face. I could see his intentions in his eyes. He was planning to impale me on the tree like a piece of succulent red meat on a roasting skewer! It was a large, black, half-dead mesquite made up of waist-high, broken, sharp old limbs. And I was about to become buzzard bait on it! About right now my body was going into adrenaline overdrive and I had about two seconds to formulate a plan of survival. Now, the two choices were simple. Either take my chances with the mesquite tree, which really wasn't much of an option, or let go of the steering wheel and risk being dragged under the back wheels of the truck.

Never having been fond of being stabbed, I opted for the back wheels and prayed it wouldn't be worse than a couple of broken legs. God must have been listening. Either that or I just don't know that much math about thrust and force. When I let go of my death grip on the steering wheel, Tequila naturally jerked it back hard the opposite direction. The truck banked away from me at the same time I hit the ground. I tucked and rolled away from the back wheels and ended up in the bottom of the mesquite tree that was to have been my final resting place. Oh, by the way, if I haven't mentioned it yet, this would be a good time: I have some lucky Irish blood running in my veins!

I shook the cobwebs out of my head and jumped up on wobbly legs. As soon as I regained my balance I careened off in the direction of the BP agent's vehicle. I proceeded past the agent, who was literally standing in the middle of the arrest scene like a frozen mannequin. To bring him back to some simulation of the living and present, I screamed at him to give me the fucking keys to his BP vehicle! Once in his vehicle I radioed all available U.S. Customs and BP agents to shoot the wheels off my vehicle before it entered into Mexico. The mannequin and I then followed the tracks Tequila was leaving with my truck.

When we arrived on scene at the border fence, I saw about four or five BP vehicles with a BP aircraft circling overhead. I figured that they had located my vehicle. What I didn't know was that my truck was south of the border fence in old Mexico by about two hundred yards. Tequila had evidently bailed out into the brush after running through the barbwire fence because there wasn't hide nor hair of his bean-infested ass around.

I knew I had to go into Mexico and get my truck back. All Customs agents' vehicles are equipped with the same government-secure coded radio as mine. If I didn't get my truck with the secrecy codes back, a lot of agents' lives would be put at risk. The dope smugglers would be able to copy all of our transmissions. There was never a doubt in my mind that it had to be done. I was going in, come hell or high water. Like I always say, don't ride your horse into a canyon you ain't willing to walk out of.

I started across the border on foot with my .45 in hand at the ready. There were a lot of surprised, opened-mouthed BP agents gawking at me when I crossed that rusty old fence. I knew I was in violation of the Neutrality Act plus about a thousand other State Department laws and regulations. But I was determined to get that radio back before I would end up being responsible for the death of one of our agents.

My boots hit the ground steady and deliberate as I stepped off toward my truck. I kept my .45 trained on the surrounding mesquites, ready for action. I figured that by now the black uniforms had responded to the area after receiving Tequila's radio transmission for help. I kept wondering when they would make their move on me.

I got to the truck with about ten extra years added to my natural age. The driver's side door was open, the keys were in the ignition, and the motor was running. It had all the characteristics of a great trap. After all, I was somewhat illegally in a foreign country and they could have whacked me without any guff from the U.S. State Department. In fact, the REMFs in D.C. would probably apologize to the Mexican government for my rudeness in attempting to recover stolen U.S. government property.

I jumped in the truck and floored the accelerator back into Arizona. I couldn't believe the black uniforms hadn't arrived yet, not that I was bitching about their tardiness. I thanked my lucky stars and the good Lord as I crossed the border fence back onto U.S. soil.

Once back, I stopped to talk to the BP agents for a few minutes while I cut some of the border fence wire from around my truck's wheels. Other than the mannequin, I thanked the remaining BP agents for their help and started to drive away. I had gone no more than fifty yards when I heard that unmistakable sound that makes you want to hold your breath and duck. We were taking automatic weapons fire from south of the fence! I jammed my vehicle into the brush line and bailed out, looking for some solid cover. I belly-flopped behind a three- or four-foot-high mound of rock and dirt. All of the BP vehicles came zipping past me headed north, shouting that they were being shot at. Deaf I'm not!

Why didn't I follow them? A couple of reasons. One, any combat veteran will tell you that it's the dumbest way to get killed. You want to keep your enemy in front of you where you can see and engage him. You never want to give him your flank or especially your back. The second reason: Remember the six black uniforms who had caught Womack and me in an ambush a few months before? Well, it's payback time and today I'm especially aggravated about my truck being destroyed and then stolen.

You can imagine how I felt right about now about our "hands across the border" friendly neighbors to the south. In just the last thirty minutes I was almost killed in a vehicular assault, almost burned to death, almost impaled on a tree, I was dragged by my own stolen vehicle, and now I was taking hostile fire from a foreign "friendly" government. I was exhausted, scared, pissed off, humiliated, and felt betrayed by every REMF in Washington who voted to give U.S. tax dollars to Mexico to fight the war on drugs! I would have to say that at this moment I was about as "postal" as any sane Customs agent could get.

I cringed behind my dirt mound as the rounds ripped the air over my head from Mexico. The only thing keeping me from getting closer to the ground were the buttons on my shirt. I kept thinking to myself, why in hell didn't I wear a tight T-shirt today? Every time I heard another round come whizzing by I tried to force my body deeper into the desert floor. The only thing I was leaving up for the shooter to hit were the cheeks of my rosy red rebel's ass.

When the smuggler eased up on spraying lead I tried to sneak a peek, hoping to locate his position. I kept probing the mesquite tree line in Mexico where the fire was coming from. I eventually got a bearing on his location from his muzzle flash. He was in a dark hole formed by the thick foliage of a large cluster of mesquite trees. I took extra .45 ammo magazines out and placed them by my weapon for quick reloading. I waited for the assailant to get to the end of his ammo magazine.

The asshole capped round after round in my direction until he was empty. When I heard him pause to reload I took full advantage of the time. I rolled over on my side, extending my .45 out to take aim from behind my dirt stronghold. I put my gunsights directly on the dark hole he was hiding in and lit his ass up! In rapid succession I pumped two-and-a-half magazines of 185-grain hollow-point blood-curdling hot lead into his position. He never fired again. Whoever this asshole was, whatever he aspired to be, I made sure he wasn't ever going to become a cop killer. This piece of shit just became another number in the drug-war history books.

I picked up my empty magazines and reloaded my .45 with a fresh magazine. I sauntered over to my truck feeling both fortunate and cocky. The autumn air cooled my sweating body as the adrenaline rush started to subside. I felt like I always do after a walk with the Reaper. A bit shaky and rattled, but more alive than I can possibly explain with mere human vocabulary. The truth be told, I felt great! Not about capping the shooter, but about surviving the battle. After all, that's the bottom line when you come right down to it.

As I started driving up the San Pedro River road toward the other Customs agents, I met Womack as he was coming down to my location to back me up. He was decked out in full battle gear with his 9mm MP-5 machine gun slung around his chest. Womack gave me a chew of Red Man and told me that Sperling and other Customs agents had managed to put the fire in the Ram out before it burned the dope load. Womack said that the Ram appeared to contain about a quarter of a ton of marijuana.

Womack was madder than a wet hen because the BP agents had left me and fled north when the shooting started. But the truth of the matter is that you can't be pissed at the BP agents themselves. It's the REMFs in headquarters who make the chickenshit no-shoot/no-pursuit policies that bind the agents from protecting our borders. And until our country really gets serious about controlling our borders and winning the war on drugs, border agents like Womack, Sperling, and me will continue to fight the drug war the only way we can: one small battle at a time. Win or lose, we'll know we fought the good fight. Why did we do it? Because it was the right thing to do.

9

Naco

NACO IS A SLOW-PACED little border town of about a thousand residents. The air possesses a scent of antiquated mesquite-burning stoves over which freshly fried tacos and warming flour tortillas are being prepared. The quaint, century-old, mud-brick pueblo struggled onto the pages of history in the early 1890s when the need arose to open a port of entry for the railroad that was being built between Cananea, Sonora, and Bisbee, Arizona. With all the aromas and flavors of the Southwest high desert, Naco embodies a peculiar atmosphere of Old West romanticism. Its dormant appearance is disarming almost to the point of enchantment. However, what you see on the surface in no way suggests the underlying enterprise of deadly dope smuggling that flourishes here. The port of entry and its accompanying border fence are the only things that separate the Arizona town of Naco from its sister city in Mexico, which is also conveniently named Naco. How they both came to be named the same is anybody's guess. Perhaps the little town rose up out of the desert hills before the border fence was built, cutting the town between the north and the south.

On the Mexican side, the pueblo sits at the bottom of the dense pine- and oak-covered San José Mountains. On the U.S. side of the border rise the rocky ocotillo- and juniper-dotted Mule Mountains, where neighboring Bisbee was founded. The Mules are so named because these mountains were at one time populated by an ample number of the stubborn critters. They had been turned loose to fend for themselves by unlucky prospectors who had gone bust in the 1880s. Although the numbers have dwindled considerably over the years, you can still see a few remaining survivors of the wild herds that once roamed the area. They still lazily feed near the border in the foothills of the San José Mountains, claiming both countries as their grazing refuge. Like the old gunfighters and prospectors, I imagine it won't be long before they, too, become extinct, vanishing from their rightful place in history.

In 1902, just outside Naco at the base of the grand old San José Mountains, Arizona Ranger Captain Burt Mossman arrested one of the worst black-hearted killers of the era. Agustín Chacón was said to have tallied some twenty-four murders on both sides of the border before being brought to justice. During the high point of his outlaw career, the crazy son of a bitch even sent word to Cochise County Sheriff "Texas" John Slaughter that he would be coming for him in Tombstone. When they finally did clash, Slaughter opened up on Chacón with both barrels from a 10-gauge shotgun. Chacón fell down into a wash and narrowly escaped becoming another notch chalked up to Slaughter's deceased-outlaw tally.

Chacón and his men had been accustomed to using the mountains of northern Sonora to cross into Arizona, robbing and killing at their leisure. Chacón's name struck fear into the hearts of Arizona residents as he became the Rangers' top priority. After his capture by Captain Mossman, Chacón swung high from an Arizona gallows. Just before he dropped to the end of the rope the outlaw said, "This is the greatest day of my life." Although they may have not been directly blood related, several subsequent desperados from Naco, Sonora, who were equally as mean-spirited would later run into my partners and me.

After cleaning the varmints out of Douglas, the Rangers moved on to the hard-core mining camps in Bisbee, where they set up head-quarters until 1908. At the end of that year the lawmen transferred their main detachment to the rowdy dust- and smoke-filled border town of Naco. The population of Naco, Arizona, was only about five hundred at that time. Naco, Mexico, had a few more people, accompanied by a good number of saloons and whorehouses that attracted the partying, criminal crowd. The area had become a hot spot for all classes of smuggling activity, such as gun running south and Chinese-alien smuggling north. The Rangers felt that local officials had joined up with the criminal element to give birth to a good deal of corruption in the area. Acts of violence had become a recurring affair, and the Rangers figured their continued presence was needed.

The Rangers never totaled more than twenty-six men at any one time, and in their brief existence from 1901 to 1909 they had only three captains. Captain Harry Wheeler was a Ranger whose expertise in gunfights had earned him the respect of his peers. After the Rangers were ordered to disband in 1909, Captain Wheeler signed on as a U.S. Customs Service officer, patrolling and protecting the U.S.-Mexican border on horseback. During his tenure as a Ranger and a Customs officer, Harry Wheeler used Naco as a base from which to pursue smugglers, rustlers, fugitives, gun runners, and other undesirables.

On April 3, 1908, Ranger Jeff Kidder rode his horse into Naco, Arizona, from Nogales, where he was stationed. He had been sent to headquarters in Naco to sign his yearly re-enlistment papers under Captain Wheeler. The captain was away rounding up outlaws in the Chiricahua Mountains, leaving Kidder with idle time to squander. Midnight found the thirty-three-year-old Ranger spreading his seed in brothels and saloons in Naco, Mexico, about two city blocks from the border. His reputation as a *pistolero* and effective lawman was already known south of the border. Two years earlier he and another Ranger had a nasty running gunfight with two Mexican Army soldiers who were smuggling guns. The Rangers gunned down both smugglers and seized thousands of rounds of ammunition and contraband.

Hearing that the young Ranger was in town, four Mexican soldiers prepared to take revenge for their fallen gun-smuggling compadres. The Mexicans ambushed Ranger Kidder in a saloon by coming at him from behind as he was preoccupied with a lovely señorita. Just before the first shot was capped, Kidder must have sensed the assassins coming up behind and turned to face them, because one of the first bullets hit the young man in the gut near his navel. The hot piece of lead ripped through his flesh, leaving a nasty hole in his back where it exited. As he went down, he returned fire with his .45 Colt and sent three of the four Mexicans to the floor breathing their last air. The badly bleeding Ranger made for the cantina's door and stumbled for the U.S. side of the border about fifty yards away. As he desperately struggled for the fence, Kidder was blocked off by mounted Mexican soldiers who were pumping lead at him with their Winchesters. The Ranger was eventually pinned down by about ten Mexicans during the ensuing gunfight. With his ammunition exhausted, Kidder was taken alive and nearly beaten and kicked to death in the dirt street by the Mexicans. He died of his wounds the following day, still in Mexican custody.

Between 1913 and 1916, Mexican armies representing opposing generals continued to fight for control of Naco, Sonora. The resulting gun battles caused the residents of Naco, Arizona, to fortify the south sides of their homes from the guaranteed stray lead. The ruckus escalated to a point that the Buffalo Soldiers of the 9th U.S. Cavalry were brought in from neighboring Fort Huachuca. This detachment of African American soldiers built and occupied Camp Newell, an outpost on the northwest side of Naco about a quarter of a mile from the border. Camp Newell was constructed with the enlisted men's barracks, officer's quarters, and stables being strategically placed in a square defensive perimeter configuration. During these years, the U.S. troop buildup in Naco was said to have been as high as 3,000 soldiers. The cavalry's primary duty in Naco was to guard the border and protect the U.S. from any armed invasion.

In December of 1916, Naco, Arizona, had the dubious honor of being dubbed the only American soil ever aerial bombed by a foreign enemy. As legend has it, Mexican General Obregón employed two American mercenaries to fly their biplane over Naco, Sonora, during one of the many sieges of the town. The gringos had been hired by General Obregón to bomb the Mexican forces of his opponent, General O'Hara, who was a Pancho Villa ally in the revolution. During their bombing run, the unpredictable high desert winds sweeping the bottom of the San José Mountains caught the airborne projectiles and swept them astray. The explosives ended up impacting about two miles north of the Naco Port of Entry, well within the United States. Subsequently, Douglas Chief of Police Percy Bowden and Ranger Captain Wheeler interviewed the two gabacho mercenaries and decided not to arrest them for the accidental bombing that demolished several houses and a couple of cars.

I've been told that U.S. residents, wanting to see the battle on the Mexican side of the border, actually got on top of the port of entry for a ringside seat. To support that story, I can tell you that back in the 1970s when I first arrived on duty with the Border Patrol in this area, I remember seeing the old bullet holes in the sides of buildings next to the Naco Port of Entry. But even better yet, I met a living, breathing confirmation of the battle for Naco, and much, much more. The leather-faced old man was about ninety when I met him. In addition to the many Ranger and Mexican gunfights he had knowledge of, the old-timer claimed that he was a veteran of the Mexican Revolution, having ridden with Villa and O'Hara. Having had a memorable, adventurous life as a young man, he was now content to live out his life in a converted stable that was part of the crumbling 9th U.S. Cavalry's Camp Newell on the edge of town.

Whenever we were assigned to patrol Naco, I and some other agents would always look in on the old man to make sure he had food and enough blankets to stay warm. He had no one else to care for him and we enjoyed spending time listening to his stories about Villa, O'Hara, Obregón, and the revolution. The old man has long since been carried home by the Reaper. I only knew him as Pancho. Whether he took that name in honor of one of his heroes or not, I can't say. I can only say that I now wish we had tape-recorded his hard-earned stories so they would be preserved and not lost in the emptiness of today's deafened ears. Even though he was getting pretty senile when we knew him in the '70s, some of our younger agents even thought that listening to his stories was better than having sex in the lusty, smoke-filled Mexican cantinas of Naco. Well, Ranger Kidder might have argued that point with us.

Both Nacos remained about the same size over the next few decades as they survived Prohibition and World War II. By the time we were in Vietnam, marijuana became a metaphor for the war protestors and hippies. With the illegal proceeds made from smuggling the flower children's chosen high, the sister Nacos started to grow a bit. On the Arizona side, two new cantinas opened up as adobe huts began being replaced by fancy modern mobile homes with running water and indoor plumbing. Right along with the rest of the country, Naco was "progressing" into the toilet, and I mean that in more than one way.

As a young Border Patrol agent in the 1970s, I saw a good bit of law-enforcement action in the small pueblo once patrolled by men such as Wheeler and Kidder. It was here that I went up against my first dope-smuggling desperado. Because I was so inexperienced, my first dope smuggler was also damn near my last.

As is customary for patrol work, it all started with just an every-day routine stop of a vehicle for questioning. The car had come careening out of the west side of Naco near the border and I didn't think that the guy really had any legitimate business for being down there. After he left the fence area he headed north on Naco Highway, where I lit him up with my flashing red lights for a brief field interrogation. The driver pulled over to the side of the road and appeared to be pretty cool and calm. On face value, it looked like I had probably stopped a guy who had been lost on his first visit to the border. No big deal. I figured I'd help him out with directions and do a little public-relations work for the Border Patrol at the same time.

I got out of my patrol car into the warm, relaxing Arizona sun and strolled over to ask if I could help the driver find what he was looking for. When I got close to the guy's side door, I could tell he was scared to death by the way his hands were shaking on the steering wheel. So much for being a good-will tour guide today. Getting a bit more aggressive in enforcement attitude, I asked the dude for his driver's license and registration. He wouldn't budge. He was as petrified as if he were posing for a family portrait. This was the first time I had ever seen a bad guy freeze up so tight without having a weapon pointed in his face. Being the dumb cherry I was, I left myself wide open for trouble by leaning into his open window to get a better look at what was under a layer of blankets on the back seat.

Until now, I had never before seen burlap-covered bundles of marijuana. When I pulled the blankets back and saw the dope, like a young dumb shit, the only thing I could think to blurt out was, "That's marijuana, ain't it!" Being that I was stupid enough to be hanging halfway inside his window, the guy did what any smart, self-respecting outlaw would do. He floor-boarded the gas pedal, thereby educating me on the finer points of remaining outside a suspect vehicle during a goddamn traffic stop!

Thank the good Lord, the luck of the Irish is a force to be dealt with. The dope smuggler had to slow down when he hit a curve in the highway, and that was all the invitation I needed to unass my death-defying circus act. I bounced across the pavement like a ping-pong ball being slammed over the table at a Chinaman's tournament. When I regained my footing I ran, half limping, in a scrambled state back to my patrol car. As can be expected, the asshole who had just tried to kill me headed south for the border like Chacón's ghost was chasing him.

Now, I really can't say if it was because the dope smuggler was in such a panicked rush to get back under the protection of Mexico that he unsuccessfully negotiated a curve in the highway big-time. Or maybe it could have been that a couple of rounds from the smoking barrel of a young, half-trashed, pissed-off Border Patrolman's .357 Magnum took a couple of his tires out. But for one or both of those reasons, the smuggler lost control of his conveyance and abandoned it in favor of proceeding on foot across this particular mesquite-choked part of the border. At least that's something like the official report went, as I remember.

A few minutes later, a now slower, wiser, and somewhat matured Border Patrolman drove up to the crumpled load vehicle as it lay smoking on its side in the cactus and rocks of the roadside ditch. He stood there, in his torn uniform and pavement-scrubbed boots, thinking how lucky he was that he hadn't been whacked. Although the arriving Cochise County deputies told me I resembled fresh roadkill, I couldn't have been happier. This was my first-ever big-time load of dope. Even though he "fugitated" into Mexico's protective arms, some five years later the driver would be picked up by Arizona cops on a child molestation charge that couldn't be proven. They found our warrant on him for the dope smuggling and justice, however slow and blind she may be, was served. The outlaw got three years for the dope load and another six years for trying to drag me to death. The upside? Innocent kids wouldn't have to fear the pervert for at least nine years.

For the next few weeks my supervisor in Douglas kept assigning me to patrol the Naco area. Like getting back on a horse once you've been thrown. I guessed that the Border Patrol chief wanted to make sure I wouldn't shy away from Naco. Whatever the reason, I took extra care when I made my next vehicle stop. You never knew who you were going to run into out there, be he friend or foe. And let me tell you, just about the time you think you're getting a handle on this job, it slips you a mickey.

So I'm back in the saddle patrolling the Naco area one afternoon when I spot a shiny new black van with dark tinted windows sitting on the side of a dirt road near the border. Now, I'll admit, I had become a tad bit gun-shy after being dragged around like a rag doll a couple of days before. Remembering that exhilarating experience, I decided to approach this situation a little differently.

I cautiously parked my vehicle behind the van and got out with my shotgun at the ready. As I approached the van I observed a guy changing a flat tire on the driver's side front wheel. From my previous angles I hadn't been able to see him before. So now I figured the whole thing looked pretty innocent. I began to drop my guard and eased up on my drop-of-the-hat-react attitude. It wasn't until I got closer to the guy that I was startled to see a second dude standing with his back to me in front of the van. Since I hadn't seen the second guy until I was right up on him, I became concerned that maybe there was something more than just a tire changing going on here. I pulled the shotgun up and cradled it across my chest.

The guy changing the tire heard me walking up behind him and turned to look. I announced my presence and asked the men what their business was so close to the border. The guy changing the tire said that they had been at a ranch in Mexico and they had just crossed the border at the Naco Port of Entry on their way back to California. I asked him if he was a citizen of the U.S. He produced a California driver's license for identification. I then turned to the man who had his back to me and asked him for his citizenship. The guy turned around to face me and I felt my face flush.

Jimmy Stewart looked a lot older in person than I had remembered him in the movies. I guess the silver screen disguises a lot of a person's real flaws and imperfections. Standing so close to him I could see the age lines and veins up under the worn, withering skin covering his cheekbones. However, whatever his true age may have been, there was still fire in his light-blue eyes. Without so much as one friggin blink of the eyes, he looked me dead center face to face, studying me and the shotgun. When he cut loose, he stuttered and drawled in that one and only Stewart accent, "Son, you, you, you know I'm an American and proud to be one! Looks to me like you're, you're packing for grizzlies there, hey." I sheepishly pulled the shotgun down to my side, trying to conceal it behind my leg. If it had been possible to do so at this point, I think I would've shoved the damn thing up my ass to get it out of sight.

Now, if this had been any other movie star, perhaps I wouldn't have felt so bad about damn near shoving a shotgun in his face. With somebody like the wartime North Vietnamese-loving Jane Fonda, I probably would have enjoyed this same scenario. But in my eyes, Jimmy Stewart was one of those good, rock-solid Americans who supported our country's government and law enforcement in general. The only thing that I could get out of my fool mouth as I promptly dismissed myself in embarrassment was, "Mr. Stewart, you ain't the grizzly I'm looking for, so ya'll have a nice day." As I drove off it all seemed so bizarre. Drug down the highway by a dope smuggler one day, and the next, pulling a shotgun on Jimmy Stewart! Shit like this could only happen on the border in Naco.

Between the '70's and '80s, my time spent working the Naco area with both the Border Patrol and Customs was usually the most interesting. Not only did I get my largest dope seizures from the area, but there were always armed confrontations and shootouts between law enforcement and the bad guys. I would have to say that if there is indeed an Old West gunplay type of town left in the U.S., it would be Naco. If the Border Patrol wasn't shooting it out with the dope smugglers, the Customs agents were. If the Cochise County Sheriff's Department wasn't being shot at by border bandits, they were having armed confrontations with the Mexican Army. What can I tell you? The place is virtually a modern-day gunfighter's turf. Other than cars replacing horses and indoor plumbing taking the place of outhouses, not a damn thing has changed since 1902!

In May of 1998, U.S. Customs special agents in Los Angeles culminated a three-year money-laundering investigation that a special agent of the Douglas office had been temporarily assigned to. The final stages of the case netted the largest seizure of dirty money in U.S. history. Depending on who you talk to and at what point during the seizures, the total amount of money seized would bounce somewhere between $100 million and $110 million. Twenty-six Mexican bankers were arrested when they crossed into the U.S. and were subsequently charged with the laundering scheme. From a U.S. law enforcement agent's point of view, it was understandable that the entire investigation was done without the "proper" approval of the Mexican government. If we had asked the Mexican feds to help us, it would have been the same as asking the fox to guard the henhouse. Because we couldn't trust the Mexican officials not to tip off their dope-smuggling cohorts, the border agents would eventually suffer the consequences when the political shit hit the fan over the case.

Intelligence from several federal law-enforcement agencies yielded reliable information that the gloves were coming off the Mexican Federal Judicial Police (MFJP). The Mexicans wanted revenge for their bankers being taken down and they felt we had slapped them in the face by not confiding in them concerning the investigation. The Mexicans put the word out on the border that U.S. agents were free for the taking, bought and paid for. Whereas this had been deemed bad business practice in the past, dope smuggling mules were now given permission by corrupt elements of the MFJP to shoot at Border Patrol and Customs agents if they had a chance. We had broken one of Clinton's new rules about not notifying Mexico of our operations down south, and the Mexican government was bound and determined to make us pay for it. Never mind that on a daily basis these same motherfuckers send armed dope smugglers across our borders in what we all should call an outrageous invasion of our sovereign soil. But when we try to do something defensively about it, to stop the poisoning of our children, the Mexicans reverse the political spin on it and we somehow are painted as the aggressors. Go figure!

On June 3, 1998, Alexander Kirpnick, a twenty-seven-year-old Border Patrol agent, was shot in the head and killed by marijuana smugglers in the hills west of Nogales. Although we had two Customs officers killed in a gunfight with dope smugglers east of Nogales in 1985, this was the first BP agent killed in this same area since 1926. It was a grim statement of how violent the border was becoming, and one would have to surmise it may have been related to the Mexican government's revenge for the arrests of its bankers. Since the beginning of the Big Sandy Wars, we had been trying to tell the REMFs in Washington that we needed better equipment and dependable weapons to deal with the rapidly escalating drug wars. Coming behind the Los Angeles money case, now more than ever, we could expect more and more armed confrontations with less and less real help from the D.C. REMFs.

Law-enforcement tempers were escalating on both sides of the border. The MFJP were pissed about their bankers taking a fall. The Border Patrol and Customs agents were enraged by Kirpnick's murder. The volatile mixture of bad feelings was boiling to a point of overflow. If you could have somehow measured the tensions in the air on the border at the time, you would have bet even pesos that another showdown was forthcoming. It was like red-hot lava in the bowels of a volcano. It was just a matter of time before it would rise to the surface and expel its pressure in a raging force. And knowing this part of the border like the back of my hand, I *knew* that the next gunfight would occur in either Naco or the Big Sandy area.

On the morning of June 4, 1998, special agents of the Douglas Customs office were engaged in a surveillance that had been going throughout the night. We were going up against the same violent bunch of armed smugglers we had previously fought to a standstill in the Big Sandy Wars. Because we had temporarily taken the Big Sandy area back from them, they had moved their operation to the east of Naco, where we were presently monitoring their activities. Four of our agents had spent the night on surveillance hiding in the desert brush waiting for the dopers to make their move on the border.

Barrett and I had recently taken supervisor jobs, which required a lot of time doing paperwork. So we weren't as apt to go out with the boys as much as we used to. We figured that the agents who had recently joined our office would have to get their feet wet sooner or later, with or without us. The four guys on this particular surveillance had each been with the Customs Service for a number of years, but they were relatively new to the Douglas and Naco area. As far as we knew up until then, they had never had their mettle tested in a gun-fight. If you work the border in Cochise County long enough, sooner or later your cherry is gonna get busted with hot lead.

Marvin Tigert had joined our office several years before, coming from the Phoenix Customs Office of Investigations (OI). He was one of a kind, a good-humored guy who often joked about his Italian-Arabic features. If he wasn't referring to himself as a sand-riding camel jockey, he would be cracking jokes about no place to tie his camel to in our parking lot. The dude stood about six plus one on a slender, sturdy, muscular frame that had been enhanced by many years of weight-lifting. He sported some of the kinkiest black hair I've ever seen on a gringo's head. The damn thing almost looked like a thick, well-used Brillo pad. Tigert had a no-retreat character about him. He had already helped put some crooked feds and border cops in prison for dope smuggling. I knew when it came down to the hard-core action he would be the first to make a stand, toe to toe, and shoot it out. I never worried about what this guy would do when it came time to showing his balls.

Terry Miller had come to us a couple of years before from Florida. He was middle-aged with silver-gray hair that looked like it was naturally permed. Most of his time had been spent doing drug interdiction on the water as a Customs agent. Not having known his history when he walked into the Douglas office, we welcomed him to the border. Miller unwittingly showed his ignorance of the situation when he quickly snapped that he already had plenty of experience working the border. When we inquired where he had been on the border, he flippantly suggested to us that the Florida seacoast and the Mexican land border weren't much different. We knew by his comparison of the two that he had a hell of a lot to learn. We watched him over the next few months and found the stocky little guy to be more mouth than bite. He proved to be easily excitable in tight spots such as vehicular pursuits and search-warrant entries. We had serious concerns about how he might react under fire.

Al Barron had also come to us from the Phoenix Customs OI. He was a short, rotund fifty-year-old with a dark, freckled complexion under a topping of short black hair. I had heard that he spoke Spanish and just assumed by his last name he was of Mexican descent. I later found out that he had learned Spanish when he had previously been an agent in the Border Patrol. Not that it mattered one way or the other, but I was really surprised to learn that he was Filipino by heritage. Al was a really quiet type of guy with a chip on his shoulder. I guess it was because he thought he had been passed over for promotion unjustly. He seemed to have a problem with the younger, aggressive agents because he was apparently concerned they would outpace him. But regardless of these personality problems, he had once helped me in a fight with mules and I knew that he would be there for you when the shit hit the fan.

Joe Gistinger was a new, spry kid still in his mid twenties. He had just come out of the U.S. Customs Service Academy for special agents and was eager to make a name for himself. He had some experience as a U.S. Customs Service air interdiction officer in Florida, but he knew nothing of the Mexican border. He was a young chatterbox who admittedly couldn't help but flap his jaws all the time. I think part of the reason he was so talkative was that he desperately wanted to learn the job and that just made him naturally a bit inquisitive. I also sensed in him a driving desire to fit into the office with the older, more experienced agents. He was a good-looking youngster with wide, questioning, brown eyes and a short-cropped buzz haircut. If you had met him in college, he was the type of fellow you would peg for being in the ROTC program. Joe was aggressive yet cautious. He was the type that would test the waters before he dove in. I had a pretty good idea of how he would react under fire. I knew he wouldn't run, but I figured he would hold back a bit.

It was about 6:00 a.m. when the outlaws made their move. Their scouts crossed the border on foot and reconned the area for the presence of Border Patrol and Customs agents. When they thought the area was clean, they cut the border fence as they brought the dope-laden vehicle up to get ready. Ever so cautiously, the smugglers eased the loaded truck through the wired barrier.

This particular part of the international boundary near Naco had recently been rebuilt by the U.S. Army Corps of Engineers. The Army gave the old border a whole new face. Because of the increased criminal activity in the area, the U.S. government had authorized the Army to build a wall on the border that stretched about one mile on each side of the Naco Port of Entry. The barrier was constructed of steel landing mats, which are commonly used by the military for making temporary aircraft landing strips all over the world. The wall was about ten or twelve feet high, and at about a five-mile viewing distance from the side of the Mule Mountains it reminded me of a long, black freight train winding through the Arizona hills.

Our four Customs agents watched as a white 4x4 Chevrolet Blazer with dark tinted windows drove around the east side of the black-walled border. Once on the U.S. side, the Blazer turned due north and then came screaming up in a cloud of dust from Mexico. It headed north for a paved highway that would have taken it directly into Bisbee's vehicle traffic pattern, where it could mingle and disappear. The boys knew they couldn't allow the smuggler to get that far because it would put innocent folks in town at risk. The agents cranked their vehicles up and made ready for the anticipated lethal pursuit. Remembering agent Kirpnick's recent death, prayers were silently lipped as they checked their weapons and spare ammo pouches, anticipating the worst. One smoked. One chewed tobacco. Two just clenched their teeth with whup-ass attitude.

When the Blazer came ripping by their hiding place, Tigert, Gistinger, and Barron jumped out on the highway behind it. It didn't take the smuggler long to see the heat was on his ass. As soon as he hit the next intersection where he had some room to maneuver, the bastard braked hard right and cut his steering wheel left, flipping a U-turn. The agents had a hard time seeing through the black smoke the Blazer's tires laid across the highway. Even though he was running like a veteran at the Indy 500, the boys managed to flip right along with him and hang near his rear end.

I had just gotten out of bed and was getting my first cup of coffee when I turned my walkie-talkie on in the kitchen. The first thing I heard was a transmission from Tigert radioing Miller to get ready with the spikes to take the asshole's tires out. Knowing that the guy would make a run for the border, the team had left Miller back at their hiding place near the highway so he could cover the smuggler's anticipated retreat south. A few seconds later I listened as Miller screamed over the radio like a calf being castrated during spring roundup. He kept jamming the air with high-pitched screams that were so sharp and annoying I had to turn my radio down.

The smuggler saw Miller standing on the side of the highway with the spikes and he didn't want to have anything to do with the game plan. The bastard figured it would be easier to just run over the agent instead of waiting for him to deploy the tire-shredding devices in front of him. The outlaw took aim with his Blazer and went for Miller's plump, round silhouette. The agent dropped the spikes and took aim at the driver with a .12 gauge pump shotgun. Looking down the business end of the .12 gauge convinced the smuggler he was about to commit a grave mistake. He quickly reconsidered his options, deciding it may be better to steer clear of his intended now-aggravated target. When the smuggler turned back down the center of the highway, Miller took revenge on his tormentor by kicking the spikes across the highway in a manner befitting a Brazilian soccer star.

Miller nailed both tires on the driver's side of the Blazer. Despite his frantic tone on the radio, he had stood his ground and done an excellent job. The other three agents gained on the now-slowing smuggler and started to pull up alongside him. As Barron pulled up on the driver's side, the outlaw in the Blazer started blasting away, releasing a stream of .40 caliber rounds at the agent. Basic survival instinct caused Barron to brake down hard and fall in line behind the Blazer's rear end. As soon as he was out of the line of fire, he hung his left arm out of his car's window and returned fire on the smuggler with his Customs-issued .223 Steyr Aug assault rifle. The running gun battle continued off the highway into the desert on a dusty red dirt road that goes directly south around the border wall into Mexico.

As the smuggler neared the border, he had to turn the Blazer around the corner of some old cattle corrals to get into Mexico. Since he had run his deflated, shredding tires to the rims, it was impossible to make the turn with no rubber on the road. The outlaw unassed the load vehicle and looked back, seeing Barron and Tigert bearing down on him. In a desperate fight for his freedom, the scumbag began capping .40 rounds at the agents from his pistol as fast as he could squeeze the trigger. Tigert and Barron hit their brakes hard on the desert road when they saw the puffs of red dust dancing between their cars. If the sleepy little border town wasn't yet awake, it certainly would be in moments.

The agents came out smoking with their .223 Augs cracking the morning's cool air. They were spraying lead all over the rear end of the Blazer, trying to take down their attacker. And just when they thought they had the motherfucker outgunned, guess who gets reinforcements. Two more bad guys appeared over the top of the border wall tossing more rounds from automatic shoulder weapons at our boys. And if this wasn't enough to turn the tide against them, Barron's fucking Aug jammed on him as he was running through his first magazine. That's right, these are the same piece-of-shit weapons most of the agents have been bitching about to the REMFs for years. They may be great for the air boys in helicopters, but they ain't for squat in a desert shoot-out!

Now in all the dust that was being raised by the speeding cars and impacting bullets, it was pretty damn hard to see your target down-range. Most everybody was going by muzzle flash and gunfire reports. Even the bad guys knew according to the shots they heard that they outnumbered the good guys by one. When Barron's Aug jammed, they may have even figured that he had been hit and they could now make a rush and take the remaining agent. Things were looking weak for Tigert and Barron until Gistinger caught up and threw down into the scrape.

I'm not saying Gistinger necessarily rode in like the cavalry and saved the day or anything. But I do believe that when the bad guys heard another automatic Aug start barking in their direction, they had to have figured more and more help would be on the way. Being the chickenshits these behind-the-border back-shooters are, any show of equal or superior force causes them to run like scared jackrabbits being chased by coyotes. Sure enough, shortly after Gistinger arrived and capped a few rounds downrange, the engagement from the border subsided as the outlaws broke brush for the safety of their adobe walls in Naco, Sonora.

Feeling like a friggin REMF because I missed this one, I called Barrett up and told him what I had heard on the radio. Knowing that the real REMFs in Washington would be having a hissy fit when they heard about yet another shoot-out, Barrett and I skipped our morning showers so as not to delay our arrival at the war zone. When we pulled up to the border wall, the boys had the dope taken out of the Blazer and stacked for transport in my truck. The total weight of the marijuana load would be set at 909 pounds. But after examining the dope I would have to say it was 900 pounds of weed and nine pounds of lead!

Neither Barrett nor I had ever seen more bullet holes in a load of dope in our entire careers on the border. The sides of the dope bales looked like the shattered walls of war-torn Beirut. But that was only the half of it. We counted damn near fifty silver-rimmed bullet holes in the Blazer. The boys literally shot the shit out of the motherfucker. Butch and I cut sign and tracked for a blood trail from the Blazer to the border wall. Although we didn't find one, I'm still of the opinion that the dickhead was hit. He may not have had a through and through bleeder, but I would bet he was fragged up nicely around his neck, back, and left arm. It appeared that because the bullets had to travel through the Blazer's walls and side panels, then through the high, tight-stacked dope, by the time the rounds reached the driver they were breaking up into fragmented pieces of shrapnel. All around in the driver's compartment we found tiny holes from pieces of lead resembling that of birdshot from a shotgun.

Now, you have to remember, we were standing in what I would classify more as a battlefield than a simple shooting scene or perhaps a crime scene. I mean, if you were a homicide dick and were called to a murder scene, there would be certain procedures of investigation you would follow to preserve evidence. While doing so, you would probably be relatively safe processing your scene and evidence because it would have already been cleared and secured by uniformed officers. But down on the border fence line, those same rules of evidence preservation and methodical investigative steps ain't gonna fucking happen.

Under the protection of our own armed agents, we searched around the scene for blood and shell casings, and photographed everything of importance that could possibly later be construed as evidence. It wasn't a meticulous search, but it was a swift and cautious one. Every time one of the guys took his eyes off the border wall to bend over and pick up evidence, he was thinking in the back of his mind that he may not hear the one that blows his brain apart like a ripe melon.

As soon as we were done we gathered, grouped, and departed the border with all eyes watching behind us. Butch and I were really proud of the boys. They had done an excellent job of taking the war to the dope smugglers' front steps. We all got back to the office where a freshly brewed pot of black coffee was waiting. The guys were towing the battle-weary Blazer into the storage lot behind the office when the phone calls started. First it was the REMFs, then the news media, then Internal Affairs. In a way we really didn't mind because we had been through so much of this kind of crap lately we were used to it. But there's always some asshole Rear Echelon Mother Fucker out there who feels it is his assigned duty to make a good thing into a bad thing.

You know, this is a good thing. Hell, this is a fucking great thing! Our boys went up against some real mean gun-toting gutter-puke outlaws from the badlands of Naco, and we won. We got the dope. We got the bullet-riddled Blazer. To boot, the scumbag driver was probably experiencing some real sharp, burning discomfort in certain portions of his anatomy. And on top of it all, as the salsa sits on the tortilla chip, none of our agents had been wounded or otherwise injured! What more could you want?

Well, if you can believe it or not, the dickheaded REMFs at Internal Affairs in Washington wanted to know where all the shell casings our agents had fired were. They were on the phone drilling us about recovering all of the fired brass that would match and identify each bullet hole in the Blazer. I didn't know whether to get pissed off or fall out of my chair laughing in hysteria. It was insane! The REMFs, sitting some 2,000 miles away, were bound and determined to pervert a great thing into a nightmare. Because the shooting had taken place on a Friday, they wanted Barrett and me to go back to the scene on Saturday and Sunday until we collected all of the spent ammo casings that were spread out in the desert sand.

I guess on this one Barrett and I would have to plead guilty to noncompliance due to temporary sanity. We told the REMFs there weren't enough tacos in Mexico to get us out there on a weekend looking like ostriches with our heads stuck down in the sand waiting to have our tail feathers plucked with lead. We countered that on Monday, if they still insisted that we do it, we would send an armed party of agents out on their urgent brass roundup. They decided to hold their Monday-morning quarterbacking until after the weekend and it all went away. We never heard from them again on the matter. I guess that sometime during the two-day cooling-off period, somebody with a little measure of common sense in Headquarters figured it wasn't worth the agents being shot at again. Whoever that REMF was, I would like to nominate the guy to become the next U.S. Customs

Commissioner. He has demonstrated more gray matter between the ears than most REMFs I've known in the last twenty-five years!

Now that we had satisfied their bitches, which were entirely ridiculous, what about ours? I'm talking about our valid concerns about the Aug assault rifles always jamming. And this particular time it couldn't have happened at a more crucial point for an agent. We had moaned and groaned with Headquarters about this on a number of occasions. Still they had refused to address the issue and discuss a change in the shoulder weapons we so desperately needed. Today was living—and at the same time nearly deadly—proof that the Augs malfunction in battle. The Colt M16/AR-15 assault rifles that our agents had been previously issued had been battle-tested in Vietnam, Grenada, Panama, and Saudi Arabia. With proper cleaning and maintenance they are a worthy and dependable weapon. Why in the world do you think our military forces still carry them today?

Barrett and I, both having experienced combat with the Colts in Vietnam, had seen enough of the Steyr Augs' inferior performance on the firing range. And now we had seen their deficiency during a border engagement. We knew we had to do something for our agents' protection. We turned to our firearms training officer and all-around military expert, Allan Sperling. He was able to get an inordinate number of 9mm MP-5 submachine guns assigned to our office. They didn't have the range the .223 Augs did, but you could fire a thousand rounds of ammo through the little black submachine guns and they would never jam. But on top of that, Sperling one-upped us. Somehow, he found out that the Customs Service had a half dozen or so M16s stashed in Fort Benning, Georgia, for special undercover ops. He was able to convince one of his buddies in charge of the secret that we were indeed working undercover.

I think the wording on Sperling's request memo may have been somewhat ambiguous as to the exact definition of undercover. Whether his description of hiding beneath desert yuccas was construed as being under the cover of brush, or working undercover in the desert, I'm not exactly sure. I guess it's possible that he may have given the reader of the memo the wrong impression. All I'm saying is that you have to take care of your agents the best way you can. It's ludicrous that we have to play friggin word games with the controlling REMFs to get the equipment and weapons we need to survive our jobs. Until they recruit agents into Washington who have "been there and done that," we in the field will continue to suffer and pay the price for their ignorance.

In 1907, Captain Harry Wheeler, the most famous Arizona Ranger and U.S. Customs Service officer who ever drew breath, asked Territorial Governor Kibbey for a .30 caliber Colt machine gun for his men. In 1908, Captain Wheeler also requested that the new 1903 Army Springfield rifles be issued to his Rangers in replacement of their aging Winchesters. In 1909, when the Rangers were disbanded, they had no machine gun and were still using their outdated 1895 Winchesters. I can't help but wonder how many gunfights Governor Kibbey had been in compared to men like Kidder and Wheeler. In fact, it would also be interesting to know how many shootings U.S. Customs Service Commissioner Von Robb had been in when he so wisely decided to dispose of our new Colt AR-15s and issue us the nonproficient Augs. If I ever have the pleasure of meeting Wheeler and Kidder on the other side, I'm gonna tell them ain't too much has changed in the last hundred years of law enforcement. The guys who *don't* live the job are still getting in the way of the guys who *do* live the job.

On June 13, 1998, just nine days after our Naco gun battle, a twenty-six-year-old Mexican named Reymundo Valenzuela-Reyes was found executed and thrown across the border near the west corrals in Douglas. He had been gut-shot and then dragged by his own belt, which was wrapped around his throat. The back of his neck and arms exhibited earlier birdshot-size shrapnel wounds on them. By the time the Border Patrol found the body there were already maggots making their home in his rotting throat and mouth. The guy had probably been dead for a couple of days, which would have put his demise somewhere around a week after our Naco gunfight. I learned from a well-placed informant in Agua Prieta that the guy had been a mafioso driver who had been involved in the loss of a large load of marijuana. When I asked the informant how big the load was, he said he had heard it was about nine hundred pounds. Justice may be blind, but the Reaper is ever so vigilant in waiting for what belongs to him!

In 1999, two rival dope-trafficking organizations in Naco, Sonora, began warring over control of border-fence smuggling avenues. After a gun battle in which the outlaws on both sides used automatic AK-47 assault rifles and TEC-9 submachine guns, three Mexican smugglers lay writhing in death from numerous gunshot wounds. As history so often repeats itself, the three dope smugglers went down in the same dirt streets that Ranger Kidder had died in while taking three gun smugglers with him. About the only thing I can see that has changed in the past century on the border in Naco is the type of lead dispensers being used by the law and the outlaw. And the one thing that is as regular as an old woman on prunes is the fact that people are still willing to forfeit their lives over this ancient business of smuggling.

Did you ever wonder which came first—borders or smuggling? Whichever you choose, there is no denying that because of the border, an otherwise insignificant, anonymous pueblo will retain its place in an Old West history that is enriched by our own fascination with violence. Naco will always be synonymous with the names of Wild West characters and their smoking gun barrels. Legendary lawmen like Arizona Rangers Kidder and Wheeler will be nearly impossible to replace. But border bandits and smugglers like Villa and Chacón just seem to be a dime a dozen on the Reaper's border.

10

The Border Bandits

WHEN I WAS A YOUNG STUD romping and stomping down in Texas, I remember that the king of chips, the Frito-Lay Company out of Houston, had this cartoon ad gimmick known as the Frito Bandito. Of course most gringos, never having been on the border or even down into old Mexico, accepted the stereotyped cartoon character as being what a Mexican pistolero would look like. He was pictured as a short Mexican vaquero with a wide-brimmed sombrero and a long, black, thick, greasy, drooping handlebar mustache. In some of the ads, he was depicted as grabbing hold of two six-shooters that were slung low beneath the ammo-laden bandoleers strapped across his chest. So if you've never seen a real Mexican bandit, except in the funny papers, well, I guess you may be one of those folks who thinks they all look like the Frito Bandito.

The cross-border counterpart of the Frito Bandito's stereotype would probably have been the Old West's dime-novel depictions of Wyatt and Morgan Earp. The two legendary brothers were usually posed with Western boots, long riding coats, Stetson hats, and six-shooters hanging from their waists. But the truth be known, there were a good number of both lawmen and outlaws who died with hot steel in their hand while wearing lace-up foot gear and similar "un-Western" garments. So what's my point about these comparisons?

Never judge a man by his appearance, especially on the border. It can be a fatal mistake.

During my time on God's green earth, I've fought hard-core, dedicated communist soldiers and guerrillas defending their home soil. I've arrested dope smugglers, thieves, cattle rustlers, murderers, assassins, rapists, child molesters, wife beaters, and terrorists. But the worst and most die-hard sons of bitches I've ever gone up against have always been, and will continue to be, the fucking bandits and burglars of the Mexican border. And when you're dealing with numbers and numbers of illegal aliens, they ain't that easy to pick out of the crowd. Odds are, they're standing right in front of you and you don't even know it.

In 1976, one of my partners in the Border Patrol in Douglas was a rowdy rooster named Theo Hudson. Theo was about a forty-year-old former Green Beret who had seen some pretty hairy combat in Vietnam, where he led a force of pygmy-size Montagnard Indians up in the mountains. The experienced ex-Special Forces soldier had become a highly proficient Border Patrolman who possessed some pretty fucking awesome hand-to-hand fighting skills. Theo kept himself in prime shape and was probably one of the best man-trackers I've ever had the privilege of cutting sign with. He was both a mentor and an idol to most of the younger agents, who understandingly admired him. Theo seemed to radiate that air of being invincible. He was the last guy at our Douglas BP station that any of us figured would ever be taken down in either a fistfight or a gunfight.

Hudson was on routine patrol on the east side of Douglas during one of our pleasant southeastern Arizona fall afternoons. It was that time of year when the distant fading autumn sun gives the high desert a hazy, lazy, tinted light. Combined with the accompanying cooler temperature, it tends to set a man at ease, or as they would say in Mexico, *en paz*. Toward the end of his shift, Theo's Border Patrol radio unexpectedly blared off a transmission that rudely interrupted the tranquil afternoon he was enjoying. He had received a sensor alert on the border in the Rose Avenue ditch behind the Douglas cemetery. This was the same area where a couple of years later I would fight two border bandits for the right to live.

In response to the sensor alert, Theo maneuvered his BP truck into a thicket of mesquites and yuccas on the north side of the cemetery. The border was no more than several hundred yards south of him as he patiently scoped it out using his binoculars. After seeing no movement of importance, Theo got out and locked his vehicle as he kept an eye on the two elevated levees that parallel both sides of the Rose Avenue ditch. Leery of the unexpected, Theo slowly and cautiously walked through the thick brush toward the ditch. His war years had instilled a subconscious stealth as he stepped over and around downed, dry twigs and mesquite limbs most people wouldn't even see. Theo moved like an Apache. He was damn near as quiet as the worm-infested residents at the bottom of the boneyard just south of him.

As Theo drew toward the barren levees of the ditch, he observed a somewhat heavy-set Mexican walking north from the border along the eastern edge of the graveyard. Theo's years of experience caused him to automatically give the guy a visual patdown. He noted that the guy wasn't packing anything and that his hands were empty. As far as the agent could see, the Mexican didn't have any kind of weapon in his belt or waistband. It looked like another routine apprehension. It looked like the guy was coming "en paz." A perfect ending for a beautiful day. It looked like the six o'clock evening news and Miller time were just around the corner.

Theo made his way out of the brush and up onto the top of the levees, where he stopped to wait for the guy. He stood there waiting with his legs slightly apart and arms folded behind him in his characteristic military "at ease" stance. A few years before, in a foreign jungle, if he had been standing there waiting in a similar fashion, you could have bet even money that some young soldier was about to get his ass chewed out royally. But today, in this desert, this particular feller from Mexico was going to get an ear-bending lecture on the errors of illegally crossing the border. Especially so close to Theo's end-of-the-shift Miller time.

The overweight but powerfully built Mexican never broke stride as he walked the middle of the levee toward Hudson. As the alien approached, Theo saw a "you win" smile on the guy's face. It was a disarming reaction that he had seen on thousands of illegals' faces over the years when they get caught with no place to hide. It's that sheepish look and accompanying body language that telegraphs messages like, "Who me? I'm just a good ol' boy looking for work. No need to worry about me. No problem. I'm just as peaceable and meek as a lamb." Theo's face turned into a scowl of profound disappointment. His well-rehearsed rhetoric about the evils of illegally crossing the border would have to wait until he caught some other alien who needed an attitude adjustment. This Mexican was just too damn nice a guy to waste all that good venom on.

As the Mexican approached, Hudson was thinking of the routine arrest procedures he was about to perform—mundane, unspoken rules of engagement attached to the cat-and-mouse game played by Border Patrol agents and aliens. Theo had executed this drill more than a thousand times. At least those were his last thoughts when his body suddenly went limp. Theo thundered to the ground with a ringing in his ears. He never even saw the bowling-ball-size fist that rocketed through the thin desert air and cold-cocked him.

The border outlaw Theo had just encountered was an ex-boxer and former soldier gone bad. The asshole possessed a one-two combination that had previously kept him out of the unemployment lines. Later, finding there wasn't too much of a job market for ex-boxers and soldiers, the heavyweight now turned to the only alternative in Mexico he knew that would keep him from having to perform stoop labor in the bean and chile-pepper fields. He worked his way up the violent rungs of the dope-smuggling ladder of success. Because of his size and his willingness to inflict pain on others, he became a capable enforcer and bloody trigger for the Agua Prieta cartel. At the end of his criminal career, this former soldier's body count would surpass by scores the twenty-five or thirty men the black-hearted Chacón had accumulated at the turn of the twentieth century. This was the beginning, the early years of Tombstone Fragoso, the most sadistic mass murderer that Sonora and Cochise County have ever known, bar none.

As Hudson lay there with his brain redlining, he tried to figure out which way gravity worked. While he was desperately struggling to get right-side-up on his haunches, his befuddled brain registered a second and more immediate threat. Fighting through the fog to regain some part of his senses, Theo felt the tug of death that some lawmen have survived, and some have not. The Mexican was trying to free Theo's heavy-framed .44 Magnum revolver from his holster. It looked like Miller time was going to be late this particular evening.

Hudson grabbed hold of his assailant's arm as the outlaw was trying to extract the death machine from its sheath. The old soldier had to overcome a twenty-or-so-year age deficit between him and his hefty younger opponent. Tombstone's prominent arms were the results of years of weightlifting and related boxing training. His physique was way beyond the capabilities of the older agent's. The only thing Theo had going for him was his Special Forces training and the mindset to survive at all costs, against all odds. Theo torqued his brain into getting pissed off. The adrenaline kicked in as the combat veteran thought to himself, "Only God has the right to take my life! And this fat fucking tamale vendor is not God! So let's get down to business and kick some serious ass!"

Theo managed to wrap his right arm around the shithead's gun arm in a martial arts move of death-defying proportion. He locked up on Tombstone's arm in a relentless grip as they went rolling and thrashing down the outside of the levee into the rocks and red dust of the desert. The brief wrestling match was a hurricane of flying desert debris mixed with flailing legs and arms. During the tussle, Hudson heard the unmistakable sound of bones popping and muscles tearing in his right shoulder. Having been pulled up and out of the socket, the useless limb now dangled helplessly from a grotesque, knotted mass of tissue. The pain was so excruciating that for a split second Hudson thought he may be better off if the son of a bitch did blow his brains out. Hell, for a another split second Theo thought about blowing his own brains out!

The helpless agent lay there writhing in agony as the outlaw continued in his pursuit to clear the .44 widowmaker from Theo's belt-holster rig. As the ruthless Mexican fought Hudson for control of the six-shooter, Theo grabbed his thick, long, black hair on the top of his head with his left hand, and violently pulled back, pushing Tombstone's vocal cords forward for exposure. The ex-Special Forces soldier had every intention in the world of delivering a well-learned killing blow that would crush the outlaw's throat. As Theo stretched his target's neck up and back with his left arm, he fought through the pain to bring his right arm around to deliver the fatal blow. Other than more pain, nothing happened. His right arm did not respond in his defense. There were no motor skills. The arm had been rendered as useless as tits on a boar hog.

Realizing his crippling disability, Theo silently prayed that his life would end in a quick head shot. He knew that within moments he would be looking down the business end of his own .44. Theo's eyes clenched shut as the stinging beads of sweat from his forehead seeped in between his pressed eyelids. Theo had often asked me if I thought you'd ever hear the one that took you down. I guess he figured he was about to find out if you felt the ripping of your gray brain tissue before or after the bursting of your ear drums.

As Tombstone's immense hand dwarfed the grip of the heavy-duty .44 pistol, his beefy index finger began to enter the trigger guard in an effort to pull the hammer into final battery for discharge. Theo was on the path to the bright shining light when a swift black Border Patrol boot drove deep into the outlaw's ribs. Hudson heard the asshole's ribs break about the same time the .44 went limp and dropped from his hand. Dragging his torn limb with him, Theo scuffled for the pistol with his good arm. He saw the black boot flash a second time and heard the report of yet more breaking bone as the *bandido* squealed like a stuck pig. Theo managed to roll himself over in time to see the outlaw's face dive into the dirt. Although not yet in complete control of his faculties, Hudson managed to force a smile at the sight of the asshole's broken, bleeding mouth.

It wasn't until after he had taken control of his own six-shooter that Theo was able to concentrate on the north end of the life-saving black boot. Top side of the boot was the welcome smiling bulldog mug of senior Border Patrol agent Ed Blankenship, the station chief. Ed had heard Theo responding to the sensor alert and on a whim had decided to wander over and give Theo a helping hand. I guarandamn-tee that if it hadn't been for this stroke of luck, Theo Hudson would have never made it to retirement.

Hudson and Blankenship scooped the future terror of Sonora up and dropped him off at the Cochise County Jail. The agents returned to the Border Patrol station in Douglas, where they ran enforcement data checks on Fragoso and learned he was wanted by the state of Arizona for escaping from one of their prisons, where he was doing time for a felony conviction. Blankenship notified the FBI in Tucson of the fugitive's arrest and assault on Hudson. Although Hudson would be laid up off duty for days in agonizing recovery, the FBI did not charge Tombstone with assault on a federal agent. Either they were too lazy to do their job properly, or they just plain didn't give a fuck about a little do-or-die fight on the border 120 miles away in Douglas. I don't know. All I know is that the FBI did not properly investigate the case. They never interviewed Theo, nor did they pursue prosecution against Tombstone for his attempt on an agent's life. Instead, they just threw the fugitive back in state prison and forgot about the incident. Hoover's boys blew it big-time. They had a free shot at making a federal felony case on a soon-to-be mass murderer, and they let it slip through their bureaucratic, paper-cut fingers.

In early 1976, I was detailed from the Douglas Border Patrol station to the San Ysidro, California, station for three months. It was one of the few times that I can remember in my government service that we actually had a non-REMF commissioner who knew what the hell he was doing in field operations. U.S. Immigration Service Commissioner Chapman was a retired Marine general who had the balls to come meet us in the dirt. At the beginning of the San Ysidro operation, which was supposed to clean up lawlessness on the border, Chapman gave us a long-winded oration that lasted about an hour. It was probably the single best go-get-'em pep talk I had ever heard a politician give. At the end of his presentation the honcho actually had the guts to publicly state, "Good luck and good *hunting* out there!" And out in

California in the 1970s, that was just like slapping the ACLU and all of the Brown Power radical folks in the face at the same time.

I reported to the San Ysidro headquarters for the first time on the evening shift about two hours before sundown. After walking through the door to get an assignment from the agent in charge, I was a tad bit stunned at the activities in the station. There were Border Patrolmen standing with prisoners cuffed and chained in what seemed like infinite numbers. Which in itself is really nothing unusual for San Ysidro. The part that snapped me to attention was that the agents looked like they had just come off a fucking battlefield. I shit you not! Their shirts were torn and hanging off their sweating, exhausted bodies from recent skirmishes down on the "war line." Some had dried bloodstains, some had fresh blood still flowing across their arms and faces, and then there were even a couple with blood-soaked wraps around their heads.

Between the complaints and moanings of both prisoners and agents, I heard a couple of Border Patrolmen requesting fresh ammo before going back out on the line. The radio was jammed with calls of shots fired and officer-assist requests. For a moment I wondered if this place was going to be as bad as Vietnam. Looking around the station, the only difference I could see so far was that the bad guys weren't in black pajamas or khaki uniforms, yet.

My assigned partner was an old Border Patrol veteran of the San Ysidro border wars. He had been stationed there for ten years and he quickly filled me in on the different radio codes and distress calls his guys used. He taught me the area we would be working and the rest came rapidly. You either caught on as you went along or the Patrol sent you back to where your permanent station was. The place was so battle-conditioned, they didn't have the time or the luxury of babysitting an ignorant or lazy agent, as is the norm today in the government service.

During my first evening of duty, before the sun could set behind the cool blue Pacific Ocean, I watched as a wall of humanity amassed at the border fence for an assault across the line. As they waited for dark, they bought tacos, tamales, and other tantalizing Mexican delicacies from the numerous Tijuana street vendors who were no doubt taking advantage of a nightly border ritual. As you watched the spectacle in its almost carnival atmosphere, you would be hard-pressed to figure out which ones were coming to feed off our welfare programs, and which ones were coming to help feed our tax base. Nevertheless, something else struck me as I stood in awe at the sheer mountain of people gathered at the fence. I had a strange, distant feeling of déjà vu. It was like one of those sensations you can feel close to you, almost like you can touch it. But when you reach out in your memory to hold it, it dissipates before you're able to mentally grasp it and dissect it. I never had a real genuine "go bonkers" flashback that I'm aware of, but this would probably have to qualify as a close call.

When I was in Army boot camp in Fort Polk, Louisiana, in 1969, the training staff of drill sergeants did a down-and-dirty one on the young, green recruits one day. It was several weeks into our training when we were herded into a large auditorium or hangar of some sort. One of the drill sergeants got up on a makeshift stage in the center of the troops and bellowed something like, "Listen up, shitheads! I have an important announcement to make! The People's Republic of China has just entered the war in support of North Vietnam. They are dispatching troops in an unprecedented number to Hanoi as I speak. Accordingly, your training will be expedited and you boys can expect to be sent to the front lines of the DMZ in Vietnam ASAP. When I turn the lights out you will be shown a film that may help save your life in combat. Be sure to pay attention, because it will probably be some of the last training you will receive here before shipping out."

Folks, I gotta tell ya'll the honest-to-God truth. My mind went stark-ass blank, my knees went weak, and my whole torso damn near went as limp as my granddaddy's ninety-year-old dick. Of course, as you may have guessed by now, it was just an Army fuck-with-your-head trick to get you to watch the goddamn movie and learn something. But to this day I couldn't tell you one lousy thing that friggin film was about. Because all I could think about, all I could imagine during the whole stupid film, was this horde of screaming red Chinese with sharp pointy bayonets charging balls to the wall at us as soon as we got off the plane over there. And although I never went up against an extremely large wave attack like that in Vietnam, here on the Mexican border in San Ysidro, it was about to really happen! Oh, sure. These aliens weren't soldiers, and they weren't *all* armed. But then again, it was just me and a few other agents, and we didn't have the whole damn U.S. Army with us, either!

After the sun dipped behind the ocean, the shit started hitting the fan. There were shots being fired every quarter- or half-hour in a 360-degree circle around our assigned patrol area. My partner and I had been assigned to work, or perhaps a better description would be "to hold," an asparagus field just east of Dairy Mart Road right down on the border fence. From where we set up our position, I could see both Border Patrol units and ambulances running Code Three, red lights glaring and sirens howling. They were screaming back and forth on roads that were still unfamiliar to me. Straight south of our assigned operational area, right on the border, I could see a dilapidated old ranch house. I asked my partner if we would be going into the house to roust illegal aliens out since it looked like a good staging area. His response was the first mention I would ever hear of the infamous San Ysidro Border Bandits.

The old Border Patrol vet explained that a group of armed Mexican bandits would cross the border every night after dark and take temporary possession of the old homestead. From there they were, for all practical purposes, free to roll and rob aliens at will. Then the old agent paused as if to study his choice of words and said, "Well, at least the lucky ones just get robbed. If the girls are good-looking they'll probably end up being gang-raped. If the old men argue over their money or possessions, they'll probably get knifed or shot, or both." I asked him why in hell was it that we weren't making an effort to take the place back and hold it. He said that the BP agents would get together whenever there was a lull in the action and make a run at the place. But it's the same old story; once the shooting stops and the assholes retreat back into Mexico, they later drift back in since we don't have the manpower to hold the homestead permanently. Sounded just like Vietnam. Take a hill and later walk away from it.

Somehow it seemed like my life was becoming intertwined with a weird repetitive cycle of America's national disappointments.

After a couple of evenings of riding with the vet, the agent in charge cut me loose in my own BP vehicle. I continued working the asparagus field, where I quickly got used to arresting fifty to sixty aliens at one time single-handedly. I'm not kidding you in the least; this was par for the course in San Ysidro. Some evenings and early mornings, the fog would roll in from the coast so thick that you couldn't even see the front end of the patrol vehicle you were sitting in. Because everyone's vision was so limited, the aliens would literally walk right into the bumpers of the agents' vehicles and raise their hands in surrender. I've even gotten out to take a leak on a couple of occasions, and while in midstream with my dick waving in the breeze apprehended thirty to fifty folks. And don't even think about dropping your pants to take a dump. Odds are you would be trampled to death before you could even wipe your ass.

After the morning sun broke across the fields, it reminded me of fish that had swum upstream and been stranded in separate pools when the water subsided. There were large and small groups of aliens hiding just about anyplace you could imagine that would afford them some kind of concealment. The problem was that because we were down in flat farming country without a lot of cover, they couldn't stand up to continue north without sticking out like a sore thumb. So all the agents had to do after sunup was drive around and collect them up as they lay in ditches and between rows of asparagus. It was during the daylight that the unforgivable sins and ravages of the Border Bandits became evident to me. It was enough to inspire a future of sleepless nights.

Other than Vietnam, I've never seen such desperation in the pleading, frightened eyes of so many people at one time. If they hadn't already been brutalized by the MFJP and cops in Mexico before crossing, the odds were they would get it from the Border Bandits after getting through the wire. You could easily spot who had and who hadn't encountered the vicious bastards during the night. The unlucky ones had torn clothes, abrasions, cuts, and the likes. If there were women in their group who had been taken by the bandits, you could tell. They wouldn't look you in the eye because they were embarrassed by what had happened to them during the night. They endured their un-warranted shame by turning their faces away when you gently asked if they had been molested. That's the way most of these poor souls had been raised down south. They were taught to be submissive to crooked police, government officials, and other armed bandidos. It tears your heart out to see folks like these. It makes you want to rip the throats out of those fucking blood-sucking predators that abuse these people. On both sides of the line!

Night after night, I would sit in my asparagus field catching folks as they drifted by me like silent ghosts in the fog. And night after night, I'd listen to the shooting and screams coming from the aban-doned old homestead south of me. It tested one's sanity. You wanted so badly to relieve your anxiety and temper by emptying a fully loaded revolver into the walls of the bandidos' hideout. But wanting and doing are two different animals.

After a couple of weeks of working the same area, my spirits were lifted when the call came over the radio to group up for an assault on the bandits' headquarters. As we got gathered up in the asparagus field, the cool, moist Pacific air seemed especially pleasing. The mouth-watering aroma of charbroiled fajitas and tacos was drifting in from Tijuana. The fog had yet to roll in, leaving a ceiling of bright, shining stars over the ocean. It seemed like it was poten-tially one of the more enjoyable evenings I would spend in San Ysidro. Maybe it was just the fact that we were about to do some-thing really good by chasing those cocksucking bandido mutants back into their stench holes in Mexico. Whatever, the chilly evening was going to be a nice one.

For the seasoned agents who had seen action before, the assault on the hideout was no big deal. It was just like getting on line and walking into a hooch or village in Vietnam. As we approached the farmhouse in the dark, we took a little bit of high and wide gunfire. We responded by opening up on the muzzle flashes with suppressive fire. Between the exchange of gunfire, you could see shadows of dark figures jumping out of windows and fleeing across the line to their safe haven in Mexico.

When we had cleared the building, there were no noticeable fatalities on our side of the fence. If somebody had dropped on the south side of the fence, we probably wouldn't have known about it anyway. Being right down on the fence in the dark, you can fully understand that not too many of the agents were interested in using their flashlights to search for blood trails. And you can imagine why there weren't any gung-ho volunteers willing to be illuminated by the Border Patrol helicopter that had swooped in to support us. So if any bandidos were hit, who knows?

But more important, at least for the few remaining hours of the night, we owned the fucking farmhouse. And if some poor soul wanted to cross through the fence, and we didn't happen to see him do it, at least he and his loved ones could do so without fear of being murdered or raped. At least just for a few hours, these people could walk like humans with some dignity and not have to worry about squirming like scared animals while pleading for their lives at the end of a knife or gun barrel. That's one thing I've learned over these many years on the border. The non-criminal aliens are never as scared of the U.S. lawmen as they are of their own Mexican border bandits and corrupt cops. Oftentimes after an apprehension, I have seen the discreet smile of relief when they learned they had run into U.S. officers instead of their own countrymen.

After my detail to San Ysidro, I learned that because of the hundreds of rapes, murders, and robberies we had been dealing with in the "war zone," the San Diego Police Department had put together a group of lawmen known as the Border Bandit Detail. The detail began operating in November of 1976 and was composed of San Diego cops, U.S. BP agents, and U.S. Customs agents. It was these lawmen that inspired Joseph Wambaugh to write his book *Lines and Shadows*.

The original detail group was headed up by a Border Patrol agent who had transferred over to the San Diego Police Department. The detail, in one form or another, has continued over the years to survive the political shifts in law-enforcement support. To date, three BP agents have been shot in the line of duty while working undercover on the teams.

The detail was still pumping out arrest stats for the REMFs to drink coffee over in 1984, when U.S. Border Patrol agent Lisandro Montijo joined the anti-bandido unit. After earning a Border Bandit notch during a gunfight in San Ysidro, Montijo would later come to the Douglas U.S. Customs Office of Investigations in 1988. He would become one of my best partners.

Lisandro Montijo had gotten out of the Marines in San Diego in 1971. He was a short, stocky, well-built specimen of machismo with black, short-cropped hair and matching mustache. He was born and raised in Benson, Arizona, which is only about twenty miles from Tombstone, where the family once had roots. There are Montijo descendants six feet under in the Tombstone cemetery, resting along-side some of the Earps' handiwork. In respect for the family's history and tenure in Tombstone, there is even a brass memorial plaque to a Montijo who was killed in action in 1969 while serving with the Marines in Vietnam.

After his time in the service, Montijo returned from the Marines to his homeland near the Mexican border, where he started a career in law enforcement as a highway patrolman with the Arizona Department of Public Safety. The thing you can't get away from with Monti is his proud Mexican heritage. Like they say, "You can take the boy out of Mexico but you can't take the Mexican out of the boy." Arizona DPS quickly realized the potential this young hombre had for undercover work posing as a Mexican scumbag. They trained him, prepped him, and Monti was off down under, riding hogs with the outlaws of the Dirty Dozen bike gang.

After almost losing his sanity and life while working the biker gang, Monti decided to resign from the Arizona DPS and return to San Diego while he was still ahead. He joined the Border Patrol in 1983 and after the academy was sent to San Ysidro. Monti broke in as a cherry taking the usual border duties as they came. When he heard about the Bandit Detail, he thought it would be a good change of pace. Always looking for a little extra spice and excitement, Monti applied for the detail and went in to be interviewed. The selecting supervisors took one look at the boy and saw the same thing the Arizona DPS had seen in him. I mean, what the fuck can you say? Monti emanates the aura of a bona fide Mexican bad guy. And with a little change in wardrobe, he also easily adapted to the role of a *pobrecito* (poor little) wetback who's ripe for the plucking. Accordingly, the Border Patrol bosses put Monti on the Border Bandit Detail as a decoy. Or maybe it would be more appropriate to say as bait.

Dressed like illegal aliens, Monti and a group of other undercover agents and cops would roam through the canyons of the San Ysidro border on a nightly basis. Disguised as easy pickings, the group walked the rank, urine-splattered and feces-laden trails near the fence. Each team member had his own way of carrying his weapon concealed, but easy access was the key factor and a must for survival. Some carried them in the waistband of their Levi's with their shirttails out. Others, like Monti, preferred to wear a side-slit full-cover serape that enabled him to palm the pistol at the first hint of trouble without being too obvious about it. Whatever the case, this group of hard-core undercover cops hunted trouble every night by mingling among the desperate masses of aliens on the move north. For eight to twelve hours a night they lived in the confrontational state known to lawmen as the "red zone." You could search the world over and probably never meet a more adrenaline-cocked, locked, and ready-to-rock bunch of shooters than these boys.

During one of his tours in this particular combat zone, Monti and his buds got a shot at testing their own mettle. They were doing their nightly mope shuffle down an alien-littered path when they heard a woman shrieking like she had just given birth to Rosemary's baby. Like a finely tuned bunch of choirboys hitting the right notes in harmony, each team member palmed his weapon and moved in to his rehearsed position on the trail. Just about the time the choir was warming up to sing, a couple of bandidos drug a woman across the trail directly in front of maestro Monti. Still giving the appearance of a harmless alien, Monti challenged the bad boys to release the distressed damsel. The bandidos looked Monti and his compas up and down before breaking into a low, muffled laughter. Apparently, at least to the bandidos, the team looked pretty meek and docile. One of the assholes pulled a .45 semiauto piece out of his jacket and plunged it straight into Monti's nose. When he finally stopped laughing long enough, the prick looked into Monti's dark browns and growled in Spanish, "Stay right here, little *pollo* (chicken), until I'm done with the girl. Then we'll see what you have for me under that pitiful excuse of a serape."

Now, taking into consideration that the bandit *knew* he had the drop on Monti, you can't help but wonder how surprised the asshole was when Monti's serape shot him. Not just once. That goddamn serape must have been loaded for bear because it shot the scum-sucking piece of shit a total of nine times. By the time Monti's serape stopped smoking, the border bandit had a belly button you could drive a diesel truck through. Just before that sorry scrotum croaked, do you think he wished he had never asked Monti what was under his dirty, stinking serape? Or do you perhaps find it entertaining to sur-mise that, just maybe, the degenerate's dying regret was that he'd robbed the meek unfortunates of this world?

The Bandit Detail boys capped the second shitbird as he was going up a hill in what can best be described as a "save my ass at all cost" retreat. Although the bandido survived, he would never rob or rape again. His cocaine-nurtured spinal cord was severed in two places. Some of the best justice never takes place in the courtroom!

Montijo transferred from the Border Patrol to the Bureau of Land Management in 1994. He landed a job in the criminal investigations section of the BLM as a special agent. Considering that most of south-eastern Arizona is federal land, and a good portion of that is in Cochise County near the border, the BLM asked if Montijo could be housed with our boys in the Douglas Customs OI. We knew we would be getting an experienced hand, and since Montijo's duties included working dope labs and marijuana grows on the national lands, it worked out real well for both agencies.

Over the next few years Monti and I pulled a couple of the same undercover ops that others and I had done before with DPS Officer

Jesse Gutierrez. We would intercept narcotics-packing mules crossing the border, take the dope, and deliver it to the bad guys ourselves. Having known Monti's history over in San Diego with the
Border Patrol, I knew he would be exceptionally good at our undercover muling ops. And when we were with him in the brush, neither
I nor Jesse nor Sperling ever doubted that Monti would pull the trigger when the time came. And that, my friends, is one of the most
comforting thoughts you can have about your partner in the pitch
dark of a black-ass night when the dope-running season is at full
speed in the desert.

Between July of 1992 and June of 1996, there were sixteen border-
bandit armed robberies committed in the Bisbee and Naco areas just
west of U.S.-Mexico International Boundary marker #90, on Border
Road. Most of them were home-invasion robberies where the victims
were beaten, terrorized, and then left in their pilfered residences,
bound and gagged like livestock waiting to be branded, slaughtered,
or both. The total number in the outlaw gang has never been fully
established that I know of. However, the information over the years
indicated there were a minimum of three central figures. And as hard
as these *pendejos* (dumb sons of bitches) were going at it, it would
appear that they were trying to challenge the ghost of Mexican outlaw
Chacón for his unsavory title as the baddest of the bad. The terrorized
victims frequently described the outlaws as Spanish-speaking young
Mexican males. The Cochise County residents, particularly the ones
living on Border Road near Bisbee Junction, were living in a continual
state of siege, always in fear for their lives.

Just think about it for a minute. It's hard enough for most folks
who live in the cities and worry about being victimized by some jerk
down the street. But if that does happen, at least in that situation it's a
good possibility that the law can come up with a suspect and track
him down, because nine times out of ten he's a neighbor or resident of
the area. But if your victims live on the border and get ripped off and
beaten within an inch of their lives, there are two other towering fac-
tors that you've got to deal with in the attempt to take the violator
into custody before he strikes again.

First, odds are that the bad guy is going to live in a foreign country under the protection of a corrupt government, and, even more important, under the umbrella of corrupt cops. Second, the biggest part of the strategic problem: Escape across the border means no arrest, no jail, no prosecution, and usually no extradition. So if you whack a U.S. citizen during the commission of your burglary or robbery, it ain't like you have to worry about any kind of a Mexican cop coming after you for your transgressions.

When I took down the two bandits behind the cemetery in the '70s as a Border Patrolman, it was common knowledge back then by Cochise County lawmen that a majority of the Mexican burglars were working for the Mexican police. Why and how in hell can that be, you may ask? The answer is simple. If you're a poor Mexican citizen and you get busted in your homeland for any large or small infraction of the law, you're headed for the *bote* (slammer) without bail. Before you get to see a judge, much less an attorney, guess what happens next? A couple of fat fucking Mexican thieves wearing badges will pay your cell a visit one night. While they're busy electrocuting your *huevos* (balls) with a hot charged cattle prod, they present two pretty convincing options to you. Work for me and live. Or don't work for me and die. If you're slow answering, get ready for more fun and games, because so far the electric shock treatment of your gonads and the unlubricated exploration of your rectum's walls shall just be considered friendly foreplay.

Next, you'll probably receive the benefits of a generous non-medicinal sinus cleansing. Two or three other sociopaths, no doubt also wearing Mexican badges, will hold you sitting down in a chair while one pulls your head so far back you'll swear you're going to end up kissing your own ass. While they hold you in this position, one of their compas will shake up a bottle of Coca Cola or seltzer water with a large amount of ground-up flaming-hot chile peppers swirling in the mix. As he pours and squirts the lava mixture up your nose, you'll pray to God you could have the cattle prod back up your ass. If you don't pass out from the pain of the burning acid and pepper literally eating your sinus membranes and tissue away, you'll scream out giving your own mother up for whatever crime of the century they want to pin her with. The next time you're able to get an audible word out of your mouth, you don't think twice and you don't ask what the job is. And once they have you working for them, they own you mind, body, and soul. I've even heard from my Mexican informants that when the first part of November rolls around, the MFJP gives its U.S.-side Christmas shopping list to its best thieves.

In February of 1996, Manuelín Cano-Martan was arrested by Cochise County deputies after he had kidnapped a woman and commandeered her car. He had allegedly been burglarizing a residence in Naco, Arizona, when he was interrupted by the law. In a failed attempt to escape officers who were pursuing his sorry, scroungy ass, Manuelín grabbed a lone female driver and her car, thereby escalating the charges that were forthcoming. While incarcerated in the Cochise County Jail, in lieu of facing his due justice, the bandido took the law into his own hands. He met the Reaper by hanging himself with a bedsheet in his cell. But there was a little ray of light that came out of the young man's miserable existence. While he was in custody, the Cochise County detectives learned the names of the three prime honchos leading the bandits. And although I didn't know it at the time, one of these mangy hombres and I had already locked horns.

Through the information they had received from Mexican authorities concerning Manuelín's partners in crime, the Cochise County detectives searched their own archives and learned they had previously arrested two of the three outlaws within the past two years. One of them, Luis Alberto Gámez-García, had been arrested for attempted auto theft.

On May 2, 1994, at 1:40 a.m., Gámez and another unidentified maniac stole a pistol from a 1987 Nissan pickup truck after a failed attempt to hotwire the vehicle. They hastily departed the area on foot after realizing the Nissan's owner had called the cops.

On the same day, starting at 5:15 AM, the lovely armed couple spent the next three hours trying to steal a total of seven other vehicles as they retreated back toward the border. Now, either hyperactivity runs in these boys' bloodline, or they must have been coked up out of their space-cadet minds. And it's a good thing these idiots made their living as bandits, because they would have starved to death as car thieves. It was most interesting to note that all seven of the vehicles they attempted to steal were exactly what the MFJP and other dope smugglers in Mexico prefer to drive: two Chevrolet pickup trucks, two Chevrolet Blazers, one Chevrolet Suburban, one Dodge pickup, and one Isuzu Trooper. Remember what I said about the Christmas shopping list of the MFJP? Well, Christmas came early this year in Mexico.

When Gámez was arrested later that day by Cochise County deputies, he was still armed with the pistol he had stolen from the Nissan truck. Since he was carrying the weapon rolled up and hidden in his jacket, he got nailed with possessing a concealed weapon on top of the attempted auto theft charges. The cokehead confessed to the attempted thefts, his prints were found in at least two of the vehicles, and the weapon was positively identified as being stolen from the first truck-jacking attempt. Gámez subsequently pleaded guilty before an Arizona Superior Court judge in Bisbee, where he received a supposedly substantial sentence for his crimes. A whopping six months in jail! I guess if he had capped the deputy with the pistol he was palming under his jacket, the lamebrain judge might have really been upset and punished him. Instead of six months, maybe the pendejo would have gotten a whole year and we could have kept him off the border for a while!

After another armed home invasion and U.S. citizen hog-tying contest in 1995, the Cochise County detectives had a stroke of luck. The victims positively identified the photograph of the second leader of the gang, Santos Javier Vásquez-Urrea, also known as "El Checo." The information on this dickhead indicated he was as unstable as gelatin dynamite sweating in the Arizona sun. He was a violent psycho who got his rocks off by going 10–8 on whoever got in his path. And if he was the least bit smart about anything in his life, he had two elementary rules he disciplined himself with. He only crossed the border to kidnap and rob. And he only crossed the border armed. If you ever kept a list of sordid assholes who really needed to be taken into custody by the Reaper, this motherfucker would have been at the top of it.

Well, I reckon it's pretty easy to understand the anguish and frustration the Cochise County residents along the border were living with. So much pressure was bearing down on Sheriff Pintek that he eventually, and reluctantly, succumbed to the wishes of some of his best detectives. For quite a while, the detectives had been saying that they needed to put a substantial reward out to nail the outlaws. By this time in the investigation, the detectives knew who the perpetrators were. The problem was that they were Mexican citizens and it was going to take some money to get an informant to set them up for a bust on this side of the border. Cochise County had one detective who could do it. And once the reward money was made available to pay the informant, that was the beginning of the end for the remaining border bandits.

Detective Carlos Cruz was at that time assigned as a narcotics agent in the Border Alliance Group working out of our U.S. Customs Office of Investigations in Douglas. He was an energetic twenty-eight-year-old who came from one of those large Mexican families with ties on both sides of the border. He had seven brothers, of whom all but one or two were cops with different state and local agencies on the U.S. side of the line. One of his brothers was an Arizona Highway Patrolman who would give his life in the line of duty several years later, suffering a horrible death I had twice escaped. DPS Officer Juan Cruz would be fatally trapped inside his burning patrol cruiser in 1998.

Carlos was around five-foot-eight, the average height for a native Arizona border rat. His medium frame supported a tough, brawny body that reflected years of competitive jostling as a kid with his older brothers. With brown hair and impish, twinkling eyes, he was a seasoned desert hunter of both wild game and bad men. Carlos spoke so low and soft that you often had a hard time hearing what he said. And when you could hear him, he spoke such a garbled dialect of border Spanglish that I hardly ever knew what the fuck he was talking about. But that didn't matter one iota. He knew what he was saying and he always got the job done.

Cruz understood the nature of the border and its outlaws. But more important, the outlaws understood Cruz and his intentions.

They knew his reputation. If you were a crook and Carlos Cruz gave you a courtesy call concerning your worn-out welcome in Cochise County, you had fair warning. If you didn't take heed, and you were foolish enough to remain in the game, Cruz would hold true to his word and take you down sooner or later. Butch and I had our eyes on him for several years. The young man started as a Cochise County Sheriff's deputy, where he excelled as a lawman. We knew that this kid was going to be something special, a law-enforcement star. We wanted to recruit him as a U.S. Customs special agent so bad we could taste it.

Being born and raised in Cochise County on Border Road, Cruz and his cop brothers maintained the best stable of informants in southeastern Arizona and Sonora. Besides the usual useful information about dope smuggling and assorted other criminal activity in general, if you needed to know, they could even find out who was fucking the mayors, judges, and city council members on both sides of the border. So when it came to formulating a plan to get the border bandits across on the U.S. side of the border to bust, it came as no surprise to any of the cops in the county that Carlos would have an informant who could accommodate the plan to a perfect T.

Being that Carlos's guy was already in good graces with the bandidos in Naco, Sonora, he directed the informant to lay out a sob-story scenario to the bad guys over a beer. So sure enough, over a brewsky with El Checo and his outlaw compadres, the snitch sniveled that he had been fucked out of a lot of money on a dope deal by a U.S. citizen trafficker in Arizona. After each beer the actor would digress into a state of more and more self-pity concerning his plight. When the informant wasn't too busy reveling in his phony grief, he would take time to emphasize how much money he had lost to the rip-off artist. Well, if the boy doesn't make it in the nonfiction crime world, he ought to become a silver-screen star in Hollywood. The bandidos bought the whole package unseen. Hook, line, and a sinker that was about to take them all the way down.

With the hook set deep in his mouth, El Checo told the informant that he was the man for the job. The way El Checo had his Mexican math figured out, 50 percent of any monies recovered would be his fee for helping the informant. When the snitch asked how he planned to handle the debtor, El Checo pulled up his shirt, proudly exposing two pistols in his waistband. Like the beaming father of newborn twins, the bandit boasted that he would use the duo for the kidnapping and subsequent murder. When the snitch pushed him on what he would do to the trafficker to recover his money *before* whacking him, El Checo said that he would use sharp pliers on the dude's huevos until he spilled where he had stashed the money. The informant set a date and time at a sleazy, scorpion-infested motel in Bisbee where he said he would have the debtor meet him. The bandit said that he would bring one of his "associates" from Mexico to assist him in the kidnapping and subsequent torture to the death. The deal was done. The players were in motion.

Now, as you probably already guessed, the intended Arizona trafficker to be tortured was none other than our one and only Carlos Cruz. And when Cruz debriefed the informant along with other detectives of the Cochise County Sheriff's Department, he wasn't too enthused to hear the part about the Mexican's pliers being applied to his family jewels. In fact, when it came right down to planning the split-second precision timing for the bust, our somewhat distraught comrade contemplated going down to the local college to borrow stopwatches from the track coaches to be issued to each bust team member. I guess Carlos wanted to ensure that everything, other than his balls, came off at the right time.

On June 11, 1996, after a reign of terror in Cochise County that spanned some four years, El Checo and his two partners in crime were about to be brought to their bony knees. The Cochise County Sheriff's Department SWAT team, and the BAG unit composed of U.S. Customs special agents and Arizona Department of Public Safety agents, hunkered down at the motel. When the wary outlaws arrived in a little sedan, they drove around the parking lot rubbernecking for any lawmen. El Checo was carrying a 9mm Sig Sauer semiautomatic pistol. Luis Gámez was carrying a .38 caliber revolver. Teodolo Gámez, who was up until this point not fully identified, was unarmed.

As they pulled up and parked in front of the room that Detective Cruz was waiting to meet them in, Carlos gave the bust signal before they were allowed to get out of their car. The SWAT team deployed bone-jarring stun grenades through the sedan's windows to knock the bandits to the floorboard of their car. Between the bright flash and the ear-shattering KA-BOOM, the bandits got a case of temporarily scrambled brains. They were so freaked out that they probably couldn't have pulled their weapons even if they had wanted to. SWAT swarmed on their asses before the smoke even had time to clear. The border bandits were miraculously taken into custody without one shot being fired.

In the car with the sadistic little fucks were a roll of duct tape, a pair of black leather gloves, and of course Cruz's nightmare come true, a shiny new set of stainless-steel pliers. And as it turned out not only were they pliers, but they were part of one of those new Gerber multi-tool kits with knives and serrated-edge saw blades of all shapes and sizes. Hell, an experienced Mexican surgeon couldn't have asked for anything better to perform a dick-slice-and-dice interrogation. As Cruz examined the Gerber he ran his fingers up and down the extremely sharp edges of the cold steel. It made him grit his teeth as a few still drops of sweat formed over his eyebrows.

And if it wasn't enough that the whole operation went off without anybody getting shot, or having their balls crushed and diced, we got an added big-time bonus. One of the bandits turned out to be an hombre I had dealt with before on a Border Road dope-smuggling operation. He was a longhair *pistola*-packing Mexican Indian dude known as "El Indio." By the looks of him I would have to guess that the raunchy son of a bitch might have been about half Apache or Yaqui. At the time I tangled with El Indio, he'd remained on the other side of the border and I was unable to bring him to justice. But now, I'm pleased to announce that he no longer roams the Sonoran mountains or the Arizonan deserts smuggling dope for the MFJP. Nor does he any longer invade Arizona homes and terrorize our residents. Luis Alberto Gámez-García, a.k.a. El Indio, is presently being cleansed of his sins within the walls of the Arizona Department of Corrections.

Teodolo Gámez, El Indio's half brother, was released due to the lack of enough physical evidence to place him at any of the aforementioned crime scenes. Although he did show up to assist in the kidnapping and torture of Detective Cruz, he was unarmed and consequently only arrested for being an illegal alien. He was turned over to the Border Patrol for deportation to Mexico, and we haven't heard a peep out of him since. Cut the rattler's head off and the remaining body will just wither up and turn to dust in time.

The Mexicans cultivate some damn hard nail-eating hombres down there in the waxy agaves of Sonora. So you know this story can't end without a little more bloodshed. And it doesn't. Facing charges of kidnapping, aggravated assault, burglary, theft, and armed robbery, El Checo committed suicide by swinging himself high in his Cochise County Jail cell the day after he was arrested. A copycat of Manuelín, or a death pact agreed upon earlier by the outlaws? Were their lives so corrupted by dope and crooked Mexican lawmen that there was no turning back? Or is this perhaps the result of a deeply rooted hatred between the haves of the North and the have-nots of the South that goes back more than a century? I really can't give you one straight, simple answer. Maybe the Reaper knows. After all, it's *his* border.

Since El Checo, El Indio, Teodolo, and Manuelín were taken down, there have been no further home invasions in Cochise County that I'm aware of. El Checo, Manuelín, and the infamous murdering Chacón all have one common bond as border bandits that a span of a hundred or so years cannot dissolve. All three Mexican outlaws died with a noose around their necks on the Arizona side of the border.

Carlos Cruz is now a special agent with the U.S. Customs Service Office of Investigations in Douglas. In 1999, he was flown to Washington, D.C., where he received the U.S. Customs Service Commissioner's Award for Integrity for his diligent undercover work during an attempted bribery investigation. To this day, he refuses to possess or even borrow a Gerber multi-tool pliers kit.

11

Blue Trucks

FOR SOME CONFOUNDED REASON unknown to me, the color blue has ended up being an integral part of my turn on this earth. They told me that when I was born I was what was known back then as a "blue baby," due to a lack of iron in my blood. In fact, they had to give me a complete life-juice overhaul just to jump-start me. After the transfusion, there ain't no telling whose blood I have coursing through my veins. Being that I ended up soldiering and enforcing the laws on the Mexican border most of my life, I reckon that hospital staff back in Texas must have shanghaied some wayward wetback deserter and put him in with the "donor group." Now, don't go getting crossways with me on what I'm saying here. If it was in fact a south-of-the-border citizen who gave this stumbling baby pup a hand, I appreciate it. I just can't help but wonder if that wasn't why I ended up being so partial to spending my life on the Mexican frontier.

When I was in the U.S. Army Infantry, their dress color was blue, as was the braided rope that you wore over the shoulder of your uniform. And of course as we all know, the Air Cavalry of Vietnam had an infatuation with blue coming from their mounted predecessors. Although the U.S. Border Patrol uniform is green, its arm patches are blue and its dress uniforms have prominent blue stripes on the jackets and legs of the pants. And for those of you who have never traveled abroad and been inspected at one of our ports of entry, all of the U.S. Customs Service inspectors' uniforms, emblems, and shoulder patches are blue. So when I finally got into plainclothes investigative work as a narcotics agent with Customs, do you want to guess what color of 4x4 pickup truck I got? Yeah, you got it. BLOOOOOOOO! Out of a whole sea of different-colored seized vehicles that Customs and the Treasury Department has access to, you'd think they could've picked another color of the rainbow, right?

But I really didn't mind it too much. The color just kind of grew on me. Anyway, for the most part I had always thought that blue had been a lucky color for me. After starting out the gate as a "blue baby," I grew up to be a fat, healthy little devil. In the Infantry Recon, I made it through a year of nonstop death-dodging without much more than superficial wounds and burns. During my time with the U.S. Border Patrol, I had my fair share of shootings, not to mention high-speed chases and fistfights. Worst-case scenario from those years was a few trips to the hospital to be sewn up. But now I'm in the Customs Service Office of Investigations with a guy named Buddy Harrison. And what may have been good luck for me seemed like it ended up being just the opposite for Special Agent Harrison.

It was some time during 1994 or so when we had this particular group of dope smugglers that wouldn't break off smuggling through the Monument #90 area of Border Road between Douglas and Naco. Now, let me take a minute here to explain to you about this monument business. Years ago the U.S. Boundary Commission went about mapping out 675 miles of border between the "have" gringos and the "have-not" Mexicans. Non-inclusive of Texas's natural muddy-creek boundary known as the Rio Grande, the land border was drawn from El Paso to the Pacific. This was done subsequent to several treaties that began with the Gadsden Purchase in 1853. The land border was later re-established by other agreements between the two countries in 1882 and 1889. Both governments sent surveyors and construction crews to hell and back, covering hundreds of miles of scorching deserts, monsoon-raging rivers, and jagged mountains. When they were done we had a seven- to ten-strand barbwire fence that ran from

Texas to California. The fence is still standing, but as we all know by now the international agreements don't mean squat.

All along this 675 miles of land barrier are 275 obelisk-shaped "line of sight" silver-painted steel monuments that are sometimes referred to as markers. Now, when I say "line of sight," it means just that. The monuments were not built as one might expect, like about every five or ten miles in an orderly row. Instead, they were grounded from wherever you could see from one to the other. It didn't matter if it was from the top of one mountain to the next, or straight across the desert in view of each other. Beginning down at the western tip of El Paso at the Gulf of Mexico, and running in escalating sequential numbers to the Pacific Ocean in Southern California, the spiked metal six- to eleven-foot-high pillars point to the heavens like a path of trail markers left by an expedition of lost steel workers from back east.

I've spent a good deal of time over the years contemplating the border. And if someone was to ask me what I actually thought of this dividing line in the dirt I'd have to say this: The border is a line of barbwire and spiked pillars that seems only to serve as a symbol of one of man's many futile lifetime endeavors, his attempts to define Mother Nature's boundaries, as well as man's national claims to a piece of what no human can ever definitely call his own possession. Politicians rally their countrymen around their flags and make decisions behind closed doors as to who will possess what lands and where the borders are to be mapped. Men will always be willing to fight and die in follies of nationalism, but they will never continually control their own borders. Whether it be the present U.S.-Mexican border or the formerly defined DMZ in Vietnam, there is only one who may truly lay claim to regulating such bloody barriers. Only this one has complete power over the mere mortals' proclaimed borders of this world. Cloaked, with a black hood, he's a bone-rattling angel who travels alone, wielding a sharp sickle. Each one of us will have the opportunity to meet him. Just once.

The Douglas special agents are responsible for enforcing the laws of our nation beginning with Monument #73, near the New Mexico-Arizona line, and continuing to about Monument #105, just west of the Cochise County line. The Monument #90 area sits about midway on the international boundary between Douglas and Naco on the dusty wild-ass frontier Border Road. It is an area of black-limbed, squatty greasewoods, whitethorn mesquites, and one of the Sonoran Desert's favorite blessings, the enchanting long, bony-fingered ocotillos. Other than that, there's nothing else but rocks and rattlesnakes crawling about with an occasional Gila monster thrown in the mix for color.

Before this particular campaign against the dope smugglers, I had quite a bit of experience in the Monument #90 area smuggling dope myself. I bet that took you by surprise, now, didn't it? Let me give you the details of my straying from my sworn oath before you get your bowels in an uproar.

Several years earlier, one of the best undercover narcotics agents I've ever had the pleasure of working with needed a little help on one of his cases. Ron Gomez was a big, muscular special agent for the Arizona Attorney General's Office out of Phoenix. He had gone over to the Arizona AG Office after retiring from a gang-busting investigative unit with the Phoenix Police Department. That was where I had first met and worked with Ron, when I was still with the anti-smuggling unit for INS in Phoenix. But our Phoenix history together constitutes stories for other times, so let's stay on this trail right now.

Ron worked at the direction of Assistant Attorney General Kip Holmes, who was himself an ex-cop and *compañero* of mine from the Yolanda Molina investigation. With Kip's legal guidance and permission, Ron had been introduced by an informant to the dope-smuggling Domínguez family of Agua Prieta, who owned a Mexican restaurant in Douglas. Ron wheeled and dealed with the traffickers until he actually silver-tongued them out of thousands of dollars that he was being paid to smuggle the Domínguezes' dope across the border for them.

I mean it doesn't get any better than this. The law is going to seize the bad guys' dope and money at the same time! Ron told these greedy pendejos that he would move their dope across the line for them, but there was only one hitch: They had to front him operational money so he could hire all the necessary drivers, shooters, safe-house operators, and here's where I came in, a crooked Border Patrol agent.

Now, believe it or not, just like the Lord had intended this one to work out for the good guys, the people the Domínguezes bought the Mexican restaurant from were also known dope smugglers of the Agua Prieta cartel. Trini Segovia, the previous proprietor, had once been arrested and convicted for narcotics trafficking in the 1970s; he also had a Border Patrolman for a son-in-law who was a suspected corrupt agent. So when Gomez started spouting the line that he had a bought and paid-for Border Patrol agent on his own payroll, it all just seemed like good business sense to the Domínguezes. It was common knowledge in those days that the majority of the Agua Prieta cartel families had some kind of crooked U.S. officials on their pay roster. If you move large quantities of dope, it was like having a prepaid insurance policy.

So after being briefed on the undercover scenario by Gomez, I called the U.S. Attorney's office in Tucson and got their permission to participate in the UC operation by assuming the role of a paid-off, crooked Border Patrol agent. After getting the okay from the feds, I rushed home and dug up some of my old green USBP uniforms. Of course, like an old World War II veteran who some thirty years later tries on his dress uniform from the mothballed cedar chest in the attic, I had more paunch sticking out of the green pants than the river belt would hold in check. Slowly but surely I stuffed my gut into the uniform and then stepped back to scope out the newfound stud in the mirror. Do you remember that movie where Arnold Schwarzenegger played the guy who was going to have a baby? Well, maybe we don't need to go all the way down that road, but the sight in the mirror was pretty gross.

I finally settled for regular olive Wrangler jeans on the bottom with a large green Border Patrol winter coat that still fit me across the chest. It all got topped off with the BP Western gray felt Stetson that I had boxed up in my closet from my youthful duty days with the Patrol. I figured as long as I didn't have to get out of the vehicle, the gabacho I was admiring in the mirror would pass for a bad-guy BP agent.

Ron gave me my marching orders and told me the traffickers would be waiting for me at Monument #90 with more than five thousand pounds of dope loaded in two vans. Gomez said that he had to go to Agua Prieta to get the last of the up-front money from the Domínguezes, and that we couldn't take delivery of the dope until he got his ass safely out of Mexico. While Gomez was in Agua Prieta, I was supposed to drive down to old #90 and tell the outlaws everything was clear as far as any other Border Patrol or Customs agents being in the area. Then I was supposed to return to Douglas and pick up two more Arizona Attorney General agents who were on the job undercover with Ron, and take them back out to Monument #90 to drive the vans across the border. I have to admit, this was one of the few times in law-enforcement history that I had ever seen one of these deals go so smooth. Well, except for a couple of little bumps.

On my first trip to Monument #90, I pulled my Border Patrol Stetson way down over my forehead, and zipped my winter coat up over my nose so no one could get a good look at the "crooked agent." I stopped the official-looking patrol car I was driving and flashed my lights a few times across the border fence into Mexico like Gomez had told me to do. An Indian-looking son of a bitch sprang up out of the brush and cleared the fence like a friggin antelope on the run. He approached my car door, and I opened my window about halfway with my left hand while I palmed my gun in my right hand under the storm jacket. As the guy leaned into the top of the window to talk, I could see a locked and cocked .45 Colt pistola sticking out from under his coat. It's times like these that one undercover phrase best describes the situation. Play it by fucking ear!

We spoke Spanish back and forth for a while with me keeping my head down enough so that the bastard wouldn't recognize me. Although I had previously heard of El Indio and knew him to be an extremely volatile and capable border outlaw, we had never met face to face. I didn't think he would've made me, but then again in those days you never knew who was passing counter-surveillance photos of U.S. border lawmen around in Mexico. Besides, this cocksucker was as squirmy and jittery as a diamondback rattler during mating season in a sun-baked bed of cactus thorns. The whole time we *hablar*ed, I kept the barrel of my pistol pointed straight into his chile-filled gut from the inside of the car. If he would have as much as twisted his eyebrow the wrong way I would have dropped the hammer on his ass and never missed a wink of sleep that night. In a mano-to-mano like this, there is no such thing as a second chance with a border killer like El Indio. None at all.

El Indio demanded a few more minutes because one of the vans had gotten stuck where it had to cross the Mexican railroad tracks about fifty yards south of steel marker #90. I played my role to the hilt, making it look like I was real pissed off and worried that we were all going to get busted because they were running behind schedule. I told El Indio that I could only guarantee safe passage for another five minutes before the next shift of BP agents came on duty. He started cussing up a desert sandstorm in Spanish. The whole time he was pitching his temper tantrum he ran his greasewood-stained fingers back and forth across the .45's grips, which protruded from his waistband. The wild-eyed Apache argued with me for more time but I knew I couldn't make it look too smooth or easy. I countered by cursing back that I was going to patrol back down Border Road and that when I returned in five minutes it would be then or never, do or die. Having popped those words somewhat prophetically into my mind and over my dry lips before I could stop them, I later wished I had never said that "do or die" part considering who the fuck I was talking to!

As I drove off I turned around on Border Road by Monument #90 and looked south into Mexico. Hell, you would have thought half of the Naco-based Mexican federal police were helping smuggle this load of grass! There must have been fifteen or twenty guys standing around the van with badges and rifles dangling off their coats and shoulders. And I couldn't help but giggle to myself a bit. It was a typical goddamn fucked-up Mexican operation. All of the armed Mexican "outlaw lawmen" were standing around watching and arguing over how to get the van off the tracks. Meanwhile, there were only three or four dope mopes lifting with steel bars around the van's embedded wheels. I swear, if these guys ever got organized they could flood the entire U.S. of A. with dope and deny the Colombians and Asians any access to the market at all!

Before returning to marker #90, I received confirmation on the radio from our agents that Gomez had just received the last payment for our transportation services and he was out of Mexico. We now had a green light to cross the dope. I picked up the two undercover agents and returned to the Monument #90 area. As luck would have it, a now evil-grinning and obviously pleased El Indio was waiting with both vans at the fence.

As we took delivery of the vans, I shook hands and Spanglished with El Indio, with each of us promising the other we would one day again do business together. At the time of this operation, I had no inkling that the Indian would end up going down several years later as a violent border bandit.

Having said our adioses at the fence, the two undercover agents and I rode off into the sunset on Border Road with more than two-and-a-half tons of grass belonging to the Agua Prieta cartel. And the whole time we were going hand-to-hand with the outlaws, every swinging dick standing in Mexico had his cocked trigger finger ready to rock and roll. The slightest fuckup during our undercover roles and it would have ended up going down as live-or-die time on the border! What a fucking adrenaline rush!

Gomez and the other Arizona agents wrote the case up, later arresting and convicting the mother and father of the Domínguez family. As an extra bonus, we had the pleasure of throwing the cuffs on some of Yolanda Molina's hired guns that had been providing security on the dope negotiations Gomez had been present at up in Chandler, Arizona. The restaurant, along with all of the permanent residing cockroaches in the kitchen, were seized by the Arizona Attorney General's Office. And believe me, the agents had a few ironic laughs over that seizure because this restaurant, like its proprietors, had a history of being filthy.

Some years earlier, the first owner of the restaurant, a convicted dope smuggler by the name of Trini Segovia, was awarded the distinguished honor of going to Washington, D.C., to put a Mexican dinner on for members of Congress. Segovia had been invited to the affair by former Arizona Senator Dennis DeConcini. How? Why? What was the relationship between an Arizona senator and a dope-trafficking felon? I'm not even going to try to go down that trail with you. But if those gullible REMF D.C. politicians had seen what we found in the kitchen when we seized the restaurant, I imagine they would probably have had the caterer re-arrested for serving food topped with *caca de cucarachas*.

Mom and Pop Domínguez were caught up in such a legal bind that they had to start cutting a deal for cooperation or spend most of their remaining lives in the *lata* (jail). When the word leaked that they were talking, the Agua Prieta cartel got a little perturbed that one of their members was breaking bread with U.S. lawmen. They didn't waste any time in sending a Mexican torch over to burn down the Domínguez residence on Tenth Street, right smack in the middle of Douglas. So all in all, I guess you could say this family of bad guys got fucked by both ends of the proverbial stick.

But it's just like a Western diamondback rattlesnake that sheds his skin each spring; you can count on it that next year he'll be back with a new, thicker hide. We had put the Domínguezes away and now another entirely different dope-smuggling outfit had taken to using Monument #90 for its own greedy stab at the U.S. market. And being that we weren't wired in on an undercover operation, we would have to do this one the hard way, with long hours of surveillance. Because of the lack of large-trunked trees and thickets in the area, it was a real bitch to find a good hidden surveillance point. But never wanting to knuckle under to a little adversity, Jesse Gutierrez and Allan Sperling pinned down a good spot after pouring some sweat into reconning the area.

The lawmen found a place up high in the overhanging red volcanic rocks, which are indigenous to the area. It was up on the side of an ocotillo-covered hill overlooking the smugglers' favorite routes for crossing the border near old #90. It was a dark, secret, cool place for a couple of agents to crawl up under to get out of the searing summer desert sun. Of course you had to beat the varmints and reptiles out of the cubbyhole first, because they, too, are looking for a shady place about that time of year. But once you ran them off, they usually wouldn't come back and try to retake the shady rock hideaway. If they did, one of the agents would usually have had an unofficial and unreported accidental discharge of his service-issued pistola. That's one of those things that supervisors never hear about for some reason.

Gutierrez, Sperling, and I would spend many a day and countless hours lying in those rocks, waiting for the outlaws. And while you may think the wait boring, the natural beauty and history of the area kept your mind busy, tumbling through the old Western tales and legends. Out in the distance about fifteen or so miles southwest of Monument #90 was the San José mountain range, where the Arizona Rangers had run down and captured Mexican bad man Chacón. At the time of Chacón's arrest, the murdering son of a bitch had become chief of police in Arizpe, Sonora, which is located about thirty or forty miles straight south of old #90. So if any of ya'll are in doubt that history repeats itself in Mexico concerning official corruption, here again is confirmation in a nutshell.

Besides the Domínguez case, during our many surveillances of the Monument #90 area, we more than once observed that the smugglers were being aided by the Mexican police. Lying in our lava-rock hole with some pretty potent binoculars, we could see the heavily armed Mexican officers in full dress uniforms as they scouted the area before the dope smugglers crossed. Then at the time of the illegal border crossing, we would watch as the officers helped cut the fence and send the dope load on its way, along with their sick black prayers to Saint Malverde.

What? You scoff at the statement about the prayers? It's absolutely true! In recent years, the Mexicans have devoted themselves to a patron saint of drug traffickers named Jesús Malverde. His image is that of an Old West outlaw with black matching mustache, hair, eyes, and scarf draped over a white cowboy shirt. In reality, Malverde was a common thief in Sinaloa who was hanged in 1909 for petty crimes. He was never a drug trafficker or a Catholic saint, yet Mexico's most powerful smugglers pay homage at Malverde's popular, crowded shrine in Culiacán every year. It is damn near paramount to devil worshiping, if you ask me.

Calling him El Narcosantón, the Big Narco Saint, the Mexicans perversely compare Malverde to our English Robin Hood. The numerous drug smugglers who frequent his shrine pray for bumper marijuana and poppy harvests, protection for their shipments of cocaine, and help in evading enemy lead. His worshippers include such infamous drug lords as Caro-Quintero and the lately departed Amado Carrillo. In cantinas near Malverde's shrine, it is not uncommon to hear *corridos* (ballads) such as "Death of a Snitch" and "White Load." Such Mexican folk ballads elevate the drug kingpins to the level of heroes who take from the decadent rich gringos and give to the poor Mexicanos they employ as mules and pistoleros. Of course, I've never heard of a corrido that told the truth of how the drug lords cheat and murder their own mules and hired guns.

Do you believe that shit? I mean, here in Mexico you have some of the most religious Catholic folks in the world, and somehow a good number of them have taken to worshiping an image in direct violation of the sacred commandments of the Bible. And even if for just a few minutes you can understand and tolerate such behavior, the image they are praying to stands for the deliverance of death and destruction to our country. Hell, it sounds more like conjuring up narco satanism than narco sainthood, if you ask me! Then again, which side of the border you were born on is going to have a lot to do with your perspective. Maybe as the decadent, arrogant *norteamericanos*, we should start questioning our own insatiable appetite for drugs. Considering that, perhaps we, too, are guilty of co-sponsoring and promoting narco satanism in Mexico. Think about it.

Like we've talked about before, Mexican police corruption on the border is an accepted way of life. It's been going on for hundreds of years and it ain't about to change now. But the one thing that got my back up against this particular bunch of Malverde-worshiping bastards at Monument #90 was that they had taken to smuggling their dope in a blue Ford pickup truck just like the one I drove. Most of us knew damn good and well that it was an intentional effort on the smugglers' part to confuse the good guys and maybe even cast a little suspicion over me. Not that I liked it, but it was a good strategic tactic on the outlaws' part. Confuse your enemy and make his own camp distrusting of each other. Divide and conquer. It's sound basic military practice.

While this smuggling operation was in business, I had been followed on more than one occasion by BP agents who had seen me come off Border Road into Douglas. I watched them in my rearview mirror as they would get right on my bumper and pick up their radio mic to call a suspicious vehicle in. When I saw them on the radio I would switch my monitor into the scan mode and listen as they ran a check on my license plate. It pissed me off to no fucking end, but I knew it wasn't their fault. Before letting it get too far out of hand with them hitting their red lights and siren, I would pull over to the side of the road and dangle my badge out of the window for the whole county to see.

Invariably, the BP agent would get out of his patrol car and come strolling up to the side of my truck with a big mile-wide shit-eating grin on his face. With that kind of embarrassed hangdog expression, they'd tell me that they had recently chased a truck just like mine into Mexico after they had seen it driving across the border in the Monument #90 area. As they would be telling me the chase story, I'd watch their eyes cut back and forth trying to get a glimpse in the bed of my truck. Even when they would attempt to be inconspicuous about looking, it made me get a sick feeling all knotted up in the pit of my stomach. Let me tell ya'll, it's a rotten-ass feeling when the outlaws are able to reverse the tables on you.

Now, the boys in the Border Patrol who knew me didn't blink an eye at the similarity between the smugglers' truck and mine. But some of the newer agents were starting to look at me in a little different light than I cared for. And considering all of the corruption on the border the dope business has been catalyst to, I can't say that I blamed them. From 1988 to 1996, the Douglas Customs special agents themselves had already put about a half dozen crooked lawmen away. Or maybe it would be better to say a half dozen fucking traitors. And the good Lord willing, we'd run that score up double or so in the years to come.

Being that I had a little more at stake here than did Gutierrez or Sperling, I spent considerably more time in the rocks waiting for a shot at these assholes who were casting suspicion upon my head. Morning after morning, I'd hit the dirt at around 4:00 a.m. and sneak out to the Monument #90 area in the cover of darkness. I'd drive down Border Road with my headlights off and hide my truck in a deep draw beneath the lava-rock hideaway. Crawling up to the lookout in the dark assured me a ringside seat before the smugglers arrived with their joy weed. Some days I'd kick back under those rocks, dipping a whole can of Skoal tobacco without seeing any activity other than a few mounted Mexican vaqueros on the south side of the fence. Other days the bad guys would have scouts crawling up and down the hills looking for unwary U.S. lawmen on routine patrols. At times the scouts would sneak so close to our rock hideout that you could damn near spit your Skoal on top of their filthy, oily curls.

After four or five days of waiting and watching the scouts recon and prepare for the crossing, they finally decided to bite the bullet and go for it. And yes, you can bet your bottom dollar that I was there to raise hell with the bastards for using a clone of my truck. When I was sure the outlaws were past the point of no return with their wicked intentions, I radioed for backup. I told my agents which way the truck would be headed and that I would be running right behind it. I took extra care to make sure that everyone understood the dope vehicle was a blue Ford pickup exactly like mine. Out of the eight or ten Customs agents who responded, our main man, Buddy Harrison, was the first to arrive at the showdown.

Not wanting the scouts to detect my presence and radio the smuggler to bring the load back safely into Mexico, I slowly slithered and skidded my way down through the cactus and lava rocks to my truck. By the time I mounted up and got out onto Border Road, the smuggler was already several miles ahead of me. He was leaving a cloud of dust as he raced away north from the fence toward the highway that would afford him safety from U.S. lawmen. I radioed Buddy that I would overtake the bad guy and shut the back door, cutting his retreat back to the border off in the event he detected the agents. Harrison radioed back that he would set up a roadblock at the mouth of the highway where the smuggler would come out. I knew the shit was about to hit the fan. My heart raced, my palms got wet, my mouth lost all moisture, and my fingers choked the rim of the steering wheel in a death grip. Lord, I love the life of a border lawman! I would have just as soon swallowed my own tongue and strangled myself than to ever have worked in an office or factory!

I stomped my boot down heavy on the gas pedal, pushing my Ford's 460-cubic-inch power plant to the optimum level of performance. I squandered no time pulling up into the funnel of the smuggler's dust cloud until I could see the bad guy's rear bumper in a seriously intimate manner. I mean, I was so close that if his truck had been a cow, and mine a bull, there would have been some breeding going on. I allowed my vehicle to get caught up in his vacuum and slacked off the gas pedal, almost coasting at times. The *contrabandista* was raising so much dust and was so worried about lawmen in front of him that he never even knew I was riding his bumper. But he wasn't the only one who didn't know the whole score. Agent Harrison had a surprise party waiting for *both* of us.

When we left the dirt road and hit the hard pavement I was still nursing on the smuggler's rear bumper. We were warping toward a curve in the road that would end up at a stop sign at the intersection of Highway 80. The asshole had just found me in his rearview mirror when we made the curve. He was so busy studying on me that he ignored looking forward at the stop sign, where Buddy was standing in the middle of the highway next to his sideways-parked LTD. By the time the smuggler looked up it was either too late for him to stop or he just plain fucking decided to make buzzard meat out of Buddy's chunky gringo ass.

Now, I've read about how fast on the draw some of the Arizona Rangers were. I've also been told about some pretty quick outlaw gunslingers. But folks, you ain't seen greased lightning until you've seen Buddy Harrison pull iron from his Levi's blue jean original sew-in holster. For years we've been after Buddy to wear a leather holster on his trouser belt. But he has always preferred to carry his pistol in the hip pocket of his jeans, swearing that it served his purposes better. Well, up until today, I didn't believe it. But after I eye-witnessed the whole affair, Harrison has finally convinced me that his sewn-in denim holster works pretty damn good.

I don't know if that hombre puts graphite or wax in that right hip pocket of his jeans. But if there was ever a doubt about how fast he could get his pistol into action, it was certainly dispelled that day. Buddy palmed that iron so fast that neither me nor the doper had time to steer clear of the shooting gallery. In a fraction of a second, there was some serious, smoking hot lead headed downrange in our direction. It all happened so quick that by the time I screamed on the radio, "Don't hit me!" Buddy had already dispatched six rounds of .357 Magnum lead on a death-seeking mission toward me and the outlaw.

Being right behind the smuggler, I could see the rounds go through his front windshield and come back toward me. Something was hitting my windshield and on the spur of the moment I just assumed it was lead. I got a quick glance of Buddy squeezing the trigger and diving sideways for his life at the same time. It happened so goddamn quick it was near equivalent to the same amount of time I reckon it would take a hummingbird to flap his wings a time or two. Without being able to detail it out completely, because it all passed in a hurried blur, the smuggler and I somehow managed to skid and slide around Buddy without opening up his guts and grinding him into the asphalt. As soon as we ceased to skid and squeal tires on both sides of Buddy and his smoking six-shooter, we were off and running again toward Douglas.

As we speed-demoned off, I radioed back to check on Buddy and learned that he was okay. Now, because it had been so hot up there in those rocks on surveillance, I hadn't been wearing my bullet catcher. For ya'll that don't know any better, that's what the boys and girls on the border call a bullet-proof vest these days. With the left hand on the steering wheel, and the gas pedal pushed to the extreme max, I ran the right hand over my torso, feeling for the telltale wetness of blood. After the preliminary check revealed no new holes, I radioed back to Buddy that I was also Code Four. Some folks may laugh at that, but I guarandamntee you it's happened more than once to lawmen and soldiers. If a vital organ isn't struck, and sometimes even if it is, a feller may not know he's been hit depending on how scared or excited he is. Now, back to the business at hand.

We chased this shithead for about ten or twelve miles toward Douglas on the highway doing speeds a little over 110 mph. Not only had he tried to whack Buddy, but he kept running innocent civilian motorists off the highway. The outlaw was in total disregard for third-party human life, which meant that he was pretty much bought and paid for as far as our Treasury Department's shooting policy is written. In other words, if we could get a good, clean shot at him without endangering innocent civilians, he was history.

Keeping in touch with each other on the radio, we tried to equal his speeds on the highway and box him in with our vehicles. The son of a bitch ended up ramming his blue truck through two of our pursuit vehicles during the course of our boxing maneuver. We couldn't get a clean shot at him because of our perilous speed and the possibility of endangering civilian traffic on the highway. We decided to squeeze him down by making a square box out of our vehicles around him. It's like a squeeze-chute action used on cattle when you work them in the corrals. The only problem is that in this kind of situation you have to set your "squeeze chute" up as you're doing an average of 100 mph. And let me tell you, that takes some serious concentration on the part of all four boxing agents.

About five miles outside the Douglas city limits, four of us got the smuggler's speed choked down and he made one last effort to break away from us. When he attempted to turn out of our squeezing box and head for the open desert, it was more than his tires could bear. Two tires popped off the rims on the same side of the truck. The loss of rubber locked him into going around and round in a circle until he was stuck in the desert sand on the side of the highway. The agents jumped from their vehicles and got to both doors on the cab of the truck at about the same time.

Surrounded by screaming, adrenaline-aggravated Customs agents, Butch Barrett was trying to pull the bleeding bastard through the bullet-shattered driver's side window. But the Mexican outlaw wasn't quite done yet. The son of a bitch fought Butch tooth and nail while he kept hitting the accelerator with the tip of his cowboy boot. The truck kept surging and spinning in a tight circle like a wounded duck with one wing shot off. I got into a spinning timing sync with the truck and dove through the open passenger's side window. I smacked the son of a bitch out of my way and turned off the ignition switch. When the smuggler realized his options had run their course, he looked up at us in tears and had the audacity to start complaining about his well-deserved gunshot wounds.

Butch and I examined the doper's wounds and with no intended gentleness informed the asshole that he was merely superficially cut by flying glass and maybe lead shards from the bullets. I don't think the dope smuggler ever realized how lucky he had been. After trying to kill our number-one pistolero, he had miraculously survived a storm of lead that a century and a score earlier would have damn near prevented the Sioux from taking Custer and his troops!

After the outlaw was in custody, we sauntered over to my truck to check for bullet holes. I was kind of surprised not to find any because looking down Buddy's flashing gun barrel had given me that sure-as-shit sensation that the rounds had been coming into the cab with me. Butch and I looked at the scratches and scrapes on my windshield and figured that it must have been the pieces of glass and disintegrating bullets that were skidding over the top of the smuggler's truck and striking the front of mine. While we were chewing the fat over the shooting and chase, some of the BP agents drove up and checked the action out. And I for one was glad that the bullet-riddled dope truck, and its accompanying bleeding Mexican outlaw, were both there for them to review. Other than the bullet holes and 250 pounds of grass in the back, the Agua Prieta cartel had purchased a truck that was almost identical to my blue government truck. I'll always believe that this bust stopped some bad scuttlebutt on me before it got started.

About a year later, on the east side of Douglas in the San Bernardino Valley, we chased and battled yet another dope-smuggling outfit. I won't bore you with all the details, but sure enough after

Barrett and I chased the smugglers cross country through the deserts and mountains for about thirty miles, this one also ended up in a shooting. And if you haven't guessed the results yet, Buddy Harrison was at the trail's end of the chase to once again pour another full revolver's load into the outlaw's modern-day steed. In a repeat of the Douglas Customs agents' blazing history, Buddy's nemesis was a second blue Ford pickup truck. I reckon blue just wasn't Buddy's lucky color.

12

Mules-R-Us

THEY SAY THERE'S A FIRST TIME for everything and I reckon that's a fair statement. Most of my first impressive whatevers have been on the Mexican border. Even when I was a kid the first piece of ass I ever poked was in a Mexican whorehouse across the muddy Rio Grande from Texas. The first time I ever came close to getting whacked as a Border Patrol agent was in 1975 on the Mexican line between Agua Prieta and Douglas. It was also the first time that I had a solo head-on encounter with dope-smuggling backpackers, or "mules" as narcotics agents so fondly refer to them. It would be one of those life learning experiences that you can't buy at any cost, nor be taught at any state or federal law-enforcement academy. The powers that be will always stress the classroom hours. But there is no comparison between the classroom and on-the-job fuckups. The tricky part is to survive the fuckups long enough to get a handle on the job.

My first major screwup as a Border Patrolman began on a dark, chilly October evening in 1975. Because the Border Patrol was meagerly staffed at that time, I was lying alone in ambush on a well-used illegal-alien crossing trail about one mile east of the Douglas Port of Entry. I was no more than twenty-five yards north of the border fence, quietly tucked down behind a large desert yucca plant. The surrounding sand-and-rock terrain was flat with numerous prickly pear cacti and stubby greasewood bushes. With binoculars I was able to scout through the fence into Mexico, where I watched the people and cars rushing back and forth on the dusty, unpaved streets of Agua Prieta. There were no lights on my side of the border in the open desert. The only illumination came from Mexico, where there were a few scattered, dim street or porch lights that barely aided my surveillance.

I had brought an old multicolored Mexican poncho to put between myself and the cold autumn ground. The BP uniform I wore was in itself insufficient for the oncoming cold weather, and the agents were at the mercy of their own imagination as to personal uniform augmentation. As I lay prone on the raw cotton blanket, I used my elbows to prop the binos up to my eyes and watch the smoky shadows in Mexico. My concentration on potential illegal entrants was on occasion interrupted by the mouthwatering smell of mesquite-grilled carne asada drifting in the wind from across the border. That was one of the things I loved about working so close to the fence in the evening: The aroma of savory Mexican food was in the air. And I loved Mexican food!

A couple of hours had passed by uneventfully and boredom had begun to take its toll on my enthusiasm. A poorly maintained Mexican cop car in dire need of a new muffler slowly rumbled by the border fence, giving the appearance of a routine patrol. The jalopy turned one block south of the border fence and pulled into a dark alley between an automobile repair garage and a dilapidated shack that wouldn't even pass for a half-ass decent doghouse in one of your neighborhoods. I watched two stoic-faced uniformed officers get out of the car and slowly meander off out of my sight into the deep haze of the tumbleweed- and beer-bottle-filled alley.

A minute or two crept by before the officers returned to their car followed by about six or seven men all dressed in dark garments. I thought to myself that it must've been some kind of low-level gambling raid and the cops had probably just emptied these guys' pockets of their own personal fines. I was chuckling to myself about the Mexican system of mordida when the cops walked over to the trunk of their patrol car. I trained my binos on the rear of their vehicle as they opened it, revealing about a half-dozen plumply filled burlap bundles. Now, I was still a little green in 1975, but I had enough sense to know that those bundles were probably dope and those cops were probably more crooked than a dog's hind leg.

I tried to use my portable handheld radio to call the Border Patrol station for help. But every time I keyed the goddamn talk button it made enough fucking noise to scare a corpse from the grave. Being the young space cadet I was back then, I turned off the radio, determined that I could handle the situation alone. My cocky John Wayne attitude quickly dissipated as I watched the armed Mexican cops slowly approach the fence directly in front of me. They somberly looked up and down the fence, methodically scouting the area before crossing the border. After they had crossed, the badge-toting outlaws crept about fifty yards into Arizona, approaching a crumbling set of wooden cattle corrals that had been left to rot from an old ranch. Very quietly, they crawled up on top of the wide corner posts, carefully balancing themselves as they stood up for an easier view into Douglas.

From their perches, the Mexican cops could see both sides of the border, giving them a two-point advantage in a three-point game. I remained in the prone position on my poncho, trying in earnest not to move more than my eyes, heart, and lungs. I watched the cops as they whistled and hand-signaled the men they had left back at their patrol car. After being summoned by the uniformed crooks toward the border fence, the smugglers each grabbed a bundle of dope from the car's trunk and headed north in an orderly single file. When they got up to just south of the perched cops, they squatted down with the bags in the brush, remaining just a few feet within Mexico.

It seemed like an eternity, but it was probably no more than a couple of minutes before I heard a car driving directly behind me south toward the border from Douglas. I slowly shifted my head just enough to see the car turn its headlights off as it continued, barely rolling in the brush toward the Mexican cops. The load vehicle eventually stopped between my yucca hideout and some other brush about a hundred yards from the border. I turned my head back toward the cops just in time to see them signaling the mules on north

toward the car on the U.S. side of the line. The mules crossed the border and proceeded past the outlaw cops into Arizona. Their mission
having been accomplished, the dope-smuggling officers dismounted
their perches and undoubtedly returned to Mexico for a well-
deserved cerveza or two.

With the "eyes in the sky" gone, I was now free to move about
between the brush and shadows. I could hear the mules coming but
couldn't see exactly where they were in the darkness. Do I go east or
west? North or south? It didn't matter. As luck would have it, for better or for worse, the smugglers were headed dead straight toward my
adopted yucca! Trying not to swallow my own drying tongue, I cautiously pulled the slit poncho over my head like a bashful turtle. Planting both boots firmly beneath my haunches, I slowly inched my way
standing straight up on the back side of the cover of the tall yucca in
an attempt to take refuge from the approaching force. Focusing on the
waiting load car, the mules blindly raced by my yucca with their bags
over their shoulders. When the last one went by, one of those dumb
John Wayne ideas took control of my faculties, resulting in a macho
brain fart of immense proportion. I fell in behind the last mule and
played follow-the-dope-smuggling-leader!

Okay, so here's the scenario. As we walked along, I rolled up the
poncho blanket just enough to make it look like a bundle of dope and
put it on my shoulder. As I palmed my .357 revolver for action and
walked with it behind my back, I took a corner of the blanket and slid
it over my chest, covering the badge. I kept my mouth shut and followed the guy in front of me, never taking my eyes off his back. Other
than that, I was dangling out there in the desert night just friggin'
winging it on Irish luck! I had absolutely no idea what I was going to
do when we all arrived at the load vehicle. Pretty fucking smart, huh?
Well, it's hard to make an intelligent decision when your juvenile,
sperm-enriched thought process is based on what John Wayne
would've done if he was in your boots.

So here we went, down the easy *verde* (green) money trail, me and
my newfound amigos. We got to the trunk of the load vehicle and we
were still stacked up in a military single-file rank with yours truly in

the rear-guard position. The car was a big old '72 Ford LTD with its motor running and the trunk open. The driver was a tall, fat Mexican/East L.A. type who, standing in the dark near the back of the car with a flat cholo hat on, resembled a stout rendition of Smokey the fucking Bear. With the trunk of the car open, Smokey had his back to us because he was bent over stacking the dope as he took one bag at a time from the line of mules.

I have to admit, it was a pretty orderly little operation. There was no cluster fuck at the rear of the car. You stood in line until your turn to advance and dump into the LTD's trunk. As I stood there and waited my turn, I kept hearing this ripping noise followed by some kind of bouncing thuds on metal. As each mule departed after dumping, he would retreat into the brush at a side angle from the trunk, where I was last in line. The questioning passing glances I got in the dark from the now southbound mules would have been funny if I hadn't been so damn scared.

After about thirty seconds, everybody else had dumped their merchandise and skittered back for Mexico, leaving me next and last up. Things were going pretty good so far. By this time I had figured out what the metal-thud-bouncing noise was. It had been the kilos of hard brick-wrapped dope hitting the bottom and sides of the car's trunk. But I still hadn't figured out what the ripping noise was all about. Smokey was still bent over the trunk of the car stacking dope when I stepped up to the batter's box. He had yet not turned around to ask for my simulated poncho bag.

As the smuggler leaned over the trunk and worked stacking the dope, he asked me in Spanish for my bag of *merca* (dope). At this point in my young career, I still spoke Spanish like a webbed-mouth gringo. So when he asked me for the bag, I didn't want to open my mouth and let the cat out of the bag just yet. Without turning around, Smokey kept requesting my bag in a hurried whisper. He finally got pissed off and turned in anger to chew me out. When he shifted his fat ass around I learned the hard way what had been making the ripping noise. In his right hand, partially glistening in the night's limited light, was a fully extended ten- or twelve-inch switchblade. The knife was no more than several inches from my belly button when Smokey looked into my face and realized I wasn't one of his dope-smuggling compas.

Talk about shit or go blind! The Bear was about to make a move in the direction of putting a toe tag on my young ass when my survival instinct took over. I pulled the balled-up poncho off my shoulder and slid it down across my chest for protection. The outlaw slashed from right to left, crossing my midsection. Only cutting the top layer of cotton weave, he countered by an extended thrust, jabbing for my gut. As I sidestepped, the Bear precariously leaned past me, leaving himself wide open and vulnerable. My turn, asshole!

I used the steel barrel of my .357 Magnum combat Smith & Wesson as if it were a dungeon-issued medieval baton of pain. One blow between his neck and right shoulder sent Smokey crashing to my boots like a rainsoaked sack of Idaho potatoes. As he went down, his grip on the knife opened and the blade shot out of his hand into the reptile-infested desert sands. I kicked the blade out of the smuggler's reach and then jumped into the middle of his shit to give him an attitude adjustment. The fight abruptly ended when I threatened to skull-cap the Bear with my Magnum if he didn't surrender.

I cuffed the guy up and radioed for help. We ended up with about six hundred pounds of grass in the back of the LTD and a sullen, moaning Bear of a prisoner. Back at the Border Patrol station my immediate supervisor severely reprimanded me for the stunt I had pulled. He scolded me for posing as a mule and mixing in with the smugglers. In true hangdog fashion, I dropped my head, agreeing with the boss that it may have been a bad idea. Without contesting the admonishment, I knew I had done what had to be done. In the heat of the moment you've got to be willing to improvise to get the job done. Sure, I was a uniformed agent not authorized to work in a semi-undercover position. But the overall technique had worked. Years later, I would draw upon that experience as a plainclothes special agent for the U.S. Customs Service.

The School of Hard Knocks has been one of my best teachers. It has given me invaluable lessons on survival. In both Vietnam and on the Mexican border, I have learned that you are one stupid son of a bitch if you don't realize the need to understand and respect your enemy. You don't have to love him, but you damn well better know him. It is imperative that you obtain and analyze every bit of data concerning your adversary if you're going to rise above him. That includes studying his habits and personality from birth to death. You need to know about his family, his personal history, his values, his morals, his country, and his country's history. All of these things can give you the insight as to what makes the guy tick. If you don't have such knowledge you won't be as apt to anticipate his moves or overcome him in a confrontation. Pure luck will take you just so far as an agent in the border drug wars.

Many years of living on the border in Cochise County helped me learn about the Mexican people and their culture. As a Border Patrol agent, and later as a U.S. Customs special agent, I have been in continual contact with the Mexican narcotics backpackers we so commonly refer to as mules. Most of these guys were usually between the ages of sixteen and twenty-five, and they were in excellent physical condition. Some of the mules were raised in the economically depressed, filthy little border towns of Agua Prieta and Naco. However, a good majority migrated to the border from small, faltering farms or ranches in the Mexican states of Sonora and Chihuahua. They were usually illiterate, having been denied the opportunity to go to school because their folks needed them to work in the fields. So in essence, their choices as to how to make a living were extremely limited by their very humble beginnings. And that is the shameful difference between the decadent gringos and the plain-Jane Mexicans. Most of these illiterate pobrecitos never even had one fucking chance right out of the gate. But so many of us have had numerous chances, and we still chose to throw them away. Sinful.

Mules, for the most part, are a hard, silent group of young men who make their living the best way they can. I'm not condoning what they do, I'm just saying that's what they do because they have to put food on the table for their families. You have to view mules as a combined product of the drug trade and border economics.

They're uneducated and living in a corrupt country where there aren't enough decent-paying jobs to even begin to go around. To put it in another light, if you had a family to feed, which option would you elect? Would you be willing to work all week in an unsafe, stifling Mexican factory for the average pittance of $15? Or would you rather make one night's hump through the desert packing a forty- to sixty-pound bundle of merca on your back for the average mule rate of about $1,000?

As a rule of thumb, these farm-boy mules aren't a hard-core bunch with a real propensity for violence. There's a lot of difference between them and the military-trained mules that we've gone up against, such as the Big Sandy organization. However, like any cornered desperado, these farm-boy types have been known to fight to the death if they think they have a chance to escape a lengthy prison term. But more times than not, these boys have enough sense to surrender when the odds are against them.

Unlike the dope lords and kingpins who cry and squirm to make a deal when they get busted, mules sit there stoically and take their medicine when you bring them before the judge. This is one of the disciplines I most admire about these fellers. They accept responsibility for breaking the law and they're ready to suffer the consequences without sniveling like a goddamn baby about it.

The Mexicans have a nickname for anybody that has a measure of common sense and natural instincts to survive the elements. "Coyote" sometimes refers to a crossing guide for illegal aliens or an experienced backpacking dope smuggler who knows his way through the mountains and desert around the border agents. Like his four-legged canine namesake, a coyote is adept at walking fifteen or twenty miles in the dark in whatever weather the heavens may throw down at him. He never uses any kind of artificial light to maneuver in the darkness, and he is able to guide off the mountain peaks using nothing more than the meekest of available starlight.

The coyote-type mules were the ones we spent most of our time pursuing east of Douglas and west of Naco. Each of these guys was able to backpack forty to sixty pounds of dope over rough terrain during a round trip of about twenty miles. The average dope-smuggling operation consisted of six to ten coyotes making up the mule train. If their stash site was a two-day walk into Arizona from Mexico, they would designate one mule to carry nothing but enough food for all of them. Usually they would carry a partial ration of water, choosing to drink from available muddy cattle tanks and water holes along the way so they didn't have to carry the extra weight.

The mules we pursued were extremely adaptable and efficient in their drug-war duties in the high Sonoran Desert. Some of the rations they concocted came right out of the Apache-raiding-days cookbook. We once caught six mules with 240 pounds of marijuana that they were backpacking in the middle of the scorching Arizona summer heat across thirty miles of the San Bernardino Valley. When we snuck up on them in their mesquite-limb hideout, they were covered from head to chest with an ivory paste as they sat eating in a circle.

Initially we thought that the heat had fried the fellers' brains and they had taken to eating a bag of caustic mine lime they had found. But upon closer examination, we found the paste to be dribbles of some kind of a "power gruel." The border outlaws had mixed raw unbleached flour into a gallon of water combined with sugar, limes, and lemons. It made a messy, thick, gooey "Mexican sports drink" that was in fact a distant relative of an old Apache energy-boosting recipe. According to Matthew Magoffin, one of our Cochise County ranchers who doubles as a U.S. Fish and Wildlife officer, Cochise's and Geronimo's raiders would mix a flour made out of ground mesquite beans with water to get them across the desert when running from the Mexicans or U.S. Cavalry. The only difference was that the sugar and citrus might have been a little hard to come by in these parts a century ago. But then again, I reckon that's why they called them "raiding parties."

Whereas most border agents have to use binos and night goggles to aid their vision in night operations, it always seemed like the mules had the edge on us when we went up against them in the dark. There's no doubt that for some inherent reason the mules have better night vision than us. I've spent hours talking it over with numerous agents, and the best answer we've been able to come up with has been handed down by some older and wiser border-war veterans. These agents think that the mules, and particularly the coyote ranks of mules, have better night-vision cones because their eyes haven't been spoiled by artificial lights like the gringos'. In other words, the ranches and farms they were raised on have no electricity. So it would stand to reason that their night vision is superior because it has been frequently used and exercised after each dusk of their lives. Just like any of your other body parts. Use it or lose it.

Over my many years of federal border enforcement, I've seen some astounding physical feats performed by mules. These guys have been known to jump six-foot fences in a single leap, outrun locomotives before they get to a railroad crossing, and even elude high-velocity bullets that were meant for them. Okay, maybe they aren't as great as Superman. But I shit you not, these little Mexican fuckers are exceptional in the mountains and deserts. How many folks do you know who after taking a dump in the desert are tough enough to wipe their asses with a goddamn lava rock? I ain't pulling your leg at all. I've seen that and much, much more.

I've seen these guys pull their boots off after going thirty miles without a stitch of socks on. I've seen these guys slash their own legs open with the sharp edge of a mesquite stick to bleed out a fresh rattlesnake bite. I've seen the fuckers sew themselves up with a common house needle and cotton thread. And yes, I've even helped scrub and bandage their war wounds, open sores, and blistered, bleeding feet. Why? Because even though they are my sworn adversaries, I can't deny the bewildered look of defeat in their eyes when they go down in chains and cuffs. They've just lost their master's dope load. At the very minimum if the boss doesn't whack them when they get out of jail and return to Mexico, it means they won't get paid for the thirty miles of rough terrain they just busted their balls over. But more than that, they know it means their kids back home probably won't eat next week, or even the week after that.

Most of these boys ain't educated enough to figure out how to push the button on an office water cooler to get a drink. Don't laugh.

It's the honest to God truth, because I've had to show them and hold the button down. Where you may think that pathetic, they have other attributes you'll never even come close to in your wildest dreams. You know how those mountain-climbing pro dudes use the picks and pitons to ascend a rocky bluff that goes straight up? Mickey Mouse crap! We've seen mules go up the same incline using only their bare fingers and tennis-shoe-covered toes. And they were doing it with sixty-pound backpacks of marijuana hanging off their asses! The only gringos I've ever seen giving such comparable performances have been the U.S. Special Forces.

After years of studying the mules and their habits, I realized that about the only way you were ever gonna be able to catch them was to be waiting for them at the end of their route north. We had tried all the other options without a lot of success. If you got behind them on their tracks and attempted to run them to ground, their rear guard would spot you a mile or two away. That gave the little shits enough time to bury the dope in a sand draw and wipe out their tracks, leaving you wandering around in circles for a day or so. The only way to catch them when you were tracking them was to be on horseback. And a lot of the time you just couldn't always be trailering a horse with you, so that wasn't a really feasible option.

Another option was to lie in ambush on the trail in the middle of their route north. This was somewhat plausible, but there were two problems with this type of operation. First, the mules were moving and "heated up" when you'd hit them. In other words, they were at their twin emotional and physical peaks for action. If you weren't in a position to jump straight down on their backs and take them to the ground in a lightning-fast strike, forget it. Once they got loose in the dark, they were like ghosts. The second problem with hitting them like this was that the elusive coyotes vacillated on which trail north they would use. They knew that if our best trackers had located their route from their last trip, we'd be waiting for them on the trail during their next run. So you could end up sitting on the wrong trail for a week or two enjoying the company of Arizona's rattlers, scorpions, and tarantulas as they tried to crawl up your goddamn boots and pants legs.

Now, the years of hard-bought experience were about to pay off. Regressing to what I had done as a young Border Patrol agent, I presented an idea to the other Customs agents. The best way to take the coyote ranks down was for us to act as mules and infiltrate their trains. We could do it when the train arrived at the stash site up north at the end of the route. But we weren't going to be able to do it half-assed. I mean we had to be dressed like mules, look like mules, smell like mules, fart like mules, and ultimately speak Spanish like mules. And these were only the easy elements of the plan.

The difficult part was toward the end of the op. Before the smuggler with the vehicle got there to pick up the load, you had to have already taken the mules down and be in possession of the dope! That was the key to making the whole op a success. Once we had the dope we would have control of the situation. We could reduce the risk of violence during the pickup. After all the damaging high-speed pursuits and shootings we had been in, we knew it was time to figure out another way of taking the drivers down without putting so many lives at risk.

Now that we'd come up with the plan, we needed the right kind of agents to pull it off. We had to have a minimum of one or two Spanish-speaking agents who could pass as fluent Mexican coyotes. We had to grow some hair, get a little grubby gross thing going, and not take a bath or shower for a night or two before the op. For real, no friggin personal hygiene. The mules had such a keen awareness about them that, if the wind was right, some of them could actually smell freshly washed gringos waiting up ahead in ambush on the trails. It's the soap and deodorant that Americans take for granted. If they'd smell or see anything out of the ordinary, the coyotes would abort the smuggling attempt by returning the dope to Mexico. Sound a little far-fetched? Not really. When our recon team would hump the bush in Nam, we knew we were in Indian country when we'd smell fish and rice cooking in the jungle. It takes a coyote to catch a coyote.

We had one agent from the Border Alliance Group (BAG) who was absolutely right-as-rain perfect for the type of op we wanted to do. Agent Jesse Gutierrez was a narcotics officer from the Arizona

Department of Public Safety (DPS). He was about the same height and size as a Mexican mule and he already looked hairy and grubby, being that he routinely worked undercover for DPS. At forty-five, Jesse was a veteran of the drug wars. He strutted about with shoulder-length, wild, curly black hair and an equally unkempt scraggly-ass beard. He was a little older than most mules, but in the dark of night the bad guys weren't going to be able to tell his age. What they would see is a Mexican dude with long, unruly hair and dark camouflage clothing just like them. Most important, what they would hear would be the selling part of our op: a fluent Spanish speaker who knew the ins and outs of the dope trade.

After we had the plan down we didn't have to wait too long for the first chance to put it into operation. A couple of days later we got a call from an informant about a load of dope that was already being muled north across the desert to a stash site near Highway 80 in the San Bernardino Valley. The snitch told us exactly where the mules were going to arrive and gave us a pretty good window of opportunity on the arrival time. Jesse and I suited up in clothing similar to that of the mules. We wore camouflage Army-issued fatigues and allowed our curly locks to drip out from under our black skullcaps. Our pistolas were stowed away under our fatigue jackets and even if I say so, we looked damn good!

We set out to the brush shortly after sundown. According to our informant, the mules were supposed to arrive at about 9:00 p.m. under a designated bridge as planned with their driver. Then any time after 9:00 p.m., the pickup man would drive through the area and make contact with the mules by flashing his headlights or honking his car horn. Jesse and I got into position under the bridge two to three hours ahead of the mule train's arrival. The wait is a little long, but if you're not early enough getting in, the train's forward scout will in all probability burn you.

That's one of the reasons that you need to hook up with a well-liked partner on ops like these. It's not unusual for us to end up spending more time with each other than our own wives. But I guarandamntee that the time I spent waiting in ambushes with Jesse was anything but boring. His sense of humor was outrageous. It seemed to go hand in hand with his unruly hair and beard. It had absolutely no boundaries. I mean you never knew what the fucker was going to come up with next. You could be sitting there in pitch black darkness being as quiet as a mouse when a billowing blue flame would singe your eyebrows. No, it wasn't the beginning of a shoot-out. Jesse had quietly positioned his expelling bowel orifice in the proper launch position and had used a Bic cigarette lighter to hurl the ignited gas flame toward your face! I'll say one thing for his adolescent antics: They kept you on your toes, and that's the way you should be on an op.

We had been hiding between the rocks under the bridge for about two hours when we heard brush breaking off in the desert about a hundred yards from our position. It was a black-ass night with no moon. The stars afforded some low-level light but your vision was severely diminished past five or ten yards. The breaking of brush became louder and louder as the mules approached the bridge. You think that you'll see them off in the distance at any moment as they slowly creep in like smoke over water. But it never is like you imagine it's going to happen. You keep hearing the noise and then all of a sudden, like an old B horror flick, you get suckered, almost wanting to gasp for breath. Seemingly out of thin air, the phantoms have landed five short yards in front of you. It scares the shit out of a guy because it's as if they just floated in!

Your heart starts pumping about 150 beats per minute. It's pounding so hard that you're scared the mules can hear it. Your mouth becomes as dry as a popcorn fart, and the palms of your hands are so wet from sweat that you're worried your pistol will slip free from between your fear-locked fingers. At this very moment your senses are racing your thoughts for control of your body. You have to slow down, concentrate, impede the irrational impulses, and draw conclusions from past experiences. You try to convince yourself that these guys are only human. As spooky as they may have appeared, they put their pants on one leg at a time like anybody else. The question now is, how many of them are armed?

Jesse and I were lying motionless with our faces down so the coyotes wouldn't see the reflection from our eyes. We had hoped that the train would check the area out and then settle down, being satisfied there weren't any immediate threats. Most of the eight mules had started to take their backpacks off and relax in the crest of the bridge. One guy who apparently was the train's leader kept walking among the mules, whispering orders, directing that the dope be stashed and covered. This guy was going to be our main problem. Being in charge of the train, it's his responsibility if the load is lost for any reason. He has to answer to the big *jefes* (bosses) in Mexico. And it was common knowledge that your chances of living were less than fifty-fifty during a Mexican drug lord's angered inquisition of "Who has our merca, *cabrón* [bastard]*?*"

Wanting to keep our faces down, Jesse and I would glance up on occasion, catching glimpses of the train's leader as he tenaciously scouted the area. You know how you get that bad gut feeling when your instincts tell you something fucked up is about to happen? I felt it rising all the way up to my throat when this coyote son of a bitch looked our way. He eventually spotted something lying out of place on the bottom of the bridge. He slowly inched his way toward us to take a better look. As he approached, he would take several steps, then pause and whisper a bluff in Spanish, "I see you, pendejos!" You could tell by the way he was going about it that he wasn't really sure we were bodies or maybe something like fallen yucca trunks. Jesse and I kept our faces down toward the ground and relied solely on our ears. Any little twitch from us and our parade was gonna be rained on big-time. Frozen in the moment, all I could think of was how fucked we were gonna be if Jesse farted right about now.

The mule train's leader twice more whispered bluffing statements toward us. Each time would be words to the effect of "I know you're there!" or "Who are you?" The challenges were each time followed by several more daring footsteps in our direction. But the third time he challenged us we didn't hear the accompanying footsteps. What we did hear was that unforgettable metal cranking sound of a semi-automatic handgun being locked and loaded! A tingling sensation coursed through my brain as my conscious state ordered my arms and legs to freeze. My asshole puckered up so fast that it nearly sucked my damn underwear out of sight. The memory of black body bags raced through my mind. The Reaper was laughing and clickin' them bones again!

My heart was pounding in my ears so loud that I would've been prevented from hearing a nuclear holocaust. The dark shadow stood there deciding if it was worth the noise or not to crank off a round to find out if we were deadwood or soon-to-be dead bodies. The only part of my body that moved was my thumb when I took the safety off my pistol. Jesse was being cool. He wasn't budging a bit to the lead mule's challenges. I wasn't worried about Jesse being ready when the shit hit the fan. I'd been in tough spots before with this Arizona DPS agent and I knew he was a reactor and not a spectator.

We were both poised and ready to strike when a second shadowy figure worked his way over to the lead coyote. The subordinate argued with the leader that it would give their position away if he capped a round at the log. Jesse and I thought for a moment that the problem would go away. But oh, no. This other shithead had a better idea. Let's throw big rocks and see if the logs move! Jesse and I buried our heads under our arms as the grenade-size rocks hit within inches of our skulls.

I didn't know what Jesse thought about this shit, but I for one was ready to cap the asshole with the Nolan Ryan pitching arm. Let me tell ya, an 80-mph rock will put your goodtime lights out! After several hard-thrown rocks had been zinged in on us, the mules stopped and looked for movement. The two dickheads quietly squabbled for a few more seconds. Jesse and I never budged, lending credibility that we were no more than logs or shadows. Both mules eventually turned their backs on us and kicked back, relaxing in the sand draw. It wasn't until they calmed down that my colon did likewise. I lay there dripping in sweat, wondering how it was that a feller named Jesse Gutierrez would have Irish blood coursing through his veins.

We waited for several more hours, sharing the sand draw and Arizona night with the dope smugglers. They rested, ate, and watered up, preparing for their return trip south. As is the accepted dope-smuggling method of operation, the head mule usually departs with most of the train to get back into Mexico before sunup. One mule will remain behind to guard the stash until the pickup vehicle arrives. This particular train of dope smugglers left two mules with the load as they departed. Not knowing how many of them were armed, Jesse and I decided that discretion indeed was the better part of valor. We let the majority of the train return south, giving us better-than-even odds of pulling the op off without getting whacked. Knowing how the Mexican chain of command works, we were fairly sure that the armed leader had left for Mexico.

As the pickup time was nearing, Jesse and I made our move on the two remaining mules as they slept near the dope load in the draw. They were rudely awakened by the sound of our pistols being cocked close to their ears. Without incident, we quietly cuffed them and shackled their legs for transport. They each had pocket knives but other than that they were unarmed. We called one of our agents who was waiting in a pursuit vehicle off the highway to come bag and tag our catch. Before we turned them over to the agent, Jesse and I swapped caps and shirts with the mules in case the driver had previously met them and knew what they looked like. Then we returned to the bridge and waited.

While we were waiting, Jesse and I decided to move the dope from the draw closer to the bridge for easier loading. This is something the mules would have done anyway about fifteen minutes before the pickup. As we humped the bags to the edge of the bridge a car approached and slowed down, pulling to the edge of the highway where it meets the bridge. The driver honked his horn three short blasts and then picked up his speed continuing on north. Showtime! We knew this was going to be our pickup guy, so Jesse and I ran back and forth with the bags of dope, piling them up on the edge of the bridge.

The smuggler drove past the bridge about a mile and then turned around, squealing his tires on the pavement. Jesse and I hunkered down low behind the bags on the edge of the highway and waited. As the load car came back to us, the edge of his headlights silhouetted our bodies lying on the side of the bridge with the load. The smuggler pulled up next to us and stopped with the trunk of the car parallel to the bags. The driver got out of the car and started cussing and berating us in Spanish. He was complaining that we were late with the load and it was going to be his ass if we got caught. He went off on a tongue-lashing fit befitting a Southern Baptist minister lecturing a group of whores on the Sabbath. I guess mules don't rate too high on the dope smuggler's food chain.

We wanted to get some good incriminating statements that would stand up in court, so Jesse engaged the guy in Spanish by asking him where he wanted us to stow the dope. The guy went off on another tangent, screaming, "You fucking dumb bean-eating pendejos know the shit goes in the goddamn trunk!" The guy was really pissed off by the time he got out of the car to open the trunk for us. The more the guy cussed, the funnier Jesse and I thought it was. I mean the whole thing was getting "we got this guy by the balls" ridiculous!

As he opened the trunk and stood by the side of the car, I was still kneeling behind the dope. We knew it was going to be a problem when I stood up because even in the dark, the bad guy would know I was too damn tall for a Mexican mule. As Jesse approached the trunk of the vehicle with a couple of dope bags, I walked behind him, using him as cover to get close to the smuggler. I bent my knees and held a couple of bags directly in front of me to hide my height. Jesse threw his bags in the trunk of the car and stood to the side, allowing me the same shot. Out of the corner of my eye I saw Jesse easing his pistol from under his camouflage jacket. We were on the edge of doing this asshole.

Still crouching, I discarded my bags in the trunk and then stood straight up like a towering Texas oak. It was too dark to see the alarm in the asshole's eyes but his voice betrayed any doubt he may have had now. After I stood up the first words out of his mouth were, "Who the fuck are you guys?" He got his answer when Jesse drew down on him, announcing the resounding phrase border outlaws have for more than a century regretted hearing: "*Policía*, freeze!" After all of these years I'm still amazed that we do that stupid shit. It's like saying, "BOO! Fight or run!" But the courts and lawyers have mandated that we have to properly identify ourselves, so we do what we gotta do to satisfy the legal beagles.

The dope smuggler went sky-high 10–8 on us and tried to take off like a scalded-ass jackrabbit. Before he got a head start, Jesse jumped on his back and put a choke hold on the guy's neck. There was a pretty good fracas going on between the two when I did the NFL line-backer number on the asshole's legs and we all went crashing into the desert gravel. The good news was that the bad guy didn't have a chance to palm his pistola. The bad news was that he fought us tooth and nail until we locked him down in a classic half nelson World Wrestling Federation move.

The outlaw was bagged, tagged, and shipped off to jail to be housed with his previously arrested compañeros. Jesse and I later learned from the prosecuting Cochise County attorney that the driver was from Los Angeles, where he was hooked up with a fairly large dope-smuggling family. It seemed like the family was rather fond of the dickhead so they hired an expensive defense attorney to fight us in court. The case never went to trial, which doesn't surprise me consider-ing who muled the grass load to the car. However, the guy's guilty plea was absolutely one of a kind for a dope-smuggling case. His slime-bag defense attorney was trying to make a deal with the prosecutor for a guilty plea based on the defense scheme of "temporary insanity." And you may not believe this, but the temp insanity was supposedly due to the guy's service in the Mexican Army! I reckon you gotta come up with a really exotic and imaginative bullshit of an excuse after ordering narcs to load your car with two hundred pounds of grass!

As you might expect, this agent-muling tactic worked out so well that we put it in our ops on a regular basis. If we had an investigative scenario that it would fit, we didn't hesitate to pull the op out of our bag of tricks. But we didn't just limit ourselves to loading vehicles after intercepting the mule trains. We later expanded the program by actually delivering the dope to farms and ranches in Cochise County. We got so brazen about doing it that we wouldn't just take the dope to its final destination, we'd also make sure we got enough incriminating actions and conversations to be used in court against the bad guys.

For instance, if we knew the train was supposed to drop the load in a barn or a garage, we'd take it a step or two further. We'd stash the dope in the yard or under a tree and approach the residence. One of us would tap on the bedroom window, waking up the guy who was supposed to receive the load. Naturally, he'd haul his ass out of bed half asleep and ask us what the problem was. We'd come up with some cock-and-bull story about not knowing where he wanted the dope stashed and ask him to come out and show us where he wanted it. Most of these guys would figure we were dumb, incompetent Mexicans who didn't know shit from Shinola. Then they'd come out of the house with that attitude of, oh well, I'm up now so I might as well handle the dope myself. Talk about burning yourself with a jury! By the time we were done muling dope around Cochise County, the bad guys became so paranoid that they were damn near asking mules for proof of identification before they'd accept delivery.

Now that I have time to look back over the years of chasing these guys, I'd have to say that border agents and mules have a good deal in common. They both work for REMFs who sit hundreds or even thousands of miles away and dictate policy without having any idea what it's like to be in the real rodeo. We share the same risks and hazards the Wild Western Sonoran Desert has to offer, while the Washington REMFs and Colombian drug lords recline in their ivory towers. I guess what it all comes down to when the smoke has cleared is this: I've got more respect for these desert-humping, ball-busting mules than I could ever have for the REMFs in D.C. Sad but true.

Theodore Roosevelt once said, "The credit belongs to the man who is actually in the arena, whose face is marred by dust and sweat and blood." I believe that's an eternally accurate statement, on both sides of the fence. Not wanting to be misunderstood on the issue, let me go on record saying that I don't necessarily like mules. Hell, until the day I draw my last breath I'll continue to go out of my way to incarcerate the dope-smuggling little bastards. But give the devil his due; I think you can now understand why I begrudgingly find them somewhat admirable.

13

The Last Trackers

THE HUNTING AND TRACKING of men and animals is an art handed down over the centuries. A century or so ago, if you didn't know how to track and cut sign, you didn't eat. It was that simple. These days, however, the modern conveniences afforded by fast-food chains and shopping centers have severely curbed the need for the skill. Still a valid hunting tool, it is only used by a dwindling number of those who are qualified to conduct and teach the art.

Even the U.S. Border Patrol, whose agents for decades have been recognized by federal courts throughout the land as expert trackers, is beginning to feel the pinch caused by modern technology. State-of-the-art electronic sensors, long-range cameras, night-vision devices, and other futuristic military hardware have most definitely diminished the desire for newly hired Border Patrol agents to learn tracking skills. It seems as though the younger agents are becoming more and more dependent on the computer-age tools the government now uses. Instead of Border Patrol, it may be more appropriate in the new millennium to rename the organization the Border Response Agency. That's basically what they do, being that a myriad of gizmos now direct them where to go to make their arrests. The true days of patrolling, cutting sign, and tracking are rapidly fading into history. I fear that within the next twenty or so years, it's quite feasible that the skill will all but disappear into our Old West past.

Oh, sure, just about any mediocre soldier, agent, or city-slicker hunter can follow solid tracks left in the dirt or sand. But that's not what I'm talking about here. What I'm talking about is the part of tracking that most people in this country know absolutely zero about: sign cutting. That means that you're trailing an animal or man without the benefit of good soil that reveals a track. In other words, you have to follow the mere disturbance in nature left by your prey. It's a matter of a pebble that's been turned over here or there. A tiny solitary broken limb of brush. A clump of grass that's lying back to one side when it should actually be lying back to the opposite side because of prevailing winds. A spiderweb that's been broken through. A single fiber of material snagged on a cactus thorn. And that's just the half of it. From those signs you have to be able to tell the direction of travel. How much weight the man or beast is carrying. How long ago they may have passed through the area. Are they walking calmly? Are they running in fear? Are they wounded, sick, or healthy? What stars, mountains, or water holes are they guiding on? I guarandamntee that this is a skill that can *never* be taught in the classroom.

Among those left in Cochise County who would be considered true artists of the skill is a cattle rancher named Matthew Magoffin. I first met Matt around 1987 when he was ranching at the southern end of the Peloncillos, east of Douglas on the U.S.-Mexican border near the Arizona-New Mexico state line. He would later go on to become a border narcotics-enforcement agent working first for the U.S. Fish and Wildlife Service, and later for the U.S. Customs Service Office of Investigations.

A red-faced Scots-Irishman with blue, burning embers for eyes, Matt is one of the best-humored Arizona cowboys I've ever had the pleasure of sitting a saddle with. He sports a turned-down, unruly mustache that tends to outline his square, jutting chin. High cheekbones and short-cropped brown hair accent a determined face that has overcome thousands of obstacles associated with living and ranching on the border. Always making his living in the sun and elements, the wiry, leather-skinned lad is never without a wide-brimmed, sweat-stained cowboy hat. His lace-up rawhide Chippewa riding-heel boots are skinned and scraped from toe to heel. They tell the story of how hard it is to hang on here. Matt is a fine example of the grit a man needs to dig in and remain in this part of the country.

At first glance, most Yankees would brand the Scots-Irishman as a redneck because of his appearance and macho, steel-clenched handshake. But the boy ain't anything like those ignorant racist sons of bitches from the South. Matt is what I would have to call a primo male specimen of the Arizona rancher. He emanates the spirit of the pioneers who settled this country. Hard as nails and as honest as the day is long, when the going gets tough and the faint of heart have flushed out on you, Matt will be there with you until the bitter end.

Matt grew up on a ranch at the northern end of the Mexican Sierra Madres, which he would one day inherit from his folks. The original ranch house had been built down in Guadalupe Canyon at the southern end of the New Mexico and Arizona Peloncillos on the Mexican border. The ranch house burned down when Matt was just a pup, and the family rebuilt, choosing to relocate a few miles to the west in the San Bernardino Valley just off Geronimo Trail. As a sprouting kid with an abundance of adolescent curiosity, Matt roamed the Peloncillos and San Bernardino Valley on foot and horseback. He hiked and rode the same trails that the Chiricahua Apaches forged in and out of Mexico during their bloody raids. It was an upbringing that would help Matt become one of the most knowledgeable trackers and self-taught historians in southeastern Arizona.

During one of our many horse patrols together, Matt took Sperling and me to an old abandoned outlaw hideout in the Peloncillos near the top of Guadalupe Canyon. Believed to have been used by vermin such as the Clantons, it was a three-walled stone hut backed up against a creek bank hidden beneath a thick stand of scrub oak. The luxuries were limited, but the view toward Tombstone across the San Bernardino Valley was outstanding. It was from that direction that any approaching posse would ride in after the outlaws. When the vermin spotted the riders' dust coming across the valley, they would simply saddle up and ride south down Guadalupe Canyon into old Mexico, where they would hide under the protection of the red, white, and green flag. Some things just never change out here in the West. To this day, the outlaws are still running south from the law and thumbing their noses at us from their sanctuary on Mexican soil.

Matt taught me and a lot of the other border agents a good deal about the history and legends of the area. Just the highlights alone would be enough for an entire book. Among other things, we learned why Bunk Robinson Peak, which is a high, knobby knoll rising in the middle of the Peloncillo range, was so named. Turned out that Bunk was one stubborn hard-ass miner who paid more heed to his "gotta find it" fever than his commonsense fear of the Chiricahua Apaches. Although his life departed this earth with the removal of his scalp, his name will never be forgotten. Every U.S. and Mexican map of the Peloncillos and Sierra Madres is branded with Bunk Robinson Peak, which is a reference point that can be seen all the way across the San Bernardino Valley.

A fine memorial for a feller who staked a claim to a mountain that he would soon be murdered on. I reckon that back in those days if you had died in a city someone might have taken the time to write you a fine obituary. But out here, where the three worlds of the Apaches, the Mexicans, and the outlaws joined, you got a mountain named after you for living and dying in a violent fashion. In fact, if you study the area long enough, that seems to be the rule of thumb. There are mountains and canyons dubbed Cochise Stronghold, Clanton's Draw, Skeleton Canyon, Mexican Camp, Geronimo Trail, Outlaw Mountain, and a whole slew of others. And each one of those landmarks has its own haunting past that Matt can spin a pretty good yarn or two about.

Sperling and I have spent a good deal of time with Matt, cutting sign and tracking down dope smugglers and other outlaws. It usually would commence with Matt calling us out to his ranch whenever he stumbled across some fresh tracks coming up out of old Mexico. But it expanded more into a professional relationship when he hired on with the U.S. Fish and Wildlife Service as an enforcement officer. His official enforcement area was supposed to have been limited to the San Bernardino Wildlife Refuge, about twenty miles east of Douglas. The refuge incorporates what used to be the rangeland owned by "Texas" John Slaughter where it bumps up against the Mexican border. But realizing just how big a hand Matt would be to us out there, we talked ourselves blue in the face persuading the U.S. Customs Service REMFs in D.C. to allow the Douglas agents to hire this premier tracker. So instead of fencing Matt into just enforcement on the refuge, he was unleashed to uphold the law in an area that practically covered the whole southeastern corner of Arizona. In fact, when you come right down to it, Matt *was* the only law in Arizona east of Silver Creek.

With the nearest lawman usually at least thirty miles away, Matt wore a lot of different badges. He enforced the laws against narcotics smuggling, cattle rustling, wildlife and game poaching, burglaries, thefts, illegal immigration, and just about any other felonious acts he happened across. Although the Douglas Customs agents performed a lot of these duties with Matt out in the southeast corner of Arizona over the years, one of the most memorable enforcement operations we worked together turned out to be a smuggled load of illegal aliens from a whole other hemisphere.

Matt had been cutting the sign of some dope smugglers who kept crossing the border just east of the San Bernardino Refuge, where he was stationed. So in response to the crossings, he bugged their route with electronic sensors and waited for their next attempt. It was only a couple of nights before the bugs sounded off, sending Matt barreling up Geronimo Trail in the middle of the night toward the refuge. While en route, Matt radioed for Sperling and me to drive out his way to lend a hand. We all *junta*ed (met up) on the trail just east of Silver Creek. It was about midnight and we were expecting to run into a group of about six to eight armed dope smugglers. So accordingly, we took the time to get all decked out in our bullet-proof vests and camouflage fatigues. We loaded our vest pockets with extra ammo and augmented our firepower with a shotgun, MP-5 submachine gun, and a Ruger

Mini-14 assault carbine. All in all, when we were fully saddled up and ready for action, I'd have to say we looked pretty goddamn grim.

We hit the brush line and headed south into the mesquites and catclaws bolstered in the belief that we were the meanest mother-fuckers in the southeastern corner of Arizona that night. Little did these bold ones know that we were about to be proven foolishly wrong. Sperling was point man with Matt and me following. We were slipping along silently in the brush at a pretty good clip toward the border when Sperling held up a clenched fist as a signal to stop and listen. We immediately dropped to our knees, training our hardware out in front of us between the greasewoods and mesquites.

Beneath the bright, starlit sky, the desert floor was drenched with a milky light that outlined the mesquites. Suspicious, contorted black shadows lay at the bottom of the mesquites and brush. Silent, on-the-verge-of-shitting-your-pants moments like this cause you to probe the depths of your most dreadful fears. Did that dark spot just move its head? Was that a slight glimmering of metal? A gun barrel? A blade? Just before the shit hits the fan, you always get that same empty, dead-silent ringing in your ears. It's like every animal, bug, and reptile are all taking in their last breath before the anticipated eruption.

As we knelt and waited with sweat beading across our fore-heads, there was that uncanny stillness in the air that usually sug-gests that an uh-oh is about to rain down on your body. The only thing that could have possibly enhanced the spookiness of the entire situation would have been for the date to be October 31. We cupped our hands to our ears and held our breath as we strained to pick up any sound of suspicious movement. For a minute or so we heard nothing more than the distant yipping of a pack of coyotes on the hunt. After they made their kill, their frantic howling subsided, returning the desert floor to an eerie, lonely, time-suspended still-ness. That stillness was suddenly broken by a rustling in the brush accompanied by limbs snapping and cracking. Someone, or some-thing, was pushing its way north toward our position. We heard a low moaning, as if a man was wounded or sick. Just before the earth shook beneath our boots like a Southern Pacific freight train was passing by, we heard an unmistakable nasty-ass snorting.

The bull's low moan had now turned into an eardrum-busting full-force bellow as he lunged toward us, tearing a path through the brush that was reminiscent of a Texas tornado. I'm still not sure if it was the glow from the bull's devilish red eyes I saw coming at me, or if it wasn't the sparks off the boots of the two assholes who were about to leave me alone in their dust. But one thing was for sure: That night in a cold, lonely, desolate desert on the U.S.-Mexican border, the three meanest motherfuckers in southeastern Arizona set some major and unprecedented track records for cross-country running in the rocks in full battle dress. And when we dove into the bed of one of the trucks, it was a miracle that no one ended up with any broken bones from all of the goddamn iron we were carrying with us.

As the three meanest motherfuckers in the San Bernardino Valley fled for their lives that night, we had no idea that we would yet encounter something this same night that would get funnier, weirder, and at the same time sadder. The snorting ton-plus piece of pissed-off beef kept us "treed" in the back of our pickup truck for about half an hour. It was damn near two in the morning before he fell in love with some cow that came trailing by, swishing her chuck-roast ass in front of his nose. As the bull followed the smell of the love juices that were easing from his newfound love's calf maker, he completely forgot about his cornered boy toys. A short time later, the bull's distant bellowing turned into an erotic low growling. As any brotherly group of the menfolk gender should be, we were collectively gleeful to see one of our male comrades of the desert score. As the lovemaking and romping progressed in the dark, we stood in the back of the truck cheering the old boy on to his grand finale. Although the beef is supposed to be by far intellectually inferior to man, we later thought about it and had to question which one of us really was the dumbest. After all, the bull was the one getting his rocks off, and we were the ones being pursued across the rocks!

After the bovine porno festival ended in a dramatic brush-breaking climax, the two sweaty steak factories departed at a fairly sluggish gait. We had our fill of excitement for the night and were getting ready to call it when the goddamn sensors went off again. Being that the rawhide Romeo and Juliet had gone off in the opposite direction, we figured there may be some validity to the sensor activity. We grabbed our shoulder weapons from the beds of the pickups and once again started south through the brush toward the border using our same aligned formation. We had slowly crept to within several hundred yards of the border fence when, for the second time that night, Sperling held his clenched fist in the air. The signal rapidly sent us down on our knees to listen. This time it wasn't cattle. We could hear human footsteps and voices. This time it was the real deal. Lock-and-load time was upon us. We radioed for air support out of Tucson as we prepared our gear and minds for combat.

The Customs Service Blackhawk helicopter was immediately launched but we knew it would take him at least forty-five minutes to an hour to get to us. We were on our own. The three of us against whatever the unpredictable Mexican border was about to throw at us. The voices and footsteps kept breaking the desert's silence as the foreign intruders walked straight toward our ambush. We fully expected a toe-to-toe gunfight since we were in such a remote area of the border. As the dark figures approached our position, we hunkered down and readied for the inevitable.

When the footsteps and whispering voices got almost on top of us, we could tell it was a hell of a lot more folks than just six or eight guys. When they came to within just a few feet of our position, we simultaneously lit them up with our flashlights in one hand as we palmed our weapons in the other. As soon as the light hit them they flushed like a covey of quail in all directions. They hit the brush so quickly it was hard to tell what we had run into. We screamed back and forth to each other that none of us had seen any weapons or bundles of dope. With a sigh of relief, we knew by the way the bodies absconded that it was probably just a large group of smuggled aliens. That usually meant things wouldn't get all that weird for us. This would be the second time that night that we would be proven wrong.

All three of us broke away from each other to track the aliens down. I started down a cattle trail heading south toward the border fence. Matt and Sperling headed east or west on their respective cattle trails. I had cut sign on a group of about four or five people and it didn't take me but a few minutes to track them down to where they were hiding beneath some yuccas and mesquites. When I came up on them they were lying face down in the dust with their hands covering the sides of their faces. I illuminated them with my flashlight and ordered them in Spanish to get up. Nobody moved.

I kept shouting for them to get up and received no acknowledgment of any kind from any of them. I thought to myself, just my luck. Out of all the smuggled aliens that are going to cross the border tonight between Texas and California, I gotta end up with the only bunch of deaf ones. I cautiously knelt to the side of one of the silent figures and firmly grabbed his elbow to roll him over. When he was facing me and sitting upright, I again ordered him in Spanish to stand up. The only response I got was some kind of hand motioning as if he was trying to draw words or pictures in the air. Now, I had thought that our communication problem couldn't get much worse. Wrong again. It now looked like I had a group of deaf-mute Mexican mimes and I didn't know jack squat about miming!

Well, as we lumbered along attempting to bridge the communication gap, I got a closer look at the mime's face with my flashlight. No wonder he didn't speak Spanish—he wasn't even from this side of the globe! When I realized what we were dealing with I immediately got on my handheld radio to Matt and Sperling. We had apparently run smack-dab into the middle of an international Chinese-alien smuggling operation. And this was just the beginning of our problems for the night.

When I tried to get the group to their feet I saw that they had a young girl with them who appeared to be absolutely terrified. I mean the poor little gal was positively shivering and shaking with fear. As I moved to help her to her feet, the men shifted their stances into defensive positions around her. I stopped and backed up a couple of steps to give everybody some breathing room. There was suddenly a hell of a lot more tension in the air than when I had first made contact with them. I tried to signal them that the girl had to get up and go with us. I guess I must have slept through that international miming class they gave in high school, because my hand signals were apparently interpreted as something completely obscene in Chinese. I'll never know what the fuck I did to trip their little triggers, but these rice eaters jumped on me quicker than Monica Lewinsky swallows.

I had kung fu-flailing little arms and hands bouncing up and down my middle-age gringo ass. But considering most of these little guys weighed no more than a hundred pounds dripping wet, no pun intended, none of their blows packed much behind them. Either that or they were just giving me a warning example of their dexterity in the martial arts. Any way you cut it, I took a couple of steps back instead of drawing down on them because I knew they were just trying to protect the female. I would later learn she was their sister.

After they calmed down, I tried yet another angle. I figured that maybe because we were in battle dress, even though we had our police-identifying patches on them, they may have thought we were some kind of soldiers, or even perhaps mercenaries. I removed my badge from within my vest pocket and slowly held it out to them. In a low soothing voice I tried to communicate that I wasn't going to harm them. Well, that approach didn't work worth a shit, either! At the sight of the badge they went fucking bug-eyed bonkers on me. For a minute I thought it just might come down to a self-defense shooting. Then I tried one more thing in a random act of total crazy-ass frustration. I stood square in front of the group, threw my arms up in the air toward the heavens, and screamed at the top of my lungs, "WELCOME TO AMERICA COCKSUCKERS!"

Well, I don't think the "welcome" part worked. And I'm pretty sure that the "cocksucker" part didn't work either. But what they did understand was the global word for a dream come true. America. When they heard that one international holy word, they simply froze and smiled at the same time. They started laughing and crying as they pointed to the ground beneath their little feet. As they jumped and danced they began chanting over and over the one magical word that

they knew out of their severely limited English vocabulary: "AMER-
ICA! AMERICA! AMERICA!" Now, normally, I don't consider
myself to be an emotional type of guy. And you would think that a big
old burly feller who has frequently walked with the Reaper would go
so sour on life that he would never again get a lump in his throat. But
this whole little drama in the desert here was what you'd have to term
as a bit of a tearjerker. It kind of made the old thumper pick up its
pace and at the same time I got chills going up and down my back and
neck. Usually I reserve those feelings for the playing of taps at Arling-
ton, or the raising of the American flag at a ball game. So all in all, not
wanting to really get bogged down in mushy emotions here, I'd have
to admit it was quite a unique, touching kind of a moment that night
in the Arizona desert. It was the kind of thing that makes a man
appreciate what we all seem to take for granted these days. I AM A
FREE AMERICAN!

After learning what they would respond to, I radioed Sperling and
Matt about the secret peaceful key to the kingdom, "AMERICA."
Shortly thereafter, each one of us was leading a long line of happy, giggling Chinese citizens out of the desert back to Geronimo Trail. As I
walked ahead of my charges across the starlit desert floor, I could see
the eastern edge of "Texas" John Slaughter's ranch to my west. To my
east I had a beautiful star-bathed view of the Peloncillo mountain
range where Geronimo spent his last days before surrendering.
Caught up in my own thoughts, I couldn't help but wonder what these
two hard men would have said about what was presently happening
on their once-coveted ranching and hunting lands.

It occurred to me that my fellow Texan would have enforced the
law no matter what the public sentiment or consequences. The law
was the law as it was written. It was our job to enforce it, and not to
question it. And then I thought about what Geronimo might have said
about the situation. After all, the Apaches occupied the land before
gringo foreigners from the east invaded and eventually crowded them
off it. Now those same eastern gringo invaders, who eventually put
the Apaches on reservations, are themselves being crowded by other
foreigners from the Far East. Do you reckon that in Geronimo's native

Apache tongue there was a way to say, "What goes around comes around"? Or how about, "You all ain't nothing but temporary boarders, so enjoy the view while you're here."

All totaled, we would later learn that we had intercepted a group of about eighty Chinese aliens who were being smuggled into the U.S. for an exorbitant $30,000 each. With Hong Kong about to go back to the Reds' Republic of China, the arrest of the Asians turned out to be interesting enough to make *USA Today* and some other press. But everything that was printed was politically expeditious for the Border Patrol REMFs in Washington, D.C. Not that I nor Sperling nor Matt gave a good hoot about what agency claimed the credit for the interception of the smuggled load of Chinese. I mean, out here smuggled alien loads are a dime a dozen. It is usually not nearly as hard or as dangerous as going up against a load of dope. But you have to understand how the REMFs roll this type of thing into a political snowball and then orchestrate their agenda to the news media.

First of all, the U.S. Customs Service and the U.S. Fish and Wildlife Service were barely, if at all, mentioned in the news releases given out by the Border Patrol. The way the bust was portrayed to the media, no arrests were made by anyone other than Department of Justice Border Patrol agents. Without actually lying too greatly about it, they mentioned that a couple of U.S. Customs agents were in the area and merely reported the sighting of a group of aliens that the Border Patrol later apprehended. In other articles, I read that local ranchers reported the sighting that led to the Chinese being tracked down and arrested by the Border Patrol. These articles were coupled with earlier ones about the landing of a couple of hundred illegal Chinese in San Francisco by ship, and voilà! You've created an invading tide of Chinese aliens headed for the U.S. mainland. Attorney General Janet Reno was in the national headlines, citing the arrests and whipping the public into a frenzy about the need to double or even triple the number of Border Patrol agents. And you know what? It worked. When I joined the Border Patrol in 1974, there were sixteen agents covering Cochise County. Today, there are about a thousand agents in the county.

Now, I'm not saying that we don't need more agents to protect our borders, because it's painfully obvious that we do. I'm just telling you how the REMFs take our enforcement actions in the field, twist them around to the news media, and end up getting exactly what they want from Congress. And what you don't get to hear is the complete truth about these people and what they go through to get to the land of milk and honey.

For example, the press never asked why these people had been so terrified of the U.S. agents who apprehended them. The reason was that they had suffered unimaginable injustices and horrors in Mexico at the hands of the fucking Mexican Federal Judicial Police. The women had been raped, the men had been beaten, and in general they had either been robbed, fucked, or just plain-ass cheated out of their last coin. No wonder they went completely, stark raving nuts when I had shown them a badge. Not knowing if they had yet crossed the border or not that night in the desert, they had evidently thought us to be MFJP agents back for a second go-around at them and their women. So it's pretty easy to understand why they scurried off into the desert, splitting up into family units, ready to defend their females to the death. Wouldn't you have done the same thing for your own flesh and blood?

14

Plight of the Mexican Aliens

For you will be His witness to all men of what you have seen and heard.

—ACTS 22:15

THE REAPER FREQUENTLY VISITED the Mexican aliens crossing the border in the Douglas area in the summer of 1997. There was more than enough death to go around. If you never had a lot of contact with these people, it may be hard for you to understand what I'm about to say. But the fact is, whether you're a border agent or not, your heart has to go out to anyone willing to face numerous perils just to feed his family. If it wasn't for the sporadic asshole-criminal types that mix in with the "working class" of alien, you'd almost want to let these guys skate. But that's really not a simple option, for numerous reasons that I'll explain a little later.

The most frequently asked question concerning illegal immigration is who to blame for the staggering influx of aliens. There's not a single response that could even come close to answering the question. In regard to people from Mexico and South America, I would have to say that it's our fault as much as the Mexican and South American governments'. Greedy U.S. business conglomerates want cheap labor that cuts down on their overhead. The American public wants lower prices in the supermarkets and retail stores. I reckon it's only human nature that everybody wants to make the almighty buck and maximize their profits. Whether that's a good or bad thing isn't for me to judge. But I will say this: In the end, the uneducated, poor aliens will always end up with the short end of the stick.

But when it comes to the majority of the blame about what causes these folks to desert their homelands, I lay that burden on the heads of the Mexican and Central American governments. Their corrupt political systems were founded on keeping only two classes of people in their countries: the filthy rich and the pitifully poor. There is no middle class as we have in the U.S. Did you know that the average factory worker in Mexico makes the equivalent of $3 to $4 (U.S.) per eight-hour day? The result is an entire population of hungry, desperate breadwinners trying to make ends meet. Do you have any idea how despondent this can make a man? If you want an education on desperation, keep reading and learn about your southern border.

On a crisp, clear summer morning in June, I hauled my butt out of bed a bit early with a strong desire to score a narcotics load. Before sunup, I was up and out the door, ready for the hunt. I headed out on Highway 80 east of Douglas to check the hot spots for any dope smuggling going on in the San Bernardino Valley. It's been my experience that most of the dope loads in this area are usually picked up by the driver right at daybreak. So I headed out rather early in hopes of getting lucky.

It was just about sunup when an eighteen-wheeler hauling a trailer passed me on the highway on his way into Douglas from the San Bernardino Valley. I flicked my headlights a couple of times at him to say hello and he responded by giving a couple of short blasts with his air horn as he continued on south down the road. I watched him travel out of sight as the sun slowly started to spread over the desert and highway behind him. When he was long gone, I checked a couple of dope stash sites and came up empty. After that, there wasn't much of a point in hanging around the area, so I headed back to Douglas about an hour behind the truck.

As I neared Douglas I saw the flashing red and blue lights of one of the Cochise County Sheriff's deputies on the side of the highway. I figured he had run up on one of the dope loads I was hunting for, so I continued on in his direction at a pretty good clip. As I neared his location I could see what looked like a couple of bundles of dope hidden in the tall, dry weeds bordering the highway. I pulled up to the bundles, wondering how much the dope load was going to weigh. It's a thing with narcs. The bigger the load, the more satisfaction we get out of taking it off the streets.

I jumped out of my vehicle and ran over to the bundles, happy that one of us had scored this morning. The deputy was standing nearby with his back to me talking on his handheld radio. I figured he must've been calling his seizure in, so I went on over to inspect the load. As I approached the dope bundles in the brush they took on an odd shape. I hadn't had my second cup of coffee yet and my brain was having a little trouble shifting into high gear. I guess that's why it took a couple of seconds for it to register that the knotted-up bundle was about 150 pounds of human flesh. A flash of "Aw, shit!" panic pushed my mind into overdrive. I wouldn't being needing that second cup of caffeine after all.

It didn't take me long to figure out that this poor soul had probably been with a group of smuggled aliens who were crossing the highway when the eighteen-wheeler came barreling by. I stood there gaping at the body, trying to comprehend what was wrong with the picture. There was something missing. Something wasn't intact. When I realized what was wrong I nearly tossed my cookies. One of the guy's legs had been ripped from his body, leaving an empty pant leg dangling from his faded jeans. It had to have been one of the cleanest amputations in the annals of Cochise County medicine. A skilled surgeon couldn't have done a better job. There wasn't a drop of blood on his jeans or on the ground. When I looked up the empty pant leg, all that was remaining was just this gray, knotted flap of skin folded over the now empty kneecap.

I looked left and right around the body. The leg wasn't anywhere to be found. I thought to myself this was somehow indecent, unclean.

We've got to find this guy's leg before the coyotes start planning their daily menu! I kept getting this vision of the guy's leg ending up as a pile of dog shit somewhere in the desert. I suddenly became preoccupied with that one line of thought going over and over in my mind. We had to find the "runaway" leg.

I turned my head away from the body with a shiver running up and down my spine. I headed over to talk with the deputy, who was now off the radio. As I crossed the blacktopped highway, I looked down at the pavement and saw a gut-wrenching sight. I was gonna have to vomit sooner or later. In between the cracks of the asphalt were healthy chunks of finely ground, bright red human flesh! It was the exact same texture and look as the hamburger you buy at the supermarket to make a meat loaf with. My stomach turned over a couple of times. The idea of tonight's supper went out the window with the second cup of coffee I didn't get this morning.

The deputy had finished his radio call and had been patiently watching me look up and down the road for the absent leg. When I finally got over to him, he just shook his head back and forth saying that he too had tried unsuccessfully to locate the absent limb. He said that he thought the leg may have been caught up under the truck and that it could well be in another state by now. Not wanting to give up yet, we divided up the area to be searched and scoured the desert for a couple of hours. By the time we were done, the Arizona summer sun had taken its toll on the ground pulp that was left on the road. As the pavement heated up, the human flesh started to cook and turn greasy brown, just like hamburger patties on your backyard grill.

After the body was carted off by the county medical examiner, I said my adios to the deputy and drove off. As I went on down the highway I began to wonder what the rest of the day had in store for me. I knew one thing for sure: No matter what else happened that day or how hungry I got, I wasn't going to eat a fucking hamburger!

In July we were having a pretty good month for dope seizures and arrests. This usually means you're going to spend a lot of time testifying in court and writing reports. One afternoon we were in the office doing the latter when we heard a call come in on the radio that a

Border Patrol agent had been shot and was down. In a New York City second, all of our agents cleared the office and were running Code Three to the ranch where the shooting had been called in.

We arrived at the ranch, about fifteen miles north of Douglas off Leslie Canyon Road. The on-scene Cochise County Sheriff's deputies requested that our special agents help secure the perimeter of a garage where the shooting had taken place. As we walked up to the site of the gunfight, a bleeding Border Patrol agent was being taken out on a stretcher to a waiting ambulance. He was writhing in a good deal of pain and I could see that he had been capped with a shotgun in his right side, over his rib cage. Although he was dripping a steady stream of blood, it appeared that his bulletproof vest had taken the brunt of the lead pellets. My immediate impression of the wound was that it wouldn't be life-threatening.

The Cochise County deputies directed us around the back of the garage, where I saw one of the damnedest sights I have ever witnessed. Inside the garage stood a still-saddled, motionless horse. The gelding was standing in a pool of rapidly accumulating blood that covered most of his unshod hooves as well as the grey cement floor. In the middle of the ever-widening circle lay the rider. It looked like he had just about finished completely pumping out his red supply of life. The deceased rider's body was partially hidden under the horse's sorrel belly.

Now, usually animals will spook at the smell of blood and pitch an ungodly flared-nostril fit. But this horse didn't even flinch as the Mexican outlaw's blood began to coagulate on its hooves. I've never in my life seen a horse react this way, especially considering all of the chaotic shooting that must have taken place minutes earlier. I mean, the animal wasn't even flicking his friggin tail! But then again, considering all of the excited lawmen running around with pistolas at the ready, maybe the gelding figured he'd better make like a wooden carousel pony so he wouldn't end up sharing the same slab of cement as his recently departed partner.

As we secured the area, we spoke with the Cochise County deputy who had been with the Border Patrolman when they went up against the outlaw. The deputy said the whole thing started when he had received a call from his dispatcher about an armed illegal alien on horseback in the area of Leslie Canyon Road. The original information was that the guy was armed with a double-barrel shotgun and had attempted to raise a fuss with a neighboring rancher's wife. The lady had asked the rider to leave but he had refused to do so, prompting her to call the deputies for help. The Sheriff's office dispatched a deputy and requested that a Border Patrol agent accompany him for assistance in tracking.

The deputy and agent arrived at the ranch and learned from the lady that the horse and rider had gone off into the desert just minutes before. The lawmen found the horse's tracks and trailed them a few miles to this adjoining ranch's garage. As they approached the garage they became alarmed when the tracks disappeared at the garage door. It was apparent to the deputy and agent that the horse had been ridden inside and the sliding door closed behind it, leaving them no alternative but to investigate. The agent bent over to raise the sliding garage door while the deputy stood off to his side at the ready.

As the agent was pulling up the door, a shotgun blast caught him square in the belly, raising him up off his feet into the air. The agent landed on his back, momentarily stunned from the bone-crushing impact. When he gathered enough wind, he screamed to the deputy that he'd been shot, as he grabbed at his bleeding side, where his protective vest had left him vulnerable. As the agent was now defenseless, the ambushing bastard with the shotgun advanced from behind the half-opened garage door determined to slam a killing blast into his wounded target.

As soon as he heard the shotgun's report, and well before the wounded agent had even thought of screaming out, the deputy jerked his .45 Colt automatic from its holster knowing he was going into a live-or-die confrontation. Before the garage door had even finished rolling to the top, the deputy dropped low into a crouch, sighting in on his rapidly advancing adversary. Calm and smooth as an Old West veteran gunfighter, the deputy double-tapped the trigger on his .45, driving hot lead deep into the outlaw's flesh and bones. The first round caught the bad man in the guts, scrambling up the last burrito and beans he would ever consume. The second round penetrated the chin, driving back hard and shattering through the facial bone. Some of the bone deflected the round down so that it exited the throat and entered the chest. The round eventually tunneled its way into the aorta, sealing the bad guy's fate. And that's pretty much how the horse ended up standing in a pool of tomorrow's dried-up corpuscles.

As it turned out, the agent was extremely fortunate that he had a partner with him. Not only had the shotgun blast ripped his side up, but it also destroyed the top of his still-holstered pistol. The shotgun pellets had mutilated his handgun so bad that he would never have been able to return fire. There was absolutely no other avenue for the deputy other than to burn the outlaw down. Because of his actions in saving the agent's life, the deputy later received the Cochise County Medal of Valor. If old Sheriff John Slaughter had still been on this side of the ground, there's no doubt that he would've been proud of this deputy and his old office.

The Cochise County Sheriff's Office interviewed the deceased outlaw's family in Mexico. The young rider was Gerardo Fierros-Grijalva, a nineteen-year-old from Agua Prieta. The Cochise detectives were attempting to learn why Grijalva had committed such a violent act. The surprised and still-mourning family couldn't explain any of it. They said that their son had always been a good boy who had never shown signs of dishonesty or violence. The only thing conclusive learned from the interview was that the family and son were all poor Mexicans just trying to get by. Excuse? Not really. Reason? If you're hungry and desperate enough, yes.

A little later in the summer another tragic border crossing unfolded that again told the story of a desperate people. In July and August our desert customarily gets its share of the rains brought by the moisture rising out of the Gulf of California. Most of the folks around here have fondly dubbed this season the "monsoons." When the humidity builds up to complement the rising heat, the results are some of the fiercest thunderstorms in the country. They are quick and unpredictable, giving birth to extremely dangerous, boiling flash flooding in the sandy draws and creeks of Cochise County. Such flash floods have swept livestock and people away to an untold number of sandy graves.

During the evening of August 5, 1997, an ill-fated group of aliens attempted to enter the U.S. via one of the numerous sewer and drainage pipes that run under Douglas. It was some time after dark when the group crawled through a hole in the border fence between Agua Prieta and Douglas. After crossing, they immediately slid down into a ten-foot dirt ditch that runs parallel east and west along the border. From this ditch they had easy access to the open drainage pipes that run north and south under the country of their dreams. It was their smuggler's responsibility to guide them underground, going north for about six or eight city blocks. After scraping along on their hands and knees, they would eventually exit the drainage system to another smuggler waiting in a vehicle to pick them up. If they evaded the Border Patrol and other law enforcement, it would be north into the land of milk and honey.

Some time during their stifling subterranean journey, a severe thunderstorm slipped over Douglas under the cover of darkness. The aliens, deep into the dank bowels of the city's foul sewage pipes, were unable to hear the warning of the thunder or see the flashes of lightning. I don't think we'll ever know if they saw a foretelling trickle or if a deluge of white, foaming water fell upon them with a sudden, bone-crushing impact. But, having stalked dope smugglers in these same cement pipes before, I suspect that they may have heard an ominous rumbling seconds before it hit. No matter what they may have tried, their efforts would have been futile as they were sucked under the surge. Secure in our homes and daily routines, we will never be able to begin to imagine the panic that filled their last thoughts. Did they have time to say their last prayers? Or was there even enough time for the last mumbling of a soon-to-be widow's name?

The following morning at about 7:30, the U.S. Customs Service port director in Douglas began to make his daily operational inspection of the port of entry. He spotted what appeared to be a log floating in the border ditch where it passes under the government facility. He leaned out over the guardrails toward the ditch and got a better look.

A few minutes later the Customs Office of Investigations received a telephone call from a shocked, tongue-tied port director.

As the Douglas Fire Department devised a plan to remove two bodies from the ditch near the port of entry, the Border Patrol and Customs agents worked together to locate all of the bodies that had washed back out of the cement pipes. We walked up and down the ditch for about a half a mile east of the port of entry. Just about the time we thought we had all of the bodies located, the water and mud levels would subside a bit more, exposing the limbs or torsos of others. We found most of the bodies face-down in the mud and sand. Their eyes, noses, mouths, and ears were completely sealed with fine sand and debris. They were bloated from the intake of so much water and their skin was morbidly pale. Their lips were dark blue and black. The Reaper's take tallied eight souls from his border on this particular morning.

I later heard that in Agua Prieta, the Mexican police had found a number of survivors from the smuggling attempt. Somehow the smuggled aliens had made their way back down the drains to the border ditch. I can't tell you if they started back before the water hit or if they rode the waves out. All I know is that the survivors later fingered the smuggler who had promised them a better way of life but in reality had sold them death. Douglas Police Department detectives were working a joint homicide investigation with federal and state authorities in Chicago. The Douglas detectives had interviewed the surviving aliens in their home states of Mexico, where they had later returned. According to the detectives, the responsible smuggler was a U.S. citizen living in Chicago and he had been located and identified. The detectives were pursuing a minimum eight-count manslaughter indictment against the bastard. It's a shame that we can't suffocate the oxygen thief for his crimes against humanity. I'm sad to report that no one was indicted for these murders.

But now starts the political chest-beating. We couldn't just let the poor souls rest. If there's political gain to be made from human misery, there are those who will take advantage of it. Any day in the news is a good day for a politician. Douglas city mayor Ray Borane, seeking to ingratiate himself with his border constituents, immediately opened his mouth and inserted his foot. He spouted off to the media that the federal government was responsible for the aliens' deaths because it was the feds' responsibility to keep the border drainage ditch clean of debris. After it was pointed out to the mayor that the feds paid the city of Douglas to maintain and clean out the ditch, he found another object of blame: The feds had a newly installed grated culvert at the port of entry that caused the ditch to back up and flood.

On August 18, 1997, the Douglas city council voted to rescind the agreement between the city and the federal government that made the city responsible for cleaning the debris from the ditch. Several weeks later the council voted to direct the city attorney to investigate possible action against the federal government to require removal of the port-of-entry grate. In a rear-guard move, Borane later declared that the City of Douglas was not going to be responsible for anymore catastrophes because they were washing their hands of the border ditch.

I never could figure out why Mayor Borane got so defensive about the aliens' deaths. Why did he find it so necessary to point a finger at the federal government? It wasn't like the feds or anyone else were pointing a finger at him or the City of Douglas. And why switch the blame to the border ditch or even the grated culvert? Granted, the majority of the bodies were found near the grate, but God only knows where the actual drownings occurred. Wouldn't it be a more correct assumption that they had expired inside the city's drainage pipes and were later washed out into the ditch? Why did anyone need to find someone to blame? The real blame here lies in one word: desperation.

The thing is that you never know what hungry, desperate men are going to do. I make this statement remembering the unusually cold winter of 1997 that followed that year's torrential summer rains. It was the beginning of the El Niño weather pattern that raised havoc all across the U.S. The summer gave us more than average rain and the winter brought below-normal temperatures accompanied by an unusual amount of snow for the desert.

It was after one of these winter storms that an informant called me about a load of dope that was stranded in the snow and ice near

Highway 80 in the San Bernardino Valley. So I saddled up in my government truck and used the four-wheel drive to slip and slide my way out of Douglas. I got about twenty miles up into the valley and leisurely set up my surveillance from the top of a hill. I got out of my truck to answer the call of nature. As my kidney-filtered coffee hit the earth it damn near turned to yellow ice on the spot. Shit! It was one of the coldest winters I had seen in about ten years.

I dipped a chew of tobacco and kicked back with my trusty binoculars, thinking how beautiful and peaceful the desert floor looked covered in the white powder. The graceful mule deer pawed through the snow, grazing on the underlying vegetation. I crawled back up in the truck's cab and turned the heater off and on as it was needed. I was set to wait and watch for several hours when a Volkswagen van with out-of-state plates pulled to the side of the highway and into the brush. It was perfect timing and I was in the right spot. Talk about luck of the Irish. The day was starting out pretty damn good so far.

I trained my binos on the van as the sliding side door opened facing into the brush. Then a Customs agent's dream came true. A mule started running from his hiding place toward the van. He was carrying a black backpack as he entered the van's open side door. High five! This one was going down right under my nose! Any prosecuting attorney would accept this case hands down. It was looking so good that I nearly got an erection! Well, maybe it wasn't that great, but when you get to be my age it's the thought that really counts.

It usually takes about fifteen to thirty seconds for the mules to load their merchandise into the smuggler's vehicle. I waited more than a minute and hadn't seen another mule head for the van. Something was wrong. But then I figured what the heck, maybe it's just a one-bagger, a small load. When you get lucky enough to watch them loading in front of you, you don't look a gift horse in the mouth. You take what you can get. Talk about reading their mail! This was a dream come true.

As the seconds eroded into minutes, so did my enthusiasm. Five minutes passed without my seeing any other activity around the van.

This was way too long for a dope-smuggling vehicle to be waiting in the load area. Something had gone wrong. Was the van broke down? Did it have a flat tire? Did the driver and mule have a doper's quarrel resulting in one or both outlaws offing each other? Where was the mule with the black backpack? I hadn't seen him come back out of the van. Murphy's Law was kicking my ass again. My easy dope take-down was slowly deteriorating into a tub of shit.

With curiosity getting the best of me, I radioed for backup and left my truck. I started sneaking up to the van by making my way down the snow-covered hill through the rocks. As I slowly walked up on the blind side of the van I could hear voices inside. One of them was that of a loud Spanish-speaking male. The other was the dis-tressed, high-pitched voice of an English-speaking female who sounded like she was about to blow a gasket. I drew my weapon and stepped into the open door of the van, identifying myself as a federal agent. John Wayne balls-up time!

As I took both people by surprise, it appeared that this Mexican guy had a frightened gringa gal hemmed in to the rear portion of her van. When he saw me, the man's expression turned to one of dismay and disappointment to say the least. The female, in contrast, displayed sheer relief as she exclaimed, "Oh, thank God, Officer! I was scared to death! I don't speak any Spanish and can't understand what this man wants." Right about now, a little imagination can go a long way.

I ordered the male to put his hands on top of his head and turn around as I trained my pistol on his back. He kept pleading in Spanish that he was starving and only wanted some food. But until I knew exactly what his intentions had been, I had to take him into custody. I cuffed the young Mexican up and pulled him out of the van back-wards by the scruff of his neck. After the lady had stopped yelling and everyone had calmed down, I started a separate interrogation of both of them to figure out what the fuck was going on.

As it turned out, the gringa lady was a Yankee gal from New Jer-sey on a solo vacation. Not very smart in my book, but that's her busi-ness. She had simply stopped in the wrong place at the wrong time to take a pee in the brush on the side of the road. She told me that she had just opened her van door to get out when this Mexican feller came running up out of the highway ditch, forcing her to take refuge in the back of the van. She said that he really didn't touch or assault her, but that he did pin her in the back of the van, not allowing her to get out. She said that he kept pointing at the food boxes and yelling at her in Spanish. I thought to myself that it must be true that God only protects drunks and fools. This Yankee gal definitely fell into the latter category for more than just one reason.

When I had finished speaking to the lady I asked her if she wanted to press charges against the Mexican for any perceived wrongdoing such as criminal trespass or attempted robbery. If she wanted, I could radio the Cochise County deputies and we could all wait a couple of hours for them to arrive. She nervously replied that she just wanted to be on her way, putting as many miles between her and the Mexican border as possible. I thought that was without a doubt the smartest thing she would probably do on her vacation. The last I saw of her and that van, they were running north up the highway like a striped-assed ape. I bet that they would be selling snowballs in hell before she'd ever take a piss again in anything but a certified public restroom along the highway! Come to think of it, she never did take a leak before she left and it was about forty miles to the next rest area.

After she was out of sight, I studied up on my prisoner and started in on his side of the story. The little Mexican feller was shivering uncontrollably. I wasn't sure if it was from the cold or from the fear of being arrested. His teeth kept clicking and snapping together, making it sound like Arsenio Hall was doing a tap dance in the bed of my truck. Despite the bouncing tooth enamel, he eventually answered my questions.

His sad story was that he was part of a group of about thirty smuggled aliens that had crossed the border illegally about five days ago. During their walk north through the San Bernardino Valley they became exhausted and stopped for a night's rest. During the evening, he and his smuggler got sideways with each other over the amount of the smuggling fee. It seemed that the original deal that was negotiated in Mexico didn't include a little extra beer money for this oxygen thief, and he was jacking our boy here for a tip. My half-frozen little buddy said that when he woke up the next morning everyone else was gone. He imagined that because he didn't go along with the extortion attempt, the smuggler had abandoned him to die in the desert's ice and snow.

The little dude told me that he hadn't eaten for four or five days and that he was feeling sick and faint from lack of food. I started to believe the poor feller's story because he never stopped shaking. It looked like he may be going into hypothermia, so I invited him inside my truck and placed him in the passenger seat. I reached under the back seat and retrieved some military MREs (meals ready to eat) that the agents carry as emergency rations in the field. When I brought the food into the front of the truck the little guy's eyes lit up like Christmas lights. I told him I would uncuff him to let him eat if he didn't give me any shit. He eagerly agreed, never taking his eyes off the plastic bags of soldier chow.

The poor little feller devoured the meal without using any of the enclosed utensils. He just ripped open the bags and sucked the cold, tasteless military slop down. When the cold food hit his stomach I thought I may have killed him. He started to shake and shudder worse than he was before. I decided that the way he was shoveling the food down was doing him more harm than good at this point. I hated to do it, but I took the food away from him. And I damn near had to do it at gunpoint! I guessed that the cold food entering his body, which already must've had a lower temperature than normal, was causing some kind of reaction. I could just see myself trying to explain this one to the bosses. "As I attempted to render aid and feed a starving lost alien, he up and croaked on me sitting in the passenger seat of my government vehicle." Oh, yeah! Like the fucking ACLU would believe that story!

I made the guy sit right under the truck's heater as I doled the food out to him a little at a time. He started to settle down a bit and the shivering slowed down. When he was done I felt so sorry for him that I offered him another MRE on the condition that he eat it slower. He promised to abide by the rule, so I dug under the back seat of my truck again.

As the little feller ate he told me his sad but true life story. Like most illegals looking for a better life, he was raised on a small farm in Mexico where the family struggled to grow enough to eat. He had only gone to school a couple of years and didn't really know how to read or write. His parents had departed north from Mexico, ending up in New York a couple of years before, and he was just trying to get up to live with them. He had sold all of his farm tools and any earthly possessions that would bring a few pesos. He had prayed that he would have enough money to pay his smuggler and personal food expenses during the trip to New York. Now he was completely broke, freezing, lost, and still two thousand miles from his family. As he now realized his desperate situation, he broke down crying as he wondered where his next meal would come from.

Folks, believe me when I tell you that it's stories like this that can rip your heart away from your duty as a U.S. Border Patrol agent. It was stories like this that had inspired me to become an INS anti-smuggling agent and later a U.S. Customs special agent. Those two positions allowed me to pursue and imprison the death-dealing alien smugglers and the dope lords who are poisoning our children. Until the day I take my last breath, I will never regret my total dedication to those two parts of my life.

No matter how much I wanted to let this feller go, I couldn't ignore my sworn oath. Besides, if I had let him go back out into the desert, where would it get him? Only frozen to death. With a heavy heart, I picked up my radio and called for the Border Patrol to come take the little Mexican off my hands. As we waited for their arrival I thought how crazy being a border agent was. In a matter of an hour or so, my contact with this guy had gone from one of possibly having to shoot him, to a situation of saving his life instead of taking it. And to compound those emotions, he was no longer a perceived enemy, but a hungry little guy that I now felt terribly sorry for.

Between 1997 and 1999, the influx of aliens illegally entering the U.S. through the desert and mountains around Douglas got completely out of hand. It was not uncommon for the Border Patrol's apprehensions of aliens over a two-week period to match the entire legally residing population of Douglas's 15,000 or 16,000. The masses of desperate, hungry folks coming to Agua Prieta, Sonora, to cross the border pushed the humble and extremely limited Mexican accommodations there right over the edge.

The simple white stucco and adobe-brick boarding houses of Agua Prieta were cramming up to forty people at a time into an unfurnished one-room daily rental. And once such rooms were overflowing, the goddamn house managers would call the Sonoran State Police to come "inspect" the potential border-crossing violators. Such "inspection" usually led to the Mexicans being dragged out in the street, handcuffed, beaten at gunpoint, and then right-out robbed by the cops. Of course the house managers later got a fifty-fifty split of the booty for the informing phone call. These poor folks were gonna get fucked coming and going on both sides of the border, no matter how they tried to avoid it.

Such a large gathering of "soft targets" on the border eventually attracted the attention of ruthless outlaws who took to the hills and deserts both east and west of Douglas. Once the vultures gathered, we had aliens being robbed, raped, beaten, murdered, and even kidnapped for ransom from family members residing further north in the U.S. I daresay that the crime rate was probably equivalent to, if not worse than, what the Arizona Rangers had to go up against when they first opened their doors in Douglas near a hundred years ago.

From the survivors' and victims' descriptions, it was evident that the majority of the perpetrators were Mexican lawmen and Mexican federal agents. It seemed that no matter what side of the border the aliens were on, they were getting hit by their own countrymen more than by Americans. One of the victims said he felt as though he was a man without a country, a piece of human trash that no one wanted. Mexican authorities beat and robbed him and then kicked him across the border telling him not to return. He hadn't gone far on the U.S. side of the line before he was accosted by a second group of bandits. When he told the second bunch of assholes he had nothing to give them because he had already been robbed, they stole his boots, then beat him within an inch of his life. Imagine that. If it's not bad enough you gotta walk barefoot in the rocks and cactus, you also get your ass kicked twice in one day, first by Mexican law and second by Mexican outlaws. The feeding frenzy was on.

In response to this, the U.S. Border Patrol brought in my old alma mater, the anti-smuggling unit (ASU). Now, one thing you have to understand about these lawmen is this: What the U.S. Cavalry was to the Chiricahua Apaches, the ASU agents were to the Mexican aliens. Both regulator and protector, the anti-smuggling unit was brought in to infiltrate those responsible for murdering and robbing the aliens. What that entailed was placing undercover agents on the most frequently traveled alien-smuggling trails on the U.S. side of the border. Dressed like regular border crossers, the agents hid in the desert brush on the edge of the trails. When a group of smuggled aliens passed by, the agents mingled in and "married up" with the group, walking to the bitter end of the trail no matter where it took them. These ASU agents were John Fucking Wayne, balls-up all the way!

Operation Disrupt was a well-planned op because not only did it enable the ASU agents to protect the aliens, but they continued on with the group to the stash house where they actually went face-to-face with the awaiting smugglers.

On the frigid night of December 15, 1999, an ASU Disrupt agent joined a group of five illegal immigrants as they passed by his hidden position on the dark outskirts of Douglas. When the group arrived in the brush at the edge of an old Mexican-American neighborhood known as Pirtleville, they lay down in the night's shadows and patiently waited in silence for their transporter. During their anxious wait, a gun-yielding figure suddenly emerged from the cover of darkness. The cretin moved swiftly, coming down on the group in the blink of an eye. It happened so quickly there was no chance for escape. And as is customary on the Reaper's line, negotiation with a border outlaw is never an option. The pobrecitos couldn't run and they couldn't make a deal. If the outlaw wanted their ass, that's the way it was gonna be.

The bandit pointed his weapon into each face as he barked orders for the Mexicans to kneel down and look only at the ground. Now, you know damn good and well that when those poor folks were staring down into the night's black desert floor, most of them probably figured it would be the last thing they would ever see on God's earth. As they prayed in the dark, waiting to hear the final cracking report of the outlaw's rifle, no one bothered to worry about the loss of bladder control as their legs suddenly were momentarily warmed from the night's frigid air.

As the small group fearfully complied one by one, the veteran outlaw thought he was indeed lucky to stumble on such an obedient flock of scared-shitless *pollos* (chickens). But when he turned and leveled his .22 caliber rifle on the ASU agent, it most likely took him a second or two to understand the full ramification of having two .40 caliber slugs channeling through his liver. In a throwback to frontier justice, the hollow points distributed pieces of the hard-core outlaw's internal organs onto various mesquites and greasewood bushes that surrounded the aliens' pickup point.

A liver shot is one of the most painful wounds to delay a feller on his way to checking out of this old world. So this soon-to-be piece of worm food probably had a few minutes to think about his misspent youth. And while I'm sure he begged God's Angel to deliver him home in the most expeditious manner possible, I bet he had a couple of last questions he would have liked to have had answered before going. For one thing, I reckon he would have liked to have known who that quiet pollo was that had capped his ass while screaming something like, "Drop your weapon! U.S. Border Patrol!" That's what I'd always loved about working undercover with the anti-smuggling unit in my younger days. The confrontational edge usually belonged to you. It made going up against the draw possible to survive.

Several hours after the shooting, Special Agent Carlos Cruz and I arrived at the scene. A couple of Border Patrol agents had been working all morning in the freezing cold to determine by tracking and cutting sign where the outlaw had originated. It was so fucking cold that the snot on their mustaches was as frozen as the bandit's blood that now graced the desert sands. As Carlos and I wagered with the agents on whether the bandit's blood would thaw before their snot-laden mustaches, the sun started to rise, beginning another Wild West day in Cochise County.

Carlos wondered about the possibility of this unknown outlaw being his fourth suspect from his previous days with the Sheriff's Department's Border Bandit Detail. But as it later turned out, the asshole was a twenty-five-year-old dope smuggler from Pirtleville we had previously busted. Bandits, outlaws, alien smugglers, and dope smugglers. They're all cut from the same cloth down here on the Mexican border.

By the summer of 2000, we really had a hell of a mess in Cochise County. Folks were complaining about aliens running through their ranches and other properties. Aliens were being accused of shooting at U.S. citizens, tearing down fences, leaving tons of trash in the desert, killing cattle, and destroying pristine national wildlife refuges. These complaints eventually caught the eye of right-wing politicians, hate groups, vigilantes, and Second Amendment militia types, all hoping to capitalize on the fright of our citizens living near the border. Once again, the aliens, and particularly the Mexican aliens, became the people designated to take a public political flogging. They were mere tools to be used by ambitious politicians and hateful vigilantes who all wanted to become national heroes. And once the bigots became the designated heroes, they could use television to advance their racist hate agendas. To be honest, when all of this shit hit the fan I couldn't tell who the Mexican aliens' worse enemy was, the American racists or the Mexican border bandits.

While all of this hate mongering and political maneuvering was going on, the Reaper's toll for the summer of 2000 climbed steadily. It seemed that every week I would hear on my company radio about one or another law-enforcement agency finding a body to be picked up by the county meat wagon. We had groups of aliens being stranded in the desert for up to three and four days without food or water because their piece-of-shit smuggler took their money and left them on their own in a strange land. We had so many dead bodies along the smuggling routes that there were reports of aliens traveling the same trail, finding a dying person down, and stealing his shoes and water before he was even dead! When I heard about this I shook my head in disbelief. I thought to myself that these people must be so desperate to stay a step ahead of death's shadow that they were now leaving their own behind to die in the desert.

I remember that the first week in August two bodies were discovered within several days of each other near Monument #90 on Border Road. When I rolled up to help Cochise County deputies load one of them into a body bag, I fully expected to see an older person who had expired from a condition associated with the Sonoran Desert heat. I was shocked to see the victim was an eighteen-year-old Mexican boy who supposedly had a heart attack.

The two deputies and I stood there under the grace of the San José mountain range shooting the shit, chewing tobacco, and smoking cigarettes. No one said a word about the boy after we initially bagged him up. After all, he was just a heart attack. No one looked at the bag or wanted to think about its contents. We were all more worried about how long we would have to stand in the hot desert sun waiting for the meat wagon. We kept looking up and down Border Road, making jokes about the mortuary folks getting lost or carjacked by a group of aliens. Anything to avoid allowing old man death to creep into our midst.

If we didn't talk about him, if we didn't look at his face, if we didn't smell his final bowel movement, and if we didn't acknowledge the hordes of flies on the now-swelling body bag, then I guess all of us civilized folks just wouldn't have to admit that our own mortality will eventually catch up to us. Besides, who wants to think about the boy's parents and the expression on their faces when they're notified? And what if they aren't ever notified in the remote hills of some underdeveloped Mexican state? How many years will they keep looking out their front door for their baby boy to return around harvest time to help them with their crops? Will he ever have a proper grave? A marker?

But then, who gives a shit? It's not like this kid was anyone of importance, now, is it? He's not a governor, an athlete, a doctor, a lawyer, or a movie star. He's not even an American. He's just a Mexican heart attack in the desert. Hell, in our society that's wasted space on the precious thirty-minute evening news where it's more important to get the NFL point spread and tomorrow's weather forecast.

So while the vigilantes and politicians were all making their TV debuts arguing for or against illegal immigration, the spiraling body count continued to go for the most part unnoticed. Hell, we weren't even close to getting an accurate count on the Mexican side of the fence. That quite possibly could have doubled or tripled the number of deceased. And the crying shame of the whole matter was that most folks were more worried about their goddamn fences being torn down than the aliens dropping like flies. It was tragic to note that no one thought about the fact that a two-fucking-yard section of fence could be repaired for five or ten lousy dollars, but a dead eighteen-year-old boy couldn't be repaired for any amount of money.

A newspaper reporter recently asked me what I thought about the Mexican illegal-alien problem and what could be done to resolve it. He also wanted to know how I felt about the Border Patrol arresting poor immigrants who just wanted an opportunity to feed their children. These are probably two of the most difficult questions to respond to on border issues. I've pondered these issues for more than twenty-five years and can tell you there's no easy answer.

Let me preface what I'm about to say by telling you this: This country has had a love-hate relationship with Mexico for damn near two hundred years now. The Mexican people have greatly affected our lifestyles and activities in almost all American walks of life. If you say no to that you are lying to yourself. Why? Well, for one thing, who do you think picked that glass of orange juice for you this morning? If it were left up to me, I would have to say that the truth of the immigration matter lies in this: Our Mexican neighbors have been traipsing back and forth across our southern border for damn near two centuries and it's not about to stop now. You might as well face up to the fact that it's time to embrace and educate them, because you will never keep the Mexicans from coming to America.

However, it will be imperative that the Border Patrol remain in charge of sorting out the outlaws, dopers, smugglers, terrorists, and other criminal elements from the crossing Mexican population. But with the good law-abiding folks, the best thing you can do is assimilate them into mainstream America, into hardworking, educated, legal residents. How many would become U.S. citizens? A minimum. From what I've seen and know about Mexicans, very few would actually choose to become U.S. citizens, because they love Mexico and the majority of them eventually gravitate back down south sooner or later.

And if you are worried about Americans' jobs, those are easy enough to protect. Considering how many useless, stupid laws we can do away with by letting the Mexicans cross easier, it's real easy to add one that will protect Americans. Write it into the law that an employer must always first hire any available U.S. citizen applicant before hiring any legally admitted alien. The Mexicans can have all the employment that Americans don't want and it will still pay them eight times more than they would earn in Mexico. Think about it. They have those jobs now anyway. What I'm saying here is that we need to allow the Mexicans the latitude of crossing the border back and forth because *they are gonna do it with or without our blessings and permission anyway!* End of story. Bottom line.

But what about the entire rest of the world that wants to come here? The Chinese, the Haitians, the Dominicans, and even the white Europeans? No fucking way in hell. It's apples and oranges, folks. The Mexicans should be the only exception to the rule.

In 1999, the U.S. Border Patrol apprehended almost two million illegal aliens attempting to enter the U.S. Out of that two million, I would estimate that at least one million were repeat offenders, having been arrested during the same week, or even on the same day, for illegal entry. You can ask any Border Patrol agent and he'll tell you that they have even caught the same guy five or six times in one day. So when you add this one guy's five or six arrests into the stats, and do that for a quarter of the others that were caught, do you have any idea how bad that inflates and perverts the *true* total arrests for the U.S. Border Patrol in a year? And I guarandamntee ya'll that about 90 to 95 percent of the aliens the Border Patrol catches each year are Mexicans.

So by knocking the Mexicans off the U.S. Immigration Service's "most wanted" list, we will free up our Border Patrol and other law-enforcement agencies from dealing with repetitive Mexican crossers, so that their resources can be better spent in the next twenty-five years getting ready to defend us from the devastating global population explosion that is just around the corner.

On October 12, 1999, the world population hit six billion people. By the year 2100, we will have twelve billion people who will suffer a difficult if not terrifying time on earth. And let me tell you a fact about human instinct if you haven't already figured it out on your own. Unwanted, displaced people don't just disappear from the face of the earth. They will find a place to migrate toward, and eventually enter the area of least resistance, wherever that may be.

In 1965 there were seventy-five million people worldwide attempting to migrate. Presently there are more than one hundred and twenty million. That is equivalent to approximately one-half of the present U.S. population.

First and foremost, we as a nation have to consider our own plight. I had heard that a few years ago the CIA conducted a study and released an opinion that the worst national threat we faced was the uncontrollable influx of illegal aliens. You thought it was drugs, didn't you? That would probably be a reasonable assumption, but the CIA set forth a viable argument and made some pretty good points.

You have to understand that the dope that comes into our country is eventually snorted, smoked, or injected. It dissipates and is gone forever. Sure, it causes crime and heartbreak, and is probably one of the principal reasons for the breakup of families. However, whereas the dope gets absorbed, the illegal human beings are still with us, depleting our nation of its natural resources.

It's a known fact that our water tables are dropping. Not only from human consumption, but from the enormous amount of irrigation needed to grow crops that are in turn needed to feed more and more people. The farmland we grow these crops on is being gobbled up by builders in an effort to satisfy our ever-growing demand for housing because of our population explosion. So what do you think? Do we need more immigrants and mouths to feed, or should we close our porous borders now? It's your choice. You have to decide on one of those two options. Take care of your kids, or take care of their kids. We simply aren't going to have the resources to do both.

Having said that, now I'm really going to put the monkey on your back to force you to mull this immigration issue over for yourself. The Bush administration is presently funding millions and millions of your tax dollars to build a steel wall on the U.S.-Mexican border. The right-wing conservatives are all for it. The left-wing liberals are all against it. And the poor illegal alien who just wants to feed his babies, as usual, is caught in the middle. So how about we all use some common sense right here and right now?

We're about to throw millions of dollars away on a wall that will never work. I know; I've lived on the Reaper's line for the majority of my life. So, I don't want to hear any mealy-mouth politician tell me what I, and hundreds of other border agents and cops like me, already know. This goddamn wall will never, ever work. They will go over it, under it, around it, and right smack dab through the middle of it. This wall is going to work about as well as a helicopter made out of recycled firing-range lead.

So what's the solution on illegal immigration? I'm not going to lie to you like the politicians competing for your votes and tax dollars do. There is none. If there were, we would already be doing it. However, the next best thing is this. Instead of pissing away the multi-millions on a wall that will never work, spend the goddamn money on helping to develop Mexico so that the folks down there can stay home and feed their babies. I know it's a hell of a row to hoe in overcoming the Mexican government corruption and getting the money in the right position to help the people. But that's what we have to figure out and get done: how to create jobs in Mexico to keep the people home. That is the only answer right now.

And what about a guest-worker program to let the Mexicans come in and work temporarily? I'll tell you the truth about that, too. It doesn't matter if Congress passes that new law or not. The Mexicans are still going to cross the border anyway, one way or another, to get work and support their families. They're going to continue to work in our kitchens, pick our produce, clean our motels, build our roads, and baby-sit your kids in your mansions.

If we're willing to spend billions on NASA putting tons of orbiting trash in space, billions of dollars going to planets we will never inhabit, and billions on forcing our government, values, and morals on countries on the other side of the globe that don't really want to be like us, why would we not spend the same amount of money building factories and creating jobs in a country that in addition to being our closest neighbor, is rich in oil reserves?

And never be fooled about this: There is no such thing as a minimum-wage undocumented Mexican alien-terrorist. Do not ever believe that bullshit from any politician. You cannot, we should not, and it would be a shameful mistake in the history of this country to let our government officials attach the terrorist issue to that of the regular illegal alien who wants to feed his starving kids. They are two separate issues and they must remain that way. We need to concentrate our federal border law-enforcement efforts on seeking out the active criminal aliens who wish to do Americans harm, not the laboring Mexicans picking produce for pennies.

And if we do go down that twisting path of conveniently marrying the two issues, if our government convinces you of that, what will be its next sell after the wall? Land mines and machine guns? And if that happens, I reckon the only other question I would have is this: Where are we going to locate the ovens and their smokestacks?

In 1998, the University of Houston's Center for Immigration Research estimated that a minimum of 1,185 illegals (the majority Mexican) died crossing the U.S.-Mexican border between 1993 and 1996. According to a Mexican newspaper's research, 785 people died trying to cross between 1998 and June of 2000. We are presently averaging about five hundred deaths each year due to summer heat, freezing cold, floods, highways, and abuse by some of the worst outlaws in the land: cold-hearted, greedy alien smugglers. Because of such deaths, it is imperative that we bring the federal guidelines for sentencing convicted alien smugglers parallel to those of convicted drug smugglers. Why does our society not consider the crime of smuggling precious human cargo as horrendous as that of illegally importing dope? Have we become that callous? And in response to my own question of callousness, let me offer you this:

In 2005, subsequent to the merger into the Department of Homeland Security, my special agents, under their new authority as U.S. Immigration and Customs Enforcement (ICE), found themselves working a human-trafficking investigation in which six people were whacked. Two of the dead were U.S. citizens. Four were illegal Mexican citizens. When I spoke with the U.S. Attorney's Office about the possibility of seeking the death penalty, under a recently enacted federal law that cited that a smuggler could receive such a sentence when people die during the act of the smuggling violation, you aren't going to believe what I was told.

Under the new law, this was the first trafficking case in my office in which the U.S. Attorney's Office was seeking permission from the Attorney General in D.C. to ask for the death penalty in federal court. However, since we had previously investigated other smuggling operations with aliens' deaths without the U.S. Attorney's Office asking for the death penalty, I asked why now? And in response, an assistant U.S. Attorney in Tucson actually told me that the courts have held that if only aliens die during the commission of a smuggling act, the prosecutors will not usually seek the death penalty. However, if a U.S. citizen dies during the same crime, the U.S. government will be more inclined to seek the death penalty. This assistant U.S. Attorney was as outraged with those guidelines as I.

So, remind me what that old saying is. "Justice is blind?" Or is it, "Justice is sometimes color blind?"

15

REMFs and the Vigilantes

ON SEPTEMBER 18, 1998, I rolled out of the sack relatively early and wolfed down a sunny-side-up with a side of refrieds. The cup of black eye-opener stimulated my senses as I reined my government gas-driven steed to the west. As the sun broke over the slopes of the Perilla Mountains behind us, it looked to be a beautiful, promising autumn morning. I left my driver's-side window down to reap the full benefit of the cool air as I drove toward Paul Spur and Border Road. The early flights of doves searching for their favorite waterhole had begun and they gracefully jetted over and around the fading green mesquites on both sides of the highway. Every few miles I would catch a glimpse of quail coveys as they darted in almost perfect straight lines across the desert floor's red dirt. It was a grand fall morning to be alive. I thought about that a lot these days. How fortunate I was to still be kicking around.

Considering all of the violence the drug trade had been producing, you'd think people would learn to stay out of this stench-of-death business. But the morning before in Ensenada, Mexico, near the border, the Reaper had already extracted his toll among the traffickers. Drug lords had ordered about twenty sleeping people to be dragged out of their beds and slaughtered as they squealed like pigs against a cactus-lined backyard wall. Just another day in the Mexican drug empire. As I watched the quail flush and fly south toward the border, I couldn't help but wonder how much time America had before we would see similar terrorist-related drug massacres in our heartland.

But then again, I reckon the death toll has in reality already begun. Our anonymity and sullen apathy allow us to ignore the miseries that are engulfing all of us more and more every day. While thousands of our kids are dying in dark alleys and vomit-coated crack houses across America, we turn our heads in indifference. We don't want to know about it. It's too much to think about. We figure it's somebody else's job to take care of this kind of disturbing shit. We have cold beer and hot, thick, juicy steaks on the table. We have mind-numbing network talk shows that are so socially redeeming that you can be convinced in an hour that your life is fucked up because it's someone else's fault. We have the vicarious Home Box Office thrill of watching Van Damme or Schwarzenegger slay the dope traffickers for us in a mere one hour and forty-five minutes. Why should we worry about the threat when someone else can do the dangerous work for us in just 105 exciting living-color minutes? It's just like being out there and doing it. Right?

We have a president telling us how great our economy is doing. At least that's what he does when he's not dodging the press about Dick Cheney's superior shooting skills, or the reason we invaded a country that was not responsible for attacking us. We have an entertainment and media industry that thrives on keeping our vegetating minds stuffed with compost so we won't contemplate the real-life issues that are snuffing freedom's light. Here we sit watching bullshit movies about our impending destruction from space invaders or asteroids, and the whole time the fate of our very existence is at this very moment in doubt on our porous borders, right in front of our open eyes.

So there's no real need to think for yourself in America. There's always someone else to do that for you. You don't *need* to know the truth. Did you know that it's virtually impossible now to seat a jury without polling jurors with family members who have either been hooked or booked for dope? How did I learn that? From the news or movies? No. From my personal experience in the courtroom when assisting the U.S. Attorney in jury selection. I bet that's something they don't show you on any HBO courtroom movie.

I had this Mexican informant who had been telling me about a new place where the Agua Prieta cartel was crossing cocaine loads, between Douglas and Paul Spur. The informant said that it was a ranch on the border that only the Border Patrol had a key to. He said that the dopers had found the key hidden near the gate and copied it. So that's where I was headed this morning. Little did I know that some shit would happen today that would remind me that this dope-chasing business is pretty much a U.S. government farce. Today's drug war fornications would be prima facie evidence that the pole jugglers in Washington, D.C., have no more intention of winning this goddamn war than we did in Vietnam.

It was 7:30 a.m. when I spotted a brown Pathfinder 4x4 traveling with a gray Dodge Caravan on the highway coming toward Douglas from the west. Being where they were, and particularly being there at the time of the morning when the Border Patrol completes its shift change—the odds to me seemed pretty fair that they could have crossed the border near Paul Spur like the informant had said they had been doing. I pulled to the side of the highway to wait for the approaching targets. When the Pathfinder passed by me, the Mexican driver glared at me and then snapped his head to attention like he had just been bee-stung in his testicles. I could damn near smell his fear in the morning air. As I flipped my truck around to follow him and the van, I radioed for help. I had that gut feeling that the shit was once again about to hit the proverbial fan.

Now ordinarily, at least down here in Cochise County, when you go up against any mobile dope load you need several pursuit vehicles for each loaded car. And if it's a load of cocaine instead of grass, you can expect a fight that's going to end up in one of three situations: a shooting, a ramming, or both. I guarandamntee that the minimum in the end is going to be a death-defying crash derby.

In response to my call for assistance, only one Customs agent out of the eighteen we had stationed in our office was on the air. Special

Agent Mark Henry was roaming about Douglas working on one of his ongoing investigations when he heard me ask for help. I followed both vehicles into town and radioed Henry where to intercept us. When the bad guys saw Henry waiting for them at the planned intersection, they split up with the Pathfinder turning south and the van continuing on east. Mark took the van and I stayed up on the Pathfinder's ass. Via radio transmissions, Henry and I coordinated the timing on our attempted stops as we hit our red and blue flashing lights at the same time. As we expected, both vehicles bolted like dragsters to an invisible finish line presumed to be anywhere federal agents weren't.

Now, any other time over the past twenty-five years, this would have been a real exciting adrenaline rush for me. But this was the first time that I can honestly say that my heart wasn't in the chase. There was no real frenzy in me. Don't get me wrong; the adrenaline was there, but I was missing something that I had never missed before. It wasn't a piece of equipment or even strategically important gear. It was something much more crucial than any of those material things. It was the fear. Over the years I had walked with the Reaper so much that he didn't scare me anymore. Now, most folks would think of that as a good thing. But to a border narc, it's just the opposite. The adrenaline drives you. But the fear guides you. You can't have one without the other and expect to win.

I knew from the git-go that this guy was going to outrun me. Besides not being freaked and frenzied for the chase, I was outgunned. Motor-wise outgunned. We had begged and pleaded with the REMFs in D.C. to send us short-bed four-wheel-drive trucks with the biggest police pursuit-package V8 motors available. What we got after all our groveling were long-bed four-wheel-drives with the smallest commercial V8 the auto company made. Why? Well, according to my sources, the U.S. Customs Service was at the mercy of the U.S. Government Services Administration (GSA). It seemed that the GSA did all of the government fleet ordering, and they did not distinguish between federal law-enforcement needs and the needs of the other civilian agencies within the government.

In other words, DEA and Customs would receive the same make and model of vehicles that the Social Security Administration would get. So if we don't get lucky and seize something from the dopers with a big V8 in it, it ain't happening for us. The REMFs cut our legs out from under us before we can even get out the starting gate. Such a vehicle mismatch between the narcs and the dopers ends up being equivalent to running a Shetland pony against a registered American quarter horse in a quarter-mile race!

Henry chased the gray van across Douglas, up and down streets and through alleys, until the van broke through the border fence and returned to Mexico safely with the dope load. My Pathfinder flipped around and fled back through Douglas and then west on the highway toward the ranch where both vehicles had illegally crossed the border. I battled back and forth across the highway with the Pathfinder's driver for a full ten minutes. The shit-for-brains outlaw kept trying to run me off the highway when I would try to get around him to brake him down. It was the usual dangerous chase that has almost become mundane to me over the years. We were going 100-plus mph and the asshole's trying to run me off the road. Here he is trying to whack me with his fucking vehicle and the goddamn government REMFs I work for say that I can't shoot his ass! It's okay if he attempts to take my life, but I am not permitted to retaliate because it may be perceived as being too harsh on our supposedly friendly southern neighbors.

And as far as getting any help goes, our Customs Service radio system in Douglas is so screwed up that you're lucky to contact anybody half of the time. And that's just talking from Customs agent to Customs agent. We have *no* communication ability whatsoever with the Highway Patrol, which by the way during this particular pursuit I blew by at warp speed *twice*. And because I couldn't call him and let him know what the fuck was going on, the DPS officer could only get out of my way and look on helplessly as my suspect zipped right past him. And although better than nothing, we had an extremely limited communication capability with the Border Patrol. In other words, here we were approaching the millennium, we had people in space and all kinds of high-power technology, but us guys going up against a deadly billion-dollar illegal empire couldn't even talk on the friggin radio to each other. Disgusting!

Back and forth on the highway, up and down through the desert, me and this dope-smuggling death merchant went at each other until I almost got whacked. It basically ended for me when a steel ranch gate that the doper crashed the Pathfinder through tore loose from the posts, went up and over the Pathfinder, and landed smack dab in the driver's side of my windshield. Part of the gate's sharp steel hinges came ripping right through the windshield, stopping just inches short of penetrating my face and chest. I stopped just long enough to pull the gate out of my windshield (and my underwear out of my tight-clenched ass) as the shitbird warped away from me for the border fence.

Sperling had heard the traffic on the radio and was en route to give me a hand when we pulled up to the border crossing at about the same time. The Pathfinder was running full throttle through the desert on the Mexican side of the border as we impotently sat on the U.S. side of the fence and watched. Then four armed Mexican scouts stood up from where they had been hiding about seventy-five yards into Mexico. Sperling and I were now standing outside our vehicles with no immediate good cover. Expecting the worst, and already armed with MP-5 submachine guns, Sperling and I cocked, locked, and got ready to rock and roll with the bad guys. We put our sights point blank on the scouts' chests. They started to back away in the brush when Allan screamed in a desperate pleading voice, "Let's light their asses up!" God knows I wanted to. I had almost been killed again doing this same useless chasing shit. But still, until these guys capped the first round we were forbidden by our government from starting the firefight. I talked Sperling out of doing the very thing we both wanted to do. No matter how many of our children are murdered by this blight, we as special agents are continually forced to remind ourselves that we're not in the revenge business.

I later talked to the informant and learned that the Pathfinder and the Dodge van had been loaded with about six hundred kilos of cocaine. Talk about frustrating! Folks, the government is going to have to change the way it does business as federal law enforcers. Or at least learn the difference between administering a business and fighting a fucking war. We can't keep trying to enforce the border and keep dope from killing American children if we don't recognize the needs of the agents in the field.

Historically, the Border Patrol and the Customs Service have been run by presidentially appointed commissioners who have no idea what federal law enforcement is all about. For the most part, their pre-appointment backgrounds have been in the administration of private businesses that had nothing to do with law enforcement, much less the border. The FBI has always been properly run like a true enforcement agency, because its directors have always been cops of some nature. The same is true for the DEA administrator. But the U.S. Customs Service, because of its dual functions as an enormous money-collecting agency for the Treasury Department and a law enforcer for the Justice Department, usually ended up with a business manager instead of the law-enforcement leader that was so desperately needed.

So here I was in September of 1998, hanging my head down in the desert dust like an old broke-dick dying mongrel dog. My truck was wrecked. Henry and I were almost whacked because of no backup. The radios didn't work. We didn't have effective pursuit vehicles. The trainees we were getting were worthless idiots. And the bad guys safely returned more than 1,320 pounds of poison to their warehouse in Mexico to wait for another day when we wouldn't be around to stop them. We had a dope-smoking president who used women's twats for his ashtray. And that's not to mention the fact that if we, as government agents, lied to a grand jury we would not only immediately lose our jobs, but we would get to intimately meet all of those butt pirates we'd put in prison over the past few years.

So just about the time that a feller figures things can't get much worse, they generally can, and they usually do. We learned from our informants that the coke load we had chased back to Mexico belonged to Agua Prieta cartel member Panchi Nuñez. She is Judge Joe Borane's standup partner as godmother from the "Douglas tunnel" Camarena baby's christening, which I mentioned in Chapter 7. In other words, that cocaine had been heading from the Mexican side where the godmother reigns as a Colombian cocaine queen, to a stash house on the U.S. side where the godfather rules, or rather did rule, as a judge. Is it any wonder that a guy can get discouraged over this shit?

In January of 1999, the U.S. Border Patrol REMFs pulled a boner of historic proportion. It was one of the dumbest moves I've seen since 1974, when I first started packing iron for the Patrol. They took 25 percent of their agents from the Douglas Border Patrol station and moved them to an interdiction operation on the border in Nogales. In the same breath, they took all of the extra aliens they arrested during the Nogales operation and bused them over to Douglas, where they were released across the border into Agua Prieta. This idiocy created a growth of refugee camps, with folks barely subsisting in cardboard boxes on the Mexican streets. I swear it was reminiscent of the bombed-out cities of Nam thirty years ago. In other words, the REMFs spent your tax money to move masses of desperate repeat crossers to an unprotected area of the border where they had just reduced their force of agents! A master operational plan like this could've only been brain-farted during a fucking D.C. Romper Room play period!

And just when you think the Headquarters REMFs have done their best to fuck something up, Congress gets involved to make matters even worse. It had come to the attention of our nation's Representatives that after they had funded the hiring of thousands more BP agents following the "Chinese horde alert" in San Francisco, there was still an alarming number of illegal aliens being arrested on the southwest border. They couldn't figure it out. In accordance with their D.C. REMF thinking, more agents on the border meant that their mere patrol presence should deter aliens from crossing. But if that's the case, why was it that the Border Patrol was now catching more illegal entrants than before D.C. spent all of that money on hiring?

So these concerns were passed on from the congressional REMFs to the chief BP agents and Border Patrol supervisors in the field. And lo and behold, a new initiative was born. The Border Patrol ordered its agents into a freshly brainstormed border defensive effort. It was called the X defensive position. And what that meant was that each agent would be assigned one particular place right on the border fence that he was to defend. It would be called his/her X! And even if a hundred aliens ran north across the border in your view, if they were not right at your X spot, you were not to leave your position to pursue them. They were allowed to enter the U.S. without a chase because it was imperative that the agents not leave their assigned X. Why? Because if the Border Patrol didn't catch any aliens, then the apparent decrease in arrests would be perceived as a success by the D.C. REMFs. And if the arrest stats went up, the congressional REMFs would be unhappy and blame the Border Patrol for not doing its job. And if that happened, there would be no more funding for more agents and equipment.

So the whole thing got so back-asswardly perverted that U.S. Border Patrol management actually mandated that their agents look the other way and let the aliens run by. And if some agent was forced to accept detained aliens that had been arrested by another law-enforcement agency, he was forced to push them south into Mexico through a hole in the fence so that the number of aliens arrested in the U.S. would never be officially recorded. I've seen it and I know of scores of former and present Border Patrol agents who can testify to it. Even some of the assistant U.S. Attorneys in Tucson knew about this fraud being perpetrated against the American public.

The Border Patrol REMFs were so radical about this deceptive program they had conceived for Congress's benefit, that agents were threatened with disciplinary charges if they left their assigned X. How did this affect the Border Patrol? Hundreds of good agents resigned or transferred to other federal law-enforcement agencies like Customs and DEA. I know of a handful of agents in Arizona who even left to go into local sheriff's departments and the Arizona Highway Patrol.

When you compounded the X program with the dumping of more aliens in an area now strapped for enforcement, the people of Douglas became the victims of a proliferating drug trade, burglaries, home invasions, robberies, property destruction, and even cattle rustling. It was not unusual for me to go for a walk in the morning in the desert behind my house and find fresh pieces of human tissue, blood, hair, and clothing on the rusting barbwire fences. There were so many hordes of aliens that they literally started tearing people's residential fences and walls down during the night when they would run rampantly through the streets of Douglas.

To give you an example of the sheer numbers, when I was a Border Patrol agent in 1974 in Douglas, we were arresting between four hundred and six hundred aliens a month. In March of 1999, the Douglas Border Patrol station, in spite of the X program, arrested 26,000 aliens. And it's easy to understand why they were anticipating an arrest record in April of more than 30,000 aliens.

The aliens got so desperate about crossing, they began to intimidate cops at the drop of a hat. One day during October of 1999, Montijo and I were driving over to Monument #90 on Border Road to check on dope-smuggling activity. As we approached the area we observed about fifty aliens illegally crossing the border into Arizona. We drove to where they crossed and started to get out of our truck to chase them back. About the time we got our truck doors closed we received the first of several barrages of fist-size rocks. Here we were standing armed to the teeth with submachine guns, and these little bastards were standing right out in the open bombing us with rocks! Why? Because they knew damn good and well that our own fucked-up government policy wouldn't allow us to defend ourselves. We were not even allowed to fire warning shots against rock throwers. I know of a few agents who have capped warning shots over rock throwers' heads and have been fired for doing it. But that's only because a REMF has never seen an agent's skull cracked opened with rocks. I have. And with that in mind, a burst of automatic fire spilled over the top of the perpetrators' heads, which gave Monti and me time to retreat without getting crippled for life.

By November and December of 1999, the influx of aliens caused by the REMFs' 2,000-mile-distant decision-making was so tremendous that certain areas of Cochise County were literally reduced to dust bowls from all the aliens' trails cutting through the desert's delicate grasses. We were already in the middle of one of the worst droughts in Arizona's history, and with all of the alien traffic tram-

pling about, certain areas of the county started to look downright dec-
imated. This unintentional destruction looked like a humongous
swarm of locusts had passed over and laid waste to certain areas near
the border. The tons of trash, plastic water bottles, and even human
feces left in their wake angered the folks of Cochise County. The
Mexicans did themselves no favor by making some of their favorite
border-crossing sites into certified waste dumps. One would be hard-
pressed to defend their actions. All you could do was to remind folks
of two things: Discarded trash can be picked up, and sooner or later
trampled grass will grow back. But a trampled, discarded soul can
never be recovered. However, there weren't too many border residents
willing to listen to that kind of rationalization.

The situation got so overwhelming that the citizens of Cochise
County started circulating a petition that could be construed as falling
within a cunt hair short of saying, "We are going to take the law into
our own hands." Whether you agree with that or not, the petition in
the end would serve as a rallying cause for the radical-right vigilante
militia types. The petition read as follows:

HEAR OUR PLEA!

We the undersigned are a group of hardworking,
law-abiding, taxpaying citizens of Cochise County, of
the state of Arizona, of the United States of America.
We share a common problem and share a common
opinion. We live in close proximity to the U.S./Mexico
border. We hope that our leaders at federal, state, and
local levels hear our plea, consider this statement, and
respond to our request for immediate action to solve
the following problems.

It is our belief that our border with Mexico has
been neglected to the point of near non-existence. We
are, because of this, being overrun by illegal immigrants from Mexico. People of many nationalities are
crossing the border in alarming numbers and are
steadily increasing at an even more alarming rate.

Because of this, the quality and security of our lives are being severely affected. Our civil rights, guaranteed by our Constitution, are being violated. Drug influx, home invasion, burglary, theft, and vandalism are on the rise. We see jobs being taken by illegal immigrants who don't pay taxes. We see non-citizens using and abusing our social security, welfare, medical, and emergency facilities. We watch as our government allows this to happen, while giving billions of taxpayer dollars to Mexico and other nations. This happens while our government spreads our military across the world to police other nations' problems. We watch all this knowing that this nation has the ability and resources to secure our border.

It is our opinion and our solemn belief that as this situation worsens and friction increases between citizens and invaders, violence and bloodshed will result. This is our greatest fear. One only needs to look as far as a school history book or current news stories from other countries to realize this is inevitable.

The Border Patrol agents in this area are overwhelmed by the sheer number of invaders and are held back by ridiculous patrol areas and regulations that indicate incompetence and lack of understanding on the part of the upper management. Then to compound the problem, our government cows to Mexico's repatriation demands, further complicating things for field agents.

We want to make it clear that this statement is not construed in any way as a racially biased statement. We do not hate these people or the country of Mexico. This country is great because of the diversity of its people and we are proud of that. However, we believe that the existence and maintenance of our border is essential to our SECURITY, LIBERTY, AND FREEDOM. Security for its citizens is the most important and fundamental responsibility of government. We believe that our government is failing in this responsibility.

If the government refuses to provide this security, then the only recourse is to provide it for ourselves. It is a sickening, dreadful thought that citizens of this nation should ever have to consider such a thing. That is why we make this common plea for immediate and decisive action. We expect a reply to this letter.

Signed:

Laurence S. Vance Jr.

and 234 concerned citizens of the USA

Now, personally, I don't blame these folks one iota for getting pissed off at the government in light of the ignoramus X program. But the problem with this kind of vigilante shit is that when it starts, the bad eggs that are looking for opportunities to further their personal agendas always seem to come out of the woodwork. And I don't mean one or two different individuals or organizations. It seemed like every jerk in southeastern Arizona came to the surface during a series of media interviews that mocked all sanity. But before the circus came to town, we had to have a little catalyst. And that sparked on the evening of April 14, 1999.

On that night, two U.S. Border Patrol agents were assigned their regular patrol duties on the west side of Douglas in what is known as the White Water Draw area. While most of the other agents were being held in town on their assigned Xs, these two lone agents were supposed to patrol the outlying areas in the desert to catch aliens who may have been trying to circumvent the Xs. Being assigned to the evening shift, the young Border Patrol agents picked a spot near White Water Draw to polish off an artery-clogging bag of burgers and fries before it got dark. After scarfing down their supper, the boys got into their mesquite- and cactus-covered surveillance positions overlooking the Mexican border. As they watched the sun go down, they pulled their binoculars out of their equipment bags and started to scan the border fence for crossers.

Each agent secretly dreamed about the life he had left some four or five state-lines away to join the U.S. Border Patrol. With thoughts of home roaming in and out of their subconscious, they began to search the horizon for the usual groups of ten to twenty aliens crossing the desert floor. But when they found their targets that night, all thoughts of home dissipated quickly. As the young agents' eyes strained through their binos in the waning evening light, their pulse rates kicked into overdrive. They kept their eyes trained on a moving black cloud mass as their sweating fingers fumbled for the walkie-talkies attached to their gun belts. "Sector, Sector, this is Delta 635. We have a large group of about six hundred aliens moving on our position! We need immediate backup!"

For the first time ever in the history of Cochise County, a huge group of Mexicans had orchestrated a simultaneous illegal invasion across the border. I imagine it looked similar to Pancho Villa's deadly nighttime attack on Agua Prieta some eighty-five years before. It was the biggest group effort ever mounted against the U.S. Border Patrol in these parts. About two hundred of the stampeding aliens were caught by the Border Patrol that night. The rest of the night's invaders retreated back into Mexico after learning firsthand that the Border Patrol was not going to be intimidated into giving up its defense of the border.

And it really wasn't too big of a deal. The Border Patrol knew how to handle a mass assault because that kind of crap has been a common occurrence in the San Ysidro area of California for the past twenty-five years. But because it had occurred just this one time in Douglas, the politicians, vigilantes, racists, hate mongers, and politically correct Hispanic civil-rights groups fell out of the sky and descended on Cochise County. Douglas was all over the television and papers in a news-media command performance of "let's whip everyone up into a heated frenzy."

Douglas Mayor Borane wanted to sue the American government to open the border up and allow all Mexicans into the U.S. With or without inspection was never clarified, that I'm aware of. The good mayor wanted to guarantee all Mexican laborers the same rights and wages that Americans were entitled to. He actually wanted to put Mexican citizens in U.S. jobs at the wage and benefits parity with our American citizens! The self-proclaimed savior of Mexico was demanding that the federal government reinstate the old Bracero Program, an antiquated and abandoned labor program that was more than half a century old. Under this outdated program, just about any Mexican, regardless of his unknown criminal record and untested diseases, could travel anywhere in the U.S. and take a job. This was the same program that our government ended in the mid 1960s because we couldn't find and deport half of the Mexicans who were supposed to go home after working under it.

Now, the decent ranching folks that surrounded Douglas were the only ones using their heads during what the press dubbed an "alien invasion." They asked Arizona Governor Jane Hull to send the National Guard in to augment the Border Patrol. It would have probably been a done deal until Mayor Borane got wind of what the ranchers were asking for. As could be expected, Borane threw a hissy fit and called Governor Hull. He told the governor that he was speaking for the people of Douglas when he said that his constituents didn't want the National Guard brought into town. Now, when he had time to poll all of the residents of Douglas on this issue is beyond me. After all, he had been spending so much time preaching about the benefits of allowing Mexicans to cross and take whatever U.S. jobs they wanted, it seemed to me he had little time left to actually run the city government.

The folks in law enforcement knew that Mayor Borane's antics to open the border, which in effect would reduce the number of federal agents in town, were greatly appreciated by a lot of different people. But they were the wrong kind of people on the wrong side of law and order. People like his brother, the now-convicted ex-judge, who for a handsome sum of drug money sold Amado Carrillo's bloodletting organization the property for the construction of the infamous drug tunnel. People like the previously convicted dope-smuggling mayor of Agua Prieta, Vicente Terán, who was virtually tied to the Boranes at the hip (in more ways than one). And then there's the rest of the Agua Prieta dope-trafficking cartel. I guess I've made my point here. Everybody's got some kind of hidden agenda to use and abuse the illegal alien with. And it wasn't just limited to the bad guys. The illegals gave all kinds of politicians an excuse to shine and the self-righteous a platform from which to squawk.

Arizona congressmen were screaming for more Border Patrol agents to be sent into Douglas. Governor Hull was thinking about how many votes she could get, or would lose, if she did or did not dispatch the National Guard. When her advisors told her it would be unwise to send the Guard in, she found solid political ground (the Arizona Hispanic vote) in backing Mayor Borane on the issue of opening the border up under the old Bracero Program. Hispanic civil-rights groups, way out of sight some 125 miles away in Tucson, were protesting that the Border Patrol was lying about the unprecedented group of six hundred invaders in order to get more funding and agents from Congress. Aligned right along with this bunch was the liberal Arizona Border Rights Project, which demanded that the U.S. Attorney's Office conduct an investigation into alleged acts of vigilantism. And naturally, to oppose the liberals, there was a conservative group raising hell. The Arizonans for Border Reform, also out of sight in Tucson, was in the news waving flags and carrying signs that read things like, "Illegal Aliens Cost You 30 Billion, F.Y. 1997" and "To Do Nothing Is Treason." And last, but not least, the vigilantes were screaming that their rights were being violated and that they were victims because the U.S. government wouldn't allow them to protect their property by taking the law into their own hands. I swear, the best of the best Looney Tunes cartoons couldn't have been nearly as entertaining or half as crazy!

When you have this much lunacy running rampant, a government agent needs to figure out the single worst threat and deal with it first. To me, the vigilantism was the most dangerous. I recalled that when I was a young Border Patrolman in 1976, old man Hannigan and his sons, who ranched near the White Water Draw area of Douglas, had been arrested and tried for violating the civil rights of illegal Mexicans. After being robbed and burglarized a few times by Mexican bandits, the Hannigans had taken it upon themselves to administer Wild

West justice to the next aliens who ventured across their ranch. They caught a couple or three Mexican fellers one day crossing their property and strung them up by ropes in a tree. Now, it didn't matter to the Hannigans that these boys were innocent "looking for work" fellers and not border bandits. All old man Hannigan could think about was extracting a pound of flesh for revenge.

So the salty old son of a bitch started a fire on the desert floor, much like the one a rancher would use for the branding of cattle. When the irons were hot, the Hannigan's Beast was exposed to the world. After the sadistic bastards were done burning and torturing the Mexicans, the redneck vigilantes unleashed a volley of shotgun blasts that ripped apart the flesh of their defenseless victims. In a state of shock, the Mexicans stumbled and dragged themselves across the desert toward Agua Prieta. They were later found in Mexico with blood-dripping gunshot wounds on top of their blistering, seared black flesh.

But even before the heinous Hannigan brutalities had transpired, I remember there was a neighboring rancher's son who'd drilled a gut shot into another illegal alien a few months earlier. The young man was about eighteen or nineteen when he shot his first Mexican border crosser. The shooter's name was Larry Vance Jr. If the name rings a bell with you, it should. He's the same feller who signed off on the aforementioned vigilante petition. Now, you may think that Vance would have learned his lesson after facing a potential grand jury criminal indictment for shooting a Mexican feller in the 1970s, wouldn't you? Well, not even an indictment ever came to pass because the undersheriff of Cochise County back then was a good old Mormon boy named Jimmy Vance Judd, Larry's second cousin.

As a matter of fact, I guarandamntee that you won't even be able to find a shred of an official report on this shooting in the Cochise County records. I couldn't. And what's more, we'll never know why Vance shot the Mexican. Did he panic when confronted by someone breaking into his ranch house? Or did he just want to see what a piece of lead would do to brown human flesh?

Now, it was a known fact that Judd was a bit of a bigot. When he became the sheriff a couple of years later his feelings on racism surfaced. During a Cochise County law-enforcement meeting concerning a particular isolated black community within his jurisdiction, Sheriff Judd's opening remarks will always be remembered: "Boys, we got us a nigger problem here in Cochise County!"

So it should come as no surprise to anyone that when Judd's kinfolk Vance got his tit in a ringer, the redneck sheriff sent a Spanish-speaking deputy to the hospital to "interrogate" the wounded Mexican citizen. During the questioning, the victim was advised that all concerned, including himself, would be better off if he finished up his bleeding in Mexico. The locked door to the prisoner's ward of the hospital was left open, the deputy turned his back, and there was a mysterious escape of a wounded alleged felon from the hospital that night. I happened to be one of several young Border Patrol agents who ended up getting called to track the Mexican's blood trail back south to the border that particular evening. It only took me about twenty-five years to learn the truth about what really happened that night. Better late than never, I reckon.

So remembering how all of this snowballed back in the '70s, I now also had to consider a recent run-in with two brothers in the Perillas Mountains over their vigilante ideas. The Barnett brothers, who stood with Vance on the issue of the vigilante declaration, had only been ranching in these mountains for the past few years. Don and Roger Barnett were big-game hunters, having gone on safaris and taken game from around the world. I have been told that they possess an ample collection of stuffed animals done up by high-dollar taxidermists. What's my point? These boys like to hunt. They like to hunt exotic animals—and more.

My former Border Patrol buddy-turned-crook, Gary Callahan, became a good friend of Don Barnett after transferring to the U.S. Border Patrol station in Naco from Douglas. At the time I never could understand the new relationship between Callahan and Barnett. But now it makes sense to me. Back in the days Callahan and I rode together, he would often tell me about his trips to South Africa to go hunting. I always thought Gary was going on big-game hunting trips until the day he confided otherwise. It turned out that Callahan was mercing out to the South African government to hunt black folks. Obviously, these two guys were peas of the same pod.

Ironically enough, the Barnetts had made a good portion of the money to buy their ranch from doing legal business with people who were, for the most part, alien smugglers from Mexico. The brothers had a towing service in Tucson and Bisbee where they somehow finagled a working relationship with the Border Patrol to hook and store the seized autos that the Border Patrol caught loaded with illegal aliens. If the government, for whatever reason, didn't proceed with forfeiture proceedings against these vehicles, the Barnetts would release them back to the registered owner at a jacked-up price for their services. In fact, it was so much like legal robbery that the Arizona Department of Public Safety investigated the Barnetts for price gouging that they found was particularly directed at citizens of Mexico.

Now, I didn't know the older brother, Roger, all that well. But I knew his younger brother, Don, and I know for sure he was a real sick redneck shithead. I knew the prick in the '70s when he was a deputy for the Cochise County Sheriff's Department and I was still in uniform for the Border Patrol. In my opinion, ex-deputy Don Barnett was a sadistic fuck when he was forced to resign, and he is probably still one now. He was the kind of lawman who liked to whip up unarmed bad guys when he had them safely handcuffed with their hands behind their backs inside the jailhouse. But give the devil his due; even Sheriff Judd wouldn't tolerate the beating of a defenseless prisoner. The redneck soon-to-be vigilante was forced to resign from the Sheriff's Office and eventually ended up in the Perillas, in my backyard.

The first time the Barnett brothers' shenanigans came to my attention, they tested my skin tone by asking for my official blessings in their planning of vigilante acts. And they specifically requested that I keep their actions a secret from the U.S. Border Patrol. It seemed that they thought if they could get me, in my capacity as a U.S. Customs Service special agent, to enroll them as government informants, that they could get paid *and* have a legal license to hunt Mexican dope mules and illegal aliens. When I asked the vigilantes what their specific "hunting" plans entailed, Don Barnett hemmed and hawed around until he finally spat it out. With a wicked, uneasy, bargaining grin he said, "Well, if we just kind of shoot over their heads, and if they are carrying dope and they drop it, you can pay us a reward for it." During their sales pitch, it was made clear to me that they had their own weapons, electronic sensors, flares, night-vision goggles, radios, and just about anything else a bloodthirsty mercenary or good vigilante would need to take the law into his own hands. And as far as that statement of just shooting "over their heads" goes, Barnett was not even close to being convincing. I think the son of a bitch intended to outright blow folks away.

On my way to contact the U.S. Attorney's Office and report the vigilantes' intentions, I couldn't help but wonder about something that was eating away at my guts. These idiots were trying to make a deal with me to hunt and shoot at Mexican dope mules for a reward. If they are willing to do that, and even though they said it was our secret thing to be kept from the Border Patrol, what other kinds of deals did the Barnetts attempt to make with the Border Patrol to hunt illegal aliens?

Upon arriving back at my office, I immediately contacted the U.S. Attorney's Office in Tucson to get some guidance on how to handle the assholes. To make a long story short, Special Agent Lisandro Montijo and I went out to meet these guys in the Perillas, where we read them the riot act as directed by the U.S. Attorney's Office. During the terse meeting, the vigilantes reiterated that they were armed to the teeth and ready to do battle with the "invaders." In no uncertain terms did Monti and I explain the federal government's position on this matter. We informed them that if they spotted aliens or dope on their ranch, they were supposed to simply call us and tell us where the activity was happening. They were told to make no unauthorized arrests or dope seizures that could possibly result in their federal prosecution for civil rights violations or possession of narcotics.

Monti and I didn't know it at the time, but these were toothless, empty bluffs that the U.S. Attorney's Office never intended to act upon. Why? Because the head U.S. Attorney in each federal district is a politically appointed position. And I guarandamntee you that until the Powers That Be tested the voting winds and constituents' sentiments in

Cochise County, the Barnetts would have a free hand in what they were planning no matter how obscene it may have seemed to you or me.

Soon after the vigilante declaration was circulated, we encountered the Barnett brothers near their Perillas Mountains ranch with a host of redneck buddies. There were about a baker's dozen of the armed dickheads riding in pickup trucks up and down Highway 80 in the San Bernardino Valley. They were stopping on the sides of the highway looking for aliens hiding in cement culverts and creek beds. They were dressed in camouflage fatigues and carrying walkie-talkies, pistols, rifles, and their own stamped badges that said "Barnett Ranch Patrol. Cochise County. State of Arizona." They even had embroidered shoulder patches similar to those of the U.S. Border Patrol. About the only difference in the patches was the fact that the vigilante version read "U.S. Patriot Patrol." In fact, they looked so much like the real thing that I couldn't even tell the difference until I handled one and closely eyeballed it. It was an obvious attempt to fool folks, probably mostly crossing Mexicans, into thinking the vigilantes were agents or at least some kind of approved representatives of the U.S. Border Patrol.

At one point Butch and I observed some of the vigilantes to have about twenty-five Mexican aliens in custody on the side of the highway. For the safety of the Mexicans, we sat off a short distance and watched them until a Border Patrolman arrived to take them off the vigilantes' hands. While we were sitting there waiting, one of the assholes drove up on us and wanted to chew the fat. Being that we're always in plainclothes, I don't think the prick knew who we were because he got awful loose-tongued. I pardoned myself to take a leak and walked out into the desert as I kept an eye on the vigilantes.

When I got back to the truck I could tell by the look on Butch's face that he wanted to evacuate the area in a hurry. We said our adioses to the vigilante and drove off. Then Butch unloaded on me. The ranch-hand vigilante had told Butch that the Barnetts had plans to build a six-room, 4,500-square-foot hunting lodge and bring in big-game safari hunters from around the world to participate in a once-in-a-lifetime hunt. You guessed it. These crazy sons of bitches were going to have safari adventures for people who wanted to track down illegal aliens! Now, we didn't know if that was idle talk coming from the ranch hand or Barnett. But either way you cut it, someone on that ranch was talking about some pretty fucking sick ideas.

The Barnetts' hunting plans so bothered me that I started doing a little research on Border Patrol calls to the Barnett ranch area. It turned out that of twenty-one times the Barnetts confronted and detained aliens, nineteen of the encounters were on weekends or a holiday. Twelve incidents were on Sunday, six on a Saturday, and one on Labor Day. The two unaccounted-for confrontations were done in the middle of the week for the benefit of an ABC news crew that accompanied the Barnetts on a filming segment. In the twenty-one incidents the Barnetts detained a total of 428 people. That we know of, the vigilantes were armed sixteen out of the twenty-one encounters, and the aliens were usually surrounded by Barnett's hunting dogs. We also know, according to witnesses, that on at least one of these armed detentions, one of the Barnett brothers fired a weapon at a running alien.

On May 30, 1999, Douglas Mayor Ray Borane announced that he wanted to put Mexican troops on the border to prevent alien smuggling. Notice that he didn't say anything about dope smuggling, which his ex-judge brother had been tied to. He just wanted to put the Mexican Army on our border to prevent alien smuggling. That's right, the Mexican Army. You know, the guys who smuggle half of the dope into the U.S. and shoot at U.S. narcotics agents while doing it. And the really funny thing is that before he made this announcement he had just come from a meeting with Agua Prieta Mayor and cartel member Vicente Terán! Now, here is a politician who just a couple of weeks before was screaming that it was a terrible, oppressive idea to put U.S. troops on the border, but now he wanted to put the dope-smuggling Mexican Army there.

Between April of 1999 and April of 2001, there were two or three dozen instances of "ranchers," inclusive of the Barnetts, making armed arrests of illegal aliens. Such detention of Mexican nationals infuriated the government of Mexico and brought great concern for

U.S. politico REMFs, especially in light of the new North American Free Trade Agreement. It seemed that if the vigilantes weren't shooting at aliens, the same rednecks were claiming they were being shot at by aliens. Out of three of these shootings I looked into with U.S. Border Patrol agents and Cochise County deputies, we could find no evidence of regular illegal "going north to work" aliens shooting at anyone. In fact, in my twenty-five or so years on the border, I had never seen or heard of a "passing through, going to work" illegal alien shooting at anyone. Besides that, these folks are so poor they couldn't even afford to buy a box of bullets, much less a gun!

Now, granted, there is no denying that there are bad *frijoles* in every bean patch. You are going to have bandits, smugglers, rustlers, and just plain-ass thieves because the good Lord created man with a hell of a lot of flaws. But it seemed to me that a conspiracy to blame the aliens for everything wrong in America was starting to form in Cochise County. I even overheard rednecks in a San Pedro bar planning to start a prairie fire and blame it on the aliens so their "cause" would have more gunpowder with the politicians in Washington. And the more I listened over a second beer, the worse it got. These incredible assholes were even talking about the lack of mule deer in the area, and how that was the fault of the crossing aliens scaring the animals away. Never mind the fact that Arizona Game and Fish would attribute the lack of game in Cochise County to the death grip of the worst Arizona drought in a decade. Oh no. We're going to blame the lack of game on the fucking aliens. And even if part of that was true, and the game did leave certain areas, they weren't killed by the aliens. They simply moved into a different area. Pointing fingers at one group of people—isn't this the way Hitler convinced the Germans that the Jews should be roasted in ovens?

In April of 2000, the extreme-right hate groups got so bad that someone had the nerve to publish and distribute the following flyer:

> NEIGHBORHOOD RANCH WATCH—This vacation is for the winter visitor who wants to help an American rancher keep his land protected while

enjoying the great southwestern desert. Good ol' western individualism spirit of private property. You are
invited to take part. Come and help at the ranches and
help keep the trespassers from destroying private
property. Be a part of the AMERICAN WAY TEAM.

Volunteers may be deputized by the Sheriff if
necessary to keep the peace and protect private property from vandalism and unlawful trespass.

VOLUNTEERISM AT ITS BEST. Serve and protect.

The second page of the flyer spelled out the particulars of the program. It stated that a volunteer would set up his RV at lookout points
on a ranch and report sighting of illegal aliens to the Ranch Neighborhood Watch Program, which in turn would notify the sheriff. The vigilantes were told to bring CB radios, binoculars, spotlights, signal
flares, horns and sirens, infrared scopes and night-vision goggles,
dogs, trip-wire flare launchers, and video cameras. All of this military-
type hardware was going to be used to ambush known paths used by
"lawbreakers."

After reading the flyer and paying particular attention to the part
about the dogs, night-vision goggles, infrared scopes, and trip flares, it
became all too apparent to me that what the ranch hand had told
Butch was true: These assholes were actually getting ready to *hunt*
illegal aliens for sport!

When later asked about the "vacation to hunt illegal aliens" flyer,
Roger Barnett stated that it was all true and that folks would be on
the way to help him. Barnett officially declared he was taking the law
into his own hands when he told a reporter that the ranchers were tired
of the illegal aliens and dope. If the government couldn't stop it, they
would. In a separate interview Barnett went on to say, "It's time for
Americans to take back the country!" If I'm not mistaken, that's just
what the KKK had been spewing at their Mississippi and Alabama rallies in 1970 during their own Klan "Border Watch" activities.

After realizing that these extremist vigilantes were about to get
out of hand, I contacted the U.S. Attorney's Office in Tucson. They

were extremely concerned that the sheriff had been mentioned in the flyer and they requested that I contact Dever and see where he stood on the matter. I knew Larry wouldn't side with these racist hate-mongers, but when I contacted him he told me his hands were tied under an old Arizona statute. And I'll bet you a dime to a doughnut that the guy who wrote the alien-hunting flyer was a former deputy sheriff who had knowledge of the statute. Maybe even someone like ex-deputy Don Barnett. In fact, when contacted by the news media, Roger Barnett stated that he *knew* the people (vigilantes) would be arriving in Cochise County in a few months. Roger refused to elaborate on how he knew this would come to pass.

The statutes that hung Sheriff Dever out to dry are Arizona ARS 13-407-408 and even 411. Although antiquated and probably written during Territorial days, these state laws make it clear that an Arizona resident can use physical force in defense of his premises and property. And in most cases you are allowed to use *deadly* force if you can simply articulate the fact that you were in fear of your life. In addition, the law plainly reads that you have no obligation to retreat from a person before capping him. Kind of like a standing gunfight in the middle of the dusty streets of old Tombstone.

So you see, the assholes who dreamed up the flyer knew the law and they knew they could use these laws to make the sheriff knuckle under to their wishes. I explained this to the U.S. Attorney's Office and my Customs *jefes* in Washington. Well, as usual, the REMFs couldn't make a decision on what to do. Now, I had two concerns here. First and foremost, my agents work in plainclothes all over Cochise County, including on the Barnett ranch. And the last thing I wanted to see was a group of trigger-happy racist vigilantes coming into town in anticipation of capping anything that moves in the brush on one of the "vacation hunting" ranches. The second was under what authority my agents could protect any aliens from being abused by such shitheads. The U.S. Attorney's Office and the REMFs weren't of much assistance on the matter. Their basic response was something we already knew. If you take hostile fire, defend yourselves. If you see an alien being beaten, assaulted, or shot, make an arrest. Other than that I could get no preventive advice or direction. I wanted a way to stop these assholes before innocent folks started dying. But according to the law, we had to wait until the vigilantes had already hurt someone before we could make a move.

So with time on my hands, I began to study my new adversaries. I got my hands on books about the American militias, the Second Amendment folks, the Klan, Neo-Nazi groups, and other hate-mongers. I queried informants, other law-enforcement agencies, the Southern Poverty Law Center, and even news reporters. In the end I connected some very interesting dots concerning the folks who had surfaced in this Cochise County border mess.

Back in January of 2000, presidential candidate Pat Buchanan came to Douglas. He hooked up with Larry Vance and Roger Barnett at different meetings and rallies. The group went up and down the border area screaming about how the aliens were ruining America. It was clear that Buchanan intended to use the aliens as the "whipping boy" part of his reform platform. At one point while out in the desert west of Douglas at the actual border fence, Buchanan proudly showboated for the extremists and vigilantes by illegally crossing on foot into Mexico, and then again by illegally crossing back into the U.S. When an accompanying Cochise County deputy sheriff advised Buchanan not to violate the law in her presence again, Buchanan stated that "if the Mexicans can do it, so can I!" Barnett and Vance looked on in hero-worshiping approval as they defiantly smirked at the deputy. After Buchanan left Douglas, a good number of folks agreed that about the only things this whole parading group of assholes was missing were white sheets and pointy white nightcaps.

Now, here is the really interesting part. Did you know that in his 1996 bid for president, Buchanan's campaign co-chairman was a man named Larry Pratt? Did you know that Larry Pratt is a former Virginia legislator who is the founder of the Virginia-based Gun Owners of America? That's a group of militia-type extremists who are so radical that they think the National Rifle Association is a bunch of limp-wristed wimps and pansies.

According to Morris Dees of the Southern Poverty Law Center and its Militia Task Force (an organization dedicated to informing law-enforcement officers of the activities of hate groups and extremists in the U.S.), Larry Pratt has raised money for anti-abortion extremists, and he is the founder of English First, a 250,000-member group that sponsors efforts to block bilingual education. His platform advocates an armed militia on the border to stop illegal aliens and drugs. Having been at the infamous "Rocky Mountain Rendezvous" in 1992, where hate-mongers and militia types gathered in Colorado, he is known as the father of the modern militia movement. It was in Colorado that plans were laid for a citizens' militia, plans that sparked a movement that led to the most destructive act of domestic violence perpetrated by U.S. citizens that our country has ever known: the Oklahoma City bombing.

Dees asserts that at the Rocky Mountain meeting, alliances were forged between Posse Comitatus, the KKK, Aryan Nation, Neo-Nazis, tax resisters, and the Second Amendment gun nuts. According to Dees, the unprecedented meeting was a "watershed for the racist right." Vigilantes and the racist right. I found myself asking how much difference, if any, there was between them. And if there are some good people with the right intentions mixed up with the vigilantes, how long would it take for them to be tainted by the racist right? I didn't have to wait long for the answer.

On May 4, 2000, Roger Barnett took an ABC news crew with him on an alien hunt. Not only were the Barnetts armed when they surrounded nine sleeping Mexican aliens, but they also used dogs on them. In a separate incident, Don Barnett boasted to *Time* magazine that he slammed an alien to the ground and threatened to kick the shit out of him, and further threatened to take a photograph of the beating to send to the victim's relatives and friends in Mexico.

On May 13, 2000, the vigilantes had a two-tier rally in Cochise County. It was hosted by Barbara Coe and her racist-right California Coalition for Immigration Reform. After going to the first part of the rally at a hotel in Sierra Vista, participants were invited to the second half at Barnett's ranch. It was during the meeting in Sierra Vista that my worst fears were proven correct. The Klan made an appearance and passed literature out. Some of the vigilantes asked them to leave, but it was too late. The fly had already gotten into the ointment and he would eventually want more.

It was later learned that at the Sierra Vista meeting, the California Coalition for Immigration Control had presented Roger Barnett with a poster of himself and a 1776 Minuteman. The racist Coalition dubbed Barnett a modern-day minuteman for his "patriotism in defending his country and our border from the illegal alien SAVAGES who kill livestock and slit the throats of dogs." Now, I've been on the border the better portion of my life and I got to tell you folks that I have never seen a cow or a horse that was killed by illegal aliens. And even if they had wanted to kill one, what the hell are they going to use to catch it, hold it down, and then butcher it up for a piece of meat? A rock? A stick? Or a friggin two-inch penknife, which is about all the utensil these impoverished fellers will have on them? This is just more of that Neo-Nazi "blame the alien for anything and everything" bullshit.

Time magazine eventually photographed Barnett standing next to a fence with his .223 caliber military semiautomatic assault rifle in hand. He was being written up and hailed as a "rancher hero" by just about every newsmagazine and paper that was hungry for a good story. Through the dozens of interviews and quotes, no one ever asked him where the money came from to buy the ranch he was now "defending." No one asked about the fact that he owned the largest tow-truck service in Arizona. A tow-truck service that tows and stores vehicles that are caught being driven by those who prey on the illegal alien: low-life, blood-sucking alien smugglers. What blatant hypocrisy. You make money off the aliens' misery one day, then turn around and blame them for the country's problems the next day!

The far right even started distributing pictures of an armed Roger Barnett standing across from Mel Gibson under the title "The Patriot." What a hero. Always armed to the teeth when he surrounded poor unarmed folks with dogs. Come to think of it, I wonder where this patriot was during Vietnam? We surely could have used a brave man like him. That is, if he didn't mind going up against others who were equally armed. I wonder why the media or the California Coalition for Immigration Control never asked "The Patriot" why he never *volunteered* for duty in Vietnam. But come to think of it, in the 1960s and early 1970s he was probably already towing alien-smuggling vehicles for a profit that would eventually gain him this ranch to "defend" as an American hero.

On May 18, 2000, an e-mail threat was sent to Arizona Governor Jane Hull's website. In fear of border violence escalation, and no doubt loss of revenue from scared-off tourists, this e-mail was never released outside the law-enforcement community. In response to the actions of the vigilantes and Barnetts, it read verbatim:

> Last Name: Human Being
> First Name: Mexico
> Feedback: Clear and Short
> For every Mexican killed by your shooters, the damned rangers [believed to mean "ranchers"], we will kill one American traveling in our country. We have too many places to do it. Acapulco, Vallarta, Cancun, who knows? Do you think are reasonable to kill all Americans living for more than ten years in some place in Mexico, only because their visas are expired. They are still illegal aliens in our country. This is not one of too many messages about it. This is real. Be careful. Arizona first, Texas second, who will be third??? Maybe an American traveling. Last moment great offer. Two American kids for the next Mexican killed by shooting. We are now 30, tomorrow maybe 50. All us are hungry and armed.
> Sincerely yours
> Mojados@yahoo.com

The Arizona Department of Public Safety noted that the word *mojados* is a derogatory term used to describe illegal aliens from Mexico. DPS also noted that Mexican citizens do not normally use this term when referring to their people. I wholeheartedly agree with that assessment. Therefore, it would be reasonable to conclude that this threat was written by someone other than a Mexican. Perhaps the type of fellers who like to blame fires on others.

By February of 2000, Roger and Don Barnett began to branch out in their pursuit of being American heroes. Because the U.S. Attorney never moved against them, their audacity and contempt for U.S. law enforcement recognized no bounds. The armed vigilantes actually began to pursue and force to a stop vehicles traveling the Arizona highways that were carrying Mexican aliens. It was reported that they would flash their headlights off and on as they followed and waved the suspect vehicles to a stop. And if we know for a fact that they did this to Mexicans, one can only wonder how many innocent citizens they stopped and detained on public roadways while hunting cars and trucks containing illegal aliens. Regardless of politics, why the U.S. Attorney's Office and the FBI did not pursue these obvious human-rights violations is beyond me.

On May 30, 2000, one week to the day after I had eavesdropped on the "fire bug" rednecks in the bar, a blaze broke out along the San Pedro River that burned two homes and the largest, oldest cotton-wood tree in the preserve, and did millions of dollars of other damage. I guess I don't have to tell ya'll who the news media blamed, now, do I? And that was the crazy part. How could they possibly attribute it to illegal aliens, since no one saw who started the fire much less the fact no suspects were identified or taken into custody? I reckon it was just easier to interview the local barfly redneck and ask him who he *thought* started the fire.

By June of 2000, Barnett and his vigilantes had everyone up in arms. Governor Hull was calling for the Mexican community to remain calm while she made statements to the press that any act of vigilantism would not be tolerated by her office. The Mexican government opted to hire American attorneys in an effort to build a case against the vigilantes. Even the fucking dope mules got into the act. I reckon the armed vigilantes' threats had the mules so rattled that they started packing pistols on dope runs across the Barnett country for self-protection. Before, it was a pretty good bet that the lead coyote may be armed. But now we were seeing others under his command packing also. That's right. The whole goddamn thing backfired on the vigilantes and put our U.S. Customs and Border Patrol agents in more of harm's way.

In June of 2000, a Texas-based group calling itself Ranch Rescue announced it would be coming to Cochise County to assist Barnett in patrolling his property. These had to have been the same folks who had distributed the "vacation to hunt aliens" flyers in April. They stated that they would be making "lawful apprehensions" of illegal aliens. On their Internet site, members were being told it was up to each individual vigilante if he wanted to make the arrests armed or unarmed. However, the implication was that the participating vigilantes would be putting their lives at risk if they were unarmed.

On June 15, 2000, the citizens of Arizona learned what most law-enforcement officers in southern Arizona already knew, that the Barnetts were for the most part just common bullies. A Tucson judge awarded $1.3 million to a broken-down trucker. The Barnetts had given him a tow and then unlawfully held his truck. Not only did they violate state law and keep the guy's truck ransom for two-and-a-half months, they also sent a previously called tow company away, then disabled the truck so they could claim it as their own tow. During the trial it also came out that in 1996 Don Barnett had been charged with two felony counts of theft and fraud, and a misdemeanor count of threatening and intimidating a Mexican guy who had come to reclaim his vehicle from the Barnett tow service. It turned out that after Barnett cussed and threatened to kick the Mexican's ass (where have we heard this before?) and ran him off, Barnett filed an abandoned title with the state of Arizona, saying that no one ever came to claim the car. This was a fraudulent effort to steal the car and sell it for a profit. In 1996, Barnett had pleaded guilty to one count of disorderly conduct "by engaging in violent and seriously disruptive behavior." Had this gone to trial without Barnett pleading guilty, a lot of other prior bad acts involving Barnett's use of his towing business to strong-arm people and force them to pay exorbitant rates would have come to light. And these are the "hero patriots" the racist-right vigilantes have chosen to hunt down the "savage" illegal aliens!

On August 4, 2000, Javier Bencomo Arreola, an illegal alien from Mexico, filed a civil lawsuit in the U.S. District Court in Tucson against two Cochise County wannabe vigilantes who at gunpoint detained and imprisoned him and other citizens of Mexico some fifteen miles north of Douglas. The suit sought $50,000 for pain and injury, and another $250,000 in punitive damages. Finally, someone was talking the language the Barnetts and other vigilante monkeys would understand. And I'm sorry to say that by the time someone learned how to head these assholes off, it was too little too late. Innocent lives had already been lost on the Reaper's line.

The record-breaking heat of the new millennium's first summer was so sweltering that even the goddamn lizards headed north. It was the worst time imaginable for the U.S. Border Patrol REMFs to conduct a politically expedient reorganization of their priorities and use of agents. Because the Barnetts were so popular with the national news folks, and because that would eventually attract more unfavorable press for the Border Patrol in light of the new funding they had recently procured from Congress, the agents were ordered to saturate the border just south of the Barnett ranch on the east side of Douglas. Where I had historically seen maybe one agent on patrol in the Barnett ranch area, there was now a force of twenty or thirty Border Patrol agents.

This REMF maneuver did two things. First, it stacked agents on the east side of Douglas and consequently restricted the manpower available to respond to patrol duties on the west side of town. And second, it pushed the crossing Mexicans further out into the rough desert terrain on the west side of Douglas, because they were aware that most of the agents were patrolling in the opposite direction. In a three-week period between the end of July and the middle of August, law-enforcement officers sadly retrieved the bodies of three dead illegal aliens west of Douglas. A fourth body was discovered by Border Patrol agents on August 24. A fifth was stumbled upon on September 3. And a sixth badly decomposed body was spotted in the desert west of

Douglas by a Border Patrol helicopter on October 19. A shameful legacy of almost one human being per week for the summer.

Could they have been saved had the Border Patrol not been so intent on pleasing one man and attempting to keep him out of the news headlines? I don't know for sure. What I do know is that we had never had five border crossers die in as many weeks on the west side of Douglas. Why was it that all the deaths were out west and none of them were on the east side near Barnett's heavily patrolled ranch? The government big shots were more worried about bad press than human lives!

On August 20, 2000, Roger Barnett detained forty-three illegal aliens on his ranch and turned them over to the U.S. Border Patrol. The agents reported that when they got there, Barnett and his wife were feeding the aliens cookies and giving them water. Is this the brother of the asshole who'd "slammed a Mexican to the ground and threatened to kick his ass" just weeks prior? Although the "patriot" was obliged to detain the Mexicans in order to keep face with the right-wing racists who applauded him in their ranks of American heroes, he had toned it down quite a bit. No doubt the August 4 lawsuit filed against one of his fellow vigilantes had put the damper on Barnett's hunting spirit. Besides, Barnett couldn't afford such a suit. He already had enough problems from riding roughshod over people in the truck-towing business.

Toward the end of August 2000, Roger Barnett filed for bankruptcy protection, seeking to reorganize his towing service under Chapter 11 pursuant to the $1.3 million judgment against him. It was a just reward for the strong-arm tactics he so desired to carry over into his vigilante activities against Mexican aliens.

The vigilantes' acts caught the attention of just about every major newspaper and magazine in Arizona and the rest of the U.S. They were plastered all over the front pages, where they heroically portrayed their illegal apprehension of Mexicans as incidental to their ranch "surveying" duties. And one of the most irritating things about the whole sordid affair was the way the gullible newspaper reporters referred to the Barnetts as "ranchers." What a pile of cow shit. In fact, these guys wouldn't recognize cow manure if they stepped in it because they aren't dyed-in-the-wool ranchers. That's something you have to be born into. You can't just go out and buy into it. There's a hell of a deep-ass canyon between owning a ranch and being a rancher. That's why the brothers had to hire a ranch manager to run it for them. And I can tell you for a fact that none of the surrounding San Bernardino Valley real ranchers thought much of the Barnetts or their actions. In fact, their sentiment was, "What real rancher has the time to chase Mexicans, and why would you want to, anyway? All they're doing is walking across God's country on their way to a better life. They've been doing it for two hundred years. What's so different about it now?"

On October 21, 2000, the alien-hunting party of the Texas Ranch Rescue showed up on the Barnett ranch. I never saw more than a half dozen people with two or three tents set up. Special Agent Allan Sperling had the opportunity to encounter one of the boogers during a routine traffic stop he made near Barnett's ranch. Although the vigilante's pickup truck had Louisiana tags, a query of his background showed that he'd moved around the Deep South before ending up in Texas. He had been previously arrested in Mississippi for possession of a concealed weapon. The Ranch Rescue volunteer had done three years in a Texas prison for forgery, and before that he had been under federal investigation for possessing and selling machine guns. After such fun and games, he came under the scope of another federal investigation when he threatened to bomb a private industry in Texas.

A second vigilante was found by U.S. Border Patrol sources to be a helicopter pilot for a free enterprise known as Angel Fire Rescue. This crazy son of a bitch offered to hunt aliens by air for a reward. Bounty hunters or mercenaries? Take your pick. And these were just two of the six Ranch Rescue heroes who showed up in Cochise County to help the Barnetts run down illegal aliens! As a federal agent it kind of makes me feel warm and fuzzy all over knowing such outstanding citizens are willing to lend a hand in upholding the law. I wonder if such high-caliber fellers had ever worked for or had at least been Southern acquaintances of Klan Wizard David Duke.

After the Ranch Rescue group had met with the Barnetts, they decided the following agenda for their militia-oriented flock would be necessary in the future: All volunteers would dress in military-style desert-tan khaki battle-dress uniforms and combat boots with matching boonie hats; firearms would be required for Ranch Rescue security services. The following military calibers were designated as the only acceptable weapons to be carried: .223 or .308 rifles, 9mm or .45 caliber pistols, and/or a .12 gauge shotgun with buckshot, slugs, or flesh-slicing fléchette rounds. All ammunition was to be the standard military full metal jacket. Military web gear and extra ammo magazines were also recommended. And that, my fair-haired friends, is pretty much how a militia/paramilitary hate group is born.

When later asked by the reporters if they were armed for the explicit purpose of hunting down illegal entrants, the Barnetts emphatically lied in denial. As usual, the news media bought it and never ventured to look further.

It's too soon to say how such acts of taking the law into your own hands will turn out for the Cochise County Ranch Patrol or the Texas-based Ranch Rescue. I'm not sure of the intentions of the U.S. Attorney's Office. To date, I know they're looking at handling Roger Barnett in a discreet manner in hopes of not turning him into a martyr for other vigilantes to follow. And I tend to think the whole vigilante initiative in Cochise County may just die now that the lawsuits have started hitting them in the pocketbooks. But I'll tell you this for sure: None of this shit would have ever transpired had it not been for the bad policy-making of REMFs who have never seen the border, and yet they come up with initiatives like the fraudulent and insane X policy that the vigilantes would later use as a tool.

In the spring 2001 issue of the Southern Poverty Law Center's *Intelligence Report,* the Barnett brothers, Ranch Rescue, and Barbara Coe and her California Coalition for Immigration Reform were awarded the detestable honor of appearing in the "Immigration & Hate" section. I found it of particular interest that David Duke and Pat Buchanan's activities were documented in the same alarming article.

Between April 4, 1999, and February 2, 2003, there were forty-eight documented incidents in which armed private Cochise County citizens threatened and apprehended individuals presumed to be undocumented immigrants. Thirty-one of these incidents are attributed to the Barnetts, who, because they were never before prosecuted, only got braver and braver as they continued their vigilante shenanigans.

On February 2 and 8, 2003, during two separate incidents, the Barnetts allegedly assaulted three federal agents in the performance of their official duties. One of the federal agents was yours truly. The assistant U.S. Attorney in Tucson who drew up the subsequent indictment charging the Barnetts with violation of 18 USC 111, assault on a federal officer, was killed in a hunting accident before he could pursue the case. As far as I know, and for whatever political reasons he may or may not have had, the U.S. Attorney for the District of Arizona declined to pursue the criminal indictments against the vigilantes. What follows, in my humble opinion, is what happens when indifference begins to rule the hearts of good men.

On October 30, 2004, Roger Barnett allegedly pointed a loaded semiautomatic assault rifle at five people who just happened to be Mexican-American U.S. citizens instead of Mexican citizens. Three of the victims were little girls between nine and eleven years old. That's right, folks, baby girls! And to this date, although a Cochise County Sheriff's deputy did cite Roger Barnett for eight felony counts of aggravated assault and ten other misdemeanor counts, no federal or state court in the land has proceeded criminally against this vigilante. It is my understanding from what I've read that during the time of the assault, Barnett, a man who has been branded "Minuteman, patriot, and hero," actually pointed the weapon at the little girls and threatened to shoot them. Goddamn! Ain't that something to be proud of.

At the time of this writing, the only court action regarding Roger Barnett's alleged assault of children is an ongoing civil lawsuit that was filed in November 2004, by the two adult Mexican-American victims. However, you have to wonder: if these children and adults had not been U.S. citizens, but rather poor unfortunate illegal aliens from Mexico, would any politicians or attorneys in our country have lifted one little finger to help them? I know the Southern Poverty Law Center out of Alabama would have. But they are an exception to the rule.

You know, if the greedy politicians in Arizona and Cochise County are so goddamn scared of repercussions from conservative voters, I can understand how vigilantes assaulting big old strong federal agents can be swept under the rug. But when these motherfucking vigilantes get so brazen as to start putting gun barrels in the faces of hysterical, crying little girls who are actually reduced to begging for their lives, we as an American society have lost our moral ground.

Although the laws of the land must be enforced, we don't need and cannot condone any form of vigilantism. Sooner or later it always gets out of hand. What the people want is simple. They want law, order, regulation, and security on our last great frontier. Without question they deserve that. However, if the U.S. government cannot provide it, then the vigilantes, racists, and hate-mongers will do so for all the wrong reasons. It's as elementary as that.

16

The West Corrals

DURING THE FIRST MONTHS of 1997, the Douglas Office of Investigations was blessed with the arrival of four new "baby" special agents. It was one of the most unusual mixes of talent and abilities I had ever seen under one roof. Arriving together were a Puerto Rican *caballero* (gentleman), an Oklahoma Indian cowboy, a Norwegian boy with Viking blood, and a Heinz 57 gringo city dude from the motor town of Detroit, Michigan. After being assigned to my team and catching a few loads of dope together, the youngsters began to bond and became the best of friends. When you are lucky enough to have such a team of diverse individuals whose completely different characteristics complement each other in the line of duty, there's no limit to what bad guys you can take down. Any good lawman will tell you that your investigative techniques are only as good as the limits of your imagination and talent.

Norman DelToro was a quick-witted Puerto Rican kid of about twenty-five. He sported a black mustache and an equally dark head of short-cropped hair that contrasted with his light complexion. He had a wicked twinkle in his brown eyes that reminded me of another mischievous kid I once knew. Me. He was a native Spanish speaker we sorely needed in our office. He was intelligent, aggressive, a super sleuth with informants, and I could tell he would rise a head above the rest as an outstanding narcotics investigator. I immediately began to turn all of my informants over to his care. I figured it was time for the old man to kick back and smell the roses a bit.

Leo Edwards was a twenty-four-year-old Okie with a good portion of Native American Indian blood surging through his veins. He spoke with a southern Texas-Oklahoma drawl that jumped right at you when he said "ya'll." You really couldn't tell he had Indian blood in him, but the Okie cowboy part stood out. He was one of those boys who just looked like he was born to wear a Stetson, blue jeans, and Justin roper boots. He lived by that Southern kicked-back pace, slow and deliberate. In a race you may get there first, but Leo would be there for the duration, even during the toughest of times.

Gary Friedli was a thirty-five-year-old Norwegian boy from Minnesota. He was a little older than the others because he had taken a longer way around in his career with U.S. Customs before becoming a special agent. He was a big, strapping Viking type with a body befitting an NFL linebacker. He stood about six-foot-three and weighed around 250 solid pounds. All muscle and no fat, Gary loved the outdoors and soon hooked up with Allan Sperling to learn how to track and cut sign on border outlaws. Gary was a thinker. He wouldn't open his mouth to ask a question or make a comment until he had thought everything through and through. I always got a chuckle out of watching him working on a problem. It was almost as if you could see the wheels of his mind turning as he processed the situation looking for the right answer.

Mark Henry was about thirty years old. He was the only one who had some experience at being a U.S. Customs special agent. He had been stationed in the foul air of Detroit, where he decided there wasn't enough law-enforcement action to suit him. He came to the Mexican border to find it. He was an unusually quiet bachelor with a somewhat pudgy build. He was smart as a whip and kind of standoffish in the beginning. An intellect and avid reader, Mark had opinions that he kept to himself until he was asked. But once asked, he'd lay into your ass with his point of view even if it was the complete opposite of the ruling majority's. I was worried that he wouldn't mix in well with the team. My fears rapidly dissipated as I began to witness him in action. He was cool and thoughtful under fire. He always maintained presence of mind and a focus on his partners' safety.

Shortly after these Four Musketeers got to Douglas, we began to work a pretty violent group of dope smugglers in an area known as the far-west corrals. These shipping pens were made of thick old oak boards supported by even older railroad ties that were buried in the ground as corners and crosses. They were located about a half a mile west of the Douglas Port of Entry, right dead center on the border. With one set of livestock pens located on the U.S. side, and one set of pens on the Mexican side, these corrals are used for the importation and exportation of cattle and horses between the two countries. For all practical purposes, I reckon you could call them the livestock port of entry.

The corrals were a natural setup for dope smugglers, being that there was a continual presence of legitimate activity to hide behind. Not only was there the constant milling of cattle and horses waiting to be loaded and shipped in semi trucks, but the dust they raised running through the corrals was equivalent to the grenade smokescreens we used for cover in Vietnam. When the livestock were running up and down those wooden chutes between the two countries, there was enough dust and dried manure in the air to choke a full-grown diamondback rattlesnake. And I reckon that was just one of many reasons the dope smugglers loved the area for illegally crossing the border.

We took a good number of dope loads from a particular group of smugglers that hung around the corrals. But, Katie bar the fucking doors, none of them came easy. These assholes were damn near as determined and dangerous as the Big Sandy smugglers. No matter what we tried to do to ensure the safety of our agents and any innocent bystanders, we always ended up in a fight when dealing with these sordid cockroaches. Some of them were armed to the teeth when we busted their ass. And you'd figure these would be the worst of the lot. But they weren't. As long as you got the drop on the mules in an ambush, they'd usually dump their guns and give it up without a fight.

I wish I could say the same thing for the drivers of dope-loaded vehicles that came out of the corral area. Believe it or not, these salsa-dipped dickheads were always the worst ones to go up against. I guess it's because in a speeding vehicle they felt invincible compared to having to hoof it on foot through the desert like the mules. Believe me, every year more and more cops die from vehicle collisions than from going down in a gunfight.

As if we didn't have enough shit going on around the west corrals, to make matters worse it was also a choice crossing-point for the hundreds of illegal aliens desperately seeking to enter the U.S. The problem this presented was one of simple math. The Border Patrol makes more arrests than any other federal, state, or local law-enforcement agency in the country. Although they may not always be felony arrests, the sheer numbers are sooner or later going to net you some real badass fugitives, terrorists, criminals, or just plain crazy assholes. Old border agents have a saying, "Only God knows what goes on at night on the border." One clear, crisp fall night we were working a narcotics surveillance near the corrals when Edwards and I heard about six to eight pistol shots ring out in rapid succession. Now, to be totally honest, this isn't unusual on the border, because the Mexicans are always having altercations of some nature or the other on their side of the line. But we could tell that these shots were not only on our side of the border, they also were close to us. I immediately radioed our other agents on the surveillance, checking on their welfare. After learning that it wasn't any Customs agents who had capped the rounds, I cranked up my vehicle and headed off in the direction of the shooting.

When I neared the area of the shots, I saw a Border Patrol vehicle stopped in the brush about a quarter of a mile north of the west corrals, off Chino Road. About the time that I pulled up and got out of my vehicle, a young Border Patrol agent came running out of the mesquites with his flashlight shining my way. I asked him if we had any agents down and he responded by pointing his light out into the brush showing me where his partner was. In between his gasps for air, he blurted out that his partner was okay but an illegal alien from Mexico had been shot. I ran off into the brush toward the shooting, shouting ahead of myself, "U.S. Customs agent coming in to help! Don't shoot!"

When I got to the shooting scene, I hooked up with a second young Border Patrol agent as he stood trembling over a downed and bleeding Mexican man. The alien was moaning and incoherently muttering in Spanish as he lay sprawled on his back on the cold desert floor. The pain he was experiencing probably led him to hallucinate that he was in limbo between hell and a worse hell. But in reality he was not only shot to shit, he was also lying in one of the most wicked thickets of prickly-pear cactus and white-thorned mesquites I had ever encountered. Talk about nothing going your way!

As we attempted to cut through the natural barrier of brush in an effort to render aid to the Mexican, the young shaken agent explained to me that the guy had gone bonkers when he'd tried to arrest him. The agent pensively looked away into the surrounding darkness toward the border as he shook his head in disbelief. He was searching for what I knew to be an elusive answer to an equally fleeting question. How the fuck did it happen so quickly? Why did he force me to shoot him?

With some simulation of composure, the young agent told me that the crazed Mexican came at him with rocks and a large piece of wood. It was painfully obvious that the kid wished he hadn't been forced to use his weapon. In a quiet, breaking voice he said that it wouldn't have been so bad if the guy had been by himself. But he was accompanied by a group of about twelve other border crossers. The BP agent said that he was scared that if the Mexican had been successful in knocking him down, the remainder of the group would have jumped in and finished him off.

He looked at me as if I was going to second-guess his decision. His eyes pleaded for an agreeing answer. In consolation, I patted him on the back and told what I believed to be a comforting truth. It wasn't his decision at all. It was the asshole's choice to bring this shit down on himself when he picked up the rocks and stick. And that in fact was the straight and narrow of the matter. There's not an agent alive who wants to cap a guy. We do what we are forced to do by the immediate circumstances. We respond to that level of resistance and force in the manner necessary to survive the confrontation. Plain and simple. Do you want to go home after your day of duty, or not?

While waiting for the paramedics to arrive, we attempted to locate the gunshot wounds without moving the Mexican around. The guy's blood continued to ooze into the desert sand and I was scared he was going to go into shock. I engaged him in conversation in an attempt to keep him from losing consciousness. I kept telling him he was going to be okay, knowing damn good and well he was losing way too much blood. Somewhere in the closing darkness around us, I felt the Reaper's presence as he crept in to make another claim.

I could see that one of the Border Patrol agent's bullets had penetrated the Mexican's elbow area and tunneled through the arm, leaving an open furrow of pink and red flesh. I gently lifted the arm and found a small, round hole in the guy's shirt over his stomach. The round had evidently continued through the arm and entered the internal organs. Ever so lightly I ran my hand across the Mexican's belly back to his ribs. Over one of the ribs I found a bulging knot about the size of a nickel. The lead was just under the skin. The round had traveled across his midsection, coming to rest as it lodged between the skin and rib. It was so close to having exited the body that it would have been possible to remove the bullet with nothing more than a small razor.

From what I could see of the wounds, there was still way too much blood surging from this guy's body. Within a few minutes, paramedics arrived and we assisted them in rolling the Mexican over as they looked for other gunshots. We found where a second round had entered the alien's right hip. The paramedics whipped out their scissors and skillfully cut the guy's pants off. I nearly choked on my own spit when I saw the pool of clotted, dark blood between the Mexican's legs directly under his crotch. We checked the dude's genitals and found them to be intact. Boy, was this guy lucky! The round had exited somewhere under his scrotum, leaving his manhood unharmed. If he lived, he probably wasn't going to be able to take an enjoyable crap for a while. But that was the price he'd have to pay for trying to take a Border Patrol agent out. Fuck with the law and meet the Reaper. It was his choice.

A couple of days after the shooting we went back into the area on another dope operation. We changed from nights to days knowing that the smugglers would do the same after hearing about the Border Patrol shooting. One early morning we set up a covert surveillance with Jesse Gutierrez hidden near the corrals in the brush. We had information from an informant that the dopers were going to make a predawn run. So Jesse dressed out in camouflage and got in position before sunup.

Right after first light Jesse began to read the bad guys' mail as the operation kicked off. He watched through his binos as a pickup truck drove south on Chino toward the corrals. The dope smugglers in Mexico could be seen as they used handheld radios to talk to the driver. They coached him into position between the corrals using the ever-present livestock for cover. The bundles of dope were packed in from Mexico and thrown into the truck as Jesse lay perfectly still under the desert brush. As the loaded truck departed the corrals and headed north, Sperling and I readied to make the intercept and arrest. We were about a half a mile north of the corrals, off Chino Road. We had hidden our trucks in a nearby shopping center parking lot where we were waiting in adrenaline-driven anticipation. The acid burned my stomach as I listened to Jesse on the radio. Showtime was just around the corner!

As Jesse radioed us the description of the drug-laden truck, we spotted it as it approached the shopping center. We knew we were in a world of shit when the truck turned into the parking lot instead of heading out of town on the highway. This usually indicates that the smuggler's counter-surveillance team has spotted us and the load driver has been radioed to abort the load and run at all cost for the border. This is where it *really* gets hairy.

As Sperling and I pulled our vehicles into position to intercept the smuggler as he entered the parking lot, the asshole went 10–8 on us, going into that ever-so-dangerous frenzied escape mode. He floorboarded the gas pedal, leaving burning rubber and screaming civilians fleeing for their lives in the parking lot. Put the women and children to bed, because that's going to be the only safe place to be!

This crazy son of a bitch started ramming into vehicles and endangering the lives of man and beast. We had a sudden and informal multiracial, multi-age, open-invitational track meet in the parking lot. Jack LaLanne would have been proud of these folks. If they weren't in shape you couldn't tell it. They sure as hell moved like it was the University of Arizona fifty-meter high-hurdle quals! People were jumping over cars in athletic form best described as terror-inspired. They were running for cover wherever they could find it. The only way to stop this scumbag was to disable his vehicle. We couldn't cap the guy because a bad shot would put civilians at risk. He had to be taken out as quickly, safely, and as soon as possible. It was imperative that it be done *now!*

In the middle of this "aw shit" situation, you have to understand that this is the type of "Action Jackson" crap that Sperling lives for. So, being the civic-minded good trooper he was, and having the biggest, oldest, baddest dually truck in the U.S. Customs Service fleet, Sperling took aim at the smuggler's broadside. As the outlaw's truck crossed in front of his bow, a shit-eating grin came over Sperling's face. With a death grip on the steering wheel, Sperling gleefully spurred his steel steed forward into mortal combat.

Wham, bam, thank you ma'am! Sperling nailed the bastard so hard that it knocked the smuggler out of the fucking driver's side clear over into the passenger's seat. Needless to say, the drug-laden vehicle came to a stop and we took the dickhead into custody without having to cap his ass. He did four or five years of federal time for the five hundred pounds of marijuana he possessed. I later heard that this dude went to see the prison dentist quite a bit. It seemed that it was something concerning a number of his teeth being jarred loose.

This was a repeated scenario with this particular group of smugglers for about a year and a half. They would ram-and-run anyone who tried to arrest them. They didn't give a flying fuck if innocent civilians got in the way. All that mattered to these assholes was evading arrest and getting back home free onto their precious Mexican soil. If it was up to me, we would have declared these fuckers a national security threat and called out the Guard, the Reserves, and maybe even the 101st Airborne.

You know, any other country in the world would authorize the use of deadly force to protect its citizens in situations like this. But according to the U.S. federal law-enforcement agencies' guidelines on the use of deadly force, you have to wait until the last possible moment before you resort to firing your weapon. You have to be absolutely positive that you, your partner, or an innocent third party are in imminent danger of being whacked before you squeeze the trigger. And as usual, the REMFs who write these policies have never had to make such a life-and-death decision. And the hardest part to explain to them is that you never have five or ten minutes, or even one minute, to decide. It's usually a decision that relies on a limited several-second response time. When it goes down it's like the blink of an eye. Right or wrong, I guarandamntee you're going to end up in criminal or civil court for doing your duty. It doesn't matter whose life you may have saved. While everyone else is grieving, the fucking defense buzzards smell blood and money simultaneously.

During another episode with the corral smugglers, the Four Musketeers took the fight to the bad guys one day in a major way. Friedli was camouflaged up and calling the shots from the brush as he watched the dope smugglers loading yet another truck in the corrals. He radioed DelToro, Edwards, and Henry about the activity. Friedli gave them a description of the truck carrying the dope and gave them the heads-up when it was on the way north. When the smuggler exited the corrals with his load, I bet he nearly pissed his pants when he saw what was waiting for him on Chino Road: DelToro, Edwards, and Henry, revving their motors and squealing their tires in anticipation of the fun they were about to have. You should have seen them as they swooped down like Wild West Indians surrounding one of the last frontier wagon trains. Somehow I wondered if this attack hadn't been planned and initiated by Edwards.

Anyway, the dude driving this particular load of dope was not only young, dumb, and full of cum, but he had a nose full of the infamous white-powder candy. The dumbshit figured he wasn't going to be taken alive on this side of the border and he let it be known to the Musketeers at the onset of the contest. At least, those were the signals his coke-burned brain cells were transmitting to the controlling parts of his anatomy as he speed-demoned off in the loaded truck. Why else would his middle finger pop up at the agents when they challenged him? You don't think it could have anything to do with a total disrespect for the law, do you?

DelToro and Edwards spun circles around the cokehead as they chased him from Chino Road back down to the corrals toward the border. Henry zipped up ahead of him, cutting off his escape route back into Mexico. The cokehead saw that he wasn't going to be able to get back to the border so he accelerated the truck toward a deep, muddy creek that runs parallel to the border near the corrals. As he approached the edge of the creek he must have been doing 40 or 45 mph when his fried brain told him to open the door and bail out of the moving truck! The Mexican was rolling and flipping end over end across the ground like a limp rag doll. His arms and legs reversed directions so many times you had to figure if he wasn't dead he would at least be ripped up beyond recognition. Before he stopped rolling across the ground, the loaded truck went over the edge and tits-up into the creek. To our utter amazement, the cokehead survived the jump, as he came up onto his feet covered from head to toe in his own blood. Mexico and freedom were no more than two hundred yards to his south.

As he ran down into the creek, which by the way was about an eight- to ten-foot drop, I saw DelToro jumping out of his pursuit vehicle and running after him. The next thing was like something out of a Spiderman comic book when I was just a kid. DelToro never broke his stride. He was totally focused and locked in on what he must've thought was some kind of a mission from God. And DelToro had target acquisition as he ran full-speed off the creek's edge, jumping straight out into space with his arms and legs extended like an Olympic swan-diving champion!

The next thing I heard was this tremendous, nasty impact of flesh on bone accompanied by a god-awful screaming and groaning. Then a dead silence followed that prompted me to pull my pistol as I held my breath. After a few seconds, and no worse for wear, DelToro slowly surfaced from the creek with his bloody trophy in tow. The whole time the Puerto Rican was dragging the scumbag back to his car, all we heard out of the crying, crumpled little bitch was, "Give me a break! Let's make a deal! There's more dope coming. I can help you!" And all of this pleading from a little turd who had just flipped off the Musketeers several minutes earlier. It's always like that. When they're cruising around town with their "bros" and drive by the law, it's that bad motherfucking push-your-chest-out shit. But when they fall to the Man, they break back to that little-sniveling-wimp shit!

This kind of crap continued for over a year. And with each life-threatening load of dope they would intercept, the Four Musketeers would gel more and more with the rest of my team. It's a combat thing. No greater bond can come between men than knocking on death's door together. I guess it would nearly be comparable to being brothers from the same womb.

In February of 1998, we took a short break from the corral smugglers to deal with another rowdy bunch of marijuana smugglers operating on the east side of Douglas. As I've mentioned, the U.S. government constructed a wall made of military-steel landing mats on the border between the city limits of Agua Prieta, Mexico, and Douglas, Arizona. It stood about twelve feet high and ran about two miles east and west from the Douglas Port of Entry. We had heard from an informant that a group of smugglers was experimenting with extension ladders to get their dope up and over the wall. We decided it would be a good "lay in ambush" opportunity for the Desert Surveillance and Reconnaissance Team (DSRT).

Edwards, Friedli, another young new arrival named Joe Gistinger, and I made up the ambush team. We dressed out in our camouflage field uniforms and strapped down our weapons and radios. We positioned ourselves in the brush about a hundred yards north of the wall after dark. This would be Gistinger's first drug bust. I didn't know it at the time, but it would be the last bust for one of the other agents. In retrospect, I'm glad I spent this night in the brush with this particular group of kids. On the border, you never know when the Reaper is gonna call for one of you.

We crawled into our surveillance spot and waited for about thirty minutes before the first Mexican scouts showed up. We heard the ladders hitting the metal wall on the south side. A few seconds later I spotted the first trafficker's head as he peered over the wall north into the darkness. I had my 10x50 power binoculars on the scouts as they slithered over the top of the wall and disappeared into the darkness, sneaking in our direction. I whispered to the team that it was just a matter of time and we'd be in the thick of it with these boys. They were gonna fall right into our hands. Maybe.

I took the lead eye on the smugglers, since they were straight out ahead of my position. Friedli belly-crawled over to me and asked if he could look at the mules through my binos. I asked him where the hell his glasses were and he sheepishly whispered that he had forgotten them on his office desk. I chewed his rookie ass out as I silently laughed to myself the whole time. Years ago I had done the same thing and had received the same ass-chewing from my mentor. In a fatherly tone, I scolded Friedli that leaving his binos behind on a surveillance operation was paramount to going to an AIDS-infested whorehouse without any rubbers. It was a matter of pure and simple survival. Did I want to rag on him? No. Was it necessary? Yes.

After the young agent pleaded a couple of more times, I gave him the binos, making him promise to maintain lead surveillance on the bad guys. Besides, at my age the back of my neck was beginning to hurt from lying on my elbows in the brush and straining to look up at the top of the wall. In fact a lot of body parts were starting to bother me back then when I was hitting the brush with the team. Of course, that's not something I'd ever admit to these kids.

As Friedli kept the dope smugglers on the wall in sight, Edwards crawled over and signaled he had a visual on the Mexican scouts that had crawled over the wall and headed our way. They were approaching our position as they probed the thickets and bushes with what looked like some kind of steel shanks. It was obvious that they were looking for any possible ambush before signaling their compadres on the other side of the border to throw the dope over the wall. I'll have to give them credit where credit is due; these guys were worthy adversaries.

A couple of scouts damn near stepped on Friedli and me. I thought one of them had seen us because he trotted off south toward the wall whispering in a high, strained voice, *"¡Hay perros, hay perros!"* ("Cops, cops!") He was warning his compas that there were agents lying in ambush in the brush. I was fucking pissed! Of all the rotten luck! This was going to be such an easy operation to bust. And then this one little shithead walks right smack into our ambush site.

Extremely disappointed and aggravated, I was ready to pull the plug on the operation when Friedli said that he had a visual on bags of dope being thrown over the wall. I scoffed and sneered at him, saying that the scout had burned us and they were taking the bags back south over the wall. Friedli stood his ground and insisted that the dope was coming north. I jerked the binos from his face and studied the movement. It looked to me like the bags were being thrown back south over the wall. I sternly informed him he was wrong. After all, he was just a wet-nose rookie with only a few busts under his belt! There was no way in hell the smugglers would bring the merchandise north at this point. Didn't he see the scout walk right over us?

It was no more than fifteen seconds after I admonished Friedli that a string of six marijuana-smuggling assholes walked right past our position headed north. I was so shocked I didn't know whether to shit or go blind. Well, obviously I was already friggin blind! In an embarrassed and somewhat humbled voice I whispered the order to break the ambush and catch up to the mules before they got too far north. I'll never forget the quiet, low giggling I heard coming from Friedli as we scurried across the desert floor toward the smugglers.

We ended up seizing about 225 pounds of marijuana and making several arrests after a bit of desert wrestling with the mules. We gathered up the bags of dope and waited for one of our other agents to come in with a truck and pick us up. I congratulated the young agents with particular regards, and newly earned respect, toward Friedli. He graciously accepted my underlying apologies without me ever having to say I was dead wrong. We Monday-morning quarterbacked the bust and the only thing we could figure was that the dopers at the wall didn't hear their scout's warning as he ran south from the ambush site. Why else would they have committed the load north?

Within one month, out of the eight team members I had in my group, four of us were about to be visited by the Reaper. He would leave three and take one for delivery into the Lord's care. It would be a month that would change the complexion and character of the team. Some would grieve. Some would mourn. But no one would forget.

On March 2, 1998, I had to be in trial in Tucson for a week plus. The Ninth Circuit Court of Appeals had reversed the conviction of a crooked U.S. Immigration Inspector, Rodolfo Molina Jr., and a Mexican dentist I had arrested in 1991 for smuggling 661 pounds of cocaine into the U.S. I didn't want to retry these convicts because it was all bullshit. The motherfuckers were guilty as sin, but the Ninth Circuit Court of Appeals remanded the case because of a technicality. They had decided that the federal judge who had presided over the trial in 1992 had erred in one of his decisions. Therefore, as usual, shit runs downhill from the gods to the peons, and the agents have to jump through hoops like clowns in our country's failing judicial circus.

I had a bad feeling about leaving my team for so long. I've been told that I mothered the kids too much. That I needed to lighten up and let them learn on their own. Well, I don't mind being called a mother hen. As long as I'm there to help and protect my team, you can make all the fun of me you want. It's the team's survival that's essential. That's the way it went with me in Nam. That's the way it goes with me on the Mexican border.

We picked a jury and began the trial on March 3. I was waiting in the courtroom for the judge to come in when the prosecuting U.S. Attorney asked me to call my office for some additional information on the case. I left the courtroom not knowing that I wouldn't return until the trial was almost complete. The Reaper was on the move.

I called the office to ask one of the guys to get a couple of files that we needed for the trial. It was like any other duty phone call until I heard the anguish in the voice on the other end of the line. Butch had answered the phone and I knew from his voice there was bad news. Two of my team members were down. Butch wanted to know if I could go to the helipad at the University Medical Center in Tucson to meet the chopper that was bringing Friedli in. I dropped the phone and headed for the hospital.

During the drive over I stayed in touch with Butch on the cell phone and learned what had happened. Sperling had received a phone call from one of our friendly ranchers east of Douglas. The rancher had seen fresh tracks of apparent dope smugglers heading north from the border. Sperling jumped in his Jeep to respond to the call. Not wanting to miss the chance to track down some dope smugglers, Friedli went with him. If I hadn't been in trial, odds are I would've gone with Sperling instead of Friedli.

As the two were traveling out east on Geronimo Trail they attempted to pass a semi hauling a trailer. The trucker didn't see the agents as they were coming past his side. The semi turned left as Sperling and Friedli attempted to pass on the left. The little Jeep was drug under the large rig. Before blacking out, Sperling radioed the office for help. Within a few minutes, DelToro and Henry arrived on the scene to find a bleeding and dazed Sperling cradling his dying partner.

Friedli had received massive head injuries from the impact with the trailer. He was med-evaced to Tucson from the Douglas Community Hospital. I met him on the helipad when he landed. As the medics took great caution in removing Gary from the chopper, I could tell by their demeanor that we wouldn't win this one. As they wheeled him away from the pad to the ER, I felt the presence of an old friend. The Lord's errand boy had been sent to bring Friedli home. The Reaper had his orders and they weren't to be changed by man or modern medicine.

We buried Friedli in Rochester, Minnesota, on March 9, 1998. It was reportedly the coldest day of the winter that year in Minnesota. In a chilly ceremony that the team will forever remember, we laid our brother to rest. The snow-covered cemetery occupied gently rolling hills with beautiful evergreen spruce trees. At the top of the hill overlooking Gary's grave, a uniformed officer played tear-inspiring "Taps" from a shiny brass bugle. After a twenty-one-gun salute, another officer played the bagpipes. After all family members had left the cemetery, the remainder of Gary's team encircled his coffin and gave a final salute. In a manner befitting a Viking's descendant, we passed around a flask. Each man took a shot, saving the last of it for our fallen brother.

Sperling was unjustly punishing himself and tunneled into a deep emotional hole. He was guilt-ridden for surviving the accident and losing Friedli. But we all knew the score. Just as sure as if they had killed him with a bullet to the heart, the dope smugglers were the cause of Friedli's unfortunate and untimely death. If they hadn't been smuggling dope, the call from the rancher wouldn't have been generated. And if there had been no call for help from the rancher, the accident would never have occurred on Geronimo Trail that fateful day.

I speak for all of the Douglas U.S. Customs Service special agents when I say that it was an honor and a privilege to have served with such a fine, outstanding young man. Friedli was a breath of fresh air to our team. He always wore a smile and extended a helping hand to his partners when life's tribulations got the best of them. He put others first and himself last. He never shirked a responsibility and consistently stood his ground when confronting a potentially dangerous situation. He was the first to volunteer and the last to go home. He was the son every father wanted.

Friedli was a loving and caring husband and father. He enjoyed spending time with his family and sometimes regretted the many long hours he had to commit to narcotics interdiction. But he knew that there was no other job as important as protecting our nation against the onslaught of narcotics. He loved being a USCS special agent. In this day and age, when corruption in politics is rampant, drug use is destroying our future generations, and continual drug-related violence stalks our nation, it is hard to find a good man who is willing to stand up and do the right thing. This one may be gone, but he will never be forgotten. Every time we take down a dope smuggler, Gary P. Friedli will be remembered. You have the team's word on that.

After burying Friedli, we returned to Arizona to lick our wounds and carry on the fight. Sperling would be out of action for a mandatory forty-five days due to his injuries. We put a memorial to Gary, in the form of various arrest and dope-seizure photographs, on a wall in our office for the world to see. In addition, his radio call sign of Alpha

1918 was permanently retired, never to be issued again to another special agent. The team's grieving was evident. Butch and I thought the best thing to do was to keep the guys busy. Keeping in mind the fact that dope smugglers were ultimately responsible for Gary's death, we decided to go back after the west-corral traffickers.

On April 3, 1998, we took the bull by the horns and initiated another enforcement operation against the corral outlaws. The day before, we'd made a run at them that ended up in another dangerous high-speed pursuit through the streets of Douglas. It got so out of hand that I ordered the team to stand down and allow the driver to take his load back into Mexico in lieu of getting someone killed on the streets. But this time we came up with a plan that we thought would ensure the safety of our agents as well as that of innocent civilians. But as can be expected on the border, Murphy's Law was about to kick us in the ass again.

Butch had a newly acquired government-seized truck that hadn't been used yet in any dope raids. The plan was that I would ride as a passenger with Butch so that I could handle a set of deployable tire-shredding spikes. We thought that we might be able to drive up alongside the bad guys and take their tires out with the spikes when they weren't expecting it. For this to work, Butch and I would have to be waiting near the expected route from the corrals that the smugglers usually took on their way north. The plan was a long shot at fifty-fifty.

The operation got off to a good start when Gutierrez and DelToro radioed they had the eyeball on the drug-laden truck as it departed the westside corrals headed north. The truck was described as a white utility work vehicle with a phony City of Douglas Public Works seal painted on the side. The driver was wearing a city-employee type of hard hat in an attempt to blend in with the locals. Because the Douglas city maintenance warehouse is located near Chino Road, you have to give the dopers their due credit. They figured out a viable way to hide right out in the open.

DelToro and Gutierrez passed the surveillance off to Special Agent Buddy Harrison, who followed the truck by staying back by two or three city blocks. The truck didn't take the expected route after it left Chino Road and drove toward downtown Douglas. Our plan of a surprise takedown was falling behind the eight ball. Butch and I were now out-of-pocket and we had to hustle to catch up to Harrison's moving surveillance of the load vehicle. There wasn't enough time for DelToro and the other guys to catch up. We knew the smuggler would spot the heat coming down in just a matter of minutes. The outlaw was studying his rearview mirror hard enough to make you think he was driving backwards!

The Douglas city employee impersonator eventually suspected the surveillance. He started rubbernecking in an effort to identify the heat. Harrison radioed that the guy was about to break and run when he made a left turn south toward the border at the intersection of E Avenue and Fifth Street. Butch and I flipped a bitch in the middle of the street and radioed Harrison that we would block the outlaw's vehicle when he approached the stop sign at the intersection of E Avenue and Fourth Street.

As we approached the intersection, the white truck was just coming up to the stop sign with Harrison behind him. We knew we would have to improvise because there wasn't enough time to get the spikes out in front of the smuggler's tires. Butch pulled his truck broadside in front of the doper's truck at the intersection. Harrison crept up on the bad guy's rear bumper. As I opened the passenger's side door to get out of Butch's truck, I was standing dead center in front of the driver, looking eyeball to eyeball.

I held up my hand and screamed "Police, stop!" The fucking asshole's face lit up 10–8 big-time. He had that wild-eyed demon-possessed expression of flight-or-fight. His eyes darted back and forth, desperately searching for an escape route for the border. But he was fenced in with no place to run. He had to make up his mind to make a stand or surrender. Then, much like the murderous mountain lion who once confronted my partner Matt Magoffin, the outlaw's eyes locked in on me. I could see the bastard had made up his mind. It would be fight instead of flight. In a cold, calculating effort to take me out, the outlaw punched the gas pedal and lurched the truck forward.

He was going to put a hurt on me in a major way. I'd seen legs crushed and amputated before.

The sudden forward attack of the truck was about as close as I ever want to come to being an amputee. As I jumped back up into the passenger's seat of Butch's truck, I was forced to quickly retract my legs somewhere up under my fucking chin! And believe me, I didn't have to close the goddamn door. The border outlaw rammed it shut with his truck's bumper. If this mama's boy had been a hair slower, I'd probably be in a wheelchair today, and every day thereafter.

After ramming my door shut, the dope smuggler slammed his gear shift into reverse. Again he punched the accelerator, crashing backwards into Harrison's sedan. By this time, Harrison was out of his car and in the smuggler's face, wrestling with him through the open window of the driver's-side door. I jumped from the safety of Butch's truck, seeing that Harrison needed some help. It was a dumb thing to do because it once again placed me between the battering rams. But what the fuck are you gonna do? Leave your partner hanging onto the side of a moving load of dope with no help? Not in my lifetime!

As I was trying to cover the distance and get from between the doper's bumper and Butch's truck, I saw something that nearly buckled my legs from fear. The smuggler's truck was still lodged against Harrison's sedan with his wheels spinning as he kept accelerating in reverse. That was the good news. The really bad news was that the asshole was trying to throw the gear shift into forward as Harrison fought with him. I knew if he hit the gear I would never be able to get out of harm's way in time.

The following tenths of a second would determine if I lived or died. There wasn't time for me to draw my weapon. I could only pray that Harrison could cap the guy before he hit the forward gear. While fighting for his own life, Harrison knew I was about to be whacked or crippled for life. Buddy had his weapon out of the holster ready to rock and roll when he did what he had to do to ensure our survival. KA-WHAM! He capped the outlaw right square in the face from point-blank range.

Just about the time I saw Butch running around the back of the truck toward Harrison, I heard the shot go off. I saw the doper's head snap to his right as he went down across the truck's seat. Simultaneously, I saw the passenger-side window of the smuggler's truck shatter. With the glass sharding and spraying out, I couldn't tell how much of it was the guy's brains and how much of it was just pieces of glass spreading out all over the street.

Butch and I both hesitated for a moment before helping Harrison get the dickhead out of the truck. Neither one of us had seen brains since Vietnam and we were in none too much of a hurry to see them again. If you've ever seen them freshly scrambled and dripping from a guy's open skull before, it's something that you don't want to look at a second, third, or fourth time. Once in a lifetime is the limit for most folks.

When we got inside the cab of the truck it was a split decision. First, we were relieved to see that Harrison had missed the brain pan and we wouldn't have to deal with the black-and-gray slippery stuff. But then on the other hand, the smuggler was bleeding like a leaky sieve. I mean at first sight I would've bet even money that this guy was going to completely pump out on us right there before an ambulance could arrive. He was absolutely free-flowing! Butch found some old rags from one of the trucks and we half-ass plugged the guy's gaping bullet hole until the ambulance crew got to the scene. When the flow of blood subsided you could see that the round had entered the lower left side of his nose and exited the right side of his face between the nose and the cheek. It would be a while before this dickhead could snort any coke.

The doper was eventually med-evaced to Tucson Medical Center, where it was decided he would live and be able to stand trial. While he was at the hospital he was given a toxicology test. When one of our Tucson agents called us with the test results it was what a toxicologist may call a "home run." Basically, the bad guy had everything in his system but tobacco. That included, but was not limited to, cocaine, heroin, marijuana, meth, and barbiturates. No wonder his eyes locked in on me when we tried to stop him! Like I said before, the border makes a desperate criminal twice as bad as he would be anywhere else. Add all this other juice to his system and the border-desperado formula triples into a law-enforcement officer's worst nightmare.

For the next several days, Harrison, Butch, and I would be writing reports, answering questions, and dodging reporters. We had the U.S. Customs Service Internal Affairs agents to contend with, not to mention the detectives from the Douglas Police Department. It wasn't enough that these guys wanted to know exactly what each one of us did and saw. They also wanted to know what we saw each other do and say. This whole assault-and-shooting scenario took about five to eight seconds from beginning to end. And there is no way in hell I could tell you everything that was said and done by each one of us in that eight or so seconds. To sum it up, the bad guy tried to take us out. Things didn't work out for him and he lost his fucking nose. Special Agent Gary Friedli would have loved it!

17
The Ghosts of Las Perillas

BETWEEN 1992 AND 1993, U.S. Customs Special Agent Allan Sperling pursued a dope smuggler known as Chemo Vásquez. The Mexican cowboy owned a small *ranchito* about twelve miles east of Douglas on the northern end of the Perillas Mountains. The ranchito was no more than a measly forty acres or so of scanty scrub brush and cactus. By Arizona standards, forty acres ain't even a spit in the ocean in coming close to being a real ranch. It is a mere fraction of the amount of land you really need to run cattle on. It was quite evident from the lack of grazing pasture and visible livestock that Chemo had hidden, illegitimate sources of income. There was no way on God's green earth that the cowboy could support a family, build a fairly decent house, and own several new trucks, all on the money he was losing, not making, on his ranchito. Noting these obvious financial discrepancies, Sperling began a slow process of sporadic surveillance by horseback and truck of Chemo's ranch and the Perillas Mountains.

Since the area of the surrounding Perillas was so vast, Sperling allied himself with the Border Patrol in keeping an eye on Chemo. Other Customs agents and I joined in the investigation as our duties allowed, but for the most part Sperling used his Border Patrol partners on this particular case. During a two-year period, the agents tracked down and seized more than a ton of marijuana in the Perillas that was making its way to Chemo's ranchito. But Chemo was no fool. He was a coyote son of a bitch who knew better than to allow himself to be linked to the dope loads. For one thing, the outlaw never allowed the mules to smuggle the marijuana right into his ranchito. He knew this would give trackers like Sperling and the Border Patrol the opportunity they needed to get on his property.

Instead of having the dope smuggled to his ranchito, Chemo would watch the Perillas from his place with binoculars. When he saw a prearranged signal being flashed from the mules, probably something like the reflection of sun off a mirror, he would know the load had arrived safely and was being stashed in a draw or cave of the mountains. Then the old boy would sit back for two or three days just watching the stash to see if any law showed up in the area. When he was sure there was no heat on the load, Chemo would drive his truck up into the Perillas and secure his illegal merchandise by taking it to one of the barns on his ranchito. He was smart to be sure that no tracks, nor violations of law, were ever found on his property.

Once Sperling and the Border Patrol figured out Chemo's method of operation, they targeted his loads in the Perillas to put him out of business. The agents knew that there was more than one way to skin a coyote, and with this particular one, they knew that they would be hard-pressed to ever catch him with the dope in his hand. Instead, the agents planned to track down and seize every fucking pound of dope that could conceivably be bound for Chemo's ranchito. They knew that if they took all of his potential illegal income, the smuggler would go into financial distress and make a mistake. In Chemo's case, the mistake would be twofold. It would be both his last and a fatal mistake.

Sperling and the Border Patrol agents were so successful in what they had set out to accomplish that Chemo eventually experienced a serious cash-flow problem. Out of desperation, Chemo was forced to sell his soul to the devil when he asked the vicious dope lords of the Agua Prieta cartel to run him a line of credit. The cartel evidently agreed to front Chemo marijuana loads that he promised to make good on after he sold them for a marginal profit to his connections in

Phoenix and Los Angeles. It was a seemingly good deal that didn't work out too well for the soon-to-be departed Mexican outlaw.

On January 14, 1994, Sperling and I responded to radio traffic from the Cochise County Sheriff's Department that there had been a gunfight at Chemo's ranch. When we arrived at the ranch we assisted a Cochise County deputy in securing a perimeter around a shooting scene in the middle of the ranch road. Other than it being just one body full of holes, if we had been a few miles closer to Tombstone, the Yankee newspapers back east might have written this one up as a modern-day O.K. Corral. In true Old West Cochise County gunfighting fashion, Chemo went out with the toes of his cowboy boots straight up, saluting the Lord.

As the outlaw lay faceup in the dust, his Stetson was still sitting square center on his head. There was one neatly cut .45 caliber bullet hole through the brim of the Stetson near his left ear. Chemo had been pumped with .45 slugs that stitched him with three perfect, neat, symmetrical round holes that the outlaw hadn't been born with: one in his gut, one in his sternum, and the last in his throat just below the Adam's apple. Spread out in a circle around his body were the telltale remains of a fatal gunfight. There were spent cartridges from the hired killer's .45, and almost the same number of empty brass casings from Chemo's 9mm pistol. It looked like both participants had done their damnedest to exchange an even amount of lead on Chemo's way to burn in hell.

As the dead man lay on his back in the dirt, a roadrunner pranced across the desert road, momentarily pausing in silence near the edge of the deceased's boot tips. When the bird was satisfied that Chemo wasn't going to move, the brown-feathered beep-beep continued on down the road, never looking back at the stiffening cadaver. Allan and I looked at each other, cracking hairline smiles. We couldn't help but note how one of nature's creatures had marked the passing of another Cochise County bad man with such indifference. It was almost as if the desert had dispatched her own messenger with these words: "Chemo, you were just a temporary visiting outlaw who wore out your welcome in these parts. Good riddance!"

From the visible evidence in the dirt, it appeared that a car or truck had driven up Chemo's ranch road toward his house and corrals. According to an informant that Sperling had within Chemo's own family, the Mexican knew he was in deep caca with his debtors because of all of the dope loads he had lost to us. He also knew that the cartel would be sending a hired gun to take him out. Romanticizing himself to be somewhat of a macho Old West gunfighter, Chemo had foolishly claimed that he could take on whoever the dope lords sent. When they arrived, not wanting anything to happen near his family, Chemo walked up the road to intercept the vehicle and its occupants. The last conversation of his life was most likely about the two most deadly combinations on the Mexican border I can think of: money and dope.

Sometime during a no-doubt intimate heart-to-*corazón* discussion, both desperados apparently decided that lead was a helluva lot more decisive than words. When the shooter in the vehicle jerked his .45 automatic, Chemo answered the challenge by pulling his 9mm pistol from inside the Western tooled belt that held up his faded blue jeans. The ensuing duel left Chemo dying from more new holes in his body than he probably gave his opponent. If the paid assassin in the vehicle was hit, we never heard about it. But you can bet one of two things happened to the hired killer. He returned to Agua Prieta, where he was either hailed by his narcotics bosses as a hero, or they allowed him to painfully croak from his wounds in some hidden shithole, after which he was dumped like a mangy dog in the desert without a fucking marker. Knowing the cartel like I do, it was probably the latter.

Chemo Vásquez died with his eyes closed and his lips parted as if he may have tried to make a last-minute apology for his wicked, brief existence on earth. As he lay on his back, one of the last things he must have seen were the Perillas Mountains surrounding his homestead. When the Reaper reached out for him, Chemo was sporting a long, turned-down handlebar mustache with complementing wide, deep sideburns. He was wearing a Western blue-and-gray-checkered shirt with a large cowboy belt buckle anchoring his pants. His boots were scuffed and rock-worn. His light-colored Stetson was faded from the Arizona sun and sweat-stained. As Sperling took his case-closing photographs of the deceased smuggler and one-time gunfighter, I looked up into the Perillas and studied their outline against the blue sky. I knew Chemo's face would join a long line of hauntings in this little mountain range of Cochise County.

The rugged Perillas Mountains are located several miles to the east of Douglas. Their knobby appearance inspired their name; the Spanish word *perillas* translates to pear-shaped or doorknobs. Their southern end bumps up against the border, where the small range is defined by a dormant dome-shaped volcano in Sonora named Cerro Gallardo. It was from a camp at the bottom of Cerro Gallardo that Pancho Villa and his revolutionary army based their failed, savage attack on Agua Prieta in 1915. Hundreds of Mexicans perished in the shadows of the Perillas during that three-day bloodbath some ninety years ago.

The little Perillas range runs straight north from the border for some ten or so miles, where it merges into the foothills of the towering Chiricahuas, which were once the domain of Geronimo and Cochise. Across the San Bernardino Valley on the east side, the Perillas are bordered by the Peloncillo Mountains. Across the Sulphur Springs Valley on the west side the Perillas face the Mule Mountains.

As far as mountains go, the Perillas aren't much to brag about, with the highest peak topping out at about 6,400 feet. However, what they lack in height they make up for in rough Southwest beauty. They are covered predominately by ocotillo and mesquites, with an occasional stand of short, scrub-oak trees scattered about at their northern end. Their reddish-pink color is particularly apparent in the bluffs that shoot up from the sides of the range's largest division, Hog Canyon. No matter what season of year, when the setting sun strikes the bluffs of Hog Canyon, they adopt a rose color that transforms into a rich lavender as the evening darkness progressively covers the mountain range.

When I was a young Border Patrol agent in the 1970s, we would frequently track illegal aliens through the Perillas Mountains. Some of them would trek north up the San Bernardino Valley on the eastern edge of the Perillas following their elusive dreams of a better life. Others would choose to cross the Sulphur Springs Valley, skirting the western edge of the knobby Perillas range. But a good number of Mexican dope-smuggling mules would choose the Hog Canyon passage for delivery of narcotics to the highway east of Douglas. It was during one of these dope-tracking operations in the late 1970s that I learned for myself that the little range and its thunderstorms were a force of nature.

During one of my many days on duty with the Border Patrol in Douglas, our office received a phone call from a rancher off Geronimo Trail in the San Bernardino Valley. He reported that within the quarter hour he had seen four or five backpacking hombres dressed in dark clothing cross out of Mexico and head north up into the Perillas through the Hog Canyon passage. The report was radioed to me since I was on routine patrol to the east of Douglas. I wasted no time in driving to the area of Geronimo Trail where the rancher reported he had seen the illegal activity. I quickly encountered the tracks of about five men headed north toward the canyon's southern entrance. By the looks of their stride, the men were wasting no time.

It was about 3:30 in the summer afternoon when I left my vehicle on foot and followed the tracks toward the southern end of the canyon. I didn't take a flashlight, figuring that I still had about four hours of good daylight remaining. Armed with only my revolver and carrying a handheld radio, I started off at a trot, trying to make up the distance between me and the outlaws. Their tracks were fresh and easy to stay on. My pace allowed me to close the gap between us rapidly, and I thought I would catch them before dark set in.

As we headed north, the walls of the canyon narrowed in places, causing the Mexicans to travel in small, sandy draws. I didn't mind it because their tracks were easier to follow in the sand than over the rocky desert floor. As I trailed them, I found where the smugglers had stopped to kill a rattlesnake and skin it out. Having had the pleasure of tasty rattlesnake steaks myself, I knew the boys would stop to cook up the delicacy toward the end of the day. I figured if I could catch up to them about suppertime, their fire's smoke would give their hideout away and that would give me the edge to take them by surprise.

As we continued north, I found two more fresh rattler skins and blood. I began to get a little concerned about the snake population in the canyon. Not about how many these dope smugglers were killing, but about just how many of the damn reptilian egg gobblers were slithering about! I knew if the dark caught me in Hog Canyon without a flashlight, I would be in a world of shit trying to negotiate around the whizzing little bastards at night. I was seriously considering turning back when I got a glimpse of about five dark figures going around a bend in the rocks up ahead of me.

I broke into a slow trot as the sun kept sinking lower in the sky. As if running out of daylight wasn't enough of a problem, the evening summer rain clouds started building a sudden and formidable thunderstorm. The more I gained on my prey, the worse the weather conditions and light got. I should've let go of the hunt, but I was young and the echoes of my sworn duties were still freshly embedded under my badge. I recklessly pushed on.

Just before dark I had pulled within a hundred yards or so of the Mexican traffickers. The shadowy figure in the rear of the group spotted me coming up behind them just about the time the rain started to break. Like ghosts, they were just in front of me one second, and gone the next. Pulling my pistol, I rapidly advanced to the last place I saw them as the rain steadily got harder. Slowly and cautiously, I searched the brush and surrounding terrain. Not a sign of life was to be found. With the rain wiping their tracks out, it was like they'd never even existed. They had Houdinied right in front of my betraying eyes. The more I thought about it, the more I started to doubt if I had ever even really seen the Mexicans. The spooky Perillas were starting to play with my mind.

The storm set in with ion-charged lightning and booming thunder bouncing off the canyon walls. It was time to resign from the chase and think about taking care of my foolish young ass. I dashed for higher ground, taking refuge in an old, dark cave that time had slowly carved in the side of a mountain. I couldn't help but think that many an outlaw and Apache had used the same place, for the same reason, ages before.

As I sat there in silence, a virtual prisoner of the storm, there was plenty of time to reflect. I pondered the mass of clouds slipping between the steep canyon walls as the storm brought them forward in a brief life of their own.

After the storm passed, Hog Canyon's serenity gradually returned. The freshly washed desert filled my nostrils with an almost intoxicating scent. Taking the good with the bad, the stars came out, as did the rattlers to cool themselves on the desert rocks. Hearing the buzzing of the little devils' tails brought me back to the reality of my situation. Instead of trying to walk out of the canyon in the dark, I radioed fellow agents for help and settled in for the night. I was picked up by one of our patrol Jeeps during the early hours of the next day.

When the agents got there I knew I would be in for some chiding and razzing about my being unprepared to overnight in the Perillas. During a good-humored ragging on my ass, they asked me what had happened to the group I was chasing. Embarrassed that I had allowed myself to become stranded overnight on foot in the canyon, I showed them the three rattler skins I had picked up on the Mexicans' trail. It was the only proof I had that somebody, other than ghosts, had been in that canyon with me.

Over the next couple of decades I would experience several more spooky events in the Perillas that have remained with me to this day. But before you can really understand how weird they were, I need to explain the way this job affects a Customs agent's life. Like in most professions, the more you produce on the job, the better you shine at promotion time. With drug agents, it's a two-edged knife. Sure, we know we're going to get credit for popping the load. And the heavier the weight of the dope load, the more you shine with your agency. But the first and probably most important thing with a drug agent about his scoring a load is the prideful aspect of protecting his country. The more dope you take off the street, the less grief and heartache some American family will have to suffer.

It's like bagging the big one at the end of a hunt. You take their dope and hurt the bad guys in the worst possible place: their wallets. We know that drivers and mules are a dime a dozen. We know that the big Colombian and Mexican drug lords are protected by their governments and immune to our U.S. arrest warrants. But when you rip their dope and burn it, all of the time and money they have invested in their illegal merchandise goes up in smoke. So the more dope we score, the better we feel about what we're contributing to the war on drugs. And as far as how we seize it goes, as long as it's legally done, we don't give a flying fuck where the help comes from— from informants, good citizens, outlaws wanting to make a deal, or even ghosts!

One of these spooky deals happened in 1994, well after I had transferred over to Customs as a special agent from the U.S. Border Patrol. Although now with another agency, I was still working narcotics interdiction near the southern end of the Perillas. I was driving east on Geronimo Trail when I came upon a car stuck in a sand draw about fifty yards off the road. Since this has historically been a bad area for dope smugglers, I radioed my location in and got out of my vehicle to investigate the seemingly abandoned car. As I warily approached the vehicle I could hear low, moaning animal grunts coming from up the draw in front of the car. The car appeared to be empty, so I turned my attention up the sand wash and drew my pistol. When I came around a bend I was stunned to see a human body being tugged at by several coyotes. I instinctively fired a couple of shots at the scavenging bastards, driving them away from the body.

As I inched near the body, still not knowing exactly what the hell I had walked into, I could tell it was a lady. She was lying on her left side with her back to me. Her legs were curled up as her left arm gently cradled the left cheek of her face. I could tell by the pale gray color of her face and arms that the Reaper had already taken her from this world. It looked as though she had lain down and curled up in a near-fetal position before crossing over. I searched the area for signs of a struggle, or possibly foul play, and found none. I radioed for the Cochise County Sheriff's Department to dispatch a deputy and remained with the lady until they arrived, in order to keep the coyotes from ripping her apart.

The next day I learned from the deputies that the lady had a history of diabetes. She evidently had failed to take her insulin on time, causing her to go into diabetic shock. She probably became disoriented as she drove down Geronimo Trail looking for an intersecting road that would have taken her to a friend's ranch. Possibly she had mistakenly taken the sand draw for a road and got stuck in the sand. It was a grim reminder of how deadly and unforgiving the desert can be. I can only say that it is regrettable that luck hadn't allowed us to find her in time. But on the flip side of that, at least someone got there in time to keep her from being dismembered by hungry predators.

Over the next few months, I continued to patrol the Perillas and Geronimo Trail for dope smugglers. Every time I passed by the sand draw I would think of the lady and feel a bit sad about the way she had departed this life. The desert can be lonely enough during the day, but at night when you're all by yourself, it can go much deeper than just lonely. I will always wonder what her last thoughts may have been. The stars up above her? The sand beneath her body? Or the terrifying sight of the coyotes as they circled her, waiting to hear her last breath? I hope it wasn't the latter.

During this same period in the Perillas, we had a group of dope smugglers that kept driving through the border fence in the San Bernardino Valley about six or eight miles east of where I had found the lady. One morning I was on the way out to surveil that area of the valley and hopefully score a load of dope. As I was crossing through the little range, I drove up over a small hill and unexpectedly came upon six or eight smugglers loading a car with dope on the side of Geronimo Trail. I don't know who was more surprised, me or them. But the expression on their faces was worth more than a million bucks! When they saw me suddenly on top of them, pure panic sent bodies zigging and zagging into the rock-filled mountains. Bundles of marijuana were being thrown half in the car, half on the side of Geronimo Trail, and some ended up being drug by the fleeing mules partially up the mountains toward old Mexico.

The load driver took off, steering his car right at me. I could see in his eyes that he couldn't figure out if he should jump and run, or piss his pants. I skidded my truck sideways in front of his car in a blocking maneuver. Exiting with a cocked and loaded .12 gauge shotgun, I pointed the barrel straight into his ugly mug through the oncoming windshield. You should have seen this guy's eyes as they damn near bulged right out of their sockets. The son of a bitch was so shook up that he literally dove straight out of the car's window, never even bothering to open a perfectly good door. The outlaw rolled several times across the gravel road, ending up in the desert brush and cactus. I reckon the poor feller had some really bad karma working for him on this particular day because things just kept going downhill from there for him. The idiot ended up face first and balls down in a pile of needle-sharp, spine-filled prickly pear cactus. That pretty much explains the bloodcurdling screams that were enough to wake the dead two counties over the mountains in New Mexico.

When I stopped laughing long enough to catch my breath, I had a choice to make. The asshole was pulling himself out of the cactus as his car was still idling down the road toward my truck. Not wanting my truck to sustain too much damage, and considering this shithead had already suffered more than any judge could possibly sentence him to, I opted to deal with the runaway load car. I pulled my truck to the side of the road and slid through the driver's-side window of the load car as it went past. I managed to steer it off the road into a draw, where the sand slowly bogged it to a stop. A couple of minutes after securing the load vehicle, I could still hear the painful screechings and cursings of the Mexican outlaw from a distance off in the mountains. Every time he pulled a cactus thorn from his genitals, he renewed my faith in officer field-discretion justice. And if you aren't familiar with the term, it's a lawman's way of saying that there are sometimes worse indignities to bear than a jury or prison.

By the time I got the load car stopped, dope bales were scattered up and down the road and draw to hell and back. From what I could tell, it was a good seizure of about three hundred pounds or so of marijuana. As I started to radio for assistance I got this strong sense of

being watched. I couldn't figure out if the mules or some of their compadres had double-backed on me to verify that I had found all of the
dope. It was a weird, uneasy feeling that I couldn't shake loose of. I
kept looking around, over my shoulder, waiting for something bad to
go down. It was enough to make me hope that it wouldn't take the
cavalry too long to arrive.

It took agents Harrison and Sperling about fifteen minutes to get
to my location after I had radioed them. We conducted a search of the
area, but as usual, all of the mules had fled south on foot into Mexico.
When we were sure the area was secure, we started to gather all of the
marijuana bundles up for transport back to our U.S. Customs office in
Douglas. We were all joking and slapping each other on the back
about how the load was scored. The guys were laughing themselves
silly when I told them the story about driving up on the smugglers in
the middle of their loading operation. Then right in the middle of the
joking and playing around, it hit me. I knew what was causing that
uneasy feeling of being watched, or maybe even déjà vu. We were
standing in the same draw, picking up dope bundles from the exact
same spot, where I had kept the dead lady from being torn to pieces
by coyotes. These Perillas are some spooky sons of bitches!

To totally appreciate the weirdness of it all, you have to understand that our eighteen or so Customs agents assigned to the Douglas
office had about 14,500 square miles of area they were responsible
for. And with all of that area to enforce the law in, each agent probably averaged about four to six personally generated dope seizures per
year. And that's just an average. I've seen some guys who have been on
the border for five or eight years and they have never scored even one
load of dope on their own initiative. Combine that with the fact that it
takes the average smugglers about ten to fifteen seconds to load their
vehicle and vamoose. In other words, to be effective in this area of law
enforcement, you have to be in the exact spot, at the exact time, to
catch these bastards in the act.

With 14,500 square miles of area to cover, and taking the aforementioned numbers of probabilities into consideration, do you realize
what the odds are of me seizing a load of dope from the dead lady's

draw must have been? About the same as O. J. Simpson finding his wife's "real killers." You tell me there wasn't some kind of assistance going on here from beyond "our borders"? And if that isn't enough to make a believer out of you, it happened again some four years later.

In 1998, when chasing a dope smuggler down through the Perillas on Geronimo Trail, Sperling and I hemmed the bad guy in between us at gunpoint. It looked like the bastard was going to make a fight out of it. Then, just as gentle as a little schoolgirl, the outlaw threw his hands up into the air off the steering wheel and surrendered. It was something we rarely saw back in those days. As he cuffed the doper up, Sperling looked at me with a twinkling appreciation in his eye and said, "You know where we're at?" I replied, "Yep. You think he gave us a hand with this one?" Sperling gently smiled for a fallen comrade.

Without either one of us being hurt, we had just scored a dope load while safely arresting a guy who was potentially dangerous. What's so miraculous about that? We were standing in the exact spot where Sperling had been with Customs Special Agent Gary Friedli when he was killed three months earlier during a narcotics inter-diction response. Say what you will, but me, well, let's just say this Texican believes he's had some help "from the other side" on more than one occasion.

18
Drex and the La Copita

ONE OF THE GRANDEST MEN I ever knew was a U.S. Border Patrol supervisor by the name of Drexel Atkinson. Born and raised in Arkansas during the Great Depression, this Southern good ol' boy was the son of a county sheriff. Drex was raised hunting in the backwoods country, where as a child he cut his teeth on guns and fishing poles. Following in his father's footsteps, he joined the Arkansas State Troopers when he came of age and went on to become a celebrated state trooper.

Drex left the Arkansas Troopers for the U.S. Border Patrol around 1955. He came west to his first and only U.S. Border Patrol station in Douglas, Arizona. The big, burly country boy quickly adapted to the border and went on to become a supervisory agent for the Patrol after a few years. I first met Drex in 1974 when I signed on with the Border Patrol as a trainee. Even back then Drex was already nearing retirement age, but before the old salty son of a bitch pulled the pin I would end up being assigned to him until 1980. In those six years I absorbed more *sabe* (savvy) about Cochise County, the border, and the Mexican culture from this one man than I would ever learn the rest of my life from a hundred other federal or state lawmen.

Drex possessed the classic characteristics and manners of a Southern good ol' boy, not to be confused with a bigoted country redneck, which is a whole different being. One of the things I found most interesting about Drex was how much he looked like the former Chiricahua Apache renegade leader Geronimo. To me, the resemblance between pictures of the Chiricahua warrior and the old gringo was simply amazing. Since Geronimo had been forced by the U.S. Cavalry onto a reservation in Oklahoma in 1886, it was enough to make you ponder the chances of him having crossed the state line into Arkansas to spread a little seed on occasion. While I seriously doubt that may have been the case, Drex's presence always taunted me into thinking about the old days out here. It was as if Geronimo had been reincarnated and brought back from Arkansas to once again rain terror over Cochise County.

Drex had short military-cut graying hair that set off a pair of cold steel-grey bluish eyes. His weatherworn face and arms testifed to years of trailing bad men and illegal aliens in the elements and unpredictable desert. Drex had those old-man gigantic earlobes, about the size of walnuts, that hung down the side of his neck almost to his shirt collar. He tightly cinched his black Border Patrol river belt up under an overhanging belly that had been earned over the years from a good number of beers and steaks. His .357 Magnum service revolver hung off his river belt on the right at a more than peculiar angle. Drex had a habit of resting his humongous, heavy right hand on top of the pistol's grip whenever he stood around shooting the shit with folks. This caused the holster to gradually end up at a crazy forward-tilting angle with the gun barrel pointing almost straight back behind the old border veteran.

To most folks the crusty old lawman was the spitting image of a cross between an Old West gunslinger and a Southern backwoods sheriff. From beneath a sweat-stained grey felt Stetson cautiously peered a wrinkled, suntanned, scouring frown. Set the squinting eyes of a wary hunter in such a face, and that usually leaves the impression of one pissed-off individual. If you didn't know him, you would take one look at him and swear he was a hate-mongering redneck from Mississippi. But he wasn't even close to being that kind of a feller.

The old man hid a heart as big as the state of Texas under his 250-pound, six-foot frame. He didn't let many folks know about it, but it was there. I learned a lot about compassion for aliens from this old man. In fact, I would have to say I learned a lot about compassion for all people under his guidance. Drex even had mercy on me on more than one or two occasions. But when he got pissed off, Katie bar the door, because you were about to be caught right smack-dab in the middle of a raging storm of biblical proportion.

A red-headed, barrel-chested Irishman by the name of Michael McMahon and I hadn't been out of the Border Patrol Academy for more than a month before we first felt the wrath of Supervisory Agent Drexel Atkinson. He had assigned us an old International four-wheel-drive Scout to patrol the border west of Douglas. The vehicle wasn't much to look at, but we got the standard "new recruit" speech from Drex about taking care of government-issued equipment. What we didn't know at the time of the speech was that the antique Scout was one of Drex's own favorite vehicles to scoot about in the desert.

Now, back in 1974–75, there weren't any designated roads along the U.S.-Mexican border fence in Cochise County. You either crawled along in a Scout at a speed equivalent to that of a blood-filled tick moving across a hound's back, or you just flat-out walked certain areas of the border. Under Atkinson's tenure and way of thinking, horses had not yet been domesticated enough for his liking, so that wasn't an option open to his agents.

So after being read the riot act on the care of government vehicles, McMahon and I started out cutting along the border fence in the Scout doing about four friggin miles per hour. It was a beautiful, sunny spring day to be cruising out in the Arizona desert. As McMahon and I decrepitly motored along, we took the time to enjoy the sweet honey smell of the yellow and purple prickly-pear-cactus blooms. The terrain really wasn't too awful for driving, but there were ample numbers of cactus and greasewood to dodge, so we had to go at it pretty easy. Now and again we would have to traverse little dirt and rock ravines that Mother Nature's rainstorms had cut through the desert's floor. Most of the ravines were no deeper than one or two feet and not much more than that in width.

McMahon and I saw a few tracks of illegal border crossers in the desert sand, but most of them were of no interest to us since they were more than several days old and long gone. Whoever they were, by now those folks were probably in Chicago or New York sitting down for supper with their relatives.

Now, you have to remember, at that time McMahon and I were about twenty-three or twenty-four years old. Not only did we become easily bored in those days, but we also had a lot of wild oats to sow yet. I mean here we were, recently graduated Border Patrol agents with shiny new badges and pistols. We were just chomping at the bit for our first shoot-out, hot pursuit, fistfight, knife fight, or whatever came our way. Hell, we were so pumped with our new authority we would've even settled for a flea-bitten coyote to try our new Magnums on. In other words, we were every money-grubbing defense attorney's dream come true, civil lawsuits looking for a place to happen.

So when we came to this nice flat piece of open border country with no cactus or greasewood to impede our pent-up energy, we decided to see just how fast a four-wheel-drive Border Patrol Scout could go. Besides, we couldn't see anymore of those damn little ravines, or Drex Atkinson. And we figured if we couldn't see the old man, how in the world could he possibly see us? Fuck it. Let's cut loose and play!

McMahon revved the motor to piston-busting capacity and popped the clutch on the transmission. The little Scout's rear end sunk down into hard, fast motion as the tires began to throw sand and rocks up in the air some fifteen or twenty feet high behind us. We finished first gear somewhere at around 30 mph. McMahon floored the motor through second and ground the stick-shifting little bitch on into third gear. We were cooking down the side of the border fence at a daredevil 60 mph by the end of third gear.

We were hooting and hollering, having a circus good old time. We both had rip-roaring smiles the width of the Rio Grande on our faces. I don't know if it was so much the speeding across the desert floor or the idea of bucking Drex's authority that pleased us. But we sure as hell figured we had earned the right to hold on to those defiant smart-ass smiles since we had passed some five-and-a-half months of stringent training at the U.S. Border Patrol Academy down in the armpit of Texas.

However, time has since taught me that there's usually a price tag attached to being a smart-ass, and McMahon and I were about to pay. The last thing I remember was grabbing my crotch with both hands upon eyeballing the size of the unexpected creek bed we were about to perform a NASA launch into. It was about a ten-foot-deep, jagged, nasty-looking break in the earth's crust that literally came out of nowhere. In those days, seat belts were unheard of in the old Scouts, so I instinctively figured that it was somehow more useful to grab hold of my balls instead of the dashboard I was about to eat. If there had been time, I would've also kissed my ass goodbye. Houston, we have a problem!

To any wandering Mexicans hiding in the nearby brush, we must have looked like a giant green piñata falling from the sky and breaking up on the creek's rock-filled bottom. When we came to rest after the bone-jarring crash, both of us were pretty shook up. We ended up with minor contusions, bruises, and scrapes from being banged up against the breaking windshield. And under circumstances like these, most folks would be whining, sniveling, and tending to each other's injuries. Not McMahon and I. We didn't feel a thing. We were too scared to feel a goddamn nerve in our bodies. We were going into shock from being scared shitless. Not from our present predicament, but from thinking of the very near future. We were going to have to go before Drex! We both wondered why God didn't just kill us on the spot and put us out of our misery.

We limped, pushed, and eventually, with the help of other laughing agents, dragged what was left of the Scout back to the Border Patrol station in Douglas. The old man was waiting. He had already heard us on the radio requesting assistance from other agents in the area. When we rolled into the driveway, Drex just stood there staring menacingly at the two soon-to-be victims of his seething anger. Like an old U.S. Cavalry officer looking over his battle-wounded mount, Drex surveyed the Scout's remains for a few solemn moments. The oil pan was torn open, leaving a black trail of fluid behind the gutted vehicle. The leaf springs were completely busted on one side, causing the Scout to list over like a capsizing ship. The windshield was shattered, the fenders were crumpled, and the radiator was spewing like an erupting volcano. To put it mildly, McMahon and I were fucked.

After studying the damages, Drex focused his attention on the two perpetrators of this dastardly deed. He never said a word. The old lawman just turned beet red and walked back inside his office as he motioned for us to follow behind him. I'm not sure, but I think the trail of smoke we saw as the old man lumbered away from us was fuming from Drex's ears. McMahon and I seriously thought about shooting each other in a quickly agreed-upon suicide pact. It might have been the coward's way out, but it was good enough for both of us at the time.

We braced ourselves for the worst as we tiptoed into Drex's office, cautious as infantrymen caught in a goddamn minefield. I'm not sure there are any decent words in the English language that could describe the profane verbal tornado we were engulfed by. It sounded like the thundering of a thousand wild buffalo roaring across the great plains from all four directions. It was so loud and resounding you could actually hear each word hit your body. Hell's bells! His voice was so hurricane powerful that it even made my bruises hurt!

At the end of the punitive assault, Drex spat something out about McMahon and me spending the rest of our days on the job patrolling the border with a wheelbarrow between us. And you know, at the time, I thought the old man was dead fucking serious. But time heals all wounds, and Drex eventually assigned McMahon and me to another vehicle. However, it wasn't a four-wheel drive and we weren't assigned out in the desert for quite a while. Gee, I wonder why?

We ended up in a patrol sedan working a good deal of our time in town where, quite understandably, Drex ordered us not to go off paved streets. During that time, McMahon and I were assigned to answer sensor alerts along the border fence in Douglas. The duty was good during the day shift with a fair amount of enforcement action. But the night shift was out-fucking-standing. That was when the shit really hit the fan. Dope smugglers, alien smugglers, burglars, wanted fugitives, you got it all on the p.m. shift. And McMahon and I loved it. Especially the continual flow of adrenaline that the evening tour of duty always brought.

One evening around ten o'clock or so, a sensor on the border behind the La Copita cantina went off. This particular badass bar was located no more than fifty yards from the border fence, and no more than a stone's throw from our own Border Patrol station. The back door of the dank, smoke-filled saloon faced south toward Mexico. That made it even closer yet to dive into from the fence after making an illegal entry into the U.S.

Now, if there was ever an establishment that one would consider as a house of ill repute, a den of thieves, a gathering of the lowest scumbuckets on the Mexican border, it would have to be the La Copita bar. If this had been a hundred years ago when the Arizona Rangers were having hell with Douglas saloons filled with outlaws and whores, one of those saloons would have been the La Copita bar.

We were constantly getting into some kind of a beef or another when we entered the bar looking for whoever had set our sensor off coming through the fence from Mexico. You couldn't ever expect to just go in and simply grab your suspect and depart in peace. Oh, no. Every drunk cocksucking jailhouse lawyer and barfly in the joint took it as a personal affront that you were an uninvited guest in their private palace of pleasure and sin.

So on this particular ten o'clock sensor alert, McMahon and I rolled over in our patrol unit and gave the bar a quick peek inside from the back door. And let me tell you something: You didn't want to go any further into this manure-filled barn than just inside the back door. It was one thing to worry about some high or drunk asshole shoving a blade in your back as you walked by. But the maggot-gagging smell of unwashed, sweating bodies combined with dry urine and stale beer was a whole other world. You absolutely couldn't tolerate it unless you were blitzed out of your ever-loving mind on booze or drugs. The stench was enough to knock a goddamn buzzard off a shit wagon at a hundred and fifty fucking yards!

The usual crowd of men and women were dancing about, groping each other's rumps and groins in pursuit of that night's perfect orgasm after closing time. They were grinding to the sad, slow beat of Mexican heroes' ballads that very few gringos can in all earnest decipher.

The La Copita had them all. Painted young Mexican whores with their pushed-up tits bubbling over the tops of blouses that were two sizes too small, desperados looking over their shoulders for the law, local dope smugglers looking to score a load, and the usual alcoholic scum that would sell their iron-deficient, syphilis-infected blood for the price of a bottle.

Neither McMahon nor I saw anyone we were really interested in questioning. No one was standing around huffing and puffing like they had just participated in the infamous fifty-yard La Copita border dash. So I told McMahon I would check from the back door on down to the border if he would keep an eye on the ruffians in the bar. McMahon nodded that he had it covered. I walked out the back door and quickly slipped into the dark shadows of the alley so that I wouldn't silhouette myself into becoming an easy target.

I held up in the dark shadows of the alley for a while, giving my eyes a chance to adjust to the change. As I silently stood there waiting, the mouth-watering aroma of sizzling fajitas and tacos drifted in the wind coming out of Mexico. Above the growling of my own stomach, I could faintly hear the soft strumming of guitars accompanied by the crackling trumpets playing in the Mexican dance halls. The music had that familiar European oom-pah-pah waltz flavor that illustrated the century-old German influence on Mexico.

When my night vision kicked into high gear, I headed off to the fence without turning my flashlight on. Before I got to the hole in the fence where this particular sensor had gone off, I heard the shuffling of boots over the rocks in Mexico approaching the border directly in front of me. I stopped dead in my tracks and studied the area while trying not to move a muscle. In the darkness I could just barely make out four or five black figures slinking slowly toward the sensored hole in the fence. They were too close for me to use my walkie-talkie and call McMahon, so I turned it off, hoping not to give my position away. The closer the figures got to the hole, the easier it was for me to distinguish that they were carrying large duffel-bag-size bundles on their backs. Shit and fall back in it! A dope load was on the way across and I was going to be badly outnumbered.

I instinctively went prone on the ground from where I stood. I was right in the middle of the trail that ran from the hole in the fence into the back of the La Copita. There was no other way this could go. They were going to stumble straight into me and I was going to have to go up against them alone. There was no place to hide, and even if there had been, there wasn't time to do it. It was one of those nightmares you can see happening in slow motion before it even starts. At this very moment nothing rang truer than a saying that I remembered from my father. When things got down to the nut cutting, the old Texan often told me, "Don't ever ride your horse into a canyon that you ain't willing to crawl out of." I'd often remembered and adhered to his words of wisdom during my tour of Vietnam. I would once again act upon those words this night.

The dope smugglers made their way through the fence and unknowingly headed dead-nut on my position. When the lead guy was almost ready to step on me, I stood up from my coveted darkness on the desert floor. My flashlight illuminated the outlaws as I jerked my Magnum from its leather, shouting, *"La Migra! ¡Alcen las manos, pendejos!"* ("Police! Hands up, you dumb sons of bitches!") The lead mule screamed a warning to his compas as the entire mule train simultaneously reversed direction practically in midstride. Assholes and elbows were flying in every direction in an attempt to save the load and get it back into Mexico. The fence was no more than ten or fifteen yards away. I knew that if I didn't get the dope load now, some other agent would end up having to face this same bunch of outlaws tomorrow night. Foolish as it may have been since I was alone, I was determined not to let the pricks get the load back into Mexico. Balls-up John Wayne time!

Without firing a shot, I holstered my pistol and jumped the mule closest to me. He had originally been the leader, which usually means he's the guy in charge of the deal. I grabbed his shoulders as I climbed on his back, riding him to the ground in a cloud of dust and broken brush. We hit the dirt and rolled with each other in a mano-to-mano death grip. Between the gouging, biting, and choking, I managed to repeatedly pound the fucker in the head with my KelLite until he was "legally subdued." Thinking that the other mules had fled back into Mexico, I rolled the leader over on his stomach and started to handcuff him. I had one cuff on him and was reaching for his other wrist when I felt the Reaper's hot breath on the nape of my neck. The pillars of hell were about to collapse on my back. The mules may have abandoned their dope, but not their compadre. It was time for somebody to die.

I'll probably never be completely sure of the count. All I can tell you is that there were three or four of them. They came out of the dark from behind me and hit all at one time like a pack of starving Mexican dogs fighting over a piece of fresh red *carnita* (meat). I was taking blows from every conceivable angle and direction. If there wasn't somebody's fist coming in on me from the right, there was a boot kicking me from the left. The bastards beat me to the ground, where I ended up on my back trying to figure out where the heavens started and the desert floor began. And then to add insult to injury, one of the pricks started using my own steel-encased KelLite on my skull.

Well, you can probably imagine how I felt right about then: like a lonely turd being washed around the edge of the toilet bowl on its way down into the crevices of the eternal cesspool. Like a feller who figured things couldn't get much worse, right? Bullshit! It wasn't even close to as bad as it was gonna get yet. As these sons of bitches beat the shit out of me, I could feel a hand trying to free my revolver from the holster. I knew it wasn't my hand, because they were both accounted for defending my face and skull from being caved in. About the same time this foreign hand was probing my gear, I felt the Reaper's hot breath turning graveyard cold. Death, darkness, and being alone. All three have a history of coming up on you riding in the same saddle.

I knew if these lawless dicks got control of my Magnum I would be seeing that bright guiding light sooner than I had planned on. The adrenaline tapped into some super fear-level octane and my body immediately kicked into a high-gear survival mode. With every ounce of strength mustered up for one final push to keep breathing, I made my move. In near-blind panic, I began kicking and kneeing my tormentors in their faces as they hovered over me on the ground. At the same time I grabbed hold of the menacing, prying fingers that were wrapped around my weapon's grip. I heard this guy's bones snap as I broke his hand backwards and away from the pistol. Once I had his hand off my weapon I didn't wait for another to replace it. I hit the thumb break on the holster and jerked the iron up and forward in one continuing motion. The cold blue steel barrel had barely cleared the leather when I started pulling and releasing the trigger as fast as my finger and brain could possibly cooperate with each other.

I was lying on my back with my gun hand extended straight out and level down my torso; the first round went a couple of inches over the top of the toes of my boot and proceeded through an unknown amount of God only knows whose human tissue. After that, I stitched the next five rounds straight up in a progressively rising arch until the pistol was empty directly over my head. I don't know how many were hit, and I really don't give a fuck to this day. All I can tell you is that when I started cranking rounds off into the middle of these animals that were in a feeding frenzy over me, they lost their appetite in a hurry. They flat-out disappeared into the Mexican border's dark night.

Oh, sure. I heard the screaming and crying, like it was in the far distance. I reckon that was because my ears were still ringing from both the beating and the enormous blasts from the Magnum. Sitting there in the dirt licking my wounds, I was in la-la land for a few seconds. I shook my head in an effort to clear the cobwebs and get a focus on who survived, and if I was indeed one of them. If you've ever experienced this kind of shit you know what I'm saying here. You ain't really sure who won and who lost for a few seconds after it's all said and done.

When I got shored up and could brace myself with my hands, pushing myself up from the ground, I sat up on my butt and looked around. The only remaining bad guy was the one I had tried to cuff before the war started. Completely out of breath and drained of energy, it was all I could do to just sit there and glare at him. He wasn't much better off. He was soaking wet from a mixture of blood and sweat. In fact, for a couple of seconds there, I wasn't sure if he hadn't been fatally shot. We eyeballed each other several more seconds and neither one of us had anything left for the other. Between the both of us we probably couldn't have mustered up enough juice to spit one drop had our lives depended on it.

After a few seconds of sucking air, the dope smuggler finally rose to his knees and started to crawl off toward the border. I opened the Magnum's cylinder and ejected the empty brass into the darkness. The shitbird heard the revolver's door swing open and that gave him enough incentive to find his feet. When he got up I started to throw the pistol at him until I felt something under me that I really felt vindictive about using on his ass. It was my steel KelLite! I dropped the empty pistol and palmed the KelLite. As the dope smuggler turned to trot away I landed a Nolan Ryan fast-pitched flashlight in the back of his fucking skull just above his neck. The cocksucker, still wearing my goddamn handcuffs, went down for the second time that night.

I propped myself up on about a fifty- or sixty-pound bag of marijuana that was lying near me. It took me several tugs on the walkie-talkie before I could remove it from my river belt. McMahon had heard the shooting and was already moving like a bat out of hell toward me. I barely breathed my location into the walkie before just dropping it to the ground. I was so exhausted that I didn't give a good rat's ass one way or the other when the bad guy started belly-crawling his way back into Mexico. My newly adopted motto just became live and let live. Either that, or who gives a flying fuck? Take your pick. Whichever it was, I was too whipped to blink my fucking eyelids.

With one handcuff on his right wrist, and the other dragging in the dirt like a broken leash, the dope smuggler slithered on his stomach south through the hole in the fence. Watching him reminded me of some old broke-dick mongrel dog trying to crawl under the fence to get home after having his ass kicked by the neighborhood pit bull. But then again, I probably didn't look that much better.

When McMahon got there he found me lying in the middle of six or seven burlap bags of marijuana totaling around five hundred pounds. He loaded me into our patrol car and headed off to the hospital. The docs patched up a head wound and sent me home with a handful of painkillers. A couple of days later after the swelling went down, I went back on duty. I figured I was gonna have to face the wrath of Drex again. I could already hear the old tutor screaming at the student about going up against a group of dope smugglers all alone. But it turned out to be quite the opposite. The ornery old fart was actually sort of compassionate toward me. For whatever reasons, the old man took me under his wing from that day forward.

I spent many a day on patrol riding the border with Drex over the next five years. Although he was a supervisor, he was never one to shun an opportunity to go out in the field with his men. On one occasion when I was patrolling the line with him out west of Douglas, we came upon a dope smuggler's truck hiding beneath a Mexican railroad bridge about fifty yards south of the border. Now, Drex had just purchased a shiny new .357 Magnum Smith & Wesson revolver. It was the Border Patrol's fiftieth-anniversary commemorative model made of stainless steel with beautiful rosy brown mahogany grips. It was his new baby and he was just itching to try her out on any unfortunate target.

We pulled up alongside the border fence directly across from the smuggler's vehicle in Mexico. Drex slowly rolled his old, stiff, rotund body out of our patrol vehicle and sauntered over to the fence looking into Mexico. I got out and joined the old man as he stood there, surveying the situation in deep concentration. Drex patiently looked east and west on the fence line, checking for any movement or activity. After he had checked both sides of the border, he focused in on the smuggler's truck and growled in his usual graveled tone, "Well, what do you think about that?"

I was just about to say something when this unexpected loud sound exploded near my eardrums. Ka-Whoom! Ka-Whoom! Ka-Whoom! Three times in rapid succession. My ears were ringing in sudden deafness. I couldn't believe it! Without any defined explanation or warning, the old fart had pulled his polished new piece and started blowing holes in the side panels and doors of the truck sitting under the railroad trestle in Mexico. I didn't know whether to shit or go blind! Had the old lawman seen a threat that I didn't? Or was it just too many fucking years riding the fence in the desert that caused him to lose his marbles?

After the third shot, the old man started cussing up a ritual satanic storm. Holding both of my ears as tight as a squirrel clutching the winter's last fallen pecan, I watched Drex as he tried to pull the trigger the fourth time. The revolver's cylinder froze up and wouldn't roll over. Drex turned as red in the face as a flame-throwing-hot New Mexico chile pepper. He started beating the side of the pistol like it was a recently returned runaway stepchild. "The goddamn steel in this worthless piece of shit Smith & Wesson swole up on me!" barked the old man. Here I stood shaking in my boots, scared to death that he had just shot, possibly even killed, some poor soul, and all Drex is concerned about is kicking the ass of some anonymous Yankee gunsmith back in Springfield, Massachusetts!

No one died on the other side of the fence that I know of, or at least that I will ever willingly fess up to. But that was the way Drex was. You never knew what the fuck he was gonna do on the spur of any given moment. Just about the time you thought you had him figured out, he'd throw you a spinning, wild-ass curve. On one hand he'd preach safety with firearms, and on the other hand he'd be pulling a weapons boner in the office.

The last time he fucked up like that, he had just cleaned his Magnum after quarterly firearms qualifications at the gun range. After scrubbing all of the lead out of the barrel of his pistol, he shut the cylinder and did a little practice dry firing to ensure it worked properly. When he was done, he reloaded his weapon and holstered it, getting ready for duty.

Larry Fort, one of the clowns and pranksters of the Douglas Border Patrol station, had walked into the office just before Drex cleaned and stowed his weapon. Now, Fort was always up and ready for a good practical joke or two. He was one of those fellers filled with the devil's ways both on and off duty. Fort knew that Drex had just been dry firing his pistol because he had heard the empty clicking sound from within the locker room. Fort also knew that Drex had just loaded the gun because he could see the edge of the rounds in the cylinder as the pistol sat in the old man's holster.

So Fort shrewdly got a casual conversation going with Drex about this and that, and how's the old lady's menopause coming along kind of crap. After a few minutes Fort pointedly started admiring the old man's new pistol. He complimented Drex on the meticulous commemorative engraving on both sides of the stainless-steel six-shooter. Sure enough, Fort had egged the old man on long enough now that Drex just had to pull the Smith & Wesson from the holster to show it off. The old man aimed the pistol at an imaginary target in the office. The bull's eye just happened to be one of the supply-and-equipment lockers in the office.

Drex was on a roll now. He was preaching to Fort about how well-balanced the pistol was, and how Fort just couldn't survive his tour on the border without the same Smith & Wesson. It was during this bragging session that senility caught up to the one-time state trooper from Arkansas. He pulled the fucking trigger. Ka-Whoom! Supervisory U.S. Border Patrol Agent Drex Atkinson killed about $300 worth of government-issued Polaroid camera film in locker No. 2! And the only thing Drex said when he fucked up and blew the round off was, "Ah, shit! I did it again!"

Fort was able to read the old man like a book. One day I was coming into the station for the evening shift change when I wandered up and found all of the agents grouped in Drex's office. The entire bunch was peering out the parking-lot window like a bunch of perverts at a peep show. They were all whispering and trying to keep a low profile like a bunch of crap shooters in a no-gambling state. There was even money changing hands. So I walked in to see what the hell was going on and sure enough Fort was right smack-dab in the middle of the group. And it didn't come as any big surprise that he was the one holding all the money.

I asked Fort what kind of dog and pony show was going on. He put his finger to his lips and made a hushing gesture toward me. With his other hand he motioned me over to look out the window. The old man was out in the station's parking lot changing a flat tire on one of the patrol cars. Now, under normal circumstances, this wouldn't be a big deal, much less a betting situation. But on this particular occasion,

Drex was changing the flat on a patrol car that had a heat-cracked rear window, which was a common occurrence during the summer in the desert.

Now, the car had been deadlined for the repair shop to replace the cracked window. And Drex had taken it upon himself to fix the tire and get the vehicle to the shop. So he was moving real slow while changing the tire in an effort to keep the rear window from shattering and falling out before he got it to the shop. Although the supervisor's office was hotter than Hades, and we were all grouped up like a herd of sweltering cattle in a slaughter pen, no one moved a muscle to leave because this was just too juicy to miss out on. As the money and odds went back and forth, everyone intently watched Drex through the window to see if he would make Fort a winner or a loser.

The old man was doing a superb job. At a turtle's pace he opened the trunk and removed the spare tire and bumper jack. He then cautiously jacked the vehicle up and changed the tire, being ever so careful not to rock the vehicle back and forth. It was almost like watching an adult bear babying one of her infant cubs. Drex was being so gentle and patient with the car that it revealed a whole other nature about him that we never knew existed.

After he got the flat off and had it replaced with the spare, he steadily let the car down off the jack with the skill of a brain surgeon. Click, click, click. The patrol vehicle was ever so gently lowered to the pavement. Next Drex gingerly placed the jack and flat tire in the trunk of the patrol car. He had to exert extreme, cautious effort when lifting the flat tire and wheel up over the lip of the trunk. Slowly up and over, and he had made it! The window hadn't fallen out yet and the boys wanted to collect their money from Fort. But Fort knew the old man all too well. Before he surrendered the bet he knew there was one more thing to be done. He knew the old man would forget just like he had done with the pistol. And sure enough it happened.

When Drex was completely done softly putting the spare and jack away, he stood back from the trunk admiring the fine job he had done. He would have purred with self-admiration had he been a kitten. Or maybe I should say a mountain lion, considering who we're talking about here. Drex dusted off his uniform, straightened his gun belt and started to walk away straight and tall, all proud of his excellent accomplishment. As he walked away from the patrol car he absentmindedly placed one of his gigantic paws on the trunk lid and slammed the fucking thing shut! The whole goddamn rear window fell into the back seat of the car. The old man stood there hotly cussing his own actions; he was fit to be tied. Inside, Fort coolly collected his bet from a room full of hysterically laughing Border Patrol agents.

It was around 1979 or 1980 when Drex decided to retire. But before he'd retire he had a score to settle. It seemed like the old man not only had a bit of a soft spot for lost lambs and such, but he also possessed the quality of taking his revenge slow and deliberate. Evidently, he had never forgotten about the ass whipping the La Copita smugglers had given me. And before Drex retired he wanted to take care of some last-minute business with those folks.

It was late October and that year's new harvest of marijuana had just hit the Mexican drug lords' warehouses in Agua Prieta. The Mexicans had a bumper crop that year and we were looking forward to being pretty busy chasing dope smugglers. Since most of your dope is smuggled during the hours of darkness, Drex had most of us working the evening shift with him. We mustered up about four in the afternoon on this one particular fall Friday. During the briefing, Drex dropped the news on us that he would be retiring within a couple of weeks. No one was happy about it. It was going to be the end of an era. This bunch would never come right out and say it, but each and every agent loved the old man like a father.

Friday nights were always jumping in a major rock-and-roll way. You could usually depend on a flurry of criminal activity to keep you running from one arrest to the next. That's why McMahon and I were surprised when Drex said *he* was going to lie in the brush behind the La Copita. It wasn't something that an out-of-shape senior citizen needed to do. But neither McMahon nor I had the balls to tell Drex he shouldn't be going into the brush on a one-man ambush operation.

Drex took McMahon and me aside from the rest of the agents on the evening shift. We were going to be his designated backup guys and he wanted to tell us his plan of action and radio codes. Drex said that he had information from an informant that a couple of hours after dark, the dope smugglers who hung out in the bar had made arrangements for about seven or eight Mexican mules to load the trunk of a car with dope in the alley behind the bar. Drex had dreamed up his very last bust plan and he was about to detail it to two guys who once thought they would be riding in a wheelbarrow for the rest of their careers.

The old man said that when he radioed Code One to McMahon and me, it meant that the Mexican mules were approaching the hole in the border fence with the dope. Code Two would mean that the mules had illegally crossed into the U.S. with their merchandise. Code Three meant that the dope smugglers were running up the desert trail toward the alley and back door of the bar. Code Four was the signal for McMahon and me to move in and help Drex bust everybody involved in the smuggling attempt, both inside and outside of the saloon.

Just before dark, the old man started getting his gear ready to get in position on the border behind the bar. Now, usually, most younger agents just take a dark cotton poncho or maybe even a serape to put on the ground and sit on. During the fall evenings in Arizona, the ground can get downright chilly after the sun sets. But even if you ain't worried about the chill, you at least ought to be thinking about the rattlers and scorpions crawling up your boots and pants leg. But when Drex readied his gear, McMahon and I noticed that instead of a poncho the old man was taking one of those little sawed-off folding chairs that older folks go fishing with.

McMahon and I knew this wasn't going to work. The old fart was going to go out there, get spotted by the bad guys, and they'd crawl up on him and beat his brains out. Risking great peril, which was the wrath of Drex, we tried to talk the senior agent into letting one of us take his place on the ambush. But he wouldn't hear of it. He swore up and down that as long as he didn't move in the dark, the dopers wouldn't see him sitting in the chair behind the greasewood and cactus. McMahon and I both knew that Drex was going to be about as inconspicuous in the brush as a two-hundred-pound Caribbean sea tortoise crossing the Arizona desert with a herd of

Mexican cattle. But the old man wouldn't have it any other way. So that was that.

As McMahon and I looked on, Drex saddled up and headed off into the dark behind the La Copita, dragging that fucking chair with him. McMahon and I were each assigned a different patrol car. We made a pact that neither one of us would get any farther away from the old man than a one-minute or so response time. All evening we kept cruising the border area of Douglas within a several-block radius of Drex's position. McMahon and I would meet up about every fifteen minutes or so and ask each other if anybody had heard Drex on the radio. We must have met fifty times that evening. We were worried to death that the old man would get hurt or, worse yet, whacked just before retiring. We would blame ourselves the rest of our lives if something like that happened.

It was about ten or eleven in the evening. Drex had been out in the brush now for some four hours. We hadn't heard as much as a peep out of him all evening on the radio. We hadn't even received as much as a Code One indicating mules were approaching or even scouting the area. McMahon and I hooked up to discuss the situation. Now we were really concerned. We started to wonder if the battery on the old man's radio had gone dead and he wouldn't know it until he desperately needed it. We were playing with all of those graveyard "what if" scenarios when Drex finally broke radio silence.

The old fart's gravel-throated voice was urgent. "Code Four, Four, Four!" Then there was a break in the transmission while McMahon and I looked at each other in pure fucking panic. As we both jumped into our patrol cars and floored the gas pedals toward Drex's location, we screamed on the radio to each other, "What the fuck happened to Codes One, Two, and Three?!"

We were running full-bore Code Three with sirens wailing and beams of our flashing red lights bouncing off the border fence. We were about one block from the old man's location when we heard his second garbled transmission. He was screaming the numbers so fast they sounded like one complete word scrambled together. "One-twothreefour! Onetwothreefour!" At the end of that transmission we heard the report of Drex's commemorative Magnum meting out its final night of justice behind the La Copita. Ka-Whoom! Ka-Whoom! Ka-Whoom!

Our hearts were somewhere up under our throbbing Adam's apples as we skidded our speeding patrol cars sideways into the alley behind the La Copita. As my headlights crossed over Drex and illuminated his Geronimo carbon-copy face, not only was I relieved to see him alive, but I viewed one of those golden photo opportunities that will be permanently framed in my brain. As the old man stood there in front of my headlights, he was swaying and laughing like old Saint Nick catching a kid sneaking an early peek under the Christmas tree. But instead of red this Santa was dressed in green. And instead of a bag of toys this jolly old fart carried a cylinder of lead.

In Drex's left hand, pointing toward the ground, was his Smith & Wesson .357 Magnum. A well-defined line of smoke was still pouring out of the barrel into the desert's crisp night air. As he held his right arm straight up, you could see he had hold of a little Mexican mule by the scruff of his shirt collar.

Drex was so large, and the outlaw was so small in comparison, that when the lawman extended his right arm up in the air, the Mexican's feet were completely off the ground. But that didn't stop the little shit from running because he was moving his feet as fast as he could go suspended in midair. Drex was holding him up there in the air looking at him and bellowing that big, bad, graveled, gotcha laugh. From behind the patrol car's headlights I got this crazy image of Santa in Florida posing by a hanging marlin he just hauled out of the Gulf. Maybe I was flashing on the fishing chair Drex had taken to the brush party that night.

There were bags of dope lying all around Drex's feet. Near the back door to the La Copita a car was parked with the trunk open and the motor still running. As I got out of my car I could hear the smugglers who had gotten back into Mexico whimpering and cursing in pain. How many of them Drex may have capped or wounded will remain one of those unsolved "other side of the border" mysteries. But one thing I'm sure of is this: Whether the turd balls knew it or not, they were fortunate. The old man's Border Patrol commemorative Magnum had swollen up on him again!

McMahon and I took the prisoner from the old man and cuffed him up. After throwing the little shithead in the back of the patrol car we policed up the area of all of the dope. Then we accompanied Drex through the back door of the La Copita where he proudly proclaimed to the occupants that the establishment was being closed down for facilitating the smuggling of dope across the border. All in all, the old man was pretty pleased with himself by the time we got back to the office.

The old man never would tell McMahon and me what the fuck had happened out there in the brush on his last dope load. Did he forget the signals? Did his radio malfunction? Did the smugglers cross the border at a different and unexpected location? He wouldn't fess up to any of these scenarios when we drilled him, so we just let it go. After all, he had shut the smuggling operation and the La Copita down. What more could you ask for from an old ball-busting lawman who should have been riding a desk? Why pop the old man's bubble by looking for what is obviously going to be an embarrassing error? We figured he had earned the right to go out on a good note. I'm sure that the old Arizona Rangers who tamed Douglas the first time would agree. Bringing law and order to the border can leave a lot of questions behind that are best unanswered for a while.

Drex returned to his native Arkansas, where he died within several years of his retirement. McMahon and I missed the funeral because we were out of touch with a lot of the boys after we both transferred out of the Douglas Border Patrol station in 1980. But we did manage to catch up to Fort in an airport bar in Georgia one year. Fort told us that during Drex's retirement party the old man and he had gotten off by themselves to knock a few cold ones back. Drex got confessingly drunk, which in the end made it easy for him to give up what had happened to our signals during the night of the La Copita bust.

The old man said that he had settled down in his fishing chair and found it to be pretty comfortable on that particular fall evening. While he was sitting there all cozy and comfy, the sandman caught up to Drex, causing him to doze off. When the old man woke up, the smugglers were hauling the dope right past him into the back of the bar. So much for the One, Two, and Three codes. But then again, I reckon other Western legends like Geronimo didn't put much faith in numbers, either. If he had, he would have surrendered much earlier.

19

Informants

CONFIDENTIAL INFORMANTS, or CIs as lawmen more commonly call them, are the most crucial tools that a narcotics agent can have. They are invaluable to every kind of law-enforcement officer I know. Whether you are a street cop, a highway patrolman, game warden, or federal agent, they can make or break a case for you. On the border their value doubles because they can cross into Mexico and operate where U.S. agents can no longer independently tread. CIs fill a critical void because agents are now forbidden to conduct investigations and enforcement operations in Mexico. For law-enforcement purposes you must look upon Mexican informants as free cross-border flowing dual-nationals. Like it or not, they are an authorized extension of you as a U.S. agent. And that is an extremely sharp double-edged sword when they fuck up.

I believe the public has a lot of misconceptions about informants. At the root of the disinformation, Hollywood has portrayed CIs as a bunch of scumbags from the slime-filled gutters. To a three-piece-suit CEO the word "informant" conjures up visions of the lowest dregs of society, the type of fellers seen guzzling a bottle of cheap wine and sleeping on a piece of cardboard behind a garbage bin.

But before you go condemning all informants as destitute scumbags, let me tell you about their potential incomes. Most of the ones I have worked with over the years averaged annual government rewards of $30,000 to $50,000. I have paid one of my better informants more than $250,000 in one year. And during the big money-laundering days down in Florida I heard of U.S. Customs special agents paying informants up to a cool million. The rule of thumb is that the informant who hooks you into an investigation is entitled to 25 percent of the seized property value. So if you seize $4 million in money-laundered proceeds or narcotics-derived property, the informant is eligible to grab a full million.

But not just anybody can be an informant. Did you ever notice how U.S. politicians and the influential American elite enact laws they expect the working folks to abide by without themselves adhering to the same statutes? Under the U.S. Customs Service qualifying criteria for being a confidential informant, former President Clinton does not qualify. That's right, because Bill Clinton perjured himself before a grand jury, the man cannot meet the criteria to be signed up as a Customs Service confidential informant.

Defense attorneys usually paint informants as Judases who would rat their own mother out for a couple of bucks. And even more curious, prosecutors treat informants as a painful but necessary black plague. Most prosecuting attorneys expect the agent to live and work with the informants as if they are part of our A team. And to be quite honest about it, I can tell you from experience, if you don't really spend a lot of time with your CI you'll never reap his full potential. It's very similar to raising children. You have to nurture and encourage them as they grow and develop.

Prosecuting attorneys usually don't want to be "contaminated" by seeing the CI face to face. I guess it's because they may have to shake the CI's hand and learn that he's a regular, living human being with a real pulse. It's easier that way for everybody but the agent. So when the CI is found rotting in a desert caustic-lime-filled hole with his throat cut and his balls in his mouth, the prosecutor won't miss a beat in his daily routine. Just the agent. You have to live with it forever. And if the truth be known, agents' lives are in the hands of informants just as much as theirs are in ours.

Jim Rayburn, John Nixon, and I had just completed the prosecution of a large-scale alien-smuggling ring in Phoenix in 1985 when we got notified by an informant that our lives were hanging out on an open contract. The smuggler who put the hit out was smoldering in a hellhole known as the Arizona State Prison in the little isolated desert town of Florence. We had put the outlaw there after taking him down during an undercover operation that lasted a year or so. The informant who came to us with the info used to "run" with the inmate in all the wrong circles. He had done some undercover operations with us before we sent his compa to la lata. Since he was willing, we wired him for sound and sent him in to see the scumbag on visitor's day at Florence.

During his visit with the human trafficker, the informant was able to coax the method of the hit out of the revenge-starved prisoner. The CI learned that the convict had three bombs buried in a south Phoenix park. One for the car of yours truly, one for Rayburn's ride, and the last one for Special Agent John Nixon's set of wheels.

Acting on the information our boy pumped from the inmate, Rayburn and I later located the bombs before they could be used to make spare parts out of us. The devices were buried under three different mesquites next to separate picnic tables in the middle of a public park in south Phoenix. Each bomb consisted of four or five sticks of "Giant Jelly" gelatin dynamite, accompanied by enough fuse for a car battery hookup, and the necessary electrical blasting caps. Each package had been buried with razor-sharp shards of broken glass covering them in an effort to dissuade anyone from digging them out of the ground. A kid playing with the wrong frequency of radio near one of the designated picnic tables would most likely have ended up like a crispy critter from a Nam napalm drop.

After slicing the shit out of the tips of our fingers, Jim and I ended up calling the Phoenix Police Department's bomb squad to assist us in removing the explosive devices. And that, folks, is pretty much how an informant came to save our lives. You may despise them. But a good number of us hold them near and dear to us. Hell, I'm closer to some of my informants than I am to some of my own Texas blood.

Jim Rayburn always taught me that you as an investigator are only as good as the CIs you surround yourself with. The more CIs in your stable, the more windows are going to open up to you. It's probably the most truthful statement about being a government agent that I know. I've worked with CIs from all walks of life, from mules at the bottom of the dope-smuggling chain, all the way up to attorneys and public officials at the top. They all have given me information at one time or another. You never know where and when you're going to be able to flip a guy to work as a CI for you. Sometimes it can come from twisting a doper you have an indictable case on. Other times it can come from a pure, simple bluff.

And that was how I got hooked up with two of the best CIs I would ever have working for me. We were tracking a load of dope from the Mexican border up through "Texas" John Slaughter's ranch in the San Bernardino Valley. After trailing the outlaws for several miles we came upon the dope stashed in a thicket of mesquite trees just off Geronimo Trail. I and a couple of other Customs agents patiently waited in ambush in the surrounding desert brush. We eventually busted a man-and-wife team when they approached the area with a good supply of food and water intended for the mules. Although they never took possession of the dope, we swooped down on the pair and stopped them shortly after they had dropped the mule provisions off near the stashed dope load.

Saul and Karina were quickly separated for questioning by the agents after being pulled out of their truck. Barrett and I went into the good cop/bad cop routine as we drilled the pair for answers concerning their supply delivery. We soon learned that the couple were Mexican citizens working under the direction of Agua Prieta dope lords. Barrett and I mulled it over and decided it couldn't hurt our CI stable to put these two to work for us on the other side of the border down in the Mexican dope-haven state of Sonora.

Although we legally didn't have a leg to stand on as far as charging these two with possession of the dope, we immediately went to work on the couple, attempting to convince them that we knew they were responsible for supplying 99 percent of the dope in Arizona to elementary-age school children. By the time Barrett and I got done with

Saul and Karina, they believed that they were about to be charged with the Kennedy assassination in addition to their dope smuggling. We got into their shit so bad that Saul started tossing his beans and Karina's legs became so wobbly she almost fell backasswards into a mound of prickly pear cactus.

After the wrath of the San Bernardino Valley narcs had subsided, Saul was able to hold some water down and Karina could sit in the truck without falling off the seat. After regaining a portion of their composure, the couple made a peace offering to us. In exchange for not being charged with dope smuggling, and/or the Kennedy assassination, they virtually promised to give us information on Mexican dope loads and smuggling activity as long as they drew breath. In fact, they were so committed to Butch and me that they wanted to know if it was okay if they named their next two *niños* (babies) after us! The love affair was just beginning.

Over the next two to three years, Saul and Karina turned about thirty loads of dope for us. All told, they gave us information that led to the seizure of several tons of grass and hundreds of pounds of cocaine. I can't even count all of the traffickers who fell to U.S. lawmen after a whisper of information from the gruesome twosome. Butch and I became somewhat attached to the pair. It wasn't just the cases they were delivering. We were actually beginning to look forward to seeing their smiling mugs when we made a meet somewhere in the Arizona desert.

Such meets were primarily for the exchange of information or for payments of money that they had earned for informing. It was during these meets that it became harder and harder to keep the relationship purely professional. I mean, sure, this is a couple of dope informants, but they have family problems and situations just like normal folks. We spent enough time together that Butch and I watched Karina go through a full-term pregnancy with medical complications. And almost every time we met them, we had to turn our collars around and become either priests or marriage counselors, according to their needs. They had marital problems and concerns about their children's future just like we all have.

In other words, Butch and I were beginning to see them as regular folks just like anyone else. The government had taught us to keep them at arm's length because they were just numbers. Even around the office, the informants were referred to on the phone and in reports as #501 or #505. But folks, it just ain't that easy. The government REMFs would like to think that. But as usual, they're out of touch with the agents in the field, not to mention our informants who are hanging their asses out on the front line.

As the years progressed the meetings weren't enough. Our home phones would ring at all times of the day or night with Karina and Saul's personal problems. Butch and I were becoming more and more father figures to them rather than controlling agents. But they were still delivering good loads of dope along with plenty of arrest stats. So how could we justify cutting them loose? We allowed the relationship to drag on and we tried to keep it on a professional basis. To keep a division in the lines. To keep it outside of our own families. Being a father to one family at a time was tough enough without adopting a whole other family in Mexico.

But like all kids, Saul and Karina didn't always take our advice or listen to us about what was best for them. Children always think they know better than dad and that they can pull the wool over the old man's eyes. Saul fell with a load of dope in Ohio that he thought he could get away with behind our backs. The Ohio state troopers called us and wanted to know what to do with him since he told them that he worked for Butch and me. We did what every controlling agent (or father) would have done given the situation: We told them to lock his ass up and throw away the fucking key. It was the only way he was going to learn his lesson.

After a couple of weeks some idiot bail bondsman in Ohio was dumb enough to throw money down for Saul's freedom. Like I figured he would do, the informant ran straight for Mexico. You can take a rat off the border but you can't take the border out of the rat. I ended up fielding dozens of calls from the bail bondsman and Ohio prosecutors. Why? Because the dumb Yankee fuckers thought that I could snap my fingers and make Saul cross the border at their whim. Let me tell you, any judicial jurisdiction on the border knows that you don't give a fucking Mexican citizen a postable bond if you ever want to see him stand trial!

For several months I became the negotiator for the bondsman, the prosecutor, and Saul in Mexico. In the end, the bondsman lost his money, because he couldn't get Saul into court on time, but I worked out a deal with the prosecutor for Saul's surrender. All he had to do was turn himself in to the Ohio authorities and the prosecutor had promised that he would get probation with no jail time. Talk about a sweet deal; they don't come any better than this. It was all set up, but just like a kid who won't listen to his old man, Saul fucked up big time. He never surrendered and the prosecutor's offer expired. I would have loved to have had the chance to kick his butt over this. I had a once-in-a-lifetime deal set for the ungrateful little shit and he blew it. Informants can be such a pain in the ass! But it wasn't over yet.

A month later, Karina got busted by Customs inspectors with a three-hundred-pound load of cocaine that she was driving across the border in Douglas. Would you like to guess the first fucking words out of her mouth? "Call Morgan and Barrett. I work for them as a CI." Can you imagine the amount of shit this put Barrett and me in? We had Internal Affairs making phone calls on us before Karina had even given a statement! And I know damn good and well that Internal Affairs was probably beating feet to the door of the U.S. Attorney in Tucson.

Barrett and I knew that the only way we would survive this kiss of death was by beating Internal Affairs to a truthful statement from Karina. I could just picture this Mexican bitch sitting in a jail cell proudly telling everyone far and wide that she was our informant! And the implications of that would be that the controlling agents either knew or were somehow involved in what she had attempted to do. Let me tell you folks out there something. The Washington REMFs, the prosecutors, the judges, and all of the other powers that be are living in an alcoholic stupor if they think an agent can control every fucking thing an informant does. It is absolutely a crap shoot at best.

The powers that be don't want to know the truth about informants because it scares the shit out of them. It's the kind of truth that
causes early gray hairs. But here it is: In order for a CI to be effective
he must participate in criminal activity. The government's official policy is, as long as the criminal activity is in furtherance of an investigation, as long as the informant is doing it with our knowledge, his
activities are sanctioned. If he conducts such criminal activity without
our knowledge, it is not sanctioned. In other words, the informant
becomes an outlaw because he either doesn't, or at the time can't,
make a phone call.

Because of its own policy, the government forces the CI to become
an outlaw to save his own life. Let me put it to you in this light. If the
CI informed on every bit of criminal activity that he was party to
when he's working for a particular organization, how long do you
think it would take the bad guys to figure out who the finger is? If the
CI was present every time one of their dope loads was seized by us, he
would be toast. The CI is put into a position where he must smuggle
some successful loads of dope behind our backs to be credible with his
organization. When you understand it in these terms, the expression
"controlling agent" screams to be redefined.

Barrett and I successfully interviewed Karina on tape; she admitted that we had no knowledge of her attempt to smuggle the load of
cocaine that she had been busted with. Her statement probably saved
our asses from having to hire defense attorneys. She never would
admit to who she was smuggling the load for, but I happen to know
from another CI that Karina had a sister who was fucking Amado
Carrillo at the time of the load. It doesn't take a brain surgeon to figure that one out. Karina ended up serving ten years in prison for the
coke load. I hated to see her pull that much time. Like I said, we had
become friends and I had watched her raise a family. But bottom line,
she chose her own fate.

Saul still calls me on occasion from Mexico to say hello and ask if
I've been up to the federal pen to see Karina. He's stuck with the chil-
dren and keeps me up to date on their health and needs. Just before
Amado Carrillo was murdered, Saul gave me his hiding location.

Through official State Department channels, we made a run at Amado on his home turf. But as can be expected, the MFJP protected him and he wasn't taken into custody. Saul knew it was Amado's dope load that had put his beautiful young Karina in prison. Although Saul is still a fugitive from U.S. authorities, he still calls me to let me know he's satisfied that Amado died on the operating table. And the reality of his death was that Amado's own flesh and blood paid the surgeon to murder him. So Amado's brother, Vicente Carrillo, took over the business and once again the Reaper became the beneficiary of narco traffickers' greed.

In 1996, Bill Gately was the Resident Agent in Charge of one of the U.S. Customs Service Office of Investigations in Los Angeles. It had been bad enough when he ran roughshod over Steve Mercado and fucked up the Douglas drug-tunnel investigation in 1990. But because the REMFs in D.C. didn't know how to control him, he was about to do it again. The only difference would be, this fuckup was going to cost the whole federal law-enforcement community, *big-time*.

Gately and his agents got tied into one of those once-in-a-lifetime informants. The guy was a go-between for one of the biggest money-laundering operations the U.S. Customs Service had ever uncovered. After some razzle-dazzle bad-guy talk to the organization's money-cleaning bosses, the informant introduced undercover U.S. Customs special agents into the operation. The agents and informant are alleged to have conducted at least ten covert forays into Mexico without official permission from the Mexican government, specifically the Mexican Attorney General.

Now, to a degree, I can see where Bill was coming from here. Had he had laid out his informant's identity and covert operational plans to the Mexicans, this whole case would have never developed or culminated. However, when you decide to break protocol and go out on your own, you have to look at the big picture in the end. Would there be any possible retaliation by the Mexicans? Could they hurt us worse than we were about to hurt them? Would future generations of federal law enforcement lose or gain anything from the investigation? Would the citizens of the United States, whom you are sworn to defend, benefit or suffer from the case? Bill didn't stop to think about these crucial questions because he was a self-centered glory seeker just like he had been during the Douglas drug-tunnel investigation. He had already authored one book concerning his previous investigations, and this money-laundering investigation was about to become his next text.

To Gately's credit, Operation Casablanca was the largest, most comprehensive narcotics money-laundering investigation in the history of the United States. The investigation was active for three years and it yielded the arrests of some twenty-six Mexican bankers in the U.S. along with about 150 dope smugglers. The U.S. Customs Service seized somewhere in the neighborhood of $110 million, two tons of cocaine, and four tons of marijuana. Now, you ask, how is it possible that the largest federal money-laundering investigation ever, which produced such positive results, could be deemed such a miserable failure? Well, Mexican President Ernesto Zedillo got so pissed off about the unauthorized U.S. operation on Mexican soil that he flat-out told the Clinton administration there would be some new ground rules or else. The "or else" part is something I'm not sure of. Maybe Zedillo threatened to go red or let Castro bring troops into Sonora. Or perhaps something else equally evil. I don't know. But the new ground rules I can tell you all about at length and in painful depth.

On July 2, 1998, the Mexican and United States Attorney Generals met in Brownsville, Texas, where they signed a document now known as the Brownsville Agreement. They addressed the document to the U.S. and Mexican presidents, and laid out the notification requirements in advance of cross-border law-enforcement operations. Why they called it "cross-border" enforcement is beyond me, when the U.S. is the only one of the two willing to enforce the border and its related narcotics laws. Hell, since the Mexican government is always involved in dope smuggling, you have to wonder what the fuck was going through Attorney General Janet Reno's brainpan when she got involved in this fiasco.

Folks, this whole meeting and resulting agreement is, in my opinion, one of the biggest political shams of the twentieth century. It probably doesn't matter too much that Mexican Attorney General

Cuéllar is a suspected corrupt official in his own right, because the next Mexican Attorney General will probably be just as bad if not worse. The point is that our government made a deal with the fox to guard the proverbial henhouse. Not only that, but when we agreed to the part about training these crooked assholes on our "sophisticated investigative techniques," we gave the Mexican fox the sacred key to the lock on the U.S. henhouse door. There's a reference to "the criminal organizations that threaten the security and well-being of our countries"? Hell's bells! It's the scum-sucking Mexican Federal Judicial Police and Mexican Army that we are talking about here!

In February of 1999, during the U.S./Mexico presidential summit at Mérida, Yucatán, the Attorney Generals signed a Memorandum of Understanding (MOU) that defined putting the Brownsville Agreement procedures into effect. The MOU was binding on all U.S. law-enforcement agencies and those working under their direction, which meant all of our informants in Mexico. For the U.S. Customs Service, the DEA, and the FBI, these agreements covered our operational activities in Mexico that involved dope trafficking, money laundering, and any other crimes related to dope trafficking. The phrase "any other crimes related" was so all-encompassing it virtually cemented us into giving up all enforcement efforts in Mexico.

One of the things you have to notice about the way the Brownsville Agreement and the Mérida MOU were written was how they stated that this restriction pertains to "all federal law-enforcement agencies or law-enforcement activity." The rich Mexicans who wield the power inside their government were very careful about how that was worded. I think it would be safe to surmise that like former Panamanian President Manuel Noriega, there are certain Mexican officials in bed with the CIA, the NSA, and other similar U.S. spook intelligence-gathering agencies. Since there have always been rumors about our national security agencies' involvement in gun and dope smuggling in Panama, you can be damn sure it's also presently going on in Mexico.

So while the Brownsville Agreement and MOU were specifically written for federal law-enforcement agencies, the spooks were intentionally precluded because they are officially our nation's federal *intelligence-gathering* agencies. Besides not being included in the agreement, we later learned from our own sources, the U.S. Ambassador's office in Mexico City runs the names of our operational informants by the spooks, or rather the State Department, as they are officially known within the U.S. Embassy. This worked out real good for the crooks running the Mexican government. The best of both worlds. They could still make tons of money in dope and guns with the CIA, and at the same time they could effectively shut down their losses of narcotics to the U.S. Customs Service, the DEA, and the FBI. For us border narcs, it's like being the only blind son of a bitch at a poker table. Everyone is reading your cards but you!

And if for one minute you think this spook/dope-trafficker connection is merely an assumption, what about this: After the Brownsville-Mérida giveaway, the Mexican news media released an article that cited possible future legislation in Washington, D.C. The Mexicans published the news that the U.S. Congress would soon pass anti-drug legislation that would give discretionary powers to the CIA for not making public the identity of major Mexican drug lords and their partners in the U.S. The legislation would also allow the U.S. president to suspend the confiscation of assets and properties of those suspected of associating with drug traffickers in the U.S. when that could risk U.S. national security.

In the simplest of terms, the Mérida MOU mandated the following restrictions and handcuffs on U.S. special agents, not to mention potential impending death certificates for our informants:

• Through our State Department at the U.S. Embassy in Mexico City, we were required to notify the Mexican Attorney General of our investigations and informants in Mexico. This notification included the informants' designated alphanumeric identity codes, operational dates in Mexico, operational locations in Mexico, the full names of the Mexican drug traffickers and targets the informants were working on, and a synopsis of the informants' past and proposed future undercover dope buys from the specifically named traffickers. (Gee, whiz! I'm surprised that Janet Reno didn't want the informants' dates of births so they would be readily available to be carved onto their fucking headstones!)

• At the discretion of the Mexican Attorney General, he would decide how far down the food chain such information was to be filtered. In other words, we could expect it to go all the way down to the corrupt MFJP agents and Mexican Army on the border where the informants' locations had been identified.

And would you like to know just how big a sellout this was? Compare it to this: Each year the president of the United States gives $6 or $7 million to Mexico supposedly to be used in the war on drugs. Would you like to know what the U.S. government gets in return? Not a fucking thing. Zero. The Mexicans don't give us an operational plan on how the funds are going to be used, or an accounting of the expenditures! There are no Mexican documents that I'm aware of that detail where these millions have gone. For all we know, and I wouldn't doubt this a bit, the Mexican government may be using your U.S. tax dollars to cultivate and harvest their own goddamn poppy fields! Yet in return, we are now giving them the heads-up on our operations and informants in Mexico!

When you combined the terms of the Brownsville Agreement and the Mérida MOU, we were all but finished in Mexico. And you may ask, why was it so important that we work down there through informants? The answer is simple: We needed to know before the dope got to the border where it was going to be smuggled across. That would give us time to shift our manpower for the bust. It was the same reason that for hundreds of years generals have sent their recon teams behind enemy lines. Before the battle, you need to know the enemy's strength, position, and direction of travel. Without that, you're just pissing in the wind when it comes to the nut cutting.

The second reason is that in the past we had been able to infiltrate some of the major Mexican smuggling organizations with informants. These informants would not only be privileged to certain conspiratorial conversations, they would participate in the planning and actual smuggling of the dope. We had inside information on stash houses, the kind of drugs being smuggled, how much, the smuggling routes, the drivers' and mules' identities, what kind of weapons they were armed with, and the names of the money couriers and launderers. The information was so crucial to our interdiction efforts that most dope organizations had continuing rewards and ongoing hunts to root out and murder our informants.

After Attorney General Janet Reno signed these agreements, the Mexicans wouldn't have to hunt our informants anymore. They were being served up on a silver platter. A peace offering to the Mexicans after Operation Casablanca. I just kept wondering when the Mexican Attorney General was going to notify the U.S. Attorney General of the next date and location that the MFJP and Mexican soldiers would be smuggling dope into the U.S. That is, in accordance with the operational agreements!

Now, at first I thought we were all gonna just lie down and get fucked by the Brownsville Agreement. When I say "we," I'm referring to Customs, which at that time controlled 60 percent of all informants operating in Mexico, followed by the DEA, the FBI, and the INS. But the more I watched what was going on around me, the more I realized most of us were still operating our informants in Mexico without notifying the Mexican government. So before any of my agents took cases into court that weren't kosher with the Brownsville Agreement, I decided to give the U.S. Attorney's Office in Tucson a call. We needed to see what their official position was concerning the agreement. Our agents in the field needed some guidelines to go by. I knew it wasn't a matter of federal law; it was a matter of foreign policy. However, the Attorney General of the United States signed the fucking thing into effect and I wanted to know what her subordinates had to say about it.

On May 21, 1999, I telephoned the U.S. Attorney's Office in Tucson. The first assistant U.S. Attorney I got hold of said she couldn't and wouldn't even dream of commenting on her superiors' position on the Brownsville Agreement. She all but made the excuse that they had just been informed of a bomb threat in the federal building and she had to get off the phone ASAP. By the time I made a follow-up phone call to her boss, the chief of the Criminal Section, the stench of a rat in the woodpile was beginning to rise up in my noggin. When I got the chief Criminal AUSA on the phone, the dead-rat odor was confirmed. When I asked this guy his position on the agreement, you could have heard a pin drop at his end of the phone. When he finally broke the silence, he said he was totally unaware of the agreement and that he would have to get back to me with an answer after he researched the new policy. It was almost like talking to Bill Clinton concerning his extramarital affairs.

Several days later, Roger Duncan, the chief Criminal AUSA in Tucson, called me back. He said he had been unable to locate any information concerning the Brownsville Agreement or the Mérida MOU. He asked me to fax him a copy of both documents so that he could study them. I found the whole situation totally fucking ridiculous. Here's a tool of foreign policy that for all practical purposes binds the hands of narcotics agents behind their backs. It had been written and signed by the Attorney General of the United States nearly four months earlier, and the U.S. Attorney's Office was telling me, a border rat, to enlighten them on their boss's decision. Ludicrous!

So my legal questions, like how much trouble would an agent be in if he brought a case in where an informant had violated the agreement, went straight into the shitter. And there was a reason for it. The U.S. attorneys knew damn good and well that their boss, Attorney General Janet Reno, had sold us all out. They knew we couldn't make superior narcotics smuggling cases without having our informants operate in Mexico. But they weren't going to come right out and say it. Everyone, including the U.S. Attorney's Office, was waiting for the first agent to fall under the new policy. Everyone wanted to see how it would play out. Would the case be thrown out of court by the federal judge? Would the defense attorneys set a new legal precedent by jamming the agreement up our ass? Would the scapegoated agent be fired or disciplined by his respective agency? Or would the State Department demand the agent be prosecuted under some stupid unheard-of law because the agent pissed Mexico off—again?

With more questions than answers, I turned to the REMFs at Customs headquarters in D.C. As much as I didn't care for these pencil necks, they were the ones living in the same rat-infested shithole as

Reno. So I figured maybe they could tell me about the Brownsville Agreement. According to their version, the agreement, although binding on all of us, wasn't all that devastating to our operational interest in Mexico. They said that the only thing the Mexican government would get from us was the location, type of activity, date the informant was operating, and the *names* of the organizations the informant was infiltrating. Like because they weren't giving the informant's *real* name out, that was supposed to make me feel better! Shit and fall back into it! There's no fucking difference here! If you give up that much information, even folks who build the walls of their submarines with adobe bricks are gonna be able to figure out who the fly in the manure is!

And if the Mexicans didn't have enough pieces of the puzzle to put together for a full picture, consider this. On each one of these operational letters we submitted to the U.S. Embassy, which would later be given to the Mexican Attorney General, we were required to put our informant's code number. Without going into how that code is set up, do you really think that these multimillion-dollar dope lords, who already hire technicians to break our deciphered radio transmissions, will have a problem with these coded location designator numbers? Not in your wildest dreams. They would know without a doubt from where the informant and investigation hailed within minutes.

Within months of the Brownsville Agreement being signed, the Mexican newspapers exposed our U.S. testicles to the narcotics traffickers. One of the articles was written by the Mexican newspaper *Universal*. The article stated that the U.S. Embassy (U.S. Ambassador and State Department) indicated that the U.S. Department of Treasury (U.S. Customs) through an official MOU with Mexico (Brownsville Agreement) requested Mexico's cooperation in an undercover operation (our informants) targeting Colombian money launderers in certain areas of Mexico. So if you were a Colombian drug lord with a money-laundering operation going on in Mexico, the Mexican press just alerted you to go under for a while. And if they weren't scared enough to lay low, the Colombians at least knew to have their people stay away from new faces while continuing to launder their loot.

And this is what the REMFs are calling "non-devastating" operational disclosure to the Mexican government! Why don't we just get the address of each known bona fide drug lord in Mexico and Colombia so we can express-mail them a certified copy of our informant list and operational plans?

In September of 1999, my office conducted one of our first operations under the Brownsville Agreement. It was an investigation into the smuggling of Mexican manufactured methamphetamines through the Douglas Port of Entry. The case was originally brought to the Customs Service by an old friend of mine who had recently been assigned to my office. U.S. Immigration Service Senior Special Agent Hummer Rodriguez was an Organized Crime Drug Enforcement Task Force member out of Phoenix. Although eligible for retirement after working the border for twenty-eight years, Hummer wasn't ready to throw in the towel just yet.

Hummer was a ruddy-faced lady's man if ever there was one. Women's eyes lit up when he walked into a room and the Mexican-American took great pride in such knowledge. The boy instinctively knew the words every class of female would succumb to. On one end of the spectrum Hummer could talk a sophisticated female judge into reversing a court decision. On the other end he could silver-tongue a five-dollar Mexican whore into giving him a free taste of her wares. Besides women, Hummer was extremely good at two other things in life: working undercover and developing informants.

While assigned to my office in Douglas, Hummer plugged into a new Mexican informant named Gordo from Agua Prieta. Not only was the guy new to our stable of CIs, but he was definitely a different kind of informant from most others that the agents in my office had been used to. Theirs was a strange and comical relationship, to say the least. Gordo was one of those pleasingly plump, happy-go-lucky homosexuals that loved to flirt with men. What can I say? At thirty-two years of age, Gordo epitomized the Pillsbury Doughboy. The only difference was that he was just a tad darker with limp wrists. I have no clue as to where or how the womanizing, macho Hummer ran into the dude. But their union joined as unlikely a pair of border narcs as you'd ever want to see. Can you imagine these two on the job together, walking down the streets of Machoville, Sonora, Mexico? Hummer would be eyeballing the traffickers, wondering who had the biggest load of dope he could score. Gordo would be scouting out the same guys but wondering who had the biggest load of cum to score!

But on the job the two learned to put their sexual orientations aside, and as can be expected, the special agent and informant became best of friends. After a couple of months of frequenting doper dives in Agua Prieta, Gordo got hooked up with some heavy-duty meth smugglers. Gordo in turn introduced Hummer to the bad guys as a major buyer from L.A. We then let nature take its course and Hummer subsequently had several undercover meetings with the meth smugglers at the Motel 6 in Douglas. Each time Hummer bought six to eight ounces of meth that the crooks had smuggled in from their Mexican lab. It was a testing of the waters for both sides.

After Hummer had won their confidence, we threw out a $160,000 flash roll at the next meeting for the outlaws to ogle over. We wanted to buy some bulk meth and put these motherfuckers on a thirty-year one-way ticket into the federal pen. We already had them nailed for a ten-year rap, but we hoped to get them in the act of selling us twenty pounds of the "brain fry," which carried about a twenty-five- to thirty-year sentence.

During the negotiations, the bad guys invited Hummer down to Mexico to party up and take a look-see at their lab's cooking operation. Never wanting to endanger an agent anymore than needed, we opted to offer Gordo the tour instead. Knowing the potential danger of what we asked of him, Gordo still gladly accepted the assignment. But because the CI had to go into Mexico and actively "participate" with the crooks, I was required as the U.S. Customs Resident Agent in Charge to notify the Mexican government under the Brownsville Agreement. I reckon you don't have to be told the whole deal fell through, because you're probably not as stupid as the REMFs who run the federal government. But it didn't stop here. It was a runaway turdball heading downhill, and when it hit bottom, as shit will, it was going to get messier and a hell of a lot deadlier for all of us.

In June of 1999, all border special agents of the U.S. Customs Service, FBI, and DEA offices received an alert. Information had come from a reliable source that the Mexican Federal Judicial Police were bringing new and additional agents to the border to assist large Mexican dope-trafficking organizations by spying on U.S. Customs, FBI, and DEA offices within the U.S. The Mex feds were supposed to be armed with specific code-breaking radio scanners and cell phone-monitoring equipment to eavesdrop on U.S. law-enforcement operations and activities.

In August of 1999, I was contacted by one of my best Mexican informants. This guy was so good that he not only contracted out to the Customs Service, he also ran with the CIA, FBI, and DEA. This dude was so smooth-talking that he could coo a confession out of an underground Nazi war criminal. So I had no problem with the veracity of the information he was about to relay. My man had been at the MFJP comandante's office in Agua Prieta, where he had the good fortune to be invited to the premiere of a new Mexican movie. It starred me, and each and every special agent in the Douglas U.S. Customs Service Office of Investigations. The Mex feds had been making surveillance tapes of the people coming and going from our office. They probably videoed all the agents, but because we meet our CIs in other locations away from the office, it would have been almost impossible for the Mexicans to get them identified. But no worry. That was something the Mex feds would easily be able to obtain under the Brownsville Agreement.

That same month, within a two-week period, the Reaper frequented the U.S. Customs Service stable of informants. Three of our CIs along the Mexico-California border were found murdered in Mexico. A fourth was listed as missing in action, which in reality meant we would most likely never find his tortured, disfigured body.

In January of 2000, after the Phoenix FBI office had argued with its D.C. REMFs about how much critical information was being disclosed to the Mexicans under the Brownsville Agreement, something proof-positive occurred. The residence of one of their informants was broken into and undercover tapes the informant had recorded were stolen. The informant had recorded the evidence while socializing with members of the Mexican government-protected Agua Prieta drug cartel. Nothing else was disturbed in the house. The next time the operative met with the bad guys in Agua Prieta, it wouldn't be a pretty sight. The death merchants had recovered their own stolen undercover tapes. Now, where do you suppose they learned that this soon-to-be-hanging-dead piece of meat was an undercover operative making covert recordings of their conversations? And it continued to get worse.

On May 8, 2000, Gordo died in a hail of gunfire as he walked out the front door of his home in Agua Prieta, Sonora. The U.S. Customs Service operative was shot three times at close range in the back by a Sinaloan shooter hired by Yolanda Molina and other drug lords of the Agua Prieta cartel. A final coup de grace round was dispatched bilaterally through Gordo's brain as he lay helplessly on his front porch in death's grip. Special Agent Hummer Rodriguez had lost a good friend. The agent would spend the next several months attempting to console and care for Gordo's grieving family. But who would ever offer to help the agent with his own deep, gnawing survivor's guilt? Who would stabilize him mentally before his next undercover operation?

Nine months before his death, Gordo had gone operational under my signature according to the Brownsville Agreement's strictly crafted procedures and notifications to the Mexican Attorney General. Since I was ultimately responsible for sending this man to his death, it fell upon me to notify the U.S. Customs Service REMFs in Washington, D.C., of the informant's demise. Would you like to know the response I got from U.S. Customs Service Commissioner Raymond Kelly's hand-picked staff of overpaid REMFs when I informed them of Gordo's assassination? They made sarcastic jokes and laughed about "just another snitch dying of lead poisoning." Their pompous language and tone enraged me beyond all civility. Later, when I cooled down, I was just flat-out ashamed to be associated with such men. As a matter of fact, I would have preferred the company of Gordo any time over that of the pencil-dick desk jockeys in D.C.

Gordo was the first, only, and last informant that I would ever send operational into Mexico under the agreement. Commanding generals sent soldiers to their deaths every day in Vietnam. We didn't win that war and we don't have the resolve to win this one, either. So why would I even dream of sending another informant to his death for what in the end will be posted in the history books as another loss for America? It would only add to the lengthy roll call of soldiers, agents, and informants that visit me late at night in the dark. Other than haunting guys like Hummer and me, I'm sorry to say that their deaths haven't accomplished a fucking thing.

Whose doorstep do you lay this at? President Clinton and his desire to keep the NAFTA benefits flowing? Or Attorney General Janet Reno because she cowed down to her boss because he was upset that we pissed the Mexicans off over the Casablanca investigation? Certainly a combination of both would be most correct. Had the president not bent over backwards for Mexican relations after Operation Casablanca, and had Reno not given away our informants to Mexico under the absolutely insidious Brownsville Agreement, these operatives would not have been murdered. And yes, even though some will say they were only scumbag informants, they were still real people with hopes, dreams, and loving families, just like you or me.

Over the years, I and many other agents in Cochise County have all lost some informants at one time or another. It's something we don't like pondering because it'll drive you over the edge. The names and faces tend to haunt you, even long after you're retired from the job. Some of them were friends, and others merely business acquaintances. Whatever they may have been, you were responsible for them. It was your job to keep them alive. It was the only word they ever really asked you to keep with them. It's a promise that knots up in your gut when you're reviewing the autopsy photos.

And if you're one of the mistaken folks who think informants are all lowlifes, let me tell you a story about one of the bravest Mexican machos I've ever known. He was an informant by the name of Benito Suárez. He had been working deep in Mexican territory for the CIA spooks when I met him in Phoenix in 1982, when I was still with the INS anti-smuggling unit. Suárez was just coming back up from the south, where he had been spying on the communist training camps in the mountains of Sonora and Chihuahua. When he wasn't doing that for the spooks, he was keeping an eye on the North Korean fishing boats off the coast of Baja California. Such ships are in reality floating communist eavesdropping communication centers that are attempting to monitor U.S. government radio traffic.

In the early 1980s, a new ruthless group of dope-trafficking cowboys came out of the mountains of Sinaloa to rule the drug trade in Mexico. Their crimes and brutalities were even more horrific than those of the drug lords of Colombia. These mountain cowboys had endured civil wars between themselves, Mexican military attacks, and numerous other enforcement efforts aimed at dismantling their drug-trafficking empires. They survived by the gun and died by the gun. They became known throughout the drug world to both crooks and law-enforcement officials as the Sinaloan Cowboys. By birth a Sinaloan, Benito Suárez had grown up with these boys.

Suárez looked every bit the part of the Sinaloan Cowboy. The thirty-eight-year-old compact Mexican always wore tight-fitting, starched jeans matched with a colorful Western shirt. Sitting on top of his well-styled cowboy haircut was the traditional light-tan Stetson straw hat that became a trademark of the dope-smuggling Sinaloans. His handsome Mexican-made lizard boots looked sharp with the silver-conchoed Sinaloan belt around his waist. Suárez's hazel-green eyes and light complexion betrayed his Mexican relatives' French and German heritage. His continual smile and charm were tools of his trade. As an informant, he was unsurpassed in talking his way into a criminal's confidence. I imagine this came from years of practice growing up in the mountains of Sinaloa. When you're facing the business end of a gun and talking a crooked line of bullshit to save your ass, you get damn proficient at being quite the charmer.

On February 7, 1985, a tragic event happened that would eventually turn Suárez's life into a nightmare. DEA agent Enrique "Kiki" Camarena was grabbed by Mexican drug lords near the U.S. consulate in Guadalajara. DEA suspected that Rafael Caro-Quintero, Miguel Félix-Gallardo, Manuel Salcido, and other members of the Sinaloan Cowboys had ordered the kidnapping. Shortly after the agent was confirmed missing, DEA began sending every available informant into Mexico in an attempt to locate Camarena while he was still breathing. When DEA learned that the Phoenix INS anti-smuggling unit had an informant who was born and raised in Sinaloa, they ended up on our doorsteps with hat in hand.

James Rayburn was the agent who had developed and controlled Suárez. Rayburn contacted Suárez about DEA's request for assistance and their accompanying proposal. They would pay for all of his living expenses in Mexico, including a rental car to get around in. On top of that, DEA promised a substantial monetary reward if Special Agent Camarena could be located.

Suárez said yes without blinking an eye. He didn't need to think it over. A U.S. agent's life was hanging in the balance and he knew the rest of us gringos would stand out like sore thumbs in the Sinaloan hills. Suárez was honored to be asked to participate in the hunt for the missing DEA agent. He told us and the briefing DEA agents that he had grown up with Cochi Loco, also known as Manuel Salcido. Aware of the deadly potential of his mission, Suárez didn't think it would be too much of a problem to re-enter his old lifestyle with the Sinaloan Cowboys.

By the time Suárez got down deep into Mexico, the U.S. State Department, the INS, the DEA, the FBI, and the U.S. Customs Service were all engaged in a concerted effort to make life miserable for the Mexican government. We knew that the Mexican government was involved with the Sinaloan drug lords on some scale. The U.S. agencies pulled out every available political and economic tool to bring the Mexicans to their knees to make them produce agent Camarena. In so doing, they got the Sinaloan Cowboys running scared.

When Suárez caught up to the boys their paranoia was at an all-time high. Without much more than a "Howdy and where the fuck have you been all these years?" the Sinaloans grabbed Suárez and a buddy who had gone with him on the hunt for Camarena. They knew that Suárez had been in Arizona for the past several years and they became suspicious of his "timely" return. Suárez and his compa were taken to the back of a residence in Jalisco, where they were repeatedly beaten and tortured during a bloody, dehumanizing interrogation. Suárez would later tell me that during this session of questioning, he believed he heard the voice of Agent Camarena in an adjoining room, where he, too, was being tortured.

After the grisly ordeal, a bleeding Suárez was placed in his rental vehicle behind the steering wheel. His compa, dying from massive, hemorrhaging head wounds and other lacerations, was placed in the passenger seat. The car had been taken to the edge of a mountain cliff overlooking a steep canyon. Before they were pushed over, Suárez looked into his buddy's pleading, dying eyes. His compa begged him that if he survived, he would take care of his wife and children back in Phoenix. Suárez agreed just before one of the hired guns crushed his buddy's face and skull into a bloody pulp with the buttstock of an AK-47.

Before going over the side of the cliff, Suárez was butt-stroked in the back of the head between the lower portion of his skull and neck. That was the last thing he remembered before being found on the side of the mountain road by some tourists. He had been miraculously thrown out of the car before it made a final rolling crash into the bottom of the canyon. Obviously, the dope traffickers didn't see Suárez being thrown clear. Either that or they thought him to already be dead from the crushing butt strokes to the back of the head. Either way it went, Suárez ended up in a hospital in Mexico, where DEA denied his existence. That's right! When DEA was questioned by the Mexican government about Suárez's claim that he was working for them, they fucking denied it.

Rayburn and I eventually learned of the situation, and we didn't waste any time getting into the middle of DEA's shit about getting Benito out of Mexico. All we got from them was empty promises and double-talk. It was political suicide, but Special Agent Jim Rayburn went around everybody in INS and the Justice Department. Rayburn placed a personal telephone call to U.S. Ambassador John Gavin in Mexico.

Now, Gavin was a cool, politically incorrect type of a guy. He was a close friend of U.S. Customs Service Commissioner Willy von Raab, and they both loved bucking the system. Jim knew Ambassador Gavin was the juice guy to go to. Not only had Gavin played an active role in helping DEA pressure the Mexicans while looking for agent Camarena, he flat-out called the Mexican government crooked to its face. That was unheard of back in those days. The State Department wanted to fire Gavin over the incident, but President Reagan backed him up. With steel *cojones* (balls) and political backing like that, we knew Gavin would help us get Suárez out of Mexico.

A couple of weeks after we got the ball rolling with Ambassador Gavin, Suárez was carried on a stretcher across Las Americas Bridge at the port of entry in El Paso, Texas. The Mexicans delivered him to anti-smuggling agents from our El Paso office, who immediately transported Suárez to a hospital where he underwent surgery. The recovery process, both physical and mental, would never be over.

When Suárez returned to Phoenix, Special Agent John Nixon, Rayburn, and I would rotate turns driving him to physical therapy. The first time I picked him up to go to the doctor, I had to choke the tears back. I hadn't seen Suárez for about six months. The last time I saw him before he went hunting for Camarena, he was a vigorous, healthy young man with fire in his eyes and a zest in his heart for life. But what met me at his apartment door on my first visit was the pitiful remains of a man I didn't recognize.

Using a cane to creep about, and bent over like an eighty-year-old grandfather, Suárez was reminiscent of a gaunt figure from the Holocaust. His former 160-pound, vibrant, muscular body was now no more than a ninety-pound, pitifully starved, broken skeleton. His once sparkling eyes had diminished into sunken, dark, seething holes indicating months of pain and despair. His sullen face was marred by unspeakably scarred flesh with protruding stitched tissue. As a boy I had seen some tormented, ripped souls in Vietnam's field hospitals. That was the only familiarity I could now find in my old friend.

DEA did nothing to help. In fact, they wouldn't even pay for the rental car that ended up burned and totaled with its bloodstained seats in the bottom of the Mexican canyon. Rayburn and I helped Suárez get congressional assistance. After years of battling the government's red tape, Suárez received some just compensation for his courageous efforts to save a U.S. agent. The rental car was finally paid for by DEA after someone in Congress chewed their asses out. All of Suárez's medical bills were paid off and mental-health assistance was authorized. On top of that, Suárez received about $150,000 cash and a free training program to become a motel manager.

I last saw Suárez in 1997 when he came to visit me at the U.S. Customs Office of Investigations in Douglas. Physically, he looked a lot better, even though he still limped with a cane and bore terrible scars over his face and neck. But on the inside I could tell my old friend was still one hurting, tormented cowboy. We talked for about an hour. And out of that entire sixty minutes, Benito sobbed and cried through about fifty minutes of our visit. He couldn't help himself and it was painfully obvious to me that the shrinks hadn't helped him, either. Some of it was over the torture and brutality that had been inflicted on him personally. But most of it was over his compa's last request to take care of his family in Phoenix. It wasn't that Suárez had not honored the request that bothered him. But, to this day, he could still see the pleading look in his compa's eyes when he'd made the dying request.

Although that was the last time I ever saw Suárez, I received one more call from him in 1998. He was sobbing uncontrollably. He had called me to tell me goodbye. He was now in the final stages of AIDS. Because he was once a macho Sinaloan Cowboy, this was a shameful secret that he had never betrayed to anyone, not even Jim or me. During his degrading and brutal torture in 1985 at the hands of the Sinaloans, Suárez had been repeatedly raped. Cringing at the thought of what his friends may have thought, Benito decided that he would rather die of AIDS than be treated for it. He was raised a proud Sinaloan hombre. He was a faithful soldier through and through, no matter what one may think of the U.S. government's war on drugs. Suárez was our compa and friend. Rayburn and I mourned his passing as much as any partner we had ever lost.

Agent Camarena's tortured, disfigured body was found along the side of a road in Michoacán on March 6, 1985. He was murdered by some of the same Sinaloan drug traffickers who today still deal with the Agua Prieta drug traffickers in Sonora. This is the same murderous scum that threatened to kill Cochise County Sheriff's Detective Arturo Bernal and me in 1989. That death threat was made during our investigation of narcotics smuggling by the Agua Prieta cartel and their facilitating money-laundering ties to Douglas Justice of the Peace Joe Borane. Because of these ties, in my opinion, Judge Borane is distantly responsible for facilitating the murder of DEA agent Enrique Camarena in 1985.

On February 21, 1986, U.S. Customs Patrol Officer Glenn Miles was tracking a group of marijuana smugglers on the Tohono O'odham Reservation southwest of Tucson when he was ambushed and murdered by the traffickers. Other Customs patrol officers ultimately tracked Miles's assailants south to the border, where they escaped into Mexico knowing that our officers could not pursue them. When I left the INS anti-smuggling unit to join the Customs service a year later, the murder was still unsolved. I was asked by my new agency to send one of my better informants into Mexico in an attempt to identify the shooters. They needed a guy like Benito Suárez. I turned a deaf ear to the request.

Like most calloused agents and cops, I too in my younger years was guilty of treating informants like inanimate objects, tools of the trade to be thrown out after their usefulness had played out. During my career I've known no fewer than ten informants who went down while in the employment of myself or one of my partners. And now at night, when I'm alone, surrounded by shadows and whispers from beyond the room's darkness, I'm troubled by the faint outlines of faces I once made promises to. Faces that force me to shamefully ask myself, "Since when does becoming a great investigator outweigh becoming a decent human being?"

A lot of folks have died, and many others will continue to forfeit their lives in the drug wars. Some go down under hostile fire, like DEA agent Camarena and Customs officer Glenn Miles. Some we lose to "in the line of duty" accidents like Customs agent Gary Friedli. Because they died while nobly attempting to save America's children from being poisoned by a foreign enemy, history will vaguely remember these men as heroes of another one of America's unpopular wars. But it's shameful to know that Benito Suárez, an authorized "unofficial" agent of the U.S. government, who in the end gave his life for our country, will only be remembered by most as just another lowly informant. To Jim Rayburn, John Nixon, and me, Suárez will always be remembered as the hero he deserves to be known as. I'm sure that Special Agent Hummer Rodriguez will recall Gordo in the same light.

On December 19, 2000, I and other federal law-enforcement officers met with Attorney General Janet Reno in Douglas, Arizona. She was touring the border on a last government-paid hurrah before President-elect Bush kicked her ass out of office. Now, I was gonna ask her point-blank about why she fucked us with the Brownsville Agreement. But when I shook her quivering, cold hand and looked into her rest-home bewildered eyes, I knew I would get the same response that a Customs agent friend of mine had received the month before at a meeting in D.C. When Special Agent Grant Murray asked Reno about the future of the Brownsville Agreement, the old gal replied with a bowed head and defeated posture, "That problem is for the next administration to figure out." If that wasn't an admission of "I fucked up," I don't know what is!

On January 4, 2001, I received a directive from the Office of the Attaché at the U.S. Embassy in Mexico City. Under the umbrella of the Brownsville Agreement, I was now being ordered to reveal information to the Mexican government that would make it even easier yet to identify the location of each Customs informant my agents had operating in Mexico. I was actually being forced to report the number of arrests, and the exact quantities and types of drug seizures each informant was responsible for during a specified period in Mexico. With the informants' locator codes, the Mexicans would be able to damn near pinpoint where and who each Customs operative was.

For me, this was the straw that broke the burro's back. To keep myself from potentially being prosecuted here, I won't tell you exactly how I handled this asinine directive. I'm just gonna say that this was the day that I targeted an early retirement date in order to safeguard my sanity. I couldn't stand to watch the REMFs get away with what essentially boils down to allowing government operatives to be murdered, while at the same time destroying a federal agent's will to continue fighting the drug wars. Not only did they destroy our will, but just as importantly, our ability. In a matter of several months my Douglas office dropped from about twenty-five active informants to just a few producers. Either the informants refused to work for us under the Brownsville Agreement, or their controlling agents were unwilling to send them into Mexico under the virtual death warrant.

The Brownsville Agreement expired on February 14, 2001. President Bush and Attorney General Ashcroft went back to the table with the Mexicans and foolishly breathed fresh life into the agreement. I wonder if these powerful men can do the same for Gordo and the others?

20
Traitors

For what profit is it to a man if he gains the whole world, and loses his own soul? Or what will a man give in exchange for his soul?

—MATTHEW 16:26

WHEN I CAME BACK down to Douglas as a special agent with the U.S. Customs Service in 1987, Butch and I figured it was as good a time as any for me to go back undercover. I had been gone for seven years and had spent most of that time doing undercover operations all over the country for the anti-smuggling unit of the INS. I was still appropriately undercover grossed out, with a good deal of long, greasy hair and a scraggly-ass ugly beard to boot. In other words, I could easily mix in with the undesirable rowdy border trash. To them, I looked like just another new player from out of town who had recently saddle-tramped in. And in Douglas during the high-rolling dope-smuggling '80s, that was nothing out of the ordinary.

As with the border outlaws who were attracted here nearly a century earlier, we again had nameless faces drifting into Douglas from the four corners of the earth. And while their faces may have been different, they all had one thing in common: They were desperately looking to score an illegal fortune in the drug trade. Butch figured I could pass for a couple of undercover deals before the bad guys figured out they were getting snakebit by the good guys.

Butch had this informant who was wired into some crooks from south of the border who wanted to trade dope for guns. Lots of guns. As luck would have it, at about the same time this CI had hooked up with these outlaws, we had begun to seize some really large loads of automatic assault rifles going south through the Douglas Port of Entry destined for a different organization of bad guys in Sonora. It was simply amazing to watch what type of hardware the dope smugglers south of the line were arming themselves with. And I don't mean little dingy .22 caliber rifles or antiquated .12 gauge pump shotguns.

If you don't understand why I call the pump .12 gauges out of date, just believe me on this one. These days, especially on the border, you don't go getting into a gunfight armed with a pump-tube spray-shooter. If you do, you probably won't even live to tell your compas how bad you fucked up. No, nowadays if you don't have an AK-47, M16, Mini-14, MP-5, TEC-9, or some other fast or otherwise long-range shooter, don't even bother coming to the party. You'll be extremely disappointed in your lead-swapping participation.

So like I said, we had been seizing these large loads of brand new Norinco AK-47s that had been manufactured in China and smuggled by ships into California. We would usually find the weapon loads in south-bound California-plated vans and motor homes that were attempting to smuggle the arms into Mexico. The contraband was consistently concealed in the false floors and walls of the vehicles. Along with the weapons you could usually find residue of cocaine that had previously been smuggled north into the U.S. in the same hidden compartments. Sometimes we would discover up to two dozen of the deadly AKs in these compartments. Most of them were still in the boxes straight from the Chinese factory. And talk about some serious armament. Strictly kick-ass military. The fucking things even came with mounted bayonets and beaucoup extra magazines! Hell, if I didn't know any better, I would have guessed that we had been interdicting some kind of semi-military-destined arms shipments. And as I would later learn during my time in Douglas, that assumption wasn't too far-fetched.

Under Mexican laws enacted in 1972, it's illegal to own or import guns in that country. And like a horse and carriage, guns and dope just naturally go together because of all the connecting inherent violence. And the old saying that "you always want what you can't have" rings all too true down south in old Mexico. So even though Mexican law states that it's illegal for the average citizen to be armed, that doesn't mean squat to a couple of special elite classes of folks down there. If you are either a filthy-rich crooked-ass politician or a scumbag dope trafficker who has bought off all of the cops and corrupt politicos in your area of operation, no sweat. You can possess all of the machine guns and rocket launchers your hired killers need.

So here's a little point to remember about how you may want to vote in the future on the different propositions in your state regarding gun control. Now, I'm not taking sides one way or the other on the issue. I'm no gun nut by any stretch of the imagination. I've had to carry them most of my life as a tool of the trade. Like a carpenter carries a hammer on his belt, a soldier or cop totes a weapon of one kind or another. And I'm here to tell you they are a pain in the ass to maintain, haul on your shoulder, or wear on your body. No, I'm not a heavy-duty gun fan at all. I'm just telling you the facts about who holds the reins in a "gun-controlled" Third World country: the powerfully rich and the violently corrupt. In Mexico those two classes of folks palm the pistolas in one hand, and hold all of the power in the other hand. The regular hard-working poor folks are just shit out of luck, as they are ultimately left at the mercy of the gun-toters. Food for thought, ain't it?

So I got hooked up with Butch's informant and had him set up a meet with the bad guys at the Motel 6 in Douglas. I picked the oldest, ugliest unmarked LTD I could find out of our Customs fleet and headed down to the seizure vault where we stored guns and dope as evidence for trial. Butch and I "borrowed" about a baker's dozen of the new AKs, still in the boxes with bayonets, extra mags, and other military hardware. After loading the trunk of the LTD with the widowmakers, we came up with a last-minute operational plan and a backup team of door-busting agents in the event the deal went sour. A couple hours later, I was out the door headed for the motel to once again waltz with the Reaper.

I parked the LTD in front of my room so I could keep a constant eye on the car's trunk from my front window. Like a hovering buzzard not letting anyone in on his roadkill, I knew the Customs Service would have my rebel-red ass in a sling if I lost the "borrowed" load of guns. I knew the backup team was out there for me. But if you've ever done this kind of work, you learn to depend primarily on yourself. While the backup guys may be the toughest gung-ho fuckers in the world, even they can't get there in the two or three seconds it takes a bad guy to kill you once he's of the mind to do so. And that's about all the time it takes for the shit to hit the fan and you to lose your ranch in one of these undercover deals.

I took time to distribute some pretty convincing props around my room to make the outlaw into a believer. A *Soldier of Fortune* magazine was strategically placed in open view under the lamp near the phone. A half-empty bottle of Jack Daniels decorated the bathroom vanity next to the ice bucket and glasses. And just for good measure I threw an old Army duffel bag, loaded with camouflage fatigues and a few boxes of ammo, at the foot of my bed. I jammed a government-model Colt .45 semiautomatic pistol inside my jeans waistband and pulled my shirt out over it, purposely leaving an obvious bulge for my future partner-in-crime to see. After all, there's no self-respecting arms smuggler on the border who would ever be caught dead without an iron on him. Not wanting to be even slightly buzzed, but wanting the bad guy to smell the booze on my breath, I rolled a few drops of Old No. 7 over my tongue. Well, maybe a little more than a few drops. What can I say? It's one of the bennies of working undercover.

As I was trying to decide if I should mix the whiskey with water, I heard a car drive up outside my door. The asshole showed up right on time. I watched him through the window as he got out of his new, shiny, decked-out doper ride and sauntered up to my room. He had that bad guy's rock-and-roll gait. It's like his body language was saying, "I'm too cool to move." Like everyone he passes on the sidewalk is just a poor dumb working stiff. And our boy here? Well, he thinks he's just way too smart to have to soil his *manos* like a regular working man. This bad guy truly believed that his shit didn't stink.

When the dickhead got to my door he beat on it like he was the bronze Tarzan of Sonora. He was gonna let me know right off the bat that one of us was the baddest man on the border. It's a Mexican thing. The asshole thought that the intimidating macho display would rattle me before we even started dancing. He was dead wrong. It pissed me off so bad that before I answered the door I figured to match him macho for macho. It's a Mexican outlaw mentality that I've learned to deal with over the years. I pulled my shirt up exposing the .45's handle before I opened the door. Why leave anything to the imagination for a cocksucker who's already aggravated you before the band has even warmed up? It was obvious that we were going to start the waltz out on the wrong fucking foot anyway, so I might as well give him an attitude check before we snuggled up to each other.

I opened the door to a long-haired Mexican *vato* (dude) of about twenty-five. His unshaven face and enchilada-stained mustache reeked of tequila shooters. His bloodshot, dilated eyes darted leerily about the room as he asked me if I was alone. I told him in Spanish that I was solo and asked him to come in as I pulled the door back so he could see it wasn't an ambush. When I broke into Spanish, the crook cut his eyes back at me trying to size up what kind of gringo or half-breed border rat I might be. Like a high desert coyote circling a baited trap, the bad guy carefully crossed through the door, going away from me as he looked back behind himself checking for a tail.

After shutting the door, I slowly crossed the room toward the whiskey bottle while offering my new playmate a drink. I poured a couple of shots in two glasses while I watched his reflection behind me in the bathroom mirror. The son of a bitch was eyeing the pistol in my belt. But the part I found alarming, or maybe I should say strange, was that he wasn't looking at it like he was scared or worried of being ripped. It was more like he was admiringly curious about it. I could tell by the look on his face that the outlaw was gonna be a gun lover. Shit! Here I am trying to get the edge in this macho game by hanging iron out for him to see, and instead of being scared, the fuckhead wants to play with my gun!

Just my luck. The dope smugglers had sent me the Mexican version of a Louisiana redneck gun nut. You know, one of those Southern
mosquito-bitten gringos that rides around up and down the highways
with rifles and shotguns mounted in the rear window of his pickup
truck. And right on the window or bumper of the truck is usually one
of those intellectual, catchy Billy Bob phrases like, "You can have my
gun when you pry my cold dead fingers off it."

I knew his type. I had been raised with them in Texas. Most of
them were gringos but that was only because the Mexicans I knew
back then were too poor to buy guns. I could tell this guy was going
to slobber all over the AKs when I flashed them. Before I could hand
the vato his drink, he began drilling me about the piece I was carrying in my belt. Being trained on the .45 in the Army, I thought it a
good time to impress the dickhead with some of that drill-sergeant-
inspired jargon concerning the pistol's nomenclature. In true military
form, I rattled off the weapon's specifications and history. When I
was done, the bad guy was holding his breath and gaping at me in
awe like he was about to cum in his pants. I would like to take this
time to tell Drill Sergeant Bacote of Fort Polk, Louisiana, that he was
wrong. I didn't have shit for brains. I actually learned and remembered some of that crap he was spouting off during basic training in
1969.

The outlaw asked me if I had been a soldier before. Not really
wanting to go there with this guy, but knowing it would sell the deal, I
told him about being a 101st Airborne sniper for the recon teams in
Vietnam. He was particularly interested in the part about the teams
working with the spooks and mercenaries. As I told the stories, his
cokehead eyes turned gleamy and glowed with interest as his defense
mechanisms started to drop. He wanted to know all about the rifles
and weapons I had used in Nam, how many people I had whacked,
and all the gory, intricate details about what napalm and explosives
do to human bodies. I was in. This guy had bought the arms-dealing
merc act hook, line, and sinker.

We talked military and merc shit for a few more minutes while
tossing shots of Old No. 7 down our windpipes. When the foreplay

was all done, he opened the door to his deal. His name was Vega. He told me that he represented some people down south who needed to arm a good number of shooters to guard marijuana fields and cocaine landing air strips. I was surprised that when I pressed him for the names of the traffickers he represented, he gave them up so easily. Apparently, he wanted to brag. It was just part of the bastard's macho world. He wanted to flash the power, to put thunder in my ears and the fear of God down in my bones. But that was fine. He needed to impress me and I needed the names. Without names, you never know how seriously wired your negotiator is. And no shit, this guy was representing some fucking heat. He rattled off names like Clemente Soto-Peña, Yolanda Molina, Tony Hernández, Amado Carrillo, Tombstone Fragoso, and some other big guns in Sonora.

I told the doper I had a sample of some of the hardware I could supply to his people in the back of my car outside. He eagerly agreed to take a look at the merchandise. We strolled out to the LTD while we both kept rubbernecking all around the parking lot for any *chotas* (cops). We saw a Cochise County Sheriff's deputy making a run through the lot and my new compa from down south began to get a little hinky on me. I told him to chill out, that it was nothing to worry about, that the deputies and the Douglas Police Department make routine patrols through all of the motel lots in Douglas looking for illegal Mexicans trying to boost cars. The deputy left after a couple of laps around the parking lot and our future NRA poster child cooled his jets.

I opened the trunk and lifted the lid just high enough for the guy to peek in. I swear, the outlaw got so excited I thought he was going to get a woody right there in the parking lot! He started breathing fast and talking as rapidly as any guy I've ever seen on speed before. He rattled on that he loved the AKs and that his bosses would be extremely pleased to see that they came equipped with bayonets. The thought of what these bastards may do with bayonets made my guts tighten up. My imagination ran a little wild with flashes of the tortured, murdered bodies these pricks had no doubt already left in their wake.

After establishing my credibility, the whole thing got even wilder. The bad guy's coked-up eyes started rolling around in his head like a fucking Vegas slot machine about to make the big payoff. When they finally stopped and he could focus on me, he dropped the bomb. The son of a bitch asked me if I would be willing to heist a load of grenades, rocket launchers, and M-60 machine guns from the U.S. Army at Fort Huachuca!

Fuck! I didn't know what to think. I had been out of touch with this particular part of the border for about seven years. Had things changed so much that the dopers were now outfitting their own small private armies? What about law enforcement at any level in Agua Prieta, Sonora? What about the Mexican Army? I mean, there is no way in hell that you can arm as many men with the weapons these people were asking me to get without complicity on the part of the Mexican authorities. Had things really gone this sour since I had been here in the 1970s with the Border Patrol? I was just beginning to learn how volatile and corrupt this whole region of the border had become.

After Vega and I had danced around and made a tentative deal for the arms his drug lords wanted, we parted company with the understanding that we would meet one more time before the final sell. I returned to my office, where Customs agents and other members of the Cochise County Sheriff's Department Border Alliance Group (BAG) were waiting to debrief me. I gave them the suspect's name to run for a criminal history check. The next thing I knew there were a couple of sheriff's detectives at the door damn near drooling. It turned out that Vega had been in on the murder of another dope trafficker several years prior and he had beaten the rap in court.

Cochise County Sheriff's deputies had found a body dumped in the brush off Washington Avenue near 23rd Street just outside the city limits of Douglas. A tip led the investigating detectives to Vega, who lived in the same area and was known to prefer an outlaw existence. He was picked up, indicted, and stood trial.

On the stand Vega admitted to having concealed the bloody corpse in a closet in his house until he could later dump it under the cover of darkness. However, his story as to his participation was a well-rehearsed rendition of "I was *victimized*!" It seemed that Vega, who should have been admitted to the Screen Actors' Guild, convinced the jury that he disposed of the body in a blind panic after watching some other dopers punch and grind a broom handle through the guy's bowels. Perjuring and squirming his way to freedom, Vega testified that two unknown Mexican hit men held him at gunpoint and forced him to watch the murder. Folks, I've said it before and I'll say it again. Our judicial system is fucked up beyond repair and it needs a complete overhaul. It seems half of the jurors we empanel have the attention span of a wet noodle and the other half believe soap operas are for real!

Now it's pretty easy to understand why the detectives showed up, ain't it? They wanted to know if there was anything they could do to give the U.S. Customs Service a hand in taking this piece of shit off the street.

I set up another meet with Vega as soon as it was feasible. The asshole never showed again. We got to going over the scenario of the last meet with Vega to see where we may have been burned. It turned out that the Cochise County Sheriff's deputy who had cruised the motel parking lot during the meeting with Vega was an officer named Leon Klute. Leon had been fucking one of the motel maids and it seems that other than the physical relationship, they also had an informational exchange thing going on. Leon had been suspected of shit before, but this time he burned himself bad. We figured out that he told the maid who I was and that something was going down in my room. The maid in turn leaked it back to Vega and the gun deal went sour. We didn't get Vega, but we got Leon. The Sheriff terminated the dirty little prick as soon as he heard the details of what had transpired. So the undercover deal wasn't completely in vain. We got one out of two bad guys. Dirty cop, or homicide suspect. I'm not sure which is worse.

In May of 1987, I had a rude awakening concerning just how far out of hand things had become in Douglas and Agua Prieta. I was contacted by a good Mormon feller who managed one of the three main banks in Douglas. I didn't know this guy from Adam, but for some reason he wanted to meet with me. I was somewhat apprehensive, not knowing the guy and all. But since coming back to Douglas I had quickly learned that whenever I was in doubt about a guy's character or motives, I could ask Art Bernal and he would fill me in on just about any local's track record. It turned out that the bank manager was on the up and up. He was just getting sick and tired of seeing Douglas turn into a dope smugglers' refuge, so he decided to do something about it.

I met the guy one evening way out in the desert away from man or beast. Now, before the Yolanda Molina investigation, I had never done a financial case. So all of this monetary jargon about the flow of money back and forth across the border was a little confusing for a farm boy from the backwoods of Texas. But even this country bumpkin grasped the seriousness of the situation the bank manger was about to explain to me.

The guy nervously looked back and forth across the desert, like we were both about to draw our last breaths. When he started talking he opened a Pandora's financial box that would reveal new corruption in the Douglas/Agua Prieta area.

According to his bank's records, from January to about the middle of May 1987, his bank had shipped $7 million to the federal reserve for deposit. The unusual part about this was that for the first time in Douglas banking history since the Arizona Rangers had cleaned up the little border pueblo at the turn of the past century, money had come north for deposit from the Mexican banks in Agua Prieta. The banker went on to explain that usually his bank had to order money from the federal reserve to take care of the payroll needs of the Mexican banks. Up until now, copper and cattle had been the cash crops rendering Douglas a boomtown compared to its little sleepy Mexican sister city just across that invisible line called the border. But now, Mexican and Colombian dope had replaced the once-coveted copper and cattle industries, thereby making Agua Prieta the head breadwinner, surpassing Douglas by leaps and bounds.

What we were looking at here was an unprecedented reversal of cash flow that pretty much proved that the Mexican banks were now accepting large quantities of drug profits deposited in U.S. currency. The writing was on the wall, and it spelled Colombian coke and Mexican grass. Since the 1960s there had always been a little dope smuggling going on here. But up until now, it had never risen to this level. You were talking about Mexican banks having more U.S. dollars than American banks! And there was no way that this was going on without the complicity of the Mexican government and its federal agents.

Let's face it, the Mexicans are the absolute and final lords of corruption. They've been elevating the tainted art of taking bribes to a professional status for hundreds of years. They ought to hand out B.A. and Master's degrees in it. It's what they do best! In Spanish it's known as *mordida,* "the bite." And the more illegal the activity you want to hide, the bigger the bite that will be taken out by the Mexican officials. The Mexican feds have a gold mine here and they're going to take advantage of it as long as Americans want dope. Obviously, they'll be doing business until Gabriel blows his horn.

So if this was also occurring at the other two main banks in Douglas, which was a good bet, we could feasibly be looking at somewhere around $21 million going to the Federal Reserve from the Agua Prieta banks in about four-and-a-half months. In a year that could easily total about $63 million. Now, when you consider that at the time Douglas had a population of about 15,000 people with an average family income of about $20,000 per year, and that the average income for their new young local and federal officers wasn't much better, what the hell do you think was going to happen with that much illicit money floating around? Corruption on a goddamn wholesale scale!

Before I left Douglas in 1980, one of my Border Patrol partners was a red-headed Mick named Gary Callahan. He was a pretty jovial feller, always with a joke rolling off his tongue and a smile perched on his Irish face. Both being Vietnam combat veterans, Callahan and I got along in the sense that we shared that peculiar bond between men who have lived through hell. On our off-duty time we would spend countless nights drinking beer and playing poker with the other Border Patrol agents. After a few drinks we would drift in conversation back to our past military lives. We talked about the good times on R&R in Australia. And of course no matter how we tried to stay off it, we always got around to talking about the bad times. We talked about meeting the Reaper in the jungle and the mark he had left on us. I guess when we talked about it, we were helping each other to heal up a bit. And that can only be remembered as a good thing. At the time I knew Callahan he was a solid trooper. Never in my wildest dreams would I have thought that he could have been turned.

I hadn't been back in Douglas more than a few weeks when I started hearing rumors that my old beer-drinking Nam brother was going astray. Other law-enforcement agencies were reporting sightings of Callahan dressed in camouflage and carrying a full automatic assault rifle as he patrolled the border alone at night. There was some speculation that he may be losing his marbles. I had even heard that the fucker had gone on leave to South Africa, where he hired on as a mercenary for the sole purpose of slaughtering black folks. After hearing all of this shit, I thought I had better pay Callahan a visit to see for myself if he had indeed lost a couple of cards from his deck.

When I got to his house, I had a pretty good idea that Callahan was fucked up. And I don't just mean mentally. He was showing way too much money for his income. It was obvious that his large, expensive residence and new vehicles didn't match the meager income of a Border Patrol agent. We talked for a couple of hours and neither one of us was comfortable with the other. When I confronted him with the rumors and what I had seen of his assets, he explained his new-found wealth was the result of hitting the California lottery. I didn't buy it, and he knew it. As I said goodbye to Callahan for the last time, he lent me a book on military snipers. It's still in my office today. Inside the book is a copy of the federal warrant for Callahan's arrest.

My old buddy fell into the trap of the most deadly combination Lucifer has to offer: women and money. He left his wife and took up with some gal who turned his world upside-down. Either she was a super piece of ass or an expert at removing a guy's brain and playing with it. I suspect it was a little of both. When a cop starts letting that little head hanging between his legs do all of the thinking, a heated bitch can talk him into assassinating the friggin Pope. And if she does-n't want the Pope whacked, well, maybe a few loads of cocaine will be enough to keep her wetting your pole.

After he started ripping coke loads off dope smugglers on the bor-der, Callahan's girlfriend directed him to a dentist she was acquainted with in Phoenix who would buy the stolen merchandise. Since the Bor-der Patrol is in the Department of Justice along with the FBI, it didn't take Hoover's boys too long to figure it out. Callahan got wind that he was about to fall and he decided to take a permanent vacation to the Australian continent. When they caught up with my old buddy, he was just about to leave New Zealand for Australia in his private yacht. The last time Callahan saw Australia he'd been a nineteen- or twenty-year-old Marine on R&R from Vietnam. He didn't know it then, but it would be the only time he would ever see the kangaroo country.

Gary Callahan, a one-time Marine, a one-time Vietnam combat veteran, a one-time Border Patrol agent, and a one-time friend of mine, was sentenced by the federal court in the District of Arizona to serve a life sentence for smuggling cocaine. The only thing I can add is that, in my opinion, my former friend should have also been tried and maybe even executed as a traitor.

Callahan was just the first of many U.S. Border Patrol agents, U.S. Immigration Service inspectors, U.S. Customs Service inspectors, and Douglas Police Department officers who would be arrested between 1987 and 1998. In a span of about eleven years we—the special agents of the U.S. Customs Service, the DEA, the FBI, the Arizona DPS, and the Arizona Attorney General's Office—would either indict, arrest, convict, or otherwise force to resign or transfer some twenty federal and local law-enforcement officers in Douglas. The charges ranged from dope smuggling to murder.

It was so bad during those years that I even had badges I thought were honest telling me about other crooked cops, but later I would find out that the badges who were telling me about the other crooks were also crooks. In an effort to throw the dogs off on the wrong scent, this ploy happened to me on more than one occasion. That's right! You needed a blood-soaked scorecard to keep up with the corruption and murders. And you couldn't ever use ink on that card because you would be erasing it the next day. You never knew who you could trust. It gave a whole new meaning to the word paranoia.

Douglas, a little border town, had become one of the most corrupt places in the United States. I have no idea how to completely research those figures across the nation. But for law-enforcement officers being arrested per capita, you would be damn hard-pressed to find any other border hellhole in the U.S. that would be more corrupt.

The way I had it figured back then, damn near one third of the inspectors at the Douglas Port of Entry were suspected of being crooked. Most of them were in the U.S. Immigration Service, but a couple of the uniformed bastards were also, and I'm painfully sorry to say, on the U.S. Customs Service payroll. I had a couple of prosecutors I was friends with at the U.S. Attorney's Office in Tucson. Together we had investigated and prosecuted some large-scale alien-smuggling cases during my previous tenure with the INS anti-smuggling unit. I told these guys in 1988 that corruption in Douglas, especially among the federal port-of-entry inspectors, was growing as rampant as a malignant cancer. They said prove it. So that's what I set out to do.

In a perfect world of law enforcement, I surmised that if every one of our U.S. Customs special agents would target and take down one of the corrupt inspectors, we could clean the Douglas Port of Entry up. But the world ain't perfect and the days of just simply convicting a crook in court have long passed us by. The appeals process is not only mind-boggling and utterly stupid, but it has swollen to a point that it takes so much time and effort that most honest cops and prosecutors don't want to stick with it. It's just too damn exhausting when you are trying to keep up on your caseloads. Taking that into consideration, there weren't a lot of special agents and prosecutors chomping at the bit to get involved.

Aside from the court system, I found that the other biggest obstacles to overcome were the unions that protect both the INS and Customs inspectors. As special agents of the Treasury Department, guys like me are afforded no protection from being fired for seriously fucking up. And that's why you don't see a lot of corruption among the special agents in either the Treasury or Justice Departments. Justice and Treasury can sort out the bad-egg agents and fire them when they suspect any wrongdoing. But with the Customs and INS inspectors, it's a whole other ballgame.

Before you can interview a federal inspector, his union shop steward tells him to keep his mouth shut until the union attorney arrives. When you're trying to pin one of them down to criminal activity, the union won't allow them to take a polygraph or submit to any other potentially incriminating situations. I've even seen inspectors who pissed positive for drug use but the fucking union kept the Service from firing them. All they had to do to retain their job was admit that they had a substance-abuse problem and go to counseling for help. Do you want to guess what would happen if a Treasury or Justice special agent pissed positive on a test? Right! Adios, motherfucker! And that's the way it should be.

Butch and I have even gone to the Douglas Port of Entry on shootings, and during the course of such investigations, we were told by the union shop steward that we wouldn't be allowed to interview the inspectors involved in the gunplay. The really hilarious part about this conversation was that the little shithead must have thought that by being the union rep he was somehow above the law. After we quoted him the law on interfering with a special agent in the performance of his duties, not to mention impeding a federal investigation, the shooters were promptly produced for their interviews. And if we had to pull our federal investigative authority just to talk to these guys, just imagine what U.S. Customs and INS management have to go through to try to fire one of these corrupt fucks. It's damn near impossible.

Now, I'm sure that the unions started out with good intentions way back in the "olden" days of unfair labor practices. But these days it seems that since the battles against such bad labor agendas have been won, the unions have nothing else to do but stay on management's ass. And in so doing, whether they realize it or not, they are shielding the crooked inspectors from being rooted out.

In 1988, I started working an investigation on U.S. Immigration Service Inspector Rodolfo Molina of the Douglas Port of Entry. He was suspected of smuggling large loads of cocaine through the port for the Amado Carrillo organization. Remembering what I had been taught by investigative mentors like Jim Rayburn, I set out to learn a little bit about my prey's background before going after him. And during this process I touched on several similarities between Molina, Callahan, and other suspected crooked cops in Douglas. You could usually look for one or more of the following road signs to corruption: The officer more than likely had been in Vietnam, the picture usually included an extramarital affair, and if you talked to the guy on a personal basis he would tell you that the country owed him something for fighting a war that nobody gave a shit about. If the suspect wasn't a Vietnam vet, he was a cop or fed who still believed the country had somehow fucked him over, be it a promotion that was given to someone else, or his income tax was disproportionately high compared to his neighbor. This type of guy always had some excuse why he was getting the shaft from the government or even the public.

Rodolfo "Rudi" Molina had been in Vietnam with the 101st Airborne. He later went into the Marines, and after leaving military service completely, he joined the U.S. Border Patrol. With the Border Patrol he was stationed in Marfa, Texas, where he ultimately ended up just down the road as a U.S. Immigration inspector at the Presidio Port of Entry. It was across the Rio Grande in Ojinaga, Chihuahua, where I figured Rudi hooked up with Amado Carrillo and his people. Carrillo had big plans for his move into the Agua Prieta and Douglas area. Amado was instrumental in the financing of the infamous Douglas drug tunnel. But why limit yourself to going under the port of entry when you can go right straight through it with a couple of well-placed, cold-blooded American traitors?

While in Presidio, Rudi found another Immigration inspector who was just as willing as he to betray his country. A U.S. Immigration Service inspector I'll call Manuel Reyes fell right into the same profile and pattern of wrongdoing. He was a Vietnam veteran and a former Border Patrol agent from Marfa, Texas. He had deserted his American wife for a Mexican girlfriend from Ojinaga. But Reyes's biggest link to the organization was that he had become good friends with a female from Ojinaga named Socorro Nieto-Ochoa. And what importance was that to the investigation? Well, oddly enough, she just happened to be not only an active narcotics trafficker, but more important, she was the mistress of Amado Carrillo.

So one by one, and I imagine at the request of drug lord Carrillo, Molina and Reyes managed to get the U.S. Immigration Service to transfer them to the most corrupt town on the U.S.-Mexican border at the time: Douglas, Arizona. My informants placed Rudi at the drug tunnel's command post in Agua Prieta. He snorted cocaine, partied with the drug lords, made phone calls to Colombia, and most important of all, he was instrumental in finalizing the plans to smuggle tons of cocaine onto the streets of America to kill our children.

On April 4, 1988, U.S. Immigration Inspector Rudi Molina was on duty in the primary inspection lane at the Douglas Port of Entry. He was performing his routine inspections when a green 1979 Ford LTD drove into the U.S. from Agua Prieta, Sonora. Now, I and other Customs special agents had let it be known to several of our most trusted U.S. Customs inspectors that Molina was suspected of waving dope loads through the Port of Entry. One of these U.S. Customs inspectors, George Campos, happened to be working in the secondary inspection area of the port on this particular day. Campos was watching Molina like a hawk when Molina simply passed the green LTD through without taking any time to inspect the driver or the car. Campos became suspicious and before the LTD could clear the port and officially enter the U.S., he stopped the driver and told him to get out and open the trunk of the car.

As the driver got out of the car, Campos could tell that the guy was extremely nervous and panicky. Customs Inspector Campos asked the driver to step to the rear of the LTD and take out his wallet with proper identification. The driver took his wallet out of his pocket as he approached Campos. As Campos was about to reach for the wallet, the driver threw the wallet at Campos's face, temporarily throwing him off balance. The driver began to run south through the port of entry for Mexico as Campos shouted to other inspectors for assistance in taking the asshole down. The driver ran within inches of

INS Inspector Rudi Molina as he escaped into Mexico. Molina never drew his pistol, lifted a finger, or even moved a muscle in an effort to capture and arrest the driver. If this had been a bank robbery, it would have been comparable to an armed bank guard holding the door open for the outlaws escaping with the money.

After chasing the driver into Mexico out of U.S. jurisdiction, Campos returned to the LTD, where he removed the keys from the ignition and opened the trunk. He discovered 661 pounds of cocaine in kilo-size bricks lying uncovered in the trunk of the car. In the dope trade, that's the same as leaving more than $45 million just carelessly lying around, because that's what 300 kilos of cocaine translates to when it hits the street. And folks, that's without even being stepped on, which means you could cut this poison at least three times and triple your blood profits to about $135 million.

The fact that there was no effort made to conceal the cocaine load in the back of the car was prima facie evidence that it was being protected by a crooked inspector who was supposed to wave the car through without opening the trunk for proper examination. In fact, because Molina was protecting it, we would later find out from an informant that the organization successfully smuggled another 1,300 to 1,400 pounds of cocaine through the port on this same occasion. Molina had agreed to wave and smuggle one ton of coke through his lane. The ton payload would be in three consecutive vehicles that were tailing each other. Because Campos was watching Molina by himself, he was only able to pick off one of the three cocaine-laden vehicles.

A couple of days later, subsequent to his being drilled with questions from U.S. Customs special agents, Molina resigned from the U.S. Immigration Service, saying that he thought he wasn't doing a good job as an inspector. It was a weak resignation letter, but he needed some excuse, any excuse, to quit his position so he could run. He knew his time in Douglas would be limited before we arrested him. So, hoping to put some mileage between himself and his crime, Molina left his wife and fled to California with his Mexican mafia-connected *novia* (girlfriend).

About a week after his criminal act and subsequent departure, we finally got a search warrant for Molina's residence. Seems a little long, doesn't it? Well, it was. Usually we can get the U.S. Attorney's Office to approve our warrant application and affidavit within just a matter of one or two hours. But because Molina wore a badge, and it was a *federal* badge, we had pure hell getting the U.S. Attorney to approve our search-warrant application. I found this to be an inherent problem when it came to going after corrupt officers. It seemed like everybody and his brother who was involved in the investigation, arrest, and subsequent prosecution of a corrupt inspector was scared to fuck up and perhaps get a little egg on his face. And one thing you have to remember about all attorneys is this: They are all egotistical maniacs and they can't stand to lose in court. And when you hitch that to the high-visibility prosecution of a fed, well, it can all be pretty damaging not only to your ego, but to your entire career if a crooked badge beats you in court.

So after we finally got the warrant and served it that late, you would think the scumbag would have taken time to clean his act up. Wrong. Molina was in such a big hurry to leave Douglas that he left incriminating evidence all over his house. The only thing he took time enough to grab was his one and only true love. A love that he was willing to die for. A love he was willing to go to prison for. A love that he had sold his soul for. A love that meant more than his wife or his children. He took his fucking money.

We found his steel safe in the garage, where it was concealed under a cardboard box. On top of the box in ink were numeric figures that would be consistent with sums of "deposits." They totaled more than a quarter of a million dollars! Now, here's a guy who took an oath to protect and defend his country and his fellow citizens. In fact, during the course of his miserable existence on God's green turf, he would take four oaths to his country: one to the U.S. Army, one to the U.S. Marines, one to the U.S. Border Patrol, and his grand finale with the Department of Justice U.S. Immigration Service. He swore four separate times to uphold the Constitution of the United States. This is the same oath that thousands of young men and women have taken before giving their lives in foreign wars and domestic troubles such as the war on drugs.

Before his resignation, Inspector Molina was legitimately earning about $60,000 per year from the federal government. Let me put it to you plain and simple. You were paying this man with taxes from your hard-earned paycheck to ultimately betray you. I understand that before we can charge a suspect with treason Congress must have declared war on the country that he is collaborating with. Well, if I'm not mistaken, every time I pick up a newspaper someone on the Hill is calling this the Mexican or Colombian drug wars. So why aren't we amending some laws that would enable us to charge shitheads like Inspector Molina with treason?

Molina left his home so fast that he didn't even pick up all of the loose change he left lying around. We found $2,000 in $100 bills in a phone book. Another thousand in $100 bills in a hat box in the closet. And for an Immigration inspector, who by federal definition is not considered to be a true law-enforcement officer, the guy had a lot of interesting toys that he had no fucking business with. He had numerous rifles and assault weapons including a .45 Thompson sub gun. He had handheld two-way radios just like the ones we have taken off dope-smuggling mules and drivers. And there were other fascinating accessories that only traitors and outlaws would need: a counterfeit-currency-detector machine, a security-monitoring device, and an electronic-surveillance detector to determine if your phone is tapped, the room is bugged, or even if you're talking to someone wearing a wire. In addition to those goodies he had a lockpick tool, a telephone attachment that codes and scrambles your conversation so no one can listen in on you, a book on wiretapping and surveillance techniques, two radio scramblers, and a wireless microphone. After viewing the spooky cloak-and-dagger shit Molina had, some of us couldn't make up our minds if the son of a bitch was a crooked badge or an employee of the CIA!

Within a few days of starting to hunt the bastard down, I and another Customs agent located Rudi at one of his relatives' residences in San Jose, California. The prick was just about to leave the house when we came bouncing up his sidewalk. Molina was standing on the front porch of the house between some kind of jubilant West Coast red *flores* hanging in pots from the rafters. When he looked up and saw us coming through the front gate I couldn't help but giggle with a warm glow down deep inside my guts. Not only did Rudi have that "ah fuck" look, but his face flushed so bad that you couldn't tell who was brighter, him or the flowers he was standing between.

After the usual "how you doing, it's been a long time" type of crap, Rudi started to regain his composure. We asked him if we could come into the house and chat a bit. He knew he was about to get drilled, but he also knew that if he didn't sit down and talk to us it would make him look worse than he already did. He led us inside through the living room and pointed to several wooden chairs circling a round table in the kitchen. After my partner and I sat down, Molina tried to act nonchalant as he crossed the kitchen floor to the sink area. He removed a clear glass from one of the cupboards and carefully filled it with water from the sink. As he started walking back over to the table you had to wonder if he wasn't getting ready to testify. He reminded me of countless defendants and alibi witnesses I've seen on the stand who get dry-mouthed from lying and have to pour a cup of water to open their vocal cords up. The next time you get picked for a jury, watch who drinks water from the pitcher that sits at the witness box. Then you decide who's lying and who's not.

During the interview my blood started to boil. The treachery Rudi displayed was on the edge of getting personal with me. This mother-fucker had disgraced some of the most cherished things in my life. He had brought shame upon the 101st Airborne, the U.S. Border Patrol, and Vietnam veterans everywhere. It took great personal restraint to keep my hands off the prick. It would have given me great personal pleasure to reach across the table and rip out his skinny throbbing Adam's apple with my bare hands. Had we still have been in Vietnam, and had he pulled an act of treachery like this, we would have kneecapped him on the spot and left him for a slow, agonizing death with the leeches and maggots. We wouldn't have even pulled his tin tags for the REMFs to send home.

Every time I asked Molina a question about what happened that day with the coke load, he just smirked and said he couldn't remember anything. In fact, all of his smirks and bullshit answers were so arrogant and rehearsed that I knew we weren't going to get him to break. How did I know he wasn't going to roll over? Because he knew that we weren't there to arrest him. If that's what we had come for, he knew we wouldn't be talking right now. He knew we would have grabbed him on the porch. But before we terminated this lying sack of shit's interview, I was overcome with a burning desire to put the fear of God down deep in his bones.

I leaned across the table we were sitting at and drew so close to his face that I could see the veins running into the back of his darting eyeballs. His breath smelled like a five-day-old napalmed corpse. The artery in his temple started to throb so hard that I could damn near hear it kicking up against his slimy, perspiring skin. Molina's smirk was now replaced with the same red flush of fear he wore earlier when we first walked up to his porch. He got so shook up that he literally spilled the whole glass of water that he was trying to sip, right down the front of his shirt into his crotch. A cow pissing on a flat rock couldn't have done a better job! He was probably wondering if I had lost control and was about to take him out. If he was, he wasn't the only one. I was so enraged from his flippant attitude that it wouldn't have taken much to push me over the edge at this point.

I tried to choke my anger back so that I could say something professional and witty. You know. Some of that clever stuff a cool modern-day federal agent is trained to say. Like, "Sir, the case is still under investigation and we would like for you to please give us an address where we can reach you at in the event we have other questions for you." But not being the modern model federal agent, something like that didn't come out of my mouth. The last thing I remember telling the insufferable prick was something along the lines of, "You're a fucking yellow-belly cocksucking traitor pure and simple. It's my job to bring you to justice and make you pay for fucking your own people over. You'll see me again. Be looking for me around every corner, because I'll be thinking about you every fucking hour of my day.

Never turn your back. I'll be coming for you when you least expect it. I'm going to be the eternal itch you can't scratch, motherfucker!" I guess the boy took my words to heart. A few days later Rudi fled California and took refuge south of the border in Agua Prieta, where he reportedly remained shacked up with his Mexican mafia *chica* (chick).

During the next couple of years, we learned that Molina owned three separate extravagant residences in San Jose that are probably worth millions by now. He had made down payments totaling more than $250,000 in cash through money-laundering straw purchasers. Most of the transactions were conducted by his brothers-in-law. But after interviewing the Realtors as to the money's origination, we knew it had come from Molina's drug-smuggling activities in Douglas. Through months of meeting informants, studying documents, and conducting personal interviews and surveillances in Agua Prieta, Sonora, and Ojinaga, Chihuahua, I eventually put the rest of the puzzle together.

The driver we were looking for was a dentist from Agua Prieta named José Amador Galván. Galván was married to the sister of another dentist in Ojinaga named Soto-Pipper. These dentists were both reported to be part of a larger group of Mexican doctors who were hooked up with Amado Carrillo. When you think about it, if smuggling is an art form, Amado was a fucking genius. Instead of using the typical uneducated Mexican dirt farmers and laborers you usually catch muling dope, he had gone to the whole other end of the human spectrum: well-educated, respectable Mexican professionals working with strategically placed corrupt U.S. government officers. This drug lord was leaving nothing to chance concerning the security of his merchandise. He had all the bases covered.

After learning the name of our dentist, we set out to locate the elusive tooth-puller. To get that kind of information out of Sonora I turned to two of my best informants in that Mexican state. One of them was a gofer for the MFJP and the other was a member of the Agua Prieta cartel. After a lot of prodding and a bit of palm greasing, they laid the whole enchilada out for me. Dr. Galván's office was in Agua Prieta on Sixth Street. The informants said that the Agua Prieta cartel used the dentist's office to stash millions of dollars of drug money at a time. And if that wasn't enough, the informants poured a zesty salsa all over the enchilada at no additional charge. They said that the office was also used as a narcotics communications and operational center for the smuggling of tons of cocaine.

When I finally located the good doctor's office in Agua Prieta, there was no doubt the informants had made a good call on this one. It was the only dentist office that I've ever seen that had more radio antennas and communications gadgets on the roof than it had patients. After previously working in Mexico with the CIA during the narco-tunnel investigation, I had become familiar with the different types of antennas the Mexican drug lords used for communications with their counterparts in Colombia. Not to my surprise, those same antennas were erected on top of Dr. Galván's office.

At great personal risk to U.S. Customs Inspector Campos, I asked him to drive into Mexico with me to the dentist's office. Once in Agua Prieta I asked Campos if he would be willing to go by himself into the office and pretend to make an appointment while looking for the driver who had run from him a couple of years earlier. Without hesitation, Campos agreed to do so as I waited in the car in the parking lot. After being in the office for just a couple of minutes, Campos shot out the front door and hurriedly trotted back to the car. His pace was so quick he almost looked like he was about to break into a full-fledged hundred-yard dash. As he got closer I could see that he was shaken. His complexion was damn near as white as a sheet. I didn't need to be told we were in trouble so I started the car and picked him up on the move as we rolled out of the parking lot. Before Campos had completely closed his door he told me to punch it for the border before we both got snatched up.

During the trip back, Campos said that the dentist was not there so he made an appointment with the receptionist for a couple of hours later. While he was talking to the receptionist Campos could see it in her eyes that she had burned him. He didn't know how, but he was sure that she knew who he was. At this point it became quite apparent that I couldn't take Campos back to the dentist's office. Knowing the way these murdering bastards worked, it was a good bet that at this very moment the bad guys were probably setting up their own trap to kidnap Campos when he came back to the office for his "appointment." This whole fucking thing was getting reversed on us. After all, we were on Mexican soil and these motherfuckers owned the law lock, stock, and barrel. That's how DEA Agent Enrique Camarena was taken. I couldn't let them take Inspector Campos the same way.

I drove Campos back to Douglas and had about an hour to come up with my next move. I knew the traffickers would have Dr. Galván at the office to positively identify Campos when he supposedly returned for his appointment. However, Campos's return to Mexico wasn't even a cunt-hair close to being considered an option. I had to come up with an alternate plan that would get me to the traitor I was after. I settled on the only one that my bosses could live with.

Dr. Galván knew Campos. His partner and our traitor, Immigration Inspector Molina, knew me. But it was about a fifty-fifty shot that Dr. Galván may or may not know my ugly mug. So that's what we went with. I changed cars and returned to Campos's Mexican dentist appointment alone. I was armed with a .38 Special in my boot and a 3mm with a telephoto lens in my lap. I parked on the street across from the dentist's office and waited. About ten minutes before Campos's appointment, I photographed several desperado-looking henchmen as they arrived in separate vehicles and hurriedly entered the office. I would later learn that two of them had criminal convictions for narcotics trafficking in the U.S. The third was known to be a hired killer for the Agua Prieta cartel.

After the shooters arrived and positioned themselves in the office, a shiny new blue Chevrolet pickup drove into the parking lot. After the driver exited the Chevy he walked in a commanding manner toward the dentist's office. He wasn't one of your regular dope mopes. He was a heavy-duty boss type. The hair on the back of my neck stood up as I realized who it was. It was him. I had been hunting this son of a bitch for two years and had never laid eyes on him until now. I shot him several times with the telephoto lens. As the camera whirled and rotated the film between shots, I chuckled to myself while flashing back a couple of decades on another continent. In the jungle it would have ended right here for the asshole at the end of the glass tube I was looking down. But here in the desert some twenty years later, the end was just beginning for this guy. These pictures would be the key to a lengthy federal incarceration for Dr. José Amador Galván-González.

After the photo "assassination," I lay over in the seat of my vehicle and waited for the criminal tide to subside. After I had sweated all over the upholstery for about half an hour past the appointment, the good doctor and his snatch team must have decided that Campos would be a no-show. The cocky smiling death merchants walked out of the office into the parking lot, where they hammed it up while slapping each other on the back. They figured that their receptionist had made a mistake and this guy, whoever he was, just looked like Campos. They had been smuggling cocaine for more than a decade with impunity. No doubt they would continue at least another ten years. To celebrate their deadly secret they probably decided to go somewhere for a shot of tequila and a snort of primo product.

After they left the parking lot I entered the office to have a look-see of my own. The only person present was an attractive, flashy receptionist slouching in a plush black leather chair behind a dark walnut desk. The walls of the office were covered with serapes and Mexican bullfighting posters. I've noticed during my years on the border that Mexican and Colombian drug lords have the worst taste in interior decorating. The dumb fucks always seem to cross-breed and confuse Euro-Mediterranean decor with Southwest contemporary. Trashy!

Now, most of the doctor's office receptionists I've ever met have been conservatively dressed professional-lady types. But this receptionist, while certainly not being a lady, was damn sure a professional.

I asked the Mexican hooker if I could see the doctor. Chomping ferociously on a piece of Wrigley's, she said that I had just missed him. I acted as disappointed as a young buck without a rubber on prom night. I told the tainted señorita that I thought I had seen the doctor just as he was leaving the parking lot in a blue Chevrolet truck. She informed me that I was correct and that Dr. Galván was driving the blue truck. And while the good doctor may have been driving the

Chevy to a party with his compas, his *segunda* (mistress or girlfriend) back at his office was driving nails in his coffin. Up until now, I wasn't absolutely positive what the guy I was after looked like. But now there was no fucking doubt that it was the heavy hitter in the blue truck.

I returned to Douglas and gave the roll of film I had just shot to Inspector Campos. I already knew what the dentist looked like. But Campos, being the main witness, had to identify the asshole on his own before I could make the arrest. We didn't have a one-hour photo development lab in Douglas, so I told Campos to drive over to Sierra Vista to have it developed. A couple of hours later Campos called to tell me what I already knew. Campos identified the driver of the blue Chevrolet pickup truck as the cocaine smuggler who had escaped from him into Mexico a couple of years earlier. Dr. Galván and former Immigration Inspector Molina were about to take a hard fall. And it was going to be a long way to the bottom of a maximum-security federal pen.

I had to return to Mexico to wrap up a couple of loose ends on the case before we were ready to make our arrests. I had learned that Molina's girlfriend and Dr. Galván were neighbors in an elite neighborhood in Agua Prieta. I also believed that a large house that shared a backyard wall with theirs was owned by dope lord Amado Carrillo. I wanted to get photos for court that would show the relationship between all of these crooks. Now, the problem was going to be how to get past all of the Mexican cops and MFJP that the cartel owned. And if I didn't get by them? Well, let's just say that I had taken steps not to end up going out like DEA Agent Camarena.

We weren't supposed to go armed into Mexico without the permission of the Mexican Attorney General. I took my .38 in my boot anyway. I mean, what the hell! We weren't supposed to work in Mexico without permission of the Mexican Attorney General, either! So why worry about a little leak in the levee when the whole fucking dam is about to break? And if the good doctor and the traitor Molina were ever going to be brought to justice, it was only going to happen at a little personal risk and some loose interpretation of international protocol. If the Mexican lawmen were just and honest we could get them to give us a hand in bringing these crooks in. But they weren't, aren't, and never will be. So fuck 'em. And while we're at it, fuck their badges, too.

It was during the last of several surreptitious excursions into Mexico that I damn near fell into enemy hands. I was cruising around the drug lords' lavishly decorated residences when the Mexican Federal Judicial Police started to tail me. By the time I made the cocksuckers in my rearview mirror it was too late to make a run for the frontera. I was not all that familiar with the streets of Agua Prieta, so these guys had anticipated my moves before I had even thought of them. When they hit their red lights I was already boxed in by one of their vehicles in front, and another in back of me. I had no choice but to pull over to the side of the street in front of Dr. Galván's elegant home. As I sat there waiting for the inevitable, thoughts of my beautiful wife and kids ran through my mind. Ask anybody that's done this kind of shit and lived through it. Those are always the ones you think of when you're about to get whacked.

As the MFJP agents got out of their cars and approached me, my mouth got cotton-ball dry and my asshole slammed up airtight. It felt like my balls were caught somewhere in my throat as I watched the Mexican agents in my rearview mirror. Their hands were palming their still-holstered weapons. I slowly inched the 35mm camera under my seat as I pulled the leg of my jeans up over my boot allowing me access to the .38. There were only two possible outcomes here. I would either end up winning an Oscar for the performance I was about to put on, or the Reaper would be paying some of us a visit after the bloodbath.

Still watching in my rearview, I saw one agent stop at the right rear of my car. He tried to stay out of my line of sight as he unleashed his 9mm Browning semiautomatic pistol from its holster. The second agent approached me at my open driver's window as I pulled out my U.S. Customs Service credentials. The gravity of my predicament set in as I felt my dick suck back to take refuge within my prostate like a panicked turtle. If they saw the surveillance camera under the seat, my

U.S. badge wouldn't deter them for a moment from taking me into custody for interrogation. Let me rephrase that. I would be taken in for interro-torturing. And believe me, well before that, the booted .38 would come into play. I may not be the brightest student of history and human nature, but let me tell you, if I've learned anything over the years it's this: In a war with a subhuman enemy, you don't wanna let them take you alive. The atrocities of Nam were in the past by a few years, but the tortured body of DEA Agent Enrique Camarena was still fresh in my mind.

I identified myself to the Mexican agent at my window. As he took my credentials for examination in his left hand, he never let his right hand leave the grip of his still holstered pistol. Off the top of my head I started ad-libbing and going with the only thing I could come up with. I remembered the name of the MFJP commander from working the Well of Death homicides a few months prior. I told the agent that I had been sent for by the comandante because he needed to see me about an investigation involving Yolanda Molina and Tombstone Fragoso.

Now, if you know anything about the Mexican culture, and especially the Mexican trafficker's code of ethics, you know that if you are sent for by any fucking MFJP comandante in Mexico, no one on this globe is supposed to interfere with your travel. It's kind of like having an *amparo,* an official letter of protection that you buy from a Mexican judge. Besides, these days on the border if a U.S. lawman is being sent for by the comandante it probably means that they have some kind of an "arrangement." And all MFJP agents know how lucrative these "arrangements" can be. There's enough for everybody. Even the gofers and *perros* (dogs) get table scraps thrown to them in this business.

As the Mexican examined my credentials, I told him that not being familiar with the streets in Agua Prieta, I had inadvertently taken a wrong turn on the way to the comandante's office. I tossed out the idea of future table scraps when I told him that I would inform the comandante of his assistance, if he could give me proper directions to the office. Since he was a Mexican cop, there had to be some tangible form of *mordida* here before I was gonna be let off the hook. And since I was a U.S. agent, he wasn't going to embarrass himself by asking for money. He wanted something better than that. He wanted something comparable to a license to steal. He wanted a border-crossing card from the U.S. Immigration Service. Why? Because Mexican crooks consider those pieces of plastic-covered American paper to be the ultimate meal ticket.

With these federal "Admit One Free" crossing cards, Mexican outlaws can drive dope loads anywhere on the U.S. side of the border. They can operate stash houses. They can cross through the U.S. Ports of Entry at night to burglarize and loot wealthy American homes. The unlawful opportunities afforded by an INS border-crossing card are only limited by the crook's own feeble imagination.

Since I was a former INS agent, this wasn't the first time one of these pricks had put the bite on me for a card. But this was the first time that knowing the INS channels to get a card probably saved my ass. I looked up at the guy and smiled. Then I told him he was in luck because I used to be with the INS and most of my friends still worked there. A card? No problem! By the time I got done spinning names, offices, appointments, and the needed INS application forms, this crooked cop all but forgot what he had stopped me for. The best-looking, hottest high-heeled hooker from the red zone of Agua Prieta wouldn't have fared as well as I did during this traffic stop. A blow job or a border-crossing card? No comparison for a Mexican crook! After a couple of swallows, a Lewinsky fades away. But you'll always have your crossing card, until you get killed or busted.

As I drove away I counted my blessings for inheriting my great-grandfather's Texan ability to talk a straight fast line of deep bullshit. Everything, other than the new brown stains in my Hanes shorts, would come out in the wash. The Mex feds didn't find the camera. I didn't have to pull the .38. There was no lead-swapping fiesta. The Reaper stayed home. My genitals returned to their designated places. And this was the last trip I ever made into Agua Prieta, Sonora, Mexico. I shit you not. I haven't been back since! And if that Mexican cop ever got his card, it wasn't with any fucking help from me!

In April of 1991, we got extremely lucky when Dr. Galván was arrested by U.S. Customs special agents in El Paso. The Texas Customs agents grabbed him for illegally attempting to export about 10,000 rounds of pistol and rifle ammunition. The fireworks were probably destined for Amado's dope-smuggling organization in Chihuahua and Sonora. Dr. Galván had enough ammo to start a small war when he was arrested. And the interesting part about the munitions he had was that they were the calibers of ammo most preferred by Mexican federal agents and other dope smugglers. Dr. Galván had a little something for every assassin in Mexico.

Galván was arrested in possession of thousands of .223 rounds, which are used in military assault rifles like the Colt M16s and the Ruger Mini-14s. He also had thousands of 7.62x39 rounds, which are for the doper's preferred AK-47, or as they call them down south of the line, the *cuerno de chivo* (goat horn). And the rest was an assortment of deadly handgun calibers like the 9mm, .45, .38 Super, .380, and last but not least, the all-time favorite of cops throughout Mexico, the .38 Super Auto. Why? Because for some weird reason, even though it is a ballistically inferior round, the Mexican cops consider it a status symbol to hold hands with a .38 Super Auto. I guess there are some things we'll never completely understand about these sunbelt folks. Go figure.

Galván was using an assumed name when he fell, so I had to fly over to Texas to identify him for removal to Arizona on the cocaine charges. As soon as I made the ID, I called Special Agent Allan Sperling and had him pop Molina as the traitor was departing his father's house near Double Adobe, Arizona. We knew that once we had Galván, Molina would probably run for the border like most other Cochise County outlaws had done for more than a century now. When Sperling caught up to him and cuffed him, former U.S. Immigration Inspector Rodolfo Molina Jr. was wearing a white sport cap. On the front of the cap was a large green embroidered marijuana plant. Beneath the dizzy weed in Spanish was written the dope traffickers' motto: "It's the Life!"

On February 4, 1992, Molina and Galván were convicted on all counts of their cocaine-smuggling indictment in federal court in

Tucson. Molina was sentenced to serve twenty-seven years and three months. Galván initially got fifteen years and six months. Five days after the convictions, my eighteen-year-old son was walking out of a convenience store in Douglas when he was approached by a Mexican mafia type from Sonora. In broken English the Mexican asked my son if his father was Lee Morgan. My son took a couple of steps back, clenched his fists and hesitantly replied that he was indeed a Morgan. The Mexican shooter pulled a .45 pistol from under his folded armpit and stuck it in the young man's face as he said, "Fuck you and fuck your whole family."

By the grace of God, the only thing that prevented my son from being capped on the spot was a carload of high school kids pulling into the store's parking lot. The shooter looked at the interrupting potential witnesses, shoved his pistol under his jacket, and then abruptly took his leave, departing in a black Chevrolet truck with frontera Sonora tags.

Now, my son was known to be quite the scrapper with his fists in high school. He had been expelled more than once for fighting. But he had to. He was one of a handful of blond-headed *güeros* (light-haired people) who had grown up on the border in this insane world of violent machismo. Of this episode he would later tell me, "Dad, the guy was shaking so bad he would have never hit me anyway. He must have been new at this hit-man gig because he was more scared than I was!" *¡Qué macho mi hijo!* What a macho son!

After they had sent shooters after my family, I vowed to do whatever it took to keep Molina and Galván locked up. And at the time, I had no idea just how hard that was going to be. Dr. Galván, being the ornery little son of a bitch he was, busted out of the federal prison in Tucson a couple of months after his initial incarceration. The U.S. Marshal's Service and the Bureau of Prisons notified me, U.S. Customs Service Inspector George Campos, and the federal prosecutor who tried and convicted Galván, Assistant U.S. Attorney Randy Stevens. They knew we were on Galván's mind. The marshals providing court security at the trial had seen the hate projected by the defendants at the prosecutor and his witnesses. Fortunately for all of us, Galván was recaptured on the same night. For his efforts to escape, the same federal judge who had handed down his original sentence tacked on another five years to serve. That left the good doctor saddled with twenty-one-and-a-half years to pay for his outlaw ways.

Subsequent to or at about the same time as our U.S. Customs case against Molina, DEA had stepped up to the plate to take a swing at Molina on a separate cocaine possession and distribution charge stemming from his dealings after he had resigned from the U.S. Immigration Service. It turned out that after we had run him out of INS, Molina hooked up with a still-employed crooked U.S. Inspector at the Douglas Port of Entry named Donald Lake Simpson. DEA got wired into Molina and Simpson's activities, and later took them both down on a conspiracy to move even more cocaine. During the time that both of the assholes were in prison on the U.S. Customs convictions, the Ninth Circuit Court of Appeals reversed DEA's case against Molina and Simpson. Now all Molina had to do was get the Customs case reversed and he could run for Mexico.

Molina and Dr. Galván's defense attorneys eventually got the Ninth Circuit Court of Appeals to nail the presiding federal judge in Tucson on a couple of reversible errors during the Customs trial. I read the decision and couldn't believe the liberal bullshit the Ninth Circuit came up with in its decision to reverse the trial. But if it's any consolation to Judge Browning, who presided over the trial of the two in Tucson, the decision illustrated that the Ninth Circuit judges themselves aren't all that bright. Continually throughout their entire decision they err in referring to Rudi Molina as a U.S. Customs inspector. Now, if you bring that to their attention, and I'm sure there are no attorneys willing to risk the wrath of the gods, these little tyrants will dismiss such an error as minor. But I and the rest of the honest U.S. Customs agents and inspectors consider it a grievous error that leaves an unnecessary black mark on a damn fine federal law-enforcement agency. How do you think the Ninth Circuit judges would like it if we compared them to Arizona Justice of the Peace Joe Borane?

But as Lady Luck would have it, even though the Customs conviction had fallen into appeal, DEA's conviction survived their appeal and that conviction was reinstated by the Ninth Circuit. The U.S. Attorney's Office surmised that since Molina had also received twenty-seven years to serve in the DEA case, they wouldn't spend the man-hours retrying him on the U.S. Customs case. However, we did have to retry Dr. Galván since he was not involved in DEA's case against Inspectors Molina and Simpson. Is it starting to ring through to you just how hard it is to prosecute a crooked badge and his cohorts?

In March of 1998, Dr. Galván's new trial began. It was during this trial that I became completely disgusted with our judicial system. First of all, some eight years after Galván's arrest, I was now being accused by the defense attorneys of planting evidence that I had supposedly illegally retrieved from Dr. Galván's office in Agua Prieta—an accusation that they neglected to bring up in the first trial eight fucking years before! Then secondly, the defense attorneys brought convict witnesses in from different prisons around the country who testified to outrageous and completely unbelievable alibis for Galván. It was a fucking joke, not to mention a mockery of our federal court system. The prosecuting assistant U.S. Attorney knew that the alibis were concocted lies. And I'm sure that the presiding federal judge also knew it down in his bones. But that's how it is nowadays. The lowlife scumsucking defense attorneys have the right to present just about any kind of bullshit story they can come up with.

Isn't it strange how the witnesses and court interpreters are always sworn by the judge to tell the truth, but *not* the defense attorneys? Have you ever seen a defense attorney take the oath to tell the truth in front of the judge? Hell, no! I've asked attorneys why it is they don't have to take the oath and you wanna know what the answer is? According to them, because they are officers of the court it is just understood that they are going to tell the truth. If you believe that one I still have that moon rock, never before touched by human hands, that I'll sell you at a bargain-basement price!

Now, you have to remember that eight years before, during the first trial, there was no question as to how and where I found evidence and there were no magical alibi witnesses. But you give the devil his due time, and guys like Amado Carrillo will funnel enough blood money to defense attorneys and convicts to pervert our system of justice. And this brings me back to something I've told you before. If we aren't careful, if we don't remain the strongest country on earth, if we aren't ever so diligent in the defense of free countries, we will all eventually fall slaves to the drug lords. Folks, we're in a war for our survival. With the Russians it was nukes and instantaneous death. With the Mexican and Colombian drug lords the Reaper will come in a slow and agonizing powder form.

On December 3, 1998, after being reconvicted in his new trial, Dr. Galván was sentenced for a second and hopefully final time. Up until that day, for the last six years, Dr. Galván had been laughing at our judicial system as he attempted to legally work his way toward freedom. During the course of these six years, Dr. Galván and his defense attorneys had managed to get a federal judge jammed up by the Ninth Circuit. They had caused the U.S. Attorney's Office to doubt the original prosecutor who, in my eyes, was the cream of the crop. And for the first time in the twenty-four years of my federal law-enforcement career, they had sullied my name and reputation in court. So here we are in court again, some ten years after the good doctor had committed his crime, awaiting a second federal judge to resentence the bastard. And the traitor Molina? Although he wormed his way out of one conviction, he still ended up getting slammed with the same twenty-seven years on the second conviction. It works for me.

Sometimes you want to pull you hair out and scream for justice. Sometimes you wonder if it has been worth all the aggravation, death threats, close calls, disappointments, and mayhem. And sometimes you get the answer. Dr. Galván wanted a new trial and he got it. His original sentence went from fifteen-and-a-half years to seventeen-and-a-half years plus the five years for escape. He had rolled the dice and lost big-time. But just when you think it's all over and some small measure of justice has been meted out, it gets snatched back from your grasp.

Just before Dr. Galván's sentencing, his slimebucket defense attorney withdrew from the case, citing some bullshit reason that he could no longer represent the dentist. This was no doubt a two-edged calculation on the defender's part. First, the attorney knew that he had fucked up and pissed the judge off when he attempted to introduce all of that false-alibi testimony in court. That meant that it was highly likely that the judge would up the doctor's sentencing after his second conviction. And that meant that the attorney would look like a big fucking loser to all of his other big-money dope clients. That ain't good. He had to disassociate himself from Dr. Galván. It could cost the counselor a lot of future business. It could even cost him his life.

Second, it set Dr. Galván up for another appeal. Citing bad counsel, the tooth maggot has already filed another appeal. Can you believe this shit? A case that has already dragged on for ten years can conceivably drag on another ten years or so. Meanwhile, the Mexicans and Colombians not only laugh at us, they continue to poison our people. If the whole thing wasn't so damn pitiful, it would be downright funny!

During my investigation of the good doctor and the corrupt inspector, the FBI started sniffing my trail. When one of their agents showed up with an assorted box of Dunkin' Donuts, a luxury we don't get in Douglas, I knew some kind of a sales pitch would be forthcoming. With the wall falling and the Reds in disarray all over the Soviet Union, the FBI didn't have a lot of domestic spies lurking around the U.S. anymore. The agency desperately needed to break into the dope arena to save their budget from getting slashed to the bone. But we always knew that their best contribution to the war on drugs would be for them to follow up on the corruption investigations. And that's just what this feller standing at my door with a box of city-bought doughnuts wanted to do.

With Molina and Galván put away, we could now concentrate our efforts on Molina's corrupt partner, who had also come to Douglas from Presidio, Texas. U.S. Immigration Service Inspector Ramon Reyes's suspected dope-smuggling activity was a carbon copy of Molina's crimes against the United States.

In April of 1990, INS Inspector Reyes waved a load of 634 pounds of cocaine through his inspection lane. The coke load was picked off right behind Reyes by an alert, dedicated U.S. Customs inspector named Dale Demmerly. As a matter of fact, Demmerly on his own had suspected that Reyes was a crook, so he had begun to dog him around the Douglas Port of Entry. Everywhere the Immigration inspector went, the Customs inspector followed. It paid off. The driver of the 634 pounds of powder was taken into custody and found to be the brother-in-law to none other than our one-time escape artist, Dr. José Amador Galván.

After his arrest and trial, Juan Soto-Pipper was sentenced to ten years in prison. He never broke the cocaine lord's code of silence. He never rolled on Inspector Reyes or any other part of Amado Carrillo's organization. But it didn't stop me and the FBI from building the same kind of case on Reyes that I had on Molina. There were so many ties and similarities between their histories and dope-smuggling activities that they could damn near be considered clones. They were both Vietnam veterans. Both had been in the Border Patrol in Marfa, Texas. Both had left their wives for Mexican women of questionable character. And they both had been U.S. Immigration inspectors in Presidio, Texas, just across the river from Ojinaga, the spawning squalor of cocaine king Amado Carrillo.

So this FBI agent and I went on a six-hundred-or-so-mile road trip to Presidio and Ojinaga. And to be quite honest, we really weren't surprised by what we learned. During the course of interviews we were told that when Reyes and Molina had been in Presidio, they would spend a lot of time in Ojinaga, Mexico. They ran with a group of Mexican doctors and dentists known to be involved in dope smuggling under Amado Carrillo. In fact, Reyes's present wife, who had been born and raised in Ojinaga, had been a patient of Dr. Joel Soto-Pipper. That's right. The brother of Juan Soto-Pipper, the now-imprisoned cocaine smuggler who had been waved through the inspection lane by INS Inspector Reyes in Douglas, Arizona, with 634 pounds of cocaine in the trunk of his car.

We interviewed a good number of Customs and Immigration inspectors at the Presidio Port of Entry, including the director of the port. We were informed that Reyes was also suspected of passing drug loads through that port when he was assigned there. The port director even went as far as to say he was relieved to see Reyes transfer to

Douglas because he was so corrupt, he was an embarrassment to the port. We also interviewed Reyes's in-laws in Presidio. From them we learned that Reyes was so sure we were going to arrest him that he gave his in-laws instructions to sell his property while he was in prison. Reyes knew we were coming, and I derived a great deal of perverted pleasure in knowing his guts were twisting and his nights were restless. Since the government wouldn't let us kill traitors like they were some kind of a plague, I'd have to settle for that.

Before leaving the Big Bend country of Texas, I spoke with a Texas DPS narcotics officer who had recently worked an undercover investigation on a doctor from Ojinaga, Mexico. During his undercover negotiations the Texas trooper learned that the doctor he was dealing with was named Carlos Colín-Padilla. During one of their face-to-face let's-make-a-deal meetings, Dr. Colín told the undercover officer that he was the personal physician to none other than Ojinaga's favorite wayward hometown boy, Amado Carrillo. At the end of the investigation, Dr. Colín was subsequently busted with 115 pounds of cocaine he was delivering to the undercover Texan.

During his trial, Dr. Colín was represented by an attorney from El Paso named Tony Chavez. You want to know the funny part about this? Tony Chavez also came to Tucson to defend INS Inspector Molina. I later checked Molina's personal telephone directory seized from his Douglas residence during the 1988 search warrant. Sure enough, there, written in Molina's handwriting, was "Dr. Colín— Ojinaga." Just like any good crime-syndicate administrator, Amado always tried to take care of his top people with the same lawyer. That way he knew in advance if anyone was going to roll out and make a deal with the feds.

When we completed our investigation in Ojinaga and Presidio, we drove on down to Houston, to which Reyes had transferred from Douglas. If I forgot to mention it, just like Molina had run to California seeking anonymity, Reyes had wormed his way with INS to Texas for the same reason. While Inspector Reyes was on duty at the U.S. Immigration office in downtown Houston, we paid his loving Ojinaga wife a visit at their home.

When Mrs. Reyes answered the doorbell and saw us standing there, the expression on her face alone was damn near enough to convict her husband. She had this confused, dazed look like alcoholics get just about fifteen seconds before they hit the floor in a nosedive. She was probably thinking to herself that we weren't playing by the rules. Like most crooks, these folks were thinking that if they transferred far enough away we would probably just forget about their transgressions against the good ol' U.S. of A. The organization wasn't used to being dogged and harassed across the country. Well, the rules were being changed. As far as we were concerned, a traitor should be shown no quarter.

Reyes's wife all but broke wide open during our interview. In fact, our visit was so damaging that about a week after we left Houston to write up our prosecution report, U.S. Immigration Inspector Reyes tendered his resignation and departed for parts unknown, relying once again on the old outlaw reasoning of "out of sight, out of mind."

We had a good case on Reyes but we couldn't find a U.S. Attorney or a state prosecutor who was willing to take the job on. And I really couldn't blame them. You had to look back at the prosecution of Dr. Galván and Inspector Molina. Who had the time and energy to go after Reyes? Like Molina, he had been a crooked badge working for one of the largest cocaine-smuggling operations this country has ever known. If you prosecuted him it would keep you tied up for a minimum of ten years. The way the prosecutors looked at it was like this: We had forced the crook to resign and run.

And since everything isn't always equal in the justice system, being rid of the traitor was halfway home. Besides, who's to say where the end will be for Reyes? He's a liability to the organization now. They know that we are on his ass. They know that if we ever do drag him into court a lot of names and secrets could be divulged. Maybe, just maybe, the organization will figure it's better to spill his blood than allow him to spill his beans. Folks, sometimes justice is simply where you find it. And I guarandamntee that you sure as hell aren't always going to find it in a U.S. courtroom.

On February 3, 1999, four former and present U.S. Immigration inspectors in Nogales, Arizona, were indicted and arrested by a federal law-enforcement task force composed of special agents of the U.S. Customs Service, the FBI, and the DEA. These INS inspectors were accused of waving twenty tons of cocaine through the Nogales Port of Entry. And guess who the traitors were working for? Well, a lot of folks down here called him "Lord of the Skies" because of all the Colombian cocaine he was flying up to the border for crossing. But to me, Amado Carrillo will always be remembered as nothing more than a sorry excuse for traitors to sell their country out. It's because of Mexican pendejos like Carrillo that we are now awash in more corruption than ever before in our country's history. And I believe such corruption will transcend more than just border-enforcement agencies. If unchecked, it will eventually soak every thread of the fabric of the jurisprudence system in our country.

On February 12, 1999, the same day that President Clinton's impeachment trial allowed him to get away with perjury and obstruction of justice, I was visited by an assistant U.S. Attorney. It seemed that the U.S. Attorney's Office in Tucson had decided that because of my many years combating drug traffickers on the border, I would make an excellent expert witness on the stand concerning dope-smuggling cases. They wanted me to testify in one of their upcoming dope trials where they would have a federal judge wave his magic wand and bless me as an "expert witness."

I didn't know whether to laugh, cry, be honored, or just flat-ass get pissed off. I mean, on this particular day, everything I had held sacred for some twenty-six years—my badge, my oath, my job, and my life—had just been defecated on by the Senate. They threw the oath of truth and honor right out the fucking window. The Senate let a man, who just happened to be the president, get away with lying to a federal grand jury. Even though he was the president, he was still just a man. And like the rest of us, according to the law of the land, he was entitled to no more and no less protection under the law.

And under these same laws, a former good friend of mine had recently been disgraced, convicted, and sentenced to federal prison. And his plight was no different than President Clinton's. He was just a man, who happened to be a federal agent. Who happened to have had sex with an informant. And who happened to have lied to a federal grand jury about his affair with the informant. My former buddy, an anti-smuggling agent for the U.S. Border Patrol, broke his oath and rightly paid the price according to the law of the land. He betrayed his word, he betrayed his oath, and most of all he betrayed his country.

Nowadays, I'm beginning to wonder about the government I've devoted my life to serving. Don't get me wrong. I will always love my country. But why is it that the government administers the laws on the regular folks, yet it defers the execution of the same laws on the rich and powerful? I reckon treachery can wear many faces. It can hide behind a badge on a chest, an attorney's credentials, or even the Presidential Seal in the White House.

Even when I was being falsely accused, and later even civilly sued for allegedly planting evidence in Molina's trial, I didn't break my oath. I had to keep telling myself that it was the traitor and not me who was on trial. It would have been so easy to lie about this event or that detail in an effort to exonerate myself. But I didn't succumb to the temptation. Even though they were hammering my ass with false accusations, I kept the oath. And I always will.

> I will support and defend the Constitution of the United States against all enemies, foreign and domestic; that I will bear true faith and allegiance to the same; that I take this obligation freely, without any mental reservation or purpose of evasion; and that I will well and faithfully discharge the duties of the office that I am about to enter. So help me God!

21

Rabbits and Greyhounds

IN 1974, THERE WERE ONLY SIXTEEN U.S. Border Patrol agents assigned to the U.S.-Mexican border in Cochise County, Arizona. During the 1970s, the Border Patrol apprehension rate of illegal aliens crossing the Reaper's line was about five hundred to six hundred per month. A little more than thirty years later, Cochise County was occupied by about a thousand U.S. Border Patrol agents covering the same area that we original sixteen agents worked. The average rate of apprehensions has now skyrocketed to about thirty thousand undocumented aliens per month. About 98 to 99 percent of these arrests have historically been folks from the economically depressed Republic of Mexico.

Now, the truth of the matter is this: Very few, if any at all, of those Mexicans returned home after their initial arrest and voluntary deportation to Mexico. They may have returned home a year or two later of their own free will. But I guarandamntee that they didn't go south after their first, second, third, or even fourth encounter with the U.S. Border Patrol. That's a fact of the cat-and-mouse game that has gone on since the dividing line was laid down between the two countries. Damn near everyone makes repeated runs at the border until they are successful at getting across. Look at it this way: After getting one or two speeding tickets, did you ever break the speed limit again? You may have slowed down for a while. But only for a while.

Never, ever think that if the Border Patrol caught six hundred people in one month or even thirty thousand in another month, that those numbers represent folks who were prevented from illegally entering the U.S. What those numbers really tell you is exactly this: 30,600 folks were merely delayed for one or two days while en route to their families and awaiting employment in Chicago, New York, or Los Angeles. And we aren't even talking about the other multiple thousands who slipped by while the Border Patrol was busy catching the 30,600. It's all a REMF numbers game. The REMFs want to portray our borders as secure safety nets, and want us to believe that their high numbers of arrests along the border demonstrate that they are in control. But in reality, they never even come close to addressing the facts of who's crossing our border northbound and how many of these same folks are some time later crossing our border south going back home. Have you ever seen any kind of report, whether it be official, estimated, or otherwise, of the numbers of illegal Mexicans who depart the U.S. of their own accord? You need to ask why not.

In 1998, the U.S. Border Patrol apprehended 1,555,776 undocumented aliens. So considering the well-known fact that we only catch about one out of every four or five illegal entrants, and the fact that the 1,555,776 are going to keep trying until they make it, you're looking at about a conservative six to eight million illegal crossings in 1998 alone. And do you really think for one minute that our country could absorb that type of influx without some serious repercussions? No way! That would mean that conceivably from 1990 to 2000 we would have had an illegal population explosion of some sixty to eighty million bodies. And I think we would have noticed that by now.

Mexicans have always crossed the border illegally, and as long as that line is in the dirt, they will continue to break that particular law. If any REMF tries to tell you different he's full of bullshit. I've seen numerous illegal-immigration studies done by both liberal and conservative groups over the last twenty-five years. And the one constant in the studies is the total illegal population living in the U.S. Because of the annual seasonal rotation between their mother country and their "second home," that number is often reported at an estimated six to twelve million and not sixty to eighty million. And I know damn good and well that most of those folks are just our backyard neighbors. Mexicans.

Most Mexicans passionately love their country. They would never think of leaving it of their own accord if it weren't a survival issue for their families. But the fact of life in Mexico is that the economy is so poor that an uneducated bottom-of-the-food-chain laborer cannot feed his family. These folks are therefore forced to emigrate to the U.S. Why? Because of the corruption of the Mexican government itself. A government that has been corrupt since its very inception. A government of which past presidents now reside in foreign countries with Swiss bank accounts filled with millions and millions they plundered from the Mexican people. A government that is unwilling to care for all of its people. What's the answer? Ask a hundred different politicians and you'll most likely get a hundred different answers.

In pursuit of the answer, I once had a lively discussion with a good friend of mine who happens to be a Mexican American lawyer with family ties to Mexican politics. I suggested to my friend that if the Mexican government wouldn't ever take the responsibility to feed its own people, then someone else would have to do it. He heatedly asked me what I meant by that and I simply told him that someone other than Mexicans needed to administer the Mexican government, be it the United Nations, the U.S., NATO, or some kind of world council. Because according to Mexican history, it has become painfully obvious that nothing else will ever work.

Well, my attorney buddy damn near blew a gasket at the idea of Mexico being subjected to anything other than Mexican rule. He said that the Mexican people had too much national pride to ever allow their flag to be disgraced by such an initiative. I was quick to point out to my friend that he was a well-to-do feller with plenty of food in his belly and a nice, dry roof over his head. That he was speaking for himself and the other small percentage of the Mexican population in his income bracket. That if he believed that Mexican nationalism was so high, I had a simple test to put it through. I asked, "How about we go down south to any one of the million Mexican shantytowns where people barely subsist in cardboard boxes, and ask them if for the one meal they might get today they would rather eat a plate of beef 'n' beans or the fucking Mexican flag?" My lawyer friend backed off. He didn't have a word to say.

We are merely pissing in the wind trying to keep Mexicans from revolving into and out of their "second home." It's a waste of U.S. Border Patrol manpower, our limited law-enforcement resources, and most of all your hard-earned tax dollars. We are worried about the mice sneaking into the barn through the cracks when we should be worried about the barn burning to the goddamn ground. Why worry about something history has demonstrated that you can't control, not to mention the fact that it has not harmed our economy, when there are bigger, more serious issues—international terrorism, worldwide criminal organizations, international fugitives, violent narcotics trafficking organizations, alien smugglers, border bandits, and the international world population explosion?

In order to survive the next century, our federal law-enforcement agencies on the border will have to concentrate on more pressing immigration problems than our routinely visiting backyard neighbors. Did you know that Mexico has become an international stepping stone of migration for people who are looking to enter the U.S. illegally from more than forty European and Asian countries? Mexico now has Chinese, Russians, Malaysians, Filipinos, Koreans, and even Thais who are continually landing in Mexican airports from Europe en route to cross the Mexican border into the United States. Since 1993, the California judicial system has added court interpreters for Cambodian, Armenian, Mandarin, Russian, Punjabi, Arabic, Cantonese, Japanese, Korean, Tagalog, and Vietnamese.

Shouldn't we be more worried about these folks from the other side of the world who have no intentions whatsoever of going back to their homeland? For some stupid reason we're more upset about the Mexican seasonal laborer who is going to go home after six or eight months of employment in the U.S.

Even U.S. Ambassador Jeffrey Davidow told the Mexican newspapers in September of 2000 that he agreed that an open border for migration is viable in the long term. The key here is to limit it to migration, and only migration, of poor Mexicans who just want to make a half-ass decent living for their families. Now, I'm by no means saying let these folks come in and take Americans' jobs. I don't think any U.S. citizen should have to stand in line behind a Mexican citizen for a job in the U.S. There are easy enough ways to prevent that from happening during the pre-employment application process. But what I am saying is that as long as the Mexican doesn't have a communicable disease, he's not wanted for any crimes in either country, and he doesn't become a welfare case supported by hard-working Americans, why not let him take a low-paying job that we don't want? He's going to do it anyway!

And are we really winning the war on drugs like the REMFs want you to believe? Well, before I get into my personal views here, let's take a look at the statistics. In 1998, 70 percent of the robberies in Phoenix and 75 percent of the robberies in Tucson were drug-related. In 1998, 53 percent of the homicides in Phoenix were drug-related. In 1999, murders involving drugs in Phoenix rose to 66 percent.

In 1991 the U.S. Customs Service nationwide seized 226,000 pounds of drugs. In 1998, we seized 1.4 million pounds of narcotics—an un-fucking-believable 420 percent increase in just seven years. By 2004, we seized more than 2.2 million pounds of narcotics. And what you need to remember here is that out of that 2.2 million total pounds, 2,153,200 pounds was grass. We only seized 44,000 pounds of cocaine and another 2,800 pounds of heroin.

Does this mean we are doing a better job? Don't be fooled. It simply means the drug lords are producing more and more poison each year. It's similar to the supply and demand of corn and wheat. More and more farmers will merely produce more of what is asked for on the world market. Besides which, we are lucky if we get one out of ten or fifteen loads of smuggled dope coming into the country every year. So if we seize two million pounds, that means about twenty-five million pounds of mind-altering product still gets to market.

In 1996, only one law-enforcement officer along the U.S.-Mexican border in Arizona was arrested for corruption as it related to narcotics smuggling. In 1997, eleven such traitors were arrested. In 1998, a record-breaking seventeen. And this backsliding of morals and integrity has continued into the present. The escalating number of dirty badges is prima facie evidence that we are going downhill into the muck of another war we are not willing to win.

Note here I said "not *willing*" to win, and not "not *able*" to win. There's a big difference. We can win it if we are willing to go the full route, if we are willing to make great personal sacrifices, giving little regard to politics and political correctness.

On the United Nations Anti-Drug Day in August of 2000, Chongqing, China, executed seventeen drug traffickers in the day's grand finale. Before that grisly public display, the red bastards shot fifty-five dope traffickers as a prelude to the celebration. That's exactly why we in America will never win the war on drugs, because we aren't willing to do exactly what the Chinese know must be done. I'm not saying that's good or bad. I'm just pointing out the facts. Dope will go the same way in America that booze did some seventy years ago. Besides, man is by nature a self-destructive mammal, and that's probably part of the reason he indulges in booze and drugs. It is simply the Beast that lies waiting in all of us.

So how can the REMFs tell you we are winning the war on drugs when each year there is more and more available dope, more dope-related violent crimes, and more corruption of our most needed and cherished profession? There can be only one tangible win for each of us in the war on drugs, and that is in exactly what Special Agent Hummer Rodriguez of the Organized Drug Enforcement Task Force once said: If you can keep yourself and your loved ones off dope, you have won the war on drugs. After twenty-five years in the trenches with Hummer, I can flat-out tell you he's *cien por ciento* (100 percent) correct.

As far as our country's recertification of Mexico's anti-drug efforts goes, let the facts speak for themselves. It is well documented that the Mexican government will not sign off on a certified U.S. Customs undercover investigation in which narcotics are going to leave Mexico and later be seized in the U.S. by our special agents. Why? Because it is more profitable for the Mexican government to seize the drugs on their own soil so that they can resell them to the highest Mexican cartel bidder. The Mex feds also want to be able to boast to their cartel bed-partners that they didn't allow the gringos to destroy their coveted merchandise. Such bragging will at a later date entitle them to a substantial "protection" reward from the cartel faction.

In addition, over the past ten or so years there have been numerous accounts of armed Mexican Army incursions into Arizona and Texas. The majority of these invasions onto our sovereign soil occurred while the Mex feds were escorting cartel dope loads. During a good number of such incidents, U.S. Border Patrol and U.S. Customs agents have come under fire by foreign troops.

And if that doesn't gall you enough, remember what I mentioned earlier: In June 1999, the U.S. Customs Service learned that the Mex feds were bringing to the border additional personnel to augment their services in the facilitation and movement of cartel dope. Such services included surveilling of U.S. law enforcement and intercepting and decoding our encrypted radio transmissions. When the Mexican agents weren't performing those treacherous acts, they were to follow special agents of the border offices of the U.S. Customs Service, the DEA, and the FBI. During such covert missions into the U.S., the Mex feds were to identify U.S. special agents and their informants. As you can imagine, this new breed of Mexican spies was directed not to report through the normal chains of the MFJP.

Sounds like KGB-CIA spook stuff, huh? And these are the same motherfuckers the U.S. president gives millions of your tax dollars to a year! Who's running this war?

And it just keeps getting worse. In August of 1999, in response to its people screaming about the need for protection from kidnappings, highway robberies, and other crimes plaguing the nation, the Mexican government ceremoniously unveiled a new federal police force called the Federal Protective Police (FPP). It was a body of more than fourteen thousand officers, including five thousand military personnel. They were directed to crack down on illegal immigration, dope smuggling, unlawful possession of firearms, and guerrilla/terrorist groups.

They were supposed to enforce the laws on the federal highways, at the ports of entry, and on the U.S.-Mexican border.

In my opinion, forming the FPP was just another excuse by Mexico City to put another corrupt bunch of cops and soldiers on the border where they could augment the dope smuggling of their MFJP brothers. In fact, we received the information about the new group of Mex feds coming to the border to surveil U.S. special agents about two months before the FPP was formed. Think about it!

In the last days of August 1999, one of my better informants from Mexico had contacted me to report that at a meeting of the MFJP in Sonora, he had viewed an interesting "documentary." As I mentioned before, it was a secretly recorded videotape of me and other special agents of the U.S. Customs Service in Douglas. The film was being shown to new recruits of the soon-to-be FPP to identify each agent in our investigative office. The new agency was so corrupt that within seven months of its formation, FPP agents in multiple Mexican states would be under official investigation for dope smuggling, alien smuggling, and theft.

In November of 1999, a whole battalion of Mexican soldiers, 570 men of the 96th Infantry battalion in Chihuahua, were put under investigation for stealing and selling six tons of "seized" cocaine. One Mexican general, Gutiérrez Rebollo, had previously been arrested in February of 1997 when he was accused of protecting cocaine belonging to the Juárez-Agua Prieta cartel's Amado Carrillo. During this same time, the Mexican government also had knowledge of fourteen other generals and forty-five high-ranking military officers who had intimate ties to dope lords.

In relation to the escalating violence on the border, believe me, you ain't getting the truth, much less the whole truth. If you did, the U.S. government believes it would be detrimental to our newly discovered second-most-popular trade partner in the world, Mexico. Because of the billions of dollars we now trade with Mexico under NAFTA, it is unlikely that we will ever decertify them as a drug-war ally. Nor will we let the American public know how fucked up things are on the border.

For instance, in 1995 there were 156 reported assaults against federal agents of the U.S. Customs Service and the U.S. Border Patrol. By 2000, those attacks ballooned to an alarming 500 incidents. Or how about this one: Did you know that on March 14, 2000, there was an armed invasion of Santa Teresa, New Mexico, by three military Humvees filled with Mexican soldiers who fired shots at U.S. Border Patrol agents on American soil? That kind of disgraceful shit hadn't happened since Pancho Villa raided Columbus, New Mexico, and killed eighteen American citizens on March 9, 1916!

Pursuant to the Santa Teresa bullet swap meet in the sand, the Border Patrol agents managed to capture nine fully armed Mexican soldiers without taking any casualties. The agents also seized one of the Mexican Humvees, along with seven .308 caliber military assault rifles, one 9mm submachine gun, and two .45 caliber pistols.

Now, I know you didn't hear about that, because it was something the U.S. government pretty much covered up. Why do I say that? Because of this: Whenever a U.S. agent is fired upon, such intolerable action immediately results in the arrest of the assailant for assault on a federal officer. It is a serious crime that I have investigated on numerous occasions during my career as a special agent. And during such an investigation, I know that you are mandated to contact the U.S. Attorney's Office and explain the incident or facts of probable cause that would warrant an arrest of the alleged shooter. The U.S. Attorney will either approve or decline the prosecution based on the facts you present. Usually prosecution of the shooter(s) is approved within five or ten minutes. But in this case, the U.S. Attorney quietly declined prosecution, and the Mexican soldiers, their military vehicle, and all of their service firearms and ammo were returned to the Mexican government!

I have been told by my contacts in New Mexico that these Mexican Army shooters were in U.S. custody for some three hours. During that time, and according to my many years of experience, I'm relatively confident that a special agent of the government contacted the U.S. Attorney for permission to prosecute the foreign invaders. And since this was a big fucking political touchy-feely vibrating international incident, I'll guess that the U.S. Attorney in either Albuquerque or El Paso contacted Attorney General Janet Reno or her office in Washington, D.C., for direction. And since Janet Reno had just given our informants away under the Brownsville Agreement, and since Bill Clinton had recently certified our second-largest world-trade partner as a willing participant in the war on drugs, guess what happened.

Ever since we backed down on the Santa Teresa armed invasion, the U.S. Border Patrol has been reporting a number of similar incursions and an escalating number of shootings at its agents. Not only that, but we have now come to a point in the drug wars where there is a standing $200,000 Mexican cartel reward for killing any U.S. Border Patrol agent or U.S. Customs Service special agent.

How can you expect to win the war on drugs when under NAFTA alone, you allow four or five million Mexican trucks and trailers to drive across the border every year with virtually no inspection by the U.S. Customs Service or anyone else? That's right. You read it correctly the first time. In 1998, four million Mexican commercial trucks entered the U.S. at designated ports of entry. Out of that number a trifling 46,000 trucks were stopped and inspected by the U.S. Customs Service. Do you believe that? A minute 1.6 percent of four million potential dope-smuggling transports were investigated for drugs! Why? Because we weren't, and still aren't, prepared to handle the flow of traffic that NAFTA and its Mexican proponents forced on us. So with that many uninspected trailers and containers crossing the border in a year, the Colombian and Mexican dope lords are virtually guaranteed they'll be unhampered while smuggling tons of dope into our great nation.

During my quarter of a century of federal law enforcement I have found that when we aren't busy shooting ourselves in the foot to appease the Mexican government, we still can stay pretty busy on the home front with self-mutilation. Although we now have the President's Office of National Drug Control Policy headed by a White House drug czar, we have never in the last century had a united effort in the war on drugs. And I don't see that changing in the near future. Why? Because the DEA is looking to control and limit the U.S. Customs Service Office of Investigations (known as ICE since the

Homeland Security merger, which I will discuss at length in the next chapter), the FBI is looking to completely devour the DEA, and since the Homeland merger, the U.S. Border Patrol is trying to control all three of these investigative agencies by limiting what they can do on the border. It's brutal, it's lunacy, and as with the drug lords that we're all out to knock down, it's all about money.

On Capitol Hill there is no drug war. There is a budget war. And the really sad part about that is all of that REMF animosity seeps down to the agents in the trenches. While we are so busy stealing arrests and seizures from each other to please our budget-conscious bosses, the Colombian and Mexican drug lords are gaining ground like Hitler's blitzkrieg during World War II.

It is imperative for the survival of America that our approach to the war on drugs be revamped. We have to look at the big picture and the threats that are on our horizon. As far as the big picture is concerned, we are rapidly headed in the direction of legalizing marijuana because we must. And there are a lot of reasons why I say this.

To start out with, we are rapidly reaching a saturation point with grass arrests and prosecutions. In the 1950s, a beatnik picked up in the Deep South with several joints of smoke ended up doing an excessive amount of years in lockup. In the '60s and '70s a hippie in California might pull a few months for the same amount in his or her possession. By the '80s it was winding down to a probational offense. And by the '90s it was no more than a small fine like a moving traffic violation. And why not? At the turn of the century we had a president *and* a vice president who admitted on national television that they had smoked marijuana. So how do you explain that to your kids when you are trying to beat it into their heads to stay off grass?

Because of the flood of dope cases, the five U.S. federal court districts that stretch the border from the northern end of California to the bottom tip of south Texas handle more than 26 percent of all criminal court filings in the United States. That means that Texas, New Mexico, Arizona, and California, just four out of our entire fifty states, account for more than a quarter of all federal criminal prosecutions in America.

We can no longer afford to fill our courts and prisons with marijuana violators. We need the resources and space for those who traffic in hard drugs that really do kill, such as smack, coke, and meth. Texas border counties are already refusing to take grass cases referred to them from the feds because it is costing the county too much of the taxpayers' dough. Even the feds are now giving misdemeanor one-week-in-jail deals to felony marijuana smugglers who five or six years ago would have ended up serving several years for the same amount of grass they are presently charged with. By April of 1999, I was seeing more and more state and federal cases where defendants who were busted with two to three hundred pounds of grass were getting off with a mere five years' probation and no jail time at all. By May 2006, the U.S. Attorney's Office in Tucson was declining prosecution of marijuana smugglers arrested with less than 500 pounds of green merca.

The threat we are going to have to deal with is guerrilla narco-terrorism. A third of Colombia is already controlled by communist guerrillas who sustain themselves through funds derived from narcotics trafficking. Mexico is rapidly spiraling down the same path, as is evident from its own anti-guerrilla/terrorist force, the FPP, which has already been corrupted by both Colombian and Mexican cartel dope money.

Now, I'm not so stupid as to think that the U.S. government hires guys like me just to enforce our nation's laws. I mean, you have to think about it like this: The Kennedy dynasty began its reign with money derived from illegal booze smuggling. So is it really too hard to imagine that a president, an attorney general, and a senator didn't want to compete with any rivals for control of "their" kingdom? Why share the power with any of a thousand up-and-coming challengers when you can hold them down by hiring guns like me and the other boys I've fought alongside over the years?

But on the other hand, I reckon it's a choice of the lesser of two evils when you consider who the competitors could be. Mark my words: Ruthless Colombian and Mexican drug lords will bring our nation to its knees. Their dark plague on our land is worse than all combined diseases and miseries we presently face. Monetarily, these pricks cost Americans $110 billion a year in lost productivity, accidents, medical benefits, and other debilitating crap. And that's not mentioning the billions of dollars in tax money we spend in drug-related law enforcement, the cost to our judicial system, and the expense to our bursting penal system. But in the long run these drug lords will cost us more than just money. We will suffer as many lost lives and casualties as we have from most of our past wars. Yet sadly enough, we as a nation lack the resolve to commit to this fight as if it really were a war. I fear to say, we may one day go silently into the night from which there is no return.

According to the Mexican government there are now sixteen leftist subversive groups operating in half of Mexico. The groups have approximately thirty thousand members. And you can damn well bet your last dime that all sixteen groups have blood ties with Mexican drug cartels as well as their Colombian guerrilla brothers. The present political atmosphere is so volatile within Mexico that the foreign-affairs minister of Belgium has continued to block an initiative to sell five hundred machine guns to the Mexican military because he is concerned they will be used by drug traffickers or guerrilla groups.

I'm not just casting idle aspersions here for your reading pleasure. The enemy is in our backyard and he is quietly waging an effective campaign against the United States. Do you remember what I told you was written on the kilo of cocaine we seized from the Agua Prieta cartel during the Douglas drug tunnel investigation? You should never forget the words. The clear and direct statement should be forever burned into your brain. "This Is Our War on the North Americans!"

This declaration of war is coming from an enemy that has enough money to actually build its own submarines. They are able to finance their own armies with better equipment than the U.S. Customs Service, the DEA, the FBI, and the U.S. Border Patrol combined. This ultimate threat is coming from a formidable, vicious foe that launders $21 billion a year through the Mexican economy, and another $5 billion a year through American Fortune 500 businesses. If these bastards can corrupt the legitimate economic base of the U.S., as they have apparently already done, do you really think we are too far from being as fucked up as Colombia and Mexico? You know good and well that $5 billion a year can buy a lot of political influence on the Hill. You can buy congressmen, senators, federal agents, and lawmakers of every persuasion. Hell, you can just about buy your own country.

In the last ten years, thirty-five thousand people have died in Colombia's war against narco-connected rebels. In 2000, a Colombian police station was completely overrun by communist guerrillas who were armed by drug lords. Thirty Colombian police officers were lined up in front of the station and slaughtered like table meat. And I'm told that these are not uncommon occurrences.

By the end of 2000, the Colombian drug lords were expected to have increased their cocaine production by 100 percent. By the end of 2001 they were expected to manufacture some four hundred tons of poison compared to a paltry two hundred tons the year before. Their cocaine production peaked in 2001, then started something of a decline that continued into 2005. But when you consider that in 2004 the new Customs and Border Protection agency (a merger of Customs and Border Patrol) seized only 2.2 tons of cocaine, does it really matter that coke production slid downhill? In fact, to keep from having a glut on the market, which would bring the price down, the drug lords may have willingly decreased production, like the OPEC nations have been known to do.

While the coke production may have peaked in 2001, the Colombian cartels started becoming major growers and producers of heroin, putting out some sixty-one tons in 1999. And their Mexican brothers aren't exactly slouching in that area, either. In 1995, I had an informant who tied me into one of the biggest Mexican heroin-smuggling organizations the U.S. Customs Service has ever dealt with. The investigation posted record seizures in 1996. By 2000, the size of our heroin loads and seizures had more than doubled. And the smack wasn't even being produced in Colombia, as one might suspect. It was being cooked in Michoacán, Mexico, where the folks of a little town called Aguadilla proudly boasted that they would become renowned worldwide as the "Medellín of Heroin."

And what about Mexico? On December 12, 2000, a Mexican newspaper reported that fifteen people, all believed to have been Mexican police agents, had been found murdered in Sinaloa and Baja California. The bold one-day massacre had allegedly been carried out by stop-at-nothing drug traffickers. And remember, this is our backdoor neighbor, not some distant South American country. Can you imagine fifteen American cops being whacked in one well-coordinated attack in Texas or Arizona? If you can't, you better start.

On January 3, 2006, one of the major American networks ran a special on the increasing drug-war violence that is bleeding over to our side of the Reaper's line. The Mexican Attorney General himself stated that in 2005 alone, the body count on the Mexican side of the line was somewhere over 1,500 people. That's right—about half of the number we lost in the 9/11 attack.

You may ask why a feller committed most of his life to a war he knew wouldn't be won. About the only way I can honestly answer that is with this story.

I once had this ugly fat wire-haired black terrier. The little mutt was about as pure-blooded as shit-mixed mud in a Louisiana hog wallow. Although the pathetic thing was damn near crippled in his rear legs and half blind in both eyes, he touched my family's very soul. He reveled in the fact that he was loved by all. For the lack of a better name, the pitiful excuse for a canine ended up being dubbed "Fat Fred." We also had a beautiful full-blood racing greyhound that had been a big winner in her heyday while she was still on the track. The two pups were about as opposite as the north and south poles. But every morning to start our day, we would all go out for our ceremonial sunrise walk in the Arizona desert.

Well, you can imagine what happened when a jackrabbit or cottontail would break brush and flush out in front of us. Off the north and south poles would shoot, both wagging their tails and loving the pursuit they so looked forward to. One effortlessly and gracefully covered the desert floor like the racing champion she was. The other painfully panted and bounced across the desert like a bloated, dying toad out of water. No matter how hard that rabbit tried to throw the greyhound off, the highbred usually caught the hare and proudly brought her trophy home to show off. And Fat Fred? Well, over the years I never saw him come close to catching even one of the elusive, furry little critters. But each and every morning that old, slow mongrel son of a bitch ran his ass off trying. Fat Fred loved the chase until the day I had to bury him. It was in his heart. It was what he lived for. It was what the good Lord intended for him—and for me.

22

The Reaper, the Beast, and the Corrupt DHS

OVER THE LAST FEW YEARS, things have gotten progressively worse. Here's how. In 2003, Customs, the Border Patrol, and INS were congressionally killed off and resurrected as the new Bureau of Customs and Border Protection (CBP) and Bureau of Immigration and Customs Enforcement (ICE), both under the Department of Homeland Security (DHS). Everybody was talking about protecting America from foreign terrorists, but by the following year I was more worried that we had all kinds of crazy armed American vigilante sons of bitches running around Douglas and Cochise County. I reckon it was because of what the Barnetts and Ranch Rescue had started with all of their shenanigans.

By the end of 2003, the whole goddamn thing started to get completely out of hand because the politicians and attorneys in Arizona couldn't figure out how to deal with it, and at the same time save their careers.

The previous year, on August 30, 2002, I had been at a meeting in Tucson with the U.S. Attorney, the chief Border Patrol agent, both sheriffs from Cochise and Santa Cruz Counties, and some other lawmen. The meeting was to figure out what to do about the vigilantes. The U.S. Attorney decided the best policy was to ignore them publicly, but watch them privately until they broke the law. With a policy like that, no one should have been surprised at how this escalated.

Santa Cruz County, to the west of Douglas, ended up with a couple of mercenary journalists who write for *Soldier of Fortune* magazine and vigilantes of the Georgia Militia all at the same time hunting illegal aliens on the border. They were armed to the teeth and wore military camouflage uniforms. It was a volatile mix of wannabe vigilante soldier-boys and Southern tobacco-stain-chinned rednecks. And over in Douglas, we had heavily armed military types from Texas take up residence on the border just west of town.

On November 25, 2003, our ICE special agents and Douglas detectives arrested one of the vigilantes on felony warrants out of Texas for aggravated assault on an illegal alien. The racist was armed when we took him down, but we never had to fire a shot. We bagged, tagged, and shipped his fat ass back to the Texas courts for adjudication.

Just a couple of months later in 2004, the same Texan was back in town with more warrants on his head. (You gotta love our courts!) This time the FBI chose to execute the warrants on their own without help from my ICE agents or the Douglas Police Department. In the end, Hoover's overrated agents ended up shooting an unarmed suspect in the Douglas Safeway parking lot. The FBI brought their own team in to investigate themselves. When the news media asked why the unarmed suspect was shot, the FBI spin was something along the lines of, "The suspect's actions forced the agent to shoot." I was later told by a Douglas detective that the guy had a bottle of water in his hand when he was capped. What's the lesson to be learned here? When in Douglas, vigilante or not, you better not leave the supermarket without bagging all purchased items when the FBI is in town.

No matter what patriotic name or spin you apply to the act, vigilantism is still just that, and it continues to make the news in 2006: amateurs, sometimes racists, taking the law into their own hands. And sooner or later these dangerous self-appointed doers of justice are going to end up breaking the law and violating the rights of human beings at the end of a gun barrel or a rope. We've seen it before on the border in Cochise County. In 1976, the Hannigans were a prime example of vigilantes' brutal torture when they hung, burned, and shot three undocumented Mexicans just west of Douglas. In the end, vigilantism can come to no good. It never does. As proof, I offer you the profound scars of vigilante heritage left on America by one of the first "patriotic" civilian groups that patrolled the U.S.-Mexican border in the 1970s: the cold-blooded KKK.

Things kept on getting worse. Here are just a couple of examples of the Reaper's handiwork: In October of 2004, an alien smuggler was fleeing at a high rate of speed from a Cochise County Sheriff's deputy when the smuggler lost control of his vehicle, which contained a heavy load of human cargo. The bloody aftermath left two U.S. citizens and four illegal aliens from Mexico dead. We ended up filling every major trauma center in Phoenix and Tucson with about fifteen critically injured people. Douglas ICE Special Agent William "Billy" Hamilton worked around the clock until he made the bad guy on DNA evidence from the steering wheel.

The smuggler, who had fled the crash scene before we could arrive, was eventually found and arrested in Phoenix. The last I heard, the U.S. Attorney's Office was going to seek the death penalty for the scumbag. Special agent Billy Hamilton would later be awarded the Fraternal Order of Police Officer of the Year Award for his diligent efforts in bringing the death-dealing smuggler to justice. I asked Billy what the hardest part of the investigation was. He said, "Other than viewing the distorted bodies of the deceased, it was telling a pregnant victim when she awoke from surgery that her baby was lost from her womb while she was under." In this job, our chosen profession, sooner or later you end up taking on the pain of others, one way or another.

In November of 2004, ICE Special Agents Matt Magoffin and Eduardo Hurtado made a traffic stop in Douglas of a vehicle they suspected to be loaded with drugs. After a high-speed pursuit, the vehicle was found to contain the body of a deceased Brazilian alien that human traffickers were attempting to get rid of. The stench of death in the back of the vehicle was so overpowering that when I later drove the vehicle back to our office I had to hang from my waist up out the driver's-side window. You would think that a 45- to 50-mph wind would wash that smell out of a feller's nose a bit. It doesn't.

Just when you think you've become so calloused that you'll never be able to cry again, a case comes along that proves you not to be the man of steel you may have thought you were. In December of 2004, Douglas ICE Special Agent Richard Flannary initiated a baby-kidnapping investigation that kept us all up for several days in a row. The young mother was an illegal alien who was being smuggled into the U.S. east of Douglas. She was crossing at night with a group of other smuggled unfortunates when several bad guys accosted her and ripped her baby from her arms. In so doing, they left her terribly wounded and disfigured for life. One of the border outlaws used a blade on the little gal. The bastard damn near cut her whole lower lip and chin off in one vicious slash. Her gums and facial bones were exposed as her flesh dangled toward her throat. When she was brought to our office to tell us what happened to her baby, we couldn't understand a word she was saying until we got a local doctor to re-attach her chin and lips. The *pobrecita* (poor little thing) will have some serious physical and mental scars to deal with for the rest of her life.

Flan and Hamilton ended up setting a trap for the bad guys in Douglas at the Motel 6 parking lot. They wired the baby's father for sound, and we watched and listened as he was supposed to pay the ransom money. Something went wrong during the meeting and the criminals detected the surveillance. We rushed to save the father's life when all hell broke loose.

We had one of the greatest Douglas detectives working with us that you ever wanted to meet. Detective Ray Rios was the coolest of the cool under fire. Of short stature and medium build, Ray was about forty years old, sporting a well-trimmed mustache accompanied by the old 1950s-style ducktailed hair on both sides of his head. Ray loved his hair. I don't care if you were in a goddamn gun battle, high-speed pursuit, or interrogation session, he would continually whip out a comb and groom that jet-black follicle factory while grinning from ear to ear like a teenager. You never saw Ray without a smile. You had to love the guy. Everybody did.

When we hit the Motel 6 parking lot, Flan and Hamilton secured the two suspects before they could whack the father. From the conversation between the baby's father and the bad guys, we had learned that there was a third suspect holding the infant at an undisclosed location in Douglas. And to make things really bad, the two bad guys had used a cell phone to make a call before we could take them into custody. Fuck! The goddamn Reaper was closing in again.

We knew we had mere minutes or even seconds before the third suspect would take the baby out into the desert to dump the "evidence" for the coyote packs to finish off. Everybody was screaming and freaking out trying to figure out how to get to the baby before she was whacked. No matter how much I and the other supervisors pleaded for the agents and officers to be calm so we could think, it got to be a pretty unruly and frenzied scene. I reckon there are paternal and maternal instincts in each and every one of us that sometimes are just going to rule our emotions. Even the hardest of the hard-core guys.

So while I watched Flan and Hamilton bouncing up and down in the parking lot, and I will maintain until this day I'm not sure if they were landing on pavement or flesh, the Grand Wizard of hair stood there combing his friggin mop, just a-smiling away without a care in the world. Pleading for some kind of assistance, I said, "Ray, this looks like fucking amateur hour out here!" Ray took a final stroke on his pride before carefully tucking his comb away behind his pistol and calmly replied, "Lee, they're just kids. They'll learn. Besides, that's what you're here for."

That was it? Were these the outstanding words of wisdom from "the cool one" I was waiting for? Well, not exactly. But because Ray emanated calmness, it was comforting to a degree. Somewhere between feeling good about being future cellmates with Ray, and thinking a judge would forgive us under the circumstances, I gathered my thoughts and moved forward in pursuit of the baby's whereabouts. From some of the actions I witnessed going on around me, I knew I was going to have to have a long talk with the U.S. Attorney's Office about "the possible violations of a suspect's rights." But how about the rights of an innocent defenseless baby? Her right to continue this journey of life she had just come into? It was like going down a slippery muddy trail in Vietnam and coming to a fork in the middle of the rotting jungle. If you go left, you may get to live another day or two. If you go right you may not. Life or death. Fuck it. We chose the path that would save the baby's life. And you know what, I can live with that decision for the rest of my days.

Flan and Hamilton eventually learned where the third bad guy was holding the baby. We all got to the location within five or so minutes of the initial contact with the first two suspects. We had Hamilton and Flan take care of securing the apartment's perimeter instead of making entry with the rest of us. We figured they needed a little time to cool off before they lost all control and just outright started kicking any and everybody's ass around them, good or bad guys, it didn't matter. These two agents really wanted this baby back right fucking now!

After our agents and Douglas police officers surrounded the apartment, Ray and I were prepared to make initial entry through the back door. ICE group supervisors Kenny Duke and Marvin Tigert hit the front door and flushed the suspect back to us. The bad guy was running with the baby wrapped up in a vomit- and feces-stained blanket when we caught him trying to escape via the back door.

After we cuffed the suspect and secured the baby, I looked down at a rat- and roach-infested, shit-covered mattress where a little body had made a tiny impression. On the filthy floor next to the little hole in the mattress was an open container of putrefied milk that the criminals had been feeding the newborn infant. I lost it. I wept like a baby. Ray gently placed his arm around my shoulder as we walked out into the dark alley from the crime scene.

On this night, just a few days before Christmas, heroes Richard Flannary and Billy Hamilton returned the infant to her mother, who had traveled from afar looking for a new home and life for her family. (Sound familiar?) Had it not been for their hard work and dedication, this baby would not be alive today. Just about everyone who worked on the case was present when we gave the baby girl back to her tearful momma. Even John Wayne would have been misty-eyed over the tenderness of it all. For those of us who were part of this investigation, Christmas will always have a reborn meaning and intensity.

We lost our beloved partner and friend a few months later. Douglas Police Detective Ray Rios died in the line of duty fighting a drug suspect on a street in Douglas not too far from the Mexican border. The biggest funeral in the history of Douglas preceded the graveside ceremony. As we drove Ray's casket through the streets of Douglas, all citizens and school children took a break from their daily routine to come outside and pay their last respects. At graveside, after the twenty-one-gun salute broke the beautiful day's silence, and the crisp notes of the bugle had last echoed, I lost it. Once again, I wept like a baby. But Ray wasn't there to lend me an arm anymore.

Well, as you can plainly see, the Reaper had been standing pretty goddamn tall in the stirrups in Cochise County over the past few months. And believe me, the son of a bitch was starting to take a toll on my ass. He was wearing me down. It got to where I would answer my phone in the middle of the night and the first thing I would ask the calling agent was, "Did anybody get killed?" It kept getting so progressively worse that I changed that first question to, "Who got killed?"

Then March 3, 2005, rolled around. It was six years to the day since our young partner Gary Friedli had died in the line of duty. Sperling and I were about to have our last dance with the Reaper. It was gonna be a helluva day.

At about 11:00 a.m., Douglas ICE Special Agent Eduardo "Eddie" Hurtado picked up a shared radio transmission that Arizona Department of Public Safety officers and Cochise County deputies were in a felony pursuit some sixty to seventy miles north of Douglas. Hurtado, a former Cochise deputy himself, had joined our Douglas office a few years prior when we were still the U.S. Customs Office of Investigations. During the time that Sperling, Magoffin, and I had worked with him, we knew Eddie to be a rock-solid law-enforcement officer. A kid of about thirty or so, Eddie sported a shaved head over a stocky 240-pound, six-foot frame. He reminded you of a cross between a young Kojak and a professional wrestler. The boy had plenty of law-enforcement savvy and to add credibility to his investigative knowledge, he had years earlier been partners with Ray Rios.

At the former Douglas U.S. Customs Service Office of Investigations, Eddie and Magoffin hooked up as partners, and they had spent a good bit of time together in border fights, high-speed vehicle pursuits, and putting hot, screaming lead downrange at bad guys. Other than that, their only pastime was giving me gray hairs and a wrinkled forehead.

After a few minutes of monitoring the radio, Eddie heard DPS and Cochise County call for immediate assistance. The bad guy they were chasing was armed with an AK-47. He had initially tried to shoot an Arizona DPS officer up on I-10 during a routine traffic stop. Since the first exchange of gunfire, DPS and Cochise deputies had had five other separate gunfights with him, and no one had yet been able to bring the outlaw down. Eddie radioed the officers that ICE special agents would be on the way to help. Without hesitation and knowing what had to be done to protect innocent lives, Special Agents Matt Magoffin, Allan Sperling, Erik Akers, James Ward, and Jesse Gonzales and Douglas detective David Rose answered the call for help.

DPS and Cochise County stayed behind the shooter as he came south off I-10 onto Highway 191. He was headed toward Douglas when I directed my agents to set up an interdiction point at mile marker 11 on 191, where we all met. Sperling took over positioning everyone on a bridge toward which we would have DPS push the fleeing outlaw. While this was being done, I got back in my truck to stop and cordon off traffic on the highway about a quarter of a mile beyond us toward Douglas. Just before I left, I told Sperling and Hurtado I would be back in a minute or so and that it was imperative that we not end up in any kind of crossfire.

Lady Luck smiled a little for us that day. I encountered three Cochise County dump trucks coming up Highway 191 from Douglas toward our roadblock. I pulled the truckers to the side and gained their cooperation in using their trucks to serve as barriers of protection for innocent citizens coming behind them. I put them in charge of stopping and concealing all traffic as I got back in my truck and raced back up to my agents.

As I was zooming back to the roadblock, I knew Magoffin was setting up a second roadblock some four or so miles south of us. If the desperado made it through us, Magoffin would be the last hope of keeping innocent folks from being murdered in Douglas. It was turning out to be a pretty FUBARed day so far.

When I returned to Sperling and Hurtado's location, I could see the bad guy being chased by DPS as he entered our planned field of fire. DPS was in radio contact with us and had agreed to stop far enough back to stay out of our background of fire. I turned my truck sideways into the roadblock and dismounted with my Colt AR-15 .223 assault rifle. Everything was looking pretty good except for two things: The outlaw was coming in faster than I had expected, and I couldn't find where my agents had positioned themselves. All I had time to do was lean up against the side of my truck and take aim.

As the outlaw sped into target acquisition, I positioned my sights on his chest and face. I was just about to trigger down when Sperling drew first blood from the wannabe cop-killer. I remember seeing the bad guy's windshield disintegrate with bullet holes and glass shards. His hands instinctively flew up in an effort to shield his grimacing face. At the same time his windshield ripped open, I heard the cracking reports of .223s, 9mms, and .12 gauge shotguns just to my immediate left. Out of the corner of my eye, I saw the bad guy going between me and a whole shitload of federal firepower whirling about to keep up with his smoking vehicle. At this point, do you really have to guess what dickhead is about to get caught right smack in the middle of crossfire? Yeah, the same idiot who kept telling his agents to make sure they stayed out of a fucking crossfire.

Now, let's take a moment to reflect here. It's March third again, not one of our favorite days because of Special Agent Gary Friedli's death. We're no longer working for the outstanding managers of the U.S. Customs Service. We're now saddled with abolished INS managers who for the most part have only been administrative desk jockeys before the Department of Homeland Security merger. And we're standing right in the middle of Highway 191, which I may have forgotten to mention used to be identified as Highway 666. That's right. We're in the middle of a fucking gunfight on a state highway named for Lucifer himself. Rosy picture, ain't it?

In about the time it takes your heart to pump one single time, the outlaw was shot to shit, I somehow dodged the few rounds that didn't connect with his sorry ass, his car crashed into and bounced off of three or four government vehicles, and then it was all over. DPS arrived in short order and they were not shy in showering their affections on the ICE agents. And somewhere between the incessant cheering and screaming, I think I heard a new song being coined by DPS officers that went something like, "ICE rocks, ICE rocks, ICE rocks!"

When everyone got down off the adrenaline, and while we were still standing over the bullet-riddled body of the outlaw, I made a cell-phone call to my new INS boss in Tucson to inform him how our day in Douglas was going so far. Now, at any other time in my career with U.S. Customs, the phone conversation from the boss' side would have gone something like this: "Great job for taking the bad guy down! Especially one that had been trying to kill cops! Are any of our agents hurt? Do you guys need some help? Do any of our agents need to go to a hospital to be checked out? Need counseling? Days off to de-stress?" But you know what I got from this former INS paper-pusher? Nothing. Not a goddamn word. No support. Dead silence.

In fact, I think my INS boss was later disappointed when the Cochise County grand jury reviewed our shooting and found it to be well within the law. I waited for weeks to get a clean bill of health ruled on this one. Because no matter what, whether I personally got any rounds off or not, because I was the Special Agent in Charge on the shooting line, every piece of lead that went downrange that day ultimately belonged to me. They were my agents and I authorized the capping of the outlaw. So in the end, my signature is on the side of each bullet no matter where it may hit. Being the Agent in Charge absofuckinglutely sucks.

It wasn't too long after the grand jury ruled it a good shoot that this same INS desk jockey just couldn't contain himself. In a visit to our office he told Group Supervisor Marvin Tigert that the interdiction and takedown of the deadly suspect was not our business, that we should have let someone else like DPS do it. He actually said that ICE's position on the action was that we, ICE, are not in the public-safety business! We were told that we would have to tell local law-enforcement that we would no longer be available to back them up in a law-enforcement situation such as this one. Can you believe it? The Department of Homeland Security will no longer back local cops up when the shit hits the fan.

So there you have it, folks. The former INS managers, who have taken over ICE under the Department of Homeland Security, are actually saying that public safety is not our business. Confused? Me too! Oh, and by the way, the shot-to-shit maniac with the AK-47 turned out to be not only a dope smuggler on his way with a stolen car to pick up a dope load at the border, but he was also an illegal alien from Mexico.

In fact, during a subsequent "interview" with the outlaw, as he lay gurgling his own blood on the side of the highway, I asked him, "What the fuck is your goddamn problem?" The prison-tattooed wannabe cop-killer locked onto my eyes and through a slur of bloody bubbles said, "I owe money to the drug bosses for a load I stole. It doesn't matter if you guys or those guys kill me. I'm dead either way. I'd just as soon it be you as them."

So with that coming out of the suicidal scumbag's own mouth, how many innocent lives do you think Sperling, Hurtado, and the other ICE special agents saved that day? With all of the extra AK-47 magazines and ammo he had on the car seat with him, there is absolutely no telling. One, ten, twenty-five, who knows? I'm just glad we didn't let him get through us, so he couldn't number the children and innocent folks of Douglas as his victims. The Douglas ICE Office of Investigations definitely cheated the Reaper out of a body count on March 3, 2005.

————

Well, at the end of the day I was pretty much drained of all caring anymore. I mean, I wasn't tuned up for the fight when the bad guy crashed into our roadblock. I had zero adrenaline flow going. And I really didn't even get too excited about standing in the middle of a partial lead and glass-shard bubblebath. It kind of just all didn't mean much anymore. The bleeding bullet holes all look the same to me nowadays. Especially when you're the one out there in the middle of it and your bosses, the REMFs, aren't willing to back you up anymore. In Vietnam the combat grunts had a saying that pretty much summed up the day if they lived through it: FTW (Fuck The World!). I got a new one now. FDHS. I'm sure you can figure it out.

So on March 3, 2005, thirty-six years after pulling down on my first trigger for the U.S. government in Vietnam, I'm done. On this day on a highway in Arizona named for Satan himself, the Reaper and my Beast came to terms with each other. For better or worse, for me, they got locked up for eternity. I was finally through with them.

————

I reckon I'll never be able to fully explain why I didn't go on and pull my last trigger that day. Was I too worried about the whereabouts of my young agents before I could cut loose with deadly lead? Were my reactions too slow from the wear and tear of gunfights over the years? Did I see the immediate terror in the outlaw's face and figure he had had enough from my kids? Or was it that I knew that although the American people may want us to protect them, as we always had over the years as U.S. Customs Service special agents, our new DHS ICE bosses were not going to allow us to do that anymore?

In May 2005, the new ICE Special Agent in Charge for the Arizona District came to Douglas to see us. One of my group supervisors told me that this same SAC, upon arriving in Phoenix, had stated, "The Wild West days in Arizona are over." From what we picked up on the radar, he was speaking of the Douglas Office of Investigations.

During the meeting with all of our special agents, the new SAC threatened to have our jobs if we didn't stop interdicting dope on the border. He said that under the DHS reorganization, dope interdiction now belonged to the U.S. Border Patrol and that Douglas ICE was to work more at immigration violations. We tried to explain that by putting the BP in charge of dope interdiction, it was equivalent to having the proverbial fox watch the henhouse. Here's why.

By 2002, between the Douglas and Naco U.S. Border Patrol stations alone, I and other U.S. Customs special agents knew of thirteen Border Patrol agents that had been arrested (in many cases by Customs agents) or convicted. We also knew of at least sixteen BP agents suspected of crimes, and two more who had died under suspicious circumstances. One of those deaths is still an open homicide investigation; the other is suspected to be related to drug smuggling. The crimes of both the suspected and arrested/convicted BP agents include homicide, drug smuggling, alien smuggling, alien harboring, transporting aliens, selling sensitive law-enforcement information and documents to drug smugglers, carrying a firearm while in the commission of a crime, child molestation, rape, etc. And in May of 2001, you had a whopping forty-five agents at the Border Patrol station in Douglas under the investigative gun for kickbacks and fraudulent schemes they were perpetrating on the U.S. government and the American taxpayer.

So now, let's take a head count here. If this ol' Texas boy's math is right I believe that comes out to no less than a grand total of seventy-six problem children carrying U.S. Border Patrol badges, guns, and Department of Homeland Security arrest authority in Cochise County alone. And when you consider that the Border Patrol has about five or six hundred agents between the Naco and Douglas stations, that means that one out of every seven or so agents has an integrity problem. And it just keeps going on and on. As late as March of 2006, I was being told by several sources that there were presently another twenty to twenty-five Douglas Border Patrol agents who were facing

disciplinary actions for misuse of government credit cards. We potentially have another Border Patrol scandal on the horizon.

But the SAC didn't want to hear it. Not only was dope interdiction the sole responsibility of the BP under the merger, but by a memo
of understanding between ICE and the BP, ICE had to give our investigative operational plans, informant-derived information, and other
sensitive issues over to the BP for their consideration and approval
before we could continue an investigation.

One of the most corrupt law-enforcement agencies in existence,
the U.S. Border Patrol, was now actually being given the authority to
tell us what we could and could not do in the enforcement of laws.
Laws that we, the former U.S. Customs Service, had been successfully
enforcing for some 214 years!

We told the new SAC that we had documented cases where we
had supplied our information to the BP while trying to work alongside
them, and that during the course of doing so the cases and investigations were compromised. We even told him that we had a stable of
informants in Mexico telling us that certain corrupt BP agents were
blowing our enforcement operations and investigations into the drug
lords. We cited that the agent in charge of the Douglas Border Patrol
station had a brother who had recently been arrested by the DEA for
smuggling a car-trunk load of marijuana.

None of this convinced the SAC, his deputy SACs, or the other
REMFs in D.C. headquarters that it would be impossible for us to
work securely and safely with the BP. None of my agents could believe
what was happening. It was a fucking nightmare. How would we ever
be able to conduct another sensitive cross-border smuggling investigation? More importantly, how would we ever be able to conduct an
international criminal conspiracy investigation when the drug lords
had BP agents on the payroll—the same BP guys who could get our
operational plans and informant information!

In late May of 2005, I was contacted by the DHS Inspector General's Office in D.C. They were doing a study of the merger for the
new DHS secretary, Michael Chertoff. A recent Heritage Foundation
study was circulating the Hill. The report determined that the

merger had, to say the least, not been a perfect marriage of law-enforcement agencies and their duties. They wanted to know what I knew about Border Patrol corruption and their continuous violations of the Fourth Amendment's search-and-seizure laws. I e-mailed them back and told the truth about the matter as I knew it to be: It was an ugly mess.

Then in late June of 2005, I had a surprise visit from a Border Patrol manager and an ICE manager out of Tucson. They said they had been sent by the ICE Special Agent in Charge, after he had received the word out of DHS headquarters, to find out why I had a problem working with the Border Patrol. From the conversation, it was evident that the corruption matters I had been speaking to the Homeland Security REMFs about were about to come back to haunt me.

To condense this a bit, I and Douglas ICE Group Supervisory Special Agent Marvin Tigert told these guys and later the deputy ICE SAC in Tucson about the Border Patrol's corruption. We told them that we would be putting our ICE special agents' lives, as well as the lives of our informants, at risk. Before this meeting the new ICE SAC had already told us that if an informant was murdered, we would "deal with it then." And now these guys were telling us that a certain amount of corruption in the Border Patrol was acceptable, and that I would ignore it and order my ICE agents to work with the BP agents even if they knew they were corrupt. Naturally, for the protection of our agents' lives, the "kids" that we loved like our own blood, Marvin and I stood our ground. We knew at that time what it would cost us in the end: our jobs.

In June of 2005, in that month alone, three known Border Patrol corruption issues made the Arizona and Washington, D.C., news. One Border Patrol agent was arrested for smuggling three thousand pounds of marijuana into the U.S. Another was arrested for smuggling or harboring an illegal alien and lying under oath. The third media event was the forty-five Border Patrol agents caught up in the Douglas "Travelgate" kickback and fraud investigation. And yet I was actually being ordered by ICE management to magically convince my ICE special agents to trust these criminals! It was absolute insanity!

Even if I had wanted to, which was not even close to the case, do you think that any ICE agent with a shred of integrity would actually entertain the idea of working with this trash? And while we are on the subject of integrity, which it seems that my new INS and Border Patrol bosses are lacking, this is written in my former Department of Treasury Law-Enforcement Code of Ethics:

> *INTEGRITY*
> *A police officer will not engage in acts of corruption or bribery, nor will an officer CONDONE such acts by other police officers. The public demands that the integrity of police officers be above reproach.*

And here are my new former INS, now ICE, managers, ordering me to violate this most sacred of codes. I may have done a lot of dirty rotten deeds in my life that I pray God will forgive me for, but I've never sold my badge, my integrity, or the trust that the American taxpayers put in me. This is where I will make my final stand. I may be done pulling the trigger for the government. But by God, I will never be done putting the truth to paper and getting it out to the American people so that they may draw their own conclusions.

On June 6, 2005, I was watching a private contractor dig for a suspected cross-border drug tunnel in Naco, Arizona, when I got a cell-phone call from my boss, the ICE Special Agent in Charge in Phoenix. I was trying to explain to him that the Naco U.S. Border Patrol had hired this guy to look for a suspected tunnel when my boss rudely cut me off and told me he was bouncing me out of my job and office. I was to report to him in Phoenix the following Monday. I was to work under his direct supervision. He told me that I would not be allowed to go back to Douglas, not even to visit my wife. This is what happens when they want to force you to retire. They keep bouncing you all around until you say uncle and go away forever.

And the whole time the SAC was telling me how he was going to rearrange my life and living conditions, I was trying to tell him a law-enforcement fact that was really important. After my "conversation" with the SAC, I walked over to my counterpart in DEA who was also observing the tunnel exploration. He could tell I had some troubling news, but it wasn't so much about my being bounced. I'd fully expected to be bounced for taking a stand on corruption. But what I told DEA Resident Agent in Charge Bogden did in fact make him stand back and say, "Oh, fuck!"

All I wanted to tell my SAC, and the DEA agent, was this: The private contractor that the Naco U.S. Border Patrol had hired for $30,000 to dig for a drug tunnel was in fact a brother-in-law of one of the biggest previously convicted drug lords in Sonora, Mexico, Vicente Terán. I wonder if my SAC would have been interested in hearing that neither the contractor, nor the Border Patrol agents that hired him, found a tunnel that day. Nah. My baby-soft, plump SAC was just getting bored with all this silly corruption business. Besides that, he had more important things to do like piss off Governor Janet Napolitano, the Phoenix Police Department, the Arizona Attorney General's Office, the Arizona Department of Safety, and others both known and unknown.

You can sympathize with me or not. I don't care one way or the other. But on June 7, 2005, I went to see my doctor for stress-related issues. He ended up sending me over to the Veterans Administration in Tucson. After the MDs got done probing and poking over old war wounds and Agent Orange scar tissue, they sent me across the hall to the shrink. When he was done, I was put out to pasture.

According to what the docs told me, there was a new study just coming to light, probably because guys like me were just getting toward retirement age. Pretty much all of the Vietnam combat veterans they had studied who went into law enforcement upon their return from the war were coming down with Post-Traumatic Stress Disorder. We had been running from our combat experiences for years, staying pumped up on law-enforcement-induced adrenaline, and now it's crash time. In World War II and Korea, they called it battle fatigue or shell shock. Like everything else these days, we gotta put a newer and nicer sounding label on it. PTSD. Sounds like a jungle or desert disease to me. So you were in some Pretty Tough Shit, Dude?

Special agents Sperling and Tigert pretty much ended up going out about the same way as did I, on sick leave. Seems there had been another shrink study done about the Rangers in Somalia who had seen serious combat. Basically the study said that most of those soldiers later crashed out because of the lack of post-support from the Army. The docs say that a soldier can put up with a lot of shit when he has to, as long as he is supported by his superiors. But when that support is nonexistent, you can expect the worst-case mental scenario to follow.

So obviously, between the government's vicious, unjust pursuit of Sperling over Friedli's death, and the non-support of the necessary shooting of the outlaw on March 3, 2005, Sperling crashed. A short time later, Supervisory Special Agent Tigert followed suit with his own lingering demons from past shootings he was never counseled for.

———

The Arizona ICE Special Agent in Charge eventually replaced me with a thirty-three-year-old Yankee who had no idea of the corruption issues on the Mexican border in Douglas. But then again, that is just what the SAC and his bosses in D.C. wanted: a yes boy, someone who through either ignorance of the Douglas situation or just plain fucking immoral indifference wouldn't rock the boat. It was easier that way. It didn't matter that it wasn't safer for my special agents and their informants. No. It was all about everyone up the chain of command being able to lie to the Hill and the President that everything in DHS was just going fine. The merger was perfect, sir, no chinks in the armor to report!

———

So, to sum it all up and put it in the correct perspective for ya'll, here it is. We're attacked by a foreign entity. We panic. Someone has to pay.

We invade Iraq instead of Saudi Arabia. While the American public is appeased that we are kicking some—any—foreign ass abroad, they are still nervous about their homeland. Quick. Let's blame someone at home. The FBI. No, too powerful, too many friends on the Hill. The CIA. No, same as the FBI. Let's fuck INS. They are screwups and we have been wanting to get rid of them anyway. Yeah. And at the same time we can take a 214-year-old federal law-enforcement agency that has done an excellent job (U.S. Customs) and mix it into the new INS when no one is looking.

Hell, we can even go as far as letting the old INS do a "Phoenix thing" and the American public won't even see it coming. A "Phoenix thing"? Sure. Let the abolished agency rise up out of the ashes and take over the whole new U.S. Customs and Border Protection gig. Yeah, but, like, didn't the old INS and their U.S. Border Patrol have a lot of corruption issues in the past? Yeah, but it's just like anything else in the government. You just gotta learn to live with so much corruption and get over it. By George, I like it. Let's get her done.

And how secure are you now, America? Well, guarding the interior U.S. you have the FBI, which fucked up in the first place and allowed the World Trade Center to get nailed. Yet, despite the arrival of the Department of Homeland Security to protect America, the FBI over in the Justice Department still commands the strongest counterterrorist law-enforcement agency in the land. They won't allow anyone to work a terrorist investigation if they can't lead it.

And on America's frontiers, protecting us from initial terrorist penetration, you have the U.S. Border Patrol, probably the most corrupt federal law-enforcement agency in U.S. history.

The recently proposed immigration legislation that continues to be debated calls for stiffer penalties on employers of undocumented aliens, and a new border wall down south. Well, let me tell you what thirty years or so of border law enforcement could teach anybody. First, it's illegal to take dope but it's a billion-dollar-a-year business in our country. So do you really think that if we make it illegal to hire undocumented aliens anyone is going to follow that law, either? The second thing: We already have a steel border wall in Douglas and Naco. About five or six years ago, the U.S. Army and Marines constructed it of tough-ass landing mats. And you know what? We have actually seen the dope smugglers cut holes in the wall with torches, hang their own doors on hinges, and then lock the fucking thing from their side in Mexico. Some of the damn things were big enough to drive vehicles through. So do you really think that's gonna work? Even if it did, they would just tunnel right under the goddamn thing!

Hello! Any lucid brains home out there? Instead of spending billions of dollars on this kind of inane crap, how about putting the same money into developing Mexico, giving the people jobs so they can feed their kids, and developing their natural resources? The only thing I can see wrong with that is that it must not benefit enough folks, and their bank accounts, up on the Hill.

In the fall of 2005, ICE Special Agent Matt Magoffin couldn't take anymore of the corrupt ICE/DHS merger. He felt so strongly about not working too closely with corrupt BP agents that he took a $30,000-a-year cut in pay to go back to U.S. Fish and Wildlife as a law-enforcement officer. Later in the year, in late November or early December, Matt set up a meeting between himself, me, and Larry Parkinson, the Under Secretary of the Department of Interior.

Larry had been down visiting with Cochise County ranchers on border issues. But before he left, he wanted to meet with us about Border Patrol issues. And one of the issues was BP corruption. We spoke for a couple of hours behind closed doors. And what amazed me was the fact that Larry was not shocked about what we were telling him. As a pre-9/11 assistant director for the FBI, he had heard it before. Between what he said and what I've been told by people in the Office of the Inspector General, most people on the Hill already are aware of the BP corruption.

Larry said that one of the reasons nothing will probably be done about it is this: "They are the only game on the border now, and Congress will probably keep throwing money and manpower at them. What are you going to do? Tear the whole Border Patrol down while you investigate it? Who's gonna watch the border while you do it?"

Not the special agents of the once-proud U.S. Customs Service Office of Investigations, that's for sure. At the turn of the last century politicians disbanded the Arizona Rangers because, in one way or another, their effectiveness was a political liability. At the turn of this century we haven't learned a goddamn thing from our own history. The USCS Office of Investigations went the same way as the Rangers.

To give you a better understanding of the continuing DHS Border Patrol corruption that I'm talking about, I offer the following criminal acts for you to mull over. On December 6, 2005, an alert Arizona DPS highway patrolman stopped a suspicious truck west of Naco near Sonoita. Two suspects bailed out and ran from the truck, leaving behind about seven hundred pounds of marijuana secreted in the bed of the truck. The Arizona DPS officer left his vehicle parked behind the dope load and gave diligent foot pursuit of the suspects, as you would expect from any good officer.

While the DPS officer was chasing the outlaws by himself in the desert brush, U.S. Border Patrol Agent Michael Carlos Gonzalez came upon the DPS dope seizure, and he stopped to—well, let's just say for now that he stopped.

Now, you would think that any agent or cop worth his salt would immediately go to the aid of a fellow officer who was outgunned by two to one in favor of the bad guys. But what you have to remember on the border in Arizona, like I've been preaching at you, is that there are a lot of crooks with badges. Especially in the U.S. Border Patrol these days.

What Border Patrol Agent Gonzalez did not know yet was that when the Arizona officer stopped the suspects with his red and blue flashing lights, a video camera within the officer's patrol car was automatically activated. So when Border Patrol Agent Gonzalez started stealing the marijuana from the Arizona state seizure, instead of giving aid to his fellow officer, he was caught on tape committing a felony while being armed. Sometimes bad shit happens to bad people. And that's how you know there really is a God.

Sickening and scary? You betcha. It's bad enough that the DPS officer could have been whacked by the two smugglers for lack of a fellow officer's help, but think about this: The officer could also have very easily been murdered by Border Patrol Agent Gonzalez had the aforementioned events strayed off course.

The DPS officer didn't review the tape in his patrol car until some time after the Border Patrol agent had left the scene. Had the officer returned from chasing the suspect earlier than anticipated, Agent Gonzalez may very well have panicked and gunned down the DPS officer in an ambush. At the very least, there most likely would have been an unfortunate "blue on blue" (cop on cop) gunfight.

Although not in Arizona, on March 9, 2006, in El Centro, California, an unsealed federal complaint alleged that U.S. Border Patrol agents Mario Alvarez and Samuel McClaren took $300,000 in bribes to release illegal immigrants and their smugglers. Both BP agents had been assigned to an alien-smuggling joint task force between the U.S. Border Patrol and the Mexican Attorney General's Office. "The agents arrested today, who are supposed to represent the very best, epitomize the very worst," said a U.S. Department of Justice official in San Diego.

Border Patrol agents Alvarez and McClaren have been charged with conspiracy, bribery, making false statements, immigrant smuggling, and filing false tax returns. Alvarez worked on the task force from November 2002 until the end of 2005. McClaren worked on it from July 2003 until the end of 2005. Can you just imagine what potential criminals and/or murdering terrorists they may have unleashed on our country? God forbid, we won't know until the next 9/11.

In March 2006, a query of Internet postings concerning corrupt U.S. Border Patrol agents revealed that between Laredo, Texas, and San Diego, California, eleven had been arrested, and two suspended from duty while under investigation. The agents had been accused of crimes ranging from drug/alien/ammunition smuggling to sexual assault of illegal aliens. These postings were not all-inclusive of the total number of agents arrested across the country; a number of the previously arrested Border Patrol agents from Arizona, for example, did not appear.

So, who's keeping track of the aggregate corruption number? I would imagine that the Office of the Inspector General in D.C. has the tally safely tucked away. But don't expect them to be forthcoming with this disgraceful information. Hell, you're talking about an administration that can't even figure out what constitutes a civil war in Iraq, much less what constitutes an unacceptable level of corruption within its own Department of Homeland Security's U.S. Border Patrol.

Epidemic proportion of corruption? If it's not, from what I've witnessed over the past three-plus decades, it's headed that way pretty damn pronto. I can assure you that in the 1970s and early '80s there was nothing comparable to the present loss of integrity and honesty.

And you must remain cognizant of this fact: These are the same federal U.S. Border Patrol agents with whom my former U.S. Customs Treasury special agents, now known as Homeland Security ICE special agents, have been ordered to share sensitive smuggling investigative information. I rest my case with you, the now-informed jury of the American people.

———

Art Bernal and I once interviewed a notorious, violent Sonoran drug lord as he rotted away in an Arizona state prison. For whatever reasons of his own, Tepiro Samaniego gave up decades of well-guarded secrets concerning corruption on both sides of the border in Douglas and Agua Prieta. For talking to us and laying the belly of the organization wide open, Samaniego would later be murdered by the Agua Prieta cartel. And although he supplied us with a wealth of investigative information, there was one particular thing I learned that day concerning how the Mexican dope lords viewed Bernal, Butch Barret, me, and our partners. When Samaniego shook my hand at the end of the interview, his rough, calloused prison-labor grip drew me eye to eye with the man. As we stared straight down into each other's souls, the fallen drug lord solemnly said, "I see it's true what they say about you and your boys." Samaniego paused, studied me, and continued as if he were a judge passing out a life sentence. "You can't be bought!" It was the greatest career compliment ever bestowed upon me and my partners.

Integrity. You're either born with it or you're not. Federal law-enforcement agencies, particularly DHS and the U.S. Border Patrol, need to embrace the concept.

So, who's going to watch the border for you? There is always one you can count on: The Reaper.